JESUIT EDUCATION

ITS

HISTORY AND PRINCIPLES

VIEWED IN THE LIGHT OF

MODERN EDUCATIONAL PROBLEMS

BY

ROBERT SCHWICKERATH, S. J.,

WOODSTOCK COLLEGE, MD.

SECOND EDITION.

ST. LOUIS, MO.
B. HERDER
17 South Broadway.
1904.

PREFACE.

Mr. Quick, the English educationist, asserts that "since the Revival of Learning, no body of men has played so important a part in education as the Jesuits." And yet, as the same author says, "about these Jesuit schools there does not seem to be much information accessible to the English reader." (*Educational Reformers*, pp. 33—34.) It is true, indeed, that during the past few years much has been said and written about the Jesuit schools; in fact, they have occupied the attention of the public more, perhaps, than ever before. However, with the exception of the excellent book of Father Thomas Hughes, S. J. (*Loyola and the Educational System of the Jesuits*, 1892), most of what has been offered to American and English readers is entirely untrustworthy. The account given of the Jesuit system in Histories of Education used in this country, as those of Compayré, Painter, and Seeley, is a mere caricature. Instead of drawing from the original sources, these authors have been content to repeat the biased assertions of unreliable secondary authorities. Some observations on American Histories of Education will be found at the end of this book (p. 649 *sqq.*). The publication of a new work on the educational system of the Jesuits may be justified at the present day. During the last decade, educational circles in this country have been greatly agitated about various questions of the utmost importance: the elective system, the value of the study of the classics, the function of the college and its relation to the high school and university, and the problem of moral and religious training. It has been the author's intention to view the Jesuit system chiefly in the light of these modern problems. These important educational questions have been treated at some length, and it is hoped that on this account the work may engage the attention of all who are interested in education.

I feel almost obliged to apologize for one feature of the book, *viz.*, the numerous quotations and references. Though aware that there is among American and English readers a sort of antipathy against many references, I have yet deemed it necessary to quote freely from various sources. This course I am forced to adopt, as I do not wish to lay before the reader my own opinions about the educational system of the Jesuits, but I want to show what this system is according to the original sources. These are, above all, the *Constitutions* of the Society of Jesus, and the *Ratio Studiorum*, which, however, must be supplemented by other documents. For, many points of the Ratio Studiorum are intelligible only in the light of the decrees of the Legislative Assemblies of the Order, the regulations of the General and Provincial Superiors, and the commentaries of prominent Jesuit educators. A great deal of this material has been published by Father Pachtler, in four volumes of the great collection *Monumenta Germaniae Paedagogica* (Berlin 1887—1894); other valuable information has been published within the last few years, in the *Monumenta Historica Societatis Jesu*, especially in the part entitled *Monumenta Paedagogica*, which appeared in 1901 and 1902. An account of these works is given in the Bibliographical Appendix, under the heading: *Primary Sources*.

Another reason which moved me to make use of numerous quotations was the desire to show what distinguished historians and educators outside the Society, particularly non-Catholics, both in America and Europe, have said on the educational system of the Jesuits. I wished also to call attention to points of contact between the Ratio Studiorum and other famous educational systems. As so many features of the Jesuit system have been misrepresented, a work of this kind must, at times, assume a polemical attitude. Painful as controversy is, the unfair criticism of many writers has compelled me to contest their positions. The style of the book may not always be as smooth as is desirable. In partial extenuation of this defect, it should be stated that a considerable amount of the material had to be translated, chiefly from the Latin, German, and French. It has been my principal aim to be faithful to the original, and in general, to write in the simplest possible language, so as to let the facts speak without attempt at literary embellishment.

I desire to acknowledge my obligation to several friends of Woodstock College, who rendered kind assistance in revising the manuscript and reading the proofs. In particular I wish to thank the Rev. Samuel Hanna Frisbee, S. J., editor of the *Woodstock Letters*, who allowed me the freest use of the *Letters* and furnished other valuable material.

R. S.

WOODSTOCK COLLEGE, MARYLAND,
March 12, 1903.

CONTENTS.

CHAPTER I.
Introduction.

Modern Criticism of Jesuit Education . . . 5

PART FIRST.
History of the Educational System of the Society of Jesus.

CHAPTER II.
Education before the Foundation of the Society of Jesus.

The Jesuit System and Early Protestant Schools   17

§ 1. *Schools at the Close of the Middle Ages.*

The Catholic Church and Medieval Education   21
Primary Schools 23
Secondary Schools 25
Schools in Italy 26
Schools in Scotland and England . . . 28
Schools in Germany, France, and the Netherlands 31
The Older Humanists in Germany . . . 34
Universities 38

§ 2. *Character of Medieval Education.*

Trivium and Quadrivium 44
Scholasticism 45
Renaissance 47
Two Schools of Humanists 49
Condition of Education on the Eve of the Reformation , , ... 55

(VII)

§ 3. Education under the Influence of the Reformation.

Luther's Alliance with the Humanists	57
Decline of the Schools	60
Luther's Endeavor to Prevent the Total Ruin of the Schools	65
Effects of the English Reformation on the Schools	69
Catholic Counter-Reformation	71

CHAPTER III.
The Society of Jesus.—Religious as Educators.

Ignatius of Loyola, his Character and Aims	73
The Society of Jesus	76
Religious as Educators	80
The Society of Jesus the First Order that Made Education of Youth a Special Ministry	87
Opposition to the Educational Labors of Religious	98
Constitutions of the Society	101
The Fourth Part of the Constitutions Treating of Studies	103
The Society and Primary Education	104

CHAPTER IV.
The Ratio Studiorum of 1599.

Plans of Studies in Jesuit Colleges Previous to the Ratio Studiorum	107
Care in Drawing up the Plan of Studies	109
Peculiar Character of the Ratio Studiorum	114
Officers of Jesuit Colleges	115
The Literary Curriculum: Ancient Languages	118
The Study of History	124
Geography	127
Study of the Mother-Tongue	129
The Philosophical Course	131

Mathematics and Sciences 133
Sources of the Ratio Studiorum . . . 136

CHAPTER V.
Jesuit Colleges and Their Work before the Suppression of the Society (1540—1773).

Rapid Spread of Jesuit Colleges 144
Superiority of the Jesuit Schools according to the
    Testimony of Protestants 145
Literary and Scientific Activity of Jesuit Colleges 148
Languages 149
Mathematics and Natural Sciences . . . 155
Geography 158
History 160
Literature 161
School Drama of the Jesuits 164
Growing Opposition to the Society . . . 173
Suppression of the Order 175
Protection of Frederick the Great of Prussia and
    Catharine II of Russia 176
Efficiency of Jesuit Colleges at the Time of the
    Suppression 178
Effects of the Suppression on Education in Catholic Countries 184

CHAPTER VI.
The Revised Ratio of 1832 and Later Regulations.

Restoration of the Society 189
Revision of the Ratio Studiorum . . . 191
Philosophy Preserved as Completion of College
    Training 195
The Ratio of 1832 not Final 197
Later Educational Regulations 198

Chapter VII.
The Educational Work of the Jesuits in the Nineteenth Century.

New Growth of Jesuit Colleges . . . 200
Jesuit Colleges in the United States . . . 201
Colleges in Other Countries 206
Efficiency of Jesuit Schools 209
President Eliot's Charges 223
Literary and Scientific Work of the Jesuits during the Last Twenty-five Years 225

Chapter VIII.
Opposition to Jesuit Education.

Laws against Jesuit Schools 239
General Charges against the Jesuit Schools . . 241
Contradictory Statements of Opponents . . 243
Special Charges: "The Jesuits Educate only the Rich and Those Who Pay" 247
"Estrange Children from the Family" . . 250
"Cripple the Intellect and Teach Corrupt Morality" 251
"Seek Their Own Interest in Educational Labors" 254
"Their Education Antinational and Unpatriotic" 255
Causes of Opposition among Protestants . . 264
Causes of Antipathy of Some Catholics . . 269

PART SECOND.

The Principles of the Ratio Studiorum. Its Theory and Practice Viewed in the Light of Modern Educational Problems.

CHAPTER IX.
Adaptability of the Ratio Studiorum.—Prudent Conservatism.

Adaptability and Adaptation 280
Necessity of Wise Conservatism 288
Lesson from Germany 289
Lesson from American Schools 292

CHAPTER X.
The Intellectual Scope.

Scope of Education: Harmonious Training of the Mind 297
Cramming in Modern Systems 300
Premature Specialization 302
Function of the College 306

CHAPTER XI.
Prescribed Courses or Elective Studies.

Electivism in the United States . . . 310
President Eliot Censures the Jesuit Colleges for Adhering to Prescribed Courses . . . 311
Criticism of the Elective System . . . 313
Dangers for the Moral Training 316
Dangers for the Intellectual Training . . 322
Wise Election almost Impossible . . . 325

Chapter XII.
Classical Studies.

Modern Discussions about the Value of the Study of the Classics	330
Distinguished Men Defend Their Value	333
Advantages Derived from the Study of the Classics for the Logical, Historical, Literary, Aesthetic, and Ethical Training	346
Beneficial Results for the Mother-Tongue	356
Objections against the Jesuit Method of Teaching the Classics	361
The Gaume Controversy and the Jesuits	366

Chapter XIII.
Syllabus of School Authors.

§ 1. *General Remarks.*

The Study of Grammar	370
Choice of Authors in Jesuit Colleges	372
§ 2. *Latin Prose Writers*	377
§ 3. *Latin Poets*	385
§ 4. *Greek Prose Writers*	392
§ 5. *Greek Poets*	399

Chapter XIV.
Scholarship and Teaching.

Scholarship in Relation to Practical Teaching	402
Decline of Teaching	404
American Scholarship	411

Chapter XV.
Training of the Jesuit Teacher.

The Candidate for the Order	415
Noviceship and Religious Training	417
Study of Languages and Philosophy after the Noviceship	422

Influence of Uniform Training on Individuality . 425
Immediate Preparation of the Jesuit for Teaching 432
Permanent Teachers 435
Work Assigned according to Ability . . . 439
Class Teachers, not Branch Teachers . . 443
Continued Self-Training of the Teacher . . 446

Chapter XVI.
The Method of Teaching in Practice.
§ 1. *The Prelection or Explanation of the Authors.*

Characteristic Feature of the Jesuit Method . 457
Accurate Pronunciation 458
Translation and Explanation 461
Repetition 466
Specimens of Interpretation 468
Soundness of the Method of the Ratio . . . 475
Amount of Reading 482
Subject and Antiquarian Explanation . . . 485
Explanation of Authors in the Vernacular . 491

§ 2. *Memory Lessons.*

Importance of Memory Lessons 493
Manner of Committing to Memory . . . 496

§ 3. *Written Exercises.*

Importance and Value of Compositions . . 498
Subjects to be Taken from Authors Studied . 499
Correction 503
Speaking Latin 506
A Lesson from Germany 509

§ 4. *Contests (Emulation).*

Emulation in School Work 511
Various Kinds of Contests, Class Matches . . 515
Academies 518

Chapter XVII.
The Moral Scope.

The Moral Training Neglected by Many Teachers
   of Our Age 522
Importance Attached to the Moral Training in
   Jesuit Schools 527
Means Employed 531
Supervision 537
Private Talks with Pupils 548
Educational Influence of Confession . . 550
Communion 557
Devotions 558
The Sodalities 560
Watchfulness in Regard to Reading . . 564
Good and Evil Results of Sports 569

Chapter XVIII.
Religious Instruction.

Religious Instruction the Basis of Solid Moral
   Training 574
Correctness of the Catholic Position in Regard to
   Religion and Education 577
Undenominational Religion an Absurdity . . 582
The Reading of the Bible not Sufficient for Religious Instruction 583
Catholic Position 587
Religious Instruction in the Jesuit System . 590
Catechisms Written by Jesuits 592
Peter Canisius, the Model Jesuit Catechist . 594
Correlation of All Branches with Religious Instruction 599
Religious Instruction Necessary also in Higher
   Schools 605

CHAPTER XIX.
School-Management.

Trials in Teaching 608
Particular Points of School-Management:
  § 1. *Authority* 610
  § 2. *Punishments* 614
  § 3. *Impartiality* 619
  § 4. *Discipline in the Classroom* . . 623
  § 5. *Politeness and Truthfulness* . . 626
  § 6. *Some Special Helps* . . . 631

CHAPTER XX.
The Teacher's Motives and Ideals.

The Chief Motive: Utility and Dignity of the Work of Education 636
Illustrated by Analogies 638
The Ideal and Model of the Teacher: Christ, the Great Master 641
Conclusion 647

Appendix I: Additions and Corrections . . 649
Appendix II: Bibliography 662
Index 671

Chapter I.

Introduction.

We are living in an age of school reforms and pedagogical experiments. The question of higher education in particular is warmly debated in England, France, Germany, and the United States. The respective merits of rival educational systems are topics of lively discussion and comment in numberless books and articles. New "curricula" are planned on all sides, and new courses are offered in the various seats of learning. Not long ago it was stated that "the American College was passing." Harvard, Yale, Columbia, the University of Pennsylvania, and other leading schools, now accept the studies of the professional schools as meeting the requirements of the last year in college. Yale University was also reported as making ready to follow in the wake of Harvard and abolish the study of Greek as a requisite for admission. The University of Michigan, abandoning the attempt to distinguish between forms of admission or courses of study pursued in the college, will give up degrees like bachelor of letters or bachelor of philosophy, and confer on all its students indiscriminately at graduation the degree of bachelor of arts, in this respect following what is substantially the procedure of Harvard. Harvard, with its system of election, election in the preparatory schools, in the college, and in the professional schools, is the forerunner in the revolution, and to the course it has laid down the other colleges and universities either have adapted themselves or are preparing so to do. "Faculties and Presidents are trying to tear down the old order which they no longer honor."[1]

For two or three decades various attempts and experiments have been made to establish a "new order." But the dissatisfaction seems rather to grow than to diminish. The man who has kept in touch with pedagogical publications knows right well that there exists in our high schools and colleges an unsettled state of affairs and a wide-spread discontent with present methods. Thus, in the *Educational Review*, we find the following statements: "It is not without reason that one so often hears the state of the educational world described as chaotic."[2] The first sentence of an article on "Latin in the High School" informs us that "even to the superficial observer it must be apparent that our secondary Latin teaching is in a state of unrest." "Further proof of this widespread feeling of insecurity lies in the susceptibility of our Latin teachers to fashions or 'fads', in a surprising readiness to adopt innovations and carry them to an extreme."[3] Many will not care much for the "dead" languages, if only the "sciences" are taught well.

[1] New York *Sun*, March 3, 1901. — However, at the last Commencement, President Hadley of Yale declared that a careful inquiry made among the masters of the secondary schools had furnished abundant evidence decidedly unfavorable to this change, and he allowed it to be understood that Greek would be required at Yale for a good while to come. The *Yale Alumni Weekly*, July 31st, 1902, pp. 430—32.

[2] *Educational Review*, 1894, p. 62.

[3] *Ib.*, p. 25.

What is said about the sciences? The same volume contains an article entitled: "The Disappointing Results of Science Teaching." Therein it is stated that "the results of the teaching of science in schools of all kinds have been very disappointing to the friends and advocates of science teaching. .... The work is unsatisfactory when the best opportunities are provided and skilled teachers devote all their time to it, indeed where they practically have everything their own way. .... This has given the advocates of the older literary studies a chance to look over their spectacles and say: 'I told you so.' It is plain that class-room science-teaching has no history to be proud of, but the reverse. Something is radically wrong when, after a generation of science-teaching, those who have had the best available teaching in it do not show some of the superiority which is claimed for it in insight, tact, skill, judgment, and affairs in general."[1] Complaints of a similar nature can be found in more recent publications.

It is evident, then, that final judgment on the modern system is reserved for the future. If we consider the results obtained within the last ten years, it appears unintelligible that many writers on education are so unreserved in denouncing systems of the past, which have a "history to be proud of." Indeed, it may be said that the present educational movement is characterized by a morbid craving for novelties, but still more by contempt of old traditions. Modern pedagogy has rightly been called a Proteus. It daily assumes new forms so that even its most ardent followers seem not to know what they are really

[1] *Ib.*, p. 485.

grappling with. In very truth, pedagogists of to-day appear to be quite certain of only one point, that "the old is worthless and that something new must be produced at any price."[1]

We do not deny that our age demands "something" new in education. Growth and development are necessary in educational systems. Every age and every nation has its own spirit, its peculiar ways and means to meet a given end, and these very ways and means inevitably exert a great influence on educational methods and call for modifications and adaptations of what has met the purpose of the past. An educational system, fitted in every detail to all times and all nations, is an impossibility. For the majority of cases it would be a Procrustean bed. It would be folly, therefore, to claim that even the best system of education in all its details were as fit for the twentieth century as for the sixteenth, or that the same system in its entirety might be introduced into Japan or China as well as into Germany, England and the United States.

For an educational system must aim not at educating men in general, but at educating the youth of a

[1] See Dr. Dittes, in *Report of the Commissioner of Education*, 1894—95, vol. I, p. 332. — From different sides complaints are heard that many educationists of to-day are conspicuous for their contempt of all that was venerated formerly. Dr. Matthias of Berlin, one of the most distinguished schoolmen of Germany, wrote recently: "Men of sound judgment point with alarm to a sort of pedagogical pride and arrogance of the younger teachers, which was unknown to the older generation." *Monatschrift für höhere Schulen*, January 1902, p. 9. — Similarly Professor Willmann of the University of Prague: "A morbid hunting after novelties and a haughty contempt of all traditions are the characteristics of the modern educational agitation." In *Vigilate*, I, p. 31.

INTRODUCTION.

certain age in a certain country. Hence the necessity of changes, of development. Education is something living and must grow, otherwise it will soon wither and decay. There are, however, certain fundamental principles, certain broad outlines of education, based on sound philosophy and the experience of centuries, which suffer no change. Unfortunately, it is some of these principles which have been abandoned by modern pedagogists, and it is for this reason that many "school reforms" of these days have proved mere "school changes" or, as Professor Münsterberg of Harvard University styles them, "school deteriorations."[1] This important distinction between what is essential and what is accidental in education, has too frequently been disregarded by those advocates of the new system who claim that the old principles and methods must be given up, because they are not suited to cope with modern conditions. What is but secondary in education, as for instance the election of courses and branches, has been proclaimed to be of vital importance, and its absence in the older systems has been considered as the strongest proof that these systems are entirely antiquated. This mistake has more than once been made by those who attack one of the celebrated old systems, the *Ratio Studiorum* of the Jesuits.

Only three years ago, President Eliot of Harvard University, in a paper read before the American Institute of Instruction, July 10, 1899, advocated the extension of electivism to secondary or high schools.[2]

[1] *Atlantic Monthly*, May 1900.
[2] The paper was printed in the *Atlantic Monthly*, October 1899.

6   JESUIT EDUCATION.

As opposed to his favorite system, President Eliot mentioned "the method followed in Moslem countries, where the Koran prescribes the perfect education to be administered to all children alike. Another instance of uniform prescribed education may be found in the curriculum of Jesuit colleges, which has remained almost unchanged for four hundred years, disregarding some trifling concessions made to natural sciences." The President further declared that "the immense deepening and expanding of human knowledge in the nineteenth century and the increasing sense of the sanctity of the individual's gifts and will-power have made uniform prescriptions of study in secondary schools impossible and absurd."

As the Jesuits, together with the Moslems, are said to uphold prescribed courses, they are implicitly charged with attempting what is "absurd," nay "impossible." In our days of critical and fair-minded research, such sweeping condemnations are beyond excuse; they show forth no careful and impartial examination of the system censured. But we have reasons to suspect that *lack of sympathy* and of *knowledge* impairs the judgment of most opponents of the Jesuits. "True criticism," writes a distinguished English historian, "must be sympathetic;"[1] where there is antipathy a false appreciation is inevitable. That lack of sympathy has led many critics into unfair discriminations in regard to the educational system of the Jesuits, can be proved by numerous instances. In the sixteenth century, Protestant as well as Catholic schools made Latin the principal subject matter of

[1] Professor Ramsay in *The Church in the Roman Empire before A. D. 170.* G. P. Putnam's Sons, 1893, p. VIII.

INTRODUCTION.

instruction, and the study of the mother tongue was well nigh neglected. In many Protestant schools the use of the Latin language in conversation, school exercises and dramatic performances was more strictly enforced than in Jesuit colleges, and those who spoke the vernacular were punished.[1] Should we not suppose that in Protestant and Jesuit schools the same reasons suggested the use of the Latin tongue? Some Protestant critics assign quite different reasons, but without proof. In a work published by order of the Prussian Ministry for Instruction,[2] we find the following: "The School System of Saxony of 1528 provided Latin schools pure and simple. Why? Because it demanded an extraordinary amount of time to make Latinists of German boys, so that little time and energy were left for other subjects. Melanchthon, for this reason, excluded even Greek from his plan of studies. As Latin, at that time, was the universal language of all Western Christendom, the official language of the Roman Church and of diplomatic intercourse, the language of the most celebrated code of laws, the only language of learning, mastery of this language was the first and indispensable condition for a career in Church and State, and for every participation in the higher intellectual life." However, when speaking of the great stress laid on Latin in the Jesuit schools, the same author does not hesitate to assert: "A more zealous cultivation of the mother tongue

---

[1] Paulsen, *Geschichte des gelehrten Unterrichts auf den deutschen Schulen und Universitäten vom Ausgang des Mittelalters bis zur Gegenwart*, p. 239. (2. ed. vol. I, p. 352.)

[2] *Deutschlands höheres Schulwesen im neunzehnten Jahrhundert*, von Professor Dr. Conrad Rethwisch. Berlin, 1893, p. 12.

would have opposed the Romish-international tendencies of the Order."[1] Here we must ask: Was not the Latin language, for Catholics as well as for Protestants, the language of learning, of diplomatic intercourse, of the most celebrated code of laws? And was not the mastery of this language, equally for the Catholics, the indispensable condition for a career in Church and State, and for every participation in the higher intellectual life? Consequently, the Jesuits had to insist on this language as well as the Protestants, and that for the very same reasons. Why, then, impute to them other motives of rather a suspicious character?

Nor are scholarly works of prominent American writers free from similar misstatements. Dr. Russell, Dean of Teachers' College, Columbia University, writes: "Catholic and Protestant schools alike at the beginning of the seventeenth century, gave little heed to the substance of the ancient civilization. Both alike were earnestly devoted to the study of the Latin language — the Jesuits, because it was the universal speech of their Order; the Protestants, because it was the first step towards a knowledge of Holy Writ."[2] No proof is given to substantiate the discrimination between Protestants and Catholics. Latin was, as

[1] *Ib.*, p. 2. There it is also stated that "the greatest Greek authors were all excluded from the Jesuit schools, and that the mother tongue and its literature received some attention for the first time in the Revised Ratio of 1832." How utterly false these assertions are will appear from later chapters of this book. Suffice it to state here that among the Greek authors studied in Jesuit schools were Homer, Sophocles, Euripides, Demosthenes, etc. See below chapter XIII, § 1, 4—5. On the study of the mother tongue see chapter IV.

[2] *German Higher Schools*, New York, 1899, p. 50.

Dr. Rethwisch affirms, "the universal language of all Western Christendom," not only the universal speech of the Order of Jesuits. Besides, as the Catholics used extensively the Latin Vulgate of the Bible, the study of Latin was for them much more than for the Protestants "the first step towards a knowledge of Holy Writ."

Lack of sympathy is the least unworthy reason assignable for President Eliot's grouping of only Jesuits and Moslems as the upholders of prescribed courses. Have not all European countries prescribed courses that resemble the system of the Jesuits incomparably more than President Eliot's electivism? Germany, for instance, although it offers various schools: classical (*Gymnasium*), Latin-scientific (*Real-Gymnasium*), scientific (*Real-Schule*), has within these schools strictly uniform curricula.[1] And yet American educators do not hesitate to say that "the organization of the higher school system, especially in Prussia, is worthy of general imitation;" that "for many years American educators have drawn professional inspiration from German sources;" that "the experience of Germany can teach us much, if we will but learn to consider it aright;" and that "*a uniform course of study for all schools of a particular grade, and a common standard for promotion and graduation, can be made most serviceable* in a national scheme of education."[2]

[1] It is only since 1901 that, in the three middle classes of the Gymnasium, English may be taken as an alternative for Greek; in the three highest classes Greek remains obligatory. Besides in these three classes English or French may be taken (just as in many Jesuit Colleges in this country French or German is obligatory).

[2] Dr. Russell, *l. c.*, pp. V, 409, 422. (Italics are ours.)— See also *Report of the Commissioner of Education*, 1888—1889,

Why then mention only Jesuits and Moslems? Considering the esteem in which German schools and scholarship are held by many, it would evidently have produced little effect to have said: "Moslems, the Jesuits and the Germans have prescribed courses."

Many writers on education have been misled in their estimate of the Jesuit system by blindly accepting and uncritically repeating the censures of a few authors who, deservedly or not, have acquired a reputation as pedagogical writers. Thus Quick, in numerous passages of his *Educational Reformers*, pays a high tribute to the Jesuit system. In a few places, especially in one paragraph, he finds fault with it. In some American works [1] we find this one paragraph quoted as Quick's judgment on the Jesuit system, and not a word is said of his hearty approbation of most points of that system. It is also most unfortunate that American teachers and writers on education place so much confidence in the productions of M. Compayré, especially his *History of Pedagogy*. For many reasons this work must be called a most unreliable source of

Vol. I, pp. 32—74, especially pp. 70 foll. where it is stated that "the superiority of German public schools over those of other nations has been acknowledged repeatedly." In another place of the same Report (1891—92), Vol. I, p. 140, the words of Dr. Joynes of the University of S. C. are quoted: "Germany has now become the schoolmistress of the world."

[1] So in the histories of education by Painter and Seeley. — I wish to state here that of all American text-books on the history of education the latest, the *History of Education*, by Professor Kemp, (Philadelphia, Lippincott, 1902) is the most impartial. The chapter on the Jesuits (XVIII.) is singularly free from the misrepresentations which are so numerous in other text-books. In one point, however, regarding "emulation," the author is mistaken. See below, ch. XVI, § 4.

information.[1] In the chapter on the Jesuits in particular, there are not many sentences which do not contain some misstatement. Whereas nearly all writers, even those most hostile to the Society, acknowledge at least a few good points in its educational system, Compayré cannot admit therein a single redeeming feature. The Jesuits are blamed alike in their failures and in their successes. It is sad to think that from such untrustworthy sources American teachers largely derive their information about the educational labors of the Jesuits and of Catholics in general. Can we wonder that so many prejudices prevail against Jesuit education, of which many know only an ugly caricature?

Indeed, lack of sufficient knowledge is at the root of most censures of the educational principles and methods of the Society. In nearly every case of adverse criticism, it is apparent that a scholarly examination of the official documents has been dis-

[1] Br. Azarias calls this work a "condensation of all virulence and hatred against everything Catholic, but ill concealed beneath a tone of philosophic moderation." *American Ecclesiastical Review*, 1890, p. 80. foll. — Another critic said recently of M. Compayré: "He misquotes and suppresses, blinded, I suppose, by a bad form of Anti-Jesuit disease. You can certainly learn from his book the fury of that malady. In France, one may fairly say, M. Compayré is recognized as meaning to attack the beliefs of Christian pupils, and as ranging himself essentially on the side of those who wish 'to eliminate the hypothesis of God' from the education of children." (This opinion was expressed in a resolution of five hundred teachers in a meeting at Bordeaux in 1901.) Mr. Stockley, of the University of New Brunswick, in the *American Ecclesiastical Review*, July 1902, p. 44. — See also the criticism of Father Poland, S. J., in the *American Catholic Quarterly Review*, January 1902.

pensed with, and that the oft-refuted calumnies of virulent partisan pamphlets have simply been repeated. Or have the assailants of the educational system of the Jesuits carefully studied the original sources: the *Fourth Part of the Constitutions*, the *Ratio Studiorum*, and the numerous other documents of the Society, treating of its educational system? Or have they themselves studied in Jesuit colleges? Have their children, relatives or friends been Jesuit pupils? Have they been sufficiently acquainted with Jesuit teachers? If not, is it fair and conscientious criticism to condemn a system about which they possess no reliable information whatever? If now-a-days one writes on the philosophy of India, on the doctrine of Zoroaster, or on the education of the Greeks and Romans, he adorns his books with an elaborate scientific apparatus. He studies the original languages or consults the best translations and commentaries, and spares no pains to let the reader know that he has drawn from trustworthy sources. How much more care should be taken if, not philosophic systems or nations of a far-off past, but a living institution is concerned? No matter how much opposed it may be to the critic's views, fair treatment and justice should never be denied, even if all sympathy is withheld. But a few years ago a Protestant writer in Germany, reviewing Father Duhr's work on the educational system of the Society, recommended the work most earnestly to the Protestant educators; for, as he said, "even our scholarly works on education betray a shocking ignorance in regard to everything pertaining to the Jesuits."[1] It

---

[1] *Central-Organ für die Interessen des Realschulwesens*, Berlin.

is needless to say that this remark has an application for America and England.

The study of this system cannot be without interest to those who devote themselves to educating youth. During the two centuries preceding the suppression of the Order, this system exerted a world-wide influence on hundreds of thousands of pupils, and, although in a lesser degree, does so at present.[1] In 1901 the Jesuits imparted a higher education to more than fifty-two thousand youths, of which number seven thousand two hundred belong to this country. The educational work of the Jesuits produced most brilliant results in former centuries and received most flattering commendations from Protestant scholars and rulers, and from atheistic philosophers.

However, the study of the Ratio Studiorum is not only of historical interest. Protestant writers admit that a close examination of the Jesuit system may teach the educators of our age many valuable lessons. According to Quick "it *is* a system, a system built up by the united efforts of many astute intellects and showing marvellous skill in selecting means to attain a clearly conceived end. There is then in the history of education little that should be more interesting or might be more instructive to the master of an English public school than the chapter about the Jesuits."[2] Davidson, in spite of some severe strictures, is not less convinced of the advantages which may be derived

---

[1] Quick prefers to speak of the Jesuit schools as "things of the past." Compayré thinks otherwise: "They are more powerful than is believed; and it would be an error to think that the last word is spoken with them." Quick, *Educ. Ref.*, p. 35, note.

[2] *Educational Reformers*, p. 59.

from the study of Jesuit education: "While it is impossible for lovers of truth and freedom to have any sympathy with either the aim or matter of Jesuit education, there is one point connected with it that well deserves our most serious consideration, and that is its success. This was due to three causes, *first*, to the single-minded devotion of the members of the Society; *second*, to their clear insight into the needs of their times; *third*, to the completeness with which they systematized their entire course, in view of a simple, well-defined aim. In all these matters we can well afford to imitate them. Indeed, the education of the present day demands just the three conditions which they realized."[1]

For many the study of one of the old systems may be the greatest novelty. So much is said now-a-days about the new pedagogy and modern psychology, that it might appear as if the past had been utterly ignorant of the true nature of the child and of the rational methods of education. Still the writer hopes to establish that, what the ablest educators, even of our own age, have pronounced *essential* for the training of the young, is contained in the educational system of the Jesuits. It is not claimed that this system is perfect. No educational system can be found which, both in plan and execution, is without defects. The Society of Jesus has never denied the possibility and necessity of improvements in its educational system; nor has it ever claimed that the Ratio Studiorum, in every detail was to be applied to all countries and to all ages. Changes were made in the course of time;

[1] *A History of Education* (New York, Scribner's Sons, 1900), p. 187.

INTRODUCTION.

and in many passages of the Ratio Studiorum it is expressly stated that the Superiors are empowered to make these changes, according to the demands of time and place. Thus the teaching of the Jesuits varies considerably in different countries, without necessitating any change in the Order's legislation on education.

A biographer of the founder of the Society says with reference to the educational system of the Order: "*It is a plan which admits of every legitimate progress and perfection*, and what Ignatius said of the Society in general, may be applied to its system of studies in particular, namely, that it ought to suit itself to the times and comply with them, and not make the times suit themselves to it."[1] The advice of St. Ignatius is undoubtedly of vital importance to the Order, if now and in future it wants to do the work for which it was instituted. In fact, the versatility of the Jesuits has become proverbial and a reproach to the Order; they are said to be so shrewd and cunning that, among those hostile to the Order, the very word "Jesuit" has come to mean the incarnation of craft and subtlety. Is it probable that the Jesuits on a sudden have utterly forgotten the all-important injunction of their founder? Is it probable that they who are said to be most ambitious and most anxious of success, have so little suited themselves to the times, as to leave their method of teaching unchanged for centuries? Is it possible that the men who, as Davidson says, had such "a clear insight into the needs of their times" do not adapt their system to the needs of our age? Or is their system not capable of being suited to modern times? This indeed is the favorite objection raised

[1] Genelli, *Life of St. Ignatius*, part II, ch. VII.

now-a-days. "The Ratio Studiorum is antiquated and difficult to reform... For nearly three centuries they [the Jesuits] were the best schoolmasters of Europe; they revolutionized instruction as completely as Frederick the Great modern warfare, and have thus acted, whether they meant it or not, as pioneers of human progress... Whatever may have been the service of the Jesuits in past times, we have little to hope for them in the improvement of education at present. Governments have, on the whole, acted wisely by checking and suppressing their colleges."[1] At any rate, the study of a system which for "centuries furnished the best schoolmasters of Europe and completely revolutionized instruction", must be interesting for the student of the history of education. For this reason we first present the history, or the development, of this system. In the second part we shall explain its principles, its theory and practice, with special reference to modern educational views.

[1] Oscar Browning in the *Encyclopedia Britannica*, article: *"Education"*.

PART FIRST.

History of the Educational System of the Society of Jesus.

CHAPTER II.

Education before the Foundation of the Society of Jesus.

The following remarkable passage is taken from the work of one who cannot be charged with partiality to the Jesuits, — I mean Frederick Paulsen, a professor of the University of Berlin, the author of the great "History of Higher Education."[1] In this work, after having described the marvellous success which the Jesuits achieved in the sixteenth century, the author asks: "What was the secret source of the power of these men? Was it that they were 'men filled with wickedness', as Raumer styles them? Or was it that they were more cunning, more unscrupulous than the rest? No, this would ascribe to lying and deceit more than it can do. . . . There is in the activity of the Order something of the quiet, yet irresistible, manner of working which we find in the forces of nature. Certainty and superiority characterize every move-

[1] *Geschichte des gelehrten Unterrichts auf den deutschen Schulen und Universitäten vom Ausgang des Mittelalters bis zur Gegenwart.* Leipzig, 1885, p. 281 foll. (2. ed. I, p. 408.)

ment. . . . Whence does the Order derive this power? I think it can arise only from a great idea, not from base and selfish desires. Now the root idea which animated all the members of this Society, and which inspired them with enthusiasm, was that their Order was the chosen instrument for saving the Church; that they were the knights, the champions, of the ruler of the Church, ready, if God should so will it, to fall as first victims in the great battle against a heathen and heretical world. . . . Lasting results cannot be achieved by an idea unless it is embodied in some external system. The system of the Society of Jesus, from the fundamental principles to the minutest details of discipline, is admirably fitted and adapted to its ends. The greatest possible power of the individual is preserved without derangement of the organism of the Order; spontaneous activity and perfect submission of the will, contrasts almost irreconcilable, seem to have been harmoniously united in a higher degree by the Society than by any other body."

These remarks of the Berlin Professor were made with special reference to the educational system of the Society, as laid down in the Ratio Studiorum. Years before another German Protestant had spoken similarly on the same subject. Ranke, in his *History of the Popes*, admits that the Jesuits were very successful in the education of youth, but he claims that this success can scarcely be credited to their learning or their piety, but rather to the exactness and nicety of their methods. He finds in their system a combination of learning with untiring zeal, of exterior pomp with strict asceticism, of unity of aim with unity of government, such as the world has never witnessed before or since.

EDUCATION BEFORE FOUNDATION OF THE SOCIETY. 19

Now-a-days a great interest is taken in the historical aspects of educational systems. The first question, then, which presents itself is: From what sources did the Jesuits derive the principles and methods by which they were enabled to obtain such success? It is evident that the Jesuit system was not altogether the original work of a few clever men who produced a system with methods previously unheard of; their Ratio Studiorum was, to a great extent, a prudent adaptation and development of methods which had existed before the foundation of the Order. It has frequently been maintained that all, or at least much, of what is good in the Ratio Studiorum, was drawn from the famous *Plan of Studies* of John Sturm, the zealous Protestant reformer and schoolman of Strasburg. Dr. Russell is convinced of this fact, when he writes: "Sturm could have received no greater compliment than was paid him by the Society of Jesus in incorporating so many of his methods into the new Catholic schools."[1] Indeed, Sturm himself expressed in 1565 the suspicion that the Jesuits had drawn from his sources.[2] As we shall see in the next chapters, both Sturm and Ignatius of Loyola drew, in all likelihood, from the same sources, namely, the traditions of the great University of Paris and the humanistic schools of the Netherlands.

It is a very common error to argue: *post hoc, ergo propter hoc*. Anything good found after the Protestant Reformation of the sixteenth century, is by many writers directly ascribed to its influence. Thus it is said that, after the Protestants had awakened a zeal

[1] *German Higher Schools*, p. 47.
[2] "*Ut a nostris fontibus derivata esse videatur.*" See Duhr, *Studienordnung*, p. 7.

for learning, the Jesuits determined to avail themselves of this zeal in the interest of the Catholic Church, and to combat the Reformation with its own weapon.[1] To the same purpose Dr. Russell writes: "The Jesuits in employing schools to check the growth of heresy and to win back to the Church apostate Germany, merely borrowed the devil's artillery to fight the devil with. And they used it to good effect."[2] Two serious errors are at the root of such statements: First, it is taken for granted that the Society of Jesus was instituted directly against Protestantism, and that it used schools and learning only to counteract this movement. In the next chapter we shall prove that this view of the Society is entirely unhistorical. The second error underlying this view is the implicit belief that, before the Protestant Reformation, education was at a very low ebb, and that there existed little, if any, zeal for learning. In order to understand the rise and progress of the educational system of the Jesuits and its dependence on other schools, it will be necessary to sketch the status of education in Western Christendom before the foundation of the Society of Jesus. This sketch must be very imperfect and fragmentary in a work like the present. Besides, there exists as yet no history of education in the Middle Ages which can be considered as satisfactory, although some valuable monographs on the subject have appeared within the past few years.[3]

[1] *American Cyclopedia* (ed. 1881), article: "*Education*".
[2] *L. c.*, p. 47. — So also Seeley, *History of Education*, p. 182.
[3] The following works are the chief ones consulted: Paulsen, *Geschichte des gelehrten Unterrichts auf den deutschen Schulen und Universitäten vom Ausgang des Mittel-*

§ 1. Schools at the Close of the Middle Ages.

The intellectual darkness of the Middle Ages has been long a favorite theme for popular writing. Many have had the fixed notion that the Church, afraid of progress, ever set her face against the enlightenment of the people, but that at length her opposition was beaten down by the craving for knowledge aroused by the principles of the Reformation, and that, in consequence of the break with Rome, various schools at once arose in Protestant countries. Such popular declamations have been disavowed by all honest Protestant historians.[1] They admit that, what may be called the darkness of these centuries, was owing to the political and social conditions of the nations after the Northern barbarians had nearly annihilated ancient civilization, but not to any hostility of the Church against learning and education. "The grossest ignorance of the Dark Ages," says an English historian, "was not due to the strength of the ecclesiastical system, but to its weakness. The improvement of education formed a prominent object with every zealous churchman and every ecclesiastical reformer from the days of Gregory the Great to the days when the darkness passed away under the influence of the

alters bis zur Gegenwart. Leipzig 1885. — Specht, *Geschichte des Unterrichtswesens in Deutschland bis zur Mitte des dreizehnten Jahrhunderts.* Stuttgart, Cotta, 1885. — Janssen, *History of the German People,* London, Kegan Paul, 1896, vol. I. — Gasquet, *The Eve of the Reformation,* New York, Putnam's Sons, 1900. — Rashdall, *Universities of Europe in the Middle Ages.* 2 vols. Oxford 1895. — See also West, *Alcuin and the Rise of the Christian Schools.* New York, Scribner's Sons, 1892. (The *Great Educators Series.*)

[1] See Maitland, *The Dark Ages.*

22   JESUIT EDUCATION.

ecclesiastical revival of the eleventh and twelfth centuries."[1]

In another passage of his great work the same author says of education before the Reformation : "It may be stated with some confidence that, at least in the later middle age, the smallest towns and even the larger villages possessed schools where a boy might learn to read and to acquire the first rudiments of ecclesiastical Latin, while, except in very remote and thinly populated regions, he would never have to go far to find a regular grammar school. That the means of reading, writing and the elements of Latin were far more widely diffused than has sometimes been supposed, is coming to be generally recognized by students of medieval life."[2]

It is now not only acknowledged that much was done for the education of the people, but also that all education during the Middle Ages proceeded from the Church.[3] Nothing but prejudice or ignorance of the

[1] Rashdall, *Universities of Europe in the Middle Ages*, vol. I, p. 27.
[2] *Universities of Europe in the Middle Ages*, vol. II, p. 602.
[3] Paulsen, *Geschichte des gelehrten Unterrichts*, p. 11.— Professor Harnack of the University of Berlin, speaking of the achievements of the Roman Church, says: "In the first place it educated the Romano-Germanic nations, and educated them in a sense other than that in which the Eastern Church educated the Greeks, Slavs, and Orientals..... It brought Christian civilization to young nations, and brought it, not once only, so as to keep them at its first stage — no! it gave them something which was capable of exercising a progressive educational influence, and for a period of almost a thousand years it itself led the advance. Up to the fourteenth century it was a leader and a mother; it supplied the ideas, set the aims, and disengaged the forces." The same

EDUCATION BEFORE FOUNDATION OF THE SOCIETY. 23

past can raise any doubts about the merits of the Church in the field of education. We cannot narrate what the Church has done to advance popular education in the earlier Middle Ages. Numerous councils, — for instance, those of Orange in France (529), Constantinople (680), Aix-la-Chapelle (802),[1] Mentz (813), Rome (826 and 1179), — exhorted the clergy to instruct the children, "without accepting anything beyond a compensation the parents should offer freely," as Bishop Arbyton of Basle (died in 821) writes. From the twelfth century on the number of schools increased considerably.[2]

Much more evidence is available about the schools of the closing Middle Ages. A great deal of it is published in the well-known *History of the German People* by Janssen.[3] Although compulsory education was unknown, we learn from many records, preserved in towns and villages, that the schools were well attended. In the little town of Wesel there were, in 1444, five teachers employed to instruct the children in reading, writing, arithmetic, and choir-singing. In the district of the Middle Rhine, in the year 1500,

author admits that even at present the Catholic Church has an important share in the movement of thought. *What is Christianity?* (Putnam's Sons, New York, 1901.) Lecture XIV, p. 247. — Well has Cardinal Newman said: "Not a man in Europe now, who talks bravely against the Church, but owes it to the Church, that he can talk at all." *Historical Sketches*, vol. III, p. 109.

[1] On the schools of Charles the Great and of the centuries following see Specht, *Geschichte des Unterrichtswesens.* — West, *Alcuin and the Rise of Christian Schools.*
[2] See Specht, *op. cit.* — Russell, *German Higher Schools.*
[3] Vol. I. (English translation), pp. 25—60.

there were whole stretches of country where a "people's school" was to be found within a circuit of every six miles. Small parishes even of five or six hundred souls were not without their village schools.[1] The Protestant historian Palacky stated that, while examining documents in the archives of Bohemia, he took note of all the teachers whose names he happened to come across, and found that about the year 1400 the diocese of Prague must have had at least 640 schools. Taking this for the average, the 63 dioceses then existing in Germany would have possessed the respectable number of over 40,000 elementary or primary schools.[2]

This conjecture may not be very accurate, but the evidence furnished by contemporary documents at least goes a great way to show that the number of schools was very large. The latter part of the Middle Ages was the time in which the burning zeal for learning led to the invention of the art of printing, and this art in turn still further increased the desire to learn and facilitated the work of education. In a pamphlet printed in Mentz, in 1498, it was said: "Everybody now wants to read and to write." In the light of such facts, who does not see the absurdity of the assertion of Compayré and other writers that the primary school, whether Catholic or Protestant, is the child of the Reformation?[3] Towards the end of the

---

[1] *Ib.*, pp. 26—27.

[2] At present the number of elementary schools in Germany is less than 60,000; there were 56,563 in 1892.

[3] "In its origin, the primary school is the child of Protestantism, and its cradle was the Reformation." Compayré, *History of Pedagogy*, p. 112. — Similarly Professor Beyschlag of Halle.

fifteenth century good and respectable parents, at least in Germany, began to consider it their duty to let their children acquire an education. This interest in education naturally led to the establishment of many new schools. Complaints are even made in some cities that too many schools are opened. The facts given so far prove also that it is not correct to say that the German "people's school" did not assume the shape of a school for the masses until the Reformation,[1] or that medieval culture was but for the few, and that it was Luther who brought the schoolmaster into the cottage.[2] Otherwise who frequented the numerous schools in towns and villages, where "everybody wanted to read and to write"?

What is now called "secondary education" was not as strictly distinguished from elementary and university training as it is now-a-days. From very early times higher education was cared for in numerous schools connected with monasteries and cathedrals. The merits of the Order of St. Benedict in preserving the treasures of classical literature are universally acknowledged. Its monks were not only the great clearers of land in Europe, at once missionaries and laborers, but also the teachers of the nations rising from barbarism to civilization.

Benedictine monasticism gave the world almost its only houses of learning and education, and constituted by far the most powerful civilizing agency in Europe, until it was superseded as an educational instrument by the growth of the universities. The period that

[1] *Report of the Commissioner of Education*, 1888—89, vol. I, p. 32.
[2] *Encyclopedia Britannica*, article: "Education."

intervenes between the time of Charlemagne and the eleventh century has been well styled the Benedictine age. And before that period the numerous monastic schools of Ireland had been frequented by so many holy and learned men as justly to win for that country the title of *Insula Sanctorum et Doctorum*, the Island of Saints and Scholars.[1] In general, careful historical research by modern scholars presents a picture of the medieval monks quite different from that given by the author of Ivanhoe and by other imaginative "misdescribers", according to whom the monk was, if not a hypocritical debauchee, at the least a very ignorant and very indolent person.

We have to sketch chiefly the condition of education at the close of the Middle Ages. It is scarcely necessary to speak of Italy which, in the fourteenth and fifteenth centuries, was the intellectual centre of Europe and at that time exhibited a literary activity such as no other period of history has ever witnessed. For it was in Italy that the *renaissance* began. This mighty movement, which marks the transition of the Middle Ages to modern times, effected a revolution in literature, science, art, life and education. From Italy it swept on over Europe and caused similar changes everywhere. What is called the classical education is the immediate outcome of the Italian Renaissance. During the first half of the fifteenth century there lived in Northern Italy one of the ablest and most amiable educators in the history of all ages: Vittorino da

---

[1] See *Ireland's Ancient Schools and Scholars*, by the Most Rev. John Healy, D. D. — Newman, *Historical Sketches*, vol. III, pp. 116—129.

Feltre.[1] He modified considerably the medieval school system of the *Trivium* and *Quadrivium*. Although the classics, carefully selected, formed the groundwork of his course, other branches, as mathematics and philosophy, were not neglected. Due attention was devoted to the physical development of the pupils, and riding, fencing, and other gymnastic exercises were greatly encouraged. Vittorino lived among his pupils like a father in his family, revered and beloved. Poor scholars were not only instructed, but also fed, lodged, and clothed gratuitously. The secret of his wonderful influence lay in his lofty moral principles and his deeply religious spirit. In his calling he recognized a noble mission to which he devoted himself zealously and exclusively, without seeking anything for himself. His contemporaries called him the "Saintly Master". His virginal purity charmed all who came into contact with him. Although not a priest, he daily recited the Divine office, frequently approached the sacraments and accustomed his pupils to receive holy communion monthly and to hear mass daily. This great educator's fame spread far and wide, and eager youths flocked to him even from France, Germany and other countries. Many customs and practices found in humanistic schools north of the Alps may have been copied from Vittorino's famous school. It is certain that his influence was felt in England, for one of his pupils, Antonio Beccaria, was secretary and "translator" of Duke Humphrey of Gloucester, the first patron of the new

---

[1] Pastor, *History of the Popes*, vol. I, pp. 44–46. — Woodward, *Vittorino da Feltre and other Humanist Educators*, N. Y., Macmillan.

learning in England,[1] and the celebrated school of Winchester, founded by Bishop Langdon, was, in all probability, modeled after that of Vittorino.[2]

It is almost superfluous to mention the keen interest in learning manifested by the Italian ecclesiastics of this period. They raised to the papacy the book-lover and enthusiastic student, Parentucelli; and he, as Nicholas V. (1447-1455), placed himself at the head of the great movement of the renaissance, and won immortal renown by founding the Vatican Library, where the glorious monuments of Greek and Roman intellect were collected under the protection of the Holy See. The second successor of Nicholas V. was Aeneas Sylvius (Pius II.), famous as a humanist scholar and author. But it is impossible here to enumerate all the ardent promoters of learning among the popes, cardinals and other church dignitaries of this time. So large a part of a churchman's life did learning occupy in Italy, that no prelate considered his household complete without a retinue of scholars.[3] — We cannot here trace the gradual spread of this mighty movement into other countries, but must confine ourselves to the bare mention of a few facts regarding the educational conditions.

What has often been said respecting the ignorance prevailing in Scotland before the Reformation, has been repudiated by the researches of Protestant historians, such as Burton, Lawson, Edgar, and others. It has been proved that this country, throughout the

[1] Einstein, *The Italian Renaissance in England* (New York, the Columbia University Press, 1902), p. 4.
[2] *Ib.*, p. 53.
[3] *Ib.*, p. 20.

latter part of the Middle Ages, possessed an abundance of educational facilities. We find here even an interesting example of *compulsory higher education*. At the instance of the clergy, in 1470, an act of parliament was passed providing that all barons and freeholders should, under penalty of twenty pounds, send their sons at the age of nine or ten years to the schools, to remain there until they had acquired a competent knowledge of Latin. They were then to attend the schools of art and law.[1]

As regards secondary schools in England, it used to be commonly asserted that Edward VI., the first monarch of the Reformed Faith, was the great founder and reformer.[2] Upwards of thirty free grammar schools founded at this time have permanently associated the reign of Edward VI. with popular education. The Schools Inquiring Commission in 1886 went further, and set down fifty-one schools to the credit of Edward. Modern historical research has broken, stick by stick, the whole bundle of old misrepresentations. "The fact is that the whole theory about the dearth of grammar schools and other schools still more elementary is a mere delusion. The immense prestige that Edward VI. has acquired as a patron of education is simply due to the fact that he refounded out of confiscated Church property some small percentage of schools which he and his rapacious father had destroyed. The probability is that England was far

[1] Bellesheim, *History of the Catholic Church of Scotland*, vol. II, pp. 326, 346.
[2] See the article: *Medieval Grammar Schools*, in the *Dublin Review*, 1899, vol. CXXV, pp. 153-178.

better provided with grammar schools before the Reformation than it has ever been since."[1]

This startling statement has been confirmed by a careful study of the records of the time of Henry VIII. and Edward VI., from which it is clear that at least two hundred grammar schools must have been in existence before Edward came to the throne. Mr. Leach raises the number by the addition of another hundred, and says that three hundred is a moderate estimate for the year 1535;[2] and this number is exclusive of elementary schools and universities. It will suffice to mention a few names of famous schools: Canterbury, Lincoln, Wells, York, Beverly, Chester, Southwell, Winchester, Eton, the school of Dean Colet in London, and the numerous schools attached to the monasteries. In regard to the great number of foundation schools established just after the Reformation, Professor Thorold Rogers maintains that it was not a new zeal for learning, but a very inadequate supply of that which had been so suddenly and disastrously destroyed.[3]

During the period immediately preceding the Reformation, England possessed a great number of distinguished scholars, most of whom were ecclesiastics. The revival of letters was heartily welcomed by the clergy. The chief ecclesiastics of the day, as Wolsey, Warham, Fisher, Tunstall, Langton, Stokesley, Fox,

[1] The Rev. Hastings Rashdall, *Harrow School*, chap. II, p. 12. (*Dublin Review*, *l. c.*, p. 156.)
[2] *English Schools at the Reformation*, p. 6; (*l. c*, p. 157).
[3] *Six Centuries of Work and Wages*, vol. I, p. 165. (*Dublin Review*, *l. c.*, p. 162.)

Selling, Grocyn, Whitford, Linacre, Colet, Pace, William Latimer, and numerous others, were not only ardent humanists, but thorough and practical churchmen.[1]

Similar conditions existed on the European continent. The Latin City Schools towards the close of the Middle Ages were numerous throughout Germany.[2] About this time, the intellectual condition of the people in Germany, the Netherlands and France was most beneficially influenced by the "Brethren of the Common Life". Founded by Gerard Groot of Deventer, this fraternity at first was employed in the transcription of books, all profane studies being prohibited. They were supposed to restrict themselves exclusively to the reading of the Scriptures and the Fathers, not wasting their time over "such vanities as geometry, arithmetic, rhetoric, logic, grammar, lyric poetry, and judicial astrology."[3] These principles were extreme, and it is some consolation to find that the founder admitted the "wiser of the Gentile philosophers," such as Plato, Aristotle, and Seneca. In 1393, a little scholar, Thomas Hammerken of Kempen, Rhineland, entered the school of Deventer; he was no other than the famous Thomas a Kempis, most probably the author of the *Following of Christ*.

Shortly after the death of Gerard Groot (1384), the labors of the Brethren were made to embrace a wider sphere, and especially to include the education of

[1] Einstein, *The Italian Renaissance in England*, pp. 18-57. — Gasquet, *The Eve of the Reformation*, pp. 36-50.
[2] On their character see *Report of the Commissioner of Education*, 1897-98, vol. I, pp. 20-23.
[3] A. T. Drane, *Christian Schools and Scholars*, vol. II, p. 335.

youth. The prohibition against profane learning disappeared, Deventer became a most celebrated institution, and numerous schools were founded all over Flanders, France and Northern Germany. The settlements of the Brethren spread gradually along the Rhine as far as Suabia, and by the end of the fifteenth century they reached from the Scheldt to the Vistula, from Cambrai, through the whole of Northern Germany, to Culm in Prussia. In these schools, Christian education was placed high above mere learning, and the training of the young in practical religion and active piety was considered the most important duty. The whole system of instruction was permeated by a Christian spirit; the pupils learned to look upon religion as the basis of all human existence and culture, while at the same time they had a good supply of secular knowledge imparted to them, and they gained a genuine love for learning and study.[1] The Brethren had been established by John Standonch, doctor of the Sorbonne, in the *Collège de Montaigue* in the University of Paris.[2] The founder of the Society of Jesus studied in this college, and some suppose that the rules of the Poor Clerks, as they were often called, furnished Ignatius some ideas for his rules.[3] This much is certain, that Ignatius had imbibed the spirit of those Brethren from the study of the works of Thomas a Kempis. It is related that at the time when he wrote the Constitutions of his Order, he had no other books in his room except the New Testament and the Following of Christ.

[1] Janssen, *Hist. of the German People*, vol. I, ch. 3.
[2] Drane, *Christian Schools and Scholars*, vol. II, p. 339.
[3] This is for instance the opinion of Boulay, the historian of the University of Paris.

EDUCATION BEFORE FOUNDATION OF THE SOCIETY.

Youth eager for knowledge flocked from all parts to the schools of the Brethren. The number of scholars at Zwolle often rose to eight hundred or ten hundred; at Alkmaar to nine hundred; at Herzogenbusch to twelve hundred; and at Deventer, in the year 1500, actually to twenty-two hundred. Other celebrated Schools were at Liège and Louvain. The instruction being free in all these schools, they were open to students of the smallest means. In many of the towns also, where they had not started actual schools, the Brethren supplied teachers for the town schools, not unfrequently paid the expenses of the poorer scholars and supplied them with books, stationery and other school materials. In 1431 Pope Eugene sent orders to the bishops that they should prevent any interference with the beneficial work of these zealous educators. Pius II. and Sixtus IV. went even further in their support and encouragement. One of their most active patrons was Cardinal Nicholas of Cusa, renowned as a mathematician and the precursor of Copernicus. Nicholas himself had been educated at Deventer, and had given this school material support by a liberal endowment for the maintenance of twenty poor students.[1]

The schools of the Brethren had been among the first of those north of the Alps which introduced the revived study of classical literature. It was in these schools that Rudolphus Agricola, Alexander Hegius, Rudolph von Langen and Ludwig Dringenberg studied the revivers of the classical studies on German

---

[1] Janssen, *l. c.*, pp. 61-62. In most of these schools the Brethren had charge only of the religious training of the pupils, while the classical instruction was given by teachers not belonging to the Fraternity. Paulsen, *l. c.*, I, 158-160.

soil, — the fathers of the older German humanism.[1] Hegius, one of the greatest scholars of the century, was rector of the schools at Wesel, Emmerich and Deventer. Erasmus, a pupil of Deventer, ranks him among the restorers of pure Latin scholarship. Hegius enjoys the undisputed credit of having purged and simplified the school curriculum, improved the method of teaching, corrected the old text-books or replaced them by better ones. He also made the classics the staple of instruction of youth.[2] Together with Agricola, Erasmus and Reuchlin, he was foremost in propagating enthusiasm for Greek in Germany. Hegius emphasized the necessity of a knowledge of Greek for all sciences:

Qui Graece nescit, nescit quoque doctus haberi.
In summa: Grajis debentur singula doctis.[3]

In Alsace flourished the school of Schlettstadt, more important even than those on the Lower Rhine. It was one of the first of the German schools in which the history of the Fatherland was zealously studied side by side with the classics. Among its most distinguished pupils were Johannes von Dalberg, Geiler von Kaisersberg and Wimpheling. Dalberg was bishop of Worms and curator of the Heidelberg University, a liberal patron of all learned men, especially of Reuchlin, the great Greek and Hebrew scholar. This noble bishop was also the leader and director of the "Rhe-

[1] See Creighton, *History of the Papacy*, vol. V, chapter I: "Humanism in Germany."
[2] Janssen, *l. c.*, p. 68.
[3] Paulsen, *Geschichte des gelehrten Unterrichts*, p. 42, (vol. I, p. 67). Further details are given by Janssen, *History of the German People:* "The Higher Schools and the Older Humanists." (English translation, vol. I, pp. 61—85.)

nish Literary Society," founded in 1491, to which belonged a host of learned men,—theologians, lawyers, doctors, philosophers, mathematicians, linguists, historians and poets, from the Rhinelands and the Middle and Southwest of Germany. The object of this society, as of many similar ones existing at that time in Germany, was the encouragement and spread of science and the fine arts generally, and of classical learning in particular, as also the furthering of national historical research.[1]

Another great pupil of Schlettstadt was Geiler von Kaisersberg (died 1510), the Cathedral preacher of Strasburg, great not only as theologian and pulpit orator, but also as an ardent promoter of humanistic studies, a friend of the learned Benedictine Johannes Trithemius and of Gabriel Biel of Tübingen, and the leading spirit of a circle of highly gifted men on the Upper Rhine. The third great scholar of Schlettstadt was Wimpheling, called the "Teacher of Germany." As Hegius was the greatest German schoolmaster of his century, so Wimpheling was the most distinguished writer on matters educational, one of the most famous restorers of an enlightened system of education from a Christian point of view. In one of his writings, the *Guide for German Youth*, (1497), he forcefully points out the defects of the earlier system of education and lays down some golden rules for improvements, especially for mastering the ancient languages. It is the first work published on rational pedagogy and methodics in Germany, a truly national work. According to Wimpheling and other schoolmen of this time, the study of Latin and Greek should not be con-

[1] Janssen, *l. c.*, p. 107.

fined to the learning of the languages, but should be the means of strengthening and disciplining thought, true gymnastics of independent judgment.[1]

There are many names of great educators and scholars of this time which deserve at least to be mentioned: Pirkheimer in Nuremberg, Cochlaeus, professor of classics and director of the school of poetry in the same city, Murmellius, co-rector of the Cathedral school in Münster, Count Moritz von Spiegelberg, provost at Emmerich.

But we must leave this interesting subject, however reluctantly, and refer the reader to Janssen's first volume. From contemporary sources this author has drawn the following conclusions: "Outside the Mark of Brandenburg, there was scarcely a single large town in Germany in which, at the end of the fifteenth century, in addition to the already existing elementary national schools, new schools of higher grade were not built or old ones improved."[2] The control of these schools was in the hands of the Church, and most of the masters were clerics. School rates were unknown. The schools were kept up by frequent legacies; for the education of the young was counted among the works of mercy, to which money was liberally given in loyal obedience to the Church's doctrine of good works. Libraries were also founded in the same spirit.[3]

All over Europe we find, therefore, a great, yea

[1] *Ib.*, p. 80.
[2] *L. c.*, pp. 80—81. Erasmus wrote to Luiz Vives: "*In Germania tot fere sunt academiae quot oppida. Harum nulla paene est, quae non magnis salariis accersat linguarum professores.*" *Opera*, III, 689.
[3] Janssen, *l. c.*, p. 81.

enthusiastic, activity in the field of learning and education. The foremost promoters and patrons of this intellectual movement are everywhere ecclesiastics. This fact is so patent that an impartial American scholar wrote quite recently: "The patronage of learning which has always been one of the proudest boasts of the Catholic Church existed especially in the Renaissance, when a genuine love for it on the part of churchmen atoned for many other shortcomings. The higher clergy, moreover, were mostly university men whose scholarly interests had been awakened early in life, and who later were placed in a position to show their gratitude. A zeal for learning and the patronage of scholars became almost an affectation on the part of the higher clergy. . . . In all ranks of the Church an interest in the new learning was shown, even by those who were to leave the Roman faith, but who in their zeal for letters continued former traditions." [1]

It may be said, in general, that nowadays all scholarly and fair-minded Protestants, on the strength of incontestable historical evidence, repudiate the traditional views of the pre-Reformation period. Professor Hartfelder of Heidelberg unhesitatingly affirms that "from 1500—1520 Roman Catholic Europe presented the aspect of one large learned community." [2] Numerous similar statements can be quoted, but we must refer the reader to special works on this subject. [3] In the face of such undeniable facts it is unintelligible how certain writers can describe the close of the Middle Ages as an age of intellectual stagnation and degeneracy, or how Mr. Painter can say that shortly before

[1] Einstein, *l. c.*, pp. 51—54.
[2] Schmid, *Geschichte der Erziehung*, vol. II, 2, p. 140.
[3] See the present work, Appendix I, Additons to chap. II.

the Reformation learning had died out among the clergy, the schools were neglected, superstition and ignorance characterized the masses.[1] Is not the ignorance rather on the part of the so-called historians who make such sweeping indictments? The greatest and most glorious achievement of the medieval Church in the intellectual sphere are the universities. These institutions have been bequeathed to us by the Middle Ages, and they are of greater and more imperishable value even than its cathedrals.[2] The universities were, to a great extent, ecclesiastical institutions,[3] they were, at least, endowed with privileges from the Holy See. They were meant to be the highest schools not only of secular, but also of religious learning, and stood under the jurisdiction of the Church, as well as under her special protection.[4] It was through the privileges of the Church that the universities were raised from merely local into ecumenical organizations. The doctorate became an order of intellectual nobility, with as distinct and definite a place in the hierarchical system of medieval Christendom, as the priesthood and the knighthood. In fact the *Sacerdotium*, *Imperium*, and *Studium* are

[1] *History of Education*, pp. 135—136.
[2] Rashdall, *Universities of the Middle Ages*, vol. I, p. 5.
[3] Of the forty-four universities founded by charters before 1400, there are thirty-one which possess papal charters. Denifle, O. P., *Die Entstehung der Universitäten des Mittelalters bis 1400*, p. 780.
[4] On this subject see: Denifle, *l. c.*; Rashdall, *The Universities of Europe in the Middle Ages*, 2 vols. — *Dublin Review*, July 1898: *The Church and the Universities*, by J. B. Milburn. — Newman, *Rise and Progress of Universities*, in *Historical Sketches*, vol. III. — For further literature see Guggenberger, S. J., *A General History of the Christian Era*, vol. II, pp. 126—129.

the three great forces which energized those times and built up and maintained the mighty fabric of medieval Christendom. The University of Paris, the first school of the Church, with its four Nations, possessed something of the international character of the Church.[1] "It may with truth be said that in the history of human things there is to be found no grander conception than that of the Church in the fifteenth century, when it resolved, in the shape of the universities, to cast the light of knowledge abroad over the Christian world."[2] These are the testimonies of Protestant historians.

As the Benedictines in the earlier ages had been the most zealous educators, so, from the twelfth century on, the *friars* or *mendicants* took the most prominent part in university education. The greatest professors in philosophy and theology were friars; to the order of St. Francis belonged Alexander of Hales, St. Bonaventure, Roger Bacon, and Duns Scotus. The last mentioned was one of the profoundest and most original thinkers that the world has ever seen, and deservedly was styled the *Doctor subtilis*. Blessed Albertus Magnus, and Thomas Aquinas, "the Angelic Doctor and Prince of the Schools," were Dominicans. Albertus Magnus and Roger Bacon were far in advance of their time in the knowledge of mathematics and natural sciences. Mr. Rashdall compares Roger Bacon with his great namesake, Francis

---

[1] Rashdall, *l. c.*, vol. I, p. 546.
[2] Burton, *History of Scotland*, vol. IV, p. 109. (Bellesheim, *History of the Catholic Church of Scotland*, vol. II, p. 346.)

Bacon, and the comparison is decidedly in favor of the monk.[1]

There existed a considerable number of universities before the year 1400, chief among them were those of Paris, Bologna, Oxford and Cambridge, Salamanca, Prague, Vienna, Heidelberg, etc. From 1400 to the Reformation many new universities were founded in Western Christendom.[2] Twenty-six of those founded between 1400 and 1500 are still existing,[3] among them Würzburg, Leipsic, Munich, Tübingen, etc., in Germany; St. Andrew's, Glasgow, Aberdeen in Scotland; Upsala in Sweden; Copenhagen in Denmark, etc. In Germany alone nine were founded between 1456 and 1506.[4] But we need not dwell further on these universities, as any information that is sought can be easily gathered from the many books that are available on this subject.[5]

The intellectual activity of the universities of the Southern European countries was nowise inferior to that of Central and Northern Europe. In Portugal there was the University of Coimbra; in Spain, there were at least twelve universities before 1500,[6] the

[1] *L. c.*, vol. II, pp. 523—524.
[2] Compayré enumerates 75 universities existing in 1482, the year before Luther's birth. "Who could deny," he says, "after merely glancing over this long enumeration, the importance of the university movement in the last three centuries of the Middle Ages?" *Abelard*, pp. 50—52.
[3] See *Report of Com. of Ed.*, 1897-98, vol. II, p. 1741.
[4] Janssen, *l. c.*, vol. I, p. 86.
[5] Janssen, vol. I. — Compayré, *Abelard and the Origin and Early History of Universities* (Scribner's Sons, New York). — Rashdall, vol. II, pp. 211—280; on the universities of Poland, Hungary, Denmark, Sweden, and Scotland, pp. 283—315.
[6] See Rashdall, vol. II, pp. 65—107.

EDUCATION BEFORE FOUNDATION OF THE SOCIETY. 41

chief among them at Salamanca. Here flourished, shortly before the outbreak of the Reformation, the famous classical scholar, Peter Martyr, Prior of the Church of Granada. He and other scholars labored with such success for the higher education of the nobility, that no Spaniard was considered noble who showed any indifference to learning. Erasmus also declares that "the Spaniards had attained such eminence in literature, that they not only excited the admiration of the most polished nations of Europe, but served likewise as models for them."[1] Many belonging to the first houses of the nobility — once so high and proud — now made no hesitation to occupy chairs in the universities. Among others Don Gutierre de Toledo, son of the Duke of Alva and cousin of the King, lectured at Salamanca. Noble dames likewise vied with illustrious grandees for the prize of literary pre-eminence; while many even held chairs in the universities, and gave public lectures on eloquence and classical learning. Some of the names of these literary ladies have been preserved: the Marchioness of Montcagudo, Doña Maria Pacheco, and Queen Isabella's instructor in Latin, Doña Beatriz de Galindo, and others.[2] With such a zeal for knowledge the

[1] *Epist.* 977. (Hefele, *Life of Ximenez*, p. 115.)
[2] Hefele, *The Life of Cardinal Ximenez*, translated by the Rev. Canon Dalton, p. 115. — Rashdall remarks on this fact: "Salamanca is not perhaps precisely the place where one would look for early precedents for the higher education of women. Yet it was from Salamanca that Isabella, the Catholic, is said to have summoned Doña Beatriz Galindo to teach her Latin long before the Protestant Elizabeth put herself to school under Ascham." *Univ. in the M. A.*, vol. II, p. 79. The education of women was not so entirely neglected as is

old schools began to be filled, and the newly endowed Salamanca excelled them all. It was called the "Spanish Athens", and was said at one time to have seven thousand students. It was there that Peter Martyr gave lessons on Juvenal (1488), before such an immense audience that the entrance to the hall was completely blocked up and the lecturer had to be carried in on the shoulders of the students.[1] It should be mentioned to the credit of Salamanca that her Doctors encouraged the designs of Columbus, and that the Copernican system found early acceptance in its lecture rooms.[2]

In the beginning of the sixteenth century other schools for higher education were established at Toledo, Seville, Granada, Ognate, Ossuna, and Valencia. But all these schools were far excelled by the new university of Alcala, founded by Ximenez in 1500. It was so magnificent an establishment that the Spaniards called it the "eighth wonder of the world." The college of San Ildefonso was the head of the new university. Moreover, Ximenez founded several other institutions, adapted to all kinds of wants. Most renowned was the "College of Three Languages" for the study of Latin, Greek, and Hebrew. For poor young students in the classics, Ximenez endowed two boarding schools, where forty-two scholars were supported three years free of expense. The students attended the lectures given by the six professors of languages,

commonly believed. See Specht, *l. c.*, ch. XI, "*Education of Women.*" Further Janssen's *History of the German People*, vol. I, pp. 82—85.

[1] Prescott, *Ferdinand and Isabella*, Part I, ch. XIX.— Peter Martyr's *Epist.*, 57. — Hefele, p. 116.

[2] Rashdall, *l. c.*, vol. II, p. 77.

who were attached to the university; at their houses, however, special exercises were given and disputations held for fourteen days. Strict examinations were required before any one could be admitted to a higher class, or to a particular course of lectures on any science. All the regulations were followed by such great results that, according to Erasmus, Alcala was especially distinguished by its able philologists.[1] — The most splendid production of the philological and biblical activity of this university is the celebrated Complutensian Polyglot of the Bible. In 1526 Ignatius of Loyola, the future founder of the Society of Jesus, attended the University of Alcala; in 1527 we find him in Salamanca.

In connection with Alcala we must mention the greatest school of the Netherlands, the University of Louvain. Especially distinguished was its *Collegium Trilingue*, founded in 1516 by Busleiden, the friend of Erasmus and Thomas More. Busleiden had visited Alcala and wished to have in Louvain a college like that of the "Three Languages" at Alcala for the study of Latin, Greek, and Hebrew. *The famous universities of Alcala, Salamanca, Paris, and Louvain furnish the connecting link between the educational system of the Jesuits and that previous to the foundation of the Society.* But the great University of Paris was really the *Alma Mater* of St. Ignatius of Loyola. There also he won his first companions, chief among them Peter Faber and St. Francis Xavier. In 1529 and 1530 Ignatius visited the Netherlands. During its infancy several distinguished members of the Order were scholars from that country, as Peter Canisius, Francis

[1] *Epist.* 755. (Hefele, *l. c.*, p. 122.)

Coster, Peter Busaeus, John Theodore Macherentius, and others. The traditions of the University of Paris and of the humanistic schools of the Netherlands undoubtedly exerted a considerable influence on the Jesuit system of education. Before narrating the foundation of the Society and the development of its educational system, it is necessary to speak of two great movements, the *Renaissance* and the *Reformation*.

§2. Character of Medieval Education. The Renaissance.

Higher education in the Middle Ages followed the course known as the study of the "Seven Liberal Arts," divided into the *Trivium:* Grammar, Rhetoric, and Logic; and the *Quadrivium:* Arithmetic, Music, Geometry, and Astronomy.[1] If we read that "grammar" was studied for several years and that many confined their studies to this part of the course, we ought well to understand the meaning of this term. By grammar was not meant, as now, the mere study of the rules of a language, its etymology and syntax, but rather a scholarly acquaintance with the literature of that language, together with the power of writing and speaking it.[2] Rabanus Maurus, the greatest pupil of Alcuin and later on Archbishop of Mentz, defined grammar as "the science of interpreting poets and historians, as well as the science of the rules of speaking and writing." Latin was the principal subject of instruction, the favorite authors were Virgil and Ovid. Hugo of Trimberg, the master of a school at Bamberg,

---

[1] On the *Trivium* and *Quadrivium*, see West, *Alcuin and the Rise of the Christian Schools*, pp. 1–39.
[2] Newman, *Historical Sketches*, vol. II, p. 460.

about 1250, enumerates the following authors whom he read with his pupils: Virgil, Horace, Ovid, Juvenal, Persius, Statius, Homerus Latinus, Boethius, Claudian, Sedulius, Prudentius, and others.[1] Of prose authors are mentioned: Cicero, Seneca, Sallust, and others. The study of Greek is met with only very exceptionally before the Renaissance. Mathematics were taught, but it is difficult to say to what extent.

In the eleventh and twelfth centuries there was a revival of literary studies, which, however, was soon replaced by another movement, *scholasticism*. Through the Arabs and the Jews, Western Europe became acquainted with the entire *Logic of Aristotle* — hitherto only his *Organon* was known, and that in the Latin translation of Boethius, — with his *Dialectics, Physics, Metaphysics*, and *Ethics*.[2] Scientific inquiry in the universities began to move in another direction than heretofore. The methods of Aristotle were introduced into the schools; henceforth there was a more rigorous form of reasoning, a dialectic tendency, and a closer adherence to the syllogism; disputations were very common. A renewed study of the Fathers of the Church, and a more correct understanding of Aristotle inaugurated the most brilliant period of scholasticism (1230—1330).[3]

[1] On the authors studied or known during the Middle Ages see Comparetti, *Virgil in the Middle Ages*. — Boutaric, *Vincent de Beauvais et la connaissance de l'antiquité classique au treizième siècle*, in *Revue des Questions Historiques*, vol. XVII, pp. 5—57. — An adequate history of the use of the classics during this period does not exist. A pretty full bibliography of monographs is given by Taylor, *The Classical Heritage of the Middle Ages*, pp. 363—365.

[2] Windelband, *A History of Philosophy*, p. 310.

[3] On Scholasticism see also Alzog, *History of the Church*, vol. II, pp. 728—784.

It cannot and need not be denied that the education imparted by the medieval scholastics was in many regards defective. It was at once too dogmatic and disputatious.[1] Literary studies were comparatively neglected; frequently too much importance was attached to purely dialectical subtleties. This education was one-sided, and a few great men of the age, as Roger Bacon, the great medieval scientist, and John of Salisbury, complained that scholasticism was too narrow.[2] The defects of scholasticism became especially manifest in the course of the fourteenth and fifteenth centuries, when much time and energy was wasted in discussing useless refinements of thought.

Another serious defect of medieval education was the lack of philological and historical criticism. This uncritical spirit has been well pointed out in the International Catholic Scientific Congress at Munich, 1900, by the distinguished Jesuit historian, Father Grisar. Speaking of the unwarranted traditions and pious legends that grew up during the Middle Ages, he says: "The age was really in infancy, so far as regular historical scientific instinct was concerned. As in other branches of knowledge, people lived on the good or bad tradition of former days, just as they had received it. . . . The scientific work of the whole epoch was devoted to those branches of knowledge that are most sublime in their matter and stand in closest relation to religion and Church. The age produced great and exceedingly acute theologians, philosophers and canonists, but in these very men the general absence of the historical sense, and of the criticism of facts, is

[1] See *Dublin Review*, 1899, vol. CXXIV, p. 340.
[2] Alzog, *l. c.*, vol. II, p. 783.

remarkable. It never occurs to them to question the heritage of traditions or the wonderful narratives that spring up. Rather in general they endeavor to find in their systems a place for the most incongruous statements without any question as to their foundation in fact."[1] This lack of criticism explains the general acceptance of such forgeries as the "Decretals of Pseudo-Isidorus", of the "Donation of Constantine", and of the works of "Pseudo-Dionysius Areopagita". The knowledge of antiquity was exceedingly vague and defective. Even such writers as Vincent of Beauvais, who wrote a cyclopedia of all branches of learning then known (the *Speculum Majus*), makes the most curious blunders. Thus Caesar's *Commentaries* he ascribes to Julius Celsus; Marcus Tullius Cicero he confounds with his brother Quintus, in saying that the great orator was a lieutenant of Caesar. Spurious works abound in his lists of ancient authors, whilst important works, as Cicero's *Epistles*, *De Oratore*, *Brutus*, etc., were unknown to him.[2]

Undoubtedly a reaction was inevitable and, at the same time, needed. It came in the *Renaissance*, or the *Revival of Learning*. However, this movement soon went to another extreme, to an enthusiasm for the ancient authors which was beyond the limits of reason. Thus humanism became not less one-sided than scholasticism had been. We shall see further on that the educational system of the Society is a combination of humanism and scholasticism. A thorough educa-

[1] Translation from *The Review*, St. Louis, May 23, 1901.
[2] See Boutaric, *Vincent de Beauvais et la connaissance de l'antiquité classique au treizième siècle*. (*Revue des Questions Historiques*, vol. XVII, pp. 5—57.)

tion in the classics is followed by a solid course of philosophy, mathematics, and natural sciences. Thus the shortcomings of both systems are effectively obviated.

Both terms: "renaissance" and "humanism", are apt to be misunderstood. If "humanism" means the true perception of man's nature and destiny, or truly humane feelings towards fellow-man and active humanitarian interest in his welfare, then the Middle Ages knew and practised humanism. Thus understood it is in no way different from the sublime principles laid down by the most humane of all teachers, the God-man Jesus Christ. If, however, it signifies a view of life and mankind which recognizes nothing but the purely natural man, which finds in the purely human its highest ideals and rejects the relation to the vision of a future beyond this life, then it was foreign to the medieval mind, as it is foreign to Christianity. For the religious, supernatural element was central in medieval life.[1] If "Revival of Learning" is meant to imply that the ancient classics were altogether unknown during the Middle Ages, it is a wrong conception. But should the word designate a more extensive study, and, above all, a more enthusiastic interest in classical learning which developed even into excessive admiration for antiquity, it is correctly applied to the period closing the Middle Ages.

At the time when scholasticism flourished most, Dante in his grand poem, which has been styled a "Poetical Summa Theologiae", represents the harmonious combination of scholastic and classic learn-

[1] Willmann, *Didaktik*, vol. I, p. 289.

ing.[1] In this immortal work classical antiquity and Christianity go hand in hand. Virgil is no less his teacher than is Thomas Aquinas, and his poetry is the beautiful expression of the union between faith and reason.[2] The whole humanistic movement which began soon after Dante, was not so much a change of the subject of learning as a change in the mental attitude towards these subjects.[3] This attitude assumed different shapes in various schools of humanists. Some of them, particularly the earlier humanists in Germany, combined enthusiasm for the classics with faithful allegiance to the Church; others assumed an attitude of indifference or scepticism towards Christianity; others again showed open hostility, not only against scholasticism, but against Christian dogma and morality. The one party, the more conservative humanists, admired the Greek and Roman writers, but looked upon the Sacred Scriptures as higher than all the wisdom of the ancients. Listen to Petrarch! "Let no subtlety of argument, no grace of speech, no renown ensnare us; they [the ancients] were but men, learned so far as mere human erudition can go, but

[1] The Vulgate is quoted or referred to more than 500 times; Aristotle more than 300; Virgil about 200; Ovid about 100; Cicero and Lucan about 30 and 40 each, etc. Taylor, *l. c.*, p. 365.

[2] Creighton, *History of the Popes*, vol. II, p. 332. — Baumgartner, *Geschichte der Weltliteratur*, vol. IV, p. 469.

[3] For the history of this movement see Pastor, *History of the Popes*, vols. I and V. — Burckhardt, *History of the Renaissance in Italy;* Symonds, *Renaissance in Italy;* A. Baumgartner, S. J., *Geschichte der Weltliteratur*, vol. IV, pp. 469–623. — On the Renaissance in England see Gasquet, *The Eve of the Reformation*, chapter II, and especially Einstein, *The Italian Renaissance in England.*

deserving of pity, inasmuch as they lacked the highest and ineffable gift. — Let us study philosophy so as to love wisdom. The real wisdom of God is Christ. — We must first be Christians. We must read philosophical, poetical, and historical works in such a manner that the Gospel of Christ shall ever find an echo in our hearts. Through it alone can we become wise and happy; without it, the more we have learned, the more ignorant and unhappy we shall be. On the Gospel alone, as upon the one immovable foundation, can human diligence build all true learning."[1]

Though Petrarch himself did not escape the influence of the dangerous elements contained in the writings of antiquity, still he never went so far as did his friend Boccaccio, whose writings breathe an atmosphere of pagan corruption. And yet not even this writer was an unbeliever, or an enemy to the Church.

As knowledge is good in itself and as its abuse never justifies its suppression, the Church considered the study of classical literature as a legitimate movement, productive of great fruit for spiritual and secular science. Thus we find so many ardent patrons of the new learning among the Popes and other ecclesiastical dignitaries. But there is a great danger in the one-sided enthusiasm for heathen literature. Everything depends on the manner in which the ancient authors are read and employed in education. They must be read and interpreted in the spirit of the Christian religion. This was not done by the radical humanists. They not only praised and admired the elegant style, the brilliant eloquence and poetry of the ancients, but wanted to effect a radical return to pagan thought and

[1] *Epist. rer. fam.* VI, 2. — Pastor, *l. c.*, vol, I, p. 2.

manners. They imitated, or even outdid, some of the most licentious writers of antiquity in vile and obscene productions. They endeavored to resuscitate ancient life, and not in its best forms. The horrible crimes which are the worst blot on the history of antiquity, of Greece in particular, were made the subject of elegant verses. And the vices which were the curse of Greece and one of the causes of its downfall, began to rage like a dreadful plague in the cities of Italy, especially among the higher class of society.[1]

One has only to recall the names of such humanists as Valla, Poggio, Becadelli and others, to understand how justly this class of writers is censured. Their writings have been called "an abyss of iniquity wreathed with the most beautiful flowers of poetry." It was against this flood of abomination that the zealous, but unfortunately impetuous and stubborn Savonarola directed his thundering eloquence, with only a temporary result. It can easily be imagined what influence this new paganism exerted on youth. What kind of moral safeguard could be expected from teachers of the stamp of Valla? No attempt was made to keep from the hands of the young books which in all ages have been proscribed as disastrous to morality. In the light of such facts the anxiety which Ignatius of Loyola, the founder of the Society of Jesus, felt about dangers arising from the indiscriminate reading of the classics, is fully justified.[2] Not a few of the humanists had lost all faith. Other defects of the majority of the humanists, especially their exorbitant

[1] Pastor, vol. I, p. 25.
[2] See below chapter XVII.

vanity and self conceit, have been deservedly chastised by various authors.[1]

It became especially the fashion among humanists to sneer at the "metaphysical juggleries" and the "barbarous Latin" of the scholastics. It is true, the all absorbing interest in philosophical and theological questions had caused a retrogression in the study of the classical authors. But this loss was counteracted by a considerable gain. At any rate, the sweeping condemnations of the humanists were not justified. Modern scholars begin to see the service rendered to science by scholasticism, and not a few defend the schoolmen against the "arrogant accusations of the humanists" as Professor Paulsen calls them. "We might just as well accept the judgments of socialists on our present conditions as reliable criticisms. It is the task of the historians to judge the past from what it was in and for itself, a task which in most cases means to defend it against that which immediately succeeded. For it is the lot of all historical institutions to be thrown aside with hatred and contempt by that which follows. Will not a time come when the philological and historical, physical and other inquiries of the present appear as dreary and barren, as to us scholastic and speculative philosophy appear?"[2]

Not only Leibnitz, but modern philosophers as Hegel, Edward von Hartmann, and the rationalistic Professor Harnack, have respected the schoolmen as the leaders in a great movement and defended them against their calumniators. Hartmann admits that

[1] For instance by Paulsen, *Gesch. des gel. Unt.*, pp. 29—31, (I, 51 foll.), and *passim*. Baumgartner, vol. IV, pp. 487 foll. — On Erasmus see Janssen, vol. III, p. 11.
[2] *Geschichte des gel. Unt.*, p. 20. (I, p. 36).

"scholasticism was an intellectual system wonderfully coherent and consistent in itself, of which only those judge slightingly who have not yet overcome their hostility to it and have not yet arrived at the objective view of history." [1]

From Italy the literary renaissance spread to Spain, France, England and Germany. The flourishing condition of the schools in England and Germany, described on previous pages, was chiefly due to this movement. The radical school of humanism, hostile to Christianity, did not enter England. The most distinguished English humanists were thorough and practical churchmen,[2] or laymen, most loyal to the Church. Two of them, Bishop Fisher and Thomas More, have been raised by the Church to the honor of the altar. In Germany, matters developed very differently. The humanistic movement began to be felt in the German universities after 1450. Its gradual entrance into the various seats of learning is well traced by Professor Paulsen.[3] However, it is the inner development of humanism in Germany which is of greater importance.[4]

The earlier humanists, as Hegius and his friends, had contemplated classical antiquity from the point of

[1] Quoted by Willmann, *Geschichte des Idealismus*, vol. III, p. 855. For an excellent criticism of scholasticism see vol. II, pp. 321—652.

[2] See above p. 30; cf. Gasquet, *The Eve of the Reformation*, chapter II, *The Revival of Letters in England*, pp. 14—50.—Einstein, *The Italian Renaissance in England*, pp. 18—57.

[3] *Gesch. des gel. Unt.*, pp. 44—127. (I, 74—170).

[4] On this subject see Creighton, *History of the Papacy*, vol. V. *The German Revolt*, ch. I. "Humanism in Germany," pp. 1—49.

view of absolute faith in Christianity. Wimpheling expressed their sentiments in these words: "It is not the study of the heathen writers in itself which is dangerous to Christian culture, but the false apprehension and handling of them, as is often done in Italy, where, by means of the classics, pagan ways of thought and life are spread prejudicial to Christian morality and the patriotic spirit."[1]

Fundamentally different from this conservative school were the *younger* or *radical* humanists. Wanton attacks upon the Holy See, the religious orders, Catholic doctrines and practices, contempt for the whole learning of the Middle Ages and for their own mother tongue, or even a worse than pagan immorality in their writings characterize the great majority of this school of "Poets" in Germany as in Italy. The chief representative of humanism in Germany was Erasmus of Rotterdam, who exercised an enormous influence on his times. The extent and variety of his knowledge in almost every branch of contemporary learning, his untiring activity in all directions, his consummate mastery and artistic treatment of the Latin tongue, and the variety and richness of his style were equalled by few. He brought forth fresh editions of the Bible, of the Greek classics and Fathers, and original treatises in every branch of literature. But he was altogether wanting in intellectual depth. He traveled through England, Italy, and France as a mere book-worm without eye or understanding for national life and character. His freedom in the use

---

[1] Janssen, vol. III, pp. 1—2. For the following see the same volume, pp. 1—79, and Guggenberger, S. J., *A General History of the Christian Era*, vol. II, p. 133.

of calumny, his talent for fulsome flattery to obtain money and presents, matched only by his malignant spite against adversaries, destroyed all proportions between his literary achievements and his character.[1] The leaders among the younger humanists who, when not fighting the theologians, devoted their energies to the composition of vapid verses and lewd poems, were Conrad Celtes, Eobanus Hessus, Crotus Rubianus, Conrad Rufus, Mutian, the dissolute Ulric of Hutten, the knight-errant of humanism, and a host of minor scribblers. In their school work they read the most profligate pagan poetry with their young pupils, and introduced a reign of unrestrained license at Erfurt and other universities and schools.

In Germany, as well as in Italy, this reaction in the renaissance took a special coloring from the circumstances of the melancholy period in which it occurred. From the beginning of the fourteenth century deplorable effects had been manifesting themselves in the Church. The authority of the Pope had been weakened, a great part of the clergy was steeped in worldliness; scholastic philosophy and theology had declined and terrible disorders were rife in political and civil life. The dangerous elements, which no doubt ancient literature contained, were presented to a generation intellectually and physically overwrought and in many ways unhealthy. It is no wonder, therefore, that some of the adherents of the new tendency

---

[1] A much kindlier view of Erasmus is taken in the highly interesting chapter on "Erasmus", in Gasquet's *The Eve of the Reformation*, pp. 155—207. There his attitude towards Luther and his loyalty to the Catholic Church are admirably set forth.

turned aside into perilous paths.[1] In particular the nepotism, worldly life, unscrupulous state policy, and scandalous appointments to high places, for which some of the Popes were responsible, and the scandals connected with the name of Alexander VI., furnished welcome weapons to diets, to princes and agitators, who, under the guise of "reform in head and members," pursued their own selfish ends and aimed at nothing less than the secularization of ecclesiastical property and the usurpation of ecclesiastical jurisdiction.[2]

Besides these abuses, affecting the Church at large, there were others threatening Germany in particular. It is true there existed a great love of learning among all classes, and piety and active charity were found among a great number of clergy and laity. As we have seen, in the lower elementary and the advanced middle schools a sound basis of popular education was

[1] Pastor, *History of the Popes*, vol. I, p. 12.
[2] Guggenberger, vol. II, p. 147. However, it is fair to mention that there were not only deep shadows in this period but also gleams of sunshine. The pagan tendencies were not absolutely general. The religious orders gave to the Church a line of saintly, brilliant, and truly apostolic preachers, who fearlessly raised their voices against the sins and failings of high and low, ecclesiastics and laymen. Nor were their efforts in vain, as may be seen from the conversion of whole towns and provinces, effected by Vincent Ferrer, Bernardine of Siena, John Capistran, Savonarola, and others. And beside the many unworthy prelates and priests of the period, the historian meets, in every country of Christendom, with a great number of men distinguished alike for virtue and learning. The number of Saints of this period, especially in the Franciscan and Dominican Orders, is exceedingly great, a proof that the Church had not lost her saving and sanctifying power. See Pastor, *History of the Popes*, vol. I, pp. 32—38.

established; the universities attained a height of distinction never dreamt of in former times. And art developed more rapidly than learning. But there were many dangerous symptoms in religious, social and political life.[1] In all departments perplexity and confusion were visible. A mass of inflammable material was ready everywhere, and it needed but a spark to set the whole mass ablaze. This spark came from Wittenberg.

§ 3. Education under the Influence of the Reformation.

Luther was undoubtedly a man endowed with the highest natural gifts. Still he was not what Protestant tradition has made him.[2] "On the part of the Protestants," writes one of Germany's historians, the Protestant K. A. Menzel, "it is an accepted maxim to represent to oneself the Reformers as lords and half saints. This prejudice is indeed broken in circles that are conversant with history, but among the large mass of the evangelical population it is still maintained, not, however, to the preservation of truth. It passes current as 'cultured', and is paraded as a mark of 'scientific investigation' to undermine with criticism and negation even the fundamental doctrines of Christianity. But woe to him who with the torch of science invades the vestibule of the temple in which prejudice

[1] These symptoms are summed up by Janssen, vol. II, *passim*, especially pp. 285—302.—Guggenberger, vol. II, pp. 146—151.
[2] See: *Luther and his Protestant Biographers*, by the Rev. H. G. Gauss in the *American Catholic Quarterly Review*, July 1900; also *The Messenger*, Nov. 1902.

and tradition have erected the throne of the 'heroes of the Reformation' and their works. The historical investigator who possesses such a foolhardiness is sure to be decried as a Crypto-Catholic."[1] Not a few Protestant historians frankly confess that the whole structure of Reformation history must undergo a change from its very foundation. One of them says: "Too great is the rubbish and garbage which, intentionally or unintentionally, the prevailing theological standpoint concerning the Reformation period has inaugurated."[2] From original documents a picture of the Reformers, very different from the traditional one, has been presented by the "fear-inspiring book of Döllinger" and by "Janssen's crushing examination of the Luther myth which produced a tremendous uproar in Germany."[3] A great deal of "rubbish and garbage" has also hidden the truth in regard to the influence of Luther and the Reformation on education.

It is a fact of no little significance that Luther's first confederates were the radical humanists. In their hatred against scholastic learning and ecclesiastical authority they welcomed Luther's audacious attacks on the Church. Luther himself had tried at an early date to ingratiate himself with the humanistic confederacy.[4] After the example of Luther the younger humanists, these inveterate enemies of all religion, now accustomed themselves to a Biblical style of lan-

[1] *Neue Geschichte der Deutschen*, vol. II, p. 44, quoted by Ganss, *l. c.*, p. 599, where similar statements of other Protestants may be found.
[2] Professor Maurenbrecher of the Königsberg University, *ib.*
[3] London *Athenaeum*, Dec. 1884, p. 729.
[4] Janssen, vol. III, pp. 100—101.

guage; they even became of a sudden scholars of divinity and delivered lectures on theological subjects. Luther did not shrink from a formal alliance with the most violent of these enemies of the existing order, the gifted but utterly corrupt Ulrich von Hutten, who at that time together with Franz von Sickingen planned a revolution against the Emperor.[1]

This was indeed a remarkable alliance. Prof. Paulsen's comment on it is worth quoting: "The humanists offered their assistance to the monk whose controversies they had shortly before despised as a monkish quarrel. 'Evangelical liberty' became their war-cry instead of 'learning and humanity'. It is only through this alliance that Luther's cause, which had begun as a 'monkish quarrel', became that tremendous revolutionary movement which unhinged the gates of the Church. A reminder of humanism is that naturalism contained in the pure gospel, that addition which appears so strange in Luther's writings, when now and then he represents the works of the flesh as divine commandments and continence as well nigh a rebellion against God's word and will: almost as if the emancipation of the flesh was to be realized through the gospel of Christ. Of course this must not be understood as though these elements had not existed in Luther's nature, in his views and sentiments, but it was only under the influence of humanism that they developed. Under different circumstances they might have remained latent."[2] Luther and Loyola have often been contrasted, the one as the leader of the Protestant Revolution, the other as prominent in the counter-

[1] Janssen, vol. III, pp. 106 foll.
[2] *Gesch. des gel. Unt.*, pp. 128–29. (2. ed. I, 174 foll.).

reformation. Luther tried to reform by a *revolution*, by a complete break with the past[1]; Loyola by a real *reformation*. Luther changed the doctrine, Loyola saw, as his first companion, Peter Faber, has it, that "not the head, but the heart, not the doctrine, but the life needed a change." Luther allied himself with the radical humanists, Loyola imitated the earlier conservative humanists.

That a Christian reformer followed the earlier humanists, who were thoroughly imbued with the spirit of Christianity, as Vittorino da Feltre, Hegius, Agricola, Wimpheling, is natural. But, as Paulsen remarks, "it is a strange phenomenon that a man (Luther) who seemed to be made to fight with Savonarola against the worldliness of the Church introduced by humanism, had to unite himself with Hutten for the extirpation of monasticism. True, it is stranger still that Hutten could make common cause with Luther against the Papacy whose representative was a Medici, against a Church which raised such patrons of learning as Cardinal Albrecht of Mentz to the highest dignities. Well might one have warned Hutten not to cut the branch on which he was sitting."[2]

The humanists had, indeed, cut the branch. — Humanism was ruined by its alliance with the Reformation, and as early as 1524 the eyes of the humanists were opened. The universities and schools were almost annihilated in the storms of religious strife. Professor Paulsen shows this in detail in regard to the

[1] Protestants frequently object to the appellation "revolution", as applied to the Reformation. However, men like Harnack openly declare that it was a revolution. See *What is Christianity?* Lecture XV, pp. 277-281. Paulsen, *l. c.*

[2] *L. c.*, p. 129. (1. ed.; cf. 2. ed. I, p. 174 foll.)

various German universities,[1] as Wittenberg, Erfurt, Leipsic, Frankfurt, Rostock, Greifswald, Cologne, Vienna, Heidelberg, etc. Ingolstadt, of all German universities, was least affected by the Reformation. Under the leadership of Dr. Eck the Lutheran invasion was energetically combated. The number of students declined somewhat, but not considerably, so that this university shows the most favorable conditions of all universities.[2] The same decline was visible in the lower schools. Döllinger has collected a long list of complaints that could be easily enlarged, about the ruin of the schools consequent upon the religious revolution.[3]

The humanist Eobanus Hessus writes from Erfurt in the year 1523: "Under the cloak of the Gospel the escaped monks here are suppressing all liberal studies. Our university is quite deserted; we are utterly despised." In the same year the Dean of the Erfurt philosophical faculty complains: "Nobody would have believed it, if it had been predicted that in a short time our university would have fallen so low that scarcely a shadow of its former lustre would remain." In the same strain lament Melanchthon from Wittenberg, and others from all seats of learning throughout Germany.

Erasmus, an eye-witness of the first scenes in the great drama of the Reformation, the intimate friend of Melanchthon and other Reformers, writes in 1528: "Wherever Lutheranism reigns, there literature per-

[1] Paulsen, *l. c.*, pp. 133–144. (I, pp. 184—195.)
[2] *Ibid.*, p. 143. (I, p. 194.)
[3] *Die Reformation*, vol. I, pp. 418–545; see also Janssen, vol. III, pp. 355–365; vol. VII, p. 11 foll.

ishes. I dislike these gospellers on many accounts, but chiefly, because through their agency literature everywhere languishes, disappears, lies drooping and perishes: and yet, without learning, what is a man's life? They love good cheer and a wife; for other things they care not a straw."[1] In a letter to Melanchthon he states that at Strasburg the Protestant party had publicly taught, in 1524, that it was not right to cultivate any science, and that no language should be studied except the Hebrew. In fact, who was to be blamed for this rapid decay of schools but the Reformers themselves? Carlstadt was not only a fanatic in his hatred of Catholic doctrines and customs, but also spoke with contempt of all human learning. He advised the students to return to their homes and resume the spade or follow the plough, and cultivate the earth, because man was to eat bread in the sweat of his brow. George Mohr, master of the boys' school at Wittenberg, carried away by a similar madness, called from his window to the burghers outside to come and remove their children. Where, indeed, was the use of continuing their studies, since a mechanic was just as well, nay, perhaps better qualified than all the divines in the world, to preach the Gospel.[2]

The Anabaptists in Münster decided that there was only one book necessary to salvation, the Bible, all others should be burned as useless or dangerous.

[1] Hallam, *Introduction to the Literature of Europe in the fifteenth, sixteenth and seventeenth centuries*, vol. I, chapter VI, p. 189, note (Harper's ed. 1842). — Janssen, vol. III, p. 357. — Döllinger, *l. c.*, vol. I, p. 470 foll.

[2] See Archbishop Spalding's *The Reformation in Germany*, chap. XIII.—Döllinger, *Die Reformation*, vol. I, p. 423.

EDUCATION BEFORE FOUNDATION OF THE SOCIETY. 63

This decision was carried out, and whole libraries with numerous precious manuscripts of Latin and Greek authors perished in the flames. Popes, bishops, and councils during the Middle Ages, had enforced the obligation of establishing schools throughout Christendom. The vandalism of some Reformers destroyed innumerable monasteries and with them schools without number. The funds for the support of these schools had been accumulated by the piety, zeal and liberality of previous ages.

No one is more responsible for this sad change than Luther himself. If, with the aid of the Holy Ghost, Scripture could be interpreted by "a miller's maid and a boy of nine years better than by all the popes and cardinals," — these are Luther's words, — of what value could human learning be in religion? Nay more, according to Luther's early teaching higher, learning was not only useless, but positively dangerous. He spoke with a fierce hatred against higher schools and human learning. Professor Paulsen admits that the vehemence of tone in which Luther spoke of the universities as the real bulwarks of the devil on earth, has perhaps never been rivalled before or after by any attack on these institutions.[1] A few specimens of these invectives may suffice.

According to Luther, everything instituted by the papacy was only intended to augment sin and error, so also were the universities. It is the devil himself who has introduced study; there reigns the damned, haughty and wicked Aristotle, from whose works Christian youth is instructed.[2] And yet "a man who

[1] *L. c.*, p. 134. (I, p. 185.)
[2] Paulsen, *ib.*

boasts the title of philosopher cannot be called a Christian." "The Moloch to which the Jews offered up their children, are the higher schools (*hohen Schulen* = universities), in which the best part of youth is sacrificed as a burnt offering. There they are instructed in false heathen art and godless human knowledge : this is the fire of Moloch which no one can weep over enough, through which the most pious and most clever boys are miserably ruined."[1] "The higher schools all deserve to be ground to dust ; nothing more hellish, nothing more devilish has appeared on earth, nor will ever appear. These schools have been invented by no one else than the devil."[2] Luther hated the universities because they exalted reason, "the light of nature", too much. To Luther reason is only "the devil's bride, a beautiful prostitute of the devil."[3] "Human reason is sheer darkness." The faithful strangle reason and say: "Hearest thou, a mad blind fool thou art, understandest not a bit of the things that are God's. Thus the believers throttle this beast."[4]

It is surprising to see that Melanchthon fell in with the tone of Luther.[5] He denounced universities, philosophy, and ethics, almost as violently as his master, but only for a time; he soon abated the violence of his sentiments, whereas Luther to the end

[1] *Luther's Werke*, ed. Walch XIX, 1430. See Döllinger, *l. c.*, vol. I, p. 475 foll. — Janssen, vol. II (German ed. 18), pp. 211–213.
[2] *Ib.*, XII, 45; XI, 459.
[3] See Döllinger, *Die Reformation*, vol. I (2nd ed.), pp. 477 foll.
[4] *Ib.*, p. 479.
[5] Paulsen, pp. 135 foll.

of his life preserved his bitterness against natural reason. Innumerable other preachers began to vie with each other in pouring forth virulent abuse against all enlightened knowledge and secular learning.

Can we then wonder that the parents, prejudiced by such inflammatory declamations, became averse not only to higher learning, as it had existed before the religious disturbances, but to schools in general? No wonder that the lower schools also began to be neglected, so that contemporary writers say: "About the year 1525 schools began to decline, and no one wanted to send his children to school, as people had heard so much from Luther's writings of how the priests and the learned had so pitiably seduced mankind." The official report of the inspectors of the district of Wittenberg, the centre and starting point of Luther's "reform", informs us in the year 1533: "The city schools which, in addition to the instruction they imparted, had given the children a material maintenance, are alarmingly decreasing."[1]

Luther himself was appalled at this desolation, for he knew full well the importance of the school. With bitter invective and reproach he lashes the indifference of the people and the avarice of the princes who, after having squandered the property of the Church and the funds of the schools, refused to do anything for establishing new schools or even for maintaining those in existence. "Formerly", he says, "when we were the slaves of Satan, and profaned the blood of Christ,

[1] Döllinger, *Die Reformation*, vol. I, p. 466 foll. — Numerous contemporary testimonies to the same effect may be seen in Janssen's *Geschichte des deutschen Volkes* (German edition, 18), vol. II, p. 322; vol. VII, pp. 11–211.

all purses were open; then nothing was spared to put children in the cloister or to send them to school. But now when we must establish good schools (*rechte Schulen*) — establish, did I say, no, but only preserve the buildings in good condition — the purses are closed with iron chains. The children are neglected, no one teaches them to serve God, while they are joyfully immolated to Mammon." But herein Luther was inconsistent. Had he not taught people again and again that good works were useless? Why should they make any sacrifice of money for a pious work like that of education? And was it a good and pious work at all? This might have been asked by those who remembered Luther's reckless invectives against higher schools.

Luther was absolutely powerless to remedy the evil which grew worse daily. Therefore he appealed earnestly to the Protestant princes and magistrates to found and support schools. He told them that it was their right, nay, their duty to oblige their subjects to send their children to school. As is evident, Luther had been forced to this step because his voice, always "omnipotent when it preached destruction and spoliation, now fell powerless when it was at length raised to enforce the necessity of liberal contribution for the rearing of institutions to replace those which had been wantonly destroyed."[1] *Compulsory education*, accordingly, is a child of the Reformation; so is also the *state-monopoly* which gradually developed in European countries.[2]

[1] Spalding, *The Reformation in Germany*, ch. 14.
[2] Another result of the Reformation has been pointed out by President Butler of Columbia University, New York:

EDUCATION BEFORE FOUNDATION OF THE SOCIETY. 67

The princes and magistrates to whom Luther appealed for establishing new schools, were slow in following these admonitions, whereas they had been most docile when told to confiscate the rich abbeys and monasteries which had maintained many educational institutions. Luther himself complained that so little heed was paid to his words. In 1528 a new "Order" for the cities of Saxony was prepared by Melanchthon. In 1559 appeared the "Church and School Order of Württemberg."[1] Very different from the attitude of Luther was that of Melanchthon towards higher studies. Luther saw in humanistic studies only a weapon for theological purposes; but Melanchthon was himself a humanist and believed that study of the ancient languages and literature offered immediate educational benefit to the student.[2] Melanchthon has been called *Praeceptor Germaniae*, and this he was for the Protestant part of that country. His system was an adaptation of the humanistic principles of Erasmus, and especially of Rudolph Agricola,[3] who was prominent among the earlier conservative humanists.

It is evident that Luther's merits in regard to education have been exaggerated. The words of the Protestant Hallam deserve to be more universally

"The separation of religious training from education as a whole is the outgrowth of Protestantism and democracy." *Educational Review*, December 1899, p. 427.—Why democracy should be a cause of this separation is not clear to me, nor are the arguments, adduced by President Butler, convincing.

[1] On the development of the Protestant schools see Paulsen, *l. c.*, p. 145 foll. (I, 209). — Ziegler, *l. c.*, p. 61 foll.

[2] Dr. Nohle, in *Rep. of Com. of Ed.*, 1897-98, vol. I, p. 30.

[3] Ziegler, *Geschichte der Pädagogik*, p. 69.

known: "Whatever may be the ideas of our minds as to the truth of Luther's doctrines, we should be careful.... not to be misled by the superficial and ungrounded representations which we sometimes find in modern writers. Such is this that Luther, struck by the absurdity of the prevailing superstitions, was desirous of introducing a more rational system of religion...., or, what others have been pleased to suggest, that his zeal for learning and ancient philosophy led him to attack the ignorance of the monks and the crafty policy of the Church, which withstood all liberal studies. These notions are merely fallacious refinements, as every man of plain understanding who is acquainted with the writings of the early reformers, or has considered their history, must acknowledge. The doctrines of Luther, taken altogether, are not more rational than those of the Church of Rome; nor did he even pretend that they were so... nor, again, is there any foundation for imagining that Luther was concerned for the interests of literature. None had he himself, save theological; nor are there, as I apprehend, many allusions to profane studies, or any proof of his regard to them, in all his works. *On the contrary*, it is probable that both the principles of this great founder of the Reformation, and the natural tendency of so intense an application to theological controversy, checked for a time the progress of philological and philosophical literature on this side of the Alps."[1] As regards the much vaunted intellectual

[1] *Introduction to the Literature of Europe*, vol. I, p. 165 (Harper's ed. 1842).— Hence it is utterly false to say that the reform of the studies in the sixteenth century was, in the first place, a Protestant work. And yet this statement is repeated again and again.

and religious liberty of the Reformers, it is well known that they very soon exercised an unbearable tyranny. Hallam was honest enough to admit this, however reluctantly.[1]

On the eve of the Reformation, England possessed a great number of secondary schools. Both these and the universities suffered greatly from the Reformation and the events connected with it. When by the order of Henry VIII. the monasteries were suppressed, numberless precious manuscripts and other contents of monastic libraries disappeared, and are now lost to the world beyond recovery. Grocers and soap-sellers bought them for their business purposes.[2] Learning, both secular and religious, rapidly declined, and deterioration was felt in all grades of education. Most of the schools at this time were closed, without provision for a substitute. Moreover, the monasteries and convents had supported scholars at the universities, or provided for young clerics until their ordination, when they supplied them with a title. This change was felt immediately. From 1506 to 1535 the average number of yearly degrees granted at Oxford had been 127. In 1535 the number was 108. In that year the operations against the monasteries were commenced. In the following year the number of graduates fell to only 44; the average number till 1548 was less than 57, from 1548 till 1553 not more than 33, but it rose again under Queen Mary to 70.[3] The University of Cambridge suffered not less than Oxford.

[1] *Ib.*, p. 200. Also Döllinger, *Die Reformation*, vol. I, pp. 546—563, and especially Paulsen I, 212—214.

[2] Gasquet, *Henry VIII, and the English Monasteries*, vol. II, p. 423.

[3] Gasquet, *The Eve of the Reformation*, p. 41 foll.

The scholars of Cambridge, in 1545, petitioned King Henry for privileges, as they feared the destruction of the monasteries would altogether annihilate learning.[1] For a time these great homes of learning were threatened with nothing less than ruin. Thus it is undeniable that the dissolution of monasteries, in 1536 and the next two years, gave a great temporary check to the general state of letters in England.

Hallam attempts to palliate this charge, but in vain. Let us contemplate the picture which Latimer, the fanatic opponent of Catholicism, drew in 1550 of the state of education in England. His words are almost identical with those of Luther.[2] "In those days (before the suppression of monasteries), what did they when they helped the scholars? Marry! They maintained and gave them livings that were very Papists and professed the Pope's doctrine; and now that the knowledge of God's word is brought to light, and many earnestly study and labour to set it forth, now almost no man helpeth to maintain them." ... "Truly it is a pitiable thing to see schools so neglected; every true Christian ought to lament the same; to consider what has been plucked from abbeys, colleges and chantries, it is a marvel no more to be bestowed upon this holy office of salvation. Schools are not maintained, scholars have no exhibitions.... I think there be at this day twenty thousand students less than within these twenty years and fewer preachers." Anthony Wood, in his History and Antiquities of the University of Oxford, writes: "Most of the halls and

[1] Fuller's *History of the University of Cambridge*, in Gasquet, *Henry VIII*, etc., vol. II, p. 519.
[2] See above, p. 65—66.

hostels in Oxford were left empty. Arts declined and ignorance began to take place again."[1]

This sketch of the status of education previous to the foundation of the Society of Jesus warrants us to draw the following conclusions. *First*, a reform was urgently needed, not only in the religious and moral sphere but also in education. There was a great literary activity all over Christendom. In the countries most affected by the Reformation, this activity was checked for a time, in Germany almost annihilated. In those countries which were less affected by the religious revolution, the educational work was not formed into a well balanced system of instruction and discipline. Further, the teaching of the classics was in many cases carried on in a pagan spirit. The Catholic reform centres around the Council of Trent. The members of a Commission preparatory to this Council, mostly refined humanists and university scholars, pointed out as one of the great abuses in the Church, that "in the public schools, especially of Italy, many teach impiety." This was stated in 1538, two years before the approbation of the Society of Jesus. In this Society "the Church of Rome, deeply shaken by open schism and lurking disaffection, was to find an unexpected strength. The Jesuits were speedily to acquire a vast influence by the control of education."[2] In fact, the Jesuits were to give to Catholic countries a uniform system of education, which was so sadly needed at the time. They were to purify and elevate the teaching of the classics, so as

[1] Gasquet, *Henry VIII. and the English Monasteries*, vol. II, pp. 519-520.
[2] Hallam, *Literature of Europe*, vol. I, p. 196.

to make it a useful means of Christian education as well as of mental training.

Secondly: The foregoing sketch proves that it is false to say: the Jesuits availed themselves, in the interest of the Catholic Church, of the zeal for learning which the Protestants had awakened.[1] It can be proved over and above that a great zeal for learning had existed before the Reformation,[2] and that this zeal was well-nigh extinguished by this movement. Melanchthon, Sturm and other reformers who worked for the establishment of schools, had received their literary education, their zeal for learning, and the greater part of their educational principles from the schools flourishing before the outbreak of the religious revolution. Their efforts were directed towards reestablishing what the religious disturbances had destroyed. Of course, we are far from denying that the Reformers introduced many improvements into the Protestant schools; but they and the Jesuits drew from the same sources.

The preceding sketch of the condition of education previous to the foundation of the Society of Jesus may seem disproportionately long. However, it was necessary to dwell on this point at some length, in order to expose one of the fundamental errors concerning the origin of the educational system of the Jesuits. It would not have sufficed to make a few general assertions — as has been done by some non-Catholic writers on the history of education — but it was necessary to quote details, in order to refute this erroneous view.

[1] See page 20.
[2] See the words of Mr. Einstein, above p. 37.

CHAPTER III.

The Society of Jesus. — Religious as Educators.

It is not our task to give a detailed history of Ignatius of Loyola, the Spanish nobleman who was wounded on the ramparts of Pampeluna, in 1521, nor of his subsequent conversion and life. This story has often been told and may be read in the numerous biographies of the Saint.[1] Nor need we enumerate all the different and contradictory estimates of his character, as given by various writers. Macaulay calls him a "visionary" and an "enthusiast, naturally passionate and imaginative," possessed of a "morbid intensity and energy, a soldier and knight errant," who became "the soldier and knight errant of the spouse of Christ."[2] Canon Littledale, in spite of his hostility against the Society, cannot help admitting that Loyola possessed "powerful gifts of intellect and an unusual practical foresight."[3]

To see with Macaulay in Ignatius a "visionary," is an utter misconception of his character. Nor is it

[1] The best for English readers are: *Saint Ignatius of Loyola*, by Henri Joly (London, 1899). *Life of St. Ignatius*, by C. Genelli. *Saint Ignatius and the Early Jesuits*, by Stewart Rose.
[2] *Essays:* "Ranke's History of the Popes."
[3] *Encyclopedia Britannica* (9th ed.), article "Jesuits." This article teems with gross misrepresentations of the Order, and it would take a volume to refute the calumnies and the ungrounded insinuations contained therein.

correct to style him a "religious enthusiast." This appellation could, at the most, be applied to him only for the first few years after his conversion. During that period, in a few instances, as in the famous meeting with the Saracen, Ignatius displays indeed a conduct singularly contrasting with his conduct in after-life and with those wonderfully wise rules which he laid down on the discernment of the good spirit from the evil one. In his *Autobiography* the Saint insists particularly on the mistakes into which he had fallen on the road to mature judgment in spiritual matters.[1] During these first few years following his conversion, Ignatius gave manifestation of the chivalrous spirit which he had imbibed from his early military training, when, for instance, in the Monastery of the Montserrat he hung up his sword beside our Lady's image, in token that henceforth his life was to be one of spiritual warfare and spiritual knighthood.

The Society, however, was not founded in this period of the Saint's life, but when the youthful fervor was completely mastered by the calmest discretion. At the time when he drew up the Constitutions of the Society, all his actions and sentiments were so entirely under his control that, although by nature of an ardent temper, he was commonly thought cold and phlegmatic. In framing the Constitutions he proceeded with the utmost care and circumspection. On points which might appear unimportant, he deliberated for days, nay for weeks and months. It was a common

[1] See *The Testament of St. Ignatius.* Introduction by Father Tyrrell, S. J., p. 7; and notes on pp. 60—61, 79—82, 197 foll.

practice of his to write down the reasons for and against in parallel columns, then to weigh their force and importance. After this he consulted the Fathers who lived with him in Rome, in order to take their advice as to changes or additions which they thought necessary or useful. Moreover, he submitted the results of his painstaking labors to the judgment of those Fathers who lived in various parts of Europe. Surely in this cautiousness we see anything but the traits of a visionary or enthusiast.

As early as 1523 Ignatius had conceived the idea of his future life-work, although only in general outlines. We find this idea embodied in his *Spiritual Exercises*, particularly in the contemplation on the "Kingdom of Christ." The generous knight, who has renounced all worldly ambition, is resolved to become a soldier of Christ. In Him he sees his King and General and, in order to defend and propagate Christianity, the Kingdom of Christ, he plans a spiritual crusade. Those who wish to become his companions in this noble enterprise must be determined to distinguish themselves in the service of their heavenly King. They are not to be satisfied with being ordinary soldiers in this army, but they are to constitute, as it were, Christ's bodyguard, hence the name of the Society: "La Compañia de Jesus," the Company of Jesus. A distinguished Protestant writer, Professor Harnack of Berlin, has recently made the following comparison which in *some* points is *not inappropriate:* "If we assert and mean the assertion to hold good even of the present time, that the Roman Church is the old Roman Empire consecrated by the Gospel, that is no mere 'clever remark,' but the recognition of the true state of the matter historically, and the most appropriate and fruitful way of describing the character of this Church. It still governs the nations; its Popes rule like Trajan and Marcus Aurelius; Peter and Paul have taken the place of Romulus and Remus; the bishops and archbishops, of the pro-consuls; the troops of priests and monks correspond to the legions; the Jesuits to the imperial body-guard."[1]

Ignatius' first intention was to convert the Turks in Palestine. So he went to Jerusalem, there to establish a society of apostolic men who, in the midst of the children of Mahomet, should open a way to new triumphs of the Church. This was without doubt a noble conception, one which the swords of Christian chivalry had not been able to realize by the efforts and enthusiasm of centuries. It was only after his endeavors to gain a foothold near Our Lord's Sepulchre had been frustrated, that Ignatius gave his new Society the more general character of defending the "Kingdom of Christ" among all classes, in all countries, and by all legitimate means. As the object of the Society was purely spiritual, not temporal or political, so also the means employed were to be of spiritual order, above all preaching and teaching.

[1] Harnack, *What is Christianity?* (New York, 1901), Lecture XIV, p. 252.—However, much of what has been written about the military character of the Society is due to a misconception. When Mr. Davidson, in his *History of Education*, says that "the Society of Jesus was a great military organization, a *Catholic Salvation Army*, with methods very much resembling those of its latest imitator," we must call this comparison absurd. For a greater difference than that between the methods of the Society and those of the Salvation Army is scarcely conceivable, not to say a word of the vast difference of their aims.

It has often been said that the prime object of the Society was and is the crushing of Protestantism.[1] This assertion is proved to be false by the life of Ignatius, and this proof is strengthened by the Constitutions, the Papal Approbations, and the whole history of the Order. The Papal Letters and the Constitutions assign as the special object of the Society: "The progress of souls in a good life and knowledge of religion; the propagation of faith by public preaching, the Spiritual Exercises and works of charity, and particularly the instruction of youth and ignorant persons in the Christian religion."[2] The Protestants are not as much as mentioned in this Papal document which states the end and the means of the Society. Pius V., in 1571, highly praised the educational work of Jesuit schools and granted them ample privileges.[3] Here again it is not said that these schools or the Society are directed against Protestantism.

The evidence is so strong that Professor Huber, one of the bitterest opponents of the Order, declares: "At the time when Ignatius conceived the idea of founding a new order, he had not heard as much as the name of the German Reformer. Even more than a decade later he seems to have paid little heed to the

[1] "To resist the encroachments of Protestantism, that followed the diffusion of instruction among the people, Loyola organized his teaching corps of Catholic zealots; and his mode of competition for purposes of moral, sectarian and political control has covered the earth in all Christian countries with institutions of learning." Compayré, *History of Pedagogy*, p. 163.

[2] In the first approbation of the Institute, by the Brief *Regimini militantis* of Pope Paul III., September 27, 1540. (Cf. *Litterae Apostolicae*, Florentiae, 1892, p. 4.)

[3] *Litterae Apostolicae, l. c.*, p. 44.

religious movement in Europe, especially in Germany."[1] As we said, it was the intention of Ignatius to convert Palestine. Frustrated in this plan, he chose Italy, Spain and Portugal as the field of labor for himself and his companions. There he endeavored to reform the morals of the people and to encourage the practice of works of charity.[2] His most powerful co-worker, Francis Xavier, he sent to East India; to Germany, he sent the first Jesuit in 1540, and that only at the urgent request of the Imperial Ambassador. In 1555, one year before the death of Ignatius, the Society comprised eight provinces: Italy had two; Spain, three; Portugal, one; Brazil, one; India and Japan, one. There was none in Germany, the cradle of Protestantism. Of the sixty-five residences of the Order in that year, there were only two in Germany: those of Cologne and Vienna. The first colleges of the Society were founded in Catholic countries at Gandia in Spain, Messina in Sicily, Goa in the East Indies. Protestant pupils were received only by exception, and in many colleges they were not admitted at all. How, then, can all this be explained, if the main object of the Society was the destruction of Protestantism and proselytism among Protestant students?[3]

When Ignatius had decided to devote his life "to the greater glory of God" and the salvation of souls, he understood the necessity of higher learning. So, at the age of thirty-three, the former gallant officer and hero of Pampeluna, was not ashamed to sit with

[1] Huber, *Der Jesuiten-Orden*, 1873, p. 3.
[2] Huber, *l. c.*, p. 26.
[3] On this subject cf. Duhr, *Jesuitenfabeln*. (Jesuit-Myths), Herder, Freiburg, and St. Louis, 1899, (3rd edition), pp. 1—28.

children on the school-bench at Barcelona, where he began to study the rudiments of Latin. After two years he went to the university of Alcala, thence to Salamanca, and last to the university of Paris, at that time the greatest centre of philosophical and theological learning.

He arrived in the French capital in 1528. There he studied philosophy and theology, and in 1534, by a successful examination, became a Master of Arts. At the University he had won six young men: Peter Lefèvre, a Savoyard; Francis Xavier, a Navarrese; the three Spaniards, James Lainez, Alphonsus Salmeron, and Nicholas Bobadilla, and Simon Rodriguez, a Portuguese. On August 15, 1534, the little band repaired to the church of the Blessed Virgin at Montmartre in Paris, and bound themselves by a vow to the service of God. This was the birthday of the Society of Jesus. The new Order received the papal sanction from Paul III., on September 27, 1540.

The aim of the Society is expressed by its motto: *Omnia ad majorem Dei gloriam*—(*All for God's greater glory.*) Hence it is the duty of the members to labor with the same zeal for the salvation of others as for their own perfection. The salvation of their neighbor they accomplish by conducting the spiritual exercises, preaching missions to the faithful, and evangelizing the heathen; by hearing confessions; by defending the faith against heretics and infidels through their writings; by *teaching catechism to children and the ignorant;* by *lecturing on philosophy and theology in the universities;* by *instructing youth in grammar schools and colleges.* Although various occupations are here mentioned, yet, as Professor Paulsen rightly observes, "education so largely prevails in the activity of the Order that it can be called in a special sense a teaching or school order."[1] "Evidently these university men, who were engaged in drawing up the Institute, considered that, if the greatest Professor's talents are well spent in the exposition of the greatest doctrines in theology, philosophy, and science, neither he, nor any one else, is too great to be a school master, a tutor, and a father to the boy passing from childhood to the state of manhood, — that boyhood which, as Clement of Alexandria says, furnishes the very milk of age, and from which the constitution of the man receives its temper and complexion."[2]

Ignatius, then, had founded a religious order which made the education of youth one of its primary objects. It will be well to speak here of a much discussed and most important question, namely, the educational work of religious orders in general, a work not favorably viewed by the majority of non-Catholics, to whom "monasticism"[3] is one of the features in the

[1] *Geschichte des gelehrten Unterrichts*, vol. I, p. 382. In another passage he styles the Society a *Professoren-Orden*.
[2] Hughes, *Loyola*, p. 43.
[3] It is common among non-Catholics to style the members of all religious orders "monks." However, this popular appellation is not correct. The general term is "religious." This word was used in this sense very early in English (v. g. by Chaucer, *Troylus and Chryseyde*, CIX, 759). It seems that after the Reformation, Protestants refused to honor members of religious orders with this title. J. L. Kington Oliphant, of Balliol College, Oxford, states in his work *The New English* (vol. I, p. 482), that "the phrase *the relygyon* is employed for monk's profession, almost for the last time" between 1537 and 1540. Protestants preferred to use the word "monk", which soon became a term of reproach. They saw in the monks the very type of laziness, uselessness, ignorance, fanaticism and

Catholic Church which they hold in special abhorrence. This antipathy is largely due to the unscrupulous slanders of the later humanists and the fierce invectives of the fathers of the Reformation. It is known what language Luther used against religious vows, which he called an "abomination, unnatural and impossible to keep, a slavery of Egypt, a sacrifice to Moloch," etc. The monks he styled "lazy drones, cowled hypocrites," etc.[1]

profligacy. Cardinal Newman has said of this Protestant view: "As a Jesuit means a knave, so a monk means a bigot." —The Catholic Church, as every other society, has the right to lay down its own terminology, which, we think, should be respected by all. (The term "religious" in this sense is recognized by the Standard and Century Dictionaries). The Church and all enlightened Catholics distinguish between Monks, Friars and Clerks Regular. *Monks* are the contemplative orders: Basilians, Benedictines, Carthusians, Cistercians and Trappists. The *Friars* or *Mendicants* were founded in the Middle Ages; they are the Dominicans, Franciscans, Carmelites and Augustinians. The *Clerks Regular*, or *Regular Clerics*, are chiefly of more recent date: The Theatines, the Jesuits etc. The difference, as regards the aim and manner of life of these classes, is well explained in *The Religious State*, by William Humphrey, S. J. (London, 1884, 3 vols.) vol. II, pp. 309—336. This work is a digest of the classic work on the religious state, the *De Statu Religionis* of the Jesuit Suarez. Father Humphrey's digest may prove of service to all who desire to have information with regard to a salient feature of the Catholic Church.—See also the excellent articles in the *Kirchen-Lexikon* (Herder, 2nd ed.): "Orden," vol. IX, 972; "Mönchthum," vol. VIII, 1689; "Bettelorden," vol. II, 561; "*Clerici regulares*," vol. III, 530.

[1] Much of what Luther said on the subject of vows, as well as of matrimony, does not bear translation. See Janssen, *Ein zweites Wort an meine Kritiker,* pp. 93—97. Professor Paulsen indignantly repudiates the vile calumnies of the humanists against the religious orders. He points out that the

However, there are many enlightened and scholarly non-Catholics who do not share these opinions. Careful historical research revealed that the monks were not lazy drones, but that they were the civilizers of Europe and the preservers of ancient literature. Then it was admitted that they were not all hypocritical debauchees. Thus, in a recent work of an American scholar,[2] we find, after the description of the monastic principles and ideals, the following statement: "The ideal monastic character was that which corresponded to these principles. And in hundreds of instances a personality with such a character did result; a personality when directing faultless in humility and obedience to God, faultless in humility and obedience when obeying; knowing neither pride nor vanity, nor covetousness, nor lust, nor slothful depression; grave and silent with bent head, yet with an inner peace, even an inner passionate joy; meditative, mystic, an otherworld personality; one that dwells in spiritual facts, writings of many humanists exhibit a licentiousness which would have made most religious throw these books aside with utter disgust. Some Protestant critics severely blamed the Berlin Professor for this defence of the outlawed monks. Professor Ziegler even accused him that, in alliance with Janssen and Denifle, he endeavored to restore the old Catholic *fable convenue*. Professor Paulsen answers this charge of his co-religionists by saying that he is entirely free from any such tendency. "I do not want to restore or maintain any fables, neither Catholic nor Protestant; but I wish, as far as possible, to see things as they are. It is true, this endeavor has led me to doubt whether the renaissance and its apostles deserve all the esteem, and the representatives of medieval education all the contempt which, up to this day, has been bestowed on them." *L. c.*, vol. I, p. 89.

[2] Taylor, *The Classical Heritage of the Middle Ages*, (New York, Macmillan 1900), p. 182.

for whom this world has passed away and the lusts thereof; one that is centered in God and in eternal life, and yet capable of intense activities; a man who will not swerve from orders received, as he swerves not from his great aim, the love of God and eternal life."
And the Protestant Professor Harnack declares that even to-day the Roman Church "possesses in its orders of monkhood and its religious societies, a deep element of life in its midst. In all ages it has produced saints, so far as men can be so called, and it still produces them to-day. Trust in God, unaffected humility, the assurance of redemption, the devotion of one's life to the service of one's brethren, are to be found in it; many brethren take up the cross of Christ and exercise at one and the same time that self-judgment and that joy in God which Paul and Augustine achieved. The *Imitatio Christi* kindles independent religious life and a fire which burns with a flame of its own."[1]

A still more remarkable reaction seems of late to take place in the minds of Protestant writers, concerning the origin and nature of "monasticism". After various attempts had been made to explain the rise of monasticism from Essene, Brahman, or Buddhist influence, not a few Protestants admit now that it logically, and, as it were, naturally, arose from Christianity. "Monasticism", says Mr. Taylor, "arose from within Christianity, not from without."[2] Professor Harnack even regrets it that the Reformation has abolished monasticism within the Evangelical Church. The words of this leader among rationalistic Protestants deserve to be quoted. After having pictured the

[1] *What is Christianity?*, p. 266.
[2] *The Classical Heritage of the Middle Ages*, p. 142.

achievements of the Protestant Reformation, he asks what it has cost. Among other "high prices" which the Reformation had to pay, he enumerates monasticism. When the Reformation abolished monasticism, "something happened which Luther neither foresaw nor desired: monasticism, of the kind that is conceivable and necessary in the evangelical sense of the word, disappeared altogether. But every community stands in need of personalities living *exclusively* for its ends. The Church, for instance, needs volunteers who will abandon every other pursuit, renounce the 'world', and devote themselves entirely to the service of their neighbor; not because such a vocation is a 'higher one', but because it is a necessary one, and because no church can live without also giving rise to such a desire. But in the evangelical churches the desire has been checked by the decided attitude which they have been compelled to adopt towards Catholicism. It is a high price that we have paid; nor can the price be reduced by considering, on the other hand, how much simple and unaffected religious fervor has been kindled in home and family life. We may rejoice, however, that in the past century a beginning has been made in the direction of recouping this loss. In the institution of deaconesses and many cognate phenomena the evangelical churches are getting back what they once ejected through their inability to recognize it in the form which it then took. But it must undergo a much ampler and more varied development." [1]

One of the "ends" of the Church is education. It is natural, then, that there should be personalities who

---

[1] *What is Christianity?*, p. 288.

live exclusively for this end, or, at least, devote themselves in a special manner to this work. In fact, from the earliest ages of Christianity, we find that religious took a special interest in the education of youth. The celebrated historian Dr. Neander of Berlin, who can not be accused of any undue leaning towards Catholicism, praises the early monks for their labor in this direction. He points out that the duties of education were particularly recommended to the monks of St. Basil. They were enjoined to take upon themselves voluntarily the education of orphans, and the education of other youths when entrusted to them by their parents. It was by no means necessary that these children should become monks; they were early instructed in some trade or art, and were afterwards at liberty to make a free choice of their vocation.[1]

St. John Chrysostom most earnestly recommended to parents to employ the monks as instructors to their sons; to have their sons educated in monasteries, at a distance from the corruption of the world, where they might early be made acquainted with the Holy Scriptures, be brought up in Christian habits, and where the foundation of a true Christian character might be laid, the fruits of which would afterwards manifest themselves in every station and circumstance of life. Dr. Neander thus comments on the appeals of St. Chrysostom: "Where men truly enlightened were to be found among the monks, as was often the case, the advice of St. Chrysostom was undoubtedly correct; and even where too great attention to outward forms,

[1] *The Life of St. Chrysostom*, by Dr. Neander. Translated from the German by the Rev. J. C. Stapleton, London 1845, p. 92.

and too little of an evangelical spirit prevailed, education among them was more desirable than in corrupted families, or the schools of the sophists, in which vanity and ostentation were in every way encouraged."[1]

It is scarcely necessary to state that other religious orders before the foundation of the Society of Jesus, especially the Benedictines and the Dominicans, had rendered inestimable service to the cause of Christian education. Cardinal Newman compares the educational work of these three orders in the following terms: "As the physical universe is sustained and carried on in dependence on certain centres of power and laws of operation, so the course of the social and political world, and of that great religious organization called the Catholic Church, is found to proceed for the most part from the presence or action of definite persons, places, events, and institutions, as the visible cause of the whole. . . . Education follows the same law: it has its history in Christianity, and its doctors or masters in that history. It has had three periods: the ancient, the medieval, and the modern; and there are three religious orders in those periods respectively which succeed, one the other, on its public stage, and represent the teaching given by the Catholic Church during the time of their ascendancy. The first period is that long series of centuries, during which society was breaking, or had broken up, and then slowly attempted its own reconstruction; the second may be called the period of reconstruction; and the third dates from the Reformation, when that peculiar movement of mind commenced, the issue of which is still to come. Now, St. Benedict has had the training of

---

[1] *Ibid.*, p. 37.

the ancient intellect, St. Dominic of the medieval, and St. Ignatius of the modern. . . . Ignatius, a man of the world before his conversion, transmitted as a legacy to his disciples that knowledge of mankind which cannot be learned in cloisters."[1]

However, none of the religious orders of the Middle Ages had taken the education of youth formally and expressly into its constitution. As regards the Benedictines, Cardinal Newman maintains that their occupation with literary and historical studies was, in a way, a compromise with the primary end of their institute. The monastic institute, as the great Benedictine scholar Mabillon says, demands *summa quies*, the most perfect quietness. Hence the studies which they pursued with special predilection, were such as did not excite the mind: the study of Holy Scripture and the Fathers, the examination of ancient manuscripts, editions and biographies of the Fathers, studies which can be undergone in silence and quietness.[2] So was also the educational work which they undertook accidental to the primary object of their institute. The Order of St. Dominic had a much closer, a more direct and explicit connection with studies and teaching. But it was chiefly the teaching of the highest branches, of theology, the "science of sciences", and of philosophy, which this order undertook. What we now understand by "education" was only remotely included in the object of the Order of St. Dominic.

St. Ignatius was the first to assume the education of youth as a special part of the work of a religious order, as a special ministry, a special means of ob-

[1] *Historical Sketches*, vol. II, pp. 365–366.
[2] Newman, *Historical Sketches*, vol. II, pp. 420–26; 452.

taining the end of his Society: the glory of God and the salvation of souls. "We can," says Cicero, "do no greater or better service to the commonwealth than to teach and instruct youth." St. Ignatius knew this full well, he also knew that it applied to the supernatural commonwealth, the City of God, the Church of Christ.

In opposition to the pagan ideas of the radical school of the humanists, he deemed it absolutely necessary that all efforts should be made to instil the principles of the true religion, together with useful knowledge, into the minds of boys; for as the Wise Man says: "A young man, according to his way, even when he is old, he will not depart from it." (*Prov.*, 22, 6.) — "Hence", as the Jesuit theologian Suarez says: "God raised up St. Ignatius, and gave to him this mind and counsel, without the motive and example of other religious orders, and it has been approved by the authority of His Vicar."[1]

This measure of St. Ignatius in taking the education of youth as a fundamental part into his order, marks an important epoch in the history of Catholic education. After the time of St. Ignatius other religious congregations were founded with the special object of undertaking the education of the young; we mention only the Christian Brothers, founded by Saint de La Salle, and the Piarists. For the education of women there are numerous congregations of sisters, which exclusively or primarily are engaged in imparting a refined and thoroughly Christian education.

[1] *De Religione Societatis Jesu.* — See the digest of the work in *The Religious State*, by W. Humphrey, S. J., vol. III, p. 167.

Of late the educational work of religious orders has frequently been objected to, even by some who call themselves Catholics. But in spite of all that has been said to the contrary, the care which religious orders take of education is a source of blessings for the pupils, the family, and the whole community. Religious, above all, try to impart a religious, a Christian education. How useful, how absolutely necessary this is for society as well as for the individual pupil, need not be discussed. Further, in the case of religious teachers a guarantee is given that persons of noble character and high aspirations devote their whole lives to the cause of education. Must we not expect that such teachers will obtain most satisfactory results in their work? At all events, it cannot be denied that the educational labors of the Society were crowned with success.

Protestant historians, as Ranke, Paulsen, and others, admit that the Jesuit schools of the sixteenth and seventeenth centuries were far more successful than their Protestant rivals. Whence the difference? Ranke finds it in the exactness and nicety of the methods of the Society. This was undoubtedly one cause of their greater success. Still it is more probable that the chief reason is to be sought in the teachers themselves. The teachers in the Jesuit colleges were, on the whole, better fitted for their work than were most other teachers. It is not difficult to prove this assertion. The social position of teachers was, during these centuries, a most undesirable one.[1] The salaries

---

[1] Many interesting details on this subject have been published in a recent book by Reicke, *Lehrer und Unterrichtswesen in der deutschen Vergangenheit*, Leipzig, Diederichs,

were so miserable that the teachers, to support themselves and their families, had to practise some other profession or trade. Professor Paulsen states that in Saxony, towards the close of the sixteenth century, the *one* schoolmaster of a small town was regularly organist, town-clerk and sexton.[1] The village schoolmasters were mostly sextons, field-guards, or tailors. As late as 1738, an order was issued in Prussia to the effect that in the country there should be no other tailors besides the sextons and schoolmasters, and later on Frederick the Great declared: "tailors are bad schoolmasters," and so he preferred to make teachers out of old soldiers, invalid corporals, and sergeants. The position of teachers in the higher schools was not much more enticing. They had to obtain some addition to their scanty salaries by a sort of genteel beggary: by dedicating books or orations to influential persons, by writing poems for weddings or similar occasions. Teachers were always far worse off than lawyers or physicians. It was always a true saying, but especially in those times:

> *Dat Galenus opes, dat Justinianus honores,*
> *Sed genus et species cogitur ire pedes,*

which may be freely rendered:

> The doctor's purse old Galen fills,
> Justinian lifts the esquire on high,
> But he that treads in grammar-mills,
> Will tread it on until he die.

The famous rector of the school of Ilfeld, Neander,

1901. Summary in *Neue Jahrbücher für das klassische Altertum*, 1902, vol. X, pp. 295—296. — See also Paulsen, *Geschichte des gelehrten Unterrichts* (2nd ed.), vol. I, pp. 326-333; 362.

[1] *L. c.*, p. 296.

was told one day by his former colleague of Schulpforta, Gigas, who had retired to a parish: "You should have had yourself flayed alive rather than stay so many years with the wicked and devilish youths of to-day." And Schekkius, who died in 1704, had the following inscription painted on the wall of the Gymnasium in Hildesheim:

"*Quis miser est? Vere miseros si dixeris ullos,*
Hi sunt, qui pueros betha vel alpha docent.

The schoolmasters have horses' and asses' labor; they have to swallow much dust, stench and smoke to boot; discomfort, calumnies, and sundry troubles, with ingratitude in *fine laborum.*"

We cannot wonder that the *desudare in pulvere scholastico* was not considered a desirable profession, and that the school career was sought only as a transitory occupation, which was abandoned as soon as a good parsonage was offered. Others again entered upon this career because, for lack of talent or other qualities, they could not expect to succeed in the ministry.[1] The changes among the teachers, in Saxony and elsewhere, were exceedingly frequent. It was very common among Protestant theologians to teach for one year, or at the most two years, and then to retire to a parish.[2]

What do we find among the Jesuits? The most talented youths entered their ranks, and after a long and solid training many taught in the colleges their whole lives, others for at least five or more years. They had not to worry about their livelihood, as the Order provided all they needed. So they could devote

[1] Paulsen, *Geschichle des gel. Unt.*, *l. c.*, p. 327.
[2] *Ib.*, p. 296.

themselves, all their time and strength, to the work of education.[1] But this was possible only because they had joined a religious order, which had taken up the education of youth as one of its special ministries. I have never found that any writers who discuss the causes of the superiority of the Jesuit schools have taken this fact into account. And yet it was undoubtedly one of the most important reasons of the great success of the colleges of the Society.

But may not even at the present day religious most beneficially be employed as educators of Catholic youth? Will not their state of life secure some advantages for the work of education? It has repeatedly been stated by non-Catholic writers that the schools of the teaching congregations in France were far more successful than the lay schools.[2] What is the explanation of this fact, so unwelcome to those who have to admit it? A recent article in an American magazine may help us to find a very plausible explanation. Professor Münsterberg of Harvard writes[3]: "The

[1] Professor Paulsen states that the Jesuit teachers changed also rather frequently; but *every* Jesuit had to teach at least four or five years after the completion of his philosophical course, and very many returned to the colleges after their theological studies. Hence there was incomparably more stability in Jesuit colleges than in most Protestant schools of those times.

[2] See for instance the *Contemporary Review*, March, 1900, p. 441, where it is plainly stated by a writer most hostile to the religious orders, that the "religious teachers do their work efficiently and successfully, their rivals with a degree of slovenliness which is incredible." See further testimonies below, chapter VII.

[3] *Atlantic Monthly*, May 1901, p. 828. However, this feature is not confined to American schools. Within the last few years serious complaints begin to be heard also in Ger-

greater number of those who devote themselves to higher teaching in America are young men without means, too often without breeding; and yet that would be easily compensated for, if they were men of the best minds, but they are not. They are mostly men of a passive, almost indifferent sort of mind, without intellectual energy, men who see in the academic career a modest safe path of life.... while our best young men must rush to law, and banking, and what not," and all this because the salaries are not high enough.[1] It is not our task to investigate or

many. There is even a serious danger apprehended for the higher schools. The commercial spirit has invaded Germany, and young men are not anxious to enter on a career which is perhaps the most fatiguing of all and offers the fewest chances for advancement. See Dr. Wermbter, *Die höhere Schullaufbahn in Preussen*, 1901; Dr. Schröder: *Periculum in Mora*, 1901. — Of the French teachers M. Bréal, Professor of the *Collège de France*, said as early as 1879: "Les maîtres d'études sont, généralement, des jeunes gens qui acceptent de fatigantes et difficiles fonctions pour avoir le loisir de se préparer à un emploi plus relevé, ... personnes sans expérience pédagogique, dont la pensée et l'activité sont tournées vers les examens qui les attendent... Je ne crains pas d'être contredit si j'affirme que l'autorité leur manque pour être les éducateurs que nous cherchons." Du Lac, *Jésuites*, p. 280.

[1] Political influence has repeatedly been pointed out as another cause that deters able men in this country from school work. "It seems to be true that high schools have not been able to attract the best men into their service, because appointments in them must be sought usually through avenues of political influence." *Educational Review*, May, 1902, p. 506. See also President Draper, in *Education in the United States*, vol. I, pp. 13, 16, 29; and Mr. Anderson's article "Politics in the Public Schools," *Atlantic Monthly*, April, 1901.

defend the correctness of these statements, which unquestionably contain a great deal of truth.

What do we find in religious orders? No doubt, the type of mind described in the preceding lines is to be met with among them; but in schools, conducted by religious, men are teaching who are "of the best minds", sometimes also men who belong to the best Catholic families in the land. The Jesuits, in particular, have even been charged with drawing the finest talents and the sons of the most distinguished families to their Order. If this were true, these talents would not be lost to society. For they are working for the noblest cause, the education of the young. Their state of life made firm and lasting by sacred vows, frees them from family cares and family troubles, and permits them to devote all their time and energy to education. The Jesuit is prevented from seeking earthly remuneration, consequently, no "better chance", no higher salary offered by other occupations, will entice him to forsake his arduous but sublime task.

In the year 1879, at the time of violent agitations against the Jesuit colleges in France, a writer in the Paris *Figaro* called attention to the fact how little a Jesuit teacher needed. In the provinces, a Jesuit teacher costs one thousand francs, in Paris, a little more, and this is for board, clothes, etc. Going from one college to another, he takes with him his crucifix, his breviary, and the clothes which he wears on his body, his manuscripts, if he has any, and that is all. And yet, as the same writer points out, among these truly poor men, among these volunteers to the noble cause of education, are men who are the sons of millionaires, others who have received the badge of the

"Legion of Honor", others who had been awarded this distinction before they became Jesuits; there are among them men who had been able officers in the army or navy. Indeed, these men must see in the education of youth something more than an occupation for gaining a livelihood.

In this country the instability of teachers has more than once formed the subject of complaints. "In Maine,[1] some time ago, four years was found to be the average time of service. The report of 1892 on the high schools of Washington (D. C.) remarks that, with few exceptions, all professionally prepared teachers who had occupied their positions four years ago had resigned to enter more lucrative positions. Better opportunities are offered not only to male but to female teachers, who also give up their positions to enter upon married life. Even well-to-do American women, generally highly educated, well informed, and at the same time enterprising, prefer to spend a few years in teaching rather than await their future inactively. The official report condenses all this in the mournful remark: In the United States the profession of teaching seems to be a kind of waiting-room in which the young girl awaits a congenial, ulterior support, and the young man a more advantageous position.' "[2]

It is evident that teaching must suffer from such instability. No professional skill is possible in the majority of teachers; experience and steadfastness, two

[1] In Illinois and other states the same has been proved. Mr. McBurney wrote quite recently in the *Ohio Teacher* that the average life of the country teacher is not over three years. See *The Review*, St. Louis, October 2, 1902, p. 601.

[2] *Report of the Com. of Education*, 1892—93, vol. I, p. 545; see also pp. 565 and 586.

important elements in education, are lacking. This latter point may be illustrated by a comparison drawn between the Catholic Sister and the Protestant Deaconess. The comparison has been drawn by a Protestant lady in Germany, Frau Elisabeth Gnauck-Kühne, who for many years was prominent in works of Christian charity. She says:[1] "The Catholic Sister has made a binding vow, she has burnt the ships behind her; earthly cares, earthly pleasures she knows no more, her conversation is in heaven. It is the same to her whither she goes, whom she attends, poor or rich, old or young, high or low, all these circumstances are immaterial; for she has balanced her account with the life on this side of the grave, she does nothing by halves. The Evangelical Deaconess in theory stands in a different position. Her church demands of her no oath of renunciation, she has not destroyed the bridge, she may at any moment return to the fleshpots of Egypt, especially when a man wants her for his wife. Then the motives which have led her to the service of the sick will hold no longer; then the needs, which, as far as lay in her, she wished to remedy, must continue to exist, she doffs the severe garb and decks herself with the orange-blossoms. Such being the case, is it not most natural that she yields more easily to the temptation of having one eye on her vocation, the other on the world? What is excluded in the case of the Catholic Sister, the desertion of her vocation and marriage, are possible for her, and why should she not find the possibility desirable? If, in addition, the wish is father to the thought, there arises

[1] From the Protestant *Tägliche Rundschau* of Berlin, Sept. 28, 1899.

consciously or unconsciously, that disposition which has been felt as a 'tinge of worldliness.' But it would be unfair to blame the Deaconess. Protestantism with irresistible consistency must produce the described disposition and half-heartedness, for it esteems married life more highly than voluntary virginity, and under all circumstances it is lawful and laudable to strive after that which is higher and better. The Catholic Church, on the other hand, while considering married life a sacred state, gives a higher rank to life-long virginity consecrated to God."

This surprising tribute to the usefulness and dignity of the religious life as practised in the Catholic Church, may be applied with equal force to the religious teachers. They, too, do nothing by halves; "their hearts are not divided."[1] "For the kingdom of heaven's sake"[2] they have renounced the joys of family life. All their affections purified, ennobled and made supernatural, are to be bestowed on those entrusted to their care. It is Christ whom they have to see in the little ones, according to the words of the Divine Master: "He that receiveth one such little child in my name receiveth me." We do not mean to imply that married men may not be excellent teachers,— thousands have been such, — nor that all religious on account of their state are good teachers. We merely wish to prove that the religious state in itself affords many advantages for the cause of education. The difficulties connected with education will be borne more patiently, sometimes even heroically, by one who has bound himself to a life of perfect obedience and self-sacrifice.

[1] I. *Corinth.* 7, 33.
[2] *Matth.* 19, 11, 12.

Besides, in a teaching order, a continuity of aim and effort is effected which is and must be wanting in individuals. Mr. Quick has well emphasized this fact: "By corporate life you secure continuity of effort. There is to me something very attractive in the idea of a teaching society. How such a society might capitalize its discoveries. The Roman Church has shown a genius for such societies, witness the Jesuits and the Christian Brothers. The experience of centuries must have taught them much that we could learn of them."[1] For this reason a change of Professors in a Jesuit College is attended by fewer inconveniences, as all have been trained under the same system, and thus have imbibed the pedagogical traditions of the Order.

A French writer has spoken of another advantage, the moral influence, which the religious exercises owing to his state. "The Jesuit teacher" — the same may be said of all religious teachers — "is not a paid official. The pupils look up to him as a loved and venerated friend. Perhaps they know that he is the scion of an illustrious family, who could have followed a splendid career in life, who could have succeeded in the world of finances and industry. But he preferred to take the black gown and to devote himself to education."[2]

The source of the growing antipathy against the educational labors of religious is either hatred of the Catholic religion or religious indifferentism. When people do not care any more for the supernatural, the education based professedly on supernatural views, seems to them out of date, antiquated, a remnant of

---

[1] *Educational Reformers*, p. 532.
[2] Albert Duruy in *Revue des Deux-Mondes*, Jan. 1, 1880.

medieval priestcraft and clerical tyranny. Be it remarked, however, that this opposition is not new to our age. The very Middle Ages witnessed a violent opposition to the teaching of religious orders. This was especially the case in the University of Paris, where, in the thirteenth century, a strong rationalistic party, headed by William of Saint-Amour, endeavored to expel the Dominicans and Franciscans from the professorial chair. William's contention was that the religious should not be allowed to teach, but should employ themselves in manual labors, as did the monks in olden times. Then it was that three able pens were employed to defend the religious orders and their work: those of Bonaventure, of Albertus Magnus, and of Thomas Aquinas. St. Thomas wrote his little work: "Against those who attack Religion and the Worship of God",[1] of which Fleury said that it had always been regarded as the most perfect apology for religious orders. In the second chapter, headed "Whether Religious may teach", and the third, "Whether Religious may be a corporate body of secular teachers", the Saint refutes the objections of William in a most lucid and powerful manner, and sets forth the advantages which the Church and society may derive from teaching by religious orders. He contends that a religious order may be instituted for any work of mercy. As teaching is a work of mercy, a religious order may be founded with the special end of teaching.[2] And as the common good is to be preferred

[1] *Contra Impugnantes Dei Cultum et Religionem.* Edition of Parma, 1864, vol. XV. *Opusculum* I. See *The Life and Labors of St. Thomas Aquinas*, by Roger Bede Vaughan, O. S. B., 1871, vol. I, pp. 625—726.

[2] See also *Summa Theol.*, 2., 2., *qu.* 188, a. 5.

to private utility a monk may leave his solitude with permission of Superiors, to minister to the general good by teaching as well as by writing.

We see from this fact that history repeats itself, and that the modern attacks on the educational labors of religious communities are by no means new. The tactics of the enemies of the religious change, the pretexts of attacks on them will vary, but the nature of the warfare is ever the same. It is conscious or unconscious opposition to the principles of Christianity. Therefore, we find that those who have the interest of religion at heart, are not among the opponents of "clerical" education.

Even Protestants frankly admit that the union of the clerical office with that of the teacher offers great advantages. Sir Joshua Fitch, the distinguished English educator, thinks that the "parents in parting with the moral supervision of their sons are not unreasonably disposed to place increased confidence in a headmaster who combines the scholarship and the skill of teaching with the dignity and the weight of the clergyman's office."[1] And Professor Paulsen, certainly not theologically biased, says that it was not without disadvantages that the theologians were replaced in the Gymnasia by philologians and mathematicians, a change which for a long time was wished, undoubtedly not without good reasons. The theologian, owing to his whole training, had an inclination towards the care of the *souls;* the interest in the *whole* man was the centre of his calling.[2]

[1] *Thomas* and *Matthew Arnold*, p. 97.
[2] *Geschichte des gel. Unt.*, pp. 628—629 (2. ed., vol. II, p. 390).

What we have said so far undoubtedly justifies us in maintaining that the measure adopted by Ignatius, in making education a special ministry of a religious order, marks an epoch of prime importance in the history of Catholic pedagogy.

The character and object of the Society, the means it applies for obtaining its object, and its system of administration are laid down in the Constitutions of the Society. These Constitutions are the work of St. Ignatius, not, as has been asserted, of his successor Lainez, although the latter was one of those Fathers whom Ignatius consulted very frequently whilst drawing up the Constitutions. St. Ignatius died in 1556; in 1558 the representatives of the Order met together and elected James Lainez second General of the Society. They examined the Constitution which Father Ignatius had left at his death, and received it with unanimity, just as it stood. They presented it to the Sovereign Pontiff Paul IV., who committed the code to four Cardinals for accurate revision. The commission returned it, without having altered a word.[1]

We must explain a few details of the organization of the Order, as certain terms will be used again and again in this work. The Order is divided into Provinces, which comprise all the colleges and other houses in a certain country or district. The Superior of a Province is called *Provincial;* he is appointed by the General for a number of years. Several Provinces form a so-called *Assistancy.* The head of the Order is the *General,* elected for lifetime by the General Congregation. He possesses full jurisdiction and administrative power in the Order. Five assistants form, as

[1] Hughes, *Loyola*, p. 55.

decrees, emphasizing the vast importance of the education of youth, and the great esteem to be had for the teaching of grammar and the classics. It is called "a special and characteristic ministry of the Society" (*Congr. 8., Dec. 8.*), "one of the most desirable occupations and most beneficial to many" (*C. 7., D. 26.*). In the Ratio Studiorum, the very first Rule reads :[1] "As it is one of the principal ministries of our Society to teach all the branches of knowledge, which according to our institute may be taught, in such a manner that thereby men may be led to the knowledge and love of our Creator and · Redeemer, the Provincial should consider it his duty to see with all diligence, that the fruit which the grace of our vocation requires, corresponds with the manifold labors of our schools." This work of teaching boys is considered so important in the Society that in the last vows it is expressly mentioned : "I vow according to obedience a special concern for the education of boys."

The branches which "according to the Institute may be taught," are chiefly those that are connected with higher education. The Society has been blamed for neglecting elementary education. Professor Huber thinks that the Jesuits did so, "first, because this task seemed to them to be more subordinate, since the hold on the people was assured to them any way by their ecclesiastical influence; secondly, because on the whole they were no friends of popular education, however insignificant ; for the complete ignorance of the masses did but fortify their control of them."[2] This is a

[1] *First Rule of the Provincial.*
[2] *Der Jesuiten-Orden,* p. 348. — Compayré repeats this charge: "The Jesuits have deliberately neglected and disdained primary education." *Hist. of Ped.*, p. 142.

flagrant injustice and sheer calumny. The Order never opposed popular education. On the contrary, the Constitutions expressly declare it to be a laudable work: "Moreover it would be a work of charity to teach reading and writing, if the Society had a sufficient number of men. But on account of dearth of men we are not ordinarily used for this purpose."[1] — This is the proper reason, and the only one why the Jesuits could not undertake elementary education. They had never men enough to supply the demands for higher education. Actually hundreds of applications from bishops and princes for erecting colleges had to be refused. As early as 1565, the Second General Congregation had to decree that "existing colleges should rather be strengthened than new ones admitted. The latter should be done only if there was a sufficient endowment and a sufficient number of teachers available."[2]

How, then, could the Society enter so vast a field as that of elementary education? Besides the whole intellectual training of the Jesuits fitted them better for the higher branches. At the present day, when the watchword is "specialization", the Jesuits should

[1] *Constitut.*, P. IV, c. 12, *Declaratio C.* — The XX. General Congregation, 1820, when asked whether elementary schools should be admitted, reverted to this passage of the Constitutions: "Such schools are not excluded by our Institute, on the contrary, it is said in the Constitutions that such teaching is a work of charity. But the dearth of men is to be taken into consideration, and care must be taken not to hinder greater good through this (admission of elementary schools). The whole matter is left to the prudence of the Provincials, who have to see what is expedient according to place and circumstances." *Decr.* XXI. Pachtler, vol. I, p. 107.

[2] Pachtler, vol. I, p. 74. (*Decr.* VIII.)

it were, his council. They are elected by the General Congregation, from the various assistancies. They are now five: those of Italy, Germany (with Austria, Galicia, Belgium and Holland), France, England and North America, Spain (with Portugal). The legislative body of the Order is the *General Congregation.* It alone can add to the Constitutions, change or abrogate. It consists of the General (after his death, his Vicar), the Assistants, the Provincials, and two special deputies, elected by each province. It assembles only after the death of a General, or in extraordinary cases at the command of the General. As was said, it elects a new General and his assistants, and it may depose the General for grave reasons. It is clear, then, that the General's power is not so absolute as it is sometimes represented to be, but is wisely limited.

In this way the greatest possible centralization is secured in the hands of the General, and yet the danger of abusing so great a power is excluded by the institution of the Assistants. Ribadeneira has well remarked that this form of government borders closely upon monarchy, but has still more in common with an oligarchy, for it avoids everything faulty in each of the two systems and borrows the best points of both. From the monarchy it takes its unity and stability; from the oligarchy the existence of a council, so that the General may command every one, and at the same time, be subject to every one (*praesit et subsit*).[1]

In connection with the Constitutions we must mention a book which is said to exhibit the "true" character of the Society, namely the so-called *Monita*

---

[1] *Saint Ignatius,* by H. Joly, p. 217.

Secreta, or code of secret instructions, supposed to have been drawn up by Aquaviva, the fifth General, for the benefit of Superiors and others who are considered fit to be initiated in the full mystery of the schemes of the Society. It imputes to the Society the most crooked designs to achieve the aggrandizement of the Order. It has been reprinted again and again, in England as late as 1850 (London), in France 1870 and 1876, in Germany 1886 and 1901. The work has repeatedly been proved to be an infamous libel, written by one Zahorowski, who had been discharged from the Society in 1611 or 1612. Even such enemies of the Society as the Jansenist Arnauld, the "Old-Catholics" Döllinger, Huber, Reusch, and Friedrich, declare it "spurious and a lampoon on the Order." Dr. Littledale calls it "an ingenious forgery",[1] it has been recently called a fraudulent squib by Protestants like Professor Harnack (1891), Tschackert (1891), and others.[2] And still, in spite of all this adverse authority, recent Protestant publications have referred to this forgery as to an authentic document. No, not the *Monita Secreta*, but the Constitutions, available to any one, contain the spirit of the Society.

The Constitutions are divided into ten parts, the fourth of which treats of studies. This part is the longest of all, and its perfect arrangement met with especial admiration. After the promulgation of the Constitutions successive General Congregations issued

[1] *Encyclopedia Britannica*, article "Jesuits".
[2] See Duhr, *Jesuitenfabeln* (3rd ed.), pp. 76–102. — *The Month* (London), August 1901, pp. 176–185: *The Jesuit Bogey and the Monita Secreta;* and especially Reiber, *Monita Secreta*, Augsburg, 1902.

rather find recognition than censure, for having wisely limited their work centuries ago. Moreover, the Jesuits *did* teach elementary branches, at least in some places, not only in Paraguay, but also in Europe. Father Nadal writes: "In the elementary class (*classis abecedariorum*), which may be opened with the permission of the General, the boys are taught reading and writing. A brother may be employed to assist the teacher if the class should be too large."[1] — Be it further added that at present, in the foreign missions, v. g. in Syria, the Jesuits conduct hundreds of elementary schools, in which most branches are taught by lay brothers or by sisters of various teaching congregations.[2]

The fourth part of the Constitutions contains only the general principles, not a complete system of education. That this more general legislation was not considered final by St. Ignatius, follows from the passage in which he states that "a number of points will be treated of separately in some document approved by the General Superior."[3] This is the express warrant, contained in the Constitutions, for the future Ratio Studiorum, or System of Studies in the Society of Jesus.

---

[1] *Monumenta Paedagogica*, 1902, p. 108.
[2] See below chapter VII.
[3] *Const.*, P. IV, cap. XIII. *Decl. A.*

Chapter IV.

The Ratio Studiorum of 1599.

The number of colleges of the Society grew very rapidly. Colleges were opened during the life-time of St. Ignatius, at Messina, Palermo, Naples, and other towns in Italy; at Gandia, Salamanca, Valencia, Alcala, Burgos, Valladolid, and Saragossa in Spain; at Lisbon in Portugal; at Vienna in Austria; and at Billom in France. After the death of the first General (1556), many more colleges were added to the list, especially in those parts of Germany and the Netherlands which had remained faithful to the Catholic Church. Thus Ingolstadt, Cologne, Prague, Tyrnau (Hungary) were opened in 1556, Munich 1559, Treves 1560, Innsbruck and Mentz 1561, etc.[1] In Belgium Audenarde 1566, Douay 1568, Bruges 1571, Antwerp 1575, Liège 1582, etc. But the Society possessed as yet no uniform system of education; the colleges in the various countries at first followed, more or less, the systems prevailing there, not however, without improving the existing methods according to the general principles of the fourth part of the Constitutions. Still, it would be altogether wrong to suppose that the Ratio Studiorum, or Plan of Studies, drawn up 1584–1599, was the first important document

---

[1] The Colleges of Germany are enumerated by Paulsen, *l. c.*, pp. 265–281 (2nd ed., vol. I, pp. 390–406); those of Germany (Austria), Poland, Belgium, the Netherlands, by Pachtler, vol. III, pp. IX—XVI.

of its kind. The recent historical researches of the Spanish Jesuits have shed much new light on this question.[1] These Fathers have published in 1901-1902 many important documents on the educational methods of the Society, drawn up before 1584. Three documents especially exhibit three complete "Plans of Studies." The first was written by Father Jerome Nadal (Latinized Natalis), probably between 1548-1552, during the life-time of St. Ignatius. Nadal was well fitted for drawing up a plan of studies. Possessed of great talent and a singular prudence, he had made excellent studies in the University of Paris. Appointed Rector of the new College at Messina, in 1548, he wrote his treatise *De Studiis Societatis Jesu*, the first plan of studies of the Society known thus far.[2] The second is an adaptation of Father Nadal's plan which was sent from Messina to the Roman College.[3] The most important is the third, written by Father Ledesma. This distinguished scholar had studied in the Universities of Alcala, Paris and Louvain. Immediately after his entrance into the Society, in 1557, he taught in the Roman College, until his death, in 1575. As Prefect of Studies in this college, he drew up a plan of studies which practically contains, at least in outline, all points which were later on laid down in the Ratio Studiorum concerning classical

[1] *Monumenta Historica Societatis Jesu: Monumenta Paedagogica*, 1901-1902. We quote this important collection as *Monumenta Paedagogica*, to be carefully distinguished from Father Pachtler's *Monumenta Germaniae Paedagogica*.
[2] *Monumenta Paedagogica*, p. 8 and p. 89.
[3] *Monumenta Historica Societatis Jesu:* "Litterae Quadrimestres", vol. I, pp. 349-358.

studies.[1] Besides these three documents there are extant fragments of plans of studies of various colleges in Italy, France, Spain, Portugal, and Germany.[2]

With the increase of the colleges, the want of a uniform system for the whole Society was felt more and more. Teachers and superiors of schools and provinces asked more urgently for the plan of studies which St. Ignatius had promised in the Constitutions. The final completion of the educational system was reserved to the fifth General of the Order, Father Claudius Aquaviva, who governed the Society from 1581-1615. His Generalate was a most stormy, but at the same time the most brilliant, epoch in the history of the Order. It was the glorious time of the English and Japanese martyrs; the time when the great missions in Japan, China, and Brazil began to flourish; the time in which learned men like Bellarmine, Suarez, Maldonatus, Toletus, de Lugo, Vasquez, Molina, Lessius, a Lapide, Peter Canisius, Clavius, and a host of other writers not only added lustre to the Society, but were held to be the foremost scholars of the age and the most renowned champions of the Catholic Church.

In 1584, Father Aquaviva called to Rome six experienced schoolmen, who had been elected from different nationalities and provinces, in order that the peculiarities of the various nations might be considered in the formation of a system which was destined to be put to practice in so many countries all over the

---

[1] *Monumenta Paedagogica*, pp. 10-12; and p. 141 foll.

[2] *Ibid.* — Father Pachtler had published one such plan, which he ascribed to Blessed Peter Canisius, probably written in 1560.

world. These men worked for about a year, consulting authors on education, examining the regulations and customs of universities and colleges, especially those of the Roman College, and the letters, observations, and other documents sent to Rome from the various provinces. The standard which guided these men in their deliberations was the fourth part of the Constitutions. In 1585 they presented the result of their labor to the General.[1] In 1586, Father Aquaviva sent the report to the provinces; and at the same time ordered that in each province at least five men of eminent learning and experience should examine the report, first in private, then in common, and should send the result of their examination to Rome.

How much liberty was granted in these remarks on the educational methods then prevailing in the Order, may be seen from the verdict given by James Pontanus (his German name was Spanmiller), one of the ablest classic scholars of the Society. He boldly censures some abuses, especially that sometimes young men were employed in teaching who were not sufficiently prepared for the work; men who were not well grounded in Greek; that too frequent changes occurred among teachers, etc. He deplores the fact that too much weight is laid on physics, metaphysics, and dialectics, and that the humanistic studies are not valued as they deserve. "Without classical education," he says, "the other branches of study are cold, dumb and dead; classical learning gives these other studies life, breath, motion, blood and language." Pontanus' memorandum was by no means free from

[1] Documents given by Pachtler, vol. II, p. 1 foll. A summary in the *Études*, Paris, January 1889.

exaggerations and unwarranted generalizations of single instances. But it is interesting to see how freely opinions could be uttered on a question of such importance.[1]

The notes and suggestions sent from the different provinces were examined by the most prominent Professors of the Roman College and three members of the committee of 1584-85, and then were used in drawing up a second plan. This new plan, after having been revised by the General and his Assistants, was sent to the provinces in 1591 as *Ratio atque Institutio Studiorum*, the *editio princeps* of the Ratio. The Provincials who came to Rome for the fifth General Congregation (1593-94), again reported on the results of the plan as practised during the last years, and demanded some changes. At length, in 1599, when every possible effort had been made, when theory and practice alike had been consulted, and every advisable modification had been added, the final plan of studies appeared under the title: *Ratio atque Institutio Studiorum Societatis Jesu* (Naples 1599), usually quoted as *Ratio Studiorum*. Well could it be said that this Ratio was "the fruit of many prayers, of long and patient efforts, and the result of the combined wisdom of the whole Order." — It has sometimes been said that the word *Ratio Studiorum* is a misnomer, as it does not propose any educational *principles*. However, as Father Eyre, S. J., years ago has pointed out,[2] Ratio, as applied to studies, more naturally means *method* than principle, and the Ratio Studiorum is essentially

---

[1] Extracts of this Memorandum in Janssen's *Geschichte des deutschen Volkes*, vol. VII, pp. 100-103. .

[2] Quick, *Educational Reformers*, p. 57.

a practical method or system of teaching. Hence the name is altogether appropriate.

How easily an author, even without ill will, may be led into mistakes regarding the Ratio Studiorum, can be inferred from the following passage which is found in a Catholic magazine.[1] "The work which caused the greatest sensation was the *Ratio atque Institutio Studiorum Societatis Jesu*, published in the College at Rome in 1586. It took nine months to print it. The part bearing on theological opinions raised a storm of opposition among the other religious orders, principally the Dominicans, who denounced it to the Inquisition. The result was that Sixtus V. pronounced against the book, and, in the following editions, the chapter *De Opinionum Delectu* was omitted." The same mistake is made by Dr. Huber.[2]

The author of the article was betrayed into making these very inaccurate statements by implicitly trusting Debure (*Biographie Instructive*, Paris, 1764). The historical truth is established by Father Pachtler,[3] and by Father Duhr.[4] The evidence given by Father Pachtler may be summed up as follows:

1. The Ratio of 1586 was in no sense of the word "published", and hence caused no "sensation" whatever. It was only the project or plan of a Ratio, and printed privately for the members of the Order. How it should have taken "nine months to print it," is unintelligible; the error arose probably from misunderstanding the fact, that it took the six fathers who

---

[1] In the *Catholic World*, April 1896: *Early Labors of the Printing Press*.
[2] Huber, *Jesuiten-Orden*, p. 352.
[3] *Mon. Germ. Paed.*, vol. II, pp. 19–21.
[4] *Studienordnung*, pp. 15–23.

formed the committee, nine months to work out the plan of the Ratio.

2. This first draft, written in the form of dissertations, is now very rare. It is known to exist at present in Trier (Treves), Berlin, Milan, and Marseilles. Father Pachtler has for the first time reprinted it entirely from the copy found in the city library at Trier (located in the former Jesuit College).

3. This private document was not "denounced to the Inquisition," but was wrongfully seized by the "Spanish Inquisition," at the instance of the Spanish Dominicans, set on by some disloyal Spanish Jesuits who were soon after expelled from the Society.

4. As soon as the seizure was reported to Rome, Father Aquaviva complained directly to Pope Sixtus V. This energetic Pope, formerly a Franciscan and by no means partial to the Jesuits, far from "pronouncing against the book," became highly incensed at the action of the Spanish Inquisition, and wrote a characteristic dispatch to his nuncio in Spain, inclosing a letter to the Cardinal Grand Inquisitor Quiroga, and bidding the nuncio deliver the letter to the Cardinal only after having read it to him. In this letter the masterful Pontiff commands Quiroga, in virtue of his apostolic power, forthwith to restore to the Society the book of the Institute (which had also been seized), and especially the Ratio Studiorum. And unless he obeyed this command, the Pope threatened to depose him at once from the office of Grand Inquisitor, and strip him of the dignity of Cardinal.[1]

5. The second draft of the Ratio was sent to the

---

[1] See Sacchini, *Historiae Societatis Jesu*, Pars V, *tom. prior*, p. 337.

Provinces in 1591. In this draft the chapter *De Opinionum Delectu* (i. e. catalogue of philosophical and theological questions which were not to be taught in the Society), was omitted, but was sent out separately for examination in the following year. Hence the statement that in the following editions the chapter *De Opinionum Delectu* was omitted, is again inaccurate.

6. The final Ratio, including, of course, the *Catalogus Quaestionum*, was, as we have seen before, promulgated in 1599.[1]

This final Ratio did not contain any discussions on the educational value of different subjects, nor any treatises why this or that method had been adopted. Such discussions had preceded, and had been contained in the Ratio of 1585.[2] That of 1599 was a code of laws, a collection of rules for the different officials, in whose hands lies the government of a college, and for the teachers of the various classes. The rules are divided as follows :

I.

Regulae Provincialis (Provincial Superior).
" *Rectoris* (President).
" *Praefecti Studiorum* (Prefect or Superintendent of Studies).

II.

Regulae Communes omnibus Professoribus Superiorum Facultatum (General regulations for the Professors of theology and philosophy).
" *Professoris Sacrae Scripturae.*
" " *Linguae Hebraicae.*
" " *Scholasticae Theologiae.*
" " *Historiae Ecclesiasticae.*
" " *Juris Canonici.*
" " *Casuum Conscientiae* (Moral Theology).

[1] *Woodstock Letters*, 1896, pp. 506-507.
[2] Pachtler, vol. II, pp. 25-217.

III.

Regulae Professoris Philosophiae.
"   "   *Philosophiae Moralis* (Ethics).
"   "   *Physicae* (Physics and other natural sciences).[1]
"   "   *Mathematicae.*

IV.

Regulae Praefecti Studiorum Inferiorum (together with regulations for written examinations and for awarding prizes).
Regulae Communes Professoribus Classium Inferiorum.
"   *Professoris Rhetoricae.*
"   "   *Humanitatis.*
"   "   *Supremae Classis Grammaticae.*
"   "   *Mediae* "   "
"   "   *Infimae* "   "

Then follow various rules: for the pupils, for the management of academies (literary and debating societies) etc.

The rules under No. I are those of the Superiors.[2] The entire government of a college is in the hands of the *Rector* (President). He is also the court of appeal, in all disputed questions among the teachers, or between the masters and the students. He is to inspect the classes from time to time, in order to inform himself of the progress of the students, and to give advice to the teachers. As far as possible, he is to take an interest in each pupil personally. Nothing of importance can be undertaken in the college without consulting him, nor can any custom of the house be changed without his consent. The subordinate officials have that amount of authority which he gives

---

[1] Was added in 1832. In the Ratio of 1599 natural sciences were treated as part of philosophy.

[2] See John Gilmary Shea, *History of Georgetown College*, 1891, pp. 83—84.

them, and they are obliged to report to him frequently on the conditions of affairs in the college. The Rector's power is, however, not absolute; he has to follow the laws laid down for him. Besides he is provided with a Board of Consultors and he is obliged to ask their opinion on all matters of greater moment, although he remains free to follow their advice or to reject it. The teachers have to carry out the decisions of the Rector, but they may always have recourse to the higher Superior, the Provincial. The Provincial visits the colleges at least once a year, and every teacher has to confer with him privately and may lay before him any complaints against the Rector. In this manner, a firm centralized government is ensured, while at the same time any arbitrariness on the part of Superiors is prevented.

Interesting are, in this regard, the words of Father Nadal: "Let the Rector have his ordinary advisers (*consultores*) and let him hold regular meetings (*concilia*). One is the meeting of 'languages', in which all teachers of the languages take part; the second of philosophy, and the third of theology. To these meetings the Rector may invite two or three other experienced men, if he thinks it necessary or useful. In order to settle a question concerning languages, or philosophy, or theology, a meeting of the respective professors should be held; if a question concerns the whole institution, a meeting of all professors should be called. However, the Rector is not so bound that he could not do anything without convoking such a meeting. For these meetings are held that he may benefit by their advice. The whole authority and responsibility of the administration rests with him; but every year the Rector shall report to the General about the college, and all officials of the college shall inform the General through sealed letters about the administration by the Rector."[1]

The chief assistant of the Rector is the *Prefect of Studies.* To him belongs the direct supervision of the classes and everything connected with instruction. He must be a man of literary and scientific accomplishments and of experience in teaching, so that both teachers and students can have recourse to him with confidence in all questions pertaining to education. It is his duty to assign the students to their proper classes, to determine the matter of examination, and to appoint the examiners, to select the authors to be read during the following scholastic year,[2] to visit every class at least once in two weeks, to admonish the masters of any defects he notices in their manner of teaching, and to direct them by other useful advice. In all this he is the instrument of the Rector, whom he has to consult in all important matters.

There is another assistant of the Rector, the *Prefect of Discipline,* who is immediately responsible for all that concerns external order and discipline. From these few details, it will appear that the government of a Jesuit college is, at once, extremely simple and highly efficient.

The regulations contained under No. II are for the theological faculty in universities and seminaries. We have to examine chiefly the last two classes: the regu-

[1] *Monumenta Paedagogica,* p. 102.
[2] "Before selecting the authors", says Father Nadal, "let the Prefect of Studies hear first the opinion of the teachers." *Mon. Paed.,* p. 130.

lations for the faculty of Arts or Philosophy, and those for the *Studia inferiora* or *Humanities*. These "lower studies" were for the greater part literary and correspond to the classical course of the high school and part of the college. The Ratio Studiorum treated languages, mathematics and sciences not simultaneously, but successively; hence the distinction between Philosophy (Arts) and *Studia inferiora*.

In the five lower classes — in many places there were six — the classical languages were the staple studies. Other branches, as history and geography, were to be treated as *accessories* or complements of the literary studies. The task for each grade is expressed in the first rule of the Professor of the respective class.[1]

LOWER GRAMMAR. The aim of this class is a perfect knowledge of the rudiments and elementary knowledge of the syntax. — In Greek: reading, writing, and a certain portion of the grammar. The work used for the prelection,[2] will be some easy selections from Cicero, besides fables of Phaedrus and Lives of Nepos.

MIDDLE GRAMMAR. The aim is a knowledge, though not entire, of all grammar; and, for the prelection, only the select epistles, narrations, descriptions and the like from Cicero, with the Commentaries of Caesar, and some of the easiest poems of Ovid. — In Greek: the fables of Aesop, select dialogues of Lucian, the Tablet of Cebes.

UPPER GRAMMAR. The aim is a complete know-

---

[1] The following translation of these rules is mostly that of Father Hughes, *Loyola*, p. 271 foll. These rules contain a few modifications of the Revised Ratio of 1832. The two Ratios may be seen separately in Pachtler, vol. II, 225 f. and Duhr, *l. c.*, pp. 177—280.

[2] On *prelection* see chapter XVI, § 1.

ledge of grammar, including all the exceptions and idioms in syntax, figures and rhetoric, and the art of versification. — In Greek: the eight parts of speech, or all the rudiments. For the lessons: in prose, the most important epistles of Cicero, the books, *De Amicitia*, *De Senectute*, and others of the kind, or even some of the easier orations; in poetry, some select elegies and epistles of Ovid, also selection from Catullus, Tibullus, Propertius, and the Eclogues of Virgil, or some of Virgil's easier books, as the fourth book of the Georgics, or the fifth and seventh books of the Aeneid. — In Greek: St. Chrysostom, Aesop, and the like.

HUMANITIES. The aim is to prepare, as it were, the ground for eloquence, which is done in three ways: by a knowledge of the language, some erudition, and a sketch of the precepts pertaining to rhetoric. For a command of the language, which consists chiefly in acquiring propriety of expression and fluency, the one prose author employed in daily prelections is Cicero; as historical writers, Caesar, Sallust, Livy, Curtius, and others of the kind; the poets used are, first of all, Virgil; also odes of Horace, with the elegies, epigrams and other productions of illustrious poets, expurgated; in like manner orators, historians, and poets, in the vernacular (1832). The erudition conveyed should be slight, and only to stimulate and recreate the mind, not to impede progress in learning the tongue. The precepts will be the general rules of expression and style, and the special rules on the minor kinds of composition, epistles, narrations, descriptions, both in verse and prose. — In Greek: the art of versification, and some notions of the dialects; also a clear understanding of authors, and some composition in Greek. The Greek prose authors will be Saints Chrysostom and Basil, epistles of Plato and Synesius, and some selections from Plutarch; the poets: Homer, Phocylides, Theognis, St. Gregory Nazianzen, Synesius, and others like them.

RHETORIC. The grade of this class cannot be easily defined. For it trains to perfect eloquence, which comprises two great faculties, the oratorical and the poetical, the former chiefly being the object of culture; nor does it regard only the practical, but the beautiful also. For the precepts, Cicero may be supplemented with Quintilian and Aristotle. The style, which may be assisted by drawing on the most approved historians and poets, is to be formed on Cicero; all of his works are most fitted for this purpose, but only his speeches should be made the subject of prelection, that the precepts of the art may be seen in practice. — As to the vernacular, the style should be formed on the best authors (1832). The erudition will be derived from the history and manners of nations, from the authority of writers and all learning; but moderately as befits the capacity of the students. — In Greek: the fuller knowledge of authors and of dialects is to be acquired. The Greek authors, whether orators, historians, or poets, are to be ancient and classic: Demosthenes, Plato, Thucydides, Homer, Hesiod, Pindar, and others of the kind, including Saints Nazianzen, Basil, and Chrysostom.

Let it not be imagined, however, that this plan was followed slavishly. The different provinces of the Order made such adaptations and introduced such changes as they thought best for their respective countries. We give here the plan which was followed in the colleges in Upper Germany, in the beginning of the eighteenth century. It is taken from the *Ratio et Via* of Father Kropf, published in 1736.[1]

LOWER GRAMMAR. *First Year.*
(First high school class.)

Latin. Grammar of Alvarez, elements, and easier rules of construction. — Reading: The easiest letters of Cicero, specially selected and separately printed. Selections from book I and II of Father Pontanus' *Progymnasmata*.[2]

Greek. Grammar of Father Gretser,[3] or of Father Bayer.[4] Correct reading and writing; accents and declensions.

Religion. Small Catechism of Peter Canisius,[5] part I—II. Explanation of the Latin Gospel.

History. *Rudimenta historica*,[6] vol. I., treating chiefly of the history of the people of Israel.

[1] In Herder's *Bibliothek der katholischen Pädagogik*, vol. X, pp 340—348.

[2] James Pontanus S. J, *Progymnasmatum Latinitas sive dialogorum selectorum libri quattuor.* Several works of this Jesuit were used in most European schools for over a century.

[3] James Gretser, S. J., wrote several textbooks: a larger Greek Grammar, and a Compendium; *Rudimenta Linguae Graecae*, both in many editions; a Latin-Greek-German and a Latin-Greek Dictionary.

[4] James Bayer, S. J., wrote a Short Greek Grammar, a Latin-Greek Dictionary, and a Latin-German and German-Latin Dictionary. Of the last the eleventh edition was published by Professor Mayer, Würzburg, 1865.

[5] On this catechism see chapter XVIII.

[6] This history, comprising six volumes, was written by Max Dufrêne, S. J., (Landshut, Bavaria). It appeared first 1727—1730; several editions followed.

LOWER GRAMMAR. *Second Year.*
(Second high school class.)

Latin. Alvarez' Grammar, book I, part II ; repetition of first year's matter; the irregular verb; first part of syntax. — Reading: Select letters of Cicero. Selections from Pontanus' *Progymnasmata.*

Greek. Grammar: repetition of declensions; comparison of adjectives; pronouns and auxiliary verbs.

Religion. Catechism of Canisius, part I—III. Explanation of Latin Gospel.

History. Rudimenta historica, vol. II : The four monarchies (Ancient history).

MIDDLE GRAMMAR.
(Third high school class.)

Latin. Grammar: The whole of syntax; repetition of irregular verbs. — Reading: chiefly Cicero's *Epistulae ad Familiares,* some parts of the *Progymnasmata.* The reading of poetical works which is customary in other Jesuit colleges in this class, is not sanctioned in this province.

Greek. Grammar: the verb completed. — As regards reading it is left to the judgment of the Prefect of Studies to prescribe the study of the Greek Catechism or Cebes' Tablet. At all events the pupils should practise the reading of these books from time to time and give an account of their reading.

Religion. Catechism of Canisius and Latin Gospel.

History. Rudimenta historica, vol. III: The Christian Emperors of Rome (Medieval history).

UPPER GRAMMAR.
(Fourth high school class.)

Latin. Grammar: the whole of syntax (repeated), rules of construction; rules of prosody. — Reading: Above all, the Letters of Cicero to Atticus and his brother Quintus; *De Amicitia, De Senectute,* etc. Selections from the *Progymnasmata,* books II and III. — Selections from Catullus, Tibullus, Propertius; Ovid; Virgil; fourth book of the Georgics; Aeneid, books V and VII.

Greek. First book of Gretser's grammar, except the dialects.—Reading: Chrysostom, Aesop, Agapetus, etc.

Religion. Catechism of Canisius. Greek Gospel.

History. Rudimenta historica, vol. IV : The States of the World (Modern history).

HUMANITIES, (Freshman.)

Latin. Rules of rhetoric from a brief compendium; rules of style, tropes, figures, etc. — Reading: Cicero's ethical works; Caesar, Livy, Curtius, Sallust, etc., or easier orations of Cicero: *Pro Lege Manilia, Pro Archia, Pro Marcello,* etc. Virgil; select odes of Horace, etc.

Greek. The whole of syntax. The teacher should see that the pupils acquire a fair understanding of the authors, and that they are able to write an easier Greek composition. The authors are orations of Isocrates, or of Chrysostom and Basil; also letters of Plato and Synesius, selections from Plutarch, poems of Phocylides, Theognis, etc.

Religion. Catechism of Canisius; the Greek Gospel.

History. Rudimenta historica, vol. V : Geography and heraldics.

RHETORIC. (Sophomore.)

Precepts of rhetoric from the oratorical works of Cicero and Aristotle. The practice of the rules is chiefly based on Cicero, particularly his orations; also the historians may be used to some extent. The rules of poetry may be drawn from Aristotle's *Poetics.* Of the poets only the best should be read: Virgil, Horace, etc.

Greek. Repetition of syntax; prosody; the dialects, a further introduction into Greek literature. The standard authors are Demosthenes, Plato, Thucydides, Homer, Hesiod, Pindar, etc.; also Gregory Nazianzen, Basil, and Chrysostom may be read.

Other Latin and Greek authors which may be given into the hands of the pupils of the class of Rhetoric and of other classes, are enumerated by Juvencius.

Religion. Catechism of Canisius (larger one). On Saturday the Acts of the Apostles are read in Greek, or an oration of Chrysostom.

History. Rudimenta historica, vol. VI: Compendium of Church history.

The school hours were not too long; two hours and a half in the morning and the same in the afternoon; in the highest class (rhetoric), only two hours in the morning and the same in the afternoon; thus the students of the highest grade were wisely given more time for home work. There was ordinarily a full holiday every week, usually Wednesday or Thursday, "lest," as the regulations of the Province of the Upper Rhine have it, "the pupils have to go to school four days in succession."[1] These holidays were frequently spent in a country house (*villa*), near the city. On the whole, study and recreation were so distributed that the complaints of "overburdening" the students could not reasonably be made in Jesuit schools.

Against the literary curriculum of the Society some serious charges have been made by modern critics. It has been said that nothing but the ancient languages was studied in Jesuit colleges, and that other branches,

[1] Pachtler, *l. c.,* vol. III, p. 398.

as history, were entirely neglected, "Preoccupied before all else with purely formal studies, and exclusively devoted to the exercises which give a training in the use of elegant language, the Jesuits leave real and concrete studies in entire neglect. History is almost wholly banished from their programme. It is only with reference to the Greek and Latin texts that the teacher should make allusion to the matters of history, which are necessary for the understanding of the passage under examination. No account is made of modern history, nor of the history of France. 'History', says a Jesuit Father, 'is the destruction of him who studies it'."[1] This last remark strikes us, and perhaps also other readers of M. Compayré's work, as ridiculous. We ask: Who is this Jesuit Father that made such a silly statement? Is he one of the framers of the Ratio Studiorum, or one of its commentators, or a Superior of the Order? No; no one knows who he is — if ever a Jesuit has said such nonsense. But granted one has said it, must not every fair-minded reader ask: Can the Jesuit Order be said to hold and defend all the views which every individual Jesuit has uttered? If a Professor of Harvard or Yale University made a foolish remark, would it be fair to hold up the two universities to ridicule?

But let us examine the facts. History is taught in Jesuit schools and was taught in the Old Society, it matters little whether this and other branches were called *accessories* or side branches — they were called so because much less time was devoted to them than to the study of language and literature. It is true, the historical studies were not then cultivated, neither in

[1] Compayré, *History of Pedagogy*, pp. 144—145.

Protestant nor Catholic schools, to such extent as is done now. But history was never neglected in Jesuit colleges, and it gradually obtained a place of honor among the literary studies. This was evidently the case in France in the beginning of the eighteenth century. We refer the reader to various works which deal with this subject.[1] In Germany we find in the Jesuit colleges, as early as 1622, special historical works assigned to various classes. In these compendia also "modern" history was treated.[2] The textbooks most in use in German Jesuit colleges during the eighteenth century, were the *Rudimenta Historica* of Father Dufrène,[3] and the *Introductio* of Father Wagner.[4] From Father Kropf's work it is evident that, when he wrote this work in 1736, history was treated quite systematically, in a well graded course, in all the classes below philosophy. This is evident from the programme given above on pages 121—125. The same author gives also a method of teaching history.[5]

[1] Daniel, *Les Jésuites instituteurs de la jeunesse aux XVII. et XVIII. siècles.* — Rochemonteix, *Un collège de Jésuites aux XVII. et XVIII. siècles. Le collège Henri IV. de la Flèche*, vol. IV., pp. 123—147.

[2] Duhr, *Studienordnung*, pp. 104—106. — Pachtler, *Monumenta*, vol. IV, p. 105 seq. — The first compendium used was that of Tursellini, reaching down to 1598. It went through many editions in Germany, and in 1682 Father Ott supplemented it by a history of the seventeenth century.

[3] Pachtler, vol. IV, p. 112 seq.

[4] Pachtler, *l. c.*, p. 118 seq.

[5] Pachtler, *l. c.*, p. 116; and German translation of Kropf's work in Herder's *Bibliothek der katholischen Pädagogik*, vol. X, p. 422.

Nor was geography neglected. In the earlier Jesuit schools it was treated more fully only in the philosophical course, in connection with astronomy, or as "erudition" in the class of rhetoric. As early as 1677 a geographical text-book, written by Father König,[1] was used in German colleges. We have proofs that geography was taught in the colleges in France, twelve years after the publication of the Ratio Studiorum. A few years ago a manuscript was found belonging to the old Jesuit college of Avignon, written in the year 1611 by Father Bonvalot. It contains, in ninety-four folio pages, a brief but complete course of geography. This course is divided into two parts: Europe, and the countries outside of Europe. Every country of Europe forms the subject of a special chapter, in which ancient and modern geography are combined. Special attention is paid to the customs of the peoples, the form of government, etc. This manuscript was used as the basis of lessons in geography, which were dictated to the pupils. It has been said that geography was not taught in Jesuit schools until long after this branch had been cultivated in the schools of the Oratory and the *Petites-Écoles* of Port-Royal. And yet Father Bonvalot wrote his course of geography the very year in which the Oratory was founded and more than thirty years before the opening of the *Petites-Écoles*. But Father Bonvalot was perhaps an exception. By no means. Documentary evidence is at hand to show that, before the middle of the seventeenth century, there was hardly a manuscript "course of rhetoric" in the colleges of Lyons, Tournon, Avignon, etc., which did not contain a course of geogra-

[1] Pachtler, *l. c.*, pp. 106—107.

phy.[1] The custom of dictating these lessons was continued until the handbooks of geography were published by the Jesuits Monet, Riccioli, Labbe, Briet, Saint-Juste, Buffier. Father Daniel, S. J., in an interesting essay of twenty-eight pages, has given many important details about the teaching of geography in Jesuit colleges of the seventeenth and eighteenth centuries.[2]

Special attention was given to the geography of the country in which the colleges were situated, but great interest was also taken in the geographical discoveries in foreign countries. The Jesuits had, during the seventeenth and eighteenth centuries, better advantages for obtaining geographical information than any other body of men. The Jesuit missionaries scattered all over the world sent regular accounts of their journeys and observations to their brethren in Europe. That much valuable geographical and ethnological information was contained in these reports may be seen from the "Jesuit Relations", seventy-three volumes of letters of Jesuits from New France, i. e. Canada and the Northern part of the United States.[3] Several Jesuit missionaries have made most important contributions to the science of geography, not only by great discoveries as that of the Mississippi by Father Mar-

[1] Chossat, *Les Jésuites à Avignon*, pp. 316—318.

[2] *La géographie dans les collèges des Jésuites aux XVII. et XVIII. siècles.* In the *Études*, June 1879.

[3] Edited by Reuben Gold Thwaites, published by Burrows Brothers, Cleveland, Ohio, 1896—1901. The letters of the missionaries were read by the students in the colleges. Father Nadal said they might be read to the boarders during dinner and supper. (*Mon. Paed.* p. 612.).

quette, but also by most valuable maps. Thus we read of Father Martini in Baron von Richthofen's work on China: "Father Martini is the best geographer of all the missioners. By his great work, *Novus Atlas Sinensis*, the best and most complete description which we possess of China, he has become the Father of Chinese geography." The first maps of North Mexico, Arizona and Lower California, were prepared by four German Jesuits, among them the famous Father Kino (his German name was Kühn).[1]

These few details taken from a mass of similar facts, show what interest the Jesuits took in geography, and even if we had no positive proof we would have to conjecture that they did not neglect its study in their schools. But the positive proofs abundantly show that another charge against the Jesuit colleges of former centuries is a sheer calumny.

Owing to the importance of Latin as the universal language of the educated world, less attention was devoted to the study of the mother-tongue. In this regard the schools of the Jesuits did not differ from those of the Protestants. However, at no time was the mother-tongue entirely neglected; and gradually it received more and more consideration. Thus, in France, rules for writing French verses appear in the dictated "courses of rhetoric" in 1663.[2] About 1600, the Bohemian Jesuits asked and received permission to open a private "academy" for the study of the Czech language.[3] As early as 1560 Father Jerome

[1] See *Notes upon the First Discoveries of California*, Washington, 1879.
[2] Chossat, *Les Jésuites, à Avignon*, p. 320.
[3] Duhr, *Studienordnung*, p. 110.

Nadal had exhorted the Jesuits at Cologne, "to cultivate diligently the German language and to find out a method of teaching it; they should also select pupils and teachers for this branch."[1] In 1567 he gave the same order in Mentz. During the Thirty Years' War, the German Jesuits Balde, Mair, Bidermann and Pexenfelder, planned the establishment of a society for the improvement of the German language; but the calamities of that horrible war, which reduced Germany to a state of utter misery, frustrated this whole plan. From about 1730 on, the German language was taught in the Jesuit schools according to fixed rules, and the pupils were diligently practised in writing prose compositions and poetry. Many valuable testimonies on this subject are given by Father Duhr.[2] The fact that many Jesuits are to be found among the prominent writers in the different modern languages is another proof that the vernacular was not neglected, much less "proscribed" as M. Compayré says.[3] One of the finest German writers of the seventeenth century was the Jesuit Spe. The sweetness, power and literary merits of his collection of exquisite poems, entitled *Trutz-Nachtigall* (Dare-Nightingale), and of his prose work *Güldnes Tugendbuch* (Virtue's Golden Book) are admired by critics of the most different schools, Protestants as well as Catholics.[4] Father

---

[1] *Ib.*, p. 109: "*Exerceant diligenter linguam germanicam, et inveniant rationem qua id commodissime fieri possit; deligantur etiam qui eam sunt docendi et quis docturus.*"

[2] *Ib.*, pp. 110—116.

[3] *History of Pedagogy*, p. 144.

[4] Duhr, *Frederick Spe*, Herder, Freiburg and St. Louis, 1901. See the writer's article "Attitude of the Jesuits in the Trials for Witchcraft," *American Catholic Quarterly Review*,

Denis, a Jesuit of the eighteenth century, was a most distinguished German writer, and has been called "the pioneer of German literature in Austria." How could all these facts be explained if what Mr. Painter says were true: "The Jesuits were hostile to the mother-tongue; and distrusting the influence of its associations, endeavored to supplant it"?[1]

After the pupil's mind had been enriched with the treasures of Latin and Greek literature, and after his native talents had been "cultivated" or "stimulated", as the Ratio very expressively designates it, the student entered on the study of philosophy.[2] This course, if given completely, comprised three years. The Ratio of 1599 prescribed for the *First Year:* Introduction and Logics; *Second Year:* Physics, Cosmology and Astronomy; *Third Year:* Special Metaphysics, Psychology and Ethics. A course of mathematics runs parallel with philosophy.

In philosophy Aristotle was the standard author. Of course, those of his opinions which were contradictory to revealed truths were refuted.[3] Special care is recommended in the correct explanation of the text of Aristotle. "No less pains are to be taken in the interpretation of the text than in the questions themselves. And the Professor should also convince the students that it is a very defective philosophy which neglects this study of the text."[4] The Professor of Philosophy

July 1902, p. 500. — This Father Spe is better known as the heroic opponent of witch persecution.
[1] *History of Education*, p. 170.
[2] See Hughes, *Loyola*, pp. 274—281.
[3] *Reg. Prof. Philosophiae*, 2.
[4] *Ib.*, 12.

is also told "to speak respectfully of St. Thomas Aquinas and to follow him whenever possible."[1] The Ratio had to encounter many an attack for not following St. Thomas more rigorously. But the composers of the Ratio wisely admitted modifications, as St. Thomas evidently could not claim infallibility in all questions.

The philosophical course comprised not only philosophy properly so called, but also mathematics and natural sciences. This *successive* teaching of literary and scientific subjects secured concentration and unity in instruction, whereas in modern systems too many branches, which have no connection with each other, are taught in the same class so that the mind of the young untrained learner is bewildered. There is another consideration which may vindicate the educational wisdom of the Ratio Studiorum in assigning mathematics and sciences to a later stage in the curriculum. Distinguished teachers of mathematics have recently pointed out that the mathematical teaching in the lower and middle classes is frequently beyond the capacity of the students of those grades. Problems are proposed which, at that stage, can at best be treated only mechanically and superficially.[2] Mathematics, says a prominent writer on this subject, makes very high demands on the mental powers of the pupils, in such a degree that only the mature age derives the full benefit from the study of this branch.[3]

[1] *Ib.*, 6.
[2] *Neue Jahrbücher für das klassische Altertum etc.*, 1901, vol. VIII, p. 201.
[3] Professor Simon, in Baumeister's *Handbuch der Erziehungs- und Unterrichtslehre*, vol. IV, "Mathematik", p. 33.

In the philosophical course of the Jesuit colleges, mathematics was by no means slighted, or treated as a branch of small educational value. It will suffice to quote what an autograph treatise written by Father Clavius, the "Euclid of his Age," has on the teaching of mathematics. "*First*, let a teacher of more than ordinary learning and authority be chosen to teach this branch; otherwise, as experience proves, the pupils cannot be attracted to the study of mathematics. . . . It is necessary that the professor have an inclination and a liking for teaching this science; he must not be distracted by other occupations, otherwise he will hardly be able to advance the students. In order that the Society may always have capable professors of this science, some men should be selected who are specially fitted for this task, and they should be trained in a private school (*academia*) in the science of mathematics. . . . I need not mention that without mathematics the teaching of natural philosophy is defective and imperfect.— In the *second* place it is necessary that the pupils understand that this science is useful and necessary for a correct understanding of philosophy, and, at the same time, complements and embellishes all other studies. Nay more, they should know that this science is so closely related to natural philosophy that, unless they help each other, neither can maintain its proper place and dignity. In order to accomplish this it will be necessary for the students of physics to study mathematics at the same time; this is a custom which has always been kept up in the schools of the Society. For if the mathematical sciences were taught at any other time, the students of philosophy would think, and not without some reason, that they were not necessary for physics, and so very few would be inclined to study mathematics." The writer then goes on to show the necessity of mathematics for the study of the movements of heavenly bodies, of their distances, of the oppositions and conjunctions of the comets; of the tides, the winds, the rainbow, and other physical phenomena. He also treats of various exercises by which the study of mathematics can best be advanced, such as lectures given by the students on mathematical and astronomical subjects.[1]

We find that in mathematics, pure and applied, the courses of the Jesuit colleges were advanced to the foremost rank; in arithmetic and geometry we notice that, as early as 1667, a single public course, under the direction of the Jesuits at Caen, numbered four hundred students.[2] The Order had among its members many distinguished mathematicians, some of whom will be mentioned in succeeding chapters.

The modern course of physics was, in those centuries, a thing of the future. But the physical sciences were taught as far as they were known; in the middle of the eighteenth century, we find physical cabinets in regular use, and experimental lectures given to the classes by the professor of physics.[8]

These testimonies will suffice to show that the Jesuits, however much they valued the classical studies, were not so one-sided as to disregard or neglect

---

[1] *Monumenta Paedagogica*, pp. 471—478.
[2] Crétineau-Joly, *Histoire de la Compagnie*, vol. IV, ch. 3. — Hughes, *l. c.*, p. 275. — See also Janssen, vol. VII, pp. 86—87.; vol. IV (16. ed.), p. 414.
[8] Pachtler, vol. III, p. 441, n. 7.

mathematics and natural sciences. What, then, should be said of Compayré's statements: "The Jesuits leave real and concrete studies in entire neglect. . . . The sciences are involved in the same disdain as history. Scientific studies are entirely proscribed in the lower classes."[1] Indeed, in the Old Society, the sciences were not taught in the five lower classes; there the Jesuits concentrated the efforts of the pupils on the languages; but in the three highest classes they applied the students with the same energy to the study of mathematics, sciences and philosophy.

Having thus far analyzed the Ratio Studiorum, we may be allowed to quote the judgment of Mr. Quick on the Ratio Studiorum: "The Jesuit system stands out in the history of education as a remarkable instance of a school system elaborately thought out and worked as a whole. In it the individual schoolmaster withered (*sic!*), but the system grew, and was, and I may say *is*, a mighty organism. The single Jesuit teacher might not be the superior of the average teacher in good Protestant schools, but by their unity of action the Jesuits triumphed over their rivals as easily as a regiment of soldiers scatters a mob."[2] This system "points out a perfectly attainable goal, and carefully defines the road by which that goal is to be approached. For each class was prescribed not only the work to be done, but also the end to be kept in view. Thus method reigned throughout — perhaps not the best method, as the object to be attained was assuredly not the highest object (*sic!*), but the method such as it was, was applied with undeviating exactness. In this par-

[1] *History of Pedagogy*, p. 144.
[2] *Educational Reformers*, p. 508.

ticular the Jesuit schools contrasted strongly with their rivals of old, as indeed with the ordinary school of the present day."[1]

If we ask to which sources the Ratio Studiorum is to be referred, we must confess that an adequate answer is not easy. There are many little brooks which by their conflux form that mighty river. Ignatius and his companions had been trained in scholastic philosophy. The Constitutions and the Ratio Studiorum adapted this philosophic system, modified, however, and perfected by the teachers and writers of the Order. Hence the central position of Aristotle in philosophy, and St. Thomas Aquinas in theology.[2]

[1] *Ib.*, p. 49.
[2] This close adherence to Aristotle has been made a subject of reproach against the Jesuit system. And yet Protestant universities followed Aristotle as closely as the Ratio. Professor Schwalbe said in the Conference on questions of Higher Education, held at Berlin in 1900: "We have grown up in the belief in the infallibility of the dogma of Aristotle. When I was a student, Aristotle was still considered the greatest scientist on earth. I have investigated this question most thoroughly, and have found that the universities, even the freest, with the one exception of Wittenberg, fined any one who dared to contradict any of Aristotle's propositions on scientific subjects. In Oxford the penalty was so high that Giordano Bruno was unable to pay it." *Verhandlungen über die Fragen des höheren Unterrichts* (Halle, 1902), p. 109. — This is a good illustration of the fact that there existed a Protestant "Inquisition" as well as a Catholic, and it should warn certain writers to speak with less religious bitterness on the regrettable Galileo affair. — Professor Paulsen states in his latest work: *Die deutschen Universitäten* (1902, p. 43), that the dread of heresy, during the seventeenth century, was probably greater in the Lutheran universities than in the Catholic, because in the former the doctrine was less certain, and dangers were apprehended not only from Catholicism

The literary course was an adaptation of the humanistic schools as they existed shortly before the outbreak of the Reformation. It is especially Paris and the Netherlands which we have to consider as the chief sources of much that is contained in the Ratio. We heard that the great University of Paris was the *Alma Mater* of St. Ignatius and his first companions. Great must have been the influence of this seat of learning on the formation of the educational system of the Jesuits. Bartoli, one of the historians of the Society, goes so far as to say: "Spain gave the Society a father in St. Ignatius, France a mother in the University of Paris." From this University Ignatius probably adopted the division of his system of studies into the three parts: Languages, Arts or Philosophy, Theology. In languages again the Constitutions, as well as the Paris University, distinguished three parts: Grammar, Humanities, Rhetoric. The school exercises, especially the disputations in philosophy, were fashioned after those of Paris. Father Polanco, secretary of the Society, himself a student of Paris, writes about the colleges of Messina and Vienna, that "exercises (disputations) were added to the lectures after the model of those of Paris (*more parisiensi*)."[1]

Ignatius himself had recommended Paris as "the

but also from Calvinism. Hence also in the philosophical faculties of Protestant universities theological orthodoxy was insisted on most rigorously. The same author says that in the frequent changes from Lutheranism to Calvinism, and *vice versa*, which took place in various Protestant states in Germany, careful inquiries were made as to whether all teachers and officials had accepted the change with due submission. *Geschichte des gelehrten Unterrichts*, vol. I, p. 324.

[1] Duhr, *Studienordnung*, p. 5.

University where one gains more profit in a few years than in some others in many."[1] In 1553 he writes to Cardinal Morone that in the *Collegium Germanicum* in Rome, the exercises in the *Artes Liberales* were the same as in Paris, Louvain, and other celebrated Universities.[2] Louvain was called by him a "most flourishing University," and he wishes to establish a college there.[3] It was pointed out before, that the "plans of study" of Nadal and Ledesma exerted a great influence on the *Ratio* of 1599. Both these men had for many years studied at Paris, Ledesma also in Louvain.

This leads us to another source of the educational system of the Jesuits: the humanistic schools of the Netherlands. We spoke of Louvain in chapter II. Ignatius had visited the Netherlands in 1529 and 1530, and a considerable number of Jesuits in the first decades of the Society came from that country. Ribadeneira enumerates 53 who became known as writers before 1600. Two of the men who were in the Commissions for drawing up the Ratio, Francis Coster and Peter Busaeus, were from the Netherlands. Others were influential as founders of colleges, for instance, Peter Canisius of Nymwegen; or as heads of famous institutions, like Leonard Kessel of Louvain, Rector of the College of Cologne.

As was said before, during his sojourn at Paris, Ignatius may have come into contact with the Brethren of the Common Life.[4] These Brethren conducted

---

[1] Joly, *Life of St. Ignatius*, p. 85. — *Cartas de San Ignacio* (Madrid 1874), vol. I, p. 76.
[2] *Cartas*, vol. III, p. 178.
[3] *Ib.*, vol. II, p. 292.
[4] See page 32.

famous schools all over the Netherlands; their college in Liège was perhaps the most flourishing school in Europe at the beginning of the Reformation. Many points conspicuous in the Ratio Studiorum, as well as in Sturm's system, were to be found in this college. Latin was the principal branch. It was taught very methodically, and the imitation of authors was insisted on. The course had eight classes; the lower were grammar classes; the fifth — and part of the sixth — was Rhetoric, the seventh and eighth taught Aristotelian philosophy and mathematics. Contests between the pupils (*concertationes*) were frequent, especially solemn ones at the distribution of prizes at the end of the scholastic year. On account of the great number of pupils, the classes were divided into *decuriae*, divisions of ten pupils each. At the head of each *decuria* was a *decurio*, to whom his ten subjects had to recite their lessons, etc.[1] All these customs are found in the Ratio Studiorum.

A result of humanistic influences was also the domineering position which Cicero held in the classical course. To the humanists Cicero had been *the* author, whose style was considered by many with almost superstitious reverence.

Humanism in the Netherlands had been much more conservative than in Italy and Germany. Owing to the influence of the Brethren of the Common Life, it had kept more faithfully the Christian views of the earlier humanists. It certainly was this Christian humanism which appealed to the religious mind of Ignatius; he always suspected the writings of the younger humanists. Very early, shortly after his

[1] See Ziegler, *Geschichte der Pädagogik*, p. 52.

conversion, the *Christian Knight* of Erasmus had fallen into his hands.[1] He conceived for this book, as well as for the *Colloquies* and similar works of the author, an aversion in which time only confirmed him. Not that he was insensible to the author's grace of style (for it is said he made extracts from the *Christian Knight* in order to familiarize himself with the niceties of the Latin tongue), nor that he found heterodox propositions in it; but he felt repulsed by the color in which things and ideas were presented, by the malicious satire, lack of feeling, vanity, and hollow scepticism which were prominent on every page. Undoubtedly even if Luther had not started his Reformation, Ignatius would have become a leader in a reform opposed to the radical school of humanists, to whose disastrous influence the immorality of the time and the worldliness of many ecclesiastics is, to a great extent, to be ascribed.

The dependence of the Ratio on the University of Paris and the humanistic schools of the Netherlands refutes also the supposition that the Jesuits have drawn from Sturm's "Plan of Studies". Sturm himself had studied, from 1521–1523, in the school of the Brethren in Liège, from 1524–1529 at Louvain in the famous *Collegium Trilingue;* from 1530–1537 he was student and teacher in Paris. A German Protestant[2] says: "The organization of the college of Liège made such an impression on young Sturm that he adopted it even in some minute details as the model for his school in Strasburg."[3] Similarly speaks Professor Ziegler.[4]

[1] Joly, *Saint Ignatius of Loyola*, p. 70.
[2] Ch. Schmidt, Director of the Protestant *Gymnasium* at Strasburg.
[3] *Jean Sturm*, pp. 5 and 86.
[4] *Geschichte der Pädagogik*, p. 75.

Thus we see that Sturm had drawn his educational ideas from the very same schools in which many of the first Jesuits had been educated, and which were considered by them as models. Is it not much more probable that the Jesuits fashioned their own system after these schools, than after that of Sturm in Strasburg? Assertions, like that of Dr. Russell, that "the Society of Jesus incorporated so many of his [Sturm's] methods into the new Catholic schools,"[1] are highly improbable, and certainly not substantiated by any positive proof. What was similar in both systems, was to be found in the humanistic schools of the Netherlands.[2]

On equally feeble grounds rests another hypothesis advanced in recent years, namely that "what is really good in the Jesuit system can be traced almost in detail to Luiz Vives."[3] In proof of this statement the fact is mentioned that Ignatius met Vives in Bruges. The Spaniard Vives was one of the most brilliant humanists of the time, and a distinguished writer on pedagogy. He, too, had studied at Paris (1509-1512), and spent a great part of his life in the Netherlands. The argument used against the dependence on Sturm, holds good in this case as well. It is asserted that Ignatius had borrowed from Vives, among other good things, "the physical care bestowed upon the young,

[1] *German Higher Schools*, p. 47.
[2] After this chapter had been finished, I found that Professor Paulsen had expressed the same conclusion in his *Geschichte des gelehrten Unterrichts* (vol. I, p. 412), where he states that any dependence of the Jesuit system on Sturm's plan is most improbable.
[3] Lange, in *Encyclopädie des gesammten Erziehungs- und Unterrichtswesens*, IX, 776. See Duhr, *l. c.*, p. 13.

the infrequency of punishment, the systematic teaching of Latin in a series of classes, the study of practical science, of history and geography, in conjunction with the explanation of the texts, the use of note books, emulation, and the like." Now many of these points were not inventions of Vives, but had been already mentioned by Quintilian.[1]

The words of a German writer on pedagogy are well worth being quoted on this point: "Strange attempts have recently been made to show that the Jesuit pedagogy which, through its unquestionably grand results, has become famous, is to be traced back to Vives. The fact that Vives met the founder of the Society once, for a very short time, must serve as a proof. But if one examines the educational principles which the Jesuits are supposed to have taken from Vives: infrequency of punishment, physical care of the pupils, etc., it becomes immediately evident that these are principles which all reasonable educators have followed at all times. We should be forced to make the absurd assumption that, until the time of Vives, Catholics never in the past had had sound pedagogical views, if we wished to trace back these self-evident principles to Vives."[2]

It really looks as though some writers are determined at least to deny all originality to the Ratio Studiorum, if they are compelled to admit that it achieved great results. We frankly and willingly admit that the authors of the Ratio borrowed much

[1] See Duhr, *Studienordnung*, p. 15.
[2] Dr. Frederick Kayser, in *Historisches Jahrbuch*, Munich 1894, vol. XV, page 350, article: "Johannes Ludwig Vives."

from existing systems, it matters little whence and how much. We must, however, claim that their experience from 1540–1599, and their painstaking efforts in drawing up the Ratio, had a considerable share in the results that attended their system.[1] Above all, what is most characteristic in the Jesuit system, the wonderful unity and organization, was not borrowed from any other system, but is the work of the framers of the Constitutions and of the Ratio Studiorum.

[1] "It may be said in general that the practical experience (of the early Jesuits) exerted a greater influence on the formation of the Order's pedagogy than the study of pedagogical theorizers." G. Müller, quoted by Paulsen, *l. c.*, vol. I, page 412.

Chapter V.

Jesuit Colleges and their Work before the Suppression of the Society (1540–1773).

Within fifty years from the solemn approbation of the Society of Jesus, the Order had spread all over the world, from Europe to the Indies, from China and Japan in the East, to Mexico and Brazil in the West. Wherever the Church was not actually persecuted, as in England, there sprang up educational institutions. Shortly after the death of the fifth General, Father Aquaviva, in 1615, the Society possessed three hundred and seventy-three colleges; in 1706 the number of collegiate and university establishments was seven hundred and sixty-nine, and in 1756, shortly before the suppression, the number was seven hundred and twenty-eight.[1] In 1584 the classes of the Roman College were attended by two thousand, one hundred and eight students. At Rouen, in France, there were regularly two thousand. Throughout the seventeenth century the numbers at the College of Louis-le-Grand, in Paris, varied between eighteen hundred and three thousand. In 1627, the one Province of Paris had in its fourteen colleges 13,195 students, which would give an average of nearly one thousand to each college. In the same year Rouen had 1,968, Rennes 1,485, Amiens 1,430. In 1675 there were in Louis-

---

[1] See Hughes, *Loyola*, pp. 69—77; and especially Hamy, S. J., *Documents pour servir à l'histoire des domiciles de la Compagnie de Jésus*, Paris, Alphonse Picard.

le-Grand 3,000, in Rennes 2,500, in Toulouse 2,000.[1] Cologne began its roll in 1558 with almost 800 students; Dillingen in Bavaria had 760 in 1607. At Utrecht in Holland there were 1000; at Antwerp and Brussels each 600 scholars. Münster in 1625 had 1300, Munich had 900 in 1602. The absolute average is not known, three hundred seems, however, the very lowest. This would give to the seven hundred and more institutions a sum total of two hundred and ten thousand students, all trained under one system. That thus the Jesuits exercised a great influence on the minds of men, is undeniable. The question is only, was their influence for good or evil? Was their teaching a benefit to the individuals, and more so, was it advantageous to the communities? Was their method considered as productive of good results? Let us listen to contemporaneous writers in high positions, to men known for their intellectual achievements, to men who, owing to their religious tenets, cannot be suspected of partiality to the Jesuits.

The testimony of Lord Bacon, the English philosopher and statesman, is well known: "Of the Jesuit colleges, although in regard of their superstition I may say, 'Quo meliores eo deteriores,' yet in regard of this and some other points of learning and moral matters, I may say, as Agesilaus said to his enemy Pharnabaces, 'Talis cum sis, utinam noster esses'."[2] Our American historian Bancroft does not hesitate to say of the Jesuits: "Their colleges became the best schools in the world."[3] And Ranke writes: "It was

[1] Du Lac, *Jésuites*, p. 297.
[2] *Advancement of Learning*, book 1.
[3] *History of the United States*, vol. III, page 120 (18th edition, Boston 1864).

found that young people gained more with them in six months than with other teachers in two years. Even Protestants removed their children from distant gymnasia to confide them to the care of the Jesuits."[1] — This last fact was more than once lamented by Protestants.

In 1625 a report of the Gymnasium in Brieg, Silesia, complains bitterly of the lamentable condition of this school. This condition is ascribed chiefly to the theological wranglings of the Lutherans and the Reformed, and to the inability of the teachers, who frequently were engaged in trades, or as inn-keepers, or acted as lawyers, and thus neglected their duties as teachers. The report then adds: "If the teachers knew how to preserve the confidence of the parents, then an interest in the school would soon be manifested by those who now prefer to send their children to the Jesuits. *For these Jesuits know better how to treat boys according to their nature, and to keep alive a zeal for studies.*"[2]

Also in the Protestant Margravate of Brandenburg the condition of the schools induced parents, noblemen, state officials, and citizens, to send their sons to foreign Jesuit colleges. But then the preachers started a violent campaign against this practice, although they had to admit that the Jesuit pupils were better trained than those educated in the Margravate. Consequently, the Elector John George issued severe decrees against sending children to foreign schools (1564 and 1572).[3]

---

[1] *History of the Papacy*, vol. I, book V, sec. 3 (Ed. London 1896, p. 416).

[2] Döllinger, *Die Reformation*, vol. I, p. 447 (note 55).

[3] Döllinger, *l. c.*, p. 543.

Professors and preachers in Lemgo, Danzig, Königsberg, and in other cities, denounced the "godless practice of Protestants who sacrificed their children to the monstrous Moloch of Jesuit schools."[1]

Wilhelm Roding, Professor in Heidelberg, in a book: *Against the impious schools of the Jesuits*, dedicated to Frederick III., Elector of the Palatinate, gives expression to the following complaint: "Very many who want to be counted as Christians send their children to the schools of the Jesuits. This is a most dangerous thing, as the Jesuits are excellent and subtle philosophers, above everything intent on applying all their learning to the education of youth. They are the finest and most dexterous of teachers, and know how to accommodate themselves to the natural gifts of every pupil." Another Protestant, Andrew Dudith of Breslau, wrote: "I am not surprised if I hear that one goes to the Jesuits. They possess varied learning, teach, preach, write, dispute, instruct youth without taking money, and all this they do with indefatigable zeal; moreover, they are distinguished for moral integrity, and modest behaviour."[2] A Protestant preacher attributed the popularity of the Jesuit schools to magical practices of these wicked men: "These Jesuits have diabolical practices; they anoint their pupils with secret salves of the devil, by which they so attract and attach the children to themselves that they can only with difficulty be separated from these wizards, and always long to go back to them. Therefore, the Jesuits ought not only to be expelled but to be

---

[1] *Ib.*, pp. 544—545.
[2] Further testimonies see Janssen, vol. IV (16th ed.), pp. 473—476; vol. VII, pp. 80—82.

burnt, otherwise they can never be gotten rid of." Of the Hildesheim Jesuits it was said that they used some secret charms to hasten the progress of their pupils.[1]

A most remarkable testimony to the ability of the Jesuits as teachers was rendered by the words and actions of two non-Catholic rulers, at the time of the suppression of the Society in 1773, namely by King Frederick of Prussia and Empress Catharine of Russia; we shall revert to their testimony further on in this chapter.

In a history of the Jesuit colleges mention must be made of the literary and scientific works published by Jesuits. The colleges of the Society were as many colonies of writers. It is impossible to give here an adequate description of this work of the Society; the Bibliography of the Order comprises nine folio volumes, and contains the names of thirteen thousand Jesuit authors — many, if not most of them, professors — who published works on almost every branch of learning.[2] Even Dr. Huber admires the literary and scientific activity of the Order: "More than three hundred Jesuits have written grammars on living and dead languages, and more than ninety-five languages have been taught by members of the Order. In mathematics and natural sciences there are among them first class scientists. Many astronomical observatories were erected by them, and directed with great success."[3] Still more striking is the testimony of the

[1] Janssen, vol. VIII, p. 650.

[2] *Bibliothèque de la Compagnie de Jésus*, par Carlos Sommervogel. Brussels, 1890—1900. On the writers of the old Society see Crétineau-Joly, *Histoire de la Compagnie de Jésus*, vol. IV, ch. IV (3rd ed., pp. 214-296).

[3] Huber, *Der Jesuiten-Orden*, pp. 418-420.

bitterest enemy of the Jesuits, d'Alembert. He writes: "Let us add — for we must be just — that no religious society whatever can boast of so many members distinguished in science and literature. The Jesuits have successfully cultivated eloquence, history, archaeology, geometry, and literature. There is scarcely a class of writers in which they have no representatives of the first rank; they have even good French writers, a distinction of which no other religious order can boast."[1]

Some of the linguistic works of the Jesuits are of the greatest importance and even celebrity in the history of the science of language. The first, not in time but in importance, is that of the Spanish Jesuit Hervas. Professor Max Müller of Oxford speaks of this Jesuit in the highest terms, and says that he wishes to point out his real merits, which other historians have overlooked.[2] While working among the polyglottous tribes of South America, the attention of Father Hervas was drawn to a systematic study of languages. After the expulsion of the Jesuits from South America in 1767, he lived in Rome amidst the numerous Jesuit missionaries who assisted him greatly in his researches.

His works are of a most comprehensive character; the most important is his *Catalogue of Languages*, in six volumes. "If we compare the work of Hervas with a similar work which excited much attention towards the end of the last century, and is even now more widely known than Hervas' — I mean Court de

---

[1] *La destruction des Jésuites*, p. 48; quoted by De Badts de Cugnac, *Les Jésuites et l' éducation*, p. 9.

[2] *Lectures on the Science of Language* (6th ed. 1871), vol. I, p. 157, note 40.

Gebelin's *Monde primitif* — we shall see at once how far superior the Spanish Jesuit is to the French philosopher. Gebelin treats Persian, Armenian, Malay, and Coptic as dialects of Hebrew; he speaks of Bask as a dialect of Celtic, and he tries to discover Hebrew, Greek, English, and French words in the idioms of America. Hervas, on the contrary, though embracing in his catalogue five times the number of languages that were known to Gebelin, is most careful not to allow himself to be carried away by theories not warranted by the evidence before him. It is easy now to point out mistakes and inaccuracies in Hervas, but I think that those who have blamed him most are those who ought most to have acknowledged their obligations to him. To have collected specimens and notices of more than three hundred languages, is no small matter. But Hervas did more. He himself composed grammars of more than forty languages. He was one of the first to point out that the true affinity of languages must be determined chiefly by grammatical evidence, not by mere similarity of words. He proved, by a comparative list of declensions and conjugations, that Hebrew, Chaldee, Syriac, Arabic, Ethiopic, and Aramaic are all but dialects of one original language, and constitute one family of speech, the Semitic. He scouted the idea of deriving all languages of mankind from Hebrew. He had perceived clear traces of affinity between Chinese and Indo-Chinese dialects; also between Hungarian, Lapponian, and Finnish, three dialects now classed as members of the Turanian family. He had proved that Bask was not, as was commonly supposed, a Celtic dialect, but an independent language... Nay, one of the most brilliant discoveries in the history of the science of language, the establishment of the Malay and Polynesian family of speech... was made by Hervas long before it was worked out, and announced to the world by Humboldt."[1]

Great are also the merits of Jesuits in regard to the study of Sanskrit. "The first European Sanskrit scholar was the Jesuit Robert de Nobili,"[2] a nephew of the famous Cardinal Robert Bellarmine. According to the words of Max Müller, he must have been far advanced in the knowledge of the sacred language and literature of the Brahmans.[3] The first Sanskrit grammar written by a European is commonly said to be that of the German Jesuit Hanxleden († 1732). However, this honor belongs to another German Jesuit, Heinrich Roth († 1668), who wrote a Sanskrit grammar almost a century before Hanxleden.[4] Father Du Pons, in 1740, published a comprehensive and, in general, a very accurate description of the various branches of Sanskrit literature.[5] Of Father Coeurdoux Max Müller writes that he anticipated the most important results of comparative philology by at least fifty years; at the same time the Oxford Professor expresses his astonishment that the work of this humble missionary has attracted so little attention, and only very lately received the credit that belongs to it.[6] Father Calmette wrote a poetical work in excellent

[1] *Ib.*, pp. 154—157.
[2] *Ib.*, p. 174.
[3] *Ib.*, p. 174.
[4] Max Müller, *l. c.*, p. 175. *Wiener Zeitschrift für die Kunde des Morgenlandes*, XV, 1901, pp. 313—320. Father Roth's grammar was extant in the Roman College, when Hervas wrote his *Catalogue*.
[5] Max Müller, *l. c.*, p. 179.
[6] *Ib.*, p. 183.

Sanskrit, the *Ezour Veda*, which gave rise to an interesting literary discussion. Voltaire declared it to be four centuries older than Alexander the Great, and pronounced it the most precious gift which the West had received from the East. On account of the Christian ideas contained in the poem, the atheistic philosophers of France thought they had found in it a most effective weapon for attacking Christianity. Unfortunately for these philosophers, an English traveler discovered Father Calmette's manuscript in Pondichery.[1]

Various important works on the dialects of India were written by Jesuits, among others several grammars and dictionaries of the Tamil language, for which the first types were made by the Spanish lay brother Gonsalves. The works written in the Tamil language by Father Beschi († 1740) have received the most flattering criticism by modern Protestant writers. The Anglican Bishop Caldwell, in his *Comparative Grammar of the Dravidian Languages* (London 1875), styles them the best productions in modern Tamil, and other scholars, as Babington, Hunter, Pope, and Benfey, concur in this eulogy.[2] Beschi's grammar and dictionary are praised as masterpieces. Father Stephens' grammar of the Konkani language is called an admirable achievement.[3] It was republished as late as 1857, and was used extensively in the nineteenth century.

[1] Dahlmann, *Die Sprachkunde und die Missionen* (Herder, 1891), p. 19.
[2] Dahlmann, *l. c.*, pp. 12—15.
[3] Truebner's *American and Oriental Literary Record*, London 1872, p. 258. (Dahlmann, *l. c.*, p. 15.)

Not less noteworthy were the labors of the Jesuits in the Chinese language. In the fourth International Congress of Orientalists, Father Matteo Ricci was called "the first Sinologue".[1] When not long ago the Protestant missionaries in Shanghai published an edition of Euclid, they took as the basis of their work the translation made by Ricci. His works were written in the best Chinese, and, according to the eminent Orientalist Rémusat, were even in the nineteenth century highly esteemed by Chinese scholars, for their elegance of diction and purity of language.[2] Father Prémare († 1736) is called by Morrison the most thorough and profound grammarian of the Chinese language. And Rémusat asserts that the two Jesuits Prémare and Gaubil have not been surpassed or equalled by any European in sound and comprehensive knowledge of Chinese, and that both belong to the number of great literary luminaries that form the pride of France.[3] Prémare's most important work, the *Notitia Linguae Sinicae*, was published in 1831, by the Protestant *Collegium Anglo-Sinicum* in Malakka. Rémusat styles this work the best ever produced by a European in the field of Chinese grammar.[4] And a German scholar writes: "We possess no work on Chinese grammar which, in comprehensive and judicious treatment of the subject, can be compared to that of Prémare's *Notitia*. Some may acquire a better understanding of the Chinese language than the French Father, but it may be said that not easily will

[1] Dahlmann, *l. c.*, p. 27.
[2] *Mélanges Asiatiques*, vol. II, p. 11. (Dahlmann, *l. c.*, p. 28.)
[3] Dahlmann, *l. c.*, pp. 40—41.
[4] *Ib.*, page 42.

any European so fully and so thoroughly master the spirit and taste of the Chinese language; nor will there soon be found an equally capable teacher of Chinese rhetoric. In this I recognize the imperishable value of this work, a value which in some quarters is recognized more in deeds than in words."[1] By the last remark the author seems to imply what another German writer has stated more explicitly, namely, that "several of the best works of these Jesuits have been published by another firm,"[2] i. e., they have been largely used by other writers without receiving the credit due to them. Other distinguished Chinese scholars were the Fathers Noel, Gerbillon, Parrenin, de Maillac, and Amyot.[3]

Great praise has also been bestowed on works of Jesuit authors on the languages of Japan, South America, etc.[4] Thus we read in the *Narrative and Critical History of America*, by Justin Winsor: "The most voluminous work on the language of the Incas has for its author the Jesuit Diego Gonzales Holguin... He resided for several years in the Jesuit College at Juli, near the banks of Lake Titicaca, where the Fathers had established a printing-press, and here he studied the Quichua language... He died as Rector of the College at Asuncion. His Quichua dictionary was published at Lima in 1586, and a second edition appeared in 1607, the same year in which the gram-

---

[1] *Zeitschrift der deutschen Morgenländischen Gesellschaft*, XXXII, p. 604. (Dahlmann, *l. c.*, p. 45.)

[2] Neumann, quoted by Dahlmann, p. 25; a specimen of such plagiarism which occurred quite recently, shall be mentioned in chapter VII.

[3] *Ib.*, pp. 29—56.

[4] *Ib.*, pp. 57—144.

mar first saw the light. The Quichua grammar of Holguin is the most complete and elaborate that has been written, and his dictionary is also the best."[1] — Similar commendations have been bestowed on the linguistic works of the Fathers Rubio, de Acosta, Barzena, Bertonio, Bayer, Febres (whose grammar and dictionary of the Auracanian dialect were republished for practical use in 1882 and 1884 at Buenos Ayres and Rio de Janeiro), Anchieta, Figueira, Ruiz, and others. Ruiz' grammar and dictionary of Guarani, in the words of Mulhall, are a lasting monument to his study and learning.[2] Many most valuable books and manuscripts of the Jesuits were ruthlessly destroyed, when the Fathers were expelled from their colleges and missions in South America. Protestant writers, as Bach and Kriegk, lament that this vandalism of the enemies of the Society has destroyed for ever most valuable literary treasures.

In the field of mathematics and natural sciences several Jesuit professors have attained to high distinction. We mention the names of a few. Clavius († 1610), who was called the "Euclid of his age", was the leading man in the reformation of the calendar under Pope Gregory XIII. Professor Cajori says with reference to this work: "The Gregorian calendar met with a great deal of opposition both among scientists and among Protestants. Clavius, who ranked high as a geometer, met the objections of the former most ably and effectively; the prejudices of the latter passed

---

[1] Winsor, *Narrative and Critical History of America*, Boston, 1889, vol. I, p. 279. See also pp. 262—264.

[2] Mulhall, *Between the Amazon and Andes*, London, 1881, p. 263. (Dahlmann, *l. c.*, p. 85.)

away with time."[1]   One of his pupils was Gregory of Saint-Vincent († 1667), whom Leibnitz places on an equality with Descartes as a geometrician. "Although a circle-squarer, he is worthy of mention for the numerous theorems of interest which he discovered in his search after the impossible, and Montucla ingeniously remarks that no one ever squared the circle with so much ability, or (except for his principal object) with so much success."[2]

Another disciple of Clavius was Matthew Ricci († 1610), the illustrious mathematician and apostle of China, who published also a vast number of valuable observations on the geography and history of China. Father Schall of Cologne († 1669), a prominent mathematician and astronomer, was appointed director of the "Mathematical Tribunal" in Pekin, and revised the Chinese calendar.

Within the last few years the attention of mathematicians has been drawn to the Jesuit Father Saccheri, Professor of mathematics at Pavia. Non-Euclidean mathematics is now recognized as an important branch of mathematics. The beginnings of this system have sometimes been ascribed to Gauss, the "Nestor of German mathematicians". But recent research has proved that as early as 1733 Father Saccheri had published a book which gives a complete system of Non-Euclidean geometry. Beltrami, in 1889, and Staeckel and Engel in 1895, pointed out the great importance of the work of Saccheri.[3]

[1] *A History of Mathematics*, by Florian Cajori, Professor in Colorado College. Macmillan, 1894, p. 155.

[2] Ball, *A Short Account of the History of Mathematics*, Macmillan, 1888, p. 275.

[3] Professor Halsted of the University of Texas published

Father Grimaldi († 1663), professor of mathematics in the College at Bologna, gave an accurate description of the moon spots, discovered the diffraction of light, and, in his work *Physico - Mathesis de Lumine, Coloribus et Iride*, advanced the first attempt of a theory of undulation. This work was the basis of Newton's theory of light.[1] Father Scheiner († 1650) was one of the first observers of the sun spots; it is disputed whether he or Galileo discovered them first. Scheiner also invented the pantograph, and, in his work *Oculus, hoc est Fundamentum Opticum*, laid down opinions of lasting value (especially on the *accommodation of the eye*).[2]

More famous than these was Athanasius Kircher († 1680), a man of most extensive and varied learning who wrote on mathematics, physics, history, philology, and archaeology. He is the inventor of the magic lantern and other scientific instruments. He was the first who successfully studied the Coptic language and deciphered the Egyptian hieroglyphics. The very variety and universality of his learning was naturally a danger, to which he not unfrequently succumbed. He often betrays a lack of critical spirit,

---

a translation of Saccheri's work in the *American Mathematical Monthly*, and Professor Manning of Brown University states that he has taken Saccheri's method of treatment as the basis of the first chapter of his recent book *Non-Euclidean Geometry*, Boston, Ginn and Company, 1901, p. 92. See also Cajori, *A History of Mathematics*, p. 303. — Hagen, *Synopsis der höheren Mathematik*, vol. II, p. 4.

[1] Meyer's *Conversations-Lexicon* (1895), vol. VII, p. 983. — Cajori, *A History of Physics*, Macmillan, 1899, pp. 88—89.

[2] *Ib.*, vol. XV, p. 400; XVI, p. 475; and *Allgemeine deutsche Biographie*, vol. XXX, p. 718.

and proposes phantastic theories. Still, in spite of these defects, his works are of the greatest importance, and his *Lingua Aegyptiaca Restituta* has been styled indispensable even at the present day for the study of the Egyptian language.[1] Father Kircher founded also the famous *Museo Kircheriano* in the Roman College, and if he had done nothing else, this alone would secure him a place of honor in the world of science. The services rendered to mathematics, astronomy, physics, and geography, by the Jesuits in China, especially by Ricci, Schall, Verbiest, Koegler, Hallerstein, Herdtrich, Gaubil, have been generously acknowledged by Lalande, Montucla, and more recently by the Protestant scholars Maedler,[2] and Baron von Richthofen.[3] On the astronomical observatories of the Jesuits a few words will be said when we come to speak of the suppression of the Order.

Of the geographical works of the Jesuits in China Baron von Richthofen writes: "If the Jesuits had not applied their scientifically trained minds to practical subjects, we would not possess the great cartographic work on China, and that country would still be a *terra incognita* for us, and the time would be very far off in which it would become possible to obtain as much as that picture of China which the Jesuits have given us, and which is now well known to everybody.... It is the most important cartographic work ever executed in so short a time, the grandest scientific achievement of the most brilliant period of Catholic missions in China." The same author says of the

[1] *Allgemeine deutsche Biographie*, vol. XVI.
[2] Mädler, *Geschichte der Himmelskunde.*
[3] Ferdinand von Richthofen, *China*, Berlin, 1877.

Tyrolese Father Martini († 1661): "He is the best geographer of all the missionaries, and by his great work, the *Novus Atlas Sinensis*, the best and most complete description which we possess of China, he has become the 'Father of Chinese geography.'" Father Du Halde gave an accurate description of Mongolia, and his great work on China (1735) is still one of the most important sources available on the geography, history, religion, industry, political organization, customs, etc., of that country.[1] Some of the geographical labors of the Jesuits in America have been mentioned previously.[2] Justin Winsor states that the *Historia Natural y Moral de las Indias* of Father de Acosta, "the Pliny of the New World," is much relied on as an authority by Robertson, and quoted 19 times by Prescott in his *Conquest of Peru*, thus taking the fourth place as an authority with regard to that work.[3]

All these works are as many testimonies to the efficiency and the *practical* character of the system under which these men had been trained; most of them had entered the Society at a very early age. How could they have produced such works, if what Compayré says, were true, that the Society devotes itself exclusively to "purely formal studies, to exercises which give a training in the use of elegant lan-

---

[1] *China*, vol. I, pp. 650–692. — See Dahlmann, *l. c.*, pp. 35–37. — Huonder, *Deutsche Jesuiten-Missionäre des 17. und 18. Jahrhunderts* (Herder, 1899), pp. 86–89.

[2] Chapter IV, pp. 127—129.

[3] *Narrative and Critical History of America*, vol. I, pp. 262–263. On the works of Father Clavigero on Mexico see *ib.*, p. 158.

guage, and leaves real and concrete studies in entire neglect"?[1]

In history the Society must yield the palm to the Order of St. Benedict, particularly to the celebrated Congregation of St. Maur. Still, some Jesuits produced works of lasting value. We mention first the *De Doctrina Temporum* by Father Petavius († 1652), of which a great authority on chronology said that it was superior to the work of Scaliger, and an invaluable mine of information for later chronologists.[2] Father Labbe († 1667) began the *Collection of the Councils* which is much used up to the present day. A more complete Collection of the Councils, in fact the most complete that exists, was published by Father Hardouin († 1729). He wrote also a most valuable work on numismatics, in which six hundred ancient coins were, for the first time, described and with wonderful sagacity used for solving intricate historical problems. In other historical and critical works he proceeded with an almost incredible boldness and arbitrariness, denying the authenticity of a great number of the works of the classical writers and the Fathers of the Church. In many questions of criticism he was far in advance of his age, but some of his hyper-critical and eccentric hypotheses have, to a great extent, obscured his reputation.[3] The greatest historical work of the

---

[1] *History of Pedagogy*, p. 144.

[2] Ideler, *Handbuch der Chronologie*, vol. II, pp. 602—604. See Weiss, *Weltgeschichte* (2nd ed.), vol. V, II, pp. 544—552.

[3] It is a rather curious fact that some have blamed the Jesuit Superiors for allowing the publication of several of Father Hardouin's works, curious I say, because it is said again and again that the severe censorship of the Order suppresses all original and independent works of its subjects. "Do what you may, we shall find fault with you," seems to be the principle guiding some critics of the Order.

Jesuits is the collection of documents called *Acta Sanctorum*, or the *Bollandists*, so named after the first editor, Father Bolland († 1668). The most distinguished of the Bollandist writers was Father Papenbroeck († 1714). Fifty-three folio volumes appeared before the suppression of the Society. This gigantic collection is a work of prime importance for the history of the whole Christian era, a *monumentum aere perennius*. Leibnitz said of it: "If the Jesuits had produced nothing but this work, they would have deserved to be brought into existence, and would have just claims upon the good wishes and esteem of the whole world."[1]

In literature we find the names of several distinguished Jesuits. The odes of Matthew Sarbiewski († 1640) were praised as successful rivals of the best lyrics of the ancients; Hugo Grotius even preferred them to the odes of Horace,[2] although we must call this an exaggerated estimate. Sarbiewski was surpassed by James Balde († 1668), who for many years taught rhetoric in Ingolstadt and Munich, and was styled not only the "Modern Quintilian", but also the "Horace of Germany". His Latin poems manifest a variety, beauty, warmth of feeling, and glowing patriotism unrivalled in that period. He was, however, not altogether free from the mannerisms of his age. Protestant critics, as Goethe and others, have admired the productions of this highly gifted poet, and Herder,[3]

---

[1] Quoted by De Badts de Cugnac, *Les Jésuites et l'éducation*, p. 34.

[2] See Baumgartner, *Geschichte der Weltliteratur*, vol. IV, pp. 642—644.

[3] Of Herder's works, the whole twelfth volume (Cotta, 1829), "Terpsichore", is devoted to Balde.

who translated a selection of Balde's lyrics into classical German, speaks of him in enthusiastic terms.[1]

The classical German writings of Denis and Spe have been mentioned previously. We may add here the name of Father Robert Southwell, who was executed for his faith in 1595. Saintsbury says of him that he belonged to a distinguished family, was stolen by a gipsy in youth, but was recovered; "a much worse misfortune befell him in being sent for education not to Oxford or Cambridge but to Douay, where he fell into the hands of the Jesuits, and joined their order."[2] Yet notwithstanding this terrible misfortune, he must have greatly profited from this education; for the same critic admits that Southwell produced not inconsiderable work both in prose and poetry; that his works possess genuine poetic worth; that his religious fervor is of the simplest and most genuine kind, and that his poems are a natural and unforced expression of it.

Father Perpinian wrote most eloquent Latin discourses, which, as the philologian Ruhnken affirms, compare favorably with those of Muretus, the greatest Neo-Latinist. The philological works of Pontanus, Vernulaeus, La Cerda (the famous commentator of the works of Virgil), and others, were held in high repute. Sacchini, Jouvancy, Perpinian, Possevin,

---

[1] The extensive literature on Balde's works is given by Baumgartner, *l. c.*, p. 645. A most flattering estimate of this Jesuit is to be found in Herzog's Real-Encyclopädie für protestantische Theologie, vol. II. (3. edition, 1897), article "Balde", by List, where it is said that "one always likes to return to the perusal of the lyrics of this God-inspired man."

[2] Saintsbury, *A History of Elizabethan Literature*, London, 1887, pp. 119—120.

Bonifacio, and Kropf wrote valuable treatises on education.[1]

We have purposely abstained from mentioning any writer on theology or scholastic philosophy. For it is admitted on all sides that the Society produced a great number of most distinguished writers in scholastic philosophy and in the various branches of theology: dogmatics, apologetics, exegesis, moral theology, etc.

Many good schoolbooks were written by Jesuits.[2] The number of grammars, readers, books on style, on poetics, rhetoric, editions of classics, etc., is very great. De la Cerda published one of the best editions of Virgil. The editions of La Rue (Ruaeus) were famous;

---

[1] Compayré asserts: "The Jesuits have never written anything on the principles and objects of education. We must not demand of them an exposition of general views or a confession of their educational faith." *L. c.*, p. 142. Voltaire called Jouvancy's *Method of Learning and Teaching* the best work written since Quintilian's famous *Institutes.* — Sacchini, Jouvancy and Kropf were published again in 1896, as vol. X of Herder's *Bibliothek der katholischen Pädagogik;* selections from the works of Perpinian, Bonifacio and Possevin in 1901 as vol. XI.

[2] Quick, *Educational Reformers*, p. 40. That also in the nineteenth century the Jesuits were able to write good textbooks may be seen from a statement of Thomas Arnold, son of Dr. Arnold of Rugby. During his sojourn in New Zealand, he used to borrow books from Frederick Weld, a Jesuit pupil of Fribourg (afterwards Governor of Western Australia.) "One of his text-books," says Arnold, "which he had brought with him from Fribourg, was a history of philosophy by the Jesuit professor Freudenfelt [the name is Freudenfeld, died at Stonyhurst 1850]. This book seemed to me more genially and lucidly written than similar works that had been put in my hands at Oxford." *Passages in a Wandering Life*, London, 1900, p. 99.

of course, they are not what we *now* consider standard works on the classics. Father Tursellini's book *De Particulis Linguae Latinae* appeared in fifty editions; the last edition was prepared by Professor Hand, the philologist of Jena. The celebrated Gottfried Hermann, of Leipsic, published a revised edition of Father Viger's *De Idiotismis Linguae Graecae*.[1] This is an honor which not many old books have received at the hand of German scholars, who boast of such achievements in the field of philology. It is needless to add that the two works of the Jesuit philologians thus singled out must be of considerable excellence.

One department of the activity of the Order deserves a more detailed treatment: the Jesuit school-drama.[2] At present there is no need of defending the usefulness of dramatic performances, given by students, provided the subject and the whole tone of the play are morally sound and elevating. Still, there were times, when the Jesuits had to defend their practice, especially against the rigorists of Port Royal, the Jansenists in general, and in the eighteenth century against several governments, which were swayed by a prosaic bureaucratic spirit of utilitarianism.[3] The principles according to which the drama in Jesuit schools was to be conducted are laid down by Jouvancy in his *Ratio Docendi*, and by Father Masen; a book on the tech-

---

[1] See Professor Dr. Lotholz, *Pädagogik, der Neuzeit*, 1897, p. 323.

[2] On this subject see Baumgartner, *Geschichte der Weltliteratur*, vol. IV, pp. 623—637.

[3] Paulsen, *Geschichte des gelehrten Unterrichts*, vol. I, p. 358.

nique of the drama was composed by Father Lang.[1] The Institute of the Society had taken precautions that the school dramas should neither interfere with the regular work, nor do the least harm to the morals of the pupils. The fifty-eighth rule of the Provincial reads: "He shall only rarely allow the performance of comedies and tragedies; they must be becoming[2] and written in Latin." The vast majority of plays were consequently given in Latin, — the language, in those times, understood by every man of culture. Many Protestant educators and preachers were altogether opposed to dramas in the vernacular "which, as they said, were good enough for the common people and apprentices, but unbecoming students." In Jesuit colleges plays were occasionally, and after 1700 more frequently, performed in the vernacular.[3] Of Latin plays a programme and synopsis in the vernacular was, at least in Germany, distributed amongst those who did not know Latin.

In many Protestant schools of this period, for instance in the celebrated schools of Sturm and Rollenhagen, and also in a few Catholic schools, the comedies of Plautus and Terence were exhibited, not, however, without strong opposition of earnest men, who rightly considered some of these plays as dangerous for

[1] Jouvancy, *l. c.*, ch. II, art. II, §3, §6.—Masen, *Palaestra Eloquentiae Ligatae Dramatica*, Cologne, 1664. — Lang, *Dissertatio de Actione Scenica* etc., Munich, 1727.

[2] That is, "the subject should be pious and edifying", as the 13th *Rule of the Rector* has it.

[3] Duhr, pp. 136 foll. — In France many dramas were given in French since 1679. Rochemonteix, *l. c.*, vol. III, p. 189. — The report of 1832 says dramas should be in the vernacular. Pachtler, *op. cit.*, vol. IV, p. 479.

young people. Von Raumer says: "It seems incredible that the learning by heart and acting of comedies, so lascivious as those of Terence, could have remained without evil influence on the morality of youth, and we find it unintelligible that a religious-minded man like Sturm did not consider Terence really seductive. If the mere reading of an author like Terence is risky, how much more risky must it be, if pupils perform such pieces and have to familiarize themselves altogether with the persons and situations."[1] No wonder that serious complaints were made against such pernicious practices.[2] The biblical and historical plays performed in Protestant schools were mostly directed against "Popish idolatry".[3]

The drama of the Jesuits stood in sharp contrast to that of the Protestants. As their whole literary education, so also their drama was subordinate to the religious and moral training. The Ratio Studiorum prohibited the reading of any classical books which contained obscenities; they had first to be expurgated; expressly mentioned were Terence and Plautus. This must reflect most favorably on the Jesuits, in a time when vulgarity and obscenity reigned supreme in literature and drama.

As the nature and function of the theatre the Jesuits considered the stirring up of the pious emotions, the guardianship of youth against the corrupting influence of evil society, the portrayal of vice as something intrinsically despicable, the rousing up of the inner man to a zealous crusade for virtue, and the

[1] *History of Pedagogy*, vol. 1, p. 272. (Janssen's *History of the German People*, vol. VII, p. 108.)
[2] *Ibid.*, p. 113 sq.
[3] *Ibid.*, p. 117.

imitation of the Saints. Even in the treatment of purely secular subjects, the plot was always of a spiritually serious, deeply tragic, and morally important nature. The aim of the comic drama was to strike at the puerilities and ineptitudes, which could be treated on the stage without any detriment to the moral conscience. Vulgar jokes and low comedy were once and for all excluded, and the Jesuit authorities were indefatigable in thus guarding the moral prestige of the plays. In general, only such plays were written and produced as were in harmony with the moral ends and moral limits of dramatic art itself: a meritorious achievement in an age when every sentiment of moral delicacy, every prescription of social decorum, every dictate of ordinary modesty — both in the school and on the stage — was being outraged. And this fact produced a healthy reaction in favor of all the fine arts in general. The intermittent efforts of Jesuit dramatists could not, it is true, completely stem the tide of public degeneracy, could not even remain altogether unscathed by the time-serving fashions and foibles of the age: from the grosser and more revolting aberrations they were happily preserved.[1]

The subjects of Jesuit dramas were frequently biblical or allegorical: as "The Prodigal Son" (Heiligenstadt 1582), "Joseph in Egypt" (Munich 1583), "Christ as Judge", "Saul and David" (Graz 1589—1600), "Naboth" (Ratisbon 1609), "Elias" (Prague 1610). Or historical subjects were chosen: "Julian the Apostate" (Ingolstadt 1608), "Belisarius" (Munich 1607), "Godfrey de Bouillon" (Munich 1596), "St. Ambrose", "St. Benno", "St. Henry the

[1] Janssen, vol. VII, pp. 120—121.

Emperor", etc.[1] Favorite subjects were the lives of the Saints with their rich, beautiful, touching and morally ennobling elements, and the Christian legends. In these the Catholic Church has preserved, as Professor Paulsen aptly remarks, a poetical treasure which in many respects surpasses the stories of the Old Testament, both in purity and dramatic applicability.[2]

Many of their dramas were exhibited with all possible splendor, as for instance those given at La Flèche in 1614 before Louis XIII. and his court.[3] But it seems that nowhere was greater pomp displayed than in Munich, where the Court liberally contributed to make the performances as brilliant as possible. In 1574 the tragedy "Constantine" was played on two successive days. The whole city was beautifully decorated. More than one thousand persons took part in the play. Constantine, after his victory over Maxentius, entered the city on a triumphal chariot, surrounded by 400 horsemen in glittering armor. At the performance of the tragedy "Esther" in 1577, the most splendid costumes, gems, etc. were furnished from the treasury of the duke; at the banquet of King Assuerus 160 precious dishes of gold and silver were used.[4]

We may now understand the following assertions of a German writer. "The Jesuits, as Richard Wag-

---

[1] Titles and programmes of dramas in French colleges by Rochemonteix, *l. c.*, vol. III, pp. 189—195 and 215—353. The names of the best Jesuit dramatists are given by Baumgartner, *l. c.*, vol. IV, pp. 627—637. — Janssen, *l. c.*, pp. 130—134.
[2] *Geschichte des gelehrten Unterrichts*, vol. I, p. 418.
[3] Rochemonteix, *l. c.*, pp. 96—99.
[4] Janssen, vol. VII, pp. 128—129.

ner in our own days, aimed at and succeeded in uniting all the arts within the compass of the drama. The effects of such dramas were, like those of the Oberammergau Passion Play, ravishing, overpowering. Even people ignorant of the Latin tongue were transported by the representations of subjects usually familiar to them, as at present no one travels to the village of Ammergau to be edified by the poetic beauties of the *text*. And no one can deny that the liturgy of the Catholic Church makes a deep impression, even on the uncultured, although the Latin language is unknown to them. It is in the first place the power of *what is seen* that affects the mind so forcibly."[1]

The concourse of people was often immense. In 1565 "Judith" was played before the court in Munich, and then repeated before the people on a public square; not only was the whole square densely crowded, but even the surrounding walls and the roofs of the houses were thickly filled with eager spectators. In 1560 the comedy "Euripus" was given in the court-yard of the College of Prague before a crowd of more than 8000 people. The play had to be repeated three times, and when further exhibitions were demanded, the Rector of the college urgently requested the petitioners to desist from such demands, as "after all it was not the task of the Society to exhibit comedies."

Catholic writers of the time speak enthusiastically of the salutary effects of such performances. "They do more good than a sermon", writes the Italian physician Guarinoni, who saw many Jesuit dramas at

[1] K. Trautmann, *Ober-Ammergau und sein Passionsspiel* (1890). "This play is an offshoot of the Munich Jesuit drama", p. 47.

Hall in Tyrol. At Munich, on one occasion, in 1609, the impression of a play — it was "Cenodoxus, the Doctor of Paris", (or the "Conversion of St. Bruno") — was overpowering. A spectator wrote that a hundred sermons could not have produced the same effect; fourteen of the foremost members of the Bavarian court, on the following day, withdrew themselves into solitude, to enter upon the "Spiritual Exercises" of St. Ignatius, and to change their manner of life.[1]

Protestant preachers lamented that "high personages, princes and counts, no less than townspeople and rustics take such delight in the dramas of the Jesuits, contribute money to them, and honor the actors, whereas ours have nothing of the kind. Thus the Jesuits have an opportunity of propagating their idolatry and of gaining the good will even of the Evangelicals."[2] This result would certainly have been impossible, if the Jesuit dramas had contained invectives against non-Catholics. They were free from insulting and abusive attacks with which those of the other side were teeming. This is established by the standard authors on this subject, Karl von Reinhardstöttner, and Holstein. The latter, speaking with offensive and bitter language of the Jesuit dramas as means of defending "idolatry", must admit that their object was exclusively pedagogical, not at all polemical. Another Protestant, Francke, states as the difference between Protestant and Catholic school dramas, that the former sank more and more to a mere form for political and ecclesiastical controversies, chiefly directed against Popery, whereas the Jesuits were

[1] Janssen, vol. VII, p. 133.
[2] Janssen, vol. VII, p. 125.

working quietly in their schools and performed their biblical and historical plays.[1]

That not all dramatic productions of the Jesuits were of very inferior quality may again be inferred from testimonies of competent Protestant critics. K. von Reinhardstöttner writes: "In the first century of their history the Jesuits did great work in this line. They performed dramas full of power and grandeur and although their dramatic productions did not equal the fine lyrics of (the Jesuits) Balde and Sarbiewski, still in the dramas of Fabricius, Agricola and others there is unmistakably poetic spirit and noble seriousness. How could the enormous success of their performances be otherwise explained? .... Who could doubt for a moment that the Jesuits by their dramas rendered great services to their century, that they advanced culture, and preserved taste for the theatre and its subsidiary arts? It would be sheer ingratitude to undervalue what they have effected by their drama."[2]

We have testimonies proving that not only in the first century of its existence did the Order produce good plays, but that it kept up a high standard to the very end. One witness is Goethe, the first of German writers, assuredly no mean critic in dramatic matters. He was present at a play given in 1786 at Ratisbon, where the traditions of the Jesuit schools were kept up after the suppression of the Order. He bestows high praise on the performance and on the skill with which the Jesuits knew how to make the various arts subservient to their dramatics.[3]

[1] Quoted by Janssen, vol. VII, pp. 120—121.
[2] Janssen, vol. VII, p. 133.
[3] Goethe writes: "This public performance has convinced me anew of the cleverness of the Jesuits. They re-

If the number of great men be taken as a just criterion of the merit of an educational system, the Society could exhibit a long roll of pupils, who in their after-life were among the most prominent men in European history: poets like Calderon, Tasso, Corneille, Molière, Fontenelle, Goldoni,) orators like Bossuet; scholars like Galileo, Descartes, Buffon, Justus Lipsius, Vico, Muratori, Montesquieu, Malesherbes; statesmen like Richelieu and Emperor Ferdinand; generals like Tilly, Wallenstein and Condé; Church dignitaries like the great St. Francis de Sales, Pope Benedict XIV, called "the most learned of the Popes." These are but a few of the host of Jesuit pupils who rose to the highest distinction in Church and State, or in the domain of science and literature.[1] However, the Society does not lay much stress on the fact of having educated these brilliant men. It might be said with Count de Maistre, that "Genius is not the production of schools; it is not acquired but innate; it recognizes no obligation to man; its gratitude is due to the creative power of God." Still, a system of edu-

jected nothing that could be of any conceivable service to them, and knew how to wield their instruments with devotion and dexterity. This is not cleverness of the merely abstract order: it is a real fruition of the thing itself, an absorbing interest, which springs from the practical use of life. Just as this great spiritual society has its organ builders, its sculptors, and its gilders, so there seem to be some who, by nature and inclination, take to the drama; and as their churches are distinguished by a pleasing pomp, so these prudent men have seized on the sensibility of the world by a decent theatre." *Italienische Reise* (Goethe's Werke, Cotta's edition, 1840, vol. XXIII, pp. 3—4).

[1] Many more are commemorated by Crétineau-Joly, *l. c.*, vol. IV, ch. III.

cation may contribute much to foster and quicken the development of genius. But the Society can justly claim to have made excellent men of pupils with only ordinary abilities, and these count by thousands, nay by hundreds of thousands: lawyers, professors, state officials, officers of the army, priests and bishops.

Considering the number and work of the Jesuit schools, we may conclude that they wielded a very great influence in the sixteenth and seventeenth centuries. This influence led to the persecution and finally the suppression of the Order; not as if the Order had abused its influence, but because the power which the Society exercised in the intellectual and moral world, was an eye-sore to the numerous enemies of the Jesuits. At last, after the middle of the seventeenth century, the hated Order fell a victim to the intrigues of its opponents. We cannot here enter on a lengthy account of the history of the destruction of the Society, but must refer the reader to special works on this subject.[1] Suffice it to mention briefly the opinions of a few impartial witnesses.

Prince Hohenlohe wrote at the time of the suppression that the destruction of the Order was *"une cabale infernale."*[2] Theiner, who was a bitter enemy of the Society, calls the suppression a "disgraceful warfare, a deplorable drama, in which too many impure elements played a leading part."[3] Many prominent Protestant historians, as Ranke, Schoell, J. v. Müller, Sismondi, Leo, declare the charges brought against

---

[1] See particularly the series of articles by the Rev. Sydney Smith, in the *Month* (London), 1902.

[2] Letter of August 4, 1773, in the Royal Archives at Munich.

[3] *Geschichte des Pontificats Clemens XIV.*, vol. I, p. 3.

the Society as calumnies of its enemies, and maintain that the suppression of the Order was not due to any crimes of the Jesuits, but entirely to the tyrannical violence of ministers of State.[1] In Portugal it was Pombal who aimed at separating his country from Rome and introducing infidelity; the Jesuits, for their unflinching loyalty to the Papacy and the staunch defence of revealed religion, were to be the first victims. Pombal hired pamphleteers to calumniate them systematically. Spain and France at the same time began to persecute the Society. In the latter country the Jansenists and Huguenots had always borne a deadly hatred to the Order. The names of the chief enemies of the Jesuits show clearly, in what direction the warfare against them tended: the Duke of Choiseul, the ill-famed Madame de Pompadour, Voltaire, d'Alembert and other French infidel philosophers. They had always regarded the Jesuits as the most formidable and dangerous enemies of their revolutionary designs. Voltaire wrote to Helvetius, in 1761, in a tone of exultant anticipation: "Once we have destroyed the Jesuits, that 'infamous thing' (the Christian religion) will be only child's play for us."[2] However, he could not and would not calumniate the hated Order in the style of others: "While doing my very best to realize the motto: *Écrasez l'infâme*, I will not stoop to the meanness of defaming the Jesuits. The best years of my life have been spent in the schools of the Jesuits, and while there I have never listened to any teaching but what was good, or seen

[1] So Körner in his *History of Pedagogy*. — See also the *Open Court*, Chicago, January 1902, p. 21 foll.
[2] Alzog, *Church History*, vol. III, p. 566.

any conduct but what was exemplary."[1] Neither could J. J. Rousseau be induced to lend his pen to decry the Society, although he confessed that he did not like the Jesuits.

Pope Clement XIV. at last yielded to the threats of the ministers of the Bourbon kings, and in 1773, by a Brief he suppressed the Society, "in order to preserve peace." "This letter", says a Protestant historian, "condemns neither the doctrine, nor the morals, of the Jesuits. The complaints of the courts against the Order are the only motives alleged for its suppression."[2] When recently Sir Henry Howorth represented this Brief as an infallible *ex-cathedra* pronouncement of the Pope, he thereby showed that he has not even the most elementary notion of what is meant by Papal infallibility. Succeeding events proved that — to use the words of one of the enemies of the Jesuits — a peace treaty was struck between the wolves and the shepherd, and that the latter had sacrificed the best watch-dogs of the flock. The dreadful French Revolution opened the eyes of many to the real purport of the persecutions of the Jesuits. True, the Church is not built on the Society, but on the rock of Peter. Still the Church suffered immensely by this sacrifice of its most zealous defenders, and well might Pope Pius VII., in the Bull of the Restoration of the Society in 1814, speak of the "dispersion of the very stones of the sanctuary," which had followed the destruction of the Society and the consequent calamities.

[1] *Ibid.*, p. 570.

[2] Schoell, *Cours d'histoire des États européens*, vol. XXXXIV, p. 83.

It was at this juncture that a Protestant and a Schismatical court rendered homage to the services of the Jesuits, and gave a brilliant testimony to their educational abilities. Frederick the Great, King of Prussia, being determined to preserve them in his kingdom,[1] wrote to Abbé Columbini, his agent at Rome, a letter dated from Potsdam, September 13, 1773, in which the following passage occurs: "I am determined that in my kingdom the Jesuits shall continue to exist and maintain their ancient form. In the treaty of Breslau I guaranteed the *status quo* of the Catholic religion; nor have I ever seen better priests, from any point of view, than the Jesuits. You may add that since I belong to a heretical sect, His Holiness holds no power to dispense me from the obligation of keeping my word, or from my duty as a king and an honest man."[2] On May 15th, 1774, writing to d'Alembert, who was dissatisfied that the Jesuits were not completely exterminated, and feared that other kings moved by the example of Prussia might demand of Frederick seed to cultivate in their own kingdoms, he replied: "I view them only as men of letters, whose place in the instruction of youth it would be difficult, if not impossible, to supply. Of the Catholic clergy of this country they alone apply themselves to literature. This renders them so useful and necessary that you need not fear any one shall obtain from me a single Jesuit." In 1770 he had written in

[1] See documents given by Zalenski, *Les Jésuites de la Russie-Blanche*, vol. I, livre II, ch. IV, "Frédéric II. et les Jésuites." Frederick strictly forbade the Bishops of his kingdom to promulgate the Papal Brief of suppression.

[2] Maynard, *The Study and Teaching of the Society of Jesus*, p. 246.

similar terms to Voltaire. Speaking of Pope Clement XIV., he says: "For my own part I have no reason to complain of him; he leaves me my dear Jesuits, whom they are persecuting everywhere. I will save the precious seed, for those who should wish to cultivate a plant so rare."[1] On May 15th, 1775, he wrote to d'Alembert: "In their misfortune I see in them nothing but scholars whose place in the education of youth can hardly be supplied by others." Again on Aug. 5, 1775: "For the good Jesuit Fathers I have a d— tenderness, not as far as they are monks but as educators and scholars, whose services are useful to civil society." Now, if the Jesuits were dangerous to the welfare of the state, as their enemies make them, how strange that the Atheist on the Prussian throne, the shrewdest and most keen-sighted monarch of his time, should have failed to see it? But he was not the man to let himself be influenced by silly prejudices.

The second ruler of Europe who endeavored to protect the Society was Catharine II., Empress of Russia.[2] In 1783 she wrote to Pope Pius VI. "that she was resolved to maintain these priests for the welfare of her states against any power, whatsoever it was." In the same year the Russian court in a note to Mgr. Archetti, Papal Nuncio to Poland, thus expressed its sentiments on the Jesuits: "The Roman Catholics of the Russian Empire, having given unequivocal proofs of their loyalty to the Empress, have thereby acquired a right to the confirmation of their former privileges. Of this number is the instruction of youth, which has heretofore been committed to the

[1] *Lettre à Voltaire*, 7. Juillet, 1770. *Oeuvres de Voltaire*, tom. XII.
[2] See Zalenski, *l. c.*, pp. 239—429.

Jesuits. The zeal animating these religious, and the success crowning their efforts, have been marked by the Imperial Government with the utmost satisfaction. Would it be just to deprive the inhabitants of White Russia of this precious Institution? In other countries where the Order was suppressed, no substitutes have been found. And why single out for destruction, among the many religious orders, that which devotes itself to the education of youth, and consequently to the public welfare?"[1]

These testimonies refute also a charge sometimes made even by Catholic writers. Theiner, for instance, asserts or implies that, for a space of time preceding the suppression, the Society had fallen away from the station it had held originally in literary and educational matters, that their system had become useless to the interests of science, that education suffered in their hands, that youth issued from their colleges unprotected against the assaults of error, etc.[2] These charges are ably refuted by Abbé Maynard in his work just quoted: *The Studies and Teaching of the Society of Jesus at the Time of its Suppression 1750–73.* But as we said, the appreciation of the Jesuits' educational labors, as shown by Frederick II. and Catharine II., exonerates them completely. These two were the most sagacious monarchs of Europe at the time, and what could have influenced them, atheists as they were, to show such favors to the persecuted Society, had it not been its superiority as an educating body? All attempts to weaken the testimonies of the words and actions of these two rulers have proved unsuccessful.[3]

[1] Maynard, *l. c.*, p. 240.
[2] *History of the Pontificate of Clement XIV.*
[3] Most flattering testimonies as to the educational suc-

Besides, Maynard points out in detail that the Jesuits at that time had among their number *hundreds* of able writers in all branches of learning. The Society could boast of great mathematicians and scientists, as the famous Roger Boscovich († 1787), who was despatched by the Royal Society of London to California to observe the second transit of Venus. During the heat of the French Revolution the French astronomer Lalande, who took pride in the title "the atheist astronomer", ventured to write Father Boscovich's eulogy in the *"Journal of Men of Science"* (February 1792). Then there was Maximilian Hell († 1792), for thirty-six years director of the Imperial Observatory at Vienna. In 1768 he was invited by Christian VII., King of Denmark, to observe in Lapland the transit of Venus. Of the result of Father Hell's expedition Lalande wrote: "This was one of the five complete observations made at great distances apart." [1] Father Hell was a worthy successor to the

cess of the Jesuits in Russia and Galicia, at the time of the suppression, are given by Zalenski, *Les Jésuites de la Russie Blanche*, Paris 1886.

[1] *Bibliogr. Astron.*, 1792, p. 722; see Maynard, p. 205. — For many decades it was suspected that Father Hell had tampered with the figures of his observations after others had been published, so as to make his square with the rest. In the *Atlantic Monthly*, Nov. 1900, Professor Simon Newcomb, of the Washington Naval Observatory, completely exonerates Father Hell from this malicious charge. The distinguished American Astronomer, who professes in his article a personal affection for the Jesuit scientist, has examined the manuscripts of Father Hell, in Vienna, and found that the accusation was groundless, and based on the assertion of a man whose sight was defective. Professor Newcomb further affirms that Father Hell's observations gave figures somewhat

great Jesuit astronomers and mathematicians Clavius, Kircher, Riccioli, Scheiner, Grimaldi, and a precursor of the famous Father Secchi, one of the greatest astronomers, at least in spectroscopy, of the nineteenth century.

Lalande, in his *Bibliographie Astronomique*, enumerates forty-five Jesuit astronomers and eighty-nine astronomical publications for the short period of 1750—1773. The same author, in the continuation of Montucla's *History of Mathematics*, pays the following tribute to the Society: "Here I must remark to the honor of this learned and cruelly persecuted Society, that in several colleges it possessed observatories, for instance in Marseilles, Avignon, Lyons, etc." There were other observatories in Rome, Florence, Milan, in fact in every country where Jesuits had colleges. Of Germany and Austria, Lalande remarks: "There were in Germany and the neighboring countries few large colleges of the Society which had no observatory." He mentions those of Vienna, Tyrnau, Ingolstadt, Graz, Breslau, Olmütz, Prague, etc., and speaks highly of the scientific work done by the Jesuit astronomers. He adds that after the "deplorable catastrophe of the Society," most of these observatories shared the fate of the Order.[1]

Quite recently Professor Günther of Munich[2] called

different from those of other astronomers, but that recent discoveries have proved the Jesuit's observations to have been the more correct ones.

[1] *Histoire des Mathématiques*, par J. F. Montucla, tome IV, achevé et publié par Jérôme de la Lande, Paris, 1802, pp. 347 foll.

[2] *Bibliotheca Mathematica, Zeitschrift für Geschichte der mathematischen Wissenschaften*, 3. Folge, 3. Band, 2. Heft, 1902 (Leipzig, Teubner), pp. 208—225.

attention to the important scientific works of three Jesuits of that period, three relatives of the name Zallinger: John Baptist, Professor in the Jesuit college at Innsbruck, who wrote a remarkable treatise on the growth of plants; James Anton, Professor in Munich, Dillingen, Innsbruck, and Augsburg, a zealous defender of the Newtonian system, who "published works of such importance that it is surprising that they could have been buried in oblivion." The greatest of the three was Francis Zallinger, who published several important works with new views, which partly are held at present, on electricity, meteorology, mechanics, and with particular success on hydrology. Professor Günther repeatedly expresses his astonishment that such works could have been so completely ignored, that no modern work on the history of sciences does justice to them. Very few mention the names of these writers. We may be convinced that careful research will bring to light many more distinguished Jesuit scientists of that period.

Also in literature, shortly before the suppression, the Jesuits had among their numbers distinguished writers. Father Tiraboschi († 1794) wrote the *History of Italian Literature*, in thirteen volumes, up to this day one of the most valuable works on this subject. In France, men like Father Porée and many others were admired even by Voltaire for their literary accomplishments. In Germany, the Jesuit Denis († 1800) rendered the so-called poems of Ossian into his native tongue, and this with such success as to win the highest praise from Goethe. About this time Father Hervas began to write his great "*Catalogue of Languages*", of which we spoke before. But as we are not writing a literary history of the Society, it is enough to have mentioned these few names. A host of other distinguished men, who flourished towards the end of the seventeenth century, may be found in Abbé Maynard's work. Thus the assertion that the Society had become useless to science and literature, is a pure calumny.

As groundless is the charge that the Jesuits had failed in their lofty mission with respect to teaching. We have heard what Frederick II. and Catharine II. thought of them. Most of the celebrated writers mentioned before were engaged as teachers in the collegiate or university establishments of the Order. A cloud of witnesses stands forth to testify that the work of education was carried on with unabated zeal and with great success, not only in languages and literature, but also in mathematics and sciences. Thus Deslandes, commissary of the navy at Brest, testified, in 1748, that the Jesuits had furnished the navy excellent professors of mathematics.[1]

It may be well to quote what the historian of the University of Paris has to say about the educational labors of the Society in France up to the time of its suppression: "If one rises above prejudices and narrow professional jealousies, how can one deny the eminent services which the Society rendered to youth and the family, from its reestablishment under Henry IV.? Those of its enemies who want to be impartial and sincere admit that its colleges were well conducted, that the discipline was at once firm and mild, strict and paternal; that the scholastic routine was improved by wise innovations, cleverly adapted

[1] De Badts de Cugnac, *Les Jésuites et l'éducation*, p. 11.

to the progress in manners and social demands; that the teachers were unassuming, devoted to their work, well instructed, and for the greater part masters in the art of elevating youth; some were perfect humanists, others, scientists of the first rank, so regular in their lives that never has any reproach of misdemeanor been uttered against them. Should one say that, in spite of showy appearances, the education given by the Jesuits lacked solidity, that they too often substituted frivolous practices or worldly exercises for serious work,— a charge frequently made by the University — the Jesuits could answer by pointing to their pupils who held honorable positions in the domain of science and literature, at the court and in the armies, in the ranks of the *bourgeoisie* and among the nobility. . . . As instructors of youth, the Jesuits were above reproach, and more worthy of recommendation than of persecution. . . . We do not inquire whether in other rôles played by the disciples of St. Ignatius, they did not allow themselves to be carried away to excesses of pride, ambition, and intolerance, which necessarily brought upon them cruel retaliation; in connection with our subject, suffice it to state that in the field of studies and public education, their activity was, in general, beneficial. The inexorable sentence which suddenly destroyed their colleges is explained, from the historical point of view, by the prejudices and the hatred existing against the Society. But after having related the biased acclamations of contemporaries, must this sentence, so sadly renowned, be confirmed by the equitable judgment of history? We think not; for it is against truth and justice in many regards, and, as the events that followed have proved, it served neither the Church, nor the State, nor even the University, in spite of the hopes which the latter had based on the ruin of its adversaries."[1] The author, in the chapter following, then describes the fatal consequences for education in France, resulting from the destruction of the Society.

This much is certain that it was not its inability, but, on the contrary, its great success for which the Society was doomed by the Catos of the eighteenth century, whose *ceterum censeo* was that the hated Order was to be destroyed. What the Jesuits had been doing for education and learning became apparent after the destruction of their Order, and it was openly declared by many that the ruin of the Society was followed by a fatal decline of learning among the Catholics. The Bishops of France represented to the King, that "the dispersion of the Jesuits had left a lamentable void in the functions of the sacred ministry and the education of youth, to which they consecrated their talents and their labors."[2] In 1803 Abbé Emery wrote: "The Jesuits have been expelled, their system of teaching has been rejected. But what substitutes for them have we discovered, and in what have the new theories resulted? Are the youth better instructed, or their morals purer? Their presumptuous ignorance and depravity force us to sigh for the old masters and the old ways."[3]

About the same time Chateaubriand in his famous work, *The Genius of Christianity*, exclaimed: "In the

---

[1] Jourdain, *Histoire de l'Université de Paris*, vol. II, pp. 298—300.
[2] Abbé Maynard, *l. c.*, p. 237.
[3] *Pensées de Leibnitz*, p. 429. (Maynard, *l. c.*, p. 238.)

destruction of the Jesuits' learned Europe has suffered an irreparable loss. Since that unhappy event education has never been in a state of prosperity." And in his *Mélanges* he expresses himself to the same effect: "The Jesuits maintained and were increasing their reputation to the last moment of their existence. Their destruction has inflicted a deadly wound on education and letters: as to this, at the present time, there is no diversity of opinion." And even Theiner does not hesitate to say that "the wound inflicted on education was incurable."[1] In Lord Stanhope's conversation with the great Duke of Wellington we find a striking passage on the same subject. Speaking at Walmer in October 1833, the Duke said to Lord Mahon: "On the whole I think it is very doubtful whether, since the suppression of the Jesuits, the system of education has been as good, or whether as remarkable men have appeared. I am quite sure that they have not in the south of Europe. It was a great mistake."[2] In Treves the Jesuits possessed, besides the novitiate and the university, a flourishing college. When the news of the suppression of the Society arrived, the Archbishop Elector, Clement Wenceslaus of Poland, is said to have exclaimed: "*Cecidit corona capitis nostri*"—"The crown of our head is fallen;"[3] and, as the historian of the Royal Gymnasium of Treves adds, his outcry of sorrow was justified. A few years after the Jesuits had left the college, the pernicious leaven of French infidelity had permeated the faculty and was undermining the faith of the young.

[1] Maynard, *l. c.*, p. 242.
[2] *Notes of Conversations with the Duke of Wellington*, by the Earl of Stanhope, London, Murray, 1888, p. 42.
[3] *Historisches Jahrbuch*, Munich 1885, vol. VI, p. 420.

And such was the case everywhere. German scepticism, French atheism, Jansenism, and Josephism began to reign supreme. Let us add here that the Protestant cause was never strengthened by any persecution of the Society; the only gainer was always infidelity. The statement of Mr. Browning, that the governments on the whole have done well to suppress the Jesuit colleges,[1] is proved utterly false by history. At the same time it advocates an intolerable state absolutism. If parents wish to send their children to the schools of the Jesuits, and of religious in general, it is a violation of parental rights, and an infringement of religious and political liberty, to make the attainment of such wishes impossible. In the light of this consideration, the legislation of M. Waldeck-Rousseau, and the recent proceedings against the teaching congregations in France must appear to all fair-minded men as tyranny and a new "reign of terror".

To all students of history who are not blinded by fanatical hatred, the downfall of such a society of men who had devoted their lives to the propagation of religion and the advancement of science, must appear most pathetic. Such it appeared to the atheist astronomer Lalande. "The mention of a Jesuit," he writes, "awakens all the feelings of my heart, my mind and my gratitude. It harrows all my sore feelings at the blindness of the ministers of 1762. Mankind has irretrievably lost, and will never recover, that precious and surprising union of twenty-two thousand individuals, devoted incessantly and disinterestedly to the functions of teaching, preaching, missions, to duties most serviceable and dearest to humanity. Retire-

[1] *Encyclopedia Britannica*, article "Education".

ment, frugality, and the renunciation of pleasure, constituted in that Society the most harmonious concord of science and virtue. I had personal knowledge of them: they were an assemblage of heroes for religion and humanity."[1]

We close this chapter with the following sympathetic lines of a recent writer: "The rise of the Jesuits had been astonishing. Their fall was august. Annihilation could not shake their constancy. No tempests of misfortune could attaint their magnificent obedience. Defamation, incarceration, banishment, starvation, death, unthankfulness, fell upon them, and could not alter, and could not dismay. To the cabals of courtiers and the frenzy of kings, to the laugh of triumphing harlots, and the rebuke of solemn hypocrites, to the loud-voiced joy of the heretic and the unbeliever, to the poisonous sneer of banded sectaries, exulting in their secret confederation, to the gibes of traitors, to the burning sympathies of unpurchased and unpurchasable multitudes, the only response of the Jesuits was superb and indomitable duty. Girt round by cruelty and frivolity, more cruel still; as in the centre of a vast amphitheatre of the antique which they had taught so well, they remained as high resolved, as unflinching as Sebastian before the archers of the Palatine, or the virgin Blandina amid the beasts at Lyons. It was hardly a marvel that the victorious monarch of Prussia, outside the Church though he was, but accustomed to see men die at the call of honor and discipline, half owned a thrill of warrior emotion, and paid a captain's

---

[1] Quoted in the *Annales Philosophiques, Morales, et Littéraires*, by M. de Boulogne, vol. I, p. 221.

salutation, to that infrangible, that devoted army. The Jesuits were not only the ablest of Renaissance schoolmasters, they were great priests, great missionaries, great civilizers, great practicians of the supreme art of persuading and leading men. And the sentence of destruction smote them in the midst of their activity, in a hundred regions where they had become indispensable or almost impossible to replace... Never was such a famous company of scholars in all the records of former civilizations, deep-read in philosophies; famous for sacred eloquence; masters of languages, editors of the lore of antiquity, of the writers of Byzantium, of the obscure dialects of Malaysia and the Upper Amazon; historians, philologists, restorers of chronology... To gain the lying promise of a lying peace, they were demanded as a holocaust to the licentious puppets on the thrones of the Bourbons, to the dark powers behind the veils of the lodge. And their loss to civilization, their loss to France, was not to be computed even by the largest enumeration of what they had done, and what they were capable of doing. The Christendom to which they had become so necessary, and which in an hour was forced to do without them, was yet to learn the unspeakable significance of such a deprivation. In proportion to the services of the Jesuits was the void of their disappearance, the calamity of their fall. When main pillars of an edifice are shattered, more may be shattered than the pillars alone."[1]

[1] The London *Tablet*, Dec. 7, 1901, p. 884.

Chapter VI.

The Revised Ratio of 1832 and Later Regulations.

The Society had been suppressed by Clement XIV. The historian Dr. Brück says: "The Pope's conduct was harsh and unjust", as he had not a single crime to lay to their charge;[1] and even Dr. Döllinger, however hostile to the Society, must have considered its suppression unjust; for he calls its restoration an act of justice.[2] Documentary evidence proves that the Jesuits heroically submitted. Even in Silesia, where Frederick II. wanted to maintain them, "they were unwilling to hold out against the papal bull",[3] and laying aside whatever was specifically characteristic of the Society, they directed the schools as secular priests. Catharine II. of Russia stubbornly refused to allow the Papal Brief of suppression to be published in her dominions. As the publication was required before the Brief could take effect, the Jesuits continued their work in the two colleges at Mohilev and Polotzk in White Russia. Five years after the suppression, in 1778, the new Pope Pius VI. granted them permission to establish a novitiate. Thus, as Frederick II.

[1] *History of the Catholic Church*, (Engl. transl.) vol. II, p. 306.
[2] See *Historische Zeitschrift*, 1900, vol. LXXXIV, p. 800.
[3] Alzog, *Church History*, vol. III, p. 571. Against Theiner's charge of disobedience see Zalenski, *Les Jésuites de la Russie Blanche*, vol. I, pp. 169—213.

expressed it, "the seed had been preserved for those who should wish to cultivate a plant so rare." In 1801, Pius VII., the successor of Pius VI., allowed the Jesuits to establish themselves as a Congregation in Russia, and in 1804 he authorized the introduction of this Congregation into the kingdom of the Two Sicilies.

At length, in 1814, Pius VII., who had been educated by the enemies of the Jesuits, reestablished the Society of Jesus. The Pope gives as the motive of this step, that "he acted on the demand of all Catholic Christendom". "We should deem ourselves guilty of a great crime towards God, if amidst the dangers of the Christian republic, we neglected the aids which the special providence of God has put at our disposal; and, if placed in the bark of Peter, tossed and assailed by continual storms, we refuse to employ the vigorous and experienced rowers who volunteer their services, in order to break the waves of a sea which threatens every moment shipwreck and death."[1] In this Bull, Pius VII. expressly says: "We declare besides, and grant power that they may freely and lawfully apply themselves to the education of youth in the principles of the Catholic faith, to form them to good morals, and to direct colleges and seminaries."

The Society immediately took up this work so dear to its founder and ever cherished by the Fathers of the Old Society. New fields had been opened in the meantime for establishing colleges, especially in England and her dependencies, and in the United States of America.

[1] The Papal Bull: *Sollicitudo omnium ecclesiarum*. This Bull and that of the suppression of the Society are translated in the *Protestant Advocate*, vol. III, pp. 13 and 153 etc.

As regards the system of studies it was found necessary, soon after the restoration of the Society, to accommodate the Ratio to the new conditions of the time. The changes were undertaken with the same calm circumspection with which the old Ratio had been drawn up under Father Aquaviva. As early as 1820 suggestions and observations were sent to Rome from the different provinces. In 1830, the General of the Society, Father Roothaan,[1] himself an excellent classical scholar and experienced teacher, summoned to Rome representatives of all the provinces. After careful deliberations the Revised Ratio appeared in 1832. It was not a new system; nothing had been changed in the essentials, in the fundamental principles. It was an adaptation to modern exigencies of the old methods which had been approved by such great success in former times.

The changes referred mainly to those *branches* of study, which had become important in the course of time. In the colleges Latin and Greek should remain the principal subjects, but more time and care should henceforth be devoted to the study of the mother-tongue and its literature, although this had by no means been neglected in the Old Society.[2] Thus to the 23. Rule of the Provincial was added: "He shall take great care that the pupils [in the colleges of his Province] are thoroughly instructed in their mother-tongue, and he shall assign to each class the amount

[1] J. A. Thym, S. J., *Life of Father Roothaan.* (In Dutch; German Translation by Jos. Martin, S. J.) pp. 110—113.

[2] See above pp. 129—131, and the chapter on the study of the mother-tongue in Jouvancy's *Ratio Disc. et Doc.*, part I, ch. I, § 3. — *Woodstock Letters*, 1894, p. 309. — Father Duhr, *Studienordnung*, pp. 107—118.

and kind of work to be done." The speaking of Latin in the lower classes was no longer possible; special care of idiom in translating is recommended, as also correctness of pronunciation of the mother-tongue. In the higher classes the cultivation of style in the vernacular, according to the best models, is insisted on. The rules concerning dramatic performances are left out; exhibitions are neither encouraged nor forbidden. In the report of the commission it is said that, if dramas are given, they should be in the vernacular.[1] For the grammar classes, other authors are introduced; in the highest grammar class, Sallust, Curtius and Livy are read besides Cicero, the elements of mythology and archaeology are to be taught. Xenophon takes the place of Aesop and Agapetus. In the middle grammar class Caesar is added; in the lowest, Cornelius Nepos.[2]

As mathematics and natural sciences, history and geography claimed more attention, the Revised Ratio prescribed accordingly that more time should be devoted to these branches,[3] although they were to be considered rather as "accessories" in the literary curriculum. For the study of more advanced mathematics and of natural sciences was even then thought to belong properly to the course of philosophy. Still the new Ratio left to Provincial Superiors considerable liberty in this matter, and the Jesuit colleges, conforming to the customs of the respective countries, have introduced some of these branches also in the lower classes.

[1] Pachtler, *op. cit.*, vol. IV, p. 479.
[2] Other changes see Pachtler, vol. IV, pp. 459—469.
[3] *Reg. Prov.*, 23, sect. 3. — *Reg. Praef. Stud. Inf.*, 8, sect. 11.

The greatest change was made in the rules concerning the teaching of philosophy and natural sciences. Aristotle, *the* Philosopher of former times, could no longer hold his place in the schools. So the Revised Ratio does not mention him, although the speculative questions of logics and general metaphysics are mostly treated according to Aristotelian principles. And rightly so; for as a modern Professor of Philosophy says, "Aristotle's doctrine forms the basis of traditional logic even to this day." [1]

It may be safely said that after the vagaries of Hegel and others, there was manifested, in the latter part of the nineteenth century, a greater appreciation of Aristotelian philosophy. The most prominent advocate of this revival, Professor Trendelenburg of Berlin, expressly declares that "the organic theory of the universe, the basis of which was laid by Plato and Aristotle, is the only philosophy which has a future before it; and that speculation done by fits and starts and by every man for himself, has proved itself to have no permanence." [2] A remark of Professor Paulsen may not be without interest. "There are people who are inclined to use the names of Thomas Aquinas and Scotus as synonymous with nonsense and craziness. To such it may be well to say that even at the present day there are men who think similarly as Saint Thomas, whom they consider the prince of philosophers, and on whom they base their whole philosophical instruction. And these are the men to whom the despisers of scholasticism give credit for a great amount, if not of wisdom, at least of extraordinary

---

[1] Windelband, *History of Philosophy*, p. 135.
[2] Erdmann, *History of Philosophy*, vol. III, p. 278.

prudence and cunning, I mean the Jesuits. Has not the See of Rome restored Saint Thomas, the philosopher whom the Society of Jesus has chosen as its guide, as the philosopher of the Church? Has this been done in order to stultify the clergy? Can this be the intention of those who, through the clergy, wish to domineer over the world?" [1]

Physics, chemistry, physiology, psychology, astronomy, geology, and cosmology are taught according to the established principles of modern science. The basis of this study is thus laid down: "The professor of physics is to expose theories, systems, and hypotheses, so as to make it clear what degree of certitude or probability belongs to each. Since in this faculty new progress is made every day, the professor must consider it part of his duty, to know the more recent discoveries, so that in his prelections he may advance with the science itself." [2] Higher mathematics (analytic geometry and calculus) are to be taught not only in one but in two, if possible in three, years of the philosophical course. We may now invite the reader to judge about Compayré's assertions: "The sciences and philosophy are involved in the same disdain as history. Scientific studies are entirely proscribed in the lower classes, and the student enters his year in philosophy, having studied only the ancient languages. Philosophy itself is reduced to a barren study of words, to subtile discussions, and to commentaries on Aristotle. Memory and syllogistic reasoning are the only faculties called into play; no facts, no real inductions, no care for the observation of nature. In all things the Jesuits are the enemies of progress.

[1] *Geschichte des gelehrten Unterrichts*, vol. I, p. 38.
[2] *Reg. Prof. Phys.*, 34—35. — Hughes, *Loyola*, p. 275.

Intolerant of anything new, they would arrest the progress of the human mind and make it immovable."[1] It seems almost impossible to crowd more falsehoods into so small a space. There are at least ten flagrant misrepresentations in these six short sentences.[2]

Philosophy has been discarded from most modern programs of college instruction, but to the great detriment of solid learning. A thorough philosophical training is of the greatest value for the lawyer, physician, and scientist, and for every man who wishes to occupy a higher position in life. Paulsen, and many other leading German schoolmen, express their regret that in the new systems philosophical training has been entirely relegated to the university. Two objections are made against this method: First, the form of

[1] *History of Pedagogy*, p. 145. — It is beyond my comprehension how Mr. Payne, the translator, can style this book "a model, in matter and form, for a general history of education", nor is it intelligible how such a superficial production could be received so favorably by the American educational public.

[2] 1. History, as has been proved before, is not disdained; 2. sciences and philosophy are not disdained; 3. scientific studies are not entirely proscribed in the lower classes; 4. there are ordinarily two years of philosophy, not one; 5. the student, entering philosophy, has studied much more than only the ancient languages; 6. philosophy is not merely a barren study of words; 7. nor is it reduced to a commentary on Aristotle; 8. facts, inductions, the observation of nature are not neglected; 9. the Jesuits are not enemies of progress in all things (see what has been said by Protestant scholars on their writers, above pp. 149—173, 179—182, and below, chapter VII); 10. far from being intolerant of everything new, the professors are expressly told to study carefully the new discoveries and to keep abreast of the advance of science; etc., etc.

instruction proper to the university is of the continuous lecture. But this method presupposes instruction in form of question and answer, in philosophy as well as in other branches. We should consider it a failure to try to teach grammar from the beginning by lectures, as given at the university. It seems as little promising of success to teach logic in this manner. Exercises in logic must be *practised* as well as must the forms of grammar. By giving a boy a definition of the Subjunctive or of the Ablative Absolute, you will not enable him to write correctly. Similarly by lecturing about the definition or by giving a definition of definition, even when illustrated by examples, you will not enable the student to handle these formulas logically. To a certain extent this applies also to psychology, ethics and civics. The elementary notions must be practised by concrete examples, so that they are ready, and as it were, handy in mind; then it is possible to use them for more complicated operations.[1]

The second reason for not relegating philosophy entirely to the university, has been well stated by Professor Elsperger. "If the gymnasia do not wish to leave to chance the sort of ideas the pupils get from a reading that is often enough desultory, and from intercourse with others, then they need, in the highest classes, a branch of study which gives them the ideas needed. This can be attained only by elementary training in philosophy. Mathematics can do nothing in this direction, the study of Latin and Greek liter-

[1] Paulsen, *Geschichte des gelehrten Unterrichts*, p. 771. (2. ed. vol. II, p. 668.) — See also Willmann, *Didaktik*, vol. II, pp. 142 foll.

ature does something, but is not sufficient, and unfortunately, religion is to some extent mistrusted by not a few teachers. Thus it happens that many of our older pupils not only suffer shipwreck in their faith, but leave college with that lamentable scepticism of the uneducated, which views every nobler idea with suspicion. This tendency of very many of our young men can be counteracted only by a branch of study which attacks that sceptical disposition, and forces the pupil to obtain a deeper view of things."[1]

It is exactly for such reasons that the Society of Jesus has kept the course of philosophy in its curriculum of higher education. It agrees with Professor Paulsen that elementary training in philosophy is possible and necessary in higher schools.[2] About the possibility, the Jesuits never could entertain the least doubt, as for centuries they carried it out successfully, and at present are giving a solid philosophical training in all their larger colleges.

The Revised Ratio of 1832 was in no way considered final. In the letter accompanying this Ratio, Father General Roothaan, writes to the provinces: "We offer to you the result of careful examinations and discussions. You must test it practically that it may be again corrected, if necessary, or enlarged, and then be sanctioned as a universal law (for the

[1] *Blätter für das bayerische Gymnasialwesen*, vol. VII, p. 41. (Paulsen, *l. c.*, II, 667.) — In recent years educators demand more and more that college education should terminate in a solid course of philosophy. See Lehmann, *Erziehung und Erzieher*, Berlin, 1901. — Paulsen, *l. c.*, II, 664—670.

[2] *L. c.*, vol. II, p. 666: "The lack of philosophical training makes itself felt more painfully every day among the scientists, and in public life."

Society).''[1] Only by a decree of a General Congregation of the Order is this sanction possible. Such a decree, however, was not passed; consequently, the Revised Ratio has not the force of a law in the Society, but is merely to be considered as a regulation of the General. So much liberty is left to Provincials that the teaching in Jesuit colleges can easily be adapted to the educational needs of all countries. In 1853, the XXII. Congregation of the Order passed a decree that "the Provincials should be free to exercise the power granted them by the 29th rule of making changes in the studies, according to the demands of various countries and times."[2] The same decree ordered that "new proposals for amendments be sent from the single provinces and that the Ratio (of 1832) be revised with the advice of learned and experienced men."

In the XXIII. Congregation, 1883, the study of natural sciences was especially recommended. Among others the following regulation was passed: "Those scholastics [the younger members of the Order engaged in studies] who seem to have a special talent for any of these sciences, should be given a fourth year, or special hours in the third year of their philosophical course, to perfect themselves in that science under the direction of a professor."[3] "It is advisable to destine select younger members of the Society for the acquisition of the degrees which empower them to act as authorized public teachers." (State examinations in the European Universities.) These special

[1] Pachtler, vol. II, pp. 228—233. There it is also stated expressly: "Some of these regulations are merely temporary"; p. 232.
[2] Pachtler, vol. I, p. 115.
[3] *Decr.* XVII., Pachtler, vol. I, p. 121.

subjects are to be pursued after the regular course of studies has been finished.[1] Finally, it was asked "that some regulations should be made as to special studies in ancient languages, philology, ethnology, archaeology, history, higher mathematics and all natural sciences." It was decreed that no "general prescription could be made in this matter, but the Provincials should confer with the General as to how these studies should be arranged in the different provinces. At the same time the Congregation decrees that, provided the customary studies of the Society, and as far as possible, the preeminence of literary studies remain intact in the classical schools, the progress and increased cultivation of those [special] branches should be earnestly recommended to the Provincials. It is also their duty to select those young men, who have a special talent for these branches, that they may devote themselves to them entirely."[2]

From all that has been said so far, it becomes evident that the Society is continually improving its system, and adapting it to the conditions of the age. It would also seem that it was inadvertence to these more recent legislations which betrayed President Eliot into the statement: "The curriculum of the Jesuit colleges has remained almost unchanged for four hundred years, disregarding some trifling concessions made to natural sciences."[3] As the Ratio of 1832 has not been ratified by a Congregation, and as a further revision has been demanded, we may expect to hear in the future of further development in the Jesuit system.

[1] *Decr.* XXII., Pachtler, vol. I, p. 123.
[2] *Decr.* XXIII., Pachtler, vol. I, p. 123.
[3] *Atlantic Monthly,* October 1899.

CHAPTER VII.

The Educational Work of the Jesuits in the Nineteenth Century.

It cannot be denied that the Jesuits have not had the same brilliant success as educators in the nineteenth century, as during the centuries preceding the suppression of the Order. How is this to be explained? The opponents of the Order are ready with an answer: "It is because the Jesuits have not kept up with the progress of the age. Their whole system is not suited to modern times." Even such as are not hostile to the Society, have said that the Old Society took with it into its grave the secret of its educational success. However, a short reflection will give us the true explanation.

The time of the suppression, a period of forty years, forms a gap in the educational history of the Society. These blank pages, as Father Hughes says, signify the total loss of property and position, with a severance in many places of the educational traditions for almost sixty years, and the entire destruction of them in many other parts.[1] Restored, the Society had to struggle into existence under altered and unfavorable conditions. The schools in about seven hundred cities and towns, which the Order had possessed before its suppression, were now largely in the hands of State authorities. And besides, the nineteenth century was not a time of undisturbed peace

[1] Hughes, *Loyola*, p. 266.

for the Jesuits. There was a persecution going on against them nearly all the time in one country or other. They were expelled from Spain in 1821, re-admitted, but driven out again in 1835 and 1868; expelled from Belgium 1818, from Russia 1820, from Naples 1820, from France 1830 and 1880, from Portugal 1834, from the Argentine Republic 1848, from Switzerland 1847, from Austria 1848, from Italy 1848 and 1859, from New Granada 1850 and 1859, from Guatemala 1871, from Germany 1872, from Nicaragua 1881, from Costa Rica 1884, harassed in Spain and Portugal during the last years, and driven out of France owing to the "Laws of Associations."

All these persecutions seriously hampered the educational work of the Jesuits. They frequently lost a number of flourishing colleges forever, others had to be commenced anew, when they were allowed to return. Besides, in many cases, expulsion meant the loss of libraries, observatories, and laboratories. Still, in spite of these difficulties, at the end of the nineteenth century, they possess a respectable number of colleges, scattered all over the world, from Zi-ka-wei in China to Beirut in Syria, from Australia to England and Ireland, from Argentina and Chili to Canada.

The development of the colleges of the Society in the United States deserves a brief sketch. The first Jesuit school in this country was opened in New York. A Jesuit was the first priest, so far as records go, who ever visited (1644) the island of Manhattan, now a part of the city of New York.[1] He was the saintly French missionary, Father Isaac Jogues, who was put

[1] Rev. Henry A. Brann, D. D., in *The College of St. Francis Xavier*, p. 1 foll.

to death in 1646 by the Mohawks at Auriesville. Forty years after the martyrdom of Father Jogues, three other Jesuits, Thomas Harvey, Henry Harrison, and Charles Gage, were invited to New York by Governor Dongan. These Fathers, true to the spirit of the Society, soon established a classical school in New York. It was situated apparently in what then was called "King's Farm;" the site was subsequently leased to Trinity Church. Governor Dongan, himself an Irish Catholic, heartily patronized this school, which was frequented by the sons of the best families on Manhattan Island; the bell of the Dutch church in the fort was rung to summon the pupils.[1] But the clergy and the people of the Church of England, not as friendly to the Jesuits as the Dutch Protestants, attacked the school, and penal laws were passed expelling the Jesuits and other Catholic priests from the island. It was enacted that priests "be deemed and accounted incendiaries, disturbers of the peace and safety, and enemies to the true Christian religion, and shall be adjudged to suffer perpetual imprisonment."[2] This law put an end to the Latin school of the Jesuits. The second attempt made by the Jesuits to found a classical school in New York occurred about the year 1808. The learned Father Kohlmann opened a little school in Mulberry Street, but in 1817 the Jesuits were recalled from New York to Washington, and it was only in 1847, that the College of St. Francis Xavier in New York was founded.

It is, however, not New York, but Maryland where the first Jesuit school in the colonies and the first

[1] Shea, *The Catholic Church in Colonial Days*, p. 91.
[2] Brann, *l. c.*, p. 2.

Jesuit college in the United States was founded. In 1634 two Jesuit Fathers landed in the province which George Calvert, Lord Baltimore, had obtained from the English crown. It was this province, Maryland, "the asylum of the Papists," as Bancroft says, "where Protestants were sheltered against Protestant intolerance."[1] But not long after, ungrateful men who had fled from other colonies, and who had been welcomed in this province, turned on those who showed hospitality to them, and a relentless war of persecution was waged against the Catholic settlers of Maryland. This hampered the development of Catholic education greatly. Still, zeal for higher studies was never lacking. In 1638, Father Poulton had been sent from England as Superior of the Maryland Mission. One of his first acts was the project of a seat of learning in the colony. This was about the same time when the initial movement was made to establish Harvard College. But how different were the circumstances in which Harvard and the Jesuit school developed! The one protected by the government, the other persecuted. And yet, amidst all the trials and annoyances, the Jesuits never ceased to labor for the intellectual training of the Catholics as well as for the religious. In 1651 we find their academy near Calvert Manor, in 1677 in or about Newtown Manor; for the trials of the times did not permit the school to be stationary. In 1746 the Jesuits were driven out of Southern Maryland; they crossed the Chesapeake Bay and immed-

[1] *History of the United States*, vol. I, pp. 244—248 (18th ed., Boston, 1864). — However, on the "toleration" in Maryland see Griffin, *Historical Researches*, 1902, vol. XIX, No. 4.

iately opened their academy on the Eastern shore, at Bohemia Manor.

In this school two men studied who became famous in the history of America: Charles Carroll of Carrollton, one of the signers of the Declaration of Independence, and his cousin John Carroll, the first Archbishop of Baltimore. As the institutions of learning in the colonies and the great universities of England were in those days closed to Catholic pupils, those who could afford it, went to the European Continent. Thus John and Charles Carroll went to the famous Jesuit college at St. Omer in Flanders, where they won a high reputation for their brilliant scholarship. After six years study in that school, John entered the Society of Jesus. Later on he spent a series of years as professor in the colleges of St. Omer, Liège and Bruges. The suppression of the Society filled his heart with the deepest grief. He went to England, where he was received most heartily by Lord Arundell and other English noblemen. But when he saw that measures were adopted by the English government, which more and more alienated the American colonies from the sovereign and parliament of Great Britain, Father Carroll patriotically resolved to return to his native country and share its trials and fortunes. The services which he rendered to the nascent republic during the war of the Revolution, especially his mission to Canada with Benjamin Franklin, Samuel Chase and Charles Carroll, need not be dwelled on here.[1]

In 1784 Carroll was appointed Prefect Apostolic for the Catholics in the United States. He immediately

---

[1] See Shea, *Life and Times of the Most Reverend John Carroll*, ch. IV.

planned the establishment of an academy for higher studies. The outcome of this plan was the foundation of the College of Georgetown, near Washington, in 1789. In 1791 the doors of the college were opened to students. The first pupil to enter was William Gaston of North Carolina, who became a profound scholar and a great orator. He entered the House of Representatives in 1813, was a distinguished member of the Federal party, and for many years adorned the judicial bench of his native state.[1] Among others of the pioneer pupils of Georgetown were Philemon Charles Wederstrandt (later on commandant of the "Argus"), Robert Walsh, an eminent writer who ably defended American affairs against the misrepresentations of English writers, and founder of the first American Quarterly: *The American Review of History and Politics*.[2] When Washington honored Georgetown College by a formal visit, Robert Walsh was chosen to address him.

The college had been founded by Ex-Jesuits. Many of the professors had joined the Society of Jesus, which had been revived in Russia, and, at last, in 1814, Archbishop Carroll and the Fathers in Georgetown received with joy and exultation the news of the complete restoration of the Society. After this event, Jesuit colleges began to multiply. In the year 1900 the Jesuits conducted twenty-six colleges, the principal ones, besides Georgetown, being in Baltimore, Boston, Buffalo, Chicago, Cincinnati, Cleveland, Denver, Detroit, Fordham (New York), New Orleans, New York, Omaha, St. Louis, St. Mary's (Kansas), San

---

[1] Shea, *History of Georgetown College*, p. 15.
[2] Shea, *l. c.*

Francisco, Santa Clara (California), Spokane, Spring Hill (Mobile), Washington, Worcester (Massachusetts). In that same year over fifty-two thousand boys were educated in Jesuit high schools and colleges all over the world, that is nearly twice as many as in Harvard, Yale, Princeton, Columbia, Cornell, the Universities of Chicago, Michigan, Pennsylvania, Wisconsin, combined.

Some of the Jesuit institutions rank very high, both for the number of pupils and for the excellent results which they exhibit. The German Jesuits, expelled from the "land of science and *Lehrfreiheit,*" impart a higher education to more than five thousand students in foreign countries. Their Francis-Xavier College at Bombay, in 1897, numbered fifteen hundred and twenty-six students; ten hundred and two Christians; two hundred and ninety Parsis; one hundred and seventy-one Hindoos; fifty-four Mahometans; nine Jews. French Jesuits have two colleges in Trichinopoli, East India. The one is frequented by eighteen hundred students, among them five hundred and fifty of the Brahmin caste. The English government in India shows the Jesuits many favors for their educational work. Not unfrequently the Viceroy, or the Governor, visits the colleges and praises the work of the teachers, and not a few Jesuits have been appointed University examiners.

In Syria, the Jesuits conduct St. Joseph's University, Beirut. They have a printing establishment there which probably holds the first rank among those of the Orient. A French admiral calls it "a creation which is the symbol of the union of the two greatest forces in the world, religion and science; an establishment which is the pride of France, as well as of the Catholic Church."[1] A Protestant Review in Germany writes: "The progress which, owing to this establishment, the Arabic literature has made, cannot be ignored."[2] The latest catalogue has four hundred and four numbers, of all sorts of Arabic and Syriac works, grammars, dictionaries, etc. Some of the works edited by these Jesuits, are at present used in the lectures in the University of Berlin.[3]

Another great Jesuit school in the East is Zi-ka-wei, near Shanghai, China. The educational labors of the Jesuits in this institution have been acknowledged by distinguished Protestant visitors. In 1898 Prince Henry of Prussia, on his first landing in Shanghai, paid a visit to this establishment. He spent nearly a whole day with the Fathers, and frankly expressed his admiration at the splendid work they were doing. In fact, he was so impressed by what he had seen, that again and again after his visit, he would return to the subject and talk about the work of "those excellent French Jesuits." It soured a few German fanatics somewhat against him, when reports began to be printed in the German papers, to the effect that Prince Henry had spoken kindly of the hated Jesuits. But this bigotry did not influence Prince Henry. Princess Irene, his wife, having the next year rejoined her husband in China, they paid a second visit to Zi-ka-wei, which is briefly related in the following terms: "On the 12th of March, 1899, Prince Henry of Prussia, and the Princess, his wife, arrived at Shanghai;

[1] *A terre et à bord*, par l'amiral Aube, 1894, p. 45.
[2] *Literarisches Centralblatt*, 1890, No. 42.
[3] Braunsberger, S. J., *Rückblick auf das katholische Ordenswesen im 19. Jahrhundert*, (Herder, 1901) p. 150.

the next morning they hastened to pay a visit to Zi-ka-wei. The Prince told us that he had said such nice things to the Princess about the establishments at Zi-ka-wei that she wished to visit them at once."[1]

The following comparison, made by an English Protestant, Laurence Oliphant, speaks well for the educational labors of the Jesuits: "I was struck with the intelligent expression of the youths' countenances in the Jesuit school at Shanghai, and at the evident affection they had for their teachers. Instead of cramming nothing but texts down their throats, they teach them the Chinese classics, Confucius, etc., so as to enable them to compete in the public examinations. The result is, that even if these native youths do not all become Christians, they have always gratitude enough to protect and love those to whom they owed their education, and perhaps consequent rise in life. A few days later I went over the school of the Protestant Bishop. The contrast was most striking. The small boys gabbled over the Creed in what was supposed to be English, but which Lord Elgin, who was with me, was firmly persuaded was Chinese. They understood probably about as clearly as they pronounced. Then instead of the missionaries living among them, and really identifying themselves with the lads, as the Jesuits do, they have gorgeous houses, wives and families. A Protestant missionary here, with a wife and four children, gets a house as big as Spring Grove, rent free, and £500 a year. And that is what they call 'giving up all for the sake of the heathen'."[2]

[1] *The Messenger*, New York, March 1902, p. 335.
[2] *Memoir of the Life of Laurence Oliphant* (New York, Harper, 1891), vol. I, p. 229.

JESUIT EDUCATION IN THE 19th CENTURY. 209

This is clearly another proof for what was said in a previous chapter,[1] that the religious state affords many advantages for educational work, at least in missionary countries. Here we must add that the educational labors of the Jesuits in those countries are not confined to higher instruction. Many lay-brothers give elementary instructions in the schools,[2] and the priests give catechetical instruction in hundreds of such schools, which in many other ways are directed by them. In February 1901, fifteen scholars of Paris, Professors in the University or members of the *Institut de France*, among them the celebrated Paul Sabatier, Dean of the Protestant Theological Faculty, issued a declaration in favor of the religious associations. A list is added about the educational work in foreign countries under the direction of French Jesuits. The total given there is 3,923 schools, or orphan asylums, with 156,256 children, and all this is done by the *French* Jesuits alone. Of their 193 schools in Syria in particular, the Protestant *Literarische Centralblatt* of Leipsic says, "that they are now the best in Syria."[3] Therefore, that the Order is doing very great work for civilization, is evident. Of the 15,160 members of the Order (in 1900) about 4000 were laboring in foreign missions; and this work, in most cases, means also work directed toward the education of the native people.

In this connection we may quote the striking tribute, paid by an American politician to the educational work of the Jesuits among the Indians. On April 7, 1900, Senator Vest of Missouri, during the

[1] See chapter III, pp. 89—98.
[2] See above pp. 104—106.
[3] Braunsberger, *l. c.*, p. 115.

14

discussion of the Indian Appropriation Bill before the United States Senate, made the following remarkable statements: "I was raised a Protestant; I expect to die one; I was never in a Catholic church in my life, and I have not the slightest sympathy with many of its dogmas; but, above all, I have no respect for this insane fear that the Catholic church is about to overturn this Government. I should be ashamed to call myself an American, if I indulged in any such ignorant belief. I said that I was a Protestant. I was reared in the old Scotch Presbyterian Church; my father was an elder in it, and my earliest impressions were that the Jesuits had horns and hoofs and tails, and that there was a faint tinge of sulphur in the circumambient air whenever one crossed your path. Some years ago I was assigned by the Senate to examine the Indian schools in Wyoming and Montana. I visited every one of them. I wish to say now what I have said before in the Senate, and it is not the popular side of the question by any means, that *I did not see in all my journey a single school that was doing any educational work worthy the name of educational work, unless it was under the control of the Jesuits.* I did not see a single Government school, especially these day schools, where there was any work done at all.... The Jesuits have elevated the Indian wherever they have been allowed to do so without interference of bigotry, and fanaticism, and the cowardice of insectivorous politicians who are afraid of the A. P. A. and the votes that can be cast against them in their district and States. They have made him a Christian and, above even that, have made him a workman able to support himself and those dependent upon him.

Go to the Flathead Reservation in Montana.... and look at the work of the Jesuits, and what is seen? You find comfortable dwellings, herds of cattle and horses, intelligent, self-respecting Indians.... I am not afraid to say this, because I speak from personal observation, and no man ever went among these Indians with more intense prejudice against the Jesuits than I had when I left the city of Washington to perform that duty.... Every dollar you give to these [Government] day schools might as well be thrown into the Potomac River under a ton of lead."[1]

When men who have been able to achieve the almost impossible, the education and civilization of the Indian, undertake the task of secondary education among civilized nations with the same zeal and energy, must we not expect that they will perform this successfully? If we add that, owing to their studies, special training and natural inclinations, they are even better fitted for the work of higher education, than for that of civilizing the Indian, is it then likely that they are so inefficient as some represent them?

Let us, then, see the results of a number of Jesuit colleges. I wish to remark, however, that the account in no respect can be called complete, or even satisfactory. What is given on the next pages, was found, sometimes accidentally, in various publications. More material was available about the schools of the British Empire, where the relative efficiency of a school can be fairly tested by the University Examinations.[2]

[1] From the *Congressional Record* for April 7, 1900, page 4120 (Italics ours).

[2] The data, unless stated otherwise, were communicated to the *Woodstock Letters*.

The *Tablet* (London), April 26, 1902, prints the following:

"The following Catholic names appear on the Classical Honours list issued in April by the Moderators at Oxford. The names appear in alphabetical order.

CLASS I.—J. W. Glasson, Corpus Christi; C. C. Lattey, Pope's Hall; I. C. Scoles, Pope's Hall.

CLASS II.—H. E. Tulford, Balliol; E. J. Kylie, Balliol; C. D. Plater, Pope's Hall.

From this it will be seen that the Jesuit students from Pope's Hall, formerly Clarke's Hall, achieved a success which, considering the size of the Hall, is probably a record in the history of the University. The Hall which has room for only a dozen students, distributed over the whole four years' course, was represented by three candidates at the recent examination, and all these were successful. Indeed, the Hall, which was opened by the late Father Richard Clarke, S. J., only six years ago, has had a history during that time of which very large colleges in the University might be justly proud. Starting with four students in 1896, of whom two broke down in health, the first examination at which the Hall presented candidates was Moderations in 1898, when one of the two obtained 1st class honours, and the other 2nd class honours in Classics. In 1899 the Hall secured one 1st class honours in Mathematical Moderations, one 2nd class honours and one 3rd class honours in Classics. In 1900 the score was one 1st class and one 2nd class honours in Classical "Greats"—the final degree examination; one 1st class in Mathematical Moderations, and one 2nd class in Classical Moderations. In 1901, one 1st in Mathematical Greats, and one 1st and one 2nd in Classical Moderations. As nearly all these young Jesuits have been educated either at Stonyhurst, at Beaumont, or at Mount St. Mary's, such excellent results, as soon as they are brought into open competition with the picked students of all the leading public schools, who are the holders of the innumerable scholarships in the University, go to show that after all our Catholic colleges are, to say the least, not so very far behind the best Protestant schools in the country, either in the soundness of their general education, or in the special culture of the classics.''

In Ireland there are several richly endowed Protestant foundations: the Queen's Colleges of Cork, Galway, and Belfast, the last, one of the best equipped institutions of learning in the British Empire; the three Colleges draw an annual revenue of about $125,000 to support a score of distinguished Professors in each. The Jesuits conduct the University College of Stephens Green, Dublin. For many years University College routed from the field the Queen's Colleges of Cork and Galway, and was surpassing gradually that of Belfast, although this one made a noble fight. In the two examinations of the Royal University of 1895, the Jesuit college won 67 distinctions, while the Queen's College of Belfast gained a total of 57. University College bore off all the first places in mathematics, the first two places in English, and the first honors in mathematical physics and chemistry, in classics the first place in First Arts, and the first and second places in Second Arts. Of the sixteen medical honors awarded, University College secured nine, the remaining seven were divided between her Majesty's privileged institutions. This despite the many disadvantages of University College through the lack of laboratories and museums, which the Government at lavish expense has provided for the Protestant rivals.[1] The success of the following year was equally brilliant. In the first and second Arts Examination of 1897 University College gained 51 distinctions, Belfast 46, Galway 18, Cork 6. Of the 51 distinctions 32 are in the first class (only 16 of Belfast's), and among them first place in no fewer than 9 subjects. In the M. A. Examination three out of the four studentships awarded, five out of the six first class honors awarded, the only two special prizes awarded, two out of the three gold medals, all went to University College. It bore away 13 out of the 18 distinctions conferred.

In the B. A. Examinations:

	1st Honors.	2nd Honors.	Total.
University College............	4	13	17
Queen's College, Belfast......	3	13	16
" " Cork...........	nil.	nil.	nil.
" " Galway....	nil.	4	4

Taking the whole of the arts examination for the Academic year, we find University College first on the list with 82 distinctions, as compared with 63 for Belfast, 25 for Galway, and 7 for Cork. And University College has a comparatively small number of students, many of whom can attend only the night classes.

In Autumn 1898 once again the little unendowed University College of the Jesuits outdistanced the endowed rivals, and this time more than ever. But it is not merely in the number of distinctions, though that exceeds the combined results of all its three

[1] *Woodstock Letters*, 1895, p. 504.

rivals, but in their quality that University College stands pre-eminent. The College got first and second places over all competitors in classics and mathematics, first place in history and political economy, and in modern literature. This last distinction is enhanced by the fact that the standard has been growing higher year after year, and this year the papers exceeded in difficulty any hitherto set.

The following list tells best the result:

AUTUMN: Honors and Exhibitions.			Scholarships.	Studentships.	Fellowships.	Total.
	1st Class.	2nd Class.				
University College............	13	4	3	1	1	22
Queen's Coll., Belfast.........	4	6	1	1	1	13
Queen's Coll., Galway.........	0	3	0	1	0	4
Queen's Coll., Cork............	0	2	1	0	0	3

JUNE AND AUTUMN COMBINED: Honors and Exhibitions.			Scholarships.	Studentships.	Fellowships.	Total.
	1st Class.	2nd Class.				
University College............	35	37	3	1	1	77
Queen's Coll., Belfast.........	25	37	1	1	1	65
Queen's Coll., Galway.........	4	9	0	1	0	14
Queen's Coll., Cork............	0	23	1	0	0	24

In 1896 the Jesuit college of Clongowes, in the Intermediate Examination, where 8877 students presented themselves, held the foremost place of all the schools and colleges of Ireland with a total of 45 distinctions. Also in 1897 it outdistanced all competitors in the highest grade, winning the "Blue Ribbon" of the examination, the highest honor in the senior grade.

From India similar results are reported from various Jesuit colleges, for instance from St. Xavier's College, Calcutta, the College of Darjeeling, St. Francis Xavier's College, Bombay. Last year (1901), the number of candidates for "matriculation examination" in the whole Presidency of Bombay was 3806; of these only 1217 passed (32 per ct.). The Jesuits of St. Francis Xavier's, Bombay, had sent for the examination 43; of these 34 passed (79 per ct.). In 1899 St. Joseph's College, North Point, Darjeeling, secured the only vacancy, at the "Opium Examination," and the first place at the "Accounts Examination," with these two ten first places at the Public Examinations, which is all the more creditable as the College is but seven or eight years old. Most gratifying successes are reported also from the Jesuit colleges in Australia.

Coming nearer home, we have to speak of little St. Boniface College, Manitoba. In 1897 it could insert the following advertisement in the *"North-West Review,"* which is carefully read by the Protestants of Winnipeg, who could not challenge the advertisement:

> "*St. Boniface College.* The only Catholic College in America that competes annually with half a dozen Protestant Colleges and Collegiate Institutions. In proportion to the number of its pupils, *St. Boniface College has won more scholarships* than any of its Protestant competitors."

The Governor's Bronze Medal has been awarded twenty-two times from 1879 to 1900. Seven out of these twenty-two times it has been won by a student from St. Boniface College. Considering that, during all these years, the candidates from St. Boniface College were in an extremely small minority — about one in twenty-two, or four and one-half per cent on an average, — this proportion of seven out of twenty-two, almost a third, struck every one, especially the opponent, as very extraordinary. Had St. Boniface won that medal, the most highly valued of all the University distinctions, once in twenty-two years, the Catholic college would have been doing well, would have had its fair share of success. Manitoba College (Presbyterian), the largest of all the colleges, which sometimes boasts of as many students as all the other colleges put together, has won the medal only three times. Then the proportionate value of Latin and Greek was lowered; the classics were a strong point at St. Boniface. But St. Boniface nevertheless secured the medal two years in succession. Then Greek, hitherto obligatory on all, was made optional after a long fight, in which St. John's College (Anglican) sided with St. Boniface against this innovation. The result of this move, coupled with the preponderance of mathematics and chemistry over Latin alone, prevented St. Boniface from winning the medal for seven years, although its students often headed the list in special subjects. But 1899 and 1900 the St. Boniface students forged ahead again, and won the medal two years running.

During the vacation of 1900, a change has occurred in the statute that concerns the University scholarships. Hitherto the winners of scholarships had been listed in the order of merit, with the mention of the college or school to which they belonged. Now all the winners were to be arranged alphabetically, with no mention of the institutions to which they belong. Several reasons were given for this change, but the suspicion has been expressed that the real motive was to prevent the Jesuit college from occupying so large a place in the public eye.[1] It may appear unfair to make such a charge; however, such suspicions have been expressed by men who are not Jesuits, nor biased towards the Society. Thus, about twenty years ago, Albert Duruy said of the movement against religious orders in France and the Jesuits in particular: "Without proofs, without thorough inspection, they slander and accuse the congregations... *They do not try to compete with them, they find it simpler to suppress them.*"[2] In fact, the recent movement in France against religious orders has been ascribed, undoubtedly with good reasons, to the same motive.

A few years ago there was an attempt made in France to introduce a Bill to suppress the religious schools, which (at the expense of the State schools) were gaining more and more in public favor. A Parliamentary commission was then appointed which was presided over by M. Ribot, and which took a quantity of very valuable evidence from various witnesses. Nothing, however, as may be seen from M. Ribot's report,[3] was established against the Jesuits or any other religious schools; on

[1] From the *North-West Review*, August 22, 1900.
[2] *Revue des Deux Mondes*, 1880, I.
[3] *La réforme de l'enseignement secondaire.* Armand Colin, Paris.

the contrary, they were in several respects held up as an example to the State schools, even by distinguished adherents of the latter. Such results were naturally deemed highly unsatisfactory by the anti-religious party, and accordingly for the time being the contemplated legislation was shelved. When M. Waldeck-Rousseau undertook it and enlarged it, he was careful to avoid anything so dangerous to his designs as another judicial inquiry into the facts.[1] Now, if any proofs could have been found showing the inefficiency of the Jesuit schools, it is certain that M. Waldeck-Rousseau would have made the best of such evidence.

The fact that he says nothing of it, is a sure sign that no such proofs are procurable even by the minutest examinations. Hence it follows that the Jesuit schools were, at the very least, as efficient as the State schools.

Instead of proofs, such hollow and absurd declarations were made: "Religious possess an independence which gradually will lead to the usurpation of all authority. They dare even the dignitaries of the Church. The education which they give separates a part of youth from the rest, and thus the moral unity of the country is rent."[2] The question ought to have been: "Are the youths, educated by religious, by Jesuits, less instructed, less moral, less patriotic?" To this question the answer has been given decidedly in the negative. We shall have occasion to speak of the patriotism of French Jesuit pupils; their morality has been most favorably compared to that of pupils of other schools — whereas in M. Ribot's report a dis-

[1] *The Tablet*, Nov. 2, 1901, p. 698.
[2] Speech of M. Waldeck-Rousseau, quoted by du Lac, *Jésuites*, pp. 88 sq.

tinguished adherent of the State school system declares that in these State schools the pupils are "*moralement abandonnés*". As regards the intellectual ability shown by Jesuit pupils, it will suffice to see the lists of the successes obtained by them in the *École Centrale*, the *Polytechnique*, the *Military Academy of Saint-Cyr*, and the *École Navale*.[1]

The following statement will illustrate how the anti-clerical press fabricated proofs of the inefficiency of Jesuit colleges; it shows also that Jesuit pupils are not behind others in branches other than classics, mathematics and sciences. In 1875 a student in the law school at Poitiers published these facts: "A short time ago the journal of M. Gambetta, the *République française*, had taken the trouble to occupy itself with the Law Faculty at Poitiers and its students. According to M. Gambetta the said school comprises two clearly distinct classes of students: those from the *Lycées*, and those from the Jesuit colleges. The latter are good for nothing and obtain no prizes, whereas the former carry off all the laurels. Now in point of fact, at the distribution of prizes in the law school for 1874–75, which took place last Thursday, the reports show the following results: In the 3rd year, the 2nd prize for French Law and the 2nd prize for Roman Law were awarded to a Jesuit pupil. In the 2nd year, of the four distinctions two were given to Jesuit pupils. In the 1st year, all five distinctions, two medals and three honorable mentions, were awarded to Jesuit pupils."[2]

[1] Du Lac, *Jésuites*, p. 250 foll.
[2] *Univers*, Paris, December 2, 1875. For high praise bestowed on Jesuit pupils by University Examiners in France,

Within the last two or three decades, neither the Jesuit colleges nor the schools of the other Congregations in France were inferior to the State schools. The very contrary is true, as may be seen from the remarkable testimony of an anti-clerical writer in the *Contemporary Review*.[1] The article, "Monastic Orders up to Date," is filled with virulence against the religious orders, the Roman Congregations, and the Catholic Church in general. Yet the superiority of the schools of the religious over the State schools is candidly admitted. Speaking of the charges brought against the religious orders in France, the writer says: "The members of these communities have, it is said, taken elementary, intermediate, and technical education into their own hands, are successfully preparing youths for schools, professions, and university degrees, and supply both army and navy with officers. The official report on the Budget of Instruction for 1899, querulously affirms that they and their schools act as a sort of drain upon the natural clients of the University. But why should they not? They are more successful than their lay competitors, and more deserving of success. If the education which they give be very imperfect, and it is sometimes this and more, it is on the whole the best that is to be had in the country. Lay instruction in France is purely mechanical, that given by the Congregations is living and human. Both aim at cramming, but the religious teachers do their work efficiently and successfully, their rivals with a degree of slovenliness which is in-

see *Figaro*, April 5 and June 2, 1879; De Badts de Cugnac, *Les Jésuites et l'éducation*, pp. 17, 19 foll.

[1] March, 1900, p. 441.

credible... Under such conditions one is not surprised to learn that the Congregations supply one-fourth of the pupils of the famous *École Polytechnique*, one-third of the students of Saint-Cyr, and one-half of the graduates of the Naval School. The religious communities have fairly won these triumphs by dint of hard work under conditions laid down by their enemies and applied by their opponents."

Twenty years ago the London *Times* had made a statement to the same effect, when Ferry tried to suppress the Jesuit schools in France. "We should have liked to see a frank admission on the part of prominent members of the Left, of the real causes of the success of the ecclesiastical schools. It is no use of putting it down to wiles and artifices of any kind. The perversity, or bad taste, or stupidity of the multitude will not explain it. The simple truth seems to be that the schools of the Jesuits and other religious bodies are better in many respects than their competitors. They satisfy parents and boys more than the *Lycées* do. The traditional skill in teaching of the Jesuits is not extinct. They are, as a rule, at more pains than lay professors, with many interests to occupy them, to know and study the nature of their pupils. It is their habit to pay attention to the morals as well as the intellectual training of the lads committed to their charge."[1] Such admissions, coming from such sources, speak volumes for the schools of the religious and of the Jesuits in particular.

These are a few facts about the results obtained by Jesuit colleges in recent years. As they concern colleges in various countries over the globe, directed

[1] London *Times*, July 8, 1879, p. 9.

JESUIT EDUCATION IN THE 19th CENTURY. 223

by Jesuits of different provinces of the Order, they bespeak certainly no inefficiency of the Jesuits' teaching. Can we not conclude that, were there a similar system of public examination in this country, the Jesuit colleges in the United States would exhibit similar success?

On December 12, 1900, the Juniors of a Jesuit Institution, of Holy Cross College, Worcester, Massachusetts, defeated in a debate the Juniors of Harvard. The victory of Holy Cross was all the more remarkable as Harvard a week before had won the debate from Yale on the very same question, "On the permanent retention of the Philippine Islands." On April 8, 1901, the Freshmen and Sophomores of the same College again came off victorious in a debate with a Freshman-Sophomore team of Brown University.[1] — Although we do not want to draw from such debates any conclusions for the superiority of the Jesuit college, still they deserve to be recorded, because the Jesuit college was victorious over Harvard, shortly after the President of Harvard University had charged the Jesuit colleges with inefficiency.[2]

[1] The judges of the debate were G. Stanley Hall, President of Clark University; Hon. John R. Thayer, member of Congress, and Professor Charles F. Adams of the Massachusetts State Normal School. President Abercombie of Worcester Academy presided. None of these gentlemen is a Catholic.

[2] The unqualified slurs of President Eliot against the Jesuit colleges were ably refuted by Rev. Timothy Brosnahan, S. J., Professor of Ethics at Woodstock College, Maryland, in his pamphlet: *President Eliot and Jesuit Colleges*, Messenger Press, New York, p. 86. The reception given to this booklet was remarkable. We refer the reader to a criticism in the *Bookman*, April 1900, by Professor Peck of Columbia University, N. Y. We quote only one little passage from

The *American Ecclesiastical Review*, August 1900, gave an account of the controversy between President Eliot and the Jesuit colleges, in which it was proved that the President's charges were not based on any facts which could justify his measures against the Jesuit institutions. Professor Eliot had declared, "we have had experience at the Law School of a considerable number of graduates of Holy Cross and Boston, and these graduates have not, as a rule, made good records at the School." Now the truth is that in the ten years preceding the time of the final decision of the Law School regarding Boston College (March, 1898), there were only three graduates of Boston College in the Law School, of whom one left after two years, one left with an excellent record after one year on account of ill-health, and one completed the course and received his diploma. In all the time before these

Prof. Peck's article: "Altogether we have not in a long time read anything which compacts into so small a compass so much dialectic skill, so much crisp and convincing argument, and so much educational good sense. We hope that President Eliot has been reading this over very carefully himself. He has been so long an autocrat in his own particular microcosm as apparently to make him somewhat careless when he addresses a larger public. In this case he has certainly been evolving argumentative material out of his inner consciousness, in the spirit of the person who first said *tant pis pour les faits;* and it is just as well that for once in a way he should have been brought up with a good round turn. As the information would probably never reach him from Harvard sources, we may gently convey to him the information that throughout the entire country professional educators, and men and women of cultivation generally, are immensely amused at the cleverness with which his alleged facts and his iridescent theories have been turned into a joke."

ten years, only two or three graduates of Boston College entered the Law School. The facts in the case, therefore, do not bear out President Eliot's statement that "a considerable number of Boston College graduates have been at the Law School and have made poor records." President Eliot has at several times given as his reason for the rejection of Boston College and Holy Cross, that their students were inferior. This charge has been answered by Father Brosnahan in his paper on *The Relative Merits of Courses in Catholic and non-Catholic Colleges for the Baccalaureate*, read before the conference of Catholic Colleges April 1901 at Chicago.[1] From the preceding data we may certainly conclude that so far the "inferiority" of Jesuit schools has not yet been proved, and that the facts do not warrant the assertions about the "inefficiency of the Jesuit system for modern times."

In connection with the educational labors of the Jesuits in the nineteenth century, we must not fail to mention briefly their literary and scientific work during that period. There are several reasons for treating of this in a work on Jesuit education. *First*, because the Jesuit scholars are a product of the Jesuit system; *secondly*, because some of them were teachers in colleges during the greater part of their lives, and all for at least five or six years; *thirdly*, because their case proves how highly the Society values, and how freely it cultivates the various departments of science. It is easy to understand that the frequent persecutions and expulsions from many countries are most injurious and

---

[1] This paper has been published separately with the title *The Courses leading to the Baccalaureate in Harvard and Boston Colleges.*

unfavorable to the cultivation of science, which requires above all what the Romans called *otium*. Moreover, as the Jesuits lost in several expulsions even their libraries, museums, and observatories, v. g. the famous *Museo Kircheriano* in Rome, and the observatory where Secchi had served the cause of science for so many years, they were greatly hampered in their researches. It is all the more remarkable to see that the Jesuits achieved so much in the various fields of science, in spite of these difficulties. It betokens almost a heroic enthusiasm for science that these men patiently continue their investigations and start new enterprises, even in countries where the hostile attitude of legislative assemblies is like the sword of Damocles hanging over them.

In this brief sketch of Jesuit scholars we mention only such as were distinguished for productive scholarship within the last twenty-five or thirty years. Among the scientists of this period we mention first Father Angelo Secchi, who was one of the foremost astronomical observers of the nineteenth century. Educated and trained from early youth by the Jesuits, he soon became known by his publications on solar physics and meteorology.[1] He wrote several important works, among them *Le Soleil*, a standard work on the sun, *Les Étoiles*, *L'Unité des Forces physiques*, and more than eight hundred articles in scientific periodicals of Italy, France, England and Germany.[2] He has been called "the Father of Astro-physics", on

[1] See *Nature*, London 1878, vol. XVII, p. 370.
[2] Bibliography in Sommervogel's *Bibliothèque*, vol. VII, columns 993—1031. Biography and criticism of Secchi's greater works, by Moigno, *Vie de Père Secchi*, Paris, 1879. — Pohle, *P. Angelo Secchi*, Cologne, 1883.

account of his spectro-scopical observations of the sun and the fixed stars. The ingenious meteorographic apparatus, a self-recording instrument for meteorological observations, which Father Secchi constructed, caused a sensation in the Paris exposition of 1867, and received the first prize (100,000 francs). The interesting instrument is now in St. Ignatius College, Cleveland, Ohio, where it is used by Father Odenbach, S. J., for meteorological observations. When the Piedmontese took Rome in 1870, the Roman College and its observatory were taken from the Jesuits. The new government did all in its power to separate Father Secchi from the cause of the Pope and from his Order. He was offered the position of Director-General of all astronomical observatories in Italy, the dignity of senator, etc. But all these flattering offers could not estrange the noble priest from his benefactor Pius IX., and his persecuted Order. He preferred to remain loyal to them, although he had to suffer mean and paltry annoyances. For the rest, the indignation roused in Italy and all over Europe, prevented the government from expelling Father Secchi from his beloved observatory. During an earlier expulsion of the Jesuits from Italy 1848–9, Father Secchi had been Professor of physics and astronomy in Georgetown College, Washington, D. C. This College possesses at present in Father Hagen a scholar who is highly esteemed in mathematical and astronomical circles. His great works, the *Atlas Stellarum Variabilium* and his *Synopsis der höheren Mathematik*, are most favorably spoken of by scientists.[1]

[1] Father Hagen's *Synopsis* has been called a "splendid contribution to the history and progress of mathematics,"

Another prominent astronomer was Father Perry, Professor of higher mathematics and Director of the observatory of Stonyhurst College, England. He is especially known, as was Father Secchi, for his labors in the domain of solar physics. The English Government and learned societies sent him frequently on scientific journeys, and at the time of his death it was stated that he had been employed on more scientific expeditions than any living astronomer. He was sent — as Father Hell in 1769 — to observe the Transit of Venus (in 1874 and 1882), further, to observe the total eclipses in 1870, 1886, 1887, and 1889. It was on the expedition of 1889, on H. M. S. *Comus*, that Father Perry died, a martyr for the cause of science. Scientific men spoke with admiration of the painstaking preparations of his expeditions, his accuracy and skill in observations, and his enthusiastic love for

Nature, London, June 7, 1894; "a colossal enterprise," *Revue Bibliographique Belge*, Sept. 30, 1891; "a really grand work," Professor Cantor, in *Zeitschrift für Mathematik und Physik (hist.-lit. Abth.)*, XXXVII, 4, p. 151. "One must be astonished how one man can master such an amount of learning," *Zeitschrift für math. und naturw. Unterricht*, XXVII, p. 43. The *American Annals of Mathematics* (1893, vol. VII, No. 3) call it a "monumental work" and say: "A more useful labor than this in the present condition of mathematical literature can hardly be imagined; moreover, it calls for all but the very highest, that is creative mathematical power; in particular, for immense erudition; an unerring logical instinct..., but above all for untiring industry, etc." — Father Hagen's *Atlas Stellarum Variabilium* was also highly praised, v. g. in the *Bulletin Astronomique*, 1900; in the *Vierteljahrsschrift*, XXXV; in the Leipzig *Litterarische Centralblatt*, 1900, No. 4, and 1902, No. 26.

science.[1] Among the living astronomers in England Fathers Sidegreaves and Cortie deserve to be mentioned.

In recent years the Society has extensively gone into the field of meteorology. Seventeen stations are devoted exclusively to meteorology, or at least making it a prominent feature. They are: Stonyhurst (England), Jersey (Channel Islands), Rome, Kalocsa (Hungary), Malta, Burgos, Manila, Zi-ka-wei (China), Calcutta, Ambohidempona (near Tananarivo, Madagascar), Bulawayo, Boroma, La Granada, Havana, Cleveland (Ohio), Saltillo, Puebla (Mexico). Some of them have a name. A few details about the observatory of Manila will interest American readers. It consists of four departments: astronomical, meteorological, seismical, and magnetic. The scientific publications of this observatory have been praised in scientific journals (v. g. *American Meteorological Journal*, vol. X, June 1893, p. 100; *id.*, vol. XII, Febr. 1896, p. 326. — *Meteorologische Zeitschrift*, Nov. 1887, p. 366; Oct. 1898, p. 64, etc.). The commercial world in Eastern Asia appreciates its typhoon warnings. During the Spanish-American War, Dr. Doberck, Director of the Observatory at Hongkong, addressed the Weather Bureau of the United States Government, saying that "the Observatory of Manila is in the hands of men who possess very little scientific education and cause scandal by communicating sensational typhoon warnings to the newspapers in Hongkong." The effect of this

[1] See the encomiums bestowed on him by Protestant writers in the *English Mechanic* (Jan. 25, 1890); *Nature*, vol. XXXXI, pp. 279–280. *The Observatory, Monthly Notices f the Royal Astronomical Society*, vol. L, n. 4.

accusation was that the Jesuits were forbidden to send out any such warnings. When matters were investigated, it turned out that the Manila warnings had indeed very often contradicted those of Mr. Doberck, but that the events invariably proved the correctness of the Manila observations. The Eastern newspapers: *The Hongkong Telegraph, China Mail, Manila Times, Daily Press,* strongly denounced Dr. Doberck, and rendered a brilliant testimony to the labors of the Jesuits, and especially their invaluable typhoon warnings. On November 2, 1898, the Rev. Jos. Algué, Director of the Observatory, received the following notice: "Rear-Admiral Dewey desires me to thank you for your courtesy in giving him such complete information concerning your typhoon predictions, which he has found in every case to be correct. (Signed) Flag Secretary." On February 2, 1899, a letter was sent to the Director of the Observatory, from the Flag-ship Olympia, which concludes: "I trust that the United States Government will make the necessary provisions for the continuance of the institution which you conduct in such an able manner, and which has proved itself to be so great a benefit to maritime interests in this part of the world. Very truly yours, George Dewey, Rear-Admiral U. S. N."[1]

The work done by the Jesuits at the Manila Observatory and all over the islands, may be seen from two volumes with accompanying atlas of thirty maps.[2]

[1] From a letter of Father Algué, *Woodstock Letters,* 1899, pp. 213–225.

[2] *A Collection of Geographical, Statistical, Chronological, and Scientific Data relating to the Philippine Isles, either collected from former works, or obtained by the personal observation and study of some Fathers of the Society*

The work treats of the geography of the islands, climatology, seismology, and terrestrial magnetism. Professor Henry S. Pritchett, the Superintendent of the U. S. Coast and Geodetic Survey, tells us that "to the admirable work of the Jesuits is due practically all of our present knowledge of the interior of Mindanao." Father Algué's work on the cyclones of the Philippine Archipelago is the standard work on that subject.[1]

In 1891 the French Academy of Sciences awarded prizes to the Jesuits in Madagascar, in recognition of their great service rendered by their astronomical and meteorological observations. Two years previous another Jesuit had received a prize of ten thousand francs for his geographical maps of the interior of the island; and last year, 1901, the very year which witnessed the expulsion of the Jesuits from the Republic, another Jesuit, Father Stanislaus Chevalier, by unanimous vote of the commission of the French Academy, received the prize of 3000 francs for his meteorological

of Jesus. Printed at the Government Press, Washington, D. C., 1900.

[1] The best recommendation for this work is the fact that the French Ministry of Marine had it immediately translated into French. In 1900 there appeared an English and a German work (Bremen and Shanghai) on the same subject, "based on that of J. Algué," as the preface has it. But as the name of the author is given that of Professor Bergholz. Now this work — it sounds almost incredible — is nothing but an abridged translation of Father Algué's work. This has quite recently been pointed out by Professor Nippoldt of the Magnetical Observatory of Potsdam, in *Petermann's Mittheilungen*, September 1902. (*Kölnische Volkszeitung*, Wochenausgabe, Oct. 23, 1902, p. 3.) This is evidently a proof of what we said above, p. 154, note 2.

and astronomical publications.[1] In a recent work, "Kiautschou", published with the co-operation of the German Emperor, a high tribute is paid to the scientific labors, *especially the astronomical and meteorological observations*, of the Jesuits in Zi-ka-wei, and the German official who bestows this eulogy on them, declares that he is not a friend of the Jesuits.

In other fields of natural sciences, the Jesuits are working most diligently, and their labors are appreciated by the scientific world. "The best book on mechanics is that of the Jesuit Jullien," so says a Protestant scholar.[2] Another writes of an Austrian Jesuit: "Father Braun, the distinguished Director of the Observatory of Kalocsa in Hungary, furnished some of the most ingenious experiments for establishing the density of the earth. His works are a remarkable proof for the scientific energy of the man, and the spirit of sacrifice for the sake of science."[3] In June 1900, Father Hillig of Canisius College, Buffalo (New York), published a catalogue of the most prominent Jesuit museums. He enumerates about sixty, scattered all over the world.

Several Jesuits are distinguished biologists, among them the German Father Erich Wasmann, one of the foremost entomologists of modern times. His numerous publications on the beetles living commensally with ants and termites, have been styled "classic" by the leading English, German and French scientific

---

[1] *Kölnische Volkszeitung* (Wochen-Ausgabe), January 2, 1902.

[2] Budde, *Allgemeine Mechanik*, vol. II, p. 496. (Berlin, 1892.)

[3] *Himmel und Erde*, Berlin, June 1898.

reviews.[1] Of his work on "Arthropoda" the *Canadian Entomologist* says: "Dr. Wasmann has given us the greatest contribution on this interesting subject ever made, and one that must become a classic in Entomology."[2] Other prominent biologists are the French Father Panthel who received the *prix de Thore* from the *Institut de France* for an anatomical work published in 1898; the Dutch Father Bolsius, an authority in microscopic anatomy; the Belgian Father Dierkx, whose important researches on morphology are published in *La Celulle* (Louvain, 1890—1900). These names suffice to prove that the Jesuits are by no means "enemies of progress and intolerant of everything new," as M. Compayré represents them.

Other departments of modern science are successfully cultivated by Jesuits. We mention only Father Strassmaier, who by experts is called one of the first Assyriologists.[3] Recently Father Dahlmann is becoming very prominent by publications on Indian and Chinese philosophy. His works have been greatly praised by Professor Max Müller of Oxford and other Orientalists. On the field of literature we call attention to a recent production of the German Jesuit Baumgartner: *History of Universal Literature*.[4] Sel-

[1] See, v. g., *Nature*, London 1901, Dec. 12, p. 136; and Professor Wheeler of Texas University in the *American Naturalist*, 1901, vol. XXXV, 414—418.
[2] *Canadian Entomologist*, January 1895, p. 23.
[3] See Oppert in *Le Télégraphe*, Nov. 27, 1887. — Dr. Bezold in *Wiener Zeitschrift für Kunde des Morgenlandes*, vol. II, p. 78. — Hugo Winkler in the *Berliner philosophische Wochenschrift*, 1888, p. 851.
[4] *Geschichte der Weltliteratur.* Up to 1900 four volumes were out: 1) *Literature of Western Asia and the Countries of the Nile.* 2) *Literature of India and Eastern Asia* (China

dom has a work been praised so highly by men of the different creeds and nationalities. Protestant reviews have been, we may say, as enthusiastic as those of Catholics, on this *"opera gigantesca"*, as an Italian reviewer has styled it. One Protestant Review (*Westermann's Monatshefte*) says: "No similar work can be compared to Baumgartner's in thoroughness, variety, and above all in directness."[1] The same author has published some splendid volumes on Goethe (3 vols.), Lessing, Calderon, Jost van den Vondel, and Longfellow. Father Longhaye's *Histoire de la littérature française au XVIIe siècle* (2 volumes) was awarded a prize by the French Academy in 1901.

A very distinguished historian is Father Ehrle, Prefect of the Vatican Library, author of the great *Historia Bibliothecae Pontificum* and co-editor of the *Archiv für mittelalterliche Geschichte und Litteratur*. Father Grisar is a leading author on Christian Archaeology. His latest work on the *History of Rome* is a worthy rival of Gregorovius's famous work.[2] The Belgian Jesuits continue the colossal work of the Old Society, the "Bollandists", or *Acta Sanctorum*, a work of prime importance for the history of the whole

and Japan). 3) *Greek and Latin Literature of Classical Antiquity.* 4) *Latin and Greek Literature of Christian Nations.* The coming volumes will treat of the Literature of Italy, Spain, Portugal, France, Poland, Russia, Holland, Sweden, Norway, Iceland, England, Germany.

[1] See some other criticisms of leading Protestant papers in *The Review*, St. Louis, June 6, 1901: "Protestant Criticism of a Recent Catholic Work."

[2] *Geschichte Roms und der Päpste*, "a publication of the very first rank, as indispensable as the work of Gregorovius." (*Allgemeine Zeitung*, Munich 1899, No. 45.) —*Neue Preussische Zeitung*, Berlin 1900, No. 608.

Christian Era. Of the sixty-two folio volumes of this gigantic collection, nine were published since 1845.[1]

As writers on Ethics we mention Father Castelein and Father Cathrein[2]; on philosophy the English Jesuits Clarke, Rickaby, Maher (Stonyhurst Series). Father Maher's *Psychology* recently received the note "Special Excellence" by the University of London, and the author, the degree of "Doctor of Literature". And this in spite of the fact that the book contains a very energetic criticism of the works most favored by the University, including, indeed, the writings of both the examiners themselves. We could add scores of distinguished writers on theology, but we wish to confine ourselves to publications which have favorably appealed to Protestants. In 1900 the Society conducted more than one hundred periodicals. Although a great number of them are chiefly religious magazines (as the ably written *Messenger*, New York), there are also several scientific periodicals. Some reviews, as the *Month* in England, the *Études religieuses* in France, the *Civiltà Cattolica* in Italy, the *Stimmen aus Maria-Laach* (with valuable scientific supplements), the *Theologische Zeitschrift* (Innsbruck), the *Razón y Fe* in Spain, the *Analecta Bollandiana* in Belgium, are representative literary and scientific periodicals.

A splendid tribute was paid, in January 1902, to the scientific activity of the German Jesuits. Deputy

---

[1] See above p. 161.
[2] Cathrein, *Moralphilosophie*, 2 vols. — *Socialism*. The English translation of the latter work is by Father James Conway, S. J. Cathrein's works are highly praised by Cossa-Dyer, *Political Economy*, London, 1893, where it is said that "they cannot easily be valued too highly."

Spahn, Judge of the Supreme Court of the Empire, and a prominent member of the German Parliament, pleaded in the *Reichstag* for the re-admission of the Jesuits into Germany. In the course of his brilliant speech he spoke thus of the literary and scientific work of the German Jesuits: "In whatever branch scientific progress has been made during the nineteenth century, the German Jesuits are distinguished contributors. In history we have Father Ehrle, Prefect of the Vatican Library, one of the editors of the *Archives for Medieval History and Literature,* and author of the great *Historia Bibliothecae Pontificum;* Father Braunsberger, whose *Epistulae et Acta Canisii* have been called by Protestant historians a most valuable contribution to the history of the Reformation. Then we have Father Beissel's numerous publications on Christian art; Father Baumgartner's magnificent *History of Universal Literature,* and many other literary productions by the same author. Father Kreiten's critical essays; the many volumes of the *Analecta Hymnica Medii Aevi* by Fathers Dreves and Blume; the five volumes on Aesthetics by Fathers Gietmann and Sörensen; the philological writings of Father Fox on Demosthenes. Father Strassmaier, the Assyriologist, deciphered over three thousand Babylonian cuneiform inscriptions, more than any German Academy has ever done in that line. Father Epping found the key to the astronomical computations and observations of the Babylonians, and his work is successfully continued by Father Kugler. Father Dahlmann is one of the very first authorities in the field of antiquities of India. In natural sciences we have the famous Father Wasmann, the entomologist. In physics Father

Dressel is eminent, and in pure mathematics and astronomy Father Hagen, director of the Georgetown Observatory, author of the *Synopsis of Mathematics* and of the *Atlas Stellarum Variabilium*. We find among these Jesuits several prominent writers on geography, and it is only a few months ago that Father Fischer, Professor of geography at Feldkirch, discovered the map on which the New World bears for the first time the title 'America'. The well-known moralist Father Lehmkuhl has written an excellent commentary on the new code of Germany, and was one of the first to advocate this new code. The various publications of the German Jesuits on the social question are continually working for the maintenance of the existing social and political order."

Many other names deserve to be added to these mentioned by Deputy Spahn. Father Meyer, by his German writings, has exerted a great influence on Catholic writers in Ethics. Father Cathrein has published various important works on the same subject, and one of the very best works extant on the social question. On the latter subject we possess several excellent works from the pen of Father Henry Pesch. Father Stiglmayr's critical studies of the writings of Pseudo-Dionysius Areopagita (he assigns these works to the fifth century), have recently been called "brilliant researches which have definitely settled this long discussed question."[1]

Between 1881 and 1900 the German Jesuits alone published six hundred and seven books, some of which are, as we heard before, classics in their respective fields. Three of these writers have, within the last

[1] Bardenhewer, *Patrologie* (1901), p. 474.

few years, been elected members by celebrated Academies of Science: Father Wasmann by the Russian Imperial Academy of St. Petersburg; Father Baumgartner by the Belgian Royal Academy of Ghent; and Father Ehrle, in November 1901, by the Prussian Royal Academy of Göttingen.

The favorable criticisms on Jesuit publications, quoted on the preceding pages, are almost exclusively by Protestant scholars of highest repute. Are these facts unknown, or are they studiously ignored, by certain writers who are so loud in belittling Jesuit education and scholarship? We readily confess that Jesuit scholarship has not yet regained that brilliant position which it enjoyed in the first centuries of the existence of the Order; the reasons for this have been mentioned. We also admit that the eulogies bestowed on the literary and scientific success of the older Jesuit institutions are not a sufficient guarantee that the Jesuit system is equally efficient in modern times. But we think this last point is proved by what has been said in this present chapter. It certainly proves that the Jesuits do not rest satisfied with the laurels of their predecessors, but that they strenuously struggle to keep abreast with the scientific progress of the nineteenth and twentieth centuries. The testimonies adduced are all the more remarkable, if we keep in mind the most discouraging circumstances under which the Jesuits had to labor, and the coldness and antipathy with which the works of the Jesuits are ordinarily viewed by non-Catholic writers. This leads us to a rather sad chapter in the history of Jesuit education, in which we have to speak of the opposition which the educational work of the Society had to encounter in all centuries.

Chapter VIII.

Opposition to Jesuit Education.

Nothing in the whole history of education after the Reformation is more striking than the difference of opinions about, and the attitude assumed towards, the educational system of the Society. We have heard that the Protestant King Frederick II. of Prussia, and the Schismatical Empress Catharine II. of Russia, protected the Jesuit schools, at a time when the Bourbon Kings ruthlessly destroyed all Jesuit colleges within their realms. In the nineteenth century the Jesuits were repeatedly expelled from Catholic countries, as from France, and were allowed to labor undisturbedly within the vast British Dominion and in other Protestant countries. However, this tolerant attitude was not always taken by Protestant rulers. The penal laws of England against the Catholics are well known. The Jesuits were always mentioned as particularly hateful. Thus one statute under Elizabeth (27 Eliz. c. 2), provided that "all Jesuits and other priests, ordained by the authority of the See of Rome, should depart from the realm within forty days, and that no such person should hereafter be suffered to come into or remain in any of the dominions of the crown of Great Britain, under penalties of high treason."

Special laws were enacted to prevent Catholics from sending their children to foreign schools. "Any other of her majesty's subjects," says the same statute, "who hereafter shall be brought up in any foreign popish seminary, who within six months after proclamation does not return into the realm, shall be adjudged a traitor. Persons, directly or indirectly, contributing to the maintenance of Romish ecclesiastics or popish seminaries beyond the sea incur the penalties of *praemunire*. And still further this statute enacts, that no one during her majesty's life shall send his child or ward beyond the sea, without special license, under forfeiture of one hundred pounds for every offence."[1] James I. had a law passed providing that "persons going beyond sea to any Jesuit seminary were rendered, as respects themselves, incapable of purchasing or enjoying any lands etc."[2] The same laws were enacted again under William III.[3] The schools of the Jesuits on the continent which were chiefly affected by these laws, were the great colleges of St. Omer and Liège.

In various places on the continent laws were made forbidding parents to send their children to Jesuit schools. Thus Duke Ulrich of Brunswick, "moved by his paternal care and affection for all his subjects, high and low, in order to counteract the cunning plans and bloody designs of the enemies of the Gospel, particularly of the Jesuits," issued a decree in 1617, strictly forbidding his subjects to send their children to Jesuit schools, as not a few had done before. Those who should in future "act so inconsiderately," were threatened with confiscation of all their property and

[1] *The History of the Penal Laws enacted against the Roman Catholics*, by R. R. Madden, London 1847, p. 154.
[2] *Ib.*, p. 169.
[3] *Ib.*, p. 232.

other penalties.[1] Similar laws, enacted in Brandenburg and Prussia, have been mentioned in a previous chapter.[2]

But the difference in public opinion is not less remarkable than that manifested by the attitude of governments and rulers towards the Society. No other institution has been so often the theme of the most high-flown panegyric and of the most bitter invective as the Society of Jesus. Its admirers, and not a few Protestants were among these, have proclaimed it as an establishment of the utmost utility to learning, morals, religion, and state. It may even be admitted that some have been extravagant in their praises of the Society and its labors. On the other hand, its enemies see in it an assemblage of ambitious men who, under the disguise of hypocrisy, aim at nothing but universal dominion, which they endeavor to obtain by most odious and criminal means, to the detriment of morality, religion and society. "Perhaps no body of men in Europe," says Quick, "have been so hated as the Jesuits."[3]

So many accusations have been advanced against the Jesuits that it would take a volume of considerable size merely to enumerate them. Years ago Bishop Ketteler of Mentz publicly remonstrated against "that continued crime of systematic calumny against the Society." The Jesuits have been defended and ex-

[1] Koldewey, *Braunschweigische Schulordnungen*, in *Monumenta Germaniae Paedagogica*, vol. VII, pp. 138—139.
[2] See pp. 146—148. However, it is but fair to add that Catholic rulers, v. g. the Dukes of Bavaria, forbade their subjects to send their sons to foreign Protestant schools. Janssen, vol. IV, (16. ed.) p. 464.
[3] *Educational Reformers*, p. 54.

onerated of the charges by thousands of prominent Catholics and by distinguished Protestants, and yet the muddy stream of calumny flows on; the old charges are repeated and new ones are fabricated almost daily, and believed. It is customary now-a-days to sneer at the credulity of former ages, at the superstition of the Middle Ages, and the witch panic of the sixteenth and seventeenth centuries. However, our age has little reason to look down superciliously on the benighted people of times gone by, for there is among us, and even in circles that lay claim to enlightenment, a great deal of superstition and credulity; only the forms and the objects of credulity are different from those of former ages. In fact, the "Jesuit panic" has been called a chronic disease of modern times, and the credulity manifested in accepting implicitly the most absurd charges against the Society is stupendous.

Whenever a person is indicted for a crime we demand that he be given a fair trial; we want to hear and examine impartially the whole of the evidence against him, before we pronounce him guilty. In the case of the Society of Jesus, we have a body of fifteen thousand men, who devote their lives to the propagation of Christianity, the civilization of savages, and the education of youth. Almost every day they are maligned in books, papers and public speeches. No evidence is asked for; the ordinary demands of prudence and justice are set aside; it is enough to hurl accusations against the Jesuits, and thousands and tens of thousands willingly believe them. This is no exaggeration. One need only read the most popular books on education to become convinced of this fact. The open calumnies and malicious insinuations against that work of the Society, which is especially dear to every Jesuit, viz. the education of youth, are simply appalling.

It is impossible for us to mention all the charges made against the educational system of the Jesuits; nor do we think it necessary. For, some accusations are so ridiculous that to hear them stated, should be enough for any thoughtful man to disbelieve them. Further, they are so clearly opposed to the fundamental principles of the Order, and so emphatically contradicted by its official documents, that it is difficult to see how men can, for a moment, consider them even probable. Lastly, they are so varied and so contradictory that they easily elude us. What one says, is directly or indirectly denied by another. It will be very instructive to put a few statements in parallel columns.

"They [the Jésuits] completely revolutionized education by fearless innovations."—Rev. W. M. Sloane (Princeton), *The French Revolution and Religious Reform*, p. 11.

"They were indeed far too much bent on being popular to be innovators."
—Quick, *Educ. Reformers*, p. 506.

The curriculum of Jesuit colleges "has remained almost unchanged for four hundred years, disregarding some trifling concessions made to natural sciences."—President Eliot, *Atlantic Monthly*, October 1899.

"The shrewd disciples of Loyola adapt themselves to the times, and are full of compassion for human weakness."—Compayré, *Hist. of Ped.*, p. 140.

Since 1832 "in mathematics and natural sciences proper attention is to

be given to the recent progress made in those branches. In the lower classes new provisions are made for learning modern languages, both the vernacular and foreign, and for the study of history."
—Kiddle and Schem, *The Cyclopedia of Education*, article "Jesuits," p. 492.

"Another instance of uniform prescribed education may be found in the curriculum of Jesuit colleges". . . . But "the immense deepening and expanding of human knowledge in the nineteenth century and the increasing sense of the sanctity of the individual's gifts and will-power have made uniform prescriptions of study in secondary schools impossible and absurd."— President Eliot (in 1899).

"A uniform course of study for all schools of a particular grade, and a common standard for promotion and graduation, can be made most serviceable in a national scheme of education."— Dr. Russell, Columbia University, (in 1899), *German Higher Schools*, p. 409.

"The Ratio Studiorum is antiquated and difficult to reform. . . . We have little to hope for them in the improvement of edu-

"A republic is a field far more inviting than a monarchy for the agency of an organization so vast, so able, so secret, so *adap-*

cation at present."—Oscar Browning, *Encyclopedia Britannica*, article "Education."

"For the Jesuits, education is reduced to a superficial culture of the brilliant faculties of the intelligence."—Compayré, *l. c.*, p. 139.

"To write in Latin is the ideal which they propose to their pupils . . . . the first consequence of this is the proscription of the mother tongue."— Compayré, *H. of P.*, p. 144.

"The Jesuits were hostile to the mother tongue, and distrusting the influence of its association they studiously endeavored to supplant it."—Painter, *A Hist. of Ed.*, p. 120.

"Preoccupied before all else with purely formal

tive as that of the Jesuits."—Prof. N. Porter, (Yale College), *Educational Systems of the Puritans and Jesuits compared*, p. 79.

"Thoroughness in work was the one thing insisted on."—Quick, *l. c.*, p. 46.

"With such standards of scholarship the methods of instruction will naturally be rigorous and thorough."— Cf. Porter, *l. c.*, p. 55.

"Instruction in the vernacular language was incorporated with the course of instruction in 1703, and in 1756 the colleges in Germany were advised to devote as much attention to German as to Latin and Greek."—Kiddle and Schem, *The Cyclopedia of Education*, p. 493.

"In mathematics and the natural sciences, he

studies, the Jesuits leave real and concrete studies in entire neglect. History is almost wholly banished from their programme."— Compayré, *l, c.*, p. 144.

"The sciences and philosophy are involved in the same disdain as history."—*Ib.*, p. 145.

"The Jesuits maintain the abuse of the memory." *Ib.*, p. 140.

"What the Jesuits did in the matter of secondary instruction, with immense resources and for the pupils who paid them for their efforts, La Salle attempted . . . for pupils who did not pay."—Compayré, *l. c.*, p. 258.

"They sought to reach sons of princes, noblemen and others who constituted

[the Jesuit pupil] will be the master of what he professes to know. . . . In logic and grammar, in geography and history he will be drilled to such a control of what he learns, that it shall be a possession for life."—Porter, *l. c.*, p. 55.

"The Jesuits wished the whole boy, not his memory only, to be affected by the master."–Quick, *Educational Reformers*, p. 507.

"Their instruction was always given gratuitously."—Quick, *ib.*, p. 38.

The Jesuit schools "were gratuitous. The instruction was imparted freely, not only to pupils of the Romish faith, but to all who chose to attend upon it." — Porter, *l. c.*, p. 29.

"Finally they imparted their instruction gratuitously."—Ranke, *History of the Popes*, vol. I.

"Faithful to the traditions of the Catholic Church, the Society did

the influential classes."— Seeley, *History of Education*, p. 185.

"They administer only the aristocratic education of the ruling classes, whom they hope to retain under their own control." Compayré, *History of Pedagogy*, p. 143.

not estimate a man's worth simply according to his birth and outward circumstances. The constitutions expressly laid down that poverty and mean extraction were never to be any hindrance to a pupil's admission . . . . and Sacchini says: 'Do not let any favoring of nobility interfere with the care of meaner pupils, since the birth of all is equal in Adam, and the inheritance is Christ.'"— Quick, *l. c.*, p. 39.

These quotations may suffice to show how little the adversaries of the Jesuits agree in their estimations of most important points of the educational system of the Society. We need not examine all charges in detail; we can leave them to themselves, reminding the reader of a passage in the Gospel of St. Mark (14, 56): "Many bore false witness against him, and their evidences were not agreeing." If in no other point, at least in this one, the Jesuits resemble him whose name they bear, and whom they profess and endeavor to follow.

A few accusations, however, must be examined here on account of their serious character. The first is that the Jesuits did not care for the instruction of the people, because they thought "the ignorance of the people the best safeguard of faith;" that they "administered only the aristocratic education of the higher classes."¹ This is utterly false. That the Jesuits could not devote themselves extensively to elementary education has been accounted for in a previous chapter.² As to the other charge, in their higher schools there were always many poor pupils; it is frequently inculcated in the documents of the Society to treat the poor pupils with equal, if not with greater, care than the rich.³ Father Jouvancy exhorts the teacher "to exhibit a parent's tender care particularly towards needy pupils."⁴ Further, the Society had special boarding schools for poor scholars; *domus pauperum*, or *convictus pauperum*, were attached to nearly all larger colleges; in Germany and Austria at Würzburg, Dillingen, Augsburg, Munich, Prague, Olmütz, Brünn etc.⁵ The Jesuits not unfrequently begged money for poor scholars. Peter Canisius in one year supported two hundred poor boys. Moreover, they had special libraries to supply books for poor students and fed poor day scholars. In several places the Jesuits were at times severely censured "for favoring too much poor students and the sons of the lower classes," as was said in Graz in 1767. In 1762 they were ordered by the Bavarian government to admit in future fewer poor scholars.⁶ The judgment of Quick

¹ Compayré, *History of Pedagogy*, p. 143; similarly Seeley, *History of Education*, p. 185.
² Chapter III, pp. 104—106.
³ *Ratio Studiorum*, Reg. Prof. Sup. Fac., n. 20; Reg. com. mag. class. inf. 50. — *Monumenta Paedagogica*, p. 814 foll.
⁴ *Ratio Docendi*, ch. III, art. 1, n. 2.
⁵ Duhr, *Studienordnung*, pp. 46—53.
⁶ Documents in Duhr, *Jesuitenfabeln*, 2d edition, pp. 86—93.

echoes the real spirit of the Society on this point: "Faithful to the traditions of the Church, the Society did not estimate a man's worth simply according to his birth and outward circumstances. The constitutions expressly laid down that poverty and mean extraction were never to be any hindrance to a pupil's admission . . . and Sacchini says: 'Do not let any favoring of nobility interfere with the care of meaner pupils, since the birth of all is equal in Adam and the inheritance is Christ'."[1]

It is said that the Jesuits "labored for those pupils who could pay them for their efforts."[2] In the Constitutions of the Society it is laid down as a strict rule that "no one is to accept anything which might be considered as a compensation for any ministry," [education included].[3] How this principle was applied to the colleges can be best seen from the following regulations made by Father Nadal: "The Rector cannot receive anything either for any instruction, or degree, or matriculation; nothing as a remuneration for the teacher, nor any present from a scholar. In short, nothing can be received, not even as alms or on any other grounds. Should the Rector hear that any one else has accepted anything, be he a teacher or an official of the school, he must see that it is returned to the person who gave it; and he must severely punish the person who received it."[4]

[1] Quick, *Educational Reformers*, p. 39.
[2] Compayré, *Hist of Ped.*, p. 258.
[3] *Summary of the Constit.* 27, where allusion is made to the words of our Lord: "Freely you have received, freely give."
[4] *Monumenta Paedagogica*, p. 102.

In fact, this regulation caused the Society many serious difficulties. The rival faculties of other schools, who received payments from the pupils, saw in the gratuitousness of instruction in the Jesuit schools a great danger. By various machinations the Jesuits were forced in some cities to accept fees from the students.[1] It is well known that at present most Jesuit schools are compelled by sheer necessity to accept a tuition fee, because few of their colleges are endowed. But it was different in former centuries, when the liberality of princes, ecclesiastics and cities furnished all that was necessary for the maintenance of the colleges. Nearly all historians testify that the Jesuits imparted all instructions gratuitously; some even blame the Jesuits for thus using an unfair means of competing with other schools.

The accusation of estranging the children from their families is as ungrounded as the former charges.[2] It is also refuted by the fact that the Jesuits opened boarding schools unwillingly and only where it was absolutely necessary.[3] They everywhere preferred day schools, because they appreciated the importance which the home influence — provided it was good and religious — has on the training of the character. Aside

---

[1] Duhr, *Studienordnung*, p. 47.—Hallam, *L. of E.*, I, 256.

[2] Compayré, *Hist. of Ped.*, p. 146. "The ideal of the perfect scholar is to forget his parents." This is a calumny; and the example which M. Compayré adduces of a pupil of the Jesuits who showed an eccentric behavior towards his mother, and the words of the biographer, do not express the principles and practices of the Jesuit schools.

[3] Thus, for instance, of the 83 colleges which the Society had in Germany in 1710, only 12 admitted boarders. Du Lac, *Jésuites*, pp. 297—298, and 890.

from cases in which a boy has to go to a boarding school for want of a higher school near his home, especially in the country, it cannot be denied that other cases are rather numerous in which it is better for young people to receive their education away from home. In not a few families the father has no time to look after the education of his sons; mothers are frequently too indulgent to control self-willed lads. In such cases it is a blessing for a boy to be entrusted to a good boarding school in which not only the intellectual, but, above all, the moral and religious training receive due attention. Besides, much may be said of the advantages derived from the discipline and subordination insisted on in good boarding schools.[1]

Of all the charges and imputations heaped upon the Jesuit schools, the most formidable is that they seek only the interest of the Order, cripple the intellect of their pupils, and teach them a corrupt morality. I am almost ashamed to refute such charges; for any such attempt seems to be an insult not only to the Society, but to the Catholic Church herself, who has so often praised and recommended the educational labors of the Society. However, as such charges are made in historical and educational works used extensively in this country, I think it necessary to say a few words about them. Hallam says: "The Jesuits have the credit of first rendering public a scheme of false morals, which has been denominated from them and enhanced the obloquy that overwhelmed their order."[2] And von Raumer, in his History of Peda-

---

[1] See Mr. Whitton's discussion: *The Private School in American Life* (a reply to Mr. Edward's strictures). *Educat. Rev.*, May 1902.

[2] *Literature of Europe*, etc. (ed. 1842, New York), volume II, p. 121.

gogy, frightens the readers with a dreadful picture of the "dismal and perfidious colleges of the Jesuits, of these men of wickedness, with their dark, treacherous tendencies, so fatal to the souls of the young." Dr. Huber, the inveterate enemy of the Society, remarks on this charge: "Raumer condemns Jesuit education from the specifically 'confessional' [*i. e.* Protestant] point of view."[1] On the other hand, the accusations which Dr. Huber himself made against the Society, are not more justified, and they have been discredited by a leading Review in Germany: "The opinion of some 'Old-Catholic' scholars, that the education of the Jesuits is a sort of diabolical system, tending to enslave the conscience and suppress every free movement of the mind, can no longer be maintained."[2]

Mr. Painter's charges are among the worst and unfairest that have ever been hurled against Jesuit education; summing up his criticisms on the Jesuit system, he says, it is "based not upon a study of man, but on the interests of the order... the principle of authority, suppressing all freedom and independence of thought, prevailed from beginning to end. Religious pride and intolerance were fostered. While our baser feelings were highly stimulated, the nobler side of our nature was wholly neglected. Love of country, fidelity to friends, nobleness of character, enthusiasm for beautiful ideals were insidiously suppressed."[3] These

[1] *Der Jesuiten-Orden*, p. 377.
[2] *Jahresbericht für klassische Altertumswissenschaft*, Berlin, 1891, p. 45 (quoted by Pachtler, *l. c.*, vol. IV, p. VIII).
[2] *History of Education*, p. 172. — Similar opinions were expressed recently by Mr. Frank Hugh O'Donnell, in his book, *The Ruin of Education in Ireland*, London, 1902. He would advise the commission on Irish University Education

terrible charges are made, but not proved. We can only ask with astonishment: How can a critical scholar, a cultured gentleman, a truth-loving Christian act in such manner? Who does not think of the striking parallel instance in ancient history, when the great teacher of Athens, whose life work it was to elevate and ennoble the youths of his city, was arraigned before a court for corrupting youth? He was condemned and had to drink the cup of hemlock. How many modern writers on Jesuit education are faithful imitators of the unjust accusers of Socrates and the unjust judges of Athens? They cannot despatch the hated Jesuits out of the world, but they poison public opinion and the minds of non-Catholic teachers. But there is another question which we cannot suppress here: How is it possible that enlightened American educators put any faith in such monstrous imputations? And how can they trust books which contain such frightful misrepresentations and calumnies? Wise people should suspect such charges, because of their very enormity; and they

to "refuse every public endowment and public monopoly to the Order of St. Ignatius. Their individual virtues and scholarship do not diminish the formidable hostility of their brotherhood to independence, to progress, to liberty, to toleration and concord between citizens of different creeds. They are the pretorians of religious despotism.... Catholic ruin and Catholic ignorance have attended everywhere the Jesuit monopoly. Where the Jesuit plants, the crops are indifference, emasculation, and decay.... Their system is ruin to the Catholic religion. They belong to an age before modern times.... They can stimulate fanaticism. They cannot develop reason. They supplant, and call it assistance and direction. They suck the brain of the lay-people," etc. — Quoted in *The Month*, September 1902, pp. 253–254.

should naturally think that, when some charges are so ridiculous, others may turn out equally groundless.

Those who are so positive in asserting that the aim of Jesuit education was "the interest of the Order," might well be advised to ponder over a page or two of the work of a scholar of the first rank,—we mean Professor Paulsen who at present is equalled by few as a writer on pedagogy, and who has studied the Jesuit system more carefully than any of those writers who have the hardihood to raise such charges. In spite of his opposition to the fundamental principles of the Society, this writer severely censures those who represent the Society as a body of egoists and ambitious schemers. "It would be a gross self-deception," he writes, "to imagine that the members of the Society were attracted to, or kept in the Order by any selfish motives or personal gratifications. He who should have sought a life of ease and pleasure in this Order, would soon have been disappointed. What was put before them on entering, was first a humble novitiate, then a prolonged course of rigorous studies, finally, the toilsome work of the classroom, or the self-sacrificing labors of preaching or giving missions. Suppose the powerful and influential position of the Order whetted the ambition of some individual; but he would soon have found out that, for every one without exception, not commanding but life-long obedience was the summary of the Jesuit's career. He had to be ready to accept any position without murmur, and give it up the moment the Superior should command. This law of absolute obedience was enforced in the case of men of such merit and consideration as Canisius, the first German Provincial... Besides, the Order would never have been persecuted and prohibited, had it served the ease of its members; associations for such purposes have never been considered dangerous; those societies only are dangerous that try to realize ideas." The author then adds: "Why do I insist so much on this? Because it disgusts me to hear again and again that men who, with the sacrifice of all personal interests, live for an idea, are accused of selfishness and ambition, and that by dull Philistines, who throughout their lives were seeking their own comfort and pleasure, or by ambitious place-hunters who think of nothing else but how to please those in power and to flatter public opinion."[1] These words sound severe; but have the men, whom they are meant for, not provoked this severity by unjust and venomous accusations?

Not a few writers call the Jesuit schools dangerous to the public welfare; one styles the whole Order "international and anti-national."[2] By the way, the same slander has been hurled against the Catholic Church; moreover, we know that long ago a great Teacher arose and founded a society. A certain class of learned men wanted to get rid of him, but did not dare to come forth with the real motive. Then they denounced the teacher as "anti-national": "He forbids to give tribute to Caesar; he makes himself king and opposes Caesar." And the judge was told that "if he acquitted that man, he was not Caesar's friend." The disciples of this Teacher were told that they would ever share the fate of their Master, and more than once in history the same futile accusations were

[1] *Geschichte des gelehrten Unterrichts*, vol. I, pp. 410–411.
[2] Ziegler, *Geschichte der Pädagogik*, p. 119.

made against those who professed to follow the great Master.

Not a shadow of proof has ever been advanced that the Jesuits in their principles and teaching are unpatriotic, but more than one testimony has been given, proving that they possess true patriotism and instil it into the hearts of their pupils, and that Jesuit students yield to none in ardent and self-sacrificing love of country. Of course, there is no lack of assertions to the contrary. But recently Sir Henry Howorth stated that the English Jesuits shared the anti-English views of their brethren on the continent, and he entreated English parents to keep their children away from Jesuit schools where they imbibed hatred against their own country.[1] A Roman Catholic layman in England wrote to the London *Times*, December 4, 1901, with reference to this attack on the Jesuits: "The moral

[1] The case of Sir Henry Howorth furnishes a good illustration of the "trustworthiness" of the attacks against the Jesuits. This gentleman asserted (*Tablet*, Nov. 23, 1901), that he had often read, in the *Civiltà Cattolica* and in two German Jesuit publications, "abominable slanders of England and its people." Sir Henry was challenged repeatedly to produce *one* passage from the two German publications containing a slander of England. One of these periodicals, the *Stimmen aus Maria-Laach*, has very often praised England and its liberal institutions; and the other (the *Theologische Zeitschrift* of Innsbruck) is a purely scientific paper which never touches political questions. After many evasions Sir Henry at last wrote (*Tablet*, March 15, 1902), that he had read the "abominable slanders" in the Berlin *Germania*, "which, as he was informed, was largely owned and written by the Jesuits." But the Jesuits have nothing to do with the *Germania*. And yet, for three months Sir Henry had maintained that he had read with his own eyes the slanders in the two mentioned Jesuit publications!

and religious teaching of the Jesuits is the same in England as on the Continent, but it does not follow that their political opinions or their estimate of public affairs in this country are identical. The English Jesuit is a loyal subject of his Majesty, and all his sympathies are with his own country. Sir Henry Howorth informs English fathers and mothers that it is nearly time they considered how much longer they are going to permit their fresh and ingenuous children to imbibe hatred and contempt for their country at Jesuit establishments. Here I can speak from personal experience of the hatred and contempt for their country which my three sons imbibed at the Jesuit College of Beaumont, near Windsor, and how it has influenced their after lives. The principles which the Jesuits inculcated upon them may be summed up in five words — 'Fear God ; honor thy king.' The result in after life was that they all three volunteered to fight for England and her Sovereign in her hour of need. One of them has fallen on the battlefield; the other two have survived to serve their country, and our name is known to-day to most loyalists in South Africa." In fact, more than one hundred students from the Jesuit College of Stonyhurst fought in the South African war; three have received the Victorian Cross, and many of them have lost their lives; and more than one hundred have gone from the College of Beaumont.[1] Another utterance, and that from a non-Catholic Review, deserves to be quoted in this connection. In the last number of the *Westminster Review*, Mr. Reade, speaking of the appointment of Dr. Parkin to draw up the scheme for the Rhodes Scholarships,

---

[1] *The Messenger*, New York, 1902, July, p. 127.

adds : "It is just possible that, if he will pay any attention to the teachings of history, he may find food for meditation in the system on which the *Propaganda Fide* and the English College at St. Omers [Jesuit College] were recruited during their best years. The latter school (now Stonyhurst) kept the English Catholics loyal English Gentlemen during the worst times of the Penal Laws. Many of them accompanied James II. into his exile at St. Germain, but it would be hard to find one who held a commission, as the Irish and Scotch exiles did, in the French service, when France was at war with his own country. We had no Regiment de *Howard* firing on the English Guards at Fontenoy, as the Regiment de *Dillon* did, and Wellington's chief secret agent in Spain was a Stonyhurst boy."[1]

The whole history of the Society refutes the imputation of want of patriotism. Is it not significant that the two shrewdest monarchs of the eighteenth century, Frederick the Great of Prussia, and Catharine II. of Russia, protected the Jesuits? Would they have done so if there had existed even the slightest doubt about their patriotism? And, as to France, Dr. Huber admits that "the greatest generals, as Condé, Bouillon, Rohan, Luxembourg, Montmorency, Villars, and Broglie, have come from the schools of Jesuits."[2] The same may be said of many great men in Austria, Bavaria, and other countries where the Jesuits conducted schools. Also in the nineteenth century their patriotism has been publicly acknowledged. We quote the words addressed to the Jesuits

[1] *Westminster Review*, October 1902, p. 325.
[2] *Der Jesuiten-Orden*, p. 384.

by King Leopold I. of Belgium. Visiting their college at Namur he praised them especially for giving the youth under their charge a truly national education. "I am much pleased," he said to the Fathers, "to be among you. I know that you give the students a wise direction. Youth needs sound principles. There is nothing more important in our days, when men endeavor to stir up the passions. It is of the greatest moment strenuously to fight against the spirit of lawlessness which now threatens all order and the very existence of the states. What pleases me most in your work is that *you impart to the young a truly national education.* If you continue to educate them in this spirit, they will become the support and the mainstay of the country."[1]

When in 1846 the French Minister Thiers publicly attacked the education of the Jesuits on similar grounds, six hundred former pupils of the Jesuits, who then held high positions in the administration, in literary and industrial circles, came forth with the solemn declaration: "Our Jesuit professors taught us, that God and His religion have to enlighten man's intellect and guide his conscience; that all men are equal before God and before the law which is an expression of God's will; that the public powers are for the nations, not the nations for the public powers; that every one has the sacred duty to make all sacrifices, even that of property and life, for the welfare of the country; that treason and tyranny alike are sins against God and crimes against society. Would that all France knew that this calumniated education is solid and truly Catholic, and that we, by learning to

[1] *Ami de l'ordre de Namur*, 1843, July 31.

unite our Catholic faith with patriotism, have become better citizens, and more genuine friends of our liberties."[1] In 1879, Ferry introduced new laws to suppress the Jesuit schools. In the *Revue des Deux Mondes* (1880), Albert Duruy asked Ferry whether the Jesuit pupils had less bravely fought against the Germans in the war of 1870, or whether more Jesuit pupils had taken part in the Commune; whether especially the ninety pupils of the one Jesuit school in *Rue des Postes*, Paris, who had fallen in the battles of that war, had been bad citizens, devoid of patriotism?[2]

The same question may be asked in every country where Jesuits are engaged in educating youth: Have Jesuit pupils ever shown less patriotism, less heroism, less self-sacrifice for their country than pupils of secular institutions? Was Charles Carroll of Carrollton less patriotic than the men who were educated at Harvard and Yale? Was Bishop John Carroll lacking in patriotism? And yet, John Carroll had been a Jesuit himself, and both had been educated in Jesuit Colleges in Europe. And we may safely challenge any one to prove that the American Jesuits and their pupils are less patriotic, less attached to the interests of their country, and less solicitous for its fair name among the nations than the teachers and pupils of other institutions. And we should like to know the facts on which the American writer has based the

[1] Similar protests of Jesuit pupils were published in 1879, when Ferry had cast suspicion on the patriotism of the Jesuits. See De Badts de Cugnac, *Le patriotisme des Jésuites*.

[2] Of the pupils of St. Clement (Metz) 31 died on the battlefield, of the College of Sainte-Geneviève 78; of the College of Vaunes 20, etc.

terrible indictment, that in Jesuit schools "love of country was insidiously suppressed."[1] However, if such a calumny must deeply wound the hearts of all American Jesuits, they will know, too, that other Americans, and such whose words count a thousand times more than the uncritical assertions of certain writers, have thought and spoken differently on the influence of Jesuit education. On February 22, 1889, at the centennial celebration of Georgetown College, Mr. Cleveland, President of the United States, said among other things: "Georgetown College should be proud of the impress she has made upon the citizenship of our country. On her roll of graduates are found the names of many who have performed public duty better for her teaching, while her Alumni have swollen the ranks of those who, in private stations, have done their duty as American citizens intelligently and well. I cannot express my friendship for your college better than to wish for her in the future, as she has had in the past, an army of Alumni, learned, patriotic, and useful, cherishing the good of their country as an object of loftiest effort, and deeming their contributions to good citizenship a supremely worthy use of the education they have acquired within these walls."[2]

If the old saying holds: "*Qualis rex, talis grex,*" and *vice versa,* then we must conclude that the teachers themselves cannot be devoid of patriotism. Fortunately, we are not confined to this *a priori* argument. Numerous instances are on record that Jesuits, especially at the time of war, sacrificed themselves in the

[1] Painter, *History of Education*, p. 172.
[2] *History of Georgetown College*, p. 422.

service of the sick and wounded and on the battlefields. Not to say a word of the many cases recorded of former centuries, we mention one of more recent date. In the Franco-German war of 1870-71, the Maltese Society of Rhineland and Westphalia sent, besides the 1567 Sisters, 342 male religious to the service of the sick and wounded. Among these 342 were 159 Jesuits. Of the 81 volunteer army chaplains sent by the same organization, 33 were Jesuits.[1] No less than 80 Jesuits received decorations, and two of them were honored with the "Iron Cross," the highest distinction for heroic conduct on the battlefield. The patriotism of the French Jesuits is not less conspicuous. In every war which was waged by France, a number of Jesuits accompanied the army as chaplains. In 1870-71 several were wounded on the battlefield, and one died at Laon.

The attitude of the Society towards national and political questions has been clearly stated by Father Beckx, General of the Society: "The public and the press busy themselves much about the Society's attitude towards the various forms of government. . . . Now the Society, as a religious Order, has nothing to do with any political party. In all countries and under all forms of government, she confines herself to the exercise of her ministry, having in view only her end — the greater glory of God and the salvation of souls, — an end superior to the interests of human politics. Always and everywhere the religious of the Society fulfils loyally the duties of a good citizen and a faithful subject of the power which rules his country. Always and everywhere she tells all by her instructions

[1] Braunsberger, *l. c.*, p. 37.

and her conduct: 'Render to Caesar the things that are Caesar's, and to God the things that are God's'."[1]

In recent years the attacks on the educational system of the Jesuits chiefly insist on the fact that it is "antiquated and unable to cope with modern conditions." We quoted the words[2] of Mr. Browning, that "little is to be hoped for the Jesuits in the improvement of education at present, whatever may have been their services in the past." A similar verdict is passed by Buckle. "The Jesuits, for at least fifty years after their institution, rendered immense service to civilization, partly by organizing a system of education far superior to any yet seen in Europe. In no university could there be found a scheme of instruction so comprehensive as theirs, and certainly nowhere was there displayed such skill in the management of youth, or such insight into the general operations of the human mind... The Society was, during a considerable period, the steady friend of science, as well as of literature, and allowed its members a freedom and a boldness of speculation which had never been permitted by any monastic order. As, however, civilization advanced, the Jesuits began to lose ground, and this not so much from their own decay as from a change in the spirit of those who surrounded them. An institution admirably adapted to an early form of society was ill suited to the same society in its mature state."[3] We think this charge has been sufficiently refuted by what was said in the preceding chapter.

[1] *L'Univers*, Paris, Jan. 20, 1879. See De Badts de Cugnac, *L'expulsion des Jésuites*, p. 51.

[2] Page 16.

[3] *History of Civilization in England*, vol. I, chapter XVI.

How is this hostility to the Jesuits to be explained? It is not so difficult to find some reasons which account for the aversion of Protestants to this Order. Time and again they have been told that Ignatius of Loyola founded this Society in order to crush Protestantism. Although it has been proved that such a view of the Society is entirely contradicted by the Constitutions and the history of the Order,[1] most non-Catholics still cling to their old prejudices and traditional views of the Jesuits. Even now many see in the Society the "avowed and most successful foe of Protestantism, and the embodiment of all they detest."[2] The Jesuits have been represented to them as notoriously dishonest and unscrupulous men, who teach and practise the most pernicious principles; they have been denounced as plotters against the lives of Protestant rulers, Queen Elizabeth, James I., William of Orange, Gustavus Adolphus. The mention of the Gunpowder plot, and the Titus-Oates conspiracy,[3] conjures up the most horrible visions of those black demons who dare to call themselves companions of Jesus. Then it has been said that the Jesuits were the cause of the Thirty Year's War, of the French Revolution, of the Franco-German War of 1870, of the Dreyfus affair.[4] All such and similar silly slanders

[1] See above chapter III, pp. 77—78.
[2] Canon Littledale in the *Encyclopedia Britannica*, art. "Jesuits".
[3] "That lie about the Titus-Oates Conspiracy," as the Protestant historian Gardiner says (*Hist. of England*, vol. II, pp. 483 and 615). An apostate priest, Chinicquy, has charged the Jesuits even with the assassination of President Lincoln!
[4] Quite recently the suspicion was expressed in French anti-clerical papers that the Jesuits were the cause of the coal strikes. Any one who wishes to see to what extreme of

have gradually formed that popular idea according to which the Jesuit is the embodiment of craft, deceit, ambition, and all sorts of wickedness. "It began to be rumored up and down," complains Bunyan, "that I was a witch, a Jesuit, a highwayman, and the like." Last year it was very correctly stated by Mr. Andrew Lang, the celebrated Scotch scholar, that this popular idea and the Protestant dislike of the Jesuits is not based on historical facts, but largely on works of fiction. There is a certain picturesqueness about the mythic Jesuit which makes him highly important in works of fiction. Accordingly, a number of writers have introduced him with great effect, as Charles Kingsley, Mrs. Humphrey Ward, and even Thackeray. Mr. Lang himself rises above that vulgar conception of the Jesuits, and he freely confesses: "The Jesuits are clever, educated men; on the whole I understand their unpopularity, but with all their faults I love them still."[1] And the words of another Protestant deserve to be meditated on by all fair-minded Protestants: "Why should a devoted Christian find a difficulty in seeing good in the Jesuits, a body of men whose devotion to their idea of Christian duty has never been surpassed?"[2]

But some Protestants will say: The Jesuits have always been the most strenuous and most successful supporters of the Catholic Church; hence they weaken the Protestant cause. — To men who argue thus apply

absurdity the calumniators of the Society have gone, may read Janssen, vol. VII, pp. 530—584. — *Dublin Review*, vol. XLI, pp. 60—86 ("Curiosities of the Anti-Jesuit Crusade"); vol. L, pp. 329—340.

[1] *The Pilot*, Oct. 12, 1901.
[2] Quick, *Educ. Ref.*, p. 54.

the words of the great Master; "You know how to discern the face of the sky, and can you not know the signs of the times?"[1] Indeed, the signs of the time point to dangers quite different from those dreaded from "Jesuitism". The dangers of our age arise from infidelity, immorality, and anarchy. What has become of the belief in the fundamental truth of Christianity, in the Divinity of Christ? That there are still millions of real Christians in the world, is chiefly due to the Catholic Church, to what they call the stubborn "conservatism" of the Romish Church. And the Jesuits make it the centre of their educational work and of all their labors, to strengthen the faith in the Divinity of Christ, and to propagate the Kingdom of God. They teach the lofty morality, the generous self-denial, which was preached to the world by the words and example of Jesus. They inculcate assiduously the most important civic virtue, obedience to all lawful authority. Therefore, all those who still believe in the Divinity of Christ, who zealously labor for the moral betterment of their fellow-men, who have the true interest of their country at heart — all those men should heartily welcome the Jesuits as helpful allies in their noble enterprise. There is, in our days, surely no reason for antipathy against the Society of Jesus.

However, considering the force of long cherished prejudices, we understand the dislike and the dread with which less enlightened Protestants view Jesuit schools. Their feelings spring from ignorance, and they are to be pitied rather than blamed. And every Jesuit will pray with Jesus: "Father forgive them, for they know

[1] *Matth.* 16, 3.

not what they do." But what should we say of men who lay claim to critical scholarship, if they, instead of examining conscientiously the documents and the history of the Order, unscrupulously copy the slanders of virulent partisan writers, as is done by so many modern historians and educationists? Some seem studiously to neglect to acquire that information which is necessary and easily available, in order to understand this system. Of others one has reason to suspect that they write against their better knowledge, from fanatical hatred, not so much of the Society as of the Catholic Church. But then let them at least be honest; let them say that they are fighting against the "Anti-Christ in Rome," against the "Scarlet Woman," as their leaders were pleased to express themselves; let them confess that it is the *odium Papae*, the old "no-Popery" and "Know-nothing" feeling which inspires them. Well has a non-Catholic periodical recently observed: "We end inevitably by recognizing that all the reproaches with which we may feel entitled to load the Jesuits, in the name of reason, of philosophy, etc., etc., fall equally upon all religious orders, and upon the Church herself, of which they have ever been the most brilliant ornament. Why then address these reproaches to the Jesuits only?"[1]

History has proved the correctness of these statements. In the eighteenth century the Jesuit colleges were suppressed. Not long after the monasteries of other orders were "secularized". In 1872 the Jesuits were expelled from Germany; two or three years after, the other religious orders had to leave the fatherland,

[1] *The Open Court*, Chicago, Jan. 1902, p. 28.

and then the secular priests were persecuted, and bishops imprisoned. Since 1879 there was a continued agitation in France against the Jesuits and their schools. This campaign has now issued in a general war against all teaching congregations, in fact against all religious orders.

But this is not all; of late radical papers begin to proclaim the real intentions of the persecutors of the religious orders. One paper wrote recently: "Now we must not forget the *Curés* (Parish priests); after the monks let us attend to them." Hostility to the Church, nay, to all religion, is at the bottom of the unjust and tyrannous proceedings against the Jesuits and other religious orders in France. For, whilst to the ordinary reader of newspapers the recent laws "appear to be a mere measure of self-defense forced upon the Republican Government by the reputed political intrigues of the Clerical party in France, it is in reality a systematic attempt to discredit religion, and to remove its checking influence upon the atheistic movement of the controlling party."[1] That influence was chiefly felt to come from the religious orders, particularly from the teaching congregations. Hence they must go. The hypocritical assertion : "We combat Jesuitism, not the Church, not religion," is a mere *ruse de guerre*, a stratagem, used to deceive more fair-minded Protestants, and short-sighted or lukewarm Catholics. That this is no exaggerated party statement, is evident from the discussions in the French Senate during the last three years. It is also frankly

[1] *American Ecclesiastical Review*, Sept. 1902, p. 824. — See especially the *Dublin Review*, October 1902: "The Power behind the French Government," where it is clearly set forth who the real instigators of this new persecution are.

admitted by the more candid advocates of the new persecution, and by not a few far-seeing Protestants.

Here, however, a serious objection is raised: Have not Catholics, even high dignitaries of the Church, opposed the Jesuits? How is this? "Protestants are not ignorant that the Society of Jesus has been the object of suspicion and attack from influential men in the Church of Rome itself; that no worse things have been said of it by Protestants than have been said by Romanists themselves; that Romish ecclesiastics have in all generations of its history, directed against it their open attacks and their secret machinations; that Romish teachers have dreaded it as a rival and intriguer."[1] However, such Protestants should not fail to examine who these "Romanists" are, and especially from what motives they act when attacking the Jesuits. We do not wish to say more on this subject, but quote only the words of a distinguished French writer, M. Lenormant, who said: "Outside the Catholic Church opinions regarding the Jesuits, as regarding other religious orders, are free, but within the Catholic Church the war against the Jesuits is the most monstrous inconsistency."[2]

The opposition of Catholic schools to the Society is frequently looked upon by non-Catholics as the surest proof of the dangerous character of Jesuit education. They point to the hostility of the *Alma Mater* of the Society, the once famous University of Paris, to the Jesuits. But a German Protestant, a pro-

[1] Professor Porter of Yale, *Educational Systems of the Puritans and Jesuits compared*, p. 90.
[2] "*Endedans du catholicisme, la guerre aux Jésuites est la plus monstrueuse des inconséquences.*" De Badts de Cugnac, *L'expulsion des Jésuites*, p. 6.

fessor in the University of Strasburg, not in the least partial to the Jesuits, writes on this subject: "This hostility evidently arose from jealousy, as the youths of Paris flocked to the schools of these dangerous and dexterous rivals, while the lecture rooms of the University were empty."[1] The same opinion is held by M. Jourdain, the historian of the University of Paris. He describes the scientific stagnation of the University in the seventeenth century, and the frightful licentiousness of the students, in consequence of which parents did not dare to send their sons to this school, but were anxious to have them educated by the Jesuits. The University combated this competition not so much by raising the intellectual and moral standing of the University, as by acts of Parliament, expelling the Jesuits or closing their colleges. The colleges of the University were on the point of being deserted, and this time the danger was all the more grievous, as a part of the Professors could attribute to themselves the decadence.[2] Still the members of the University never ceased from accusing the Jesuits of being corrupters of youth and disturbers of the public peace. It is admitted also that the teaching in the University was most defective. But they reproached the Jesuits for inefficiency and faulty methods. The University, although tainted with Jansenism, charged the Jesuits with spreading doctrines prejudicial to the Catholic faith, with "rendering faith a captive to vain human reason and philosophy." The historian here justly exclaims: "How often, in later days, has the Society

---

[1] Ziegler, *Geschichte der Pädagogik*, 1895, p. 121.
[2] Jourdain, *Histoire de l'Université de Paris au XVII. et au XVIII. siècle.* Paris 1888, vol. I, pp. 1—59.

reversely been accused of being the implacable foe of philosophy and reason!"[1]

The hostility of the Paris University was, therefore, merely the outcome of jealousy. At all times monopolies were jealous. Richelieu had perceived that clearly. Frequently urged to expel the Jesuits from Paris, he did not yield; on the contrary, towards the end of his life he handed over to the Jesuits the *Collège de Marmoutiers*. "The Universities," he said, "complain as if a wrong were done them, that the instruction of youth is not left to them exclusively. But as human frailty requires a counter-balance to everything, it is more reasonable that the Universities and the Jesuits teach as rivals, in order that emulation may stimulate their efforts, and that learning being deposited in the hands of several guardians, may be found with one, if the others should have lost it."[2] In another passage Jourdain does not hesitate to state that the competition of the Jesuits soon turned into a blessing for the University itself, as it was forced to exercise a more active supervision over masters and students, which was beneficial both to discipline and instruction.[3]

In Germany also and in other countries the Jesuits had to encounter the opposition of the old universities. The reason has been given by Professor Paulsen: "The old corporations at Ingolstadt, Vienna, Prague, Freiburg, Cologne, resisted with might and main, but it was all in vain; the Jesuits were victorious everywhere. The old corporations who were in possession

[1] *Ibid.*, p. 282.
[2] *Ibid.*, p. 272.
[3] *Ibid.*, vol. II, p. 299.

of the universities have often raised the charge of "imperiousness" of "desire of ruling" against the Jesuits, and many historians of these institutions have passionately repeated this charge, certainly not without good cause. But it must be added that it was not the desire of ruling that springs from arrogance and rests on external force or empty titles, but the desire that arises from real power which is eager to work, because it can work and must work."[1]

Another reason for the cold treatment of the Society by Catholics must be sought in unfair generalizations of individual cases. The Jesuits had always the privilege — or the misfortune — of being the subject of the constant pre-occupation of the public mind. They are watched closely, and they are, too often, watched with a magnifying glass. But if faults are discovered in an individual, is it fair to censure the whole body? Well has an English writer said: "The most splendid and perfect institution, if it grow, and occupy a large space, if many join it, will have among its members imprudent and therefore dangerous men — men who offer so fair a pretext to the malevolent for attacking it, that the combined learning and prudence of many years will hardly make good the damage done. The mass of men do not make fine distinctions; to distinguish with them, means casuistry, and casuistry they consider to be next door to systematized imposture. Point out some telling scandals against some member of a large organized body; be they only three or four, or true or false, repeat them often enough — and the public will pass the verdict of

[1] Paulsen, *l. c.*, p. 281 (vol. I, p. 407).

guilty upon the whole, and condemn both the system and him who sins against it."[1]

Sometimes, indeed, it may be that individual Jesuits have, by their unfaithfulness to the principles of their order, deserved the ill-feeling with which they have been regarded. But in a large majority of cases, it is due either to prejudice or ignorance on the part of their adversaries, or else to an imperfect grasp of the Jesuit system, especially to the false impression that the Jesuits exercise an influence which interferes with the work of others and that they are a rival power in the government of the Church.[2]

The utter falsity of the impression referred to has been proved more than once. In 1880 all the French Bishops, with two or three exceptions, addressed letters of protest to the President of the Republic against the decree of expulsion of the Jesuits. These letters form a splendid testimony, not only to the educational success of the Jesuits, but also to their loyalty to the ecclesiastical authorities.[3] The Cardinal Archbishop of Paris uttered these striking words about the Jesuits, so many of whom labored in his diocese: "Among the religious institutes, there is one which has been more before the world than the others; which has done splendid service in education, which has shed lustre on literature, which has formed *savants* of the first rank in every branch of science... Marked

---

[1] R. B. Vaughan, *Life of St. Thomas*, vol. I, p. 629.

[2] See Father Clarke, S. J., in the *Nineteenth Century*, August 1896.

[3] See *Dublin Review*, 1880, July, pp. 155—183. — Again in October 1902, of 79 French Bishops 72 (in a joint petition to the Senate) declared their solidarity with the religious orders.

out by its importance and success as an object of the hatred of the enemies of religion, the Society of Jesus has always confounded calumny by the splendor of its virtues, its intellectual power and its work. . . . To zeal, these generous priests have always united prudence. In the midst of the dissensions which trouble the country, just as the whole of the clergy have kept themselves rigorously within the limits of their spiritual ministry, the Society of Jesus has been scrupulously exact in avoiding all interfering with politics. Those who deny this, make assertions without proof. A Bishop like myself who has under his jurisdiction the chief Jesuit establishments in France is in a position to know the truth in a matter like this."

Cardinal Bonnechose testified as follows: "The Jesuits devote themselves to the laborious and often thankless task of education. They open colleges; experience justifies their efforts; families entrust their children to them with the utmost confidence; year by year, public opinion and the government itself, testify to their success; year by year, they send forth into every career young men who have been taught to respect authority, who are penetrated with the idea of duty; who are fitted to become brave soldiers, conscientious functionaries, and honorable and useful citizens, and who are, every one, devoted to their country and ready to die for France." — The Archbishop of Cambrai, Cardinal Regnier, spoke in the same strain: "Here I must make particular mention of the Jesuit Fathers, who are to be treated with special severity. On my conscience and in the name of truth, President of the French Republic, I bear witness that these religious men, who have so long been abused, spit upon, and calumniated by the anti-Christian press with a malice which no authority has ever attempted to restrain — who are devoted day by day to the hatred and violence of the mob, as though they were an association of malefactors — that these religious are esteemed and venerated in the highest degree by the clergy and by every class of the faithful, and that they are in every way most worthy of it. Their conduct is exemplary; their teaching can only be blamed by ignorance and bad faith. Many of them belong to the most distinguished families of the country. The house of superior education which they carry on with such brilliant success at Lille, was entrusted to them — I may almost say, forced on them — by fathers of families who had themselves been brought up by them, and who were determined to provide for their children an education which their own experience taught them to value. I fulfil a duty of conscience and of honor in addressing to you these simple and respectful observations."

The testimony of the Archbishop of Lyons will be of special interest. Cardinal Caverot writes: "It is the privilege of the children of St. Ignatius to be in the front of every battle. I know how hatred, and still more how ignorance and prejudice, have accumulated calumnies against the Society. But I owe it to the truth to declare here, that in the course of a ministry of well-nigh fifty years — twenty as priest, thirty as bishop — I have been able to satisfy myself, and I know that these worthy and zealous servants of God have well deserved the distinction given to the Society by the Church, when she proclaimed it, in the

Council of Trent, a 'Pious Institute, approved by the Holy See.' I admire these men in their work of teaching, and in the labors of their apostleship. Nowhere have I met with priests more obedient to ecclesiastical authority, more careful of the laws of the country, more aloof from political conflict; and I affirm without fear of contradiction, that if these decrees which strike at them have not made any charge whatever against their life and teaching, it is because not a charge could be made which would survive an hour's discussion."

There in no room for further extracts from these letters. The *Dublin Review* remarks that these manifestoes of the French hierarchy are precious documents for the religious orders; "but the Jesuits, in particular, will be able, from these utterances, to collect a body of episcopal testimony to their ability, devotedness, and deference towards the Bishops such as perhaps they have never before received from a great National Church during the whole course of their existence."[1]

In modern times it has sometimes been said that religious orders, in general, were admirably equipped for former ages, but time has progressed so fast that the orders were left behind and are now "out of date." One Philip Limerick, who, as he affirms, was at one time himself in a monastery, states this view plainly in the *Contemporary Review* (April 1897). This writer admits that the Monks were the benefactors of mankind, by teaching the arts of civilization to the rude tribes of the North, and that the monastic institutions were the homes, for a long time even the only ones, of learning. But, he says, "*omnia tempus habent*, and

[1] *L. c.*, p. 175.

monks are now rarely met with, and of the later orders, the Regular Clerks, only one has left a deep impression on the Latin Church and obtained a place in history — the Society of Jesus. This Society owes its still vigorous life to its wider scope and more efficient administration." Although this writer assigns an exceptional position to the Society, others include also this Order in the general doom. "We can do without the Jesuits," was a saying of Dr. Döllinger, and his opinion is shared by some so-called Liberal Catholics.

That the present Pope Leo XIII. has other sentiments about religious orders in general is evident from his numerous letters. In his letter to the Archbishop of Paris, December 23, 1900, he enumerates all the benefits religion and society receive from their hands. He says that "the religious are the necessary auxiliaries of the bishops and the secular clergy." "In the past their doctors shed renown on the universities by the depth and breadth of their learning, and their houses became the refuge of divine and human knowledge, and in the shipwreck of civilization saved from certain destruction the masterpieces of ancient wisdom. *Nor is their activity, their zeal, their love of their fellow-men, diminished in our own day. Some, devoted to teaching, instruct the young in secular knowledge and the principles of religious virtue and duty*, on which public peace and the welfare of states absolutely depend. Others are seen settling amongst savage tribes in order to civilize them. Nor is it an uncommon thing for them to make *important contributions to science* by the help they give to the researches which are being made in such different domains as the study of the differences of race and tongue, of history, the nature and products of the soil, and other questions.[1] Of course we are not unaware that there are people who go about declaring that the religious congregations encroach upon the jurisdiction of the Bishops and interfere with the rights of the secular clergy. This assertion cannot be sustained if one cares to consult the wise laws published on this point by the Church, and which we have recently re-enacted."[2]

On more than one occasion Leo XIII. gave expression to the high esteem in which he holds the educational work of the Jesuits, from whom he himself had received his early training. In the year 1886 he solemnly confirmed once more the Institute of the Society and its ecclesiastical privileges, exhorting the sons of Ignatius courageously to continue their work in the midst of all persecutions.[3]

Before closing this chapter we may mention one explanation for the widespread animosity against the Society at which some may be inclined to smile. It is recorded that the founder of the Society, St. Ignatius of Loyola, used to beg of God continually that his sons might always be the object of the world's hatred and enmity. He knew from the words of Our Divine Master: "If the world hate you, know that it hated me before you," and from the history of the Church that this persecution for the sake of Jesus has always

---

[1] On the services rendered by Catholic missionaries, mostly religious, to the knowledge of languages, especially to *Comparative Philology*, see Max Müller's *Lectures on the Science of Language*, vol. I, and Father Dahlmann: *Die Sprachkunde und die Missionen*, (Herder, 1891).

[2] Translation from *The Messenger*, New York, February 1901.

[3] Pachtler, vol. IV, p. 581.

been an essential condition for every victory won for the sacred cause of Christianity. No doubt, this prayer of St. Ignatius has been heard. Whether it be the Courtiers of Queen Elizabeth, or the Reformers in Germany, the infidel Philosophers of the eighteenth century, or the Atheists of our own days, the Communists of Paris, or the Revolutionary party in Italy, the Bonzes in Japan, or the fanatical followers of Mahomet, all who hated the name of Catholic concentrated their deadliest hatred on the unfortunate Jesuits. And what was more painful to them, even within the pale of the Catholic Church, they have sometimes met with misunderstanding and opposition. The Jansenists in France were their bitter enemies. The Liberal Catholics invariably stood aloof from them. At times even Bishops and Archbishops treated them coldly. Still, these persecutions were not without some good results. They kept the sons of Ignatius ever on the alert; and for this reason, the prayer of St. Ignatius manifests a wonderful insight into human affairs. Constant attacks prevent a body of men from stagnation and security.

> "And you all know security
> Is mortal's chiefest enemy." [1]

[1] *Macbeth* 3, 5.

PART SECOND.

The Principles of the Ratio Studiorum. — Its Theory and Practice Viewed in the Light of Modern Educational Problems.

CHAPTER IX.
Adaptability of the Ratio Studiorum. — Prudent Conservatism.

In the "Introductory Chapter" we quoted this remark of a biographer of St. Ignatius: "The Ratio Studiorum is a plan of studies which admits of every legitimate progress and perfection, and what Ignatius said of the Society in general may be applied to its system of studies in particular, namely that it ought to suit itself to the times and comply with them, and not make the times suit themselves to it."[1] We assert, then, that this is the first principle of the Jesuit system: that it should adapt itself to the different times and countries. We do not treat here of single colleges; it is possible that some have not adapted themselves sufficiently. The question to be discussed here is a general one: namely about the *system* as such.

That the Jesuit system has not suited itself to the times is the criticism of some. Others go even further, maintaining that it cannot be suited to the times, or only with great difficulty, as it is altogether "anti-

[1] Genelli, *Life of St. Ignatius*, part II, ch. VII.

quated." Here we may be allowed to ask whether men who make such assertions are sufficiently acquainted with Jesuit education. Some of them seem to have seen Jesuit colleges only from the outside; but an educational system cannot be fairly judged unless one has watched its practical working. It is very easy to make a caricature of a system which one does not know.

But let us, for fairness sake, assume that the opponents of the Jesuit system take the trouble of reading the Constitutions of the Society and the Ratio Studiorum, even then they may be led into serious mistakes, unless they pay attention to a few regulations which are usually overlooked. To say: the Jesuits teach only what is mentioned in the Ratio Studiorum and neglect what is not put down there, is altogether false. The Constitutions and the Ratio Studiorum leave great liberty in the matter of changes and adaptations. In his Constitutions Ignatius himself says: "Let public schools be opened wherever it may conveniently be done. In the more important studies, they may be opened *with reference to the circumstances of the places* where our colleges exist. And because *in particular subjects, there must needs be much variety*, according to the difference of places and persons, we shall not here insist on them severally; but this may be declared that rules should be established in every college which shall embrace all necessary points." [1]

Conformably to this fundamental law of St. Ignatius, the Ratio Studiorum emphasizes the lawfulness,

[1] Part IV, ch. VII. The translation is that of the Protestant translator (London, 1838).

nay, the necessity of changes and adaptations. In the first part of the Ratio, in the *Rules for the Provincial Superior*, it is expressed not less than six times. Thus one rule reads: "As according to the difference of country, time and persons, there may be a variety in the order of studies, in the hours assigned to them, in repetitions, disputations and other school exercises as well as in the vacations, if he [the Provincial] should think anything more conducive to the greater advancement of learning in his province, he shall inform the General in order that, after all, special regulations be made for all the particular needs; these regulations should, however, agree as closely as possible with our general plan of studies."[1] This is evidently a most important regulation, proving that the arrangement of studies is practically committed to the Provincial Superior. A distinguished commentator on the Institute of the Society, in a recent work, could write: "We do not deny that in their methods of teaching, the members of the Order differ in many points from the Ratio Studiorum as we have explained it. It cannot be otherwise, since in the various provinces, owing to different conditions, it is necessary to make different regulations, without interfering with the general principles on which the Institute rests. We have already mentioned that St. Ignatius not only permitted but ordered various regulations to be made, according to the various conditions of time and place. This is much more necessary in our days, when so many educational schemes, good ones and bad ones, have been advanced. The Society, far from considering her own system absolutely perfect and unalterable, on the con-

[1] *Rules of the Provincial*, 39.

trary grants that *many things are merely temporary and can be improved.*" [1]

This is what the Society itself thinks of its educational system. If the system has not been changed for three hundred years — it existed three hundred years, not, as President Eliot thinks, four hundred, — the Society has proved false to the principles of its founder. That the Society has changed its teaching in the course of time, is proved by its history. We referred in a previous chapter to the Revision of 1832 and later additions, and showed that the revision of 1832 was not considered final. But this general change is slight as compared with the many important changes, which were made in the different provinces. The four volumes of Father Pachtler's work exhibit a considerable number of adaptations made in the provinces of Germany in the old Society. As an instance of such a change we must consider the systematic teaching of geography and history, which was gradually introduced in the 17th century, although it was not expressly prescribed by the Ratio. [2] Greater in number and more far-reaching were the changes made in the new Society.

In this regard the demands and suggestions for a revision of the old Ratio Studiorum, sent to Rome before 1832, are highly instructive. There we read: "As the philosophy of Aristotle is no longer suited for our age, it should not be introduced into our schools... Natural sciences were formerly taught as part of philosophy; but in order to conform with the exigencies of our times, all these sciences must be taught

[1] Oswald, S. J., *Commentarius*, no. 204, *nota*.
[2] See above ch. IV, pp. 125—129.

separately... Ethics are not to be treated according to the commentaries on Aristotle, but according to the best modern works... The elements of Euclid do not suffice now-a-days, but in our age we must teach algebra, geometry, trigonometry, conic sections, differential and integral calculus, and the scientific applications of all parts of mathematics... In the lower classes special care must now be had of the mother-tongue; the pupils must be diligently exercised in the use of their native language, and must be acquainted with the best authors in the vernacular... In our times it will not suffice to explain the principles of rhetoric according to the precepts of Aristotle and Cicero, but according to modern authors; besides, now-a-days it is necessary to give instruction in aesthetics... In the lower classes we must now teach history, geography, as well as mathematics; in the higher classes also archaeology."[1] These demands were attended to in the Revised Ratio. This may suffice to show that the Jesuits do not shut their eyes to the needs and exigencies of the times. In 1830 the General of the Society wrote to the superiors of the different provinces that they should not fail to call attention to the commendable practices of other schools in their countries; they should also be careful to mention, whether certain things were to be introduced in their respective places, even if they were contrary to the common customs of the schools of the Order.[2]

The Society has never denied that vast progress has been made in all branches of learning, especially in natural sciences, history, and philology. It does

[1] Pachtler, vol. IV, pp. 392—444.
[2] *Ib.*, p. 407.

not wish a return of the conditions of former centuries, but gladly makes use of the advantages afforded by modern science, in order to qualify the pupils for the necessities of our times. If one compares the curricula of Jesuit schools in America, England, France, Belgium, Austria, and other countries, he will find the greatest variety. He will discover that it is a groundless charge against the Jesuits, that they cling with blind stubbornness to every detail of their Ratio. No, as far as it is compatible with thorough education, they have adapted their teaching to the customs of the respective countries in which they are laboring. As was said before, these changes and modifications are not added to the printed Ratio as amendments or bylaws; this is not necessary, since, as was stated above, the Ratio itself admits the necessity of having "different regulations as regards studies, according to the different conditions of time and place." The changes and modifications are laid down in the customs and directives for the different Provinces or Missions. Now, the writers outside of the Society are, as a rule, utterly ignorant of the particular regulations of the various provinces; hence, they are easily led into the same mistake which a foreigner, coming to the State of New York, would make if he imagined there existed no law except the Constitution of the United States. As the General, and to a great extent the Provincial Superiors, by the Constitution of the Order, are empowered to make all changes which they deem necessary, it cannot be said that the Ratio Studiorum is so difficult to reform.

But it may be objected here, that what remains is no longer the Ratio Studiorum. This is not correct. .

All the essential points remain; it is only important to know what is essential. The assailants of the Ratio usually suppose that it is the preponderance given to certain subjects, especially the classics, or the order and succession in which the different subjects are taught. Others again seem to find the essentials of the Ratio in minor details, concerning the manner in which the subjects are taught. We admit that it would be altogether impracticable to carry out the prescriptions of the Ratio in their entirety. Thus the Latin idiom can no longer be insisted on as the language of conversational intercourse among the students, as was done in the 17th century, nor is it possible to use it as the medium of instruction in all the lectures. Neither is it possible to devote the same number of hours to the classics, as much time and labor is requisite for the study of modern literature, mathematics, and the sciences. We admit further that some details of the Ratio, for instance the system of *decuriones* (boy supervisors and assistants of the teacher), certain solemnities at the distribution of prizes, the use of the grammar of Alvarez, etc., are really antiquated. But they are exactly those points which have been abandoned long ago, and which have never been regarded as essential.

The present General of the Society, Father Martin, who, if any one, is unquestionably warranted to speak authoritatively on this subject, declared on January 1, 1893: "There are men who think that the Ratio Studiorum was good formerly, but that it is no longer so in our times. He who maintains this position does not understand the Ratio Studiorum; he looks only at the *matter*, not at the *form* [the *spirit*] of the system...

But the matter is not the essential feature of this system."[1] Neither is the order, the sequence, in which the different branches are taught. The subject matter as well as the order is in many countries prescribed by the governments. Although this prescribed order may not always be the best, still it can be adopted, as the order is not the characteristic feature of the system of the Society.

Now, may it not be said that modern conditions merely forced the Society and its General to this broad interpretation of the Ratio, to make, as President Eliot would express it, some further "trifling concessions"? By no means. The utterances of Father Martin are neither novel nor alien to the Ratio or the Constitutions of the Society, as is shown by a comparison with the quotations we gave before from these two documents. One point is made clear, *viz.*, that the Ratio admits of a very broad interpretation, and leaves especially ample room for innovations as regards various branches of study. If it is useful and advisable to teach a new branch : economics, civics, local history, biology, or Spanish, or any other subject, there is no difficulty on the part of the Ratio Studiorum. If the Jesuits exclude certain branches from their curriculum, it is not because they are not mentioned in the Ratio, but because they consider these branches of less educational value; if they uphold certain other branches, as the classics, it is because they expect the most from them for the training of their pupils; if they defend the successive teaching of different branches in preference to the simultaneous treatment of a multitude

---

[1] The *Woodstock Letters*, vol. XXII (1893), p. 106. — Quoted also by Chossat, *Les Jésuites à Avignon*, p. 258, n. 8.

of unconnected subjects, they act according to approved pedagogical principles; if they do not admit the extravagant electivism of some modern school-reformers, it is because they consider it injurious to solid education, not because it is opposed to their system. We venture to say, they could adopt electivism to a very great extent, without entirely abandoning the fundamental principles of their Ratio. We shall speak of these principles in the next chapter. Suffice it to quote here the words of a writer in a first class literary review in Europe on the Ratio: "The regulations and principles of that system of studies, viewed in the light of modern exigencies, need not shun any comparison, and the pedagogical wisdom contained therein is in no way antiquated."[1]

Although the teaching of the Jesuits has not remained unchanged for centuries, it is true, on the other hand, that the Society was never rash in adopting new methods. The Jesuits did not experiment with every new-fangled theory, with every pedagogical "fad", no matter how loudly praised and held up as *the* system of our age. Herein they acted wisely. For, first of all, there may be several systems, equally good, and the Jesuits possessed a system of their own, which had been approved by a remarkable success in former centuries. And that in recent times the teaching of the Society has not been unsuccessful, is sufficiently proved by what we said in the preceding chapter.

Whilst the efficiency of her old and approved system justifies the conservative spirit of the Society in educational matters, another striking proof of its wisdom in this respect is furnished by the fate of the

[1] *Oesterreichisches Litteraturblatt*, Vienna, 1897, No. 4.

modern school reforms themselves. No sooner has one startled the world, than it is followed and overthrown by a newer, later, more modern system. To each of them may be applied the words of St. Peter to Saphira, which a German philosopher used with reference to modern philosophical theories: "Behold the feet of them who have buried thy husband are at the door, and they shall carry thee out."[1] We have an instance in Germany. In 1892, a new plan of studies was introduced in Prussia, and at about the same time in the other states of Germany.[2] The classical studies lost a great number of hours. Although this plan was introduced at the urgent wish of the young Emperor and through his "energetic personal interference,"[3] it met with great opposition on the part of the majority of teachers. No party was satisfied. The strict advocates of the ancient classics complained of the reduction in the classical instruction. The friends of the scientific schools were not satisfied with the concessions made them.[4] On all sides the cry was heard: "Reform the Reform of 1892."

In 1895 the Ministry of Instruction allowed the directors of the gymnasia to add, in the three higher classes, one hour a week, which should be devoted to

---

[1] *Acts* 5, 9.

[2] A very good account of this reform is given by Dr. Russell, *German Higher Schools*, ch. XX. See also *Educational Review*, September, 1900. The best and most comprehensive sketch of the "Berlin Conference of 1890" is contained in the *Report of the Commissioner of Education*, 1889—90, vol. I, pp. 343—398, by Charles Herbert Thurston of Cornell University.

[3] *Report of the Comm. of Ed.*, *l. c.*, p. 363.

[4] *Rep. of Com. of Ed.*, *l. c.*, p. 398.

the old grammatical and stylistic exercises.[1] Still more complaints were heard in the following years. In 1899 even Professor Virchow, one of the most determined opponents of the gymnasium in its old form, admitted that the graduates after the reform manifested a notable decline in grammatical and logical training. It was found necessary to convoke a new conference, which met in Berlin, June 1900. Here some of the ablest schoolmen were outspoken in demanding a partial return to the system existing before 1892. Dr. Matthias, the referee of the Ministry, stated that all official reports and the most experienced men of the Kingdom complained about the serious decline of Latin scholarship which had manifested itself after 1892. The cause of this decline he suspected to be the excessive use of inductive methods, so much encouraged by the reform. Efforts were to be made to check this decline; above all it was necessary to secure again greater grammatical knowledge, and it seemed better to introduce again some of the old methods, especially frequent translations from the German into Latin and speaking Latin.[2] He thus recommended what the most zealous of the reformers had ridiculed as antiquated. Professor Kübler and Professor Harnack were not less outspoken on this point. The latter said that writing Latin was to be insisted on, and that the discarding of this exercise in 1892 was a mistake.[3] The result of these discussions was a strengthening of the Latin course, by adding

[1] Messer, *Die Reformbewegung*, p. 155.
[2] *Verhandlungen über die Fragen des höhern Unterrichts*, Berlin, June 1900, p. 128.
[3] *Ib.*, p. 294.

one hour weekly from the third class on, therefore an increase of seven hours Latin weekly in the whole gymnasium. The new "School Order" of 1901 demanded most emphatically a thorough grammatical training. Books for translating from German into Latin, which in 1892 had been done away with almost entirely, were again introduced into all the classes.[1] By these regulations, the Prussian Ministry, taught by the experience of nine years, and convinced by the arguments of the foremost schoolmen of the Kingdom, acknowledged that the "reform" of 1892, in several important points had been a mistake, a deterioration. It was thus proved that some of the much decried old methods were, after all, the best and safest.

Within the last decade a novel experiment has been made in Germany, that of the "Pioneer Schools" or "Reform Gymnasia." These schools are to be the common foundation of all higher schools: *Gymnasium* (classical), *Real-Gymnasium* (Latin scientific), *Real-Schule* (scientific). During the first three years one modern language is taught, French in the schools of the *Frankfort-type*, English in those of the *Altona-type*. In the fourth year the schools separate. Latin is begun in the *Gymnasium* and *Real-Gymnasium*, English in the *Real-Schule*. In the sixth year the *Gymnasium* introduces Greek, the *Real-Gymnasium* English.[2] Whilst a great number of educators vigorously oppose this system — some say "the experiment should never have been allowed" — the most advanced "reformers of the universe" expect great things of it; to them it

[1] *Lehrpläne und Lehraufgaben für die höhern Schulen in Preussen*, 1901. pp. 28—30. — Messer, *l. c.*, p. 157.
[2] See Russell, *German Higher Schools*, ch. XX. — Viereck, in *Educational Review*, Sept. 1900.

is "the school of the future." Be it remarked, as a curious fact, that this modern system is not new at all, but a mere revival of the system of Comenius (1592—1671).[1] The future has to show whether this system is practicable or not. So far its value has not been sufficiently demonstrated.

Our own country furnishes significant phenomena, — similar to those witnessed in Germany. People had been told that our educational system was well nigh perfect. American children, at the age of ten or twelve years, now learn things of which in former generations men of twenty-five knew little or nothing, be it physiology, biology, hygiene, civics or what not. And all this they learn without exertion and coercion; for, agreeably to the free spirit of the country, the young citizens are to be given, as early as possible, full liberty of choosing those branches which suit their good pleasure, or, as our moderns express it, their natural abilities. Indeed, what system can be more perfect? Now on a sudden people are rudely awakened from their pleasant dreams by most distinguished men, who tell the people that there is something wrong, some say "radically wrong," in our educational system. Not a few of these critics begin to point out that one of the fundamental defects of American schools is the very thing which was vaunted as our greatest educational achievement: the elective system in secondary schools. Others discover the greatest danger in the hasty experimenting, in the rash accep-

[1] "No less a person than Comenius, the father of our new philosophical education, outlines in his *Great Didactic* a system which in its principal features agrees with that now in vogue in our pioneer schools." *Educational Review*, Sept. 1900, p. 173.

tation of novelties so common in our modern schools.[1] "There is too much agitation, unceasing change, and consequent uncertainty in the operations of our American schools. There is too much *individualism* in laying plans and arranging courses and in methods of teaching, too burning a desire to say something new or to do something novel for the sake of prominence in the teaching body. Of course it will be said that this has brought us where we are. But we might be quite as well off if we were not exactly where we are."[2]

Within the last month (October 1902) severe strictures were made on some of the very latest educational "improvements," and that not by Jesuits, nor by professional philologists, who stubbornly defend their long-cherished classics, but by such as may eminently be called men of affairs. The *Electrical World* spoke of President Eliot's efforts to lift the American college to the plane of a foreign university. "The chief effect has been to push the college into the existing dilemma. It is crowded from above by the necessity for more time in the professional schools, and for a nether millstone it finds the secondary school that its own hands have fashioned. And truth to tell, *the college is losing heart.* It has virtually surrendered its last year to professional electives, but *the sacrifice has not served its purpose.* The latest suggestion from no less eminent a source than that of Professor Butler, of Columbia, is

[1] "In America we are unfortunately too prone to view with favor any new idea, educational or other, and to embark precipitately in experiments which involve serious consequences." Professor Bennett of Cornell University, in *The Teaching of Latin in the Secondary School*, p. 80.

[2] President Draper of the University of Illinois. *Edutional Review*, May 1902, p. 457.

for a two-year college course, leading to post-graduate training, and a parallel four-year course for such as may desire it. We hope this experiment may not be tried, for its success would mean the disintegration of the college as it has been, and the introduction of nothing to take its place. . . . If the American college is still to remain a part of our educational system, *it must stand by its old ideals and neither retreat nor compromise.* . . . If the college would do the greatest possible service to education it should sharpen its ax, not to decapitate itself according to the present program, but to hew out of its curriculum the courses that demand a diffuse preparation in the secondary schools, and out of these latter the time-wasting requirements."[1] The utterances of another man deserve to be quoted in this connection, I mean Mr. Cleveland, the former President of the United States. On October 25, 1902, at the inauguration of the new President of Princeton University, he earnestly warned against "false educational notions," "a new-born impatience which demands a swifter educational current and is content with a shallower depth." Mr. Cleveland declared *"Princeton's conservatism is one of her chief virtues,* and that we of Princeton are still willing to declare our belief that we are better able to determine than those coming to us for education, what is their most advantageous course of instruction, and surely every phase of our history justifies this belief."[2] It is hardly necessary to point out what "false educational notions" are hinted at. From these criticisms of the latest

[1] *Electrical World,* October 25, 1902.
[2] From the *Evening Bulletin,* Philadelphia, October 25, 1902. (Italics are ours, also those of preceding quotation.)

"school reforms" we are justified in drawing the following inferences:

First, not all school changes and innovations are real improvements. Secondly, a great deal of sound pedagogy was contained in the old systems, which was rashly and wantonly abandoned by many modern school reformers. Thirdly, the Jesuits acted prudently in not accepting in their totality these new methods which, to a great extent, are but haphazard experiments.

The Society believes in a sound *evolution* in educational matters, but is averse to a precipitous *revolution*. Those who recently have called the educational system of the Society antiquated or absurd, because it repudiates their own pet theories, have acted very rashly, all the more so that these very theories have been condemned by many competent judges. The man who lives in a glass house should not throw stones at other people.

In every important movement, the ardent desire of progress must be tempered and controlled by a goodly amount of conservatism. Otherwise the *rerum novarum studiosi* will sacrifice much of what is of fundamental importance. At the time of the famous Gaume controversy in France about the classical studies, an English Catholic writer characterized the attitude of the Jesuits in the following words: "Though essentially conservative, that remarkable Society has never held itself so far behind the current of Catholic thought, as to lose its influence over it; nor has it placed itself so much in the advance, as to become an object of general observation. It has, as a rule, firmly, cautiously, and with a practical wisdom, manifested to so great an extent by no other order in the Church, kept pace with the general movement, and influenced its direction; and when it has not been able, through the unmanageable nature of the elements with which it has had to do, to lead, it has had the sagacity to bide its time and follow. It is this instinct which, though it may to 'carnal men' savor of human prudence, to men who see things through a spiritual eye, manifests the workings of a governing Providence through one of the most able human instruments which has ever undertaken God's work upon the earth."[1]

The extent and limit of the Society's progressiveness and conservatism in educational matters, has been clearly enunciated by Father Roothaan, General of the Society, in 1832: "The adaptation of the Ratio Studiorum means that we consult the necessities of the age so far as not in the least to sacrifice the solid and correct education of youth." Accordingly, the Society will ever adapt its system in all and to all that is conducive to the great end of its educational labors: the thorough *intellectual* and *moral* training of its pupils.

[1] *Dublin Review*, 1866, vol. VII, (p. 208): "The Gaume controversy on Classical Studies," by R. B. V. — I think the writer is Roger Bede Vaughan, O. S. B., later on Archbishop of Sydney, Australia.

Chapter X.

The Intellectual Scope.

In the preceding chapter we mentioned a statement of the present General of the Society, "that the characteristics of the Ratio Studiorum are not to be sought in the subject matter or in the order, but in what may be called the form or the spirit of the system." Father Martin explained in what this form consists: "It consists chiefly in the training of the mind, which is the object, and in the various exercises, which are the means to attain this object." In these words we have the intellectual scope of the Ratio Studiorum, in fact the intellectual scope of every rational system of education. This training of the mind means the gradual and harmonious development of all the higher faculties of man, of memory, imagination, intellect, and will.

The very meaning of the word confirms this view: to "educate" signifies to exercise the mental faculties of man, by instruction, training and discipline in such a way as to develop and render efficient the natural powers; to develop a man physically, mentally, morally, and spiritually.[1] The mind is *educated* when its powers are *developed* and disciplined, so that it can perform its appropriate work. In speaking of one as *educated*, we imply not merely that he has acquired knowledge, but that his mental powers have been developed and disciplined to effective action. Education is, consequently, the systematic *development* and

[1] *The Standard Dictionary.*

(297)

cultivation of the mind and faculties. In these definitions we see that education signifies development, and rightly so, as its original meaning is to "draw out." The fundamental mistake of many modern systems is the utter disregard of this truth. Father Dowling, S. J., of Creighton University, has expressed this very well in the following words[1]: "Unfortunately education, which ought to signify a *drawing out*, has come to be regarded as the proper word to denote a *putting in*. Properly it supposes that there is something in the mind capable of development, faculties that can be trained, implicit knowledge which can be made explicit, dormant powers which can be awakened. The main end of education should be to unfold these faculties. It means not so much the actual imparting of knowledge, as the development of the power to gain knowledge, to apply the intellect, to cultivate taste, utilize the memory, make use of observations and facts. It is not essential that the studies which produce these results should be directly useful in after life any more than it is necessary for the athlete in the development of his powers to wield the blacksmith's hammer, instead of using dumb-bells or horizontal bars, none of which play any part in his subsequent career; he puts them all aside when the physical powers have been developed."

The Germans express the same idea admirably by the name they give to their colleges. They call a college a *gymnasium*. Indeed, this is what a college should be, a place of mental gymnastics, of training,

[1] *The Catholic College as a Preparation for a Business Career*, p. 7. — See also *The Month*, February, 1886: *Education and School*, by the Rev. John Gerard, S. J.

not for the muscles, but the mind. Education ought not to be merely an accumulating of knowledge, of data from various sciences, of bits of learning gathered here and there. This, alas, it now is in too many modern systems. "Give the pupils facts, broad information, varied instruction," is their watch-word. And yet, facts, information, instruction, are only a means of educating, not education itself; they are, to use the above mentioned metaphor, the dumb-bells, the horizontal bars, the pulleys of this mental gymnasium, by the use of which the mind acquires that agility and nimbleness, that quickness of action, and last, but not least, that gracefulness and refinement which we call taste, the noblest result of a well balanced education. A mind thus trained and developed may then take up any special study. A young man thus educated has his intellectual tools sharpened and ready for use. He will accomplish more, and will do more thorough and successful work, in any line of professional or practical work, than the one who from the beginning took up special studies. Undoubtedly, the latter will get an earlier start in life; when twenty-five years old he is earning money, while the former has just finished his long course of training. But wait until they are thirty-five, then, *ceteris paribus*, the one who laid a deeper and broader foundation of general education, will be known as the more successful lawyer, physician, or teacher, perhaps even the more prosperous business man, and certainly the more cultured and more refined gentleman, one who exercises an elevating and ennobling influence on all who come into contact with him.

It may safely be said that one of the worst features

of modern educational systems is the tendency to cram too much into the courses of study, too much that is considered "practical" in one way or other. As Professor Treitschke of Berlin has expressed it, "the greatest danger that threatens the education of modern man lies in the infinite distraction of our inner life, in the superabundance of mental impressions of every sort that rush upon us and hamper the one prerequisite of all great work: recollection of soul, concentration of mind." Hence he thinks it absolutely necessary that youths should be educated as simply as possible, and should not be mentally overfed by many and various things.[1] It is, indeed, a most serious mistake to think that a person who knows all sorts of things is educated; no, sciolism is not culture. Consequently, that school is by no means the right one which "coaches" or "crams" for the future profession, — we are not speaking of the professional schools, — but that which trains the *man*, trains the mental faculties, develops clear logical thinking, cultivates the imagination, ennobles the sentiments, and strengthens the will. This, indeed, is educating, that is, "drawing out" what lies hidden and undeveloped in the soul. Instead of this, many modern schools aim at further expansion, which, considering the limited capacity of the youthful mind, is inseparable from shallowness. What is gained in extent of knowledge, is necessarily lost in depth, thoroughness, and mastery of the knowledge acquired. What is sadly needed now-a-days is concentration, a wise restriction of subjects which leads to depth and interior strength.

The educational system of the Society always aimed

[1] *Neue Jahrbücher*, 1901, vol. VIII, p. 474.

at a thorough general training in a few branches. Four characteristic points are discernible in this training: it is to be thorough, prolonged, general, simple. It is to be *thorough;* for superficial knowledge, smattering, is not training. It must be *prolonged;* for thoroughness cannot be effected in a short time. Time is as essential for maturing a man's mind and character, as it is for ripening a choice fruit; one may bake an apple in a few moments, but one cannot ripen it in that time. Education must, in this regard, follow the laws of nature. Time and prolonged and patient efforts are absolutely necessary in order to produce any success in education. In the third place this training is to be *general,* not professional; its aim is the man, not the specialist; it is the foundation on which the professional training is to be built up. It is, in other words, a *liberal* training; it has to cultivate the ideal, that which is really human and permanent in life. What is useful and practical will be cared for in time, and, as a rule, is sufficiently looked after. Lastly, this training must be *simple,* that is, it must be based on a few well-related branches; if too many disconnected subjects are treated, thoroughness becomes absolutely impossible.

The modern tendency in education is in the opposite direction. It aims at the useful and practical rather than the general training, or, at best, allots too short a time to the general education. Hence the very foundation of the practical training is weak. Besides, it comprises too many various subjects, the consuming of which does not effect a healthy mental growth, but an intellectual hypertrophy.[1] It is showy

[1] "The educational system [of America] is undertaking too much, at least in the grades below the college. 'Research'

in the extreme, and dazzles the eye of the public, and even of some whose education and position in the world of culture should be a safeguard against such delusion. For these very reasons it is most detrimental to true progress. Far-seeing men, in this country as well as in Europe, realize the dangers of this tendency, and warn all educators against them most emphatically.

In an address on the occasion of the 27th annual commencement of the Jesuit College, Buffalo, N. Y., 1897, the Right Rev. James E. Quigley, D. D., Archbishop of Chicago, said: "We Americans are a practical people, but we are also impatient. We cannot arrive at our goal quickly enough. We send the boys to a high school for three or four years, and then we call them away and send them to the study of law or medicine. Now I would tell the parents: if you want to make a lawyer or a doctor of your son, let him finish the college course, he will be the better for it in his profession. We have now lawyers and doctors enough, what we need is better lawyers and better doctors."

Dr. McCosh, for twenty years President of Princeton College, says: "There is a loud demand in the present day for college education being made what they call *practical*. I believe that this is a mistake. A well known ship-builder once said to me: 'Do not try to teach my art in school; see that you make the youth intelligent, and then I will easily teach him ship-building.' The business of a college is to teach scientific principles of all sorts of practical application.

is attempted where drill is what is needed." President Draper of the University of Illinois, *Educational Review*, May 1902, p. 455. — See also the words of Ex-President Cleveland, referred to on p. 294, and the *Electrical World, l. c.*

The youth thus trained will start life in far better circumstances than those who have learned only the details of their craft, which are best learned in offices, stores and factories, and will commonly outstrip them in the rivalries of life. He will be able to advance when others are obliged to stop."[1]

Professor Münsterberg of Harvard University, in his article on *School Reform*,[2] speaks admirably on the same subject. He points out the various fallacies underlying the system that advocates the earliest possible beginning of specialization. He ably proves that the pretensions of this system are wrong, and its calculations superficial, even from the merely utilitarian and mercenary standpoint. But above all, this system is to be condemned from the standpoint of liberal education. The Harvard Professor writes: "The higher the level on which the professional specializing begins, the more effective it is. I have said that we German boys did not think of any specialization and individual variation before we reached a level corresponding to a college graduation here. In this country, the college must still go on for a while playing the double rôle of the place for the general education of the one, and the workshop for the professional training of the other; but at least the high school ought to be faithful to its only goal of general education without professional anticipations. Moreover, we are not only professional wage earners; we live for our friends and our nation; we face social and political, moral and religious problems; we are in

---

[1] *The Life of James McCosh*, edited by W. M. Sloane, p. 204.
[2] *Atlantic Monthly*, May 1900, p. 662 foll.

contact with nature and science, with art and literature; we shape our towns and our time, and all that is common to every one, — to the banker and the manufacturer, to the minister and the teacher, to the lawyer and the physician. The technique of our profession, then, appears only as a small variation of the large background of work in which we all share; and if the education must be adapted to our later life, all these problems demand a uniform education for the members of the same social community. The division of labor lies on the outside. We are specialists in our handiwork, but our heart work is uniform, and the demand for individual education emphasizes the small differences in our tasks, and ignores the great similarities. And, after all, who is able to say what a boy of twelve years will need for his special life work? It is easily said in a school programme that the course will be adapted to the needs of the particular pupil with respect to his later life, but it would be harder to say how we are to find out what the boy does need; and even if we know it, the straight line to the goal is not always the shortest way."

Mr. Clement L. Smith is not less outspoken on this topic[1]: "An education which aims to equip men for particular callings, or to give them a special training for entering upon those callings, however useful it may be, is not the liberal education which should be the single aim of the college. It should be the aim of the secondary school, too, — if not for all pupils, certainly for those who are going to college. For those who turn away, at the end of the school course, to

[1] "The American College in the 20th Century," *Atlantic Monthly*, Feb. 1900.

train themselves for some technical pursuit, let appropriate technical schools be provided, and let them be held in all honor. But they should not masquerade as institutions for liberal education. Above all, they should not invade the province of the college, introducing confusion, and turning it into a place where there are a number of unconnected and independent educations going on at the same time, instead of a place where, though there are many paths, they all lead to a single goal. For the essence of a liberal education lies in the aim, not in the studies pursued,[1] — not in letters, not in science. These are the materials with which it works; and employs them, not to make professional or technical experts, but to make men and women of broader views, of greater intellectual power, — better equipped for whatever profession or employment they may undertake, and for their equally important function of citizen and neighbor."

The Honorable James Bryce, a man excellently fitted to express his opinion on American, as well as on European, questions, a few years ago, while advocating a special commercial training, warns against shortening the time allotted to general education, whether elementary or secondary. On the contrary, the further the general education can be carried, the better for the young man, and more would be lost by curtailing the time spent on the subjects which everybody should learn, than would be gained by any special preparation for a particular employment. He reminds the people of England and the United States that the demand for a commercial education might do more

[1] Almost literally what Father Martin declared to be the essence of Jesuit education. See above p. 286 and 297.

harm than good, "were it to lead to a shortening or to a commercializing of general school education, or were it to dispose us to ignore the supreme importance of securing that the teaching of the commercial subjects themselves shall be so directed as to arouse and stimulate the faculties no less than to inform the memory of the learner."[1]

Long before this, Arnold had spoken in similar terms: "It is no wisdom to make boys prodigies of information, but it is our wisdom and our duty to cultivate their faculties, each in its season, first the memory and the imagination, and then the judgment, to furnish them with the means and to excite the desire of improving themselves."[2] The most enlightened and experienced German educators insist on this point as strongly as any of those whose authority is cited above.[3] It is needless to point out the fact that these writers clearly and strikingly express the same opinion about the intellectual scope of education as the Jesuits, namely, that real education does not consist in merely imparting information, but in training the mental faculties, in the *efformatio ingenii*, as the General of the Society called it in 1893.

In this country the question about the intellectual scope of education is closely connected with the other most important question: What is the function

[1] *North American Review*, June 1899.
[2] Fitch, *Thomas and Matthew Arnold*, p. 61.
[3] See especially Weissenfels, *Die Bildungswirren der Gegenwart*, Berlin, 1901. — Matthias, *Aus Schule, Unterricht und Erziehung*, 1901. — Professor Weissenfels, throughout his book, expresses his deepest anxiety at the ever increasing spirit of utilitarianism in German schools.

of the high school and college? Aside from the champions of extreme electivism, there is no educator of note who does not consider *general culture* the function of the high school. A great number of prominent educators do not hesitate to assign the same function to the college, relegating specialization, the acquisition of scholarship, or professional skill, entirely, or for the main part, to the university. The college should concern itself with the final stage of secondary education; it ought to stimulate general culture and to train character, rather than to impart specific instruction. A college President declared that the first step towards a betterment is the reassertion of the aim and nature of college life. The university, demanding for entrance a bachelor's degree, is the crown of our educational system. Its province is higher education, the cultivation of advanced scholarship and research. But "the college should give itself no airs. It should not pretend to be a university."[1]

It needs scarcely be stated that the Jesuits' view of the college is exactly the same. They assign no other function, no other aim to it than general culture, harmonious training of the mind.

[1] President Jones of Hobart College, in the *Forum*, January 1901: *Is the College Graduate Impracticable?*—The greatest difficulty in this country lies in the fact that pupils go too late to the high school or college. The study of Latin should be commenced at the age of ten or twelve years, instead of thirteen or fourteen. See Dr. Stanley Hall, *Forum*, Sept. 1901; and below ch. XVI, § 1.—The same is advocated by Professor Nightingale in the *Report of the Conference on English*, read before the National Association of Education, at Ashbury Park, N. J., 1894. German boys begin with nine or ten years, why should not the clever American boy be able to begin with ten or eleven?

How is this training of the mind to be obtained? The Jesuit answers: By *exercise*, that is, by the different exercises, such as are laid down in the Ratio Studiorum: exercises of the intellect — translations, compositions; exercises of the memory — recitations and declamations; debates (academies), etc. These exercises have sometimes been styled "mechanical"; still how can any training be effected except by devices according to strict rule? Certainly not by the mere lecture of the teacher, however scholarly or interesting it may be. No one becomes an athlete by attending lectures on gymnastics, and no one becomes a perfect soldier by reading the U. S. Infantry Drill Book; but practice, drill, exercise is required. No one's mental faculties will ever become really developed, unless he is trained and drilled. The insisting on this fundamental principle is probably the most characteristic point in the educational system of the Society. Practice and exercise run all through the different grades, beginning from the teaching of the elements of Latin up to the highest course of theology. It is the same great principle of the necessity of self-exertion, self-activity which Ignatius so forcibly insists upon in that admirable little book, which he justly calls the "Spiritual Exercises." As there the exercitant is exhorted to act for himself, and not merely to suffer himself to be acted upon, so here the pupil is required from the beginning to act, not merely to listen, to exert himself in the various prescribed exercises.

As these exercises will be spoken of in a later chapter of this book,[1] we need not discuss them here. Suffice it to say that the ablest educators of the nine-

---

[1] Chapter XVI.

teenth century have recommended exercises which are essentially the same as those of the Society. So Dr. Arnold, the famous head-master of Rugby; Dr. Wiese, for decades one of the most influential men in the Prussian Ministry of Education; Dr. M. Seyffert, the great Latinist. In the introduction to his excellent *Scholae Latinae*, Dr. Seyffert has the following: "I thought this work, the fruit of twenty-five years experience, was something new. However, I had scarcely finished, when through the information of a friend of mine, I found out that there was nothing new under the sun. The merit and honor of the invention belongs, as I know now, to the seventeenth century, and, as hardly can be expected otherwise, to the diligence of the Order of the Jesuits, who were unwearied in preparing pedagogical helps and means. I shall be satisfied if my work finds only one tenth of the approval which their work found, and as I think, most deservedly found." Another great educator of Germany, K. L. Roth, said: "Exercise was the secret of the old college-systems; it forced the pupil daily to use for the formation of his judgment the material accumulated to excess in his memory."[1]

[1] In his *Gymnasial-Pädagogik;* see Duhr, p. 119.

Chapter XI.

Prescribed Courses or Elective Studies?

Intimately connected with the subject of the last chapter is a question now much discussed in pedagogical circles, namely, whether the "old-fashioned" prescribed courses are the best way of attaining the object of education, the training of the mind, or whether the elective system should claim the monopoly in the education of our nation.

Not many years ago the secondary school programmes offered a single course of study, or at most two courses which were to be pursued in order to obtain the diploma of the school. The principal course consisted of Latin, Greek, history and mathematics. At present we find in most secondary schools a number of parallel courses, and the disposition is growing to regard the different courses as of equal value and dignity. It has been said by advocates of the new system that "the old narrow course, with its formal contents and mechanical routine, is doomed; and a richer course of study, with a broader and more inspiring conception of the elementary school-teacher's responsibilities and opportunities, is taking its place."[1]

Whence these changes? Not from the conviction of teachers that the old system was bad and inefficient; but, as Professor Hanus says, these changes are chiefly the result of external demands of parents and

---

[1] Hanus, *Educational Aims and Educational Values* (1900), pp. 76, 78.

sons and daughters. They have not been stimulated by the marked encouragement of the colleges; for, at the present day, several important colleges still decline to regard any pre-collegiate course of study as comparable in value to the traditional classical course.[1] Would it not have been the duty of the "leading" schools of the country to lead public opinion, and not allow themselves to be guided by it? When some large and influential schools adopted many parallel courses, the majority of the smaller and less important schools imitated the larger ones, or were practically forced to do so. After these schools had yielded to external demands, it was but natural that there "has also come a desire on the part of all to justify such programmes by an appeal to reason."[2]

This appeal has been made most forcibly by President Eliot on various occasions. We have heard that his most serious charge against Jesuit colleges is their adherence to prescribed courses. To this indictment the President added: "Nothing but an unhesitating belief in the Divine wisdom of such prescriptions can justify them; for no human wisdom is equal to contriving a prescribed course of study equally good for even two children of the same family, between the ages of eight and eighteen. Direct revelation from on high would be the only satisfactory basis for a uniform prescribed school curriculum. The immense deepening and expanding of human knowledge, in the nineteenth century, and the increasing sense of the

[1] *Ibid.*, p. 78. — However, a writer in the *Electrical World* (Oct. 25, 1902) maintains that "the present anomalous status of the college is due perhaps more to its own laudable but ill-judged ambition than to the pressure of the times."

[2] *Ibid.*, p. 26.

sanctity of the individual's gifts and will power, have made uniform prescriptions of study in secondary schools impossible and absurd. We must absolutely give up the notion that any set of human beings, however wise and learned, can ever again construct and enforce on school children one uniform course of study. The class system, that is, the process of instructing children in large groups, is a quite sufficient school evil, without clinging to its twin evil, an inflexible programme of studies. Individual instruction is the new ideal." [1]

If this new ideal of individual instruction should be carried out consistently — and the patrons of this electivism certainly ought to work at the realization of this ideal state — we might in the twentieth century see the day, when for five thousand students at Harvard there will be no less than five thousand instructors. No wonder that all these pupils will turn out geniuses, such as the world has never seen before. It seems certain that great results are anticipated by President Eliot. For he concludes his paper with the words: "These gains are noiseless but persuasive; they take effect on five hundred thousand pupils every year. Have we not here some solid ground for hopefulness about the Republic, both as a form of government and as a state of society?"

Not less amusing is the absolute certainty with which President Eliot affirms that electivism is the *only* system which can claim a right to exist. He says: "Direct revelation from on high would be the only satisfactory basis for a uniform prescribed school curriculum, and nothing but an unhesitating belief in

---

[1] *Atlantic Monthly*, Oct. 1899, p. 443.

the Divine wisdom of such prescriptions can justify them." Does not the President himself claim almost a superhuman infallibility when he straightway asserts: "Uniform prescriptions in secondary schools have been made *impossible* and *absurd*. We must *absolutely* give up the notion that any set of human beings, *however wise and learned*, can *ever* again construct and enforce on school children one uniform course of study."[1] Could any one, whether prophet or pope, speak with more certainty, than President Eliot does in this passage? How can uniform prescriptions be styled *impossible* and *absurd*, when they are exacted in whole countries, and not only among half-civilized Moslems, or "decaying" Latin races, but also in "Teutonic" States, for instance in Germany, a country which leads in scholarship and of late years has so rapidly advanced also in industrial and commercial enterprise, that it is considered a formidable rival of American industry and commerce? The absolute certainty with which President Eliot proclaims his views is all the more unwarranted if we compare them with what other distinguished scholars think on this subject.

We quoted before the words of Professor Russell of Columbia, that the experience of Germany can teach us much, especially that "a uniform course of study for all schools of a particular grade, and a common standard for promotion and graduation, can be made most serviceable in a national scheme of education."[2] Mr. Canfield, in his interesting book *The College Student and his Problems*, cautions the student in the following terms: "The more specialized your course,

[1] The Italics are ours.
[2] *German Higher Schools*, p. 409. See above p. 9.

the more certain ought you to be that the end is that which you desire. It is quite necessary, therefore, that you know yourself and your purposes, something quite definite of your capacity and powers, if you are to make a wise selection of your work. In the inefficiency or inexactness of such knowledge the college finds one weakness and one danger in multiplying courses or in enlarging the number of electives within a course. For very few young men know themselves at the age at which they enter college, and I think that others know them less. . . . It is because of this uncertainty of purpose and this ignorance of self that the wisest educators and the most thoughtful students of mankind have always given such loyal adherence to the general culture courses, and especially to the classical courses. This adherence does not mean that all culture power is denied to other courses. It is simply an insistence upon that broad and humanizing work which has been and which ever will be one of the best and surest foundations for large and generous life."[1] Nothing less is contained in these statements than a condemnation of President Eliot's electivism. For, if a choice of a specialized course without perfect knowledge of self is a great danger to the college student, how much more to the pupil in the high school? Or, if very few know themselves when entering college, how many can be expected to know themselves when entering the high school? Another remark is most significant. President Eliot asserts that "Moslems and Jesuits" uphold the old

[1] *The College Student and his Problems,* by J. H. Canfield, formerly chancellor of the University of Nebraska and President of Ohio State University. (New York, MacMillan, 1902) pp. 44—46.

prescribed courses; the former President of Ohio State University does not hesitate to say, that for the most weighty reasons, "the wisest educators and the most thoughtful students of mankind have always given loyal adherence to the general culture courses, and especially to the classical courses," that is practically, to the old prescribed courses.

But to return to the Jesuit system. President Eliot is perfectly correct in stating that it defends a prescribed curriculum. However, it does not exclude, but in many places admits distinct *parallel courses;* beside the classical course there may be offered an English course, consisting chiefly in English, history, modern languages, some of the natural sciences and mathematics; or a Scientific course in which mathematics and natural sciences are the principal subjects taught. But these courses have to be followed as laid down, at least in the main subjects. Nor do the Jesuits exclude a certain amount of election in *secondary* branches. We say secondary, as there can be no reasonable doubt that not all branches are of the same educational value. For who would have the hardihood to say, that music and drawing, or even botany and zoology, are as well fitted to develop the mental faculties as the old-fashioned course of classics and mathematics? The Society at least does not dare to affirm it, and in this she is at one with the best educators of all ages, our own not excepted. Dr. McCosh said years ago in the famous debate with President Eliot: "At Harvard a young man has two hundred courses from which he may choose, and many of these courses, I am compelled to call dilettante. I should prefer a young man who has been trained in an old-fashioned college, in rhetoric, philosophy, Latin, Greek, and mathematics, to one who had frittered away four years in studying the French drama of the eighteenth century, a little music and similar branches."[1] Again Dr. McCosh maintains "there should be required studies for all who pursue a full course for a degree, and the required studies should be disciplinary, affording true mental training. Such studies are English, Greek, Latin, German, French, history, mathematics and physical science."[2]

The objections of the Jesuits to the extreme electivism are mainly two. The first is that they apprehend serious dangers for the intellectual training from this new system. As was said in the preceding chapter, the *intellectual* scope of the Jesuit system is a thorough general training of the mind. There are the gravest reasons to fear that this training can scarcely be expected from the elective system as practised in many schools. The second objection arises from the conviction that the *moral* training of the students will be injured if the choice of studies is to any great extent left to them, especially if they are allowed to change the branches which they find difficult and disagreeable. For, greatly as the Jesuits value the intellectual training of their pupils, they attach far greater importance to the moral training, to the training of the will and the development of character.

President Eliot implicitly asserts that the Jesuits, as upholders of prescribed courses, violate the sanctity of the individual's will-power. This is a serious charge. In answer to it we may first quote the words

[1] *Life of James McCosh*, p. 201.
[2] *Ibid.*, p. 200.

of a prominent educator who in the strongest terms makes the same charge against systems like that of President Eliot. Professor Weissenfels of Berlin wrote in 1901: "In our times the moment comes relatively early when the special gifts and abilities of the individual try to assert themselves. But let it not be forgotten that there are brilliant abnormities. The talent for a special science, particularly mathematics, or for a special art, particularly music, even in childhood, gets a tyrannical ascendancy over everything else. Shall we give free play to it and foster it? Or shall we at first endeavor to counteract it, or at least keep from it all that could stimulate still more the inclination which is in itself too strong? Among the tolerably intelligent there is but one opinion: they distrust precociousness. . . . . It is justly considered want of common sense, nay more, a sin against the child's soul, to make advances to the impatience with which the special aptitude is trying to assert itself, and thus to add fuel to the fire."[1] The author further calls this system a criminal mutilation of the soul, and maintains that the special talent, if unduly and prematurely fostered will be like a rank weed that stifles every other inclination and thus destroys all harmony of mind and character.

We hear now-a-days so much about the "sanctity of the individual's will" that one's idea of human nature may easily get confused. True, there is something sacred in human nature, because it is the image and likeness of its Maker. Still, that sanctity of man is not pure and unalloyed, that image is not altogether

[1] Weissenfels, *Die Bildungswirren der Gegenwart*, pp. 324—329.

intact and spotless. Divine revelation, the world's history, daily experience and our innermost conscience tell us that there are disorders and derangements, that there are not only holy and divine, but also animal desires, not only upward, but also downward tendencies in our nature. The great Apostle testifies to this truth, when he exclaims: "For I know that there dwelleth not in me, that is to say, in my flesh, that which is good. For to will is present with me; but to accomplish that which is good, I find not. For the good which I will, I do not; but the evil which I will not, that I do."[1] Now this "law of sin which fights against the spirit" manifests itself differently according to the different dispositions and the age of the individual. In youth, it assumes generally the shape of love of pleasure and enjoyment together with a tendency to idleness, and "idleness is the fruitful mother of many vices." The old educational systems believed in Allopathy, and thought that these moral diseases could be cured effectively only by means which directly attack the root of the evil. So they tried seriously to occupy a boy's mind, to accustom him to hard, steady work, to fight against his dislikes, to do his duty and to break his will. But, we are told, that was all wrong, it was only the outcropping of the severe and gloomy asceticism of former ages. Our modern pedagogues have discovered that Homoeopathy alone will do in education. "The poor children are overburdened, make it easy for them. Give full vent to the pupil's inclinations and do not force him to anything he dislikes. For this would be interfering with the sanctity of the individual!"

[1] *Romans* 7, 18.

If the old view of life and youth and education savors of asceticism, the new one is sheer materialism. But setting aside all supernatural considerations, we must condemn the extreme electivism of the modern system on merely natural grounds. Nor is this attitude peculiar to the Society of Jesus; it is firmly maintained by educators who in their religious tenets differ widely from ourselves. Professor Münsterberg has well pointed out the damage which results from this system to the *character* of the child, to the "formal side of education," as he styles it. "A child who has himself the right of choice, or who sees that parents and teachers select these courses according to his tastes and inclinations, may learn a thousand pretty things, but never the one which is the greatest of all: to do his duty. He who is allowed always to follow the paths of least resistance never develops the power to overcome resistance; he remains utterly unprepared for life." To do what we like to do, — that needs no pedagogical encouragement: water always runs down hill. Our whole public and social life shows the working of this impulse, and our institutions outbid one another in catering to the taste of the public. The school alone has the power to develop the opposite tendency, to encourage and train the belief in duties and obligations, to inspire devotion to better things than those to which we are drawn by our lower instincts. Yes, water runs down hill all the time; and yet all the earth were sterile and dead if water could not ascend again to the clouds, and supply rain to the field which brings us the harvest. We see only the streams going down to the ocean; we do not see how the ocean sends up the waters to bless our fields. Just so do we see in the streams of life the human emotions following the impulses down to selfishness and pleasure and enjoyment, but we do not see how the human emotions ascend again to the ideals, — ascend in feelings of duty and enthusiasm; and yet without this upward movement our fields were dry, our harvest lost. That invisible work is the sacred mission of the school; it is the school that must raise man's mind from his likings to his belief in duties, from his instincts to his ideals, that art and science, national honor and morality, friendship and religion, may spring from the ground and blossom."

According to Dean Briggs of Harvard,[1] no people lay themselves more recklessly open to *reductio ad absurdum* than advocates of the elective system. They wish to put enjoyment into education, without being sure that such education is robust enough. He quotes the example of Dr. Martineau, who gave double time to the studies he disliked, in order to correct the weak side of his nature rather than to develop its strong side. Now it is not necessary to go to such length; studies need not be imposed *because* they are difficult and unpleasant, but if they are of real educational value they should be imposed *although* they are hard and unpleasant. Still, no branch is of any educational value, unless it presents difficulties; the mental powers are called into action and are trained only if they have to overcome obstacles.

Some pedagogists sneer at the idea that resistance, the overcoming of obstacles, plays an important part in education. Herein, however, they manifest their shortsightedness. The old adage, "Fast gotten, fast

---

[1] *Atlantic Monthly*, October 1900.

gone," might be expressed in somewhat different form: "Easily gotten, easily gone." Dr. Stanley Hall, President of Clark University, whose fame as an educator is widely acknowledged, has well said: "Only great, concentrated and prolonged efforts in one direction really train the mind, because they alone train the will beneath it." President Jones of Hobart College speaks to a like purpose: "The college must not always follow the line of least resistance. The intellectual life has also its athletic exercises, and mental slouchiness is no less to be regretted than physical insufficiency. The youthful will needs cultivation no less than the growing body."[1]

On the same head Mr. Townsend Austen wrote most appositely in the *North American Review* (May 1898). He severely censures those systems of education which attempt to remove as far as possible the obstacles from the course of study. He rightly maintains that the finest nature is the one out of which the dross has been squeezed by painful pressure, and the precious metal has been hammered and beaten into shape. The human being rarely works more than he has to. He appreciates by instinct an easy thing — what college students call a 'snap'. Some of the strongest points of our nature are best called out by resistance. This element in education should never be overlooked. To eliminate the element of difficulty from a study is an act of dishonesty; it deceives the student. The practice side of almost any study is not interesting, but is often rather tedious and must be so: for instance, to spell correctly, to write good English, to draw well, to reason clearly. — This repugnance

[1] *The Forum*, January 1901, p. 592.

constitutes one of the numerous forms of resistance offered to success in human endeavor; drudgery is the bridge to success. The honors of this life must be won, as the Germans say (and how well the progress of that nation illustrates it), *"mit saurem Schweiss,"* and by the application of another German proverb: *"Geduld bricht Eisen"* (patience breaks iron). In the development of character in the youth the wise instructor finds the application of this principle most useful and efficient. Will power is acquired. The acquisition of self-control, by which I mean not only the ability to control the passions, but also to compel the action of the mental powers upon a given subject, is aided. The German historian, von Ranke, has stated as a principle in human development, that "all progress is through conflict." The results become of value, because they have a value in work.[1]

Now this last principle was the favorite one of the founder of the Society of Jesus, which he used to inculcate on every occasion, quoting the words of Thomas a Kempis: *Tantum proficies, quantum tibi ipsi vim intuleris* — "The greater violence thou offerest to thyself, the greater progress thou wilt make." But the "make-it-easy" method — and such is the elective system as advocated by its foremost champions — is pernicious to the formation of the character.

Not less serious is the harm done to *instruction*, as distinguished from moral education. If the choice of subjects is left to the personal likings of the pupils, in many, if not in most cases, such branches will be chosen which seem to be the easiest, no matter what

---

[1] Peter Townsend Austen: "The Educational Value of Resistance," *North Am. Rev.*, May 1898.

their educational value is. No one who knows human nature will deny this. But that the subjects left to the choice of the students are not all equally capable of giving a thorough mental discipline, is quite evident; and the easier the subject, the less is, as a rule, its educational value.

There are several false assumptions in the contentions of the advocates of electivism. They state without hesitation that the first and foremost object of modern education is to develop the special aptitudes of the pupils, and they apply this not only to college but also to high school education. But this is a most serious mistake. The application of the pupil's talent to specialties belongs to the university and the professional school; but in the secondary schools, and even in the college, special aptitudes may and should be left to themselves. They will assert themselves when the occasion offers, and the wise teacher will be more solicitous to prevent them from warping the whole course of education than to promote their abnormal development.[1] Special aptitudes must be developed after the general education is completed.

The premature and excessive development of such special aptitudes will invariably result in products which have been called "lop-sided". It is Lowell who said: "I had rather the college turn out one of Aristotle's four-square men, capable of holding his own in whatever field he may be cast, than a score of lop-sided ones developed abnormally in one direction." The outcome of such education, or rather instruction, is a sort of mental deformity: one faculty is over-

[1] See Francis J. Barnes, M. D., *Catholic Education*. A Lecture delivered at Boston, April 28, 1901.

developed, while the others are suffering from atrophy. If the "special aptitude" of the student lies in the field of natural sciences or technics, he is liable to neglect altogether literature, history and philosophy, branches which are indispensable for the real culture of the mind. He becomes a narrow specialist, he swells the host of those men who even now afflict the community, men who are incapable of forming a sane opinion on any question which cannot be decided by a laboratory experiment. Such men have no perceptions of the relations and interrelations of the various branches of knowledge; they lack all appreciation of what is noble and sublime; above all they are most liable to ignore, or even to deny, that beyond the narrow limits of natural science lie truths of the utmost importance, unattainable by any process of synthetic reasoning. It is such warped specialists that Goethe ridicules in the famous passage in *Faust* (part 2, act 1):

> "Herein you learned men I recognize:
> What you touch not, miles distant from you lies;
> What you grasp not, is naught in sooth to you;
> What you count not, cannot you deem be true;
> What you weigh not, that hath for you no weight;
> What you coin not, you're sure is counterfeit."

There is always a danger that science leads to pride, particularly to that kind of pride which the Germans call *Gelehrtenstolz* and *Professorendünkel*. This danger is especially great in the case of specialists. Professor Paulsen quotes a passage from Kant, in which the philosopher of Königsberg speaks of "Cyclopses of science," who carry an immense weight of learning, a "load of a hundred camels," but who have only one eye, namely that of their own specialty.[1] They lack

[1] *Die deutschen Universitäten*, Berlin 1902, p. 219.

entirely the "philosophic eye," with which they see the relations of things to one another. Of such men Schopenhauer, in his wonted forcible but not over-polite manner, has said : "The man who, disregarding everything else, studies one branch, will in this branch be superior to the rabble (*vulgus*), but in all the rest he will belong to it. If to this specialization is added a thing which now-a-days becomes more and more common, namely, the neglect of the ancient languages, in consequence of which the general humanistic culture is dropped, then we shall see scientists who, outside their special branch, are real oxen." This danger can be obviated only by a solid general training. But the earlier the specialization begins, the greater shall be the temptation to disregard all other branches, and to despise all those who know little about this special subject, no matter how much they know in other branches. This is intellectual pride, as contemptible as it is ridiculous.

After having described some of the effects which must necessarily result from electivism, as defended by some, we now turn to a plain question, which has been well stated by Professor Münsterberg. "Are elective studies really elected at all? I mean, do they really represent the deeper desires and demands of the individual, or do they not simply express the cumulation of a hundred chance influences? I have intentionally lingered on the story of my shifting interests in my boyhood; it is more or less the story of every half-way intelligent boy or girl. A little bit of talent, a petty caprice favored by accident, a contagious craze or fad, a chance demand for something of which scarcely the outside is known,—all these whir and buzz in every boyhood; but to follow such superficial moods would mean dissolution of all organized life, and education would be an empty word. Election which is more than a chance grasping presupposes first of all acquaintance with the object of our choice. Even in the college two thirds of the elections are haphazard, controlled by accidental motives; election of courses demands a wide view and broad knowledge of the whole field. The lower the level on which the choice is made, the more external and misleading are the motives which direct it. A helter-skelter chase of the unknown is no election. If a man who does not know French goes into a restaurant where the bill of fare is given in the French language, and points to one and to another line, not knowing whether his order is fish, or roast, or pudding, the waiter will bring him a meal, but he cannot say that he has 'elected his course.' From whatever standpoint I view it, the tendency to base the school on elective studies seems to me a mistake, — a mistake for which, of course, not a special school, but the social consciousness is to be blamed."[1]

[1] *Atlantic Monthly*, May 1900, pp. 665–666. — To judge from numberless comments in newspapers and magazines, Prof. Münsterberg's article seems to have caused a great stir, as coming from one of the most prominent Professors of Harvard, the centre of the movement towards electivism. The New York *Nation*, on May 17, page 379, said as follows: "If Professor Münsterberg's article on 'School Reform' in the *Atlantic* cannot be answered effectively, something is radically wrong with our scheme of education." Various attempts were made to answer the Professor's indictments of the elective system, v. g. in the *Educational Review*, June and September 1900. But the answers were anything but effective. The *Nation* had said, "what we are most curious

The same truth has been expressed in very plain language by other American educators. We mention a few utterances of more recent date. President Draper, of the University of Illinois, declared recently: "Children are being told that they should elect their studies. They cannot elect."[1] Professor Peck of Columbia University, reviewing Father Brosnahan's answer to President Eliot's charges, speaks of the latter's "theories which have made Harvard into a curious jumble of college and university, and which President Eliot would like to see carried down into the schools, in the apparent belief that babes and sucklings have an intuitive and prophetic power of determining just what is going to be best for them in all their after life."[2] Mr. Tetlow, of Boston, calls the elective system "elective chaos, and philosophical anarchism," and he lays down these propositions: the students are not competent to direct their own studies; most of the parents are utterly incompetent to make an intelligent choice, too many will readily accept the choice made to know is what they think about it at Harvard." A Graduate Student wrote soon after from Harvard: "I wish to call attention to a result of the elective system which he [Prof. Münsterberg] has not mentioned, and which might even strengthen his argument—a result most disgraceful, yet most common, and whose truth cannot be ignored. I refer to the undisguised custom of electing 'snap courses,'—courses in which, for various reasons, good marks can be made without much work. For the desire for honors, and the fear of being thought a 'dig', are two very potent factors in determining a choice." (*Nation*, May 24, p. 396.) This statement is not at all surprising; it confirms what intelligent men had expected from such a system.

[1] *Educational Review*, May 1902, p. 455.
[2] *Bookman*, April 1900.

by the children; the principals and teachers are in most cases incompetent to make a wise choice for the pupils, as they are hardly ever sufficiently acquainted with the individual scholars.[1] Indeed, to make such a choice for the individual would require nothing less than "direct revelation from on high," as no man knows sufficiently the talent and possibilities that may lie dormant in the mind of a young student. If this system is the outcome of the much vaunted child study and pedagogical psychology, we have little reason to boast of this modern science. And we think those are amply justified who, against this "apotheosis of individual caprice," defend the old system which prescribes those branches that give a solid general training and thereby prepare the mind for taking up successfully any specialty in due time. The philosophical basis of this system is undoubtedly sound, whereas the elective system fully deserves the stigma of "philosophical anarchism".

We have purposely dwelt longer on the question of "electives," as a serious charge has recently been raised against the educational institutions of the Jesuits for not accepting the electivism of some modern reformers. After having quoted the opinions of leading educators on that subject, we may ask: Was

[1] *Educational Review*, January 1901. We may be excused for quoting the following lines from the same Review, May 1900, which not unaptly travesty the elective system:
    Most pupils, like good-natured cows,
    Keeping browsing and forever browse;
    If a fair flower come in their way,
    They take it too, nor ask, "what, pray?"
    Like other fodder it is food,
    And for the stomach quite as good.

that charge justified? — It is superfluous to ask, whether the Society will ever adopt that excessive electivism advocated by several educationists. The Society considers this system as destructive of thorough education.

As early as 1832 the General of the Order, in an encyclical letter on education addressed to his subjects, thus spoke of new inventions: "As to the methods, ever easier and easier, which are being excogitated, whatever convenience may be found in them, there is this grave inconvenience: *first*, that what is acquired without labor adheres but lightly to the mind, and what is summarily gathered is summarily forgotten; *secondly*, and this, though not adverted to by many, is a much more serious injury, almost the principal fruit of a boy's training is sacrificed, which is, accustoming himself from an early age to serious application of mind, and to that deliberate exertion which is required for hard work."[1] A comparison with former quotations shows an almost literal identity of these remarks with those of Prof. Münsterberg and other American educators. This agreement, in our humble opinion, is no discredit to either party. Before concluding this chapter, we repeat once more that the Jesuits are not absolutely opposed to the election of courses or branches. But they think with many other educators that the elective system could work well only with *many* limitations and safeguards. Such limitations are nothing else but prescriptions of certain branches.

[1] Hughes, *Loyola*, p. 291.

Chapter XII.

Classical Studies.

Much has been written within the last few decades for and against the value of the study of the classical languages and literature.[1] Some writers, especially fanatical advocates of "modern" culture, see in the humanistic school only a gloomy ruin of the time of the renaissance, which stands in the midst of the grand structures of modern culture, half monastery, half pagan temple. Latin and Greek philologists have built their nests in its dilapidated walls, like owls that shun the bright light of day, and in the dusk they flutter about to frighten and torment poor children with their cries of monstrous Latin and Greek forms. Others, the one-sided ad-

[1] There exists a vast literature on this subject. Of more recent publications we mention only those of a man whose opinions must be of special interest to American educators, viz. those of the United States Commissioner of Education, W. T. Harris: *A Brief for Latin — On the Function of the Study of Latin and Greek in Modern Education — Place of the Study of Latin and Greek in Modern Education*, and *Herbert Spencer and what to Study (Educational Review,* September 1902). In this last article Commissioner Harris very ably refutes Spencer's attacks on the study of the classics. — Of older works we wish to call attention to one of an American ecclesiastic, which is almost unknown: *Bishop England's Address on Classical Education (Bishop England's Works,* vol. V, pp. 13—31), in which the advantages of a classical education are set forth with admirable force and lucidity.

CLASSICAL STUDIES.

mirers of the "practical" studies, above all of the natural sciences, decry the classical studies as useless, because they do not teach the rising generation how to build bridges or war vessels, how to make aniline colors, or how to utilize best the oil fields of Texas, or the Western prairies. These men do not appreciate classical studies because, to use the words of Brownson, they cannot reduce them immediately to any corresponding value in United States currency. They would rather fill their pockets with Attic *oboli* and *drachmae* than their brains with Attic thought. In a word, to them education is only the wild race after the hen that lays the golden eggs. All other requirements they count for nothing. Such views are based on an utter misconception of the intellectual scope of education, and on sheer ignorance of the educational value of the classics. This point we endeavor to illustrate in the present chapter.

The Society of Jesus has always valued classical studies most highly. In the preface to his *Ratio Discendi et Docendi*, Father Jouvancy says: "Any one acquainted with the Society of Jesus knows how highly she always esteemed the classical studies." Of late the Society has even been censured for clinging tenaciously to them, as to a venerable, but now out-of-date, curriculum. Be it remarked from the very outset, that the Society upholds the classical curriculum not because this is the old traditional system, but because it has so far proved the best means of training the mind, which is the one great end of education. The various branches of studies are the means to this end. Should other means prove better than the classical languages, the Jesuits would not hesitate to accept them. They would teach, let us say French and German, instead of Latin and Greek.[1] They would not have to change their system, they would apply it only to the new branches. And the much lauded new method of teaching modern languages by practice and exercise, is essentially what the Ratio Studiorum has insisted on all along. However, the Jesuits are not so short-sighted as to claim for the classical studies the educational monopoly which these studies held in former ages. It cannot be denied that the so-called modern high school, which has a curriculum of English, some other modern languages, mathematics, and natural sciences, answers to particular needs of our age. It is especially fitted for those who want to devote only a few years to study after the completion of the elementary course. For this reason the Jesuits have opened in various countries such "modern high schools," v. g. the *Institut St. Ignace*, Antwerp. In some of these schools they employ for many branches secular professional teachers, for instance in the successful "army class" attached to the College at Wimbledon, England. Still they think that the best preparation for the professions and for all who wish to exert a far-reaching influence on their fellow-men, is the complete classical course, together with mathematics, history, and a certain amount of natural sciences. They think, and with much reason, that the classical studies even at present should form the backbone of liberal educa-

[1] As early as 1843 in the College of Freiburg, Switzerland, besides Latin and Greek, French, German, English, Italian, and Spanish were taught, some as obligatory, others as optional branches. Pachtler, vol. IV, pp. 546 ff.

tion. They think, with many other prominent educators, that the humanistic studies train the *man*, whereas the sciences train the *specialist*.

This is not the place to discuss fully the question of the value of the study of Latin and Greek for liberal education or general culture. Still, we cannot refrain from enumerating a few testimonies in their favor; and that they may be the more effective, we shall exclude those of professors of classical languages, who in this matter might be looked upon as prejudiced witnesses who speak *pro domo sua*. Many interesting statements were made some ten years ago by the ablest schoolmen of Germany in the famous Berlin Conference preparatory to the "New Plan of Studies" for the Higher Schools of Prussia, which was promulgated in 1892.[1] The relative educational value of the various branches was discussed most thoroughly, and it is surprising to find what professors of mathematics, natural sciences, and medicine have to say in favor of classical studies. Dr. Holzmüller, Director of a commercial and industrial school, said: "I am a mathematician and professor of mathematics, a thorough Realist, but I sound a warning against exaggerating the educational value of mathematics in higher schools. The range of thought and ideas in mathematical studies is narrow; whereas the linguistic studies have many more forms of thought at their disposal."[2] Professor Helmholtz of the University of Berlin, one of the leading scientists of the nineteenth century,

[1] See *Report of Commissioner of Education*, 1889—90, vol. I, pp. 343—398; and especially Schmid, *Geschichte der Erziehung*, vol. V, Abteilung I, pp. 357—422.

[2] Duhr, p. 89 foll.

said in the same conference: "The study of the ancient languages alone has so far proved to be the best means of imparting the best mental culture."[1] As a proof he gives his own experience in the physical laboratory of the Berlin University, where the students that had made the classical course, after one year's laboratory work surpassed those who had made the so-called science course (*Realschulen*), although the latter had studied much more natural science than the former. Professor Virchow, one of the greatest medical authorities, although strongly opposed to the then prevailing methods of the gymnasium, made a plea for the classical studies, saying that "the dropping of Latin would prove most dangerous and injurious to the medical profession." It is a well known fact that this famous pathologist, who died but a few months ago, was an enthusiastic student and admirer of Greek Literature. The verdict of these scholars was based on personal experience made at the University of Berlin some years before. In 1899, seven years after Latin had suffered a severe loss in consequence of the School Order of 1892, Professor Virchow bitterly complained in the German Parliament, that "grammar had been kicked out of the gymnasia, and with it logic."[2]

The graduates of the German schools which deal with practical subjects, and prepare students for commercial pursuits, or for entrance into polytechnic institutes, were at first debarred from entrance into the universities, being considered unqualified for university work; but in 1870 they were admitted, on equal terms with the graduates of classical schools, to

---
[1] Schmid, *l. c.*, p. 379.   (*Rep. of C. of Ed.*, *l. c.*, p. 372.)
[2] Schmid, *l. c.*, p. 443.

the philosophical department of the universities. After ten years trial of this plan the philosophical faculty of the University of Berlin addressed to the Ministry of Instruction a memorandum, which is declared to be the most powerful plea ever made in behalf of classical studies. They declared unhesitatingly that the students of the practical schools were not fitted to pursue a university course on a par with the graduates of the classical schools, and that, if the plan was reversed, German scholarship would soon be a thing of the past. Even the representatives of science and modern languages in the faculty joined heartily in this judgment. In specifying the reasons why the admission of the non-classical graduate was injurious to the interests of higher education, the thirty-six professors mentioned slower development, superficial knowledge, lack of independent judgment, inferiority in private research, less dexterity, want of keenness, and defective power of expression.

Since 1890 new and significant results were obtained in Germany, which prove that the classical course, besides the better liberal training which it imparts, is no less fitted as a preparation for technical studies than the courses pursued in the *Real-Gymnasium* and the *Oberrealschule*. This was attested in the last Berlin Conference (1900), by professors of the Technical Institutes. The Professors of the Technical Institutes, v. g. of Aix-la-Chapelle, adduced statistics to this effect from their respective schools.[1] Professor

[1] *Verhandlungen über Fragen des höheren Unterrichts*, 1902, pp. 10, 18. Be it said, however, that Professor Slaby of Charlottenburg maintained that the graduates of the Gymnasium in *his* school were not as successful in the sciences as those of the scientific schools. *Ibid.*, p. 378.

Launhart of the Technical Institute (*Hochschule*) of Hanover stated that, from 1890-99, 1209 candidates were examined; 583 from the humanistic gymnasium, 588 from the *Real-Gymnasium*, and 31 from the *Oberrealschule*. The results of the examinations proved that the different courses had been equally efficient in preparing pupils for the technical studies. Be it remembered that the humanistic gymnasium devotes less time to mathematics and natural sciences, studies specially required for the technical schools, than the other two kinds of schools. This result, therefore, speaks very well for the solid mental training of the classical schools.

Still more interesting are the statements of Dr. Vogt, who is professor of mathematics in parallel classes of the humanistic *Gymnasium* and the *Reform-Gymnasium* at Breslau. This position gives him an exceptional opportunity to compare the results of the two systems. In the lower classes of the Reform-School French is taught, in the humanistic gymnasium Latin. Professor Vogt and his colleagues made the following observations in the third class (*Quarta*): In 124 hours of the Reform-School they could not achieve more than in the 84 hours of the Latin course. Age, talent, and other conditions of the students were compared, and it was found that all in all the two classes were equal. Does it not necessarily follow from this fact that French does not afford the same mental training as Latin? Professor Vogt maintains in general, that the pupils of the gymnasium acquire less in mathematics than those of the *Real-Schulen*, if the *extent* of knowledge is considered, but that their knowledge of mathematics is more *intense*, more thorough. This he ascribes to the more intense and more thorough training that Latin affords.[1] In fact, this contention is amply proved by the above mentioned results obtained in the Technical Institutes.

The following testimony of a distinguished German writer, who had a large experience in this matter, may claim the attention of all educators. Dr. Karl Hildebrand writes: "If it were conceivable that a youth should entirely forget all the facts, pictures, and ideas he has learned from the classics, together with all the rules of Latin and Greek grammar, his mind would still, as an instrument, be superior to that of one who has not passed through the same training.[2] To give an example, I may state that in my quality of inspector it was my duty to visit a very large number of French *lycées* and *colleges*, each of which is usually connected with an *école speciale* or *professionelle*, and here I found that the classical pupils, without exception, acquired more English and German than the others, in less than a quarter of the time. (The time devoted to living languages was six hours a week for four years in the special, and only one hour and a half a week for three years in the classical schools.) The same fact struck me in my visits to the German,

---

[1] *Die Mathematik im Reform-Gymnasium. Neue Jahrbücher*, 1901, vol. VIII, pp. 190—218.

[2] The same idea is well expressed by Edw. Thring in his *Theory and Practice of Teaching:* "The trained mind is like a skilled workman with his tools, the mind merely stocked with knowledge is like a ready made furniture shop. The one needs but a small outlay to equip, and when equipped he can always produce the things he wants. The other is costly to provide, and when provided is good only for the exact articles it contains." *The Month*, February 1886.

Belgium, Dutch, and Swiss colleges. . . . A similar experience may be gathered from practical life. One of the first bankers in a foreign capital lately told me that in the course of a year he had given some thirty scholars — who had been educated expressly for commerce in commercial schools — a trial in his offices, and was not able to make use of a single one of them, while those who came from the grammar schools, although they knew nothing whatever of business matters to begin with, soon made themselves masters of them."[1]

The same evidence may be given for England. English papers, on the experience of leading English firms, combated the idea that a university degree was of no use to a man intended for business.[2] Mr. Bryce, no mean authority on this subject, concludes the article in which he advocates a special commercial training, with this significant remark: "This paper is not designed to argue on behalf of what is called a modern or non-classical education. I am not one of those who think that either the ancient languages, or what are called 'literary' or 'humanistic' subjects, play too large a part in our schools, either in England or in the United States. On the contrary, I believe (basing myself on such observations as I have been able to make) that Latin and Greek, when properly taught, are superior as instruments of education to any modern language, and that 'literary' subjects, as history, are on the whole more efficient stimulants to the mind (taking an average of minds) than mathematics or natural science."[3]

[1] *Contemporary Review*, August 1880.
[2] See *The Month*, Febr. 1886, pp. 170—176.
[3] *North American Review*, June 1899.

If Mr. Huntington, the late railroad king, disapproved of colleges, because their training unfitted the young men for practical life, and discounted their chances for becoming millionaires, the right answer seems to have been given by President Jones of Hobart College. "Boys who have followed science, mathematics, and literature to their best results, are not, upon graduation, anxious to be brokers' runners or bank clerks at five or ten dollars per week, and do not exhibit a dawdling inaccuracy, whatever their pursuits. The fresh graduate Mr. Huntington complained of has usually 'skinned through college,' and has been unsatisfactory there also."[1] He was one of the "students" who found football reports more enticing than the Latin and Greek classics; hence "their shortcomings and their commercial inefficiency are evidently not the results and handicaps of scholarship."

Here we must add that the popular argument against the classical studies is very superficial. We

[1] *The Forum*, Jan. 1901, p. 584. However, in the Report delivered at the Commencement of Yale 1902, President Hadley could quote the following words of a leading employer of railroad labor: "When I want a college man, I want a man who knows that it is hard work to use books that are worth anything; and, as a preparation for railroad service, I would rather have a man who has used one hard book without liking it — a Greek dictionary if you please — than a man who thinks he knows all the experimental science and all the shop work which any school can give him, and has enjoyed it because it is easy." The *Yale Alumni Weekly*, July 31, 1902, p. 433. — And the *Electrical World* said recently (October 25) in the article "The College and Business": "In our profession such doubts are settled once for all by the great electrical companies in demanding a college education in those who cast their lot with them for technical training."

hear it often said: Of what use are these studies? Men in after life mostly throw aside Latin and Greek; there are exceedingly few who after leaving school take a classical author into their hands. Let us grant it. But does it not follow, then, that the study of mathematics and natural sciences is equally useless except for those who become engineers or chemists? Or who, except a professional mathematician, ever in after life looks at logarithms, equations and the like? But there are many instances on record of men in prominent positions who with pleasure returned to the classics, which they had learned to cherish in college. We may quote one instance of a Jesuit pupil, whose name is indelibly engraved in the annals of American history, we refer to Charles Carroll, of Carrollton. Bishop England says of him: "I have known men who, during protracted lives, found in the cultivation of the classical literature that relaxation which improved, whilst it relieved the mind. The last survivor of those who pledged their lives and fortunes, and nobly redeemed their sacred honor in the achievement of our glorious inheritance of liberty, was a striking instance of this. When nearly fourscore years had passed away from the period of his closing the usual course of his classical education — after the perils of a revolution, after the vicissitudes of party strife, when the decay of his faculties warned him of the near approach of that hour when he should render an account of his deeds to that Judge who was to decide his fate for eternity, from his more serious occupations of prayer and self-examination, and from the important concern of managing and dividing his property, would Charles Carroll, of Carrollton, turn for refreshment to those classic authors with whom he had been familiar through life: — his soul would still feel emotion at the force of Tully's eloquence, or melt at Virgil's pastoral strain."[1]

This much is certain from what has been said so far, that the advocates of "practical" studies indulge in a grave delusion when they object to the classical studies. Their usefulness even for a commercial and political career is undeniable, as President Stryker of Hamilton College pointed out in 1901. He said, it should be remembered that the best preparation for a practical and useful life is in the high development of the powers of the mind, and that, commonly, by a culture that is not considered practical. The great parliamentary orators in the days of George III. were remarkable for the intellectual grasp and resource they displayed in the entire world of letters, in the classics, in ancient and modern history. Yet all of them owed their development to a strictly classical training in the schools. And most of them had not only the gift of imagination necessary to great eloquence, but also had so profited by the mental discipline of the classics, that they handled the practical questions upon which they legislated with clearness and decision. The great masters of finance were the classically trained orators, William Pitt and Charles James Fox. Such an education puts no premium upon haste, nor does it discount future power by an immature substitution of learning for training. It is structural towards the whole man, and seeks to issue him, not "besmeared, but bessemered." It considers the capable metal more

[1] *The Works of Bishop England*, vol. V, p. 85.

than the commercial false edge. Self-realization is the end.[1]

The testimonies given so far undoubtedly outweigh the contemptuous charges which sometimes are hurled against colleges and higher education, by a few "self-made" men, who boast of their ignorance and proudly point to the millions which they were able to amass without any liberal education. These men and some other worshippers of the 'golden calf' frequently ask: "Of what use is the study of the classics? What can I do with Greek?" We have heard that the study of the classics is of very great use, also for practical life, and the fact that a few have become rich without them, does in no way prove against their usefulness. But let us for a moment entirely abstract from the utilitarian point of view and rise to higher conceptions of life. Too much has the spirit of the market place invaded the field of education; and the interests of a liberal training have too often been sacrificed to an insatiate commercialism. Is the highest goal of intellectual and social life nothing but the rearing of a few millionaires? No, there must be a higher aim of education, for the nation as well as the individual. A nation that aims at nothing but industrial and commercial expansion, neglecting the higher ideals of mankind, may flourish for a time, but will not contribute much to real civilization. History has proved this. Take the Carthaginians; for a considerable length of time they held the commercial supremacy among the nations. Even intellect there was in the service of capital. The economical principles of a later and more advanced epoch are found by us in

[1] See *Buffalo Commercial*, June 29, 1901.

Carthage alone of all the more considerable states of antiquity.[1] But not this "nation of shop-keepers" has civilized the world, but poor Greece, whose culture, continued into the literature of Rome, together with the studies which it involves, has been the instrument of education, and the food of civilization, from the first times of the world down to this day.[2] May we not find a lesson in this fact? This country has made marvellous strides in industrial and commercial enterprise, but should it not aim at becoming a leader in the world of science, literature and art? In order to assume this leadership, the country must aim at thoroughness in education, and at solid, productive scholarship.[3] Now, so far the classical studies have proved the best basis of thorough education and solid scholarship, and doubtless will continue to do so in the future. The inference from this seems to be evident.

Fortunately, in this country, a reaction seems to have set in against the realistic tendency of our secondary schools, and people who have the real education of the nation at heart, are more and more converted to the conviction that the classical studies are most useful, if not necessary, for a liberal culture. It will be interesting to hear what the great journalist, Charles A. Dana, thought of the relation of classical studies to journalism. In a lecture delivered at Union College, Schenectady, N. Y., October 13, 1893, he said: "Give the young man (who is entering upon journalism) *a first class course of general education:* and if

[1] Mommsen, *History of Rome*, vol. II, ch. 1.
[2] Newman, *Idea of a University.*
[3] See Professor Münsterberg's article in the *Atlantic Monthly*, May 1901.

I could have my own way, every young man who is going to be a newspaper man, and who is not absolutely rebellious against it, should learn *Greek* and *Latin after the good old fashion*. I would rather take a young fellow who knows the *Ajax* of Sophocles, and who has read Tacitus, and who can scan every Ode of Horace — I would take him to report a prize-fight, or a spelling match, for instance, than to take one who has never had these advantages." [1]

Professor West of Princeton University stated in 1899 that a change of profound significance is taking place in our secondary schools.[2] This change is an improvement, but in reality it is a return to the 'old-fashioned' classical courses, and the writer aptly styles it a 'New Revival.' As one important cause of the change now in progress he assigns dissatisfaction with former school programmes of study. There were too many studies crowded into the programme. In other words, American opinion is moving steadily, and irresistibly, toward the sound elementary and elemental conviction that the best thing for the mass of pupils in secondary schools is a programme consisting of a few well-related studies of central importance, instead of a miscellany.

Is there sufficient evidence, then, that this tendency of things is becoming strongly marked among us? Is attention being more and more concentrated on a few well-related leading studies which have been important in the best modern education? Let us see. Take out all the secondary studies for which statistics are available from 1889-90 to 1897-98:

[1] *Buffalo Courier*, Oct. 16, 1893.
[2] *Educational Review*, 1899, October.

CLASSICAL STUDIES.

Studies.	Enrollment in '89-90.	Enrollment in '97-98.	Perc't'ge of Increase.
1. Latin	100,144	274,293	174
2. History (except U. S.)	82,909	209,034	152
3. Geometry	59,781	147,515	147
4. Algebra	127,397	306,755	141
5. German	34,208	78,994	131
6. French	28,032	58,165	107
7. Greek	12,689	24,994	94
8. Physics	63,644	113,650	79
9. Chemistry	28,665	47,448	65

The importance of the figures is the more evident when we bear in mind that the rate of increase in the total enrollment of pupils from 297,894 in 1889-90 to 554,814 in 1897-98 is 86 per cent. But certain studies are growing faster than this; some of them much faster. *Latin, to the surprise of many, heads the list with its literally enormous gain of 174 per cent., a rate fully double the 86 per cent. which represents the eight year increase in the total number of pupils.* Next comes history with 152 per cent., then the two mathematical disciplines (geometry with 147 and algebra with 141), and then German with 131. After these we find French with 107, and Greek with 94. All these and only these exceed the average. Physics and chemistry close the list somewhat below. Prominent educators all the world over hail this "new revival" as one of the most promising signs of the educational movement in America.

The foregoing pages contain sufficient proof that the Ratio Studiorum does not need any defence for giving such prominence to the study of the classical languages, especially to Latin. On the contrary, it speaks well for the educational wisdom of the Jesuits that for about a century, despite the sneers of many modern school reformers, they firmly upheld that method to which the more prudent educators steadfastly adhered, and to which others, after roaming about far and wide, now wish to return.

It may be asked why the study of the classical languages is the best means of intellectual training and universal culture. The reasons are manifold. The *first* is the very fact for which this study is frequently attacked, namely, that these languages are *dead* languages. "They are not the language of common life. They are not picked up by instinct and without reflection. Everything has to be learned by system, rule, and formula. The relations of grammar and logic must be attended to with deliberation. Thought and judgment are constantly exercised in assigning the exact equivalents of the mother tongue for every phrase of the original. The coincidence of construction is too little, the community of idiomatic thought too remote, for the boy's mind to catch at the idea, by force of that preestablished harmony which exists among most modern tongues. Only the law of thought and logic guides him, with the assistance of a teacher to lead the way, and reassure his struggling conception."[1]

This, then, is the first point of the study of the classical languages: *logical training*, training that leads to correct and clear thinking, to close and sharp reasoning.[2] The study of Latin is better adapted to

[1] Hughes, *Loyola*, p. 251.
[2] See above, pp. 333—339.

accomplish this effect than any other language; for, whereas Greek is more delicately organized, more beautiful and poetic, the Latin is perhaps the more systemically elaborated tongue. In its severe syntax it participates in some of the striking qualities of the Roman character, which seems to have been fitted to legislate, to govern, and to command, as the great poet has it:

> "O Rome, 'tis thine alone with awful sway
> To rule mankind and make the world obey."[3]

The study of Latin requires such application of various rules and laws that it forces the student to the closest attention, to rigorous mental discipline. The processes of reasoning which are, at least implicitly, to be gone through, in translating an English sentence into Latin, are ample proof of this statement. Suppose a pupil has to render the following sentence into correct Latin: "As soon as you arrive at Philadelphia, give him the letter, to prevent him from going to New York." He will probably start: *As soon as: ubi primum; arrive* is *pervenire*, or *advenire*. Now what tense? *Ubi primum*, together with *postquam*, etc., is construed with the Perfect Indicative. But wait, does it always take the Perfect? No, only when a single past fact is related; is this the case here? That depends on the tense of the verb in the principal clause: it is *give*. What tense? It is properly the present tense, but has reference to the future. Therefore, the whole clause does not express a past but a future fact. In English *arrive* is present tense, but in Latin the use of tenses is much more accurate; if the action of principal and dependent clauses are both

[3] Virgil's *Aeneid*, VI.

future, they must be expressed by a future tense. Now *arrive* has a future meaning; therefore a future tense. But which of the two? First or second? That depends on the nature of the action; if the verb of the dependent clause denotes an action antecedent to that of the principal clause, it must be put in the tense which denotes antecedence. Now, let us see: the *arriving* at Philadelphia necessarily antecedes the *giving* of the letter; consequently I have to use the second future, the *futurum exactum: ubi primum — venio,* Perfect *veni* — well: *perveneris.* At *Philadelphia; at* is *in;* however, names of cities are construed without a preposition, they are used in the *locativus,* which in singular nouns of the 1st and 2nd declensions is like the Genitive case, therefore *Philadelphiae.* But is there not a rule about *advenire, pervenire, congregari,* etc.? They mean *going towards, into,* therefore I must use the construction answering the question: *whither,* therefore *Philadelphiam.* Very well. Now: *give him the letter; give: trade, da; him: eum,* but stop — *eum* is direct object, while in the given sentence *him* is indirect, so it must be *ei, trade ei epistolam.*—*To prevent,* is the infinitive, here it expresses a purpose. Clauses denoting purpose are not expressed by the infinitive in Latin prose, but by *ut, causa* with the gen. of the Gerund, or *ad* with the accusative, etc.; take *ut:* but attend to the sequence of tenses! — *impedias eum;* from going: *a proficiscendo?* No! but: *quominus* or *ne proficiscatur.* To New York — *Neo - Eboraco?* — Very often pupils use the Dative, not having been instructed from the beginning about the difference of *to,* meaning *towards, into,* and *to,* meaning *for the benefit, in the interest of;* here *Neo-Eboracum.* Now the sentence is complete : *Ubi primum Philadelphiam adveneris, epistolam ei trade ut impedias eum, quominus Neo-Eboracum proficiscatur.*

Is it not surprising how much intellectual labor is spent, and well spent, in translating that little sentence?[1] How many syllogisms were formed, or are at least implied? Père Fabri, a French Jesuit teacher, wrote in 1669: "Besides literary accomplishments gained from the study of the classical languages there are other advantages to be derived, especially an exquisite power and facility of reasoning. For in the writing of verses, in the examination of words and contents, a constant analysis and combination is required which helps the mind wonderfully to sound reasoning."[2] Indeed, the study of these languages is a course of applied logic. Immanent logic has been called the characteristic of the Latin language and its grammar.[3] "Latin grammar," says Dr. Karl Hildebrand, "is a course of logic presented in an almost tangible form. Let us only remember how an idea so abstract as that of subject and object is rendered palpable by the *s* and *m*." We said, the labor was well spent. For, a student who has thus been trained will acquire the habit of clear thinking. When a doctor, he will in a given case reason similarly, though not in that cumbrous form, but pass in a moment, unconsciously, because from habit, through various syllogisms, and examine whether this or that remedy will have the desired effect. A patient should natur-

---

[1] Professor Bennett, in his *Teaching Latin in the Secondary School*, pp. 12—22, points out the mental processes to be gone through in translating from the Latin into English.

[2] *Euphyander*, p. 157; Chossat, *l. c.*, 295.

[3] Willmann, *Didaktik*, vol. II, 115.

ally have much more confidence in such a doctor, than in one who has not had the advantage of the same logical training. The results will be similar in the case of a lawyer, a politician, a business man, a writer. The father in the fable told his sons that there was a treasure hidden in his vineyard. They began to dig the vineyard once, twice, and oftener, in the hope of finding the treasure. No chests of gold, no bags filled with good coin, appeared; but in the following year the vineyard yielded immeasurably more than ever before. Here was the treasure the wise father meant them to seek after. The same holds good in education. The man in later life may never again use his Latin or Greek, still the study of these languages has turned up the soil in the field of his intellect, fertilized it, and if now it yields a rich harvest, the result is to a great extent due to that patient digging, although he himself may not, and in most cases does not, realize to what source his success in life is to be ascribed.

But the logical training acquired by translating from or into the ancient languages, although a most important result, is by no means the only benefit of the study of those languages. There is, besides this formal side, the *historical*. The Latin and Greek literatures present to us at first hand all the great masterpieces of antiquity, which have inspired directly or indirectly most of what is really great and noble in modern literature. Most deservedly, therefore, have the classical studies been styled the ABC of all higher studies.[1] Latin especially is, as Professor Paulsen styles it, "the gate to the great historical world. No

[1] *Verhandlungen.* (*Transactions of the Berlin Conference 1890.*) See Duhr, p. 91.

one who wishes to move in wider circles of historical life can do without Latin." For similar reasons Director Jäger maintained the necessity of classical lore for the man who wishes to possess a title to real scientific preparation for higher studies. In the last Berlin Conference on higher education, 1900, there was probably no point so strongly insisted on as the necessity of Latin for all men who lay any claim to culture. Professor Harnack claimed that the humanistic training seemed to him especially necessary for all who had any great influence on their fellow-men and on the social and political life of a nation.[1] Arnold had expressed a similar opinion when he said: "Expel Greek and Latin from your schools, and you confine the views of the existing generation to themselves and their immediate predecessors, you will cut off so many centuries of the world's experience, and place us in the same state as if the human race had first come into existence in the year 1500."[2]

There is, in the *third* place, what we may call the *literary* and *aesthetic* momentum. When through means of grammatical studies the pupil is sufficiently prepared, he begins to read the greatest masterpieces of literature. Gradually he becomes intimately acquainted with some of the maturest minds of all ages, provided the teaching is carried on in the proper form, i. e. if the authors are read not to furnish merely material for grammatical drill, but in such a manner that the contents of the authors form the central part of the whole instruction, that the author begins to live, that the persons seem to act and speak before the

[1] *Verhandlungen*, 1900, p. 17.
[2] Fitch, *Thomas and Matthew Arnold*, p. 85.

eye of the student. He is thus introduced to one great author after another. First comes Caesar, whose plain but vigorous style is the true image of the great Roman general and statesman, who changed the greatest of republics into an Empire. Then appears Xenophon with his lifelike descriptions; Livy with his eloquent history of Rome, full of ardent patriotism; then Cicero, the most gifted and versatile of all the Romans, with his brilliant style, his sparkling wit, his cutting irony and stern denunciation of corruption. Then the student admires Ovid's elegant verses, Virgil's grand and stately lines, Horace's refined and tasteful stanzas. Then rises before him the great philosopher Plato, who portrays in fascinating dialogues the wise man of heathen antiquity, Socrates. If properly taught, but then only, the student is sure, after the struggle of a few months, to form an intimate friendship with the 'Father of Poetry', immortal Homer. He will soon realize the greatness of the blind old man, who lived in the mouths of a hundred generations and a thousand tribes; who, as Cardinal Newman says, "may be called the first apostle of civilization;" whose Odyssey and Iliad formed a source of purest enjoyment to many of the greatest men of history: to Alexander the Great, Napoleon, Newman, Gladstone, and countless others. We could continue and mention the powerful harangues of the prince of orators, Demosthenes, the grand and soul-stirring tragedies of Aeschylus and Sophocles. But we have enumerated enough to show what wealth and variety of intellectual food is placed before the classical student in the course of a few years. By these studies his aesthetical sense is developed, he acquires imperceptibly that precious gift, which we call taste.

Sometimes we hear it said that a good *translation* of these Greek authors would give us all the advantages we may derive from the study of the original. Any one acquainted with classical literature knows what to think of this assertion. Translations are, at the best, what the reproduction of a grammophone is compared to the original concert or solo. Father Jouvancy has well observed: "Translations of Greek authors, even if they are accurate, seldom render the force, beauty, and other striking qualities of the original. It is always better to draw drinking water from the source; the further it runs from the source, the more it is contaminated, and the more it loses its original taste."[1]

This opinion is confirmed by the judgment of many modern writers. Thus Sterne says: "The most excellent profane authors, whether Greek or Latin, lose most of their graces whenever we find them literally translated. In the classical authors, the expressions, the sweetness of numbers, occasioned by a musical placing of words, constitute a great part of their beauties."[2] Mr. Genung, Professor of Rhetoric in Amherst College, speaks thus of the "Untranslatable" in literature: "In all the higher achievements of literature there must necessarily remain a great deal that, in spite of the utmost skill, cannot be adequately reproduced in another language. The thought may indeed survive, though marred and mutilated, but the subtle spiritual aroma, the emotional essence perishes in the transmission. This is preeminently true of

[1] *Ratio Discendi*, ch. I, art. I.
[2] Quoted by Cardinal Newman in his *Idea of a University*, p. 271.

poetry. George Henry Lewes, in his *Life of Goethe*, says: 'In its happiest efforts, translation is but approximation; and its efforts are not often happy. A translation may be good *as* translation, but it cannot be an adequate reproduction of the original.'"[1] To single out one instance: there exist numerous translations of Homer's Iliad and Odyssey, in prose and verse. And yet, any one familiar with the most important poetical monument existing[2] can trace but few remains of the graces which charmed him in the original. Cowper and Wright have failed in rendering Homer's rapidity; Pope and Sotheby have failed in rendering his plainness and directness of style and diction; Chapman has failed in rendering his plainness and directness of ideas; and for want of appreciating Homer's nobleness, Newman has failed more conspicuously than any of his predecessors. Some passages of Pope's translation exhibit the translator's prodigious talent. But as Bentley said: "You must not call it Homer." Chapman's translation is praised by Coleridge, who, however, is forced to add: "It will give you a small idea of Homer." Dr. Maginn's Homeric Ballads are vigorous poems in their own way, but as a Homeric translation very often nothing more than a travesty.[3] Similar objections may be raised against any of the other translations of classical poems.

A fourth advantage which the classical studies possess over mathematics and natural sciences, consists in the moral or ethical element, in the many examples they present of the natural virtues, examples

---

[1] *Practical Elements of Rhetoric*, p. 320.
[2] Matthew Arnold: *On Translating Homer*.
[3] Arnold, *l. c.*

of heroic patriotism, of filial devotion, and dutifulness. The example of Socrates, dying in obedience to what he considers the voice of God, of chaste Penelope, of faithful Eumaeus, and of many other characters depicted so vividly and graphically with the inimitable simplicity and skill of the ancient writers, cannot fail to produce an elevating, ennobling and purifying effect on the hearts of the young; these examples show us that the sense of moral beauty was left in mankind even in the midst of the darkness and corruption of paganism. What have the other branches of study, mathematics and natural sciences, to offer that could be compared to this? Mathematics is an excellent means of developing logical thinking, but there its efficiency stops, it has, as professors of mathematics have said, "a narrow range of thoughts and ideas." It certainly does not inspire, does not elevate. Or whose heart has ever become warmed or ennobled by fully grasping the Pythagorean system, or by developing $(a+b)^3$ or any other algebraic formula? Whose aesthetic or moral sense has been refined by analyzing $FeS + H_2SO_4 = FeSO_4 + H_2S$, or other chemical equations? Mathematics and natural sciences are justly called by the Germans *Realfächer;* they impart practical, useful knowledge, but not ideal, not liberal culture. Newman has well expressed this difference: "When an idea, whether it is real or not, is of a nature to interest and possess the mind, it is said to have life, that is, to live in the mind which is the recipient of it. Thus mathematical ideas, real as they are, cannot be called living, for they have no influence and lead to nothing."[1] The same applies

---

[1] Newman, *Development of Christian Doctrine*, ch. 1.

more or less to the natural sciences, whereas the very opposite holds good of the study of literature and history.

In the *fifth* place' we mention the gain classical studies yield to the *mother-tongue*. This is very important for a thorough and scholarly understanding of the English language, as two thirds or more of the English vocabulary are words derived from Latin. But the principal gain in knowledge of the mother-tongue is derived from careful, idiomatic translations into the vernacular. If translations are made regularly and accurately, there is little need of giving special instructions on English grammar and style. In the Berlin Conference of 1890 some of the leading men, among them Professor Helmholtz, emphasized this point, saying that "good and idiomatic translations are an instruction in the German language, which cannot be appreciated highly enough."[1] The great Prussian schoolman Dr. Wiese had long before expressed himself to the same effect, referring to the example of Dr. Arnold of Rugby, who saw in good translation the best preparation for writing excellent English. "Whenever it is attended to," says Dr. Arnold, "it [translation] is an exercise of exceeding value; it is in fact one of the best modes of instruction in English composition, because the constant comparison with the different idioms of the languages, from which you are translating, shows you in the most lively manner the peculiar excellence and defects of your own."[2] In another passage he writes: "Every lesson in Latin and Greek may, or ought to be made

[1] *Transactions;* see Duhr, p. 117.
[2] Stanley, *Life of Arnold,* vol. II, p. 112; and Fitch, *Thomas and Matthew Arnold,* p. 44.

a lesson in English; the translation of every sentence in Demosthenes or Tacitus is properly an exercise in extemporaneous English composition; a problem how to express with equal brevity, clearness and force in our own language the thought which the original author has so admirably expressed in his." "The practice of translating," says James Russell Lowell, "by making us deliberate in the choice of the best equivalent of the foreign word in our own language, has likewise the advantage of schooling us in one of the main elements of a good style — precision."[1] "The old theory is now reviving *that the teaching of English in the modern fashion is of little value*, and that the old method of teaching Latin grammar, and allowing English to take care of itself, is really sounder and more practical."[2]

Similar are the words of a prominent schoolman of this country, Mr. Nightingale, Superintendent of High Schools, Chicago. In the *Report of the Conference on English*, read before the National Association of Education at Ashbury Park, N. J., 1894, he says: "I would have children at the age of ten or eleven years commence the study of that language which in the fields of persuasion and philosophy, of literature and law, is so largely the progenitor of the English — the incomparable Latin. If we would be strong we must contend with something — resist something — conquer something. We cannot gain muscle on a bed of eiderdown. Toying with straws will only enervate

---

[1] *Democracy and Other Addresses*, p. 126; quoted by Genung, *Practical Elements of Rhetoric*, p. 320.

[2] Professor Mahaffy, *Irish Endowed School Commission Report*, p. 244.

the faculties. The blacksmith's arm becomes mighty through his ponderous strokes of the hammer on the anvil. The very facility of the acquisition of the modern languages precludes the possibility of discipline. Put Latin into our common schools, and the puzzling problem of English Grammar will be nearing its solution, for the *why* that meets the pupil at every step, the very laboriousness and difficulty of the task, will open the intellect, develop the powers of discrimination and adaptation, enlarge the vocabulary, enable the student to write a better English essay, use a more terse and trenchant style of speech, and grasp with more avidity and keenness any promulgated form of thought, than if he should spend quintuple the time on the study of the English Grammar alone."

Is it not significant that nearly all the great English writers and orators were ardent admirers and students of the classical languages? A Pope, a Dryden, an Addison, a Milton, a Burke, a Pitt, a Tennyson and a Newman, and others? The younger Pitt gives a student the following advice: "The practice of rendering the Greek and Roman classics into English, and of committing to memory the most eloquent passages which occur in reading, is the best exercise in which the young student can engage. It imparts a command of language, aids him in acquiring a forcible style, affords the best mental discipline, strengthens the memory, cultivates his taste, invigorates his intellect, and gives him a relish for the sublime and beautiful in writing." Further, the whole of English literature is so saturated with classical allusions, that without a fair knowledge of the more important works of Greek and Roman writers, it is impossible to appreciate fully, or even to understand the finest productions of English literature. This being the case, we have another proof that our modern pedagogists, by exaggerating the claims of the natural sciences beyond all reasonable bounds, are doing great harm to literature and liberal culture.

Having reviewed the various advantages which the study of the classics affords, we may well say with one of the greatest minds of the nineteenth century: Modern methods and sciences, and "their inestimable services in the interest of our material well-being, have dazzled the imaginations of men, and since they do wonders in their own province, it is not unfrequently supposed that they can do as much in any other province also. But to advance the useful arts is one thing, and to cultivate the mind another. The simple question to be considered is how best to strengthen, refine, and enrich the intellectual powers; the perusal of the poets, historians and philosophers of Greece and Rome will accomplish this purpose, as long experience has shown; but that the study of experimental sciences will do the like, is proved to us as yet by no experience whatever. Far indeed am I from denying the extreme attractiveness, as well as the practical benefit to the world at large, of the sciences of chemistry, electricity, and geology; but the question is not what department of study contains the more wonderful facts, or promises the more brilliant discoveries, and which is in the higher and which is in the inferior rank; but simply which out of all provides the most robust and invigorating discipline for the unformed mind. . . . Whatever be the splendors of the modern philosophy, the marvellousness of its disclosures, the utility of its acquisitions, and the talents of its masters, still it will not avail in the event, to detrude classical literature and the studies connected with it from the place which they have held in all ages in education."[1] Goethe, realizing what debt he himself owed to the classics, exclaimed: "Would that the study of Greek and Roman literature forever remained the basis of higher education."[2]

These are the reasons why the Society of Jesus always gave such prominence to classical studies. She considers them to be among the "few well-related studies of central importance;"[3] to them she would apply the words of Dr. Stanley Hall, quoted before: "Only great, concentrated and prolonged efforts in one direction really train the mind." The mind can never be trained by that miscellany of studies crowded into the programme of our modern systems. Their effects on youth were ably pointed out seventy years ago by the General of the Society, Father Roothaan.[4] "In the lower schools [he means grammar schools and colleges], the object kept in view is to have boys learn as many things as possible, and learn them in the shortest time and with the least exertion possible. Excellent! But that variety of so many things and so many courses, all barely tasted by youth, enables them to conceive a high opinion of how much they know, and sometimes swells the crowd of the half instructed, the most pernicious of all classes to the sciences and the State alike. As to knowing anything

---

[1] Cardinal Newman, *Idea of a University*, p. 263.
[2] *Sprüche in Prosa.*
[3] See page 344.
[4] Letter of 1832. Hughes, *Loyola*, p. 290.

truly and solidly, there is none of it. *Ex omnibus aliquid, in toto nihil:* Something of everything, nothing in the end. In the method of conducting the lower studies, some accessory branches should have time provided for them, especially the vernacular tongues and literatures. But the study of Latin and Greek must always remain intact and be the chief object of attention. As they have always been the principal sources of exhibiting the most perfect models of literary beauty in precept and style, so are they still."

Here it is necessary to meet some objections to the Jesuit system. It is said that, however much the Jesuits insisted on the classical studies, they directed them to a wrong end. They aimed only at "formation of style." "To write in Latin is the ideal they propose to their pupils... They direct the pupil's attention, not to the thoughts, but to the elegancies of language, to the elocutionary effort; in a word, to the form." Thus M. Compayré.[1] Mr. Painter tells us even that the Jesuits' "plan" says: "The study of classic authors can have for us only a secondary end, namely, to form the style, we wish nothing else. Style will be formed essentially after Cicero."[2] What answer can be given to this serious charge? The answer is a very simple one: the first sentence of Mr. Painter's quotation is untrue. That statement of his is nowhere contained in the whole Ratio, neither literally nor equivalently.[3] The Ratio and its commentator Jou-

[1] *History of Pedagogy*, p. 144.
[2] *History of Education*, p. 169.
[3] I do not wish to imply that Mr. Painter has consciously committed this blunder. I suspect it is based on an entirely false translation of the first Rule for the Professor of Rhetoric, which says that Latin style should be modeled chiefly after Cicero.

vancy state expressly that *various* things are to be considered in these studies: knowledge of language, of grammar, of syntax, precepts of rhetoric, style, and varied erudition.[1] Jouvancy, in the *schemata* for explaining the authors, has five or six points, the first is always the interpretation of the meaning, the *contents*, the linguistic and logical explanation; then rhetorical or poetical precepts, then general erudition, and lastly Latinity.[2] This proves how untrustworthy are the quotations of Mr. Painter and of other critics of the Ratio. The perusal of the commentary of Jouvancy refutes also in general the charge of "mere formalism." However, if by "formal" is meant the general linguistic training,[3] the Society has always laid great stress on it. Many scholars begin to deplore the fact that this "formal" training is being neglected too much in the new schools. "The great linguistic and logical training which results from solid and properly conducted instruction in grammar, especially in another language, particularly in Latin and Greek, has of late been undervalued — the *nemesis* for it has come already."[4]

It is true that in the sixteenth and seventeenth centuries the Jesuits did not enter as fully into the explanation of the contents as is demanded at present. But who can blame them for this? It is true also that

[1] See below chapter XVI, also *Reg. Prof. Rhet. I.* — *Reg. Hum. I.*, etc.
[2] *Ratio Docendi*, ch. II, art. 4. See below ch. XVI, § 1.
[3] This is the meaning of the term "formal" in many letters of the Generals, as in that of Father Beckx quoted by M. Compayré, page 145, where this author misinterprets the phrase "pure form".
[4] Dr. Hirzel, in *Neue Jahrbücher*, 1902, vol. X, p. 53.

they insisted very much on speaking and writing Latin, much more than is advisable in our days. But so did the Protestant schools.[1] For this mastery of Latin was at that time of foremost practical importance, as Latin was the universal language of Western Christendom, the language of law and science, and the necessary organ of international intercourse. As it was necessary, therefore, to teach Latin in such a manner as to enable the pupils to write it, the Jesuits endeavored to do this as well as possible; hence they insisted much on a good Latin style, and imitated most of all that of Cicero, a choice which only some radical critics of the school of Mommsen can condemn. If even at present the writing and speaking of Latin is one of the exercises in the Jesuit schools, it is not for the same practical purpose as formerly, but these exercises are directed towards the logical training of the mind. Besides, much less time is devoted to these exercises now than heretofore. — That the writing and speaking of Latin was never the only object of teaching this language, is proved from the manner in which the authors were explained; it is also sufficiently clear from the fact that Greek was always taught in the Jesuit schools, certainly not for the practical purpose of speaking it, but for purposes of general training. One of these purposes was to acquaint the pupils with the classical writers, with their thoughts and ideas.

But here M. Compayré has discovered another defect in the Jesuit system. "It is to be noted, besides, that the Jesuits put scarcely more into the hands of their pupils than select extracts, expurgated editions.

[1] See Paulsen, *Gesch. des gel. Unt.*, vol. I, p. 352 and *passim*.

They wish in some sort to efface from the ancient books whatever marks the epoch and characterizes the time. They detach fine passages of eloquence and beautiful extracts of poetry, but they are afraid, it seems, of the authors themselves; they fear lest the pupils find in them the old human spirit—the spirit of nature."[1] There are several fallacies in this assertion. First of all the terms "select extracts" and "expurgated editions" apparently are used by M. Compayré as synonymous; but this is not correct. An expurgated edition, v. g. of the Iliad, the Odyssey, the Aeneid, gives the whole work with the omission of but a few objectionable passages. Such editions are certainly not to be called select extracts from these authors. The Jesuits used to read select extracts from some authors, whose works are of such a character as to make it impossible to read them entire, as Juvenal, Tibullus, Catullus, etc. But they read the great works, the Odyssey, the Iliad, the Aeneid, some of Plato's Dialogues, the works of Cicero, etc., in expurgated editions in which only a few indecent passages were left out. These editions did not efface what characterized the time, or marked the spirit of the authors. On the contrary, it would have been directly against the principles of the Jesuits to suppress all this. For, whereas the Protestant Reformers and the Jansenists taught that man, unaided by grace, was utterly corrupt and unable to do anything good, that the seeming virtues of the pagans, of a Socrates and others, were but gilded vices, the Jesuits always maintained firmly that fallen man remained capable of performing some good works. The Jesuits were more

[1] *History of Pedagogy*, p. 144.

than once styled Pelagians or Semipelagians, because, as their adversaries said, they extolled human nature too much. The Jesuits could, consistently with their philosophical and theological doctrine, propose to their pupils the example of the natural virtues of the pagans.

On the other hand, they were most anxious to show the immense superiority of the religion of Christ to the philosophical systems of the ancients; they pointed out the helplessness of Greek philosophy to raise man above the baser elements of nature, and they showed into what an abyss of corruption the human race, left to itself, had fallen. All this instruction they could impart only if they left in the authors what was characteristic of their time and spirit, except such passages as on account of their obscenity were not fit to be read by youths. Here we have the meaning of the saying frequently used by Jesuit educators: "So interpret pagan authors as to make of them heralds of Christ." The religious and moral principles of the ancients were to be judged by the standard of Christian principles; what manifested the human spirit in its divine likeness, the testimony of the *Anima naturaliter Christiana*, as Tertullian says so beautifully, was approved and recommended; what exhibited that spirit of nature which is "the enemy of Christ," was condemned. If M. Compayré reprehends the Jesuits for doing this, they must be proud of such reproach; for it is a contumely suffered for defending the teaching of Christ against the doctrine of rank naturalism.

The Jesuits were never afraid of the ancient authors themselves. History has proved this. If they had been afraid, they would have introduced the Christian Latin and Greek authors instead of the pagan classics.

As they possessed almost an educational monopoly in Catholic countries for about two centuries, it is certain that they would have succeeded, had they attempted such a change. But they never attempted this change; on the contrary, they strongly opposed such attempts. It suffices to allude to the famous controversy carried on with so much vigor by Abbé Gaume in France, about fifty years ago. This zealous scholar maintained that the pagan classics infected the schools with pagan ideas; indeed, he saw in their use in the schools the "fatal cancer which preys upon the vitals of Christianity."[1] Christian Latin and Greek authors should, therefore, be substituted for the pagan classics. Many distinguished Catholic scholars and writers, such as Montalembert, Louis Veuillot, Donoso Cortes and others sided with Abbé Gaume. Among those who most strenuously defended the classics were the Jesuits, foremost among them Father Daniel. In a most elegant and learned book[2] this Jesuit proved overwhelmingly that, from the earliest centuries, the majority of the great Doctors of the Christian Church were not opposed to the classics, on the contrary that most of them favored their study, and that the severe language of a few Fathers is directed not against the classics as such, but against the idolatry and obscenity contained in many of them.[3]

[1] Gaume, *Paganism in Education*, translated by Robert Hill, Loudon, Dolman, 1852.

[2] Charles Daniel, S. J., *Des études classiques dans la société chrétienne.* Paris 1853.

[3] On this subject see two interesting articles in the *Dublin Review:* "The French Controversy on the Use of Pagan Literature in Education," vol. XXXIII, Dec. 1852, pp. 321—336; and "The Gaume Controversy on Classical Studies," vol. VII (new series), 1866, pp. 200—228.

There was, as far as I can ascertain, only one Jesuit writer who ranged himself prominently on the side of Abbé Gaume in this controversy.[1] The Jesuits, as a body, "the greatest of all educational communities," as a writer at the time called them,[2] stood up for the defence of the classics. They did not deny that the classics contained dangerous elements, which could work evil in men of bad hearts, or weak heads. But they thought that it was the vicious organization of the individual, or a pernicious system of teaching, as that of many humanists, that extracted the poison from the classics and rejected the sound aliment of intellectual food contained in the ancient literature. This danger cannot exist for all, and it can be effectively remedied by wise teaching. As the afore-mentioned writer declared, "put education into proper hands, and the greatest step [towards obviating

[1] *La Natura e la Grazia*, Rome 1865. — The fact that this Jesuit publicly opposed the views held generally by his fellow-religious, may furnish material for an important reflection. It is so often asserted that the Jesuits have to follow, like humble sheep, a certain system or set of opinions prescribed for them, and that any utterance of individual views is practically excluded. The whole history of the Order proves the contrary. Even in theological opinions, as Cardinal Newman said, the Order is not over-zealous about its traditions, or it would not suffer its great writers to be engaged in animated controversies with one another. (*Historical Sketches*, vol. II, p. 369.) We shall have more to say on this subject in chapter XV, when we treat of the training of the Jesuit teacher. Whenever the Jesuits as a body defend certain opinions, they do so on the *intrinsic* strength of the arguments for these opinions, not for the *extrinsic* reason of a tradition of their Order.

[2] *Dublin Review*, December 1852, p. 322.

possible evils] is achieved. The present position of the Jesuits in France is for us a more hopeful sign than would be the introduction of the very system called for by Abbé Gaume."[1]

In 1894 M. Jules Lemaître renewed the attacks on the classics, directing his accusations especially against the Jesuit schools. "I find," he writes, "in the pagan authors read in schools voluptuous naturalism, Epicurean principles, or that Stoicism which is not virtue but pride. The consequences of this anomalous state of affairs are incalculable. We cannot wonder that the Jesuit colleges have produced so many pagans and freethinkers, among them Voltaire."[2] Now this is very amusing. This writer accuses the Jesuits of fostering a heathen, free-thinking spirit, by means of teaching the classics; and M. Compayré charges them with suppressing the characteristic spirit of the classical writers. This is one of the numberless contradictions into which the opponents of the Society have been betrayed. If the classics were taught in the spirit of M. Compayré, there is little doubt that, as Abbé Gaume and M. Lemaître apprehended, freethinkers would be produced. But the Jesuits teach them in quite a different spirit. Hence the charges of these writers are wide of the mark. Nor did the Jesuits give mere anonymous fragments, mere travesties of the classics, as M. Compayré claims. They expunged obscene passages from their editions, as conscientious non-Catholic editors have done, and that is all.[3] The reasons for doing this are so obvious that

[1] *Ibid.*, p. 335.
[2] *Revue bleue*, Jan. 1894. Chossat, *l. c.*, p. 330.
[3] We do not intend by any means to say that all Jesuit editors of such texts have kept to the golden mean. On the

there should be no need of defending this practice. However, we shall say more on this subject when speaking of the "Moral Scope of Education." (Chapter XVII.)

One more word about selected extracts. One of the greatest Greek scholars of our age, Professor von Wilamowitz-Moellendorf of the Berlin University, has just published, at the recommendation of the Prussian Ministry of Instruction, a Greek reader consisting of selected extracts from different authors and different kinds of literature.[1] The object of this book is to give the students of the higher classes of the gymnasium, by means of characteristic selections from various kinds of writings, a conspectus of the whole range of Greek literature. We do not wish here to attempt a criticism of such a plan; what we want to state is that, even at present, great scholars think selected extracts of great value especially for acquainting the students with the spirit of a great nation, as expressed in its literature. If, then, the Jesuits had read chiefly selected extracts—which is not the case—M. Compayré would not be justified in blaming the Jesuits in particular for doing this, unless he could prove that their selections were destitute of all educational value.

contrary, we admit that some have gone to extremes. But we do not deal here with individual cases, but with the general principle.

[1] *Griechisches Lesebuch*. Berlin, Weidmann, 1902. Two volumes text, two volumes commentary. See on this reader, *Transactions of the Berlin Conference*, 1900, pp. 205-215. — *Neue Jahrbücher*, 1902, vol. X, pp. 270-284. — *Monatschrift für höhere Schulen*, Berlin, March 1902, pp. 158-160, and October. In the April number of this new educational review, p. 301, it is stated that an English edition of this work is in preparation.

CHAPTER XIII.

Syllabus of School Authors.

§ 1. General Remarks.

The Ratio Studiorum divides the literary curriculum into five classes. Father Jouvancy speaks of six,[1] adding that the sixth is sometimes combined with the fifth. Father Kropf in 1736, in his programme, has six. Most Jesuit colleges in this country have six classes in the literary course, to which are added two years of philosophy with higher mathematics, natural sciences and economics. These eight classes correspond to the high school and the college course. The four lower or grammar classes are equivalent to the high school, whereas the four higher classes: Humanities (Freshman), Rhetoric (Sophomore), Junior and Senior Philosophy, correspond to the American college, with one essential difference, "that the work of the Jesuit college is not professional study, but general culture and preparation for professional study."[2]

When in the following pages we speak of the study of the authors, it is understood that a systematic study of grammar has preceded and partly accompanies the reading of the authors. Of late there is a tendency to begin reading too early, almost from the beginning,

[1] *Ratio Docendi*, ch. II, art. 7.
[2] Rev. F. Heiermann, S. J., in *Woodstock Letters*, 1897, p. 376: "The Ratio Studiorum and the American College."

and to study the whole grammar inductively. Such reading cannot be fruitful. Let us hear two German schoolmen on this question. Director Jäger of Cologne said in the 41st Conference of the German Philologians and Educators (Munich, 1891): "The reading of the authors should remain the principal object of the classical training, but it must be an intelligent reading, reading that is understood because of solid grammatical training imparted previously. Only thus can the study of a language become a means of scientific knowledge. Therefore, sufficient time must be devoted to the grammatical training." Professor Seeliger makes the following very timely observations: "One point in the linguistic training must not be lost sight of: namely, that the understanding of the authors must be solid; but a solid appreciation of the authors can be built only on the foundation of a knowledge of grammar. Teachers now-a-days try too much to keep this end out of sight for fear of public opinion; some weakly yield to the *Zeitgeist* and hush it up altogether, to proclaim the more loudly that the reading of the authors is the only object of classical instruction. But I think grammatical discipline is very salutary, even for the youth of the present age, indeed, a remedy against many dangers of our time. And any one of us teachers who conscientiously endeavors to make instruction effective should fearlessly profess to be a *grammaticus*, and act according to this profession."[1]

The Ratio Studiorum prescribes the authors to be studied in the various classes, and in Jouvancy's commentary and similar documents, other authors are mentioned which may be read alongside or instead of

[1] *Neue Jahrbücher*, 1898, vol. II, p. 83.

those enumerated by the Ratio. As we have seen, the matter and the order in which the different subjects are to be taught are not essential to the Ratio. Consequently it is not necessary to follow strictly the given list. If in any point the Ratio can and must be adapted to the times, it is in the choice of authors. Therefore, those which are generally read in other classical institutions of the country, should be preferred and taught according to the spirit and method of the Ratio. In fact, all authors read in the modern classical schools are mentioned in the Ratio or by Jouvancy.

In different ages we find different tastes and opinions. We must not, therefore, be surprised to find authors recommended as school books which do not suit our taste. We give here a list of authors as contained in different documents of the Society.[1] When the Ratio enumerates many authors for one and the same class, it is understood that the choice was left to provincial or local superiors.

FIRST GRAMMAR CLASS (first high school class): *Latin:* easy selections from Cicero, if possible in separate editions; Fables of Phaedrus, Lives of Nepos.

SECOND GRAMMAR CLASS. *Latin:* Ratio Studiorum: the same as preceding. Jouvancy: somewhat more difficult letters of Cicero, Virgil's Bucolics, selections from Ovid and other poets. — *Greek:* Fables of Aesop.

THIRD GRAMMAR CLASS. *Latin:* Ratio Studiorum: Letters of Cicero, Caesar's Commentaries, easy poems of Ovid. Jouvancy: Cicero's *Somnium Scipio-*

---

[1] From various rules of the Ratio Studiorum, and Jouvancy, *Ratio Docendi*, ch. II, art. 7.

nis, Virgil's Georgics, especially books I and IV. Ovid's Metamorphoses. — *Greek:* Fables of Aesop; the Tablet of Cebes; select dialogues of Lucian.

FOURTH GRAMMAR CLASS. *Latin:* more important letters of Cicero; *De Senectute, De Amicitia* etc.; select elegies and epistles of Ovid, or selections from Tibullus, Catullus, Propertius, and Virgil's Eclogues; or the fourth book of Virgil's Georgics, the fifth and seventh book of the Aeneid etc. — Jouvancy: Caesar, Cicero's *De Officiis.* — *Greek:* St. Chrysostom (select Homilies), Xenophon. — Jouvancy: Orations of Isocrates.

HUMANITIES (Freshman). *Latin:* Cicero, especially ethical writings and easier orations. Caesar, Sallust, Livy, Curtius etc.; of the poets, above all Virgil (Aeneid); Odes of Horace, etc. — *Greek:* Orations of Isocrates, St. Chrysostom, St. Basil, Epistles of Plato,[1] and Synesius, selections from Plutarch; of the poets: Homer, Phocylides, Theognis etc. Nadal prescribes besides Aristophanes.

RHETORIC (Sophomore). *Latin:* Rhetorical works and orations of Cicero; Quintilian; historians. Jouvancy: Livy, Tacitus, Suetonius etc.; poets (not specified by the Ratio); Jouvancy: Seneca, Juvenal etc. — *Greek:* Demosthenes, Plato, Thucydides, Homer, Hesiod, Pindar etc.; also St. Gregory Nazianzen, St. Basil, and St. Chrysostom. — Jouvancy: Sophocles or Euripides. — Nadal prescribes Demosthenes, Thucydides, the tragedians, Pindar, and "all the more important and more difficult authors."[2]

---

[1] Now universally considered spurious, although even in the 19th century scholars were not wanting who defended their genuineness, as Grimm and Grote. .

[2] *Monum. Paed.,* p. 92.

From this last statement, and in fact from the whole list, it appears that all the important authors were included in the Jesuit plan, and that those who made the sweeping assertion that "the greatest Greek authors were all excluded from the Jesuit schools,"[1] have not looked at the documents of the Society. All the most important authors were explicitly prescribed. It is evident that not all the authors which are mentioned could be read. The different provinces of the Society drew up lists, or catalogues of authors, which varied in different years. Thus in the Province of Upper Germany in 1602—1604 a *catalogus perpetuus* was drawn up, i. e. a list of authors to be read every four or five years. We subjoin the list of the books for Rhetoric class.[2]

A. D. 1604: Cicero, *Orator ad Brutum;* orations, vol. II. The Annals of Tacitus. The Tragedies of Seneca. — The Philippics of Demosthenes. The ἔργα καὶ ἡμέραι of Hesiod.

A. D. 1605: Cicero, *Partitiones Oratoriae;* orations, vol. III. Livy, I. decade. Juvenal — The Olynthiacs of Demosthenes. Homer, Iliad, books I and II.

A. D. 1606: Cicero, *De Oratore,* three books; orations, vol. I. Livy, III. decade. Statius, Thebaid. — Isocrates, Panegyric. Euripides, Hecuba.

A. D. 1607: Cicero, *De Optimo Genere Oratorum;* orations, vol. II. Tacitus, *Historiae*. Claudian and Herodian. — Aristotle, Rhetoric. Sophocles.

[1] See above p. 8, note 1.
[2] Pachtler, vol. IV, pp. 1—29.

A. D. 1608: Cicero, *Partitiones Oratoriae;* orations, vol. III. Statius, *Sylvae.* — Xenophon, Cyropaedeia. Homer, Odyssey, I and II.

In the Province of the Rhine in Rhetoric class were read:

A. D. 1629: Cicero, *Partitiones;* orations, vol. I. *De Claris Oratoribus.* Horace, Odes, b. III. Seneca, *Hercules furens.* Livy, I. decade. — Demosthenes, Olynthiacs. Chrysostom, *De Sacerdotio,* b. IV. Homer, Iliad, b. IV. Greek epigrams.

A. D. 1630: Cicero, orations, vol. IV. *De Inventione; Orator.* Horace, b. IV. and Epodes. Livy, III. decade. Seneca, Thyestes. — Homer, Iliad, b. V etc.

These lists represent a considerable amount of reading from the best authors. Modern writers object to some of the authors recommended by the Ratio. However, to avoid unfairness, it should not be forgotten that the opinions held in former ages about certain authors were different from those current at present. The same objections can be made against Protestant school plans of former centuries. Thus Melanchthon, as well as the Jesuits, considered the smaller poems formerly attributed to Homer, v. g. the Batrachomyomachia, as a fit school classic. Also Hesiod, Aratus, Plutarch, and Lucian are recommended by Melanchthon.[1]

Catullus, Tibullus, Propertius, the *Disticha Catonis,* Aurelius Victor, Eutropius, Lucan, Pliny, Pru-

[1] Hartfelder, *Philipp Melanchthon als Praeceptor Germaniae,* vol. VII of the *Monumenta Germaniae Paedagogica.* Berlin 1889, pp. 360—397.

dentius, Publilius, Sedulius, Seneca, Severus, Vellejus, Aelian, Aesop, Cebes, Hesiod, Lucian, Phocylides, Plutarch, Pythagoras, Theognis etc., were read in the Protestant schools of Brunswick and other countries.[1] Besides, in these schools the works of the Neo-Latinists, as Buchanan, Castalio, Eobanus Hessus, Erasmus, Lotichius, Sabinus, Sleidanus and others, were read more extensively than in the Jesuit schools, which confined themselves almost exclusively to the ancient classics. As the ancient authors possess a far superior educational value, the choice of the Jesuits betokens great pedagogical wisdom.

It is evident that authors like Theognis, Phocylides, etc. are not read in modern Jesuit schools. In fact the Jesuits have, in the choice of authors, suited their schools to the times.

It may also be questioned whether it is advisable to read selections from Cicero's letters in the lowest classes, as they can be given only piecemeal; they furnish an excellent subject for higher classes, after the students have become acquainted with Roman history. For the lowest class good connected pieces, short stories from history, mythology etc., as found in Latin Readers, will serve the purpose better than Cicero's letters. In the next class the Lives of Nepos may be taken up, followed by the study of Caesar's Commentaries in the third. Such a plan was suggested by the German province as early as 1830. In the propositions sent to Rome in that year it was said that Cicero's letters, with very few exceptions, require a considerable knowledge of Roman history and should

---

[1] Koldewey, *Braunschweigische Schulordnungen*, vol. I and VIII of the *Monumenta Germaniae Paedagogica, passim*.

be replaced by select historical passages etc. from the writings of the same author.[1]

Father Jouvancy, in several chapters of his *Ratio Discendi*, gives brief notes on the most important Latin and Greek authors and their characteristics, "to show," as he says, "in what order they should be read and what fruit may be derived from their study."[2] A few of his remarks, as is to be expected, cannot stand in the light of modern philological and historical criticism. However, for the greater part his observations are most judicious and correct. We shall embody the substance of these chapters of Jouvancy in the following notes on the authors, supplementing them from the splendid *History of Universal Literature* of Father Baumgartner,[3] and comparing them with the opinions of other prominent scholars.[4]

§ 2. Latin Prose Writers.

CICERO is first and preeminently prescribed by the Ratio for every grade. And rightly so, if we except the lowest classes. For he is the master of the Latin language and the best representative of ancient culture, indeed, as regards Latin oratory, the only representative.[5] In former times, particularly during the

[1] Pachtler, vol. IV, p. 442.
[2] *Ratio Discendi*, ch. I, art. 1, § 2; art. 2, § 5; ch. II, art. 2, § 7, and art. 3, § 3.
[3] *Geschichte der Weltliteratur*, especially vol. III, which deals with the classical literature of Greece and Rome; on this work see above p. 233—234.
[4] We quote chiefly from Nägelsbach, *Gymnasial-Pädagogik* (3. ed.); Dettweiler, *Didaktik und Methodik des Lateinischen* and *Didaktik und Methodik des Griechischen;* Willmann, *Didaktik als Bildungslehre*; Anthon, *Class. Dictionary*.
[5] Dettweiler, *Did. des Lat.*, p. 193.

Renaissance, Cicero was overestimated; now, after the sweeping condemnations of Drumann, Froude, and Mommsen, it has become the fashion to treat him with contempt. Cicero finds a more sympathetic, and we think more just, treatment at the hands of the great Cardinal Newman, in his *Personal and Literary Character of Cicero*,[1] where the life of this gifted Roman, his works, and his style are admirably described. Cicero's style is so splendid and masterly that the greatest of the Romans, Caesar, could not help admiring his inventive powers, which, as Newman says, "constitute him the greatest master of composition that the world has seen." Of late years a healthy reaction has set in against the vagaries of such radical critics as Mommsen and Froude. Quite recently Professor von Wilamowitz of the University of Berlin, stated emphatically: "In spite of Mommsen, Cicero must remain the centre of Latin instruction."[2]

Which works of Cicero are to be read? The Ratio Studiorum and other documents mention his epistles, orations, philosophical and rhetorical works. Some specimens of all these should be studied.

I. Of his *orations* the following deserve especially to be read.[3]

1. *Verrinae* I, IV, V; in the fourth, *De Signis*, the marvellous grouping of the material is highly instructive. 2. *De Imperio Cn. Pompei* (*De Lege Manilia*), has a most lucid disposition. 3. *In Catilinam*,

[1] *Historical Sketches*, vol. I, pp. 239—300.
[2] Transactions of the Berlin Conference 1900, p. 207. — See also Weisweiler, *Cicero als Schulschriftsteller*, and Zielinski, *Cicero im Wandel der Jahrhunderte*, Leipsic, Teubner.
[3] Cf. Dettweiler, *l. c.*, p. 193 sq. — Nägelsbach, *Gymnasial-Pädagogik*, p. 123.

especially the first and third exhibit a splendid eloquence. 4. *Pro Milone*, distinguished by masterly argumentation. 5. One or other of the *Philippicae* (the second seems to be the best). 6. *Pro Ligario*. 7. *Pro Marcello*. 8. *Pro Archia Poeta* (contains a magnificent passage on the Liberal Arts). — Cicero's invectives (against Catiline and Anthony) are sometimes wanting in gravity, and are too declamatory; his laudatory orations, on the other hand, are among his happiest efforts. But all abound in descriptions full of life and nature, and his skill in amplification is unsurpassed.

II. *Philosophical writings:*

1. The finest part is his *Somnium Scipionis*, on the immortality of the soul, (in his *De Republica*, which cannot well be read on account of the many gaps in the text).[1] 2. *Cato Major*, or *De Senectute*, is clear and easy, and is better than *Laelius: De Amicitia*.[2] 3. *De Officiis* is well fitted for the highest classes. 4. The *Disputationes Tusculanae*, especially lib. 1, form good and relatively easy reading.[3]

III. *Rhetorical Works*. *De Oratore*, *Orator ad Brutum* etc., are read in Rhetoric class (Sophomore).

IV. The *Letters* of Cicero form the most valuable, as well as the largest, collection of letters (870 pieces)

---

[1] There exist good separate editions of the *Somnium Scipionis*, for instance, Reid's (Pitt Press Series).

[2] In the introduction to his excellent commentary on the latter work, Professor Seyffert says: "*De Senectute* may be read in Tertia (fourth class), *De Amicitia* should not be taken up before Upper-Secunda (sixth class)."

[3] See Dettweiler, p. 200. — On Cicero's philosophy see also Döllinger, *The Gentile and the Jew*, vol. II, p. 118 sq.

we possess of any of the ancients. They are the most important source for the history of this remarkable period. In a very pleasant manner the writer exposes all his good and weak points: his honest, although short-sighted patriotism, his affectionate heart, his fickleness, inconstancy and vanity. Drumann and Mommsen, who take his naive confessions in a wrong light, are too severe on Cicero. Professor Mommsen is altogether biased against Cicero in favor of his hero Caesar. Mr. T. Rice Holmes has well said with reference to Mommsen: "Historical imagination is a great quality, but it should not be allowed to run riot."[1]

These letters are an excellent subject for study in the middle or higher classes. A selection can easily be made so as to illustrate Cicero's stormy career from 62—43 B. C., as well as to reflect the whole history of that period fraught with events, which were to change the world's history. For this purpose the following selection used to be read in a Jesuit college of this country: *Ad Fam.* V, 1; V, 2; *Ad Att.* II, 22; *Ad Fam.* XIV, 4; *Ad Att.* IV, 1; *Ad Fam.* VII, 1; XIV, 4; *Ad Att.* VII, 11; *Ad Fam.* XVI, 12; *Ad Att.* VIII, 3 (Cicero's opinion of Pompey and Caesar); *Ad Att.* IX, 18 (a highly interesting description of Cicero's interview with Caesar); *Ad Att.* XII, 18; *Ad Fam.* IV, 5 and 6; *Ad Att.* XIV, 12; *Ad Fam.* XI, 27 and 28; XI, 1; IX, 14; XII, 4; X, 28, *etc.*[2]

[1] *Caesar's Conquest of Gaul*, p. 755 (see also p. 803).
[2] On "Cicero's Letters as Class Reading," see the excellent article of Dr. O. E. Schmidt in *Neue Jahrbücher*, vol. VIII, pp. 162—174. This author wishes them to be read, after the orations against Catiline, *De Senectute*, or *De Amicitia* have been studied. He adds also a plan for a new selection of the letters.

The translation of Cicero should be exquisite and polished, as is the noble and refined diction of the original.[1]

CAESAR. Of the character of this "greatest of the Romans," Mommsen has given a splendid delineation in his *Roman History*, although this sketch is overdrawn and entertaining rather than convincing. We have here to do with Caesar only as historian, particularly as the writer of the *Commentaries* on the Gallic War. For simple straightforward historical style these commentaries remain up to this day, an unsurpassed model.[2] Caesar's style is remarkable for clearness, ease, perfect equality of expression, and a simplicity bordering on severity. There is something of the *imperator* or the *dictator* in his very language. He commands style and language as he does his legions. After the first difficulties are overcome, the reading ought to be quick, as that of all histories and epics in general. Continual references are to be made to the maps. Drawings and plans, illustrating the descriptions of battles and sieges, will arouse interest and facilitate the understanding of the text. The translation of this author, quite different from that of Cicero, should be plain and forcible, like the original itself. From the historical standpoint it must not be overlooked that Caesar's Commentaries are not an unbiased historical work, but one written for a political purpose, *viz.*, the justification of his proceedings in Gaul. The great general was also a skilled strategist in writing, a master in the art of grouping events, so

---

[1] See also various works on Cicero, by Middleton, Forsyth, Trollope, Collins, Boissier, etc.

[2] Father Baumgartner, vol. III. p. 383.

as to represent his measures as justified without losing the appearance of strict historic objectivity. In particular the speeches are frequently clever partisan writings. From the ethical point of view it will be also necessary to indicate occasionally the brutality of this great imperialist in dealing with the Gallic and German tribes. Roman military antiquities should be studied in connection with the reading of the Commentaries,[1] while the civil, political and social antiquities are best treated in connection with the study of Cicero. So it was done in the Jesuit schools under the name of "general erudition."

Livy's great history of Rome is not a critical work, but a popular narrative, written with the warmth of an enthusiastic patriot. His Latin is not as elegant and grand as Cicero's, but is, as Jouvancy says, "forcible and dignified."[2] In a period of moral decadence he upheld the old *virtus Romana* which had made Rome the queen of the world. Of special beauty are the speeches which Livy makes his heroes deliver in important moments. They form part and parcel of his narrative and dramatically exhibit the inner feelings of the principal personages. Books I and II should be read; but above all XXI and XXII, the glowing account of the second Punic War, especially Hannibal's daring exploit in crossing the Alps.—Care must be taken to analyze his periods and to render them into shorter English sentences.

Sallust, in his *Bellum Jugurthinum* and *Conjuratio Catilinae*, of which latter event he was a contem-

---

[1] A magnificent and most helpful work for the study of the Commentaries is T. Rice Holmes' *Caesar's Conquest of Gaul*. London, Macmillan, 1899.

[2] *Rat. Disc.*, ch. 1, art. 2, § 5.

porary, gives an insight into the political machinations and the corruptions of Roman society. His style is carefully formed after that of Thucydides, and is distinguished for vigor and conciseness, but becomes sometimes sententious and abrupt. He is also censured for archaic expressions, and on the whole, lacks graceful ease and smoothness. The delineations of character, (e. g. of Catiline, Jugurtha, Marius), have always been considered masterpieces. Jouvancy rightly says: "Sallust exhibits an abundance of material and a wealth of ideas."

TACITUS is the greatest historian of Rome, if not of antiquity.[1] He was a stern Roman of the old stamp, an enthusiastic admirer of the *virtus Romana*, which in his time had almost totally vanished. But the sad condition of his time made him gloomy, pessimistic, and one-sided. "Tacitus and Juvenal paint the deathbead of pagan Rome; they have no eyes to see the growth of new Rome, with its universal citizenship, its universal Church (first of the Emperors, afterwards of Christ). . . . The Empire outraged the old republican tradition, that the provincial was naturally inferior to the Roman: but this, which is the greatest crime in the eyes of Tacitus, is precisely what constitutes its importance in the history of the world."[2] Tacitus' sympathetic description of the simple and incorrupt manners of the Germans, in his *Germania*, was intended to set the Roman corruptions in a more glaring light, and is evidently too much idealized. In psychological depth, warmth of feeling, and vigor of expression, Tacitus surpasses even Thu-

[1] See Father Baumgartner, vol. III, pp. 531—538.
[2] Ramsay, *The Church in the Roman Empire*, p. 175.

cydides. His style is dignified, manly, studiously devoid of everything feminine and merely ornamental; it is so brief and concise, as to be often obscure. Jouvancy says most appropriately: "His sentiments are striking and profound, so that only deep reflection can fathom them, and mere reading is not sufficient."[1] For these reasons his *Annales* and *Historiae* are the proper reading only for the highest classes and for mature men.

Of other Latin prose authors not much need be said. CORNELIUS NEPOS' *Biographies of Great Generals*, written in a simple style, form easy and instructive reading for the lowest classes. — During the Middle Ages, as well as in the first centuries of the Christian era, one of the favorite authors was SENECA. The reason is obvious. No philosopher of antiquity has approached the Christian view of life as closely as Seneca, so that a legend sprang up that the Roman had become acquainted with St. Paul and Christianity. Tertullian says: *Seneca saepe noster*, and Augustine, Jerome, and Lactantius appeal to his testimony. His letters contain the loftiest moral sentiments, — in sharp contrast with the author's life—; "whole letters, with few changes, might have been delivered in the pulpit by Bourdaloue and Massillon."[2] However, it is questionable whether Seneca's works are suitable reading for young pupils. A distinguished critic says: "Seneca is not to be read. His every sentence must have a sharp

---

[1] Father Baumgartner, *l. c.*, vol. III, p. 534, speaks of the "*markige, lapidare, ur-römische Stil des Tacitus.*"

[2] De Maistre, *Soirées de St. Pétersbourg*, IX. — On the spurious *Letters of Seneca to St. Paul*, see Bardenhewer, *Gesch. der altkirchl. Literatur*, vol. I (Herder, 1902), p. 470.

point, a striking antithesis. This is no wholesome food for boys."[1] Jouvancy seems to say the same, when he speaks of the "abruptness and ruggedness of Seneca's style."

§ 3. Latin Poets.

PHAEDRUS wrote several books of fables, partly translations, partly imitations of the famous fables of *Aesop*. The gracefulness, precision, elegance, and simplicity of style, make the fables of Phaedrus excellent reading to start with in lower classes. Besides, his sound moral precepts afford other pedagogical advantages.

OVID is the most gifted of Roman poets, more brilliant than Virgil, unsurpassed in his power of describing and "painting," and in his ease and fluency of versification. Father Jouvancy, in a few words, expresses the best judgment that can be passed on this writer: "Would that he were as chaste and pure as he is elegant and pleasing." This is only too true. Therefore, his works must be read with great caution. There are some of his productions of whose existence young students should be ignorant. The *Amores, Ars Amandi, Remedia Amoris*, cannot be condemned in too strong terms. The poet himself confesses: "*Nil nisi lascivi per me discuntur amores.*" Critics, who cannot be suspected of squeamishness or religious prejudice, have severely censured the erotic poems of Ovid, as "gems of frivolousness, handbooks of lasciviousness, which on young readers must produce the effects of sweet poison that enters into the

[1] Nägelsbach.

very marrow."[1] In some parts of the second and third book of the *Ars Amandi*, the poet burns a firework, the stench of which leaves no doubt as to where we are. The poison is all the more dangerous as it is offered sweetened with the virgin honey of genuine poetic diction.[2] But even the *Metamorphoses* contain many seductive passages, for which reason only selections should be in the hands of the pupils.

The *Metamorphoses* are the most important work for class reading. There is, on the whole, not very much depth of feeling or thought, but myth after myth is related, in a marvellous variety of detailed description, in a most fascinating style, and in a truly Homeric naiveté. Indeed Ovid has little of the stern Roman character; he has more of the gay, imaginative Greek. As regards his style, the elegance and unlabored ease of his versification is unrivalled. He says himself of his facility in writing verses: *Et quod temptabam dicere, versus erat.*[3] The brilliancy of his imagination, the liveliness of his wit, the wonderful art of bringing every scene distinctly before the eye, whether he describes the palace of the Sun-God or the cottage of Philemon, have been universally admired. If properly treated, Ovid will please and delight boys. Above all, the account of the primeval chaos and creation should be read. It is, as Father Baumgartner says, "clear and grand and forms the noblest and most beautiful cosmogony which classical antiquity and the pagan Orient have handed down."[4]

[1] O. Ribbeck, *Geschichte der römischen Dichtung*, vol. II, pp. 217, 265.
[2] Schanz, *Geschichte der römischen Literatur*, vol. II, p. 147; see Baumgartner, vol. III, pp. 466—488.
[3] *Tristia* IV, 10, 26.
[4] Vol. III, p. 478.

Then should be read the four ages of the world, the war with the giants, the deluge, Phaeton (perhaps the most splendid and highly poetical of his efforts), Niobe, and the lovely idyl Philemon and Baucis.

The translation of Ovid should be easy and fluent. The students should be encouraged to translate Ovid into English verse. The study of Greek and Oriental mythology can easily be connected with the study of the Metamorphoses. Father Jouvancy, in an appendix to his edition of select stories from the Metamorphoses, gives a short, but useful account of the various deities.

Nägelsbach thinks it foolish to torment boys of fourteen or fifteen years with the *Tristia* or *Epistolae ex Ponto*, as a youthful mind could not take interest in those perpetual lamentations. A few pieces, however, may be read with advantage, v. g. the departure from Rome, or the poet's autobiography (*Ep. ex Ponto* IV, 10), etc.

VIRGIL is "the Prince of Latin poets" (Jouvancy), "the greatest poet of the Augustan age, the most celebrated imitator of Homer, the master and model of Dante,[1] the favorite of Augustus and Maecenas, the friend, whom Horace calls 'the half of my soul',[2] and the *anima candida*, the stainless soul, the 'Virgin poet', as he was styled in Naples."[3] His language is not as easy and as fluent as that of Ovid, but is grand, noble and stately; but in his ideas and lofty sentiments, Virgil is infinitely superior to Ovid.

In modern times Virgil has been severely censured

---

[1] Dante, *Inferno*, I.: "*Lo mio maestro et lo mio autore.*"
[2] *Odes* I, 3: *animae dimidium meae.*
[3] Baumgartner, vol. III, p. 415.

— for not being Homer. Indeed, he is inferior to Homer in many, in very many points. But let it not be forgotten that his epic is an entirely different species of poetry. it belongs to the *artistic* or *literary* epic, whereas Homer's is *primitive* epic. Hence it would be unfair to judge both according to the same standard. Virgil is an imitator of Homer, and did not come up to his master. For this the critics censure him, but they should remember the words of Voltaire: "Homer has made Virgil, they say; if this be true, it is undoubtedly his finest work." [1]

In his *Eclogues* or *Pastorals* Virgil imitates the Greek idyls of Theocritus. But he is not as varied, lively and natural — at the same time not as coarse — as his Greek model. Theocritus' Idyls are genuine Pastorals, full of rural simplicity of thought and unadorned style, whereas Virgil's Pastorals are rather political allegories. For a full appreciation they require much learning, and hence they are less fitted for younger boys. The first, however, and above all the celebrated fourth Eclogue, should be read. On account of this fourth Eclogue, the poet was considered as a prophet during the Middle Ages. The mysterious prediction of the son, with whose birth — as the Sybils foretold —, the golden age was to return, naturally reminds us of the prophetic passages of Isaias. Virgil evidently refers to the son of a noble Roman, most probably of Asinius Pollio; but it is highly probable that he borrowed the idea and some details from Old Testament writings, whose contents, especially the expectation of a Redeemer, had become

---

[1] *Homère a fait Virgile, dit-on; si cela est, c'est sans doute son plus bel ouvrage.*

known through the Jews in the dispersion.[1] Pope's *Messiah*, a *Sacred Eclogue*, should be read in connection with this fourth Eclogue of Virgil.

The four books of the *Georgics* are the best didactic production in Roman literature. They have been styled poetical essays on the dignity of labor, as set against the warlike glory, that was the popular theme of the day. This is Virgil's most characteristic work, which breathes the genuine air of Italy. The language is magnificent, superior to that of the Aeneid. The work abounds in beautiful descriptions and contains charming episodes. It is not advisable to read the whole work, as the student will not be satisfied with such a topic. Select passages, however, may be studied in class, especially from book II, and book IV (the life of the bees: their little state, character, pursuits, and wars).

Virgil's greatest work, the *Aeneid*, is in many points an imitation of both *Iliad* and *Odyssey;* but in its spirit it is a national poem in the best sense of the word, "a reflection and an echo of all the grandeur of the history of Rome,"[2] a *prophetia post factum*. By a most ingenious device, the poet succeeded in exhibiting, and, as it were, foreshadowing the greatness of historical Rome in its legendary history. How bold and successful, for instance, is it to connect the legendary ancestor of the Roman rulers with Dido,

[1] See *Neue Jahrbücher für das klassische Altertum* etc., 1898, vol. I, pp. 105—128: "Every unbiased mind must admit that Hellenistico-Jewish sources furnish the best explanation of this eclogue." Cf. Isaias 11, 6–8. Lactantius, *Div. Inst.*, VII, 24, 11. — Josephus, *Bell. Jud.*, VI, 312. — Suetonius, *Vesp.*, 4.

[2] Nägelsbach.

the foundress of Carthage. Her imprecation: "*Exoriare aliquis nostris ex ossibus ultor,*" is the most clever and most poetical conception of the Punic wars. Then take the sixth book, where Aeneas, in a grand vision, sees all the future splendor and glory of Rome, and show in Homer's poems, or in any other work, a passage of nobler, more majestic and more poetical character. It is true, the hero of the poem, Aeneas, does not inspire the reader. He lacks the fiery passion and impetuous vigor of Achilles, the chivalrous spirit of Hector, the inventiveness and cunning of Odysseus. But he is more than all that: he is the chosen instrument of Divine Providence for bringing about the greatest achievement in human history: "the settlement of that race in Italy, from which were to spring the founders of Rome." Only narrow prejudice, therefore, can depreciate Virgil's immortal work. Rightly has a Jesuit said: "This grand picture warmed with strong national and religious enthusiasm, elevated by the consciousness of Roman majesty and dignity, illumined by the light of a higher world, outweighs many a beautiful passage of the *Iliad.* This is not merely frosty imitation, not studied artifice, this is poetry, as it can well forth only from the inspired heart of a true poet. This noble idealism and genuine enthusiasm is the soul and the life-inspiring principle of the whole poem."[1]

I think it is Nägelsbach who says, that every classical scholar should study carefully all the works of Virgil. For the pupils, of course, selections must suffice. But, as far as possible, these selections should give a view of the whole poem. The I. book, the II.

---

[1] Baumgartner, vol. III, p. 436.

(compare Lessing's Laokoon), the V., and above all the VI., should not be omitted. In reading the sixth book, references to Dante's *Inferno* should be given throughout. The translation of Virgil is no easy task; it ought to be noble and dignified.

HORACE is the great lyric poet of Rome. His *Epistles* and *Satires*, carefully selected, make good reading for Freshman Class, his *Odes* for Sophomore. There is a great variety in his poems. All show good sense, clear judgment, extraordinary taste and elegance. His descriptions of nature are true, portrait-like, vivid and very effective. With the greatest candor he opens his heart to his friends, without disguising his weaknesses. His shorter poems are light, graceful and tender. The patriotic Odes are very different. They show the poet's aim at effecting some large social or political purpose and consequently rise to a grander and more dignified tone. Although reckoning himself among the followers of Epicurus (*Epicuri de grege porcum*), he rises above the coarser tenets of that school, and many of his sayings contain much practical wisdom. He is, as Lord Lytton says, the most "quotable" of authors.[1] He is not easy of translation.

The comedies of PLAUTUS and TERENCE, as Jouvancy says, are written in pure Latin, but contain many impure things, for which reason they should be studied in expurgated editions. This point is strongly insisted on by the Ratio Studiorum.

[1] See Father Baumgartner's sympathetic sketch, vol. III, pp. 437—457.

§ 4. Greek Prose Writers.

Before speaking of the Greek authors, it may be well to make a few observations of fundamental import. There is a difference between the study of Greek and of Latin, which seems to be well expressed in the "Prussian School Order" of 1892 and 1901. There we find as the object of studying Latin: "The understanding of the principal authors and logical training;" as the object of the study of Greek: "The understanding of the principal classical authors." A similar distinction was made centuries ago by the Jesuits. As early as 1669 Father Fabri wrote: "To write and to speak Greek is not necessary. An educated man must, according to the adage, speak Latin, understand Greek, and read Hebrew. *Latine loquatur, Graece intelligat, Hebraice legat.*" [1] It is evident that the study of Greek contributes also to the logical training of the mind, but it ought not to be sought so directly as in Latin. The Latin language with its rigorous syntax seems to be better fitted for that purpose. It is different with Greek. In a former chapter,[2] we mentioned that Latin grammar was eminently logic, and its study a course of applied logic. "Greek on the other hand, might almost be called a course of aesthetics, by means of which we learn to distinguish a thousand gradations of meaning which our barbarous languages will not allow us to accentuate."[3] However, the principal object of the study of Greek is the

---

[1] Fabri, *Euphyander* (1669). — Chossat, *Les Jésuites à Avignon*, p. 286.

[2] Chapter XII, *Classical Studies*, p. 347.

[3] Dr. Karl Hildebrand; see *The Month*, 1886, Feb., p. 167.

reading of the Greek classics. "The Greeks are for us not *one* of the civilized nations of antiquity, but *the* civilized nation (*das Kulturvolk*), which has given us the models for all kinds of literary productions."[1] And Father Baumgartner observes: "The intellectual culture of the Greeks became a power which not only survived their political decadence, but for all coming centuries exercised a decisive influence on the development of the world's culture."[2]

In order to attain this object of the study of Greek, the reading of authors should be begun as soon as possible. Etymology should be limited to the essentials occurring in the authors which form the staple reading in colleges. The old grammars contain many forms which never or quite exceptionally are met with in the course of reading. To this class belong many rare forms of declension, comparison, exceptional augments and reduplications, and, above all, numerous irregular verbs. They should be left out, as has been done in the best modern grammars.[3] The Jesuits always favored brief textbooks, "*perquam breves,*" says a document in 1829.[4] This was in accordance with their fundamental principle: *Pauca praecepta, multa exempla, exercitatio plurima.*

Greek syntax may at first not be taught systematically but inductively, incidentally, as the rules are

[1] Dettweiler, *Didaktik und Methodik des Griechischen*, p. 11.

[2] Baumgartner, vol. III, p. 5.

[3] Perhaps one of the best modern grammars is the *Small Greek Grammar* by Professor Kaegi, which has been recently translated into English by J. Kleist, S. J. (Herder, St. Louis, 1902.)

[4] Pachtler, vol. IV, p. 404.

met with in reading. Then the various rules are to be put together systematically. Important rules (the use of Subjunctive and Optative, the position of the article, and the like) should be learned with the practice of the forms. The various conditional clauses, the meaning of tenses (especially of the *Aorist*), and the use of the participles must be well explained. These points are the whole Greek Syntax *in nuce*.[1] The study of vocables should be a direct preparation for the future reading of authors. Many vocables, found in exercise-books in vogue during the last century, are altogether useless to this end. This evil arose from the system of confining Greek reading for two years to translating unconnected sentences. According to the spirit of the Ratio, the reading of connected pieces, easy narratives and easy authors, should be begun as soon as possible.

The best author to begin with is XENOPHON. For the sweetness and graceful simplicity of his language he was styled the "Attic Bee." In former times his *Cyropaedia* was the favorite book, also in Jesuit colleges. But this work is not as easy, nor as interesting as the *Anabasis*. The *Anabasis*, or *The Retreat of the Ten Thousand*, is a book most fit for youth,[2] and a good preparation for Herodotus. The speeches which are interwoven with the narrative prepare for the reading of Demosthenes. The geographical and ethnographical details about Asia Minor will prove use-

[1] "Also the epic dialect should not be studied systematically before reading Homer, but incidentally, and afterwards systematized." (*Prussian School Order.*)

[2] "*Ein rechtes Jugendbuch.*" Dr. Dettweiler. See this author on Xenophon, *Didaktik des Griechischen*, p. 29; also Willmann's *Didaktik*, vol. II, p. 519.

ful for the study of the *Acts of the Apostles* (Travels of St. Paul) and of the Crusades. Books I—IV should be read with maps, and with the plans of battles drawn on paper or on the blackboard. If this is done, and the reading is not too slow, the boys will take a real interest in the clear and simple narrative of battles and marches through the countries of hostile tribes. Boys delight in warfare and travels. — Whether the *Memorabilia* should be read is questionable, as a better picture of Socrates will afterwards be given in Plato's works. After the *Anabasis* selections may be read from the *Cyropaedia* and the *Hellenica*.

HERODOTUS, the "Father of History", as Cicero styles him, is a most attractive author. He seems not to have been read in the colleges of the Old Society. In modern times, in many plans of study, he receives more attention; some selections may well be read, especially such stories as have been taken into the literatures of all civilized nations. In their original garb they will exercise a special charm on account of their naive character.

THUCYDIDES, the "Father of Pragmatic and Political History," wrote the history of the first part of the Peloponnesian War. He ranks very high as historian, being distinguished for critical spirit, accurate research, and severe impartiality. His style is concise, often so concise as to degenerate into obscurity. This conciseness and the depth of thought make him a difficult author for young students. In the highest class, choice passages may be read: v. g. the plague in Athens, the funeral oration of Pericles. Demosthenes was an ardent admirer of the harangues of Thucydides, and the two great Roman historians, Sallust and Tacitus, have taken him for their model.

PLATO. Plato is recommended in the Ratio as one of the authors for Rhetoric class; in modern Jesuit colleges Plato is mostly read in Freshman class, for which he is an excellent author. In the words of a Jesuit critic, "Greek philosophy is one of the choicest fruits of Greek culture which, together with Greek poetry, history and oratory, was destined to form the basis of the culture of the Western nations."[1] Plato, one of the greatest thinkers of all ages, vaguely felt and presaged some of the grand religious and moral truths which were to be clearly revealed by Christ. Thus he became the παιδαγωγὸs εἰs Χριστόν. No philosopher, in fact no writer of antiquity, exerted a greater influence on the early Christian writers. His many errors, mixed with some Christian truth, gave rise to numerous heresies in the earlier centuries, and misled even gigantic intellects like that of Origen. On the other hand, as Father Baumgartner observes, "numerous minds, searching after truth, have through his writings been raised out of the depths of materialism to the purer heights of idealistic speculations."[2]

In Plato, there is, in the words of his disciple Aristotle, "a middle species of diction, between prose and verse," and Cicero said: "If Jupiter were to speak in the Greek tongue, he would use the language of Plato."[3] Some of his dialogues are so sublime, so harmonious, so rhythmical, that they may truly be

[1] Father Baumgartner, vol. III, page 268. Further references see in Histories of Philosophy, v. g. by Zeller, Brandis, Ueberweg, Windelband; Willmann, *Geschichte des Idealismus*. Döllinger, *The Gentile and the Jew*, vol. I, pp. 304—332.

[2] Father Baumgartner, vol. III, p. 277.

[3] *Brutus* 31; *Orator* 20.

styled poetical. There are not many which, both for contents and style, can be read in colleges. Best suited for this purpose are the Apology and Crito. The *Apology*, or *Defense of Socrates*, the only work of Plato which is not in the form of a dialogue, probably contains the substance of the answer Socrates made to the insidious charges of his accusers. The tone is throughout fearless, at times even defiant, the accused merely pleading that, whatever he did, was done at the bidding of the divinity, who spoke to him through a mysterious inner voice, and that all his doings were directed towards improving the minds and morals of his fellow-citizens. It is, on the whole, grand and elevating reading. A Jesuit professor and distinguished critic, Father Stiglmayr, wrote recently: "What a pity, if youths should no longer drink inspiration from such a source!"[1]

In the *Crito* we find Socrates in prison, during the interval between his condemnation and death. Crito advises him to fly, Socrates refuses, "as it was not allowed a good citizen to withdraw from proper authority and violate the laws of the state." The dialogue contains very fine passages.

The *Phaedo* is one of the most remarkable of Plato's dialogues. It relates a conversation held shortly before the death of Socrates, in which the great Athenian undertakes to prove the immortality of the soul. The last chapters narrate in a touching manner, how, when

[1] A beautiful appreciation of the Apology is given by this Professor in two articles in the *Stimmen aus Maria-Laach*, vol. LXII, 1902. — Professor Bristol, in his *Teaching of Greek in the Secondary School*, thinks the Apology not a suitable introduction to the study of Plato. His arguments are not convincing.

the summons came, Socrates with much composure and tranquillity of mind, drank the fatal cup, in the midst of his weeping friends. This dialogue may be read, as Nägelsbach says, with a good class of students. It is always advisable to read the *Apology*, then the *Crito*, and finally the last chapters of the *Phaedo*. Thus the students will get a clear picture of the whole life and the heroic death of the most remarkable man of antiquity.

DEMOSTHENES. Rhetorical talent was a gift common to all Greeks. The splendid speeches in Homer's poems are not accidental fictions, but the expressions of old traditions, of national manners and peculiarities. The diplomatic Agamemnon, the subtle Odysseus, the passionate Achilles, the conciliatory Nestor are oratorical types which were renewed in the life of the Greeks from generation to generation.[1] Greek oratory reached its zenith in Demosthenes, the "prince of orators". The Ratio Studiorum assigns his masterly orations to the highest class of the literary curriculum, which is, indeed, the proper place for this author. One or other of the *Olynthiacs* or *Philippics* should be studied, as was done early in Jesuit colleges. It may be questioned whether it is possible to do justice to the oration *On the Crown*, except with a very good class of pupils. This speech is not only the masterpiece of Demosthenes, but is regarded as the most perfect specimen that eloquence has ever produced.

A word must here be said on the reading of the GREEK NEW TESTAMENT. Professor Bristol says that the present ignorance of the Greek New Testament on

---

[1] See Father Baumgartner, vol. III, p. 257. — As a confirmation of this statement take the IX. book of the Iliad with its magnificent speeches.

the part of the people who have had a classical education is little short of disgrace, and he wishes that it should be read an hour a week.[1] This is exactly what was done in many colleges of the Old Society, as may be seen from Father Kropf's programme of 1736, in which the reading of the *Greek Gospel* (chiefly that of St. Luke), is prescribed for every Saturday in the fourth and fifth classes, and the *Acts of the Apostles* for Rhetoric (Sophomore).[2]

§ 5. Greek Poets.

HOMER is "the Father of Poetry." He was truly the "educator of Greece" and influenced the literature of all coming ages as no other writer ever has done. To dwell on his excellence, would merely be, as the Greek adage has it, γλαῦκ' εἰς 'Αθήνας. The *Odyssey* and *Iliad* should be read so as to give the pupil a perfect view of the whole. There are but few passages which cannot be read with boys. Homer is very naive and outspoken, as, in general, ancient literature is more honest, direct, and straightforward than modern literature, which often merely suggests what is offensive. But this very suggestiveness makes modern writings more insidious, as the mind is set thinking to find out what is meant. Homer is never licentious; the song in the Odyssey which is most objectionable is put into the mouth of another bard, and even in this song there is no glorification of sin, no mistake as to what is right or wrong. This straightforwardness in delicate matters must not offend the mature reader, or he must also

---

[1] *The Teaching of Greek in the Secondary School*, pp. 267—268.

[2] Kropf in Herder's *Bibliothek der katholischen Pädagogik*, vol. X, pp. 341—344. — See above pp. 123—124.

object to Holy Scripture. It is evident that not all passages of Scripture are to be read by the young, no more than many of the profane writers. As to Homer, Jouvancy says very appositely: "A few comparisons which are somewhat low, and other traces of primeval simplicity and of a *naiveté* no longer known, must not shock any one. Every sensible reader will also make allowances for the lies and other crimes which the pagan writer imputes to his gods."[1] If single lines with rather objectionable contents occur, the only way is to translate them correctly, but in careful and decent expressions, which have to be thought out beforehand; to omit them would almost surely lead some pupils to study them out at home. To give a wrong translation is dishonest, and "the end does not justify the means." Besides, as all sorts of translations may be had from our public libraries, and actually are in the hands of the students, such a fraud would be detected and would surely undermine the confidence of the pupils in their teacher. When the first passage is met with, the teacher may call attention to the above mentioned characteristics of ancient literature, sacred as well as profane. If a few prudent and grave remarks of this kind are made, the pupils will not suffer any harm from such reading.

We have said above that the epic dialect is to be studied inductively. When the first difficulties are overcome, the pupils will begin to like Homer, provided the teacher is what he ought to be. The introductions of the Odyssey and Iliad, as also other passages from Greek and Latin poetry, should be learned

[1] *Ratio Disc.*, ch. I, art. 1, § 2. — See also Nägelsbach's *Homeric Theology.*

by heart. As of Virgil's Aeneid, so also of the Odyssey and Iliad, the whole cannot be studied. But care should be taken that the selections are such as to give the pupils a clear view of the whole work.[1] The translation of Homer must be simple and natural. Anglo-Saxon words ought to prevail.[2] It has been previously stated, and it is self-evident, that the teaching of antiquities, descriptions of the life and manners of the heroic age, should accompany the reading of Homer.[3]

It is not necessary to dwell on the GREEK TRAGEDIES, and their importance for the higher classes of the literary curriculum. The Ratio does not mention them in particular; but Sophocles and Euripides are recommended by Jouvancy, and they were read in the colleges, as appears from the catalogues given on previous pages.[4] — The amount of the world's best literature, with which the student in the Jesuit Colleges was made acquainted, is certainly not insignificant.

[1] Professor Bristol, in his excellent work *The Teaching of Greek in the Secondary School*, suggests that books IX—XII of the Odyssey should be read first, then V, VI, VII, VIII, and part of book XIII. I must confess that such an inversion seems not advisable. Why not follow the author? I doubt also whether of book I. not more than the first 79 verses should be read. The whole first book is interesting and important for the correct appreciation of the whole.

[2] A good help for class translation is found in the prose translation of the *Odyssey* by Butcher and Lang; of the *Iliad* by Lang, Myers and Leaf.

[3] Works by Jebb, Gladstone, Mahaffy, Grote, Nägelsbach, etc — A splendid literary appreciation of the *Iliad* and *Odyssey*, see Baumgartner, vol. III, pp. 19—63.

[4] See pp. 373—374; see also Baumgartner, vol. III, pp. 133—244.

Chapter XIV.

Scholarship and Teaching.

The aim proposed by the *Ratio Studiorum* is a great and noble one, which tasks the undivided energy of able and experienced men. Does the Society fit the teachers for this work? This is a most important question. However good and excellent a system may be, it is of little avail if the teachers know not how to apply it, or if they apply it badly. Professor Münsterberg rightly insists on the truth that all effective school reform must start with a reform of teachers. "Just as it has been said that war needs three things, money, money, and again money, so it can be said with much greater truth that education needs, not forces and buildings, not pedagogy and demonstrations, but only men, men, and again men, — without forbidding that some, not too many of them, shall be women. The right kind of men is what the schools need; they have the wrong kind. They need teachers whose interest in the subject would banish all drudgery, and they have teachers whose pitiable unpreparedness makes the class work either so superficial that the pupils do not learn anything, or, if it is taken seriously, so dry and empty that it is a vexation for children and teachers alike. To produce anything equivalent to the teaching staff from whose guidance I benefited in my boyhood, no one ought to be allowed to teach in a grammar school who has not passed through a college or a good normal school; no one ought to teach

(402)

in a high school who has not worked, after his college course, at least two years in the graduate school of a good university; no one ought to teach in a college who has not taken his doctor's degree in one of the best universities; and no one ought to teach in a graduate school who has not shown his mastery of method by powerful scientific publications. We have instead a misery which can be characterized by one statistical fact: only two per cent of the school teachers possess any degree whatever."[1]

It would certainly be an ideal state, if all teachers came up to the Professor's requirements, as laid down in this proposition; but one may justly object to the importance assigned to the doctor's degree and the scientific publications, as necessary requisites for teaching. Although this degree and productive scholarship are very desirable, still we must consider it a mistake to expect from them alone or even chiefly the men needed in our educational institutions. The present writer, in his own school days, had some teachers who neither possessed the doctor's degree — of course they all had undergone the "State examinations" — nor had published any books, and yet as teachers were far superior to others who possessed the doctor's degree and had published books. Scholarship and capability for teaching are by no means identical. Too much weight has been given of late to scholarship in preference to practical experience, combined, as is understood, with a sufficient knowledge of the matter to be taught. The documents of the Society insist strongly that the teacher should thoroughly master the subject which he is to teach. Father Ledesma wrote

[1] *Atlantic Monthly*, May 1900, p. 667.

three hundred years ago: "In all classes the teachers should be such that they could teach a much higher class" [than that which is actually assigned to them],[1] and Father Nadal said: "All the professors should be distinguished in their respective branches, and no one can teach in the classes of Humanities and Rhetoric (Freshman and Sophomore) who is not a Master of Arts."[2] In these words Father Nadal virtually lays down as a postulate what Professor Münsterberg wants, namely, that the professors in the college course should have the doctor's degree. But the Society attached still greater weight to skill in teaching than scholarship, and we think rightly so.

Within the last two years this question of the relation of scholarship to teaching has received more attention than before, and some articles in leading reviews and periodicals found one of the reasons of the decline of teaching exactly in the excess of scholarship. It was especially the New York *Nation* which in the spring of 1900 brought the topic before the eyes of the public. On March 8, 1900, the *Nation* had an editorial on *The Decline of Teaching*, in which we find this statement: "It is at least a curious coincidence that the development of the modern science of pedagogy, with its array of physiological and psychological data, should have been accompanied by a distinct decline in the prominence of the teacher. No one, we suppose, will question that the number of great teachers is less now than it once was, and that the depleted ranks are not being adequately filled up. While this dearth of teaching power, notwithstanding the persis-

[1] *Monumenta Paedagogica*, p. 156.
[2] *Ibid.*, p. 104.

tent efforts to overcome it, is characteristic of all departments of education, it is especially noticeable in the colleges and universities; perhaps in no single respect, indeed, does the average college of the present day contrast more sharply with the college of a generation or two ago." On March 22, the *Nation* published the following correspondence. "Your editorial upon the Decline of Teaching ought to arouse very general solicitude throughout the profession : it gives notable emphasis to the condition which some of us have perceived for several years, although, so far as I am aware, stress has not hitherto been laid upon it in any public way. Your statement of the facts implies, without directly asserting, both the magnitude of the evil and its causes. Possibly both of these should receive, at the proper time and place, more extended and more exhaustive consideration. . . . In the upper schools — high schools and colleges — the evil which has brought about the decline of teaching is an entirely different one. There is no evidence that the pseudo-pedagogy has won any hold on these men, except as subjects for wise admonitions to elementary teachers. The evil here is that original research has been confounded with true teaching. Original research is an independent profession, worthy of all honor and respect, but its processes are not in any essential or fundamental way those of education. We can never bring back to our colleges the nobler ideals of character and culture until we separate them from an ideal which is purely that of a trade or profession. We should have a very analogous confusion if our lawyers were to contend that education consisted in mastering the process and methods of the law. In so far as our colleges are converted into workshops where 'the bounds of knowledge' are widened, their real and greater function becomes restricted, if not forgotten."[1] Dean Briggs of Harvard College shortly after wrote as follows: "Another doubt about the new-fashioned education concerns the abnormal value set on the higher degrees. That a teacher should know his subject is obvious; but the man of intelligence and self-sacrifice who bends his energy to teaching boys will soon get enough scholarship for the purpose; whereas no amount of scholarship can make up for the want of intelligence and self-sacrifice."[2]

Many years ago Arnold had expressed the same opinion. In a letter of inquiry for a master he wrote: "What I want is a Christian and a gentleman — an active man, and one who has common sense and understands boys. I do not so much care about scholarship, as he will have immediately under him the lowest forms [classes] in the school; but yet, on second thoughts, I do care about it very much, because his pupils may be in the highest forms; and besides, I think that even the elements are best taught by a man who has a thorough knowledge of the matter. However, if one must give way, I prefer activity of mind and an interest in his work to high scholarship, for the one can be acquired more easily than the other."[3]

The views of prominent German educators are not less pronounced on this subject — and yet, no nation insists more on scholarship than the German. Says

[1] Mr. Frederick Whitton, Michigan Military Academy.
[2] *Atlantic Monthly*, October 1900.
[3] Fitch, *Thomas and Matthew Arnold*, p. 69.

one: "We have no more educators in the true sense of the word."[1] The opinion of Professor Paulsen is especially worthy of notice. We summarize what he says on this subject in his *History of Higher Education*. It cannot be doubted that scholarship of the teacher, as a rule, tends towards raising teaching. But it should not be overlooked that the success of a teacher depends not only upon the amount of his scientific knowledge, but as much on his inclination and practical skill for teaching. Do the latter qualities increase in proportion with the teacher's scholarship? This is not always the case. It should be expected that, the richer, the clearer and the deeper the knowledge is, the stronger the inclination, and the facility of imparting it to others. But between philological scholarship proper and elementary instruction in Latin grammar and style, we find rather the reverse proportion. Scholarship can become an obstacle to teaching. *First*, it weakens the liking for it, or rather it strengthens the aversion to it. For the "drilling" in the elements of a language is undoubtedly one of the least attractive tasks to a man who feels in himself an inclination to educate the souls of the young. — *Secondly*, scholarship easily leads to introducing into class-instruction things that are important for the teacher's own scientific grasp of the subject. Hence the common complaint: the more grammar and the study of antiquities increase, and the more deeply the teachers enter into these sciences, the less the pupils learn; or rather the more the pupils learn of these things, the less thoroughness and facility they acquire

---

[1] Lehmann, *Erziehung und Erzieher*, Berlin, Weidmann, 1901. — *Neue Jahrbücher*, 1901, vol. VIII, p. 237.

in reading and writing; but this last is exactly what they need. From this it appears that it was in part disadvantageous to replace theologians in the gymnasia by philologians and mathematicians, a change which for a long time was wished for, undoubtedly not without good reasons. The theologian, owing to his whole training, had a tendency towards caring for the souls; an interest in the *whole* man was the centre of his calling, — if indeed he was an honest theologian, — not an interest in science, nor an interest in the student as student. Everything leads the theologian and the true philosopher to be an educator; the scholar, the learned specialist, may content himself with being an instructor. Add to this that the theologian through his studies was everywhere led to view things philosophically. And, after all, it is philosophy and religion alone that impel a man to communicate what he knows. He who has no philosophic views of life and of the world, has nothing to communicate; it is only the relation to some such ultimate object which gives learning pedagogical power and motives.[1] Be it remembered that the man who says this is no ecclesiastic, but a layman, one of the foremost professors of the University of Berlin.

In his latest important work,[2] he speaks still more emphatically on the drawbacks and dangers that menace teaching, even in the university, from scholarship. The professor, he says, considers himself in the first place not so much a teacher as a scholar, as the man

[1] *Geschichte des gelehrten Unterrichts*, pp. 628—629. (2nd ed., vol. II, pp. 389—391.)
[2] *Die deutschen Universitäten und das Universitäts-Studium*, Berlin 1902, pp. 213—222.

of science, and so scientific research appears to him nobler and more important than instruction. Consequently, it happens very easily that he becomes indifferent about perfecting himself as teacher, he devotes scarcely the necessary time to preparing his lectures, he loses interest in teaching, which is an unwelcome interruption of his researches. It is evident that no great success is to be expected from such teaching or lecturing. There are also dangers on the part of the students. Not unfrequently they are introduced too early to the specialized treatment of the sciences, before they have acquired general information about their subject. This danger is the greatest for the most talented and zealous students. If afterwards they are teachers in a *gymnasium,* they feel altogether out of place; nearly all they had to study in the university is inapplicable in this present position, and it takes very long before the mental equilibrium is found again. The author then points out the dangers for science. If manifestation of scholarship is required for obtaining a position as teacher, the unavoidable consequence will be a kind of "pseudo-productivity" and other evils.

Of recent utterances from England the following of the Hon. George C. Brodrick (Warden of Merton) will suffice. In an article, "Amateur Nation," he says: "Strange to say, the higher branches of the great educational profession in England are strongholds of amateurism. The masters and mistresses of elementary schools are now well trained, and even when they teach mechanically, they teach as persons who have grasped the difficulties of teaching, and mean business, as most professionals do. But what of masters at the great public schools, grammar schools, and private academies, or of the great multitude of private tutors who keep boarding houses or 'coach' pupils in their own houses? Not a twentieth of them have received any training whatever, or have the smallest idea that anything beyond a certain amount of scholarship and a certain power of commanding attention is required for teaching young people." The writer then states what he thinks is needed: "*It is teachers of average ability instructing* pupils of average industry, not individually, but in classes, who specially need training — not of necessity in training colleges, *but through close attention at lessons given by masters of tried experience.*"[1]

This is exactly the idea of the Ratio Studiorum. The aim is to provide teachers, who are "men of intelligence and self-sacrifice, who *possess, besides an excellent general culture, a good knowledge of their subject,* and who are trained through close attendance, by masters of tried experience." Before attempting to prove this from the Constitutions of the Society and the Ratio Studiorum, we beg to make one remark. The Society does not undervalue scholarship, but, on the contrary, appreciates it highly and wishes always a considerable number of her members to possess it to an eminent degree. This is proved beyond doubt by the list of distinguished Jesuit writers given in two preceding chapters (V and VII). The Society recognizes also the value of university studies. We have quoted previously the decree of the 23rd General Congregation of the Order (1883, *Decretum* XXI): "It is

[1] *The Nineteenth Century*, October 1900. Italics ours.— As early as 1880 Father Pachtler had enunciated, almost literally, the same principles, in the *Stimmen aus Maria-Laach*, vol. XIX, p. 167.

expedient to send select members to the universities to obtain the degrees which empower them to teach in the public [i. e. Government] schools."[1] We learn that the English Jesuits in late years have opened a Hall at Oxford (Pope's Hall), to afford young members an opportunity of attending the university lectures and of taking the degrees. We learn further that a number of Jesuits from other countries are there pursuing linguistic and scientific studies. The same is done in Ireland, Belgium, Holland, Austria, France and other countries. In some places, as in Austria, several Jesuit colleges are wholly under the supervision of the government, and all the teachers have made the prescribed studies at the universities and passed the rigid "state examinations". One of the professors of the Jesuit college at Feldkirch, Austria, has been chosen as "one of the seven prominent Latinists who are working at the great *Historical Grammar of the Latin Language.*"[2] It is evident that in all professional schools conducted by Jesuits, as in the Medical and Law Departments of Georgetown University, Washington, D. C., the instructors and professors are able professional teachers.

As far as America is concerned there existed peculiar handicaps to the cultivation of scholarship especially in Catholic institutions. Throughout the nineteenth century missions had to be established, chapels and churches built, and missionaries found to care for the spiritual wants of a rapidly increasing population.[3]

[1] Pachtler, vol. I, p. 123. See above pp. 198—199.
[2] Körting, *Handbuch der romanischen Philologie* (Leipzig 1896), p. 247.
[3] See the remarks of the Right Rev. Th. Conaty in the *Catholic University Bulletin*, July 1901, p. 305.

This work claimed the greatest part of the interest of the Catholic Church in general, and a comparatively large share of the time and energy of the members of the Society. But a teacher overburdened with work cannot devote himself to original research. Add to this the general poverty of the Catholic population, who had to support not only their churches, but also their schools, and it will be easy to understand that Catholic colleges had serious difficulties in acquiring the libraries, museums and laboratories which are essential for higher studies, and much more so for scholarly work. How much better situated are the secular institutions of learning in this country! "The National Government has, from the very beginning, made enormous grants of land and money in aid of education in the several states. The portion of public domain hitherto set apart by Congress for the endowment of public education amounts to 86,138,473 acres or 134,591 English square miles. This is an area larger than the New England States, New York, New Jersey, Maryland, and Delaware added together, as great as the kingdom of Prussia. The aggregate value of lands and money given for education by the National Government is nearly $300,000,000.[1] Besides, of the three hundred and fifteen million dollars given by private individuals within the last nine years for educational purposes,[2] very little has gone to Catholic institutions.

[1] *Education in the United States.* Edited by Professor Butler of Columbia University, Albany 1900, pp. VII—VIII.

[2] See *Educational Review*, May 1902, p. 492. In 1901 the educational gifts were not less than 73 million dollars. Mrs. Stanford leads the list with 30½ million to the Leland Stanford Jr. University. In 1900 the private gifts amounted to 48 million, and in 1899 to 63 million dollars.

In spite of the liberal national and private assistance granted, the public institutions have, until a short time ago, not been overconspicuous for scholarship, as is openly declared in a number of recent articles on this subject, by Professor Münsterberg of Harvard,[1] Mr. Carl Snyder,[2] and Professor Simon Newcomb of the Naval Observatory, Washington.[3] These writers repeat the complaints which Professor Rowland of Johns Hopkins had uttered more than twenty-five years ago.[4] Professor Münsterberg, in the said article of the *Atlantic Monthly*, repudiates the charge that America has no scholarship at all; he affirms that the situation is infinitely better than Europeans suppose it to be — in certain branches of knowledge excellent work has been done. Nevertheless the author is compelled to continue: "And yet I am convinced that the result stands in no proper relation to the achievements of American culture in all the other aspects of national life, and the best American scholars everywhere frankly acknowledge and seriously deplore it. . . . American publications cross the ocean in a ridiculously small number; in the world of letters no Columbus has yet discovered the other side of the globe."[5] Years ago, Dr. McCosh had passed a similar verdict: "The scholarship of the great body of the students is as high in America as in Europe; but they rear in Great Britain and Germany a body of ripe scholars to whom we have nothing equal in the New World."[6]

[1] *Atlantic Monthly*, May 1901.
[2] *North American Review*, Jan. 1902.
[3] *North American Review*, February 1902.
[4] See *Popular Science Monthly*, June 1901.
[5] *Atlantic Monthly, l. c.*, p. 615.
[6] *Life of James McCosh*, p. 204.

Can we, then, be surprised to find that the Catholic institutions could not yet develop productive scholarship? However, as was said by many distinguished writers, productive scholarship is by no means the first requisite for an efficient teacher, much more essential are "intelligence, self-sacrifice, and close attention to lessons given by masters of tried experience." In the next chapter we shall show that the training prescribed by the Ratio Studiorum for the young Jesuit is excellently suited to furnish him with these requisites, and thus to make of him a good teacher.[1]

[1] On p. 409 it is said that a sort of "pseudo-productivity" is likely to attend the excessive emphasis laid on scholarship. This statement finds a striking confirmation in the latest *Report of the Com. of Ed.* (1901, vol. I, pp. 127—128). In a brief article "Higher Education made in Germany," we read among other things: "To deplore the fact that our scholarship has a strong German tinge would be like apologizing for the loins from which we sprang. And yet it is a question if of recent years we have not followed German methods too exclusively and too unintelligently." The Germans themselves often misuse the scientific method on trivial subjects. "Scholarship suffers from an enormous overproduction of monographs in which an ambitious method stretches a thin substance to the cracking point. There is a craze not to prove something valuable, but to prove something." A few remarkable instances of such "scholarly" productions of American graduate students are given in the same article.

CHAPTER XV.

Training of the Jesuit Teacher.

It is generally admitted that even at present the Jesuits exercise considerable influence in the world. What is the secret of their hold on Catholics? What the source from which their power springs? The real secret of the Jesuits' influence is to be found in their training. Dr. Freytag in his review of Father Duhr's work on the Ratio Studiorum remarked: "After the perusal of this learned work, one will understand that only highly talented young men can join that Order; for what is demanded of them [in the line of studies] is extraordinary."[1] We have to see how far this training of a Jesuit is a satisfactory preparation for his work as teacher in high schools and colleges, how far it tends to make the Jesuit teacher — in the words of the Hon. G. C. Brodrick—"a man of self-sacrifice," and whether it gives him a "solid knowledge of his subject and the art of teaching, through close attendance from a master of experience."

The first requisite is, that the original material, the candidate for the Order, is good. The statue, however deftly carved, will not be a success if the marble has serious defects. Therefore, such only are to be admitted into the ranks of the Society, as are capable of receiving the Jesuit 'form,' only those who show a capacity for imbibing its spirit and submitting

[1] In the *Centralorgan für die Interessen des Realschulwesens.* Berlin.

(415)

to its discipline.¹ The Constitutions of the Society are quite explicit on this point. They say that the person having the power of admission "should not be turned by any consideration from that which he shall judge most conducive in the Lord to the *service of God* in the Society; to promote which he should not be too eager to grant admission."² The Provincial Superior is further exhorted "to watch that his subjects are not too anxious (*ne nimii sint*) to attract people to the Society, but by their virtues they should endeavor to lead all to Christ."³ The teachers in particular are told "even in private conversations to inculcate piety, but without attracting any one to the Order."⁴ Now what qualities does the Society require of those applying for admission? The Constitutions want men endowed with the highest gifts of nature. In order that they may be able to benefit their fellow creatures, the candidates of the Society should be endowed with the following gifts: as regards their *intellect*, they should possess good judgment, sound doctrine, or the talent to acquire it. As to *character*, they must be studious of all virtue and spiritual perfection, calm, steadfast and strenuous in what they undertake for God's service, and burning with zeal for the salvation of souls. In *externals*, facility of language, so needful for the intercourse with fellow men; besides, the applicant should possess good health and strength to undergo the labors of the Institute.⁵

¹ See Father Clarke's article in the *Nineteenth Century*, Aug. 1896.
² *Const. Soc. Jesu*, Pars I, cap. 1, 4.
³ *Reg. Prov.*, 33.
⁴ *Reg. com.*, 6.
⁵ *Constitutions of the Society*, P. I. c. 2.

Such is the material of the future Jesuit; no mean material indeed. How does the Society carry out the modelling of the young members? How does she — to confine ourselves to the question of training teachers — train them to become efficient instructors and educators? To understand this better, it will be good to follow a young Jesuit through the course of his training. Take a young man, a student of a college, perhaps of a university. May be, he has been educated in a Jesuit college, he has seen the Jesuits working for education, has heard them preaching and lecturing, he feels attracted by their work: he wants to become one of them. Perhaps he has never seen a Jesuit, but he has heard of them, has read of the great achievements of the famous missionaries of the Order, beginning from St. Francis Xavier down to our days; he has come across a book written by a Jesuit, he hears how much they have done in the defense of Christianity, above all how they are hated and persecuted by the enemies of the Church: the ideal inspirations of his heart grow stronger, and he inquires where he can find these men so much spoken of. It is a fact that during the *Kulturkampf* in Germany, the German Province of the Society almost doubled its numbers. Many students, who had never seen a Jesuit, left the gymnasium or university to join the exiles, just because of the singular hatred of which the outlawed Order was the object. They concluded that a body of men thus singled out, must possess something extraordinary, something especially praiseworthy, as they could not believe that the calumnies spread by the enemies of the Jesuits could have any foundation. The student, frequently the brightest of his class, travels to the nearest place, perhaps to a foreign country, where he finds a house or a college of the Order.[1] He is introduced to the Superior, to whom he expresses' his desire of joining the ranks of the sons of St. Ignatius. He is strictly examined as to his studies, his character, the motives which led him to apply for admission to the Society, and above all, whether any one, especially a Jesuit, has influenced him to take this step, which latter fact would be considered an impediment to his admission. The hardships of the religious life, the long course of studies prescribed by the Society, the sacrifices to be undergone, the obedience to be rendered, all this is explained to him. But suppose these representations do not deter him, then after a careful examination conducted by several Jesuits, if the student is thought to possess sufficient talent, and a good moral disposition, he is received as a novice of the Society.

Perhaps the young candidate expected soon to be sent to the missions, or to be employed in teaching or writing, but the Society holds to the old principle that he who is to teach, is first to learn. Above all, he has to learn the most necessary science, expressed by the old *Nosce teipsum:* "Know thyself," and that not in a merely speculative, but in a severely practical manner. By this intense self-knowledge, the young religious is enabled to understand the characters of others and to deal with them successfully. During the first two years, in strict seclusion from the world,

---

[1] The entrance into religious life and the happiness enjoyed in the novitiate, is beautifully told by the German Jesuit Denis, translator of Ossian's poems, and by the French Jesuit Ravignan, famous for his conferences at Notre Dame, Paris.

he learns that self-knowledge, self-control, and "self-sacrifice," which are necessary to the future missionary, and no less so, to the future teacher. It is a religious, a spiritual training which the future educator receives first as the foundation of all other training. Education and reform must begin at home. The teacher is to instruct his pupils in the principles of true and solid morality. If he does not possess and practise these principles himself, he will be a corrupter of youth instead of a father and friend, "a blind leader of the blind, and both shall fall into the pit," as the Divine Teacher expresses it. If without practising these principles he endeavors to teach them, he is a hypocrite; his deeds will belie his words, and the eyes of the young are sharp and their perception is keen; they will soon discover the discord between the teacher's action and his precepts, and the former will have a more powerful influence on them, than the latter, as the Latin adage has it: *Verba movent, exempla trahunt.* Even the pagan rhetorician Quintilian insists on this point: *Ipse (magister) nec habeat vitia, nec ferat:* "The teacher should neither have nor tolerate faults."[1] The teacher is daily for hours with his pupils, speaking to them, moving before them, his every word, his every gesture, his every smile is watched by a set of keen critics. All this must imperceptibly exercise a deep influence on the youthful mind. How perfect, therefore, ought the teacher to be, how faultless, how exemplary! But this moral perfection cannot be acquired except by severe self-control, by rigorous self-discipline, the acquirement of which forms the great end of the religious noviceship.

[1] *De Inst. Orat.*, II, 2.

It was St. Ignatius' oft-repeated maxim, not only: *Nosce te ipsum*, but, *Vince te ipsum:* "Conquer thyself." This is the way of training men, characters, of whom there is greater need than of scholars.

In frequent meditations on the end of man, on the life of the Divine Master, the young religious beholds the true dignity of man, the true "sanctity of the individual," which consists in his relation to God, his Creator. These truths brought home to the religious by daily reflection will inspire him with that genuine zeal, that pure love of man, which is ready to undergo any hardship, to spend time, talent, health, and life, in order to make his neighbor's soul good and noble on earth and happy throughout eternity. To the practical study of the character, of the life, of the words and actions of the Divine Master, not only the novice, but every Jesuit, devotes an hour every day in his morning meditation. In this school he learns to deal with pupils, seeing with what patience, kindness and love Christ dealt with little ones and with His disciples whose "slowness of grasp and understanding" (Luke 24, 25) would have been too much for any teacher, except him who was so "meek and humble of heart" (Matt. 11, 29). From Christ, the poor, and the friend of the lowly, he learns to "slight no one, to care as much for the progress of the poor pupils as of the rich," as his rule enjoins him.[1] From Christ, who sacrificed the most tender relations on earth to the will and service of God, in order to be "about his father's business" (Luke 2, 49), the future teacher must learn how to control the affections of his heart, so as not to show any partiality, any special

---

[1] *Reg. com. mag. schol. inf.*, 50.

love to particular pupils. All these qualities and virtues, so necessary for the teacher, the young religious endeavors to acquire during the time of his preparation. The new school of educators may sneer at this "asceticism," still we know that godliness, although not sufficient for everything, is nevertheless profitable for everything,[1] especially so for education.

The first two years of the life of the young Jesuit are principally devoted to this religious and moral training. However, his future life work is not lost sight of even during this time. Many exercises and practices of the novitiate have a direct bearing on his scientific preparation. As a rule, the students are admitted only after they have finished their classical course, in Germany and Austria for instance after completing the gymnasium, which is a classical course of nine years; in this country, after Sophomore class, which amounts to four years academic or high school work and two years of college properly so-called. Of course, there are exceptions to this rule, not a few enter after having finished a course of philosophy or after having taken special courses at a university, in addition to their classical studies, while sometimes students are admitted who have not completed the whole college course. During the first two years, novices have frequent oratorical exercises, they receive theoretical instructions on explaining Christian doctrine, and still more frequently — in accordance with the fundamental maxim of the Society, that practice and exercise are most important means of training — they have to give catechetical instructions. This exercise is an excellent preparation for explain-

[1] I *Tim.* 4, 8.

ing any subject in a simple and intelligent manner, a thing most valuable for instructors in lower classes. Their conversations throughout a great part of the day are to be carried on in Latin. Besides, there are several hours a week devoted to regular schools in Latin, Greek, and the mother tongue; thus the knowledge of languages is at least kept alive, if not perfected.

After the two years novitiate, the young Jesuits have to repeat the classical studies for one, two or three years — the time varies according to the studies made previous to admission to the Society. Special attention is paid to the precepts of aesthetics, poetics, and rhetoric, and to various practical applications of these precepts. Then follows a three years' course of philosophy, mathematics and natural sciences, especially physics, chemistry, biology, physiology, astronomy and geology. The system pursued is entirely different from that followed at our universities, where the student listens to the lectures of the professor, takes down notes and studies them at home, and then goes up for examination at the end of the year. Not so with the Jesuits. The lectures of the professor are not the only, perhaps not even the most important part in the philosophical and scientific training. Characteristic and most essential are again the exercises, foremost among them the *disputations*, for which three or four times a week a full hour is set apart. In what do they consist? One of the students has to study carefully a thesis previously treated in the lectures, in order to expound and defend it against the objections which are being prepared in the meantime by two other students. On the appointed day the *defender* takes his place at a special desk in front of the class, opposite him the two *objectors*. The defender states his proposition, explains its meaning, and the opinions of the adversaries, ancient and modern, then gives proofs for it, in strictly syllogistic form, all this in Latin. After a quarter of an hour, the first objector attacks the proposition, or a part of it, or an argument adduced in its proof, all this again in syllogisms. The defender repeats the objection, then answers in a few words to *major*, *minor* and *conclusion*, by conceding, denying, or distinguishing the various parts of the objector's syllogism. The opponent urges his objection, by offering a new subsumptive syllogism to the defender's solution. After a quarter of an hour the second objector does the same for fifteen minutes. During the last quarter, either the professor, or any student present, may offer objections against the defender's proposition.

These disputations are regular intellectual tournaments, the objectors trying to show the weak points of the thesis, the defender striving to maintain his proposition. "This system of testing the soundness of the doctrine taught, continued as it is throughout the theological studies, which come at a later period of the young Jesuit's career, provides those who pass through it with a complete defense against difficulties which otherwise are likely to puzzle the Catholic controversialist. It is a splendid means of sifting truth from falsehood. Many of those who take part in it are men of ability and well versed in the objections that can be urged against the Catholic teaching. Such men conduct their attack not as a mere matter of form, but with vigor and ingenuity. . . . Sometimes the objector will urge his difficulties with such a semblance of conviction as even to mislead some of those present. . . . So far from any check being put on the liberty of the students, they are encouraged to press home every sort of objection, however searching and fundamental, however bold and profane (e. g. against the existence of God, free will, immortality of the soul, Divinity of Christ, the Catholic Church etc.), that can be raised to the Catholic doctrine. In every class are found to be men, who are not to be put off with an evasion, and a professor who was to attempt to substitute authority for reason, would very soon find out his mistake. This perfect liberty of disputation is one of the many happy results of the possession of perfect and unfailing truth."[1]

Every six or eight weeks, all the more important theses discussed during the preceding time, are defended in the monthly disputations, at which all the different classes of the institution and all the professors of the faculty are present. Sometimes more solemn disputations are held, to which frequently professors from other institutions are invited, and any one is free to offer objections which the defender has to solve. There can be no doubt that this method has many great advantages. First of all, it forces the student to study his proposition most thoroughly; for he is not aware what objections shall be made. Therefore, both defenders and objectors have to prepare most carefully, to examine closely the proposition on all sides, to know its exact meaning, to understand the arguments, and to discover its weak points. The professor, of course, is present, sees that strict syl-

[1] Father Clarke in the *Nineteenth Century*, August, 1896.

logistic form is kept, and in case the defender is unable to solve the difficulties, has to give the final decision. At the same time it forces the professor to be most careful and accurate in the opinion he holds, and especially in the arguments which he proposes, as fullest liberty is given in attacking every point, and as the students, frequently mature men and highly gifted, try their very best to show any weak point in the argumentation of the text book, or in the professor's propositions. Professor Paulsen observes on the disputations of the medieval schoolmen, of which the disputations of the Jesuit schools are a modification: "As regards the disputations, it may be said that the Middle Ages were hardly mistaken. They were undoubtedly fitted to produce a great readiness of knowledge and a marvellous skill in grasping arguments."[1]

It has frequently been asserted that this uniform training of the Jesuits crushes out all individuality. Professor Paulsen says: "Great individualities do not appear in the history of the Order," and Cardinal Newman writes: "What a great idea, to use Guizot's expression, is the Society of Jesus! what a creation of genius in its organization; but so well adapted is the institution to its object that for that very reason it can afford to crush individualities, however gifted; so much so, that, in spite of the rare talents of its members, it has even become an objection to it in the mouth of its enemies, that it has not produced a thinker like Scotus or Malebranche!"[2]

Does uniform training necessarily result in uniformity of character? Certainly not. If all those

[1] *Geschichte des gel. Unt.*, vol. I, p. 38.
[2] Newman, *Historical Sketches*, III, p. 71.

JESUIT EDUCATION.

trained had the same disposition, the same nature to be worked upon, perhaps it would. Does the same nourishment given to a number of children produce the same result, the same complexion, the same color of hair, the same seize? Why should mental food? Does the same training in a military academy produce a perfect likeness in all? The military system of the "Great Powers" gives the most uniform training in the world. Does it crush out individuality of the generals and officers in tactics and strategy? Jesuit pupils will be surprised at being told that their teachers have all the same mould of character and are destitute of individuality. But no one smiles more at the above mentioned assertion than Jesuit Superiors, whose hardest task it is to unite all the different characters in one common effort, without interfering too much with their individuality. They know too well that the crushing out of the individuality would mean the crushing of energy and of self-activity so much insisted on by St. Ignatius in his *Spiritual Exercises*. It was St. Ignatius who told those who have charge of the spiritual training of the members of the Order: "It is most dangerous to endeavor to force all on the same path to perfection; he who attempts this does not know how different and how manifold the gifts of the Holy Ghost are."[1]

If one studies the works of the great writers of the Society, he will be struck by the variety and difference of opinions held by professors and writers of the same period, v. g. Suarez and Vasquez.[2] It is amusing to read

[1] *Selectae S. Ignatii Sententiae*, VIII.
[2] However, these two theologians did not teach *together* in the same university, as is often said. See the dates given by Fathers Frins, S. J., and Kneller, S. J., in the *Kirchenlexikon*, XI, 923, and XII, 634.

how one attacks and refutes the other, speaking of "the opinions of a certain modern author which cannot be maintained at all" etc. Cardinal Newman says in his *Historical Sketches:* "It is plain that the body is not over-zealous about its theological traditions, or it certainly would not suffer Suarez to controvert with Molina, Viva with Vasquez, Passaglia with Petavius, and Faure with Suarez, de Lugo and Valentia. In this intellectual freedom its members justly glory; inasmuch as they have set their affections, not on the opinions of the Schools, but on the souls of men."[1] Professor Paulsen seems to have forgotten his own statement: "Greatest possible power of the individual is preserved without derangement of the organism of the Order, spontaneous activity and perfect submission of the will, contrasts almost irreconcilable, seem to have been harmoniously united in a higher degree by the Society, than by any other body."[2] A recent English writer,[3] speaking of the "crushing of individuality practised by the Jesuits," seems to trace it to the pernicious influence of the spirit of the Latin races. The Latins "keep men in leading strings;" "liberty to Latins means license;" "true Latins cannot understand the principle of personality." The Spaniards, in particular, are regarded with special horror. The Roman Curia is said to have adopted the system used by the Spaniards, "who could not endure discussion or publicity; centralization

[1] *Hist. Sketches*, vol. II, p. 369. Does not this great writer, by so true a statement of facts, refute what, in another passage, he quoted about crushing out individuality?
[2] See above p. 18.
[3] Father Taunton, *A History of the Jesuits in England*, 1901. See *Month*, May 1901, p. 505.

was the ideal; routine the practice," and so on. "The Jesuit system of blind obedience was founded to bring about the absolutism of authority;" this "makes them akin (strange though it may seem) to that Puritan strain so often found in those doing or desirous of doing great things." This is strange indeed, but far stranger are the absurdities and contradictions into which prejudiced men are led. The Jesuits are said to be deprived of personality and individuality, and in the same breath it is sometimes asserted that everywhere they know how to adapt themselves to the most different circumstances: In England, America, Germany, Spain, France, Russia, China, Japan, Paraguay, Abyssinia. It is said the General wants a man for some secret mission. He opens his list and there he finds a man especially fitted to influence the court of St. Petersburg, or the Padisha in Constantinople; then one who knows so well how to ingratiate himself with Cromwell as to become his friend, dine at his table, play chess with him;[1] then one who is fitted for guiding his Celestial Majesty in Pekin; here one to rouse the starving peasants of Ireland to enthusiasm for their 'Romish' faith, then one who by all sorts of devices tames the savages of Paraguay; one who disputes with the bonzes in Japan, or becomes a Brahmin in India, as the famous Robert de Nobili; there is one who is best suited to conquer the refractory Professors at the University in Louvain, and the Doctors of the Sorbonne, then another who wins the confidence of the townspeople and villagers in Switzerland, the Tyrol, and Germany — in short men for

[1] Taunton, *l. c.*

every possible mission.[1] Such are the opinions of the adversaries of the Society. But is not the greatest variety of characters needed for all these employments? And yet, they are supposed to be deprived of individuality! Or is that *unpersonal* trait which is *infused* into every Jesuit so universal that all other individualities are contained in it, as the scholastic philosophers express it, *eminenter*, in a subtle and mysterious form? Is every Jesuit a sort of Proteus, who could change himself into a lion, a serpent, a pard, a boar, a tree, a fountain? A wonderful system of training, indeed, for which the diplomats of our modern courts might envy the Jesuits. To be serious, that depriving of personality, attributed to the Jesuit system, is nothing but one of the numerous Jesuit myths.

We have left our young Jesuit in his philosophical course. But what becomes in the meantime of the study of the classical languages? It is not neglected during the course of philosophy, at least the Ratio Studiorum provides special means to foster and promote this important branch of study. The lectures in mathematics and natural sciences are given in the mother tongue, but the lectures and disputations in philosophy are all conducted in Latin, so that the young Jesuit is in the habit of speaking Latin and may speak it with ease and fluency. It is true, the Latin of these disputations and lectures in not exactly Ciceronian, still it is by no means as barbarous as the

[1] There was a time "when behind every Roman Catholic Court in Europe there stood a Jesuit confessor, and a Jesuit emissary ascended the back stairs of every Protestant palace." *English Review*, vol. V, 1846, p. 65.

opponents of this system represent it. Some of the Latin text books on philosophy are written in accurate Latin.[1] It is not, however, this custom of speaking Latin which we wished to adduce as a provision of the Ratio Studiorum, to advance the study of Latin during the course of philosophy. But we find in the Ratio, among the rules for the Prefect of the higher studies, the following clause: "He shall give every student of philosophy a classical author and admonish him not to omit reading it at certain hours."[2]

[1] "Monkish Latin" has become a byword from the days of the humanists on to our age. The technical terms introduced by the scholastics are, it is true, not found in the writings of the ancients. Still we cannot deny that the schoolmen had a right, for the sake of greater brevity and precision, to form new words, from old roots, in order to avoid the cumbrous circumlocutions of a Cicero. Many modern scholars view the scholastic Latin much more favorably than was customary a few decades ago. Thus Mr. Leach, who is anything but friendly to the scholastics, says: "The medieval schoolmen sinned no more against pure Latinity, than the modern scientific writer sins against English undefiled, if such there be." And Mr. Rashdall writes: "Among the students of a University and among the clergy generally much villainous Latin was no doubt talked, just as much villainous French is or was encouraged by the rule of French-speaking in English Seminaries for Young Ladies. But the Latin which was written by the theologian, or historian . . . was not as bad as is commonly supposed by those who have only heard it abused. J. S. Mill has rightly praised the schoolmen for their unrivalled capacity in the invention of technical terms. The Latin language originally rigid, inflexible, poor in vocabulary, and almost incapable of expressing a philosophical idea, became in the hands of medieval thinkers, flexible, subtle, rich." *Univers. of the M. A.*, vol. II, pp. 595-596. See also Paulsen, *l. c.*, vol. I, pp. 45-48.

[2] *Reg. Praef. Stud.* 30.

In this manner six or seven years of training have been spent in the Society in addition to about the same number of years devoted to higher studies previous to the admission into the Order; thus, before the Jesuit begins his work as teacher, twelve years, on the average, have been spent in studies after the completion of the elementary or public school course. The Jesuit teacher is then employed in the academical or high school department. His training compares favorably to that of the high school teachers in this country, at least as far as the length of time is concerned. In Massachusetts (1897) one per cent of high school teachers were graduates of scientific schools, thirteen per cent of normal schools, sixty-six per cent of colleges, twenty per cent unclassified. — In the State of New York (1898) there were thirty-two per cent college graduates, thirty-nine per cent normal school graduates, nineteen per cent high school graduates, ten per cent had other training.[1] Thus the average of higher studies is certainly not more than eight years, against the twelve years of the Jesuit teacher.

It may be asked how far the Jesuit's studies are preparatory to his work as teacher? The repetition of the classics in the two years "Juniorate" previous to the study of philosophy, is not only considered as part of the general culture, but is especially viewed as a preparation for the Jesuits' work as teachers. Quick has correctly said that the Juvenats or Juniorates were the training schools where the young Jesuit learned the method of teaching.[2] That this was the aim of this course is apparent from what the General Visconti

[1] From *Education in the United States*, vol. I, p. 190.
[2] *Educational Reformers*, pp. 86—87.

said: "Immediately after their novitiate they [the young Jesuits] must have the most accomplished professors of Rhetoric [by which word is understood general philological knowledge], men, who not only are altogether eminent in this faculty, but who know how to teach and make everything smooth for the scholars; men of eminent talent and the widest experience in the art; who are not merely to form good scholars, but to train good masters."[1]

But there are other most important regulations concerning the direct training for teaching. Towards the end of the philosophical course, before going to the colleges, there should be an immediate preparation for those who in the near future are to enter on the momentous career of teaching boys. The outline of the Ratio Studiorum of 1586 demands the following course:[2] "It would be most profitable for the schools, if those who are about to be preceptors were privately taken in hand by some one of great experience, and for two months or more were practised by him in the method of reading, teaching, correcting, writing, and managing a class. If teachers have not learned these things beforehand, they are forced to learn them afterwards at the expense of their scholars; and then they will acquire proficiency only when they have already lost in reputation; and perchance they will never unlearn a bad habit. Sometimes such a habit is neither very serious nor incorrigible, if taken at the beginning; but if the habit is not corrected at the outset, it comes to pass that a man, who otherwise would have been most useful, becomes well-nigh useless. There is no describing how much amiss preceptors take it, if they

[1] Pachtler, vol. III, pp. 130—131. — Hughes, p. 184.
[2] Pachtler, vol. II, p. 154. — See Hughes, p. 160.

are corrected, when they have already adopted a fixed method of teaching; and what continual disagreement ensues on that score with the Prefect of Studies. To obviate this evil, in the case of our professors, let the Prefect in the chief college, whence our professors of Humanities and Grammar are usually taken, remind the Rector and Provincial, about three months before the next scholastic year begins, that, if the Province needs new professors for the following term, they should select some one eminently versed in the art of managing classes, whether he be at the time actually a professor or a student of theology or philosophy; and to him the future masters are to go daily for an hour,[1] to be prepared by him for their new ministry, giving prelections in turn, writing, dictating, correcting, and discharging the other duties of a good teacher."[2] Professor Ziegler, commenting on this regulation, says: "To the Jesuits must be given the credit of first having done something for the pedagogical preparation of the future teachers in higher schools; and of having paved the way for the *Probe-* und *Seminarjahr* of our days."[3]

Another regulation laid down in the Ratio of 1599, as a duty of the Provincial,[4] is of the greatest importance: "In order to preserve the knowledge of classical literature, and to keep up a Seminary of teachers, he shall try to have in his Province at least two or

[1] In the final *Ratio Stud.* of 1599, it was laid down as a duty of the Rector to see that this was done, but the time was limited to three hours a week. (*Reg. Rect.* 9.)
[2] Pachtler, vol. II, p. 154, no. 6. — Hughes, p. 160. — Duhr, p. 39.
[3] *Geschichte der Pädagogik*, p. 111.
[4] *Reg. Prov.* 22.

three men distinguished in these branches. This he shall accomplish, if, from time to time, he takes care that some of them who have a special talent and inclination for these studies, and are sufficiently trained in other branches, devote themselves exclusively to this vocation, so that, through their efforts and industry, a stock of good teachers is formed."

In order to give the young teachers, who were to be trained in this Seminary, a reliable guide, the general assembly of the Society, in 1696-97, passed a decree that, "besides the rules whereby the masters of literature are directed in the manner of teaching, they should be provided with an Instruction and proper Method of Learning, and so be guided in their private studies even while they are teaching."[1] Father Joseph de Jouvancy (Latinized Juvencius), one of the greatest authorities on education of his age, was ordered to revise, and adapt to the requirements of this decree, a work which he had published five years previously. This book, after a careful examination by a special commission, appeared in 1703, as the authorized handbook for the teachers of the Society, under the title: *Magistris scholarum inferiorum Societatis Jesu de ratione discendi et docendi.*[2] The General Visconti in 1752 wished the little book to be in the hands of all Jesuit

[1] Pachtler, I, pp. 101-2. — Duhr, p. 40. — Hughes, p. 162.
[2] A German translation of this work, with introduction and notes, by Robert Schwickerath, S. J., was published in 1898, in Herder's *Bibliothek der katholischen Pädagogik*, vol. X, pp. 207-322. — An excellent sketch of the life and the works of this "model of a Jesuit Professor" is contained in the *Études religieuses*, Paris, November and December 1872. — The correct form of the name is *Jouvancy*, not Jouvency, which latter originated from the Latinized Juvencius.

teachers.[1] The little work has been styled a pedagogical gem, and it was highly praised by Rollin and Voltaire.[2] Dr. Ernst von Sallwürk said of it a few years ago that its importance reaches far beyond the Jesuit schools. "We may consider it a reliable source for information of what Jesuit pedagogy at his time aimed at and achieved. Besides, this book is one of the most prominent works on college pedagogy (*Gymnasial-Pädagogik*)."[3] In the following chapters we shall frequently refer to this excellent work of Father Jouvancy.

The account we have given so far of the training of the Jesuit teacher furnishes an answer to the charge, which is brought forward now and then, that the Jesuit teachers were too young. No matter how things stood in the Old Society, at present, according to the above data, the average age of the Jesuit teacher when he begins teaching cannot be less than twenty-four years. Besides, every college, according to the Ratio Studiorum, ought to possess a number of *magistri perpetui*, permanent teachers, i. e. of men who spend their whole lives in teaching. This is clearly stated in the rules of the Provincial: "He shall procure as many as possible permanent teachers of grammar and rhetoric. This he shall effect if, at the end of the casuistic or theological studies, some men who are thought to fulfil the duties of the Society better in this ministry than in any other, are resolutely (*strenue*) destined for it, and admonished to devote themselves wholly to so salutary a work, to the greater glory of

[1] Pachtler, vol. III, p. 132; IV, pp. 401, 435.
[2] See above page 163, note 1.
[3] In Schmid's *Geschichte der Erziehung*, vol. IV, Abteilung I, pp. 460 and 538–543.

God."[1] Father Sacchini devotes the fourth part of his *Protrepticon* to encouraging the members of the Society first, to offer themselves to the arduous but noble work of education: "The education of youth for many reasons deserves to be preferred by a zealous Jesuit to all the other ministries of the Order." He quotes the words of Pope Paul III., in the Bull of the confirmation of the Society: "They [the members of the Society] shall have expressly recommended to them the instruction of boys and ignorant people. . . . For it is most necessary that the General and his council diligently watch over the management of this business; seeing that the edifice of faith cannot be raised in our neighbors without a foundation, and there may be danger among ourselves lest, as each is more learned, he may endeavor to evade this duty [of instructing the young], as at first sight perhaps less engaging: whilst in fact none is more productive, either of edification to our neighbors or of the practice of the duties of charity and humility to ourselves."[2] Father Sacchini says that this volunteering and application for the work of education, far from being in any way opposed to obedience, on the contrary, is the most beautiful flower and

[1] *Reg. Prov.* 24. — By a very curious mistake some writers (as Professor Müller in Schmid's *Geschichte der Erziehung*, vol. III, Abteilung I, page 41) represent these "permanent teachers" as a separate and inferior grade in the Society, "who received only a special drill in pedagogical courses and were not much esteemed." And yet the Ratio Studiorum, in the rule just quoted, states explicitly that the members of the Society should be appointed as *magistri perpetui* after the completion of their *theological* course. Therefore the priests are meant.

[2] English transl. from *Constitutions of the Society of Jesus*, London, 1838.

perfection of that virtue, which St. Ignatius recommended when saying, one should not wait for the Superior's *command*, but should anticipate his very suggestions and silent wishes.

In the second place Father Sacchini exhorts the teacher to devote generously his whole life to this great work. Some writers on the history of education have stated that the Jesuits, after having been admitted to Priest's Orders, did not teach the grammar classes, but gave only the higher instruction.[1] Compayré goes so far as to assert that "in their establishments for secondary instruction they entrust the lower classes to teachers who do not belong to their Order, and reserve to themselves the direction of the higher classes."[2] This is utterly false. Lay teachers are only employed when the insufficiency in the number of Jesuits makes it necessary; or for certain branches, as commercial branches, or in professional courses, as in the faculties for Law and Medicine, preparatory schools for Army and Navy, in short, wherever lay experts are needed. The history of Jesuit schools, old and new, refutes the statement of Compayré and other writers. Many priests have taught the lower classes for many years, some for their whole lives. Besides, if priests did not teach these classes, the regulations of the Ratio about "permanent teachers," the earnest appeals of Sacchini and other Jesuit writers, would be altogether meaningless.

Father Sacchini, in order to encourage the Jesuits to devote their whole lives to this noble work, enumerates the various emoluments accruing from this perseverance to the teacher himself, as it gives him

[1] Quick, *Educational Reformers*, p. 36, note a.
[2] *History of Pedag.*, p. 143.

facility, interest, and experience in his work. He further points out the advantages of this stability for the pupils and for the Society. He cites in this connection the words of *Ecclesiasticus*[1]: "Be steadfast in the covenant, and be conversant therein, and grow old in thy work. Trust in God and stay in thy place." The Greek text has, instead of " place", πόνος, *i. e.* "hard work, toil, drudgery," a word admirably suited to express the toilsome labor of education. Therefore: "stay in thy place, bear patiently the toil and drudgery necessarily connected with teaching," is the advice given to the teacher of the Society. In fact, numerous Jesuits have heeded this advice, and have spent thirty, forty, fifty, and more years in college work. Not to speak of times long gone by, or of foreign countries, we mention the following fact. In 1888, died at Spring Hill College, near Mobile, Alabama, Father Yenni, author of a Latin and a Greek grammar, who for fifty years had been teaching boys, and, at his special request, always in the lowest classes.

The Ratio speaks more explicitly of the training of the teachers for the literary curriculum; it is understood that those who have to teach mathematics, sciences, etc., receive a special training in their respective branches. Other documents of the Society state this principle in the clearest terms. In the memorandum of Father Clavius, written more than three hundred years ago, it is said: "In order to have always in the Society able teachers of these sciences, some who are especially fitted for this task should be selected and trained, in a private course, in the various

[1] *Eccli.* 11, 21, 22.

mathematical branches."[1] In another document we read: "The best way, perhaps, is that those who are chosen for this office [teaching mathematics] should, after the course of philosophy, study for a *whole year* the branches which they will have to teach."[2] This special course, in addition to the general training in mathematics received in the course of philosophy, was certainly a sufficient preparation for the amount of mathematics which was taught in former centuries.

It is evident, then, that both the general and special training of the Jesuit teacher were well attended to before he was sent out to teach.

Several weeks before the beginning of a new scholastic year, the young Jesuit arrives at the college which is to be the first field of his educational labors. After some time, during which the Rector of the college and the Prefect of Studies have formed acquaintance with the new-comer, a certain class is assigned to him for the next year. It is according to the spirit, not only of the Ratio Studiorum, but of the whole Institute of the Society, that great care be taken that the positions in colleges, as well as elsewhere, are assigned according to the talent, the knowledge and the practical abilities of the individuals. To quote only a few regulations of the Institute, the Constitutions declare: "Every one should be trained according to his age, talent, and inclinations," of course always considering "where the common good can be advanced best."[3] The Provincial is told "to take care that those who have a special inclination for a certain

[1] *Monumenta Paedagogica*, p. 471.
[2] *Ibid.*, p. 475.
[3] *Pars* IV, *cap.* V, *Declar.* C.

branch of study, in which they can distinguish themselves, spend more time in this branch,"[1] — certainly for no other reason than that they should use this knowledge for teaching, or if circumstances require, writing on this special subject. Specialization is, accordingly, no new invention of modern times, but was recognized as important centuries ago, but a specialization which presupposes the solid foundation of general culture. Unless this be done, the educational structure becomes "top-heavy"; "time, money, and labor are put on the superstructure at the expense of the foundation," as an American writer complains of modern educational systems.[2] The specialties to be provided for by the selection and fostering of special talents, are, in the terms of the second last general assembly of the Order (in 1883), "ancient languages, philosophy, ethnology, history, higher mathematics, and all the natural sciences."[3] The Institute emphasizes the necessity of selecting the teachers according to their abilities: "In universities and colleges learned and able professors are to be appointed,"[4] and the Provincial Superior is exhorted "to consider in due time what teachers are to be taken for the single branches, and look out for those that seem best fitted, who are learned, studious, and assiduous (*docti, diligentes, assidui*), and intent upon the progress of the pupils."[5] Now, there is scarcely any studiousness or

[1] *Reg. Prov.* 55 (No. 55 of the Rules in the *Institute*, not of the *Rat. Stud.*).
[2] *Is our Educational System Top-heavy?* By Elliott Flower, in the *North American Review*, February 1898.
[3] See Pachtler, vol. I, p. 123.
[4] *Reg. Prov.* 47. (*Institute.*)
[5] *Rat. St.*, *Reg. Prov.* 4 and *Const.*, *Pars* IV, cap. VI, 6.

assiduity possible, unless a man takes a natural interest in the subject which he has to study or teach. True, the Jesuit is told by his Institute to do everything from a supernatural motive; still in the special field of studies "great success is hardly possible if one possesses no natural liking for such work," as a distinguished living Jesuit used to tell the younger members of the Order.

Different documents of the Society state the same principle most emphatically. We have heard that those men were to be appointed as teachers of mathematics, who were especially fitted for this task, and who felt an inclination and a liking for this branch.[1] A second document says: "Those should be chosen who, all other things being equal, are superior to all others in talent, diligence, inclination for these subjects, and in the method of teaching.... For it happens sometimes that some, proficient enough in other branches, are not mathematicians, be it for want of study or of natural talent for this branch."[2] The same principle was, of course, applied to other subjects. Father Nadal had laid it down as a general rule of the Prefect of Studies, to see that all the younger members of the Society receive a solid general training, and that special talents should be diligently cultivated. "He must take pains to discover what talent our young men have, and endeavor to advance them accordingly. If one is fitted for the study of rhetoric, see that he is

[1] "*Necessarium etiam videtur, ut praeceptor habeat inclinationem quandam et propensionem ad has scientias praelegendas.*" In the treatise: *Modus quo disciplinae mathematicae in scholis Societatis possent promoveri.* See *Monumenta Paedagogica*, p. 471.

[2] *De re mathematica instructio.* (*Mon. Paed.*, p. 476.)

given a longer and more accurate training in the humanistic studies and oratory. The same care must be taken if one is thought to have a talent for poetics, for Greek, for philosophy, theology, Sacred Scripture, the Fathers of the Church, the Councils, and Canon Law. On the other hand, if one seems not to be fitted for a certain branch of study, he should not be detained therein longer than is necessary for acquiring an ordinary knowledge."[1]

Thus it is clear that the Constitutions of the Society and the documents directly concerning the studies, from the very beginning, insisted on the necessity of assigning each teacher's work according to his natural abilities. The General of the Society, Father Visconti, inculcated this principle later on, saying that "special care should be taken to assign the classes to the teachers according to their talent, knowledge and practical skill."[2] This must be emphasized much more in our days. For in the sixteenth century, the subjects taught in colleges were fewer, and it was not so difficult to appoint teachers. But in our times, other branches must be taught. This cannot be done effectively by the same man who teaches languages and literature. There are exceedingly few men who can excel in many branches, or can be good teachers in several of them.

Here, however, there is another danger which must

[1] *Ordo Studiorum*, in *Mon. Paed.*, p. 133. It appears from the whole context that by "talent" a "special" talent is meant. Be it added that by "oratory" and "poetics" we have to understand all the studies pursued in the two classes "Humanities" and "Rhetoric".
[2] Pachtler, vol. III, p. 131.

be avoided : that of splitting up too much the work of teaching in the same class. This is most injurious to education properly so-called, especially in the lower and middle classes. One teacher should have a prominent position in the class; he should be *the* teacher, and, in the first place, *the educator* of his pupils. For this reason he should teach as many subjects as possible in his class — provided he masters them —, all those branches which are more closely connected, as Latin, Greek, also English, in short, languages and literature. With Latin and Greek it is natural to combine also Roman and Greek history. Medieval and modern history may be taught by a special teacher. Mathematics and natural sciences go well together and can easily be taught by the same teacher. In a word, the Society wishes to have *class* teachers preferably to *branch* teachers. As is well known, the class system is, to a certain extent, prevalent in Germany. For some time the branch system had been favored, but experience proved that the old class system was unquestionably better. So the "New School Order" for Prussia, 1901, strongly recommends the strengthening of the influence of the class teacher as distinct from the branch teacher, in order to secure, above all, better education. "The splitting up of the teaching in the lower and middle classes among too many teachers, as well as frequent changes of teachers, are considered an obstacle to any enduring educational influence. To put a stop, as far as possible, to these evils, the provincial school authorities are strictly bound to see to it that a professor proposed as a *class teacher* be suitable for the position, *and that he teach in his class as many subjects as possible*, so far as his scholastic attainments and practical experience allow it."[1] The advantages of this system for education need not be demonstrated. It is the only system which gives the teacher a thorough knowledge of the pupil and influence on the formation of his character.[2]

There is another practice of Jesuit colleges which had for its end the strengthening of the educational influence of the teacher. According to the Ratio Studiorum, it was customary that the teacher should not always remain in the same grade, except the professors of the two highest literary classes, of Humanities and Rhetoric, where more erudition is required. But the young teacher should begin with the lowest class, then year after year advance with the better part of his pupils to the next higher grade, at least for three or four years. Thus the students have not to pass so often from one master, and consequently from one kind of management, to the other; master and pupil understand each other, and if the teacher is a good religious and a fairly efficient teacher, he will have won the esteem, the affection, and the confidence of the pupils, all which gives him inestimable advantages for the real and thorough education of his charges. On the other hand, frequent changes interfere considerably with the training of the pupils. As early as 1583, Father Oliver Manare, visiting the colleges of the German provinces by the General's authority, laid it down as a directive that "frequent changes were burdensome to the students, because they were forced to

[1] *Lehrpläne und Lehraufgaben*, 1901, p. 75. See *Messenger*, New York, Sept. 1901.

[2] On this subject there is a splendid article, written by Father Pachtler in the year 1880, in the *Stimmen aus Maria-Laach*, vol. XVIII, pp. 49—66.

accommodate themselves often to new teachers and prefects."[1]

If, for want of a sufficient number of men, some of the regulations laid down for the training of the teacher, were, perhaps, not everywhere and always complied with, the Ratio Studiorum is not to be censured on that account, nor the Society as such, as by wise legislation she endeavored to obviate any such shortcomings.[2] Moreover, the uniformity of the previous training of the Jesuit teachers, as well as the uniform system of teaching in the colleges of the same province, has the effect that, although teachers are changed, there is no change in the method of teaching. Besides, is not every institution, secular or ecclesiastical, however well organized, open to such or similar temporary defects? Exceptional shortcomings must naturally be expected in any system, as there is nothing on earth altogether perfect and ideal. Deficiencies in individual Jesuit teachers, or in single colleges, do not prove anything against the system, no more than the inefficient administration of one Governor or President proves the worthlessness of the constitution of a State or the Republic. Our contention is only that excellent teachers are trained if the regulations of the Jesuit system are followed.

The young teacher has received his appointment, let us say for one of the high school classes, to teach Latin and Greek. He knows his grammar well, he

[1] Pachtler I, 415. — Father Ledesma made the regulation that in the beginning of the scholastic year substitutes should be appointed, who had to be ready to step in if a teacher should, by sickness or some other cause, be compelled to discontinue teaching. *Mon. Paed.*, p. 144, 156.

[2] *Reg. Provinc.* 4, 22, 24, 28, 30, etc.

has in the course of years read many classical authors. Is anything still wanting? Indeed very much: an intimate acquaintance with the authors, facility in handling their languages, skill in explaining the grammar and the authors. All this he has to acquire by a system of *continued self-training*, under the direction of the Rector or Prefect of Studies. Above all he must study the classic authors themselves. Secondhand knowledge will not suffice for the teacher. Reading over the regulations of the Society in former centuries concerning the preparation of the teachers,[1] one must be surprised to see what an amount of reading was required of the young teacher, in Latin, Greek, and history. Thus the teacher of the second lowest Grammar class (*Media Grammatica*) had to study, besides the authors he explained in class, *all* the philosophical writings of Cicero (the epistles he had read the year before), and some of the orations of the same author; the poets Claudian, Catullus, Tibullus, Propertius, Martial, the first ten books of Livy, Justin, Valerius Maximus, Velleius Paterculus, and the whole of Caesar. In Greek, Aelian, Aesop, and Xenophon's Cyropaedia. Various books on style, poetry, and rhetoric.[2] The teacher of the third class was to study all the orations of Cicero with a commentary; Horace, Seneca, and other poets; some more books of Livy, Curtius, Sallust; the Philippics of Demosthenes. — Every minute was to be utilized in order to master these authors. Catalogues of books on philology and antiquities were printed from which the young teacher might find assistance in studying and explaining the

[1] Pachtler, vol. IV, pp. 175—235.
[2] Pachtler, vol. IV, pp. 203—204.

authors.[1] The young teacher has to look not so much for pedagogical theories, as for practical knowledge. He is to read carefully the authors, closely observe peculiarities of their style, accurately translate and intelligently expound their meaning. It is exactly the system, according to which Professor Hermann of Leipsic trained his philologians. This practical method of self-activity and self-training we find explained in the first part of Jouvancy's commentary on the Ratio Studiorum, in *The Method of Learning*.

As the object of this training is to form practical teachers, not a word is said about higher criticism and the like; but Father Jouvancy urges the teacher to acquire in the first place a thorough mastery of three languages: Greek, Latin, and the vernacular. The means of gaining this mastery are plentiful reading of the best authors, and practising compositions of various kinds: letters, orations, essays.

The second part of the learning proper to the master of literature consists, according to Jouvancy, in the thorough knowledge of certain sciences. "The erudition of a master is not confined to mere command of languages; it must rise higher to the understanding of some sciences which it is usual to impart to youth in the classical schools. Such are rhetoric, poetry, history, chronology, geography, philology."[2]

[1] See Pachtler, vol. IV, pp. 12—19, where lists of such books, recommended in the Old Society, are given.

[2] *Ratio Discendi*, ch. II.—It has been proved in chapter IV, pp. 124—129, that history and geography were never neglected in the colleges of the Society. In the mean time I found that the Protestant writers of Schmid's great *Geschichte der Erziehung* (1884–1901), in sharp contrast with the assertions of M. Compayré, candidly admit the services

As regards history, it is superfluous to speak of its usefulness for a higher education. History is, indeed, a *magistra vitae*, a teacher and mirror of life, a school of practical wisdom. Of particular importance for the teacher is the thorough knowledge of the history of Greece and Rome. A scholarly appreciation of the classics is impossible without an intimate acquaintance with the history: political, social, religious, and literary, of these nations.

Here we must say a few words on the teacher's attitude towards ancient history. The religious teacher's viewpoint of history is radically different from that of the agnostic. To the religious teacher historical events are not merely the products of natural agencies. He sees rather in history, to use the words of the Jesuit Kropf, "the wonderful manifestation of God's power and a revelation of the wisdom of a

rendered to history and geography by Jesuit schools and scholars. Thus Dr. von Sallwürk says: "The study of history was considerably advanced by Jesuit writers, but the colleges of the University [of Paris] did not imitate the example of the Jesuits." *Geschichte der Erziehung*, vol. IV, Abteilung I, p. 436. "The Fathers Sirmond, Petavius, and Labbe have well deserved of historical studies and of the teaching of history in the schools.... Geography was henceforth zealously cultivated by the Jesuits.... Of great practical importance were the labors of the remarkably diligent Father Buffier; especially on geography and grammar he has written good books, in which the traditional scholastic *tone* is happily avoided.... His *Philosophy and Practical Grammar* was for a long time considered the only useful grammar of the French language.... In the schools of the Oratory we find geography as a branch of study; but to the Jesuits must be allowed the merit of having taught this branch before the Oratorians. In their College at Amiens was trained Nicolas Sanson, the 'Father of Geography'." *Ibid.*, p. 456 and 466.

Divine Providence."[1] History, in this sense, is a record of the development of mankind under the providential guidance of God; or, more precisely, a record of the systematic training and improvement of the human race by divinely appointed means as a preparation for the birth of Christ, that God might, through the coming of His Son, secure from man a spontaneous homage, a worship worthy of Himself. The coming of Christ, in this view, gives a definite character to history, and the periods both before and after that event — the greatest in history — constitute its two grand divisions,[2] the one the preparation for the coming of Christ, the other the spread and struggle of Christ's kingdom, to the final triumph on the day of Judgment. Christ, therefore, is the central figure of all history, "the stone which was rejected by the builders, which is become the head of the corner."[3]

From this standpoint, then, the Jesuit masters will study and teach the history of Greece and Rome. Of this viewpoint he will not lose sight when reading and explaining the classic authors. It need not be feared that this view will prevent the teacher from doing full justice to these two great nations. On the contrary. In the Greeks he will acknowledge those brilliant gifts of nature which made them the foremost promoters of human art, human knowledge, and human culture. In the history of Rome he will admire that wonderful talent for ruling the world, and

[1] *Ratio et Via*, chapter V, art. 9. (German translation p. 423.) The new Prussian School Order of 1901 uses the same words in regard to Church history, p. 16.
[2] Alzog, *Church History*, vol. I, p. 6.
[3] *Acts* 4, 11.

that system of jurisprudence which exercised so potent an influence on the formation of later codes of laws. However, the Christian view of history will prevent the teacher from sharing that one-sided admiration of antiquity which was so disastrous among the humanists during the Renaissance, and which is found sometimes in the ranks of professional philologists. The Greeks were indeed a race endowed with exceptional gifts of body and mind. However, we need not and cannot shut our eyes to their many moral defects, especially to that frightful kind of immorality which has received its name from the Greeks, and which manifests itself even in the finest pieces of their literature.

Nor is the Christian teacher's attitude towards imperial Rome very different. At the time when Christ appeared on earth, Rome under Augustus had risen to the zenith of her glory, and the poets sang that the golden age had returned on earth. But under a glittering surface lay hidden the misery of slavery, universal corruption, scepticism and despair. In the midst of this darkness appeared the "Light to the revelation of the Gentiles."[1] Yet the darkness did not surrender without a fierce struggle, the greatest which the world has ever seen. The history of this struggle between Christ and Caesar, between Christianity and paganism, between faith and infidelity, is the keynote of the first three centuries, nay more, of the nineteen hundred years which have since elapsed.

The Christian historian, although objecting to Gibbon's explanation of the spread of Christianity from merely natural causes,[2] admits that, apart from

[1] *Luke* 2, 32.
[2] Gibbon, *Decline and Fall of the Roman Empire*, ch. XV. See Newman's criticisms on these chapters in *Grammar of Assent*.

the intrinsic worth and positive character of Christianity as a divinely revealed religion, external circumstances also contributed to the rapid propagation of the religion of Christ. He discovers that the coming of the *Desired of Nations* had been prepared directly, through "the Law and the Prophets," among the chosen people of Israel, *indirectly* also among the Gentiles. This indirect preparation was first a negative one; the ancient world had to realize the limitation of the natural powers; it had to experience that all progress in philosophy, art and politics could neither quiet the mind nor satisfy the heart, and was utterly unable to save either the individual or the family, the state or society.[1] But there was also a more positive preparation of the Gentile world. The Greek methods of philosophy, especially those of Plato and Aristotle, in spite of their many shortcomings, became efficient means with which the early champions of the Church successfully combated the errors and absurdities of paganism and logically defended the doctrines of Revelation. Thus Plato, in the words of Clement of Alexandria, was a παιδαγωγὸς εἰς Χριστόν, a teacher who prepared the way for Christ. Origen, Eusebius and St. Augustine see a special providence of God in the conquest of the world by the Roman Empire. It is this tracing of God's working in history which Father Kropf suggested to the teacher, and it is in this light that he has to study the history and literature of Greece and Rome.

With ancient history and the classics, the teacher has to connect the study of antiquities. Those who have heard it said again and again that the Jesuit

[1] Alzog. *Church History*, vol. I, pp. 127—135.

system aims at nothing but "mere formalism, at cleverness in speaking and disputing," will naturally ask in surprise, whether the Jesuits had any place for these subjects in their course of instruction. However, a mere glance at the Ratio, the commentary of Jouvancy and other sources will convince any one that the teaching of antiquities is even prescribed in the colleges of the Society. Under the name of *eruditio*, i. e. general erudition or general learning, the study of antiquities forms an essential part of the explanation of the authors. The professor of Rhetoric (Sophomore) is told that "one of the three principal points of this grade consists in general erudition. This is to be drawn from the history of the nations and their culture, from the best authors and from every field of learning; but it is to be imparted sparingly and according to the capacity of the pupils." The fifteenth rule of the professor says that "for the advancement of erudition, sometimes, instead of reading the historical author, other subjects might be treated, e. g. hieroglyphics, and symbolic signs, epitaphs,[1] the Roman or Athenian Senate, the military systems of the Romans and Greeks, the costumes, gardens, banquets, triumphs, sibyls, etc., in short — as the Revised Ratio has it — archaeology. The first rule of the professor of Humanities mentions the same. But that it was intended for all classes, though naturally not to the same extent, is evident from Jouvancy's treatise "On the Explanation of Authors," which we shall give in substance in the next chapter. There it will also be explained why antiquities,

[1] In 1830 the German Jesuits declared these three points to be antiquated. (Pachtler IV, 439.)

according to the Ratio, should be imparted "sparingly."

If antiquities are to be taught in Jesuit colleges, the teacher must carefully study them. This is done partly in the two years of philological studies which follow the novitiate. One of the great teachers of the first century of the Society, Father Bonifacio, who for more than forty years labored in the Spanish colleges, writes: "In the philological seminaries, our young men, besides studying Latin, Greek and Hebrew, should acquire an intimate knowledge of history and classical antiquities."[1] However, this archaeological learning has to be acquired chiefly throughout the course of teaching. It will always form a part of the preparation of the authors which are, at the time, read in class. Father Jouvancy advises the young teacher to devote especially the holidays to this study, which he calls a useful and, at the same time, pleasant change.[2]

In the Old Society there existed special lists or catalogues of various works, from which historical and antiquarian information could best be obtained. Very interesting in this regard is the *Catalogue* of the province of Upper Germany of the year 1604.[3] In an introductory remark it is stated that the list of philological helps is not made for the old and experienced professors, but for the young masters, for the beginners; and a great number of works is given that every

---

[1] Father Bonifacio's pedagogical works lately appeared in a German translation, together with those of Father Perpinian and Father Possevin: in the *Bibliothek der kathol. Pädagogik*, vol. XI. — Herder, Freiburg, and St. Louis, 1901.

[2] *Ratio Discendi*, ch. III, art. 2.

[3] Pachtler, vol. IV, pp. 12—19.

one might suit his own taste and select those authors whom he likes best. The first part of the catalogue contains the best commentaries on the classical authors. The second enumerates works on Roman Law, which will help towards a better understanding of the writings of Cicero. The third gives the titles of about sixty works on antiquities: Roman and Greek games, triumphs, chronology, religion and sacrifices, mythology, banquets, costumes, the army and navy, numismatics, measures and weights, architecture, the triumphal arches, the circus, the amphitheatre, topography, geography, etc.[1] Several works on these subjects were written by Jesuits. It will appear, then, that although antiquities were to be taught but sparingly, the information of the teacher on these subjects was supposed to be thorough. Jouvancy, at the end of his *Method of Learning*, reminds the young master that "he must beware of superficiality; he must not be satisfied with a smattering but should endeavor to master thoroughly, to exhaust, if possible, that branch to which, by his natural gifts and God's will, he is destined to apply himself. Above all he must be constant in his studies and devote all his time to earnest self-training. Should he trifle away his time, he would seriously fail in

---

[1] These works were in the 17th century of the same importance as at present the standard works on antiquities, such as Guhl and Koner, *Life of the Greeks and Romans;* Schömann, *The Antiquities of Greece;* Mahaffy, *Social Life in Greece;* Ramsay, *Antiquities;* and the works of Mommsen, Becker, Lang, Lanciani, Boissier, Friedländer, Marquardt etc. They took also the place of our modern Classical Dictionaries and of such great collections as Iwan von Müller's valuable *Handbuch der klassischen Altertumswissenschaft.*

his religious obligations; for God's glory and the honor of the Society demand of him as much progress in learning as he can possibly attain, and one day God will ask of him a rigorous account of his time and his work."

This is the training which the Society gives its young teachers. It is a solid and practical training, one, we think, fitted for forming competent teachers.

Chapter XVI.

The Method of Teaching in Practice.

It was said before that the intellectual scope of the Jesuit system is the general training of the mind; the means for obtaining this end are the various exercises. In this chapter we shall treat the exercises of the literary course, and this for several reasons. *First,* because the study of languages and literature should form the backbone of, at least, the secondary schools and of part of the college course. *Secondly,* because the Ratio Studiorum treats the exercises in languages and literature very minutely, whereas it makes only a few suggestions concerning the exercises in mathematics and natural sciences. *Thirdly,* because it is especially in the literary studies that there exists a danger to neglect the exercises, as is, in fact, the case in some modern systems. No one will doubt for a moment that for the successful teaching of mathematics continual exercises are absolutely necessary. In natural sciences, particularly in physics and chemistry, the equivalent of the exercises are the experiments and especially the laboratory work.[1] On teaching physics and chemistry the Ratio has one very important remark, viz., the professor should not treat

---

[1] On this subject see the able article: *The Teaching of Science*, by Father De Laak, S. J., Professor of Physics in the St. Louis University, in the *Report of the Commissioner of Education*, 1901, vol. I, pp. 904—916.

them merely theoretically and mathematically, so that no time is left for the experiments; nor should he, on the other hand, spend so much time on the experiments that the teaching seems to be purely experimental; but sufficient time should be devoted to the principles, systems, theories, and hypotheses.[1] The object of all these exercises, be they scientific or literary, must be clear from what has been said in previous chapters, especially in the chapter on the *Intellectual Scope*. There we compared the different branches of study to the tools of the artisan or the dumb bells of one who takes a course of physical training; the exercises are the practical handling of these instruments, not by the teacher, but by the pupil. The teacher has to show how they are to be handled, but then the pupil has to lay hold of the intellectual tools and handle them himself. Thus, and thus only, not by merely listening to the lectures of a teacher, will the youthful mind be trained and acquire that readiness and nimbleness which is the object of true education. The literary exercises laid down in the Ratio Studiorum shall be treated under four headings: the "prelection", memory lessons, compositions, and contests.[2]

§ 1. The Prelection or Explanation of the Authors.

The typical form of Jesuit instruction is called *praelectio*. This word is largely the equivalent of "lecturing" in the higher faculties;[3] of "explanation"

[1] *Rules for the Professor of Physics* 33, 34.

[2] For many observations contained in this chapter I am indebted to the *Woodstock Letters*, especially the valuable papers in volumes XXIII—XXV, 1894—96.

[3] Its equivalent is used in German, *Vorlesung*, for the lectures in the universities.

in the lower. In either case, however, it is something specific.[1] For this reason the word may be used in an English dress, as "prelection". We are here not concerned with the lecture in the higher faculties, but with the prelection or explanation in the literary or classical course. This prelection is two-fold: one is upon the authors, the other upon the precepts of rhetoric, poetry, and style in the higher classes, of grammar, prosody, etc., in the lower classes. The Ratio gives some useful hints as to teaching the principles of rhetoric in connection with the reading of the authors. Taking up a passage, let us say of Cicero, the professor will, in the first place, make clear the sense of the text; secondly, analyze the artistic structure; thirdly, explain the force and meaning of the rhetorical precept contained in the passage; fourthly, adduce other examples which are similar in thought or expression, especially famous and striking ones; cite other orators or poets, whether in the classics or the vernacular, in which the same principles are employed; lastly, weigh the words singly, comment upon the propriety of their use, their rhythm, variety, beauty. The comparison of Latin and Greek authors with those of the vernacular, that treat of similar subjects, was especially recommended by the Jesuits in Germany, in 1830.[2]

The method of explaining authors is sketched admirably in the 27th of the common rules. The first thing the professor is told to do is to read the whole passage through, unless it be too long. There is a very good reason for this. It makes an impression on the

[1] Hughes, *Loyola*, p. 232.
[2] See Pachtler, vol. IV, p. 439.

ear of the pupils, and accustoms them to the rhythm of the language. Again, the reading is calculated, better than the rules of prosody, to impress on them the correct quantity of Latin syllables. Remember that the boys are understood to be employing Latin words a year, two years, before they learn the prosody; they are surely not supposed to be pronouncing incorrectly all that time. How, then, do they acquire accuracy in this important detail? Simply by imitating their professor. He reads every lesson for them before explaining; they read every lesson before translating, when they repeat next day. The rules of prosody afterwards only complete the work. Jouvancy observes that the teacher should accustom the pupils from the very beginning to distinct and articulate reading[1]; the same holds good of the recitations. From the first lesson in Latin and Greek the teachers should insist on the correct quantity, particularly of the final syllables (*os, es, is,* etc.). If in the lowest classes the students acquire a faulty pronunciation, they will never get rid of it in later years. Some modern teachers go to an extreme in insisting too much on quantity and other points. This is affectation. Years ago many colleges used the English pronunciation of Latin: *pueri* = pyueray, etc.; others follow more or less the (European) continental system; of late the high schools and most colleges have adopted the ancient or Roman pronunciation: *Cicero* = *Kikero*, etc. This is not the place to enter on a discussion

[1] *Ratio Docendi*, ch. II, art. 8, 2. — The same is inculcated in other documents, v. g. in *Mon. Paed.*, page 297: "*Germanam pronunciationem iam tum ab ipso literarii aedificii vestibulo a discipulis suis praeceptorum quisque exigat.*"

about the relative value of the different systems. The opinions of leading educators differ considerably.[1]

The reading of the text is not merely intended for correctness of pronunciation; the passage should be so read that the sense may fully appear, and that the sentiment may be rendered expressively. Inflection, tone, quality of voice, all the elements of elocution applicable to reading should be carefully attended to, and represented faithfully. A distinguished Jesuit professor even went so far as to employ gesture in this part of his prelection. What is easier in an oration than to put that spirit into the reading which shows the pupils that they are not examining a dead series of words, but a living organism with life and feeling in it, that they are studying the actual expression of real human feelings? One would not be too venturesome in asserting that the reading of the passage well done is the very best introduction to the matter studied. Of course, the repetition of this excellent reading should be exacted immediately, as often as possible; the next day at all events. It will prove the easiest and surest means of teaching elocution. The Rule

[1] President Eliot says: "A second interesting result of effective leadership in a few American colleges and schools is to be seen in the adoption of the so-called Roman pronunciation of Latin, which being recommended by two or three Professors of Latin in leading institutions, spread rapidly over the whole United States, and is now the accepted pronunciation in most schools and colleges." *Educational Reform*, p. 298. — But Professor Bennett of Cornell University calls it a "fundamental blunder and its retention a serious mistake." *The Teaching of Latin in the Secondary School*, p. 66. — See *Latin Pronunciation, a Brief Outline of the Roman, Continental and English Methods*, by D. E. King (Boston, Ginn and Company, 1889. — *The Roman Pronunciation of Latin*, by Francis Lord (Boston, Ginn, 1895).

does not say *legat*, nor *recitet*, but *pronunciet; legat* or *recitet* would be satisfied by any reading, monotonous or not; *pronunciet* necessarily implies delivery, the attempt at elocutionary finish.

The delivery of the passage well done — and, when possible, exacted immediately, — the professor proceeds to sketch the *argumentum*, or gist of the passage. This he does briefly. Father Jouvancy, in his Odes of Horace, gives us examples of *argumenta* which are all that could be desired; other instances, found in the *Ratio Docendi*, will be given below. Of course, the professor gives the argument mostly from his notes, and he usually, or often, dictates it, — a reason for his writing it out at home. It should be brief, pithy, striking, and clear, and given in Latin in the higher classes, in the vernacular in the lower classes.

Then, when the passage is connected with the preceding, the professor has to set forth the nature of the connection; this refers especially to points of history, and, in general, to such references as come under the head of *eruditio*. It will seldom be necessary when, as often occurs in the lower grades, the passage for prelection is the whole of a short story. In Freshman class and Sophomore, on the contrary, it may require some time to explain this connection.

The professor next passes on to consider each sentence by itself. He explains each one, shows the grammatical or rhetorical connection or dependence of its successive members and phrases, and, in general, clears up any obscurities or difficulties which the words contain. If the explanation is in the vernacular,[1] he

[1] "In our times, besides the Latin interpretation, there is to be added the interpretation in the vernacular, also in the class of Rhetoric." Pachtler, vol. IV, p. 435.

is careful to keep at first, as far as possible, the order of the Latin words, to accustom the ear to the *numerus* of that language. If this cannot be done, then he first translates nearly word for word, almost regardless of vernacular excellence, then afterwards returns and gives a version, with all attention to the elegancies of diction. This last translation must be a model of the vernacular, the very best the professor can do. Jouvancy says that all translations and dictations in the vernacular must be in strict accord with the most exact rules of the language, and free from any defect.[1] The Ratio of 1832, in the eighteenth rule for the teachers, insists on the same.

By all odds the better way for the teacher, as Jouvancy has said, is to elaborate his version for himself. It is a risky thing to rely on printed translations; many of them, especially the "Handy Library Translations" and the like, are frequently done in awkward and slovenly English. Further, as now-a-days the pupils have easy access to libraries, they will soon detect what sort of translation the teacher uses. In consequence the professor will lose a great part of his authority, the first element of which is esteem for the teacher's learning. Besides, as soon as the students have discovered the source of the teacher's translation, the careless and lazy ones will no longer pay any attention in class. Of course, the most conscientious and painstaking teacher has sometimes to have recourse to translations. But he should procure the most scholarly translations, and use them with discretion.

There can be no objection to the teacher's reading

[1] *Ratio Discendi*, ch. I, art. 3.

the translation from his paper; by which means he will be ensured against slips and sins against idiom, such as otherwise can hardly be avoided. If he chooses, after his own version, he may read a printed translation, which is especially useful in the case of such works as Butcher and Lang's Homer.

Notes and remarks are now to be given. Many professors prefer the alternative suggested in the Rule, of putting these in here and there, where they belong, in the course of the explanation. This plan, and that of presenting all the remarks together at the end, have both their own advantages. The former is more in keeping with unity, the latter affords a good opportunity of going over the passage again, and gives the pupils an occasion to make a little review of what has been done so far. Repetition is always good: it impresses and enforces. It is for this reason that the second rule of the several classes orders that immediately after the prelection a short repetition be "exacted" of the students. While the matter is still fresh, this can be done more easily and will have a more lasting effect.

The notes given should be made brief and striking and should be carefully worded. *Littera scripta manet.* The Grammar classes are not to write unless bidden. This evidently supposes that the higher classes may write when they choose. They are considered to have acquired discretion enough to guide them in their choice of what to note down from the professor's explanation. The lower grades are not to do this for themselves, because, as Father Hughes[1] says, "it happens now and then that, with much labor, waste

[1] Hughes, *Loyola*, p. 239.

of time and to no good purpose whatever, the boys take down and preserve with diligence a set of notes which have not been thought out very judiciously nor been arranged very carefully, notes simply trivial, common, badly patched together, sometimes worse than worthless, and these notes they commit to paper in wretched handwriting, full of mistakes and errors. Therefore let the dictation be only of a few points and those extremely select."

The *Trial Ratio* of 1586 bids the professor and the Prefect look over the students' note books occasionally.[1] This examination ensures the notes being written neatly and in order. It must not be forgotten that one great advantage of notes in general is the habit of system which they tend to foster; hence they must be diligently seen to. The teacher leads the way, as in every other detail of class work, by being orderly himself; he exacts the same care of his pupils.

The Ratio strongly recommends careful *preparation* on the part of the professor. He is not to give the prelection *ex tempore*, but after careful thought and even writing. What a splendid thing it would be if every teacher could so thoroughly make himself *ready* as to go to class with nothing but the text of the author and give his prelection, reading, argument, explanation, version, notes, dictation and all without so much as looking on his book before the boys! This would be the perfection of preparation and has been attained in the Society, old and new, but would possibly require too much time of professors of but a few years' teaching. At any rate, the one who wishes to

[1] Pachtler, vol. II, p. 165.

be successful in his work and do it faithfully, will not only have taken the pains to have studied carefully beforehand — the long vacation is the best time to do this — the book or oration which he is to explain, but will never come to class without having prepared, at the very least, some notes put in order as he designs to give them to the pupils.

These notes may be more or less *in extenso:* if the professor has sufficient fluency in expressing himself, they can be simple jottings, mere hints of what he is to say, and in what place. He will also have carefully fixed such points as he means to dictate. It will seldom be necessary for one to write out the entire prelection word for word. Such a practice would be good at times, no doubt, by way of exercising oneself in neatness and accuracy, and in style; but ordinarily mere notes will suffice. What will they consist of? That will depend largely on the passage under discussion. Now they will include a bit of history, the narration of which is called for by the passage for prelection; now geography; at other times archaeology; oftener grammatical or rhetorical precepts will enter, and similar passages from other authors, ancient and modern, may be quoted. When possible, these notes should embrace such moral hints as may be brought in naturally. The teacher will depend to a great extent on such occasional hints for his moral influence on his pupils.

A prelection written one year, even if the same author is read, will rarely do another if not modified. The circumstances of the class will have changed. A prelection has this in common with an oration, that it must suit the present audience. Contemporary events, to which reference is at times in order, will differ. These and other circumstances will naturally make the prelection matter different, even on the same passage. Each lesson should, therefore, be prepared for each class especially. This is the chief work which a teacher has to attend to during his free hours each day. It is rarely good to make this preparation a week ahead of time; unless the professor reviews and adapts his notes shortly before delivering them. It is evident that to prepare a prelection in this manner is a serious thing, a work by no means trifling; but easy or not, it must be gone through. It supposes that the professor spends his hours free from class in honest preparation.

Repetition has been called the *mater studiorum*, and in truth, few points are of more vital importance. The Ratio insists on repetition throughout the course, but particularly in the lowest classes. Without constant, steady, persistent drilling on the same matter in the beginning of the student's career, no solid foundation for the future literary edifice can be hoped for. Perhaps it is owing to inadvertence to this necessity that in some instances the fruit does not correspond to the labor of the professor. It has been well said that young teachers think mainly of stimulating their pupils' minds, and so neglect the repetition needed for accuracy.[1]

The 25th rule enjoins explicitly two distinct repetitions, one of yesterday's lesson, the other of the lesson just explained. A short repetition should immediately follow the prelection. This is of great importance; it shows the professor whether his mean-

[1] Quick, *Educational Reformers*, p. 506.

ing has been well grasped by the pupils, and, moreover, brings home to their yet untrained minds the salient points of the previous explanation. This particular repetition should not be omitted in the lower classes. It does not require much time, ordinarily a very few minutes will suffice. The chief result to be gained is that the pupils should really understand what has just been said. In this it differs from the repetition of the lesson which was explained on the preceding day; for the principal end of this exercise is so to fix the matter in the boys' minds that it may really become their own. The more advanced students may be called to give the short repetition at the end of the prelection, whereas the duller, or perhaps the more indolent ones should be asked especially for the fuller repetition of the lesson of the previous day. But never should the teacher follow the order in which the pupils are seated, or the alphabetical order of the names. Jouvancy thinks that the teacher, before going to school, should go over the names of the boys and reflect whom he is to call up for repetition.[1] Every one should have his turn, but duller and indolent ones should be called more frequently, as they need it most.

The 26th rule establishes an excellent principle, namely "to repeat on Saturday everything that was seen during the week." Monday or any other *fixed* day will do as well. By *everything* is understood a thorough and careful review of the more important parts of the matter taught, especially the rules of grammar, precepts of style and rhetoric.

Jouvancy has drawn up several *schemata* or speci-

[1] *Rat. Doc.*, c. II, art. III, § 1.

mens of a prelection on Cicero, Virgil and Phaedrus as adapted to different classes.[1] We give the substance of two. Be it remarked, however, that the same order need not and cannot be followed strictly in all details in every prelection. They are specimens exhibiting a general rule, which is to be applied with discretion. Professor Willmann has well observed: "As all similar *schemata* also Jouvancy's *canon explanationis* is useful if applied properly, whereas if it is carried through pedantically in all subjects and with stereotyped regularity, it makes instructions mechanical."[2]

A. *Explanation of a Passage from Cicero in Rhetoric (Sophomore).* Take the exordium of Cicero's second *Philippic* from *Quonam meo fato* to *Cui priusquam.* We distinguish five parts in the explanation.

I. *Argumentum.* (Willmann: "In this part Jouvancy recommends a paraphrase of the contents, whose place is now taken by the translation.") — When Cicero had delivered his first *Philippic,* Mark Anthony attacked him vehemently. To this attack Cicero replied in this oration, the second *Philippic,* showing that Anthony's invectives were groundless, and that Anthony himself, because of his crimes, deserved the severest reproaches.

We explain the exordium of the oration in which Cicero declares that he has incurred the enmity of many; but that Anthony's animosity was unfair and less called for, than that of his other adversaries, as he had never offended him as much as by a single word. But Anthony believes he could demonstrate

---
[1] *Rat. Doc.*, c. II, art. IV.
[2] *Didaktik*, vol. II, p. 387.

his enmity to the Republic by being an opponent of Cicero.

II. *Explanatio*. (Willmann: "Linguistic and logical.") *Quonam meo fato*. This may have a double meaning; either: to what misfortune shall I say that I have been born; to what destiny of mine is it owing, by what fate of mine does it come to pass, that on me alone light all the arrows with which our enemies try to harm the country; or: what a happy and enviable lot that all who attack the Republic believe they must become my enemies. Either meaning is apt to gain the good will of the audience. — *His annis viginti*, i. e. from the beginning of his consulship, the year 690 A. U. C. — *Nec vero etc.* Cicero points to men like Catiline, Clodius, Piso, etc. .... *Tuam a me alienationem commendationem tibi ad impios cives fore putavisti*. Construe: *Putavisti alienationem tuam a me fore tibi commendationem* [*gloriae*] *ad impios;* literally: You thought your alienation from me would be a recommendation for you to the wicked, i. e.: You thought to gain in the estimation of the destructionists, if you turned away from me and became my enemy.

III. *Rhetorica*. Attention is called to all that pertains to rhetoric in the highest class, to poetry in the next, to grammar, syntax in the other classes. For the class of Rhetoric this explanation may run as follows: This is the *exordium* of an excellent oration. The exordium or introduction has to prepare the audience for the coming speech. It has to gain their good will, and to make them attentive and docile. Let us see how Cicero complies with these three requirements of the exordium.

Good will may be gained in three ways. *First*, by

showing that the speaker is possessed of a respectable character. *Secondly,* by manifesting interest for his hearers' welfare. *Thirdly,* by cleverly predisposing them against his adversaries. The first Cicero effects by pointing to his character to which all feeling of revenge is alien, to his previous career, and to the flattering testimony of the senate with regard to his consulship. — The second he effects by stating that all enemies of the Republic had ever become his personal enemies. — The third, by imputing to Anthony a passionate character, hatred against his country, and intimate friendship with the very dregs of the population.

The orator gains *attention* by telling how important the point at issue is: how the enemies of the country have become his enemies, etc.

He makes his hearers *docile* by briefly stating what he is going to speak about: little in his own defense, much against Anthony.

Fine exordiums of other orations may be mentioned, and also the faults which are easily made in the introduction. The rhetorical figure of *subjectio: Quid putem,* its force and use, may be explained.

IV. *Eruditio* ("General learning;" Willmann translates it appropriately by "antiquarian and subject-explanation, *antiquarische, also Sacherklärung.*") In the beginning occurs the word *fato.* Explain what the pagans understood by this and what we Christians have to think of it. — *His viginti annis.* Say (or better: ask) in what year Cicero was born, when he was made consul, when he died. — *Bellum indixerit.* Explain how the Romans used to declare war. (The solemnities of the *Fetiales*). — The word *maledictum* affords an opportunity to show the difference between *maledictum, convicium* and *contumelia.* — *Mihi poenarum plus* etc. A few words may be said on revenge, how little it becomes a noble character. For this end copious material may be taken from the 13th Satire of Juvenal and from the *Adagia* of Erasmus. Illustrations may also be taken from the treasure of Christian doctrine and Church History.

V. *Latinitas*. (Willmann: "The gain for vocabulary and phraseology, in short the proper technics of the pupils.").

Bellum mihi indixerit, add a few other meanings of this verb. Mention the *indictiva funera*, i. e. funerals which were publicly announced. — *Perhorrescere*, give a few examples illustrating the force and meaning of compound words.

Verbo violatus, similarly: *corpus violare vulnere, ebur ostro; fidem, foedus, jura sacra violare*.

The second specimen is on Virgil's Aeneid XII, 425—440. At its close Jouvancy adds: "In the second highest class, called Poetry or Humanities (Freshman), the same order is observed except that here more attention is paid to poetics. The strictly rhetorical part should be sparingly dealt with. In the highest Grammar class, grammar and beauty of expression claim more attention. In the two lowest classes the difference is still more striking. Here the teacher has to sail along the coast and only seldom may he venture out into the sea (of longer explanations). He must beware of the reefs along the shore, i. e. he must not become disgusted at, nor neglect, what they call trifles. To explain even one little fable will require great skill and is a sign of considerable talent."

The third specimen is the explanation of a little fable of Phaedrus in the lowest Grammar class. The fable is: "*Personam tragicam forte vulpes viderat: O quanta species, inquit, cerebrum non habet.*" The teacher explains in the vernacular.

I. *Contents* of the Fable.

II. *Explanation: Vulpes*, a fox; *viderat* (translate), *forte* (translate); *personam*. *Persona* now means "person," but originally meant a "mask," as used in carnival masquerades, and at mask-balls. (*per*—through; *sonare*, sound, speak; speak through); *tragicam*, as it was used by the players in Greek and Roman tragedies. Similarly explain all the other words, *and not once only, but twice or three times, if necessary*.

III. *Grammar*. Give declension, gender of nouns and adjectives; conjugation, tense, mood etc. of every verb. This should be done as much as possible by putting questions to the pupils. *Vulpes* is a noun of the third declension; like . . . . ? — *Proles, clades*, etc. mention such as are known already to the pupils. Then give the rules of declension, gender. *Viderat*, is a verb. What form? Third person singular Pluperfect Active. Present tense? *video.* — Like? *doceo.* . . . . Perfect: *Vidi.* Conjugate: *Vidi, vidisti*, etc. — Why third person? — *Forte:* is an adverb. Adverbs are words which . . . . — *Personam.* What case? — Why accusative? Because it is the direct object of *viderat.*[1] — *Tragicam*, why not *tragicum*, or *tragica?* Explain the rule. . . .

[1] English speaking students have at first great difficulties in grasping the rule of the object, because neither the article nor the noun shows any case ending. However, it can be explained easily with pronouns. Thus say: "*Who is*

IV. *General Erudition.* Could not a short description of the cunning fox be given? Or could not a littte story be told? Or the adage: *cum vulpe vulpinandum,* be explained?

Tragicam. A short easy explanation of tragedy might be given. — *Cerebrum.* The Latin words for other parts of the head should be added.

V. *Latinity.* Show the order of words and let the pupils imitate it in other sentences, e. g. *Fratrem tuum nuper videram,* which is better than *Fratrem tuum videram nuper.*

A short theme may be written in Latin: *Fratrem tuum nuper videram. O quanta eruditio, dixi, mercedem non habet.*

VI. *Morals.* The teacher may show that prudence and common sense are preferable to other natural possessions. A short story illustrating this may be told, which could be translated into Latin and repeated by one of the better pupils.

For the sake of comparison we add a *schema* drawn mostly from the writings of Nägelsbach and Willmann. A careful examination will prove that it is not so different from that of Jouvancy, as might appear at first sight.

I. *Preparation.* — 1. The passage which is to be prepared by the pupils for the following day, is assigned in class. The teacher gives extensive hints on difficult points, on which the pupils otherwise might lose too much time. (In the lower and middle classes the whole text should be translated. See p. 478.)

there? Who is subject. *Whom* did you see? Whom is object. — *He* is there. I saw *him*. It would be bad English to say: Who did you see, or I saw he. So it is bad Latin to say: *Vulpes viderat persona.*" These examples of *whom* and *him* are especially fitted, as they show an ending similar to the Latin.

2. At home the pupil tries to find out the meaning of the whole text. Dots on the margin should mark the passages which he could not make out.

3. In class the text is read by a student.

II. *Translation.* — 1. The boy who has read the text translates, the teacher and the other pupils correct the translation.

2. Explanations, linguistic and logical, are given to understand the text fully.

3. A correct and fluent translation is repeated by a boy with the help of the teacher and other boys. — The translation has to be different according to the authors: plain in Caesar and Xenophon; simple and direct in Homer; elaborate and dignified in Virgil and Cicero, etc.

III. *Handling of the Text.*

1. *Explanation* of contents. (*Realerklärung. Explanatio* and *eruditio* of Jouvancy.)

2. Pointing out of *ethical momenta* (*quae ad mores spectant.* Jouvancy).

3. *Technics* of rhetoric, poetry and style. (*Rhetorica* of Jouvancy.)

4. *Latinity* etc.: vocabulary, phrases, grammatical rules. (*Latinitas.* Jouvancy.)

IV. *Repetition.* — 1. Let the student translate and explain the text.

2. Frequently let the pupil, instead of a strict translation, give the contents in Latin, in a simple clear style.

3. Always see whether everything is understood.

4. Put questions of such a kind as force the boys to group and view things in a new manner. Thus they are led to reflect on the subject at home. This advice

is also given by the Jesuit Kropf in his *Ratio et Via* (ch. V, art. 9): "The repetition ought to be conducted partly in the form of an examination etc."

A few remarks about the prelection must be added:

1. *After the whole work has been studied*, a retrospective view is to be taken; the work is to be estimated as a whole, with its leading ideas; as a masterpiece of art; as a product of a certain age or school, from the aesthetical, philosophical, and historical point of view. This should be done especially in higher classes; — but *ne quid nimis*, and everything, in the words of the *Ratio:* "sparingly and according to the capacity of the pupils."

2. *Longer explanations* should not interrupt the translation, but should be put off to the end; occasionally, however, they might be given earlier in the prelection, if the text without the explanation would be hardly understood.

3. The first preparation done by the pupils at home ought not to be the principal part of the work; the principal part consists in the handling of the text in class.

This principle of the prelection of the Ratio Studiorum is also advocated by an able English schoolman. Sir Joshua Fitch says in his *Lectures on Teaching*, that home work should be "supplementary rather than preparatory." It should have a bearing on the school teaching of the previous day, "the best part of it is supplementary," and the chief value of home lessons, also of written exercises, is to give definiteness to lessons already learned (in class), and to thrust them home into the memory rather than to break new grounds."[1] And Professor Bain of Aberdeen Univer-

[1] American edition, pp. 147—149.

sity writes: "I hold to this principle, in a still severer view of it — namely, that the teacher should not ask the pupil to do anything that he himself has not led up to, — has not clearly paved the way for. The pupils should not be called upon for any species of work that may not have been fully explained beforehand — that their own faculties, co-operating with each one's known attainments, are not perfectly competent to execute. A learner should not be asked even to show off what he can do, outside the teaching of the class."[1] Dr. Stanley Hall said recently[2]: "As to the dead languages, if they are to be taught, Latin should be begun not later than ten or eleven, and Greek never later than twelve or thirteen. Here both object and method are very different. These languages are taught through English, and the one-hand circuit should have much more prominence. Word matching and translation are the goal. The chief reason why the German boy of fifteen or sixteen in *Unter-Secunda* does so easily here what seems to us prodigious, is because he is taught to study; and the teacher's chief business in class is not to hear recitations, but to study with the boys. One of the best of these teachers told me that the boy should never see a dictionary or even a vocabulary, but the teacher must be a 'pony'. The pupil should never be brought face to face with an unknown sentence, but everything must be carefully translated for him; he must note all the unknown words from the teacher's lips, and all the special grammatical points, so that home study and the first

[1] *On Teaching English*, ch. 3, p. 27. (N. Y., Appleton, 1887.)
[2] In *The Forum*, September, 1901. Article: "The Ideal School as based on Child Study."

part of the next lesson will be merely repetitions of what the teacher has told and done."

The statement that this is the practice of the German schools, needs considerable modification. It may be partly so at present, but it certainly was not common before 1890. On the contrary, in German higher schools, throughout the greater part of the nineteenth century, it was generally insisted on that the students should prepare the translations without any or much help from the teacher. In fact, most professors[1] assigned some chapters in the author which were to be prepared for the next lesson without giving as much as a hint about a difficult passage. The next day a fairly good translation was expected, and by many teachers exacted rather rigorously. It was said that this system stimulated self-activity and independent thought; and more than once the opposite system, as followed by the Jesuits, was condemned, because, as it was asserted, it did not develop independence and the spirit of research. But did the results of the German system come up to expectations? The less diligent pupils had recourse to all sorts of "ponies", — in fact, the less talented were often practically forced to use other helps, as it was impossible for them to give a translation of many passages. In this way a spirit of dishonesty was fostered. The more scrupulous and eager students lost much time on difficult passages, often without finding a satisfactory translation. All this time might have been spared by

[1] These remarks are based on the writer's own experience. Of all his professors *none* ever called attention to a difficult passage, but the students had to do all by themselves at home. This was before the reform of 1890—1892. To judge from educational publications things have changed of late.

a few remarks of the teacher, pointing to the solution of the difficulty. Above all, too much time was wasted unprofitably by thumbing the dictionary. No wonder that at length serious complaints were made. Besides the six hours spent in class, the average student had to devote at least four hours to hard home work, if he wanted to do all his tasks conscientiously.

Of late years there is a decided change of opinion among educators, and this change is, to a great extent, a return to principles which were always followed in the Jesuit system. Thus writes Professor Schiller, Director of the Pedagogical Seminary in Giessen, one of the most celebrated German educators: "In the middle classes the preparation of the new translation is to be done in class, and even in the higher grades this can be done usefully." Further, "the more difficult passages, and those which contain many unknown words, should be explained beforehand."[1] In general "new material is added only in class; the object of home work is to strengthen, practise and apply, what has been given by the class instruction."[2] The new Prussian School Order of 1901 has laid down the general rule, that "directions for the preparation of new and difficult passages are to be given in all classes; even in the higher grades the preparation of a new author is, for some time, to be done entirely in class."[3] Is not this a striking justification of the wise conservatism of the Jesuit system? After a cen-

[1] Schiller, *Handbuch der praktischen Pädagogik für höhere Lehranstalten*, Leipzig, Reisland (3rd edition 1894), pp. 456 and 476.

[2] *Ibid.*, pp. 42 and 152; see also Willmann, *Didaktik* vol. II, p. 391.

[3] *Lehrpläne und Lehraufgaben*, pp. 24, 25, 32, 34.

tury of severe criticism and condemnation, it is thought necessary to return to what is essentially the Jesuit method of preparing the authors. And this return has been made in the country that prides itself on its school system.

According to the Jesuit method the teacher studies with the pupils, and thus shows them how to study. We need now no longer defend the Ratio against the charge frequently raised in former years, that it does too much, in fact everything for the pupil. It does not do everything; neither does it overtax the pupil's abilities. It follows the wise middle course, which will effect a solid training without giving reasonable cause to complaints of overwork.

However, some preparation of the new text, on the part of the pupil, is useful and stimulates self-activity, especially in the upper grades. It is prescribed for the higher studies by the Ratio which enjoins the students of the Society "to be diligent in *praevidendis lectionibus,*" i. e. in preparing the new lesson of the day.[1]

Before concluding the discussion on the prelection, I quote a passage from the *Woodstock Letters* (1898). The question had been put: *Has the method of prelection advocated by the Ratio, especially the plan of translating the author for the student, been used in any of our American Colleges not belonging to the Society? If so, with what success?* — On October 31, 1898, the Editor of the Letters, the Reverend Samuel Hanna Frisbee, S. J., a graduate of Yale (1861), and a pupil of the matchless scholar, Professor Hadley, answered as follows :

[1] *Reg. Scholasticorum 4.*

"The professor who used the method of the Ratio, and especially the prelection, was Arthur Hadley, well known as the author of *Hadley's Greek Grammar.* He was professor of Greek for many years at Yale and was known as a fine Greek scholar. Though he was *the* professor of Greek — there were several tutors in Greek — and far the best Greek scholar in the university, he was appointed to teach the Freshmen during the first term, from the middle of September to Christmas. It was thought best they should have an experienced teacher, one who would train them thoroughly and thus give them a good start. During the rest of the scholastic year he taught Greek to the Junior class. What concerns us at present is the method he adopted for training these Freshmen. It was as follows, and from its description you can easily judge how much it resembled the method of the Ratio.

The author to be read was Homer's Iliad, and in our year, 1857, the fourteenth book of the Iliad was the book assigned. The students used to say that some book after the first six was chosen, because Anthon's copious notes to these six books amounted to a translation. The real reason which was given to us at the time I have forgotten, but it was doubtless because this book is one of the most characteristic of the Iliad. Whatever was the reason, the Freshmen of our year were told that the fourteenth book was to be read. The class — numbering 120 — was divided into three divisions. The first division went into Greek for the first hour, 7 A. M., the second division at 11, and the third at 5 P. M. Professor Hadley had thus three hours of class daily, but to each division he explained the same matter.

We came to class, then, with the fourteenth book of Homer, and to our amazement, Prof. Hadley asked no recitation — for we had been already told to prepare some lines of this 14th book — but, after giving a short history of Homer, and of the places which claimed him as their son, he carefully read through the first five lines, reading according to the accent, and then scanning them. Then he gave a literal translation of these five lines, and coming back to the first word he parsed it, gave the different dialectic forms of it and, if it was a geographical word, he explained where it was to be found on the map, and if the name of a person, he gave a short account of his life. This occupied a half hour and then the class was dismissed. The next day a half hour was spent in recitation. One was called up to scan, another to translate, and several to parse the different words, nothing being asked which had not been explained the preceding day. Then the second half hour was taken up by the professor who translated five more lines, parsing and explaining each word. It is an old Yale custom to repeat each day the lesson of the preceding day, so that we really had ten lines to translate and parse, five which some students had already recited in class. This second translation was recommended to be more elegant than the first which was literal, and only the important words were asked for parsing, etc. This manner of teaching was continued all the term — three months — only five lines of new matter being translated and explained each day. Besides we were made to review thoroughly the important parts of the grammar. A small book of a few pages containing the declensions, conjugations and a few rules, was given to each student, and it was repeated till it was known by heart. The students used to call it 'Hadley's Primer.'

As the results of this method, those who studied — for you know only about ten per cent of the students are really studying in earnest, the honor men — acquired such a facility in reading Homer that they could read the rest of the Iliad with comparative ease, while the moderate students had no difficulty in preparing the lesson assigned during the second term, which was fifty lines daily in another book of the Iliad, the eighteenth, if I mistake not. Then we took up Herodotus, at the rate of two pages a day, after an introduction about the author and his book. This was also accompanied on some days of the week by recitations from an excellent book on Greek History — Wheeler's if I mistake not.

Professor Hadley was the only one in the University to follow the method of the prelection of the Ratio, but he followed it most thoroughly. He was regarded in his time as one of the very best professors in the University, and he merited this reputation.''

It remains for us to investigate *how much* is to be read. The first question which presents itself is: Should the reading of the classics be slow or quick, *stationary* or *cursory?* It has been said that in stationary reading the boys *read* little, in cursory they *learn* little or nothing. What, then, is to be done?

It all depends *first,* on the *text,* whether difficult or easy; *secondly,* on the *character* of the book. Epics and historical works, as a rule, should be read more rapidly, because they are in themselves slowly progressing, whereas lyrics and drama should be dwelled upon. — The Ratio Studiorum of 1599 expresses quite clearly the principle enunciated by schoolmen of the nineteenth century. The 28th rule says: "The historical books [and epic poetry is of a historical character] should be read more rapidly (*celerius excurrendus*)." *Thirdly*, in every case it depends on the pupils' knowledge, capacity, practice and age. But above all these two principles should not be forgotten: *in medio est virtus*, and *non multa, sed multum*.

How much, then, is to be read in one prelection?[1] In many modern institutions, in fact in most of them, the students are to read and translate whole pages of the classics for a single lesson. The Ratio calls for a thorough study of a few lines. In the 6th rule for the lowest class, the old Ratio says four lines should be explained in one lesson, for the next class seven lines — of course the teacher should not stop in the middle of the phrase. In the Revised Ratio no number of lines is mentioned. If we keep in mind that in these classes the pupils are gradually to be initiated into the reading of authors there is nothing surprising about this small number of lines. They are to be explained to perfection, learned by heart for the following day and to be employed for an imitation theme. For the higher grades the old Ratio did not state the exact number of lines, neither does the Revised Ratio. Still, on reading the rules for the prelection it becomes evident that fifty or sixty lines cannot be studied so thoroughly in one hour. But are ten lines all that must be read in class? Is this to be understood as the full demand of the Ratio? "At the rate of ten lines a

---

[1] On this question we take some suggestions from an article in the *Woodstock Letters*, 1898, p. 185 sq.

day it would require fourteen months to translate Cicero's oration *Pro Milone*, so that to finish even the single speech within a year many parts of it must be run over more or less rapidly. At this rate of ten lines a day, it would require more than five years to translate the *Aeneid*, and twelve years to translate the *Iliad*, or two years longer than the siege of Troy lasted. The Ratio cannot, therefore, wish to bind the student and professor down to these few lines."[1] It wishes merely to show the student how to read and study the classics, how to do thorough work. Many more lines are to be read in a lesson, but the few should serve as the model. The *schemata* of Father Jouvancy do not want more. Nor is it to be inferred that all the lines are to be explained with the same thoroughness and at the same length. This would be impossible.

Moreover, we are led to the same conclusion from the programmes of some of the celebrated colleges of the old Society. They prove with certainty that the thorough study of a limited number of lines was not considered sufficient to make a student a classical scholar. In the history of the college of La Flèche,[2] we find programmes of the astounding work done by the students. Perhaps the plan of the Ratio has never been carried out more thoroughly than it was at this college, which for a long time was a rival of the great University of Paris. Here, too, one of the best commentators of the Ratio, Father Jouvancy, taught and

[1] *Woodstock Letters*, 1898, p. 186.
[2] *Un collège de Jésuites aux XVII et XVIII siècles. Le collège Henri Quatre de la Flèche, par le Père Camille de Rochemonteix.* See vol. IV, pp. 165 and 388—403.

wrote. When, therefore, we see the students of this college, studying hundreds of pages of the classics in one year, we must grant that such a method comes within the scope of the Ratio.[1] For the rest, it remains unintelligible how any real benefit can be derived from the reading of hundreds of lines in one hour. Jouvancy well observes, the teacher should remember that the minds of young pupils are like vessels with a narrow orifice. If you pour water in great quantity upon them, it quickly runs off; if you pour it upon them slowly, they will be filled in a shorter time. Recently German schoolmen speak to the same effect: "We must limit the amount of reading matter and work on less material, but must try to make capital out of it by a thorough and exhaustive treatment. Only in this way can the 'intellectual growth' be expected. Limitation is the first principle of our art. A clear understanding of the classical authors must be obtained by labor (*das Verständniss ist zu erarbeiten*). For this reason the modern tendency of increasing the amount of reading excessively must be combated."[2] This holds good of English reading as well as of Latin and Greek.

One part of the prelection is called "eruditio". We heard that Professor Willmann translated it, and rightly so, by "antiquarian explanation." For some time past there was a tendency, particularly in German schools, to devote too much time to the explanation of antiquarian allusions, a method which was detrimental to the linguistic and literary study of the

---

[1] *Woodstock Letters*, *l. c.*, p. 190.
[2] See *Neue Jahrbücher*, 1898, vol. II, p. 82.

authors. Last year a writer[1] said that it was about time to recover again the real authors, Virgil, Horace, etc., who were almost lost in a mass of archaeological, historical, and critical details. In fact, the "Homeric Question" absorbed the interests of some teachers to such a degree that the grand poems themselves were nearly lost sight of. Antiquities should not be taught in high schools and colleges *ex professo*, for this belongs to the university, but incidentally, as some antiquarian subject occurs in the reading. Thus, while reading Caesar, Roman military antiquities are explained: the legion, weapons, military roads, etc. Xenophon's Anabasis affords an opportunity for giving details on Greek and Persian warfare. Cicero's various works will call for explanations of the Roman constitution, courts, elections, of the different offices of Consul, Praetor, Tribune, Aedile, Pontifex; for descriptions of the forum, villas, family life, etc. Plato's Dialogues demand a fair knowledge of Athenian life and manners; Homer's epics can be made interesting by details of the life and customs of the heroic age of the Greeks, which may be compared with similar traits found in the epics of other nations: the Anglo-Saxon *Beowulf* and the German *Nibelungenlied* (a good translation should be read).

The practical method of teaching antiquities in Jesuit schools we learn from Jouvancy. Thus speaking of the word *fatum*, which occurs in a sentence, he says: explain the meaning which this word had with the ancients, and what we Christians have to think of it. *Bellum indixerit*. Explain the manner in which

[1] Professor Plüss, in *Neue Jahrbücher*, 1901, vol. VII, page 74.

the Romans declared war. This is described in Rosinus,[1] Abram,[2] and Cantel,[3] etc. — Speaking of an explanation of Virgil's Aeneid XII, 425-440, Jouvancy says: "In the fourth place, as to erudition : *Major egit Deus:* Explain which gods were called *Dii majores* or *majorum gentium*, which *minorum gentium*. — When you come to the word *clypeus*, describe the different kinds of shield, show the difference between *parma, pelta, scutum,* etc., and explain how the soldiers formed the *testudo*, etc. — Speaking of the ninth chapter of Cicero's *De Senectute*, he wants some explanation of the Roman warship and navy, descriptions of how the votes were taken in the senate, etc.

Another very instructive document shows how much was comprised under the term "general erudition." In 1710, the text book of the third class (*suprema grammatica*) of the College of Aix in France was Cicero's *De Senectute*. The pupils had to answer the following questions: Who and what was Cicero? What is the subject of his book on *Old Age?* Why was Cato chosen as speaker on this topic? Which motives induced Cicero to compose this work? Who was Atticus, and how did he obtain this name? Who was Flaminius? What victory is recorded of him? Who were Titon and Ariston? What does the legend say of the former? What did the Stoics mean by saying that we must follow nature? What were the consuls, praetors, aediles, and quaestors among the

---

[1] Lutheran preacher, died at Naumburg, Germany, 1626, author of *Antiquitates Romanae*.
[2] Jesuit, died at Pont-à-Mousson, 1655.
[3] Jesuit, died at Paris 1684, wrote *De Republica Romana ad explicandos Scriptores antiquos.*

Romans? What the tribunes of the people, and the augurs? What opinions were held about omens? What was the *Lex Cincia?* By whom and on what occasion was it madè? What do you know about the war to which Cato urged the Romans so persistently? What was the senate? What is the derivation of the word? Who was Naevius? Relate what you know about his poems, his exile, and his death. Who was Cyrus? Narrate the foundation of the Persian kingdom, etc. What was the *Summus Pontifex*, the dictator, the military tribune? Describe the legion. What did the Romans understand by clients? What were the sentiments of the Romans about patriotism? What do you know about Thermopylae, Tarentum, Capua, Mount Etna, Picenum, Cisalpine Gaul? What was the Rostra? What do you know about the Olympian games? etc., etc. [1]

It is clear, then, that the history of literature, the history of manners, customs, and political institutions, biography, mythology, and geography, found a place in the explanation of authors. This field was so wide and so attractive that there was a great danger lest the teachers, especially the younger, should spend too much time in antiquarian details, to the detriment of the less interesting, but more necessary linguistic and literary training of the pupils. It is for this reason that both the Ratio and Jouvancy exhort the teacher to give such explanations but "sparingly". By this it is not implied that the information should be meagre, but that it should be moderate, not excessive. The preceding testimonies prove also how unjustly Huber, Compayré, and others have asserted that the Jesuits

[1] Chossat, *l. c.,* pp. 337—339.

aim at mere literary dilettantism, cleverness of speech; that they direct the pupil's attention not to the thought but to form.[1] This is what they call "Jesuitical formalism." However, it is not Jesuitical at all. The above-cited questions certainly were directed towards the understanding of the thoughts of the authors. This method of questioning the pupils about the contents, the ideas of a literary work, was also eminently fitted to stimulate in the pupils self-activity and independent thinking. For this reason Quick's judgment on the Jesuit system is not correct, when he says that it "suppressed originality and independence of mind, love of truth for its own sake, the power of reflecting and of forming correct judgments."[2] Should he, however, take independence of thought in the sense now usually attached to it, as unrestrained rationalism which places private judgment above the teaching of the Bible and the whole deposit of Divine Revelation, then we admit that the Jesuits are opposed to this independence of thought; for it is the proud spirit of rebellion against God. Yet this is no longer an educational, but rather a philosophical and theological question, and those authors have unwarrantably dragged this discussion into their books on the history of educational methods.

We stated before that the linguistic training must always remain a more prominent part of the prelection than the antiquarian and other information. Here, however, another mistake must be avoided, which easily creeps into the teaching of the classics, a mistake which was not uncommon in the German schools

[1] Compayré, *Hist. of Ped.*, p. 144.
[2] *Educ. Ref.*, p. 50.

before the recent reforms, namely, to make the authors the means of studying, repeating, or "drilling" the rules of grammar, etymology, and syntax. This makes the reading unpleasant, as every now and then a grammatical rule is asked, paradigms are repeated, etc., so that the author merely becomes subservient to the grammar, whereas the very contrary ought to be the case, especially in the higher classes. This faulty practice is altogether opposed to the Ratio, which assigns a special time every day for repeating, studying, and drilling grammar or the precepts of rhetoric and poetry.[1] The 27th rule of the teachers, which lays down the method of explaining authors, does not even mention among the various suggestions the asking of grammatical rules. Nor is this grammatical drill contained in the *schemata* of Jouvancy for the higher classes among the five or six points to be observed in the prelection of authors. There is one called *Latinitas*, but an examination of what is said there shows that it is not a repetition of grammar, but, as Professor Willmann says, it deals with the technique of language, phraseology, etc. Jouvancy remarks that in the *lower* classes more attention is to be paid to grammar, which at this stage is not yet mastered by the pupils. This is in perfect accordance with the Ratio. The teacher of the lowest class is told when repeating the lesson of the previous day, *"often* to have words declined, or conjugated, and to ask questions about grammar in various directions."[2] The teacher of the next following class should *sometimes* do the same.[3] This is a wise prescription, as in the low-

---

[1] See the second rule of all the classes.
[2] *Reg.* 5.   [3] *Reg.* 5.

est classes the pupils are to be introduced slowly into the reading of the authors, and the grammatical part must be treated more extensively. But the corresponding rules of the third class no longer mention this point. Certainly in the higher classes, particularly Freshman and Sophomore, it is an abuse to make the classics the vehicle of teaching grammar. An occasional question is, of course, not excluded, on the contrary necessary, whenever it appears from the student's translation that he does not understand the etymology, or the syntax of a phrase. But this is by no means the abuse to which we referred.

This, then, is the prelection, the most important and most characteristic point in the practical application of the Ratio Studiorum. It is scarcely necessary to add that the Society needs no apology for this part, nor has she any reason to attempt any change of it.

As this manner of explaining authors is so much in accord with sound reason, we cannot be surprised that the Ratio insists on following the same system — of course, *mutatis mutandis* — in the teaching of the mother-tongue. The authors in the mother-tongue should be explained in nearly the same manner as the ancient writers.[1] The very same principle is emphasized by some of the best teachers of English, as for instance by Professor Bain. This writer distinguishes two methods of teaching higher English. The one a systematic course, in which "an exemplary lesson would consist in the statement and illustration of some rhetorical point or rule of style — say, the figure of hyperbole, the quality of simplicity, or the art of expounding by example. This, however,

[1] *Ratio Studiorum: Reg. com.* 28, § 2.

I deem a superfluous lesson; it would be little better than making an extract from a rhetorical treatise. There is another kind of lesson which does not exclude the methodical teaching of rhetoric, but co-operates with that in the most effectual way. It is the criticism of authors, with a view to the exhibition of rhetorical merits and defects as they turn up casually. An outline of rhetoric is almost essential to the efficiency of this kind of lesson; yet with only an outline it may successfully be carried out. It suffices to raise the questions most proper to be considered in English teaching."[1]

The second method which this writer advocates is that of the Ratio. Professor Bain illustrates his principle by various examples from leading authors: Macaulay, Samuel Bailey, Carlyle; and he develops these examples exactly as Jouvancy did in the case of Cicero and Virgil. The Scotch Professor finds fault with the "too much" of explanation on archaic forms, sources of the play, etc., in the modern editions of Shakespeare.[2] Is not this again the principle of the Ratio which insists on such details being given *sparingly?* Naturally the treatment of passages varies according to the character of the book, that of a sketch from Irving must be quite different from that of a play of Shakespeare, just as a chapter from Caesar or Nepos is explained differently from an Ode of Horace, or a Chorus of Sophocles. We may add a *schema* for reading an English author.[3] The principles are the same as those in the preceding *schemata*.

[1] *On Teaching English,* ch. V, p. 48 foll.
[2] *Ibid.,* ch. VI, page 85 foll.
[3] See Fitch, *Lectures on Teaching.*

How to read English authors, v. g. a drama of Shakespeare?

1. Read first the whole piece, quickly, uncritically, to gain a knowledge of its contents; or induce the pupils to do it at home, but in this case examine whether they do so. — 2. Explain then part after part: all archaic words, difficult constructions, until everything is understood. — 3. Explain historical and literary allusions. — 4. Explain the plot, the tragic idea, the chief characters (in an oration, the proposition and the argumentation). — 5. Criticise the work as a whole. Show its excellences and shortcomings. — 6. Have choice passages learned by heart, and delivered well. Besides, for each lesson make the pupils write something on the lesson previously explained: let them give the contents of a scene, write a synopsis, criticise a passage, or explain a beautiful sentence. Otherwise there is a danger that some will not even look at the author at home.

§ 2. Memory Lessons.

The nineteenth rule prescribes the regular recitation of memory lessons. These frequent practices of the memory in Jesuit schools have often been censured by modern writers.[1] But renowned teachers as Dr. Arnold of Rugby,[2] in fact, all educators that are not mere theorizers, strongly insist on the necessity of these exercises.

Why should we exercise the memory of the pupils?[3] The answer to this question in general is: because we

---

[1] "The Jesuits maintain the abuse of memory." Compayré, *l. c.*, p. 140.

[2] Fitch, *Thomas and Matthew Arnold*, p. 50.

[3] See *Woodstock Letters*, 1894, p. 325 sq.

must train the whole man. An old adage has it: "*Tantum scimus quantum memoria retinemus.*" Boyhood is the best season for memory work, and also the time when that faculty should be thoroughly drilled. Professor Schnell, quoted by Father Kleutgen,[1] says: "The school of the second period of childhood (10 to 14) is before everything else a school of memory, and during it more will and must be given to and absorbed by the memory than during any other period of life." And Father Pachtler[2] observes: "The lower the class the more is exercise of the memory to be insisted on." Again: "The mental power which is first developed is the memory. It is the strongest in boyhood and in the first years of youth, and decreases gradually with the development of the body, until, in old age, it is confined to the impressions produced in youth, and is remarkably weak in retaining impressions fixedly. We must strike the iron whilst it is hot, and so make use of boyhood for the acquisition of those subjects which require the most memory, the learning of grammar and the languages which are the foundation of a college career."

If it is asked what should be learned by heart, it is not easy to give an adequate answer. This much is certain that the more important rules of grammar must be committed to memory; then choice passages from the best authors in English and Latin, and a few from the Greek. Among the finest *loci memoriales* in Latin are the orations of Livy, v. g. that of Hannibal to his soldiers, the *exordia* of the orations of Cicero, striking passages from Virgil, some odes of Horace,

[1] *Alte und neue Schulen*, p. 57, note.
[2] *Stimmen aus Maria-Laach*, vol. XVIII, p. 242.

the account of the "four ages" from Ovid's Metamorphoses, etc. In Greek it will be well to have the *exordia* of the Odyssey and Iliad learned by heart; Greek *gnomes* are also χρυσᾶ ἔπη, truly "golden words"; they may serve to fix easily certain important rules of syntax in the mind of the pupils. At the same time, they well illustrate — as in fact the adages and proverbs of every nation — the most common ethical and every day life principles. To make clear what we mean, we may be allowed to quote a few of these Greek gnomes; they should be compared with similar English proverbs, if such exist, or with those of other nations, or with the sayings of Scripture and great authors.

Ὁ μὴ δαρεὶς ἄνθρωπος οὐ παιδεύεται.

Ζήσεις βίον κράτιστον, ἂν θύμου κρατῇς.

Ἐν ταῖς ἀνάγκαις χρημάτων κρείττων φίλος.

(A friend in need, a friend indeed.)

Οὗτοι ποθ' ἅψει τῶν ἀκρῶν ἄνευ πόνου.

(*Per aspera ad astra.* — No pains no gains.)

Σοφίας φθονῆσαι μᾶλλον ἢ πλούτου καλόν.

Κακοῖς ὁμιλῶν καὐτὸς ἐκβήσει κακός.

Ἀρχὴν σοφίας νόμιζε τὸν θεοῦ φόβον.[1]

It is not necessary to give specimens from the English. In general, such passages should be chosen whose contents are worth remembering, be it from the ethical, aesthetical, poetical, or historical point of view. The most beautiful and most elevating thoughts from the world's literature, treasured up in the memory, will also afford considerable help for the writing of essays.

[1] The excellent *Greek Exercise Book* by Professor Kaegi (English edition by James Kleist, S. J. — Herder, St. Louis, 1902) contains a great number of such gnomes.

A few suggestions may be added about the *manner* of learning by heart. Passages from good authors are to be known word for word. The same will ordinarily apply to the rules of grammar; the precepts of rhetoric and of poetry may either be gotten in the same way, or the sense simply may be exacted. The matter which is to be committed to memory should be understood. It will be most useful to instruct the pupils how to memorize. They should not try to learn the lesson as one whole, but rather they should memorize one or two lines at a time, a sentence, or a clause; then the second sentence or line of poetry. After two are well known they should be repeated together. Then a third sentence is learned and again united with those learned previously. The principle of the old Romans: *Divide et impera,* will here be applied. These suggestions may appear minute, and it may be objected that each individual has a way of his own which is just right for him. However, a little questioning of pupils will show that their method of memorizing is very frequently erroneous, and that instruction on such matters will be far from amiss. One great mistake of students is to try to learn by heart when their minds are bothered and distracted. Memory work is best done when body and mind are quiet; impressions then made are deeper and will last. This is the fundamental secret of the various much vaunted systems of memory which have been paraded about in different times. Concentrate the mind, is their motto, and then you will memorize with ease and tenaciously. Very few people, boys or not, have the self-control to concentrate their minds when they are disturbed. This is one of the reasons why it is best to learn by heart in the early morning, before the thoughts and feelings of a new day crowd upon one. Father Sacchini[1] recommends the pupil to go over his task when walking or alone, the same principle, as is clear, being involved.

When should the lessons be recited? By looking into the Ratio, in the second rule for the several classes, we find that the beginning of both sessions is set aside for the recitation of memory lessons. On Saturday the lessons of the whole week are to be repeated. Father Sacchini[2] speaks of monthly and yearly repetitions by heart. He adds an exhortation to the professor never to omit the recitation of memory lessons, and to exact them to the letter. It is hardly possible, in this case, to hear everything from everybody, so the professor may call on a few only, or ask but a part from each. It is very useful to have, say a whole exordium, or an entire description, thus repeated. Another such recitation is held when a whole speech or book has been seen. This public recitation is to take place from the platform; it might be made an item in the entertainments given one another by the different classes. It is incomparably more advantageous to the pupil to deliver thus by heart and declaim with the pomp and ceremony of public elocution a masterpiece of literature which he has been taught through and through, than to fit gestures and modulate his voice to some half-understood and often inferior composition which he has not had the time, nor the patience, nor the ability to make his own.

The habit of giving memory lines, for punishment,

[1] *Paraenesis*, art. 8, sec. 3.
[2] *Paraenesis, ib.*, sect. 2.

from passages which the offender does not understand is to be seriously deprecated. If it produces no other evil effect, it at least is a great loss of time, seeing that the hours so spent might have been devoted to learning something that would educate all the faculties.

It seems very important that the pupils should be directed to be careful to give their memory lessons according to the sense and feeling; in reciting poetry attention is to be paid to the quantities and, above all, to the *caesuras;* then the lines will sound like music. This is unquestionably the surest way of making good speakers, and is far superior as an elocutionary practice to any weekly or less frequent class of elocution. It is also for this reason of the utmost importance that the professor should read the authors well, and see that the pupils read according to the sense of the passage.

§ 3. Written Exercises.[1]

Themes, in the broadest sense, including imitation exercises and free essays, are of the greatest importance. They force the pupils to concentration of thought, and give them patience and facility in writ-

[1] In a recent article in the *Fortnightly Review*, November 1902 ("Are the Classics to Go?"), Professor Postgate, a distinguished English scholar, writes: "If the 'dead' languages and literatures are not to retire into the background, they must be taught as if they were alive" (p. 878). — "Translations from English into Latin or Greek is a most valuable training and necessary part of classical training; but it ought not to have superseded original composition.... From the first, speaking and writing Latin should go hand in hand with reading" (pp. 879–880). Professor Postgate calls these "improved methods"; improved, surely, if he speaks of nearly all systems in vogue during the last century, not however in regard to the system of the Society of Jesus, which always practised this system, as will appear from the next pages.

ing. As we said before, it is most advisable, also in the teaching of English, to make the students write at least some sentences every day. A short Latin theme should be given almost daily, and a Greek theme at least once a week. It is a good custom in many Jesuit colleges in this country to give an English composition for Monday. If the principle maintained by St. Ignatius in the "Spiritual Exercises" is true, that one advances according to the amount of his own self-exertion, not that of his director merely, then these provisions for much and frequent written work were well made. It is not easy to conceive, in the light of this rule, how any one can complain that in the Jesuit system the pupil has nothing to do. He rather has everything to do; the professor goes before him, indeed, and shows him how, but then demands personal application, and that of not the lightest kind, from the pupil who means to advance.[1]

The subject of Latin and Greek themes, whether they are a translation of the teacher's dictation or a free work of the pupils, should be taken, as far as possible, from the authors read in class. Shorter single sentences must be translated especially in the lower classes, in order to apply and practise the rules of grammar. But the exercises should as early as possible consist of connected pieces, descriptions, narrations etc. and should contain the vocables of the Latin and Greek authors read during that period; in short, the exercises should be based on the authors read in class. During the greater part of the last century there was an excessive use of so-called exercisebooks, consisting either of unconnected sentences, or

[1] *Woodstock Letters*, 1894, p. 329.

of such connected pieces as had no relation to the authors studied at the time. Of late years this practice is condemned more and more, and we think rightly so. The new "Prussian School Order" prescribes the former system.[1] And recently an American writer could state that "the grammatical training is now brought into more vital connection with the study of classic literature. The writing of Latin verse is generally discarded. Prose composition is receiving increased attention, and is now more imitative in its character than formerly, being commonly based on the Latin and Greek masterpiece which the class is studying at the same time."[2] Is this a new invention? It is exactly the method prescribed by the Ratio. Thus the 30th of the Common Rules reads: "The theme should be dictated not off-hand but after careful consideration and generally from a written copy. It ought to be directed, as far as possible, to the imitation of Cicero." Two things are contained in this rule: First, the teacher is to write out the dictation himself, not to take it from an exercise book; secondly, the dictation is to be based on the author studied at the time. Cicero is mentioned because he was formerly the author read with preference. Besides, other rules say that the dictation may follow other authors, especially historians.[3] The rules for the teachers of the different classes enjoin that the same method be followed.[4] Thus the professor of Humanities is told that "it is often advantageous so to compose the

[1] *Lehrpläne und Lehraufgaben,* 1901, pp. 23, 25, 29, etc.
[2] *Education in the United States,* (1900), vol. I, p. 185.
[3] *Reg. Prof. Rhet.* 1. — *Reg. Prof. Hum.* 6.
[4] *Reg. Prof. Rhet.* 9. — *Prof. Hum.* 6. — *Prof. Supr. Gram.* 6.

theme that the whole may be gathered here and there from passages already explained."

Indeed, this system affords many great advantages. The reading is made useful for the writing, and the writing helps considerably for the thorough understanding of what has been read. The students will have to ponder over the author, to examine the words, the figures, the phrases, and so they imbibe little by little the genius of the language. Thus imitation-exercises are made useful and easy at the same time. The dictionary need not be consulted for every expression, a custom which entails much waste of time with relatively little fruit. We quoted Dr. Stanley Hall's words,[1] that "one of the best German teachers told him that the boy should never see a dictionary or even a vocabulary, but the teacher must be a 'pony'." This is the old principle of the Ratio. The teacher is told that "after the dictation of the theme he should straightway call for the reading of the theme. Then he should explain anything that may be difficult, suggest words, phrases and other helps."[2] Is not here the teacher, what modern educators want him to be in their 'ideal school,' the boy's dictionary, vocabulary and 'pony'? But above all this practice produces unity in the various exercises. It is needless to say that the same principle can be followed with best success in the teaching of English. The compositions ought to be based on the work studied in class.[3]

[1] From *The Forum*, Sept. 1901; "*The Ideal School.*"
[2] *Reg. com.* 30.
[3] How this can be done may be seen from a little book recently published by a Jesuit: *Imitation and Analysis; English Exercises based on Irving's Sketch Book*, by F. Donnelly, S. J. (Boston, 1902, Allyn and Bacon.)

The imitation exercises should, however, not be a slavish imitation of the author; there may be a great variety in these exercises. Father Jouvancy gives some valuable hints on this subject.[1] "Translate," he writes, "a passage, say from Cicero, into the native tongue; afterwards, without looking at Cicero, retranslate it into Latin. Then compare your Latin with that of Cicero and correct yours wherever it is necessary. Experience has proved that many have greatly benefited by this excellent practice. Another time you may write out a sketch of an argument or write down the train of thought found in the original author, then work it out, clothe, as it were, this skeleton with flesh and nerves. This being finished the new production is to be compared with the original; not only will the difference appear but also many improvements will be suggested. There is a third way of imitating authors. Take a beautiful passage from an author, change the subject matter into one similar or opposite. Then, following in the foot-steps of the author, use, as far as possible, the same figures, periods, connections, transitions. Thus in the oration against Piso, Cicero shows that a seditious mob is not to be honored with the name of the 'Roman people.' In a similar manner it may be shown who really deserves to be styled a Christian, a gentleman, a scholar." Jouvancy justly remarks that this method of self-training is the best substitute, if another instructor and guide cannot be obtained. For the great authors themselves become the teachers, guides and correctors of the student.

[1] *Ratio Discendi*, ch. 1, art. 2, 4. — Cf. Quintilian, *Inst. Or.* X, 2.

That such imitations may be masterpieces in themselves, is proved by more than one instance. A great number of the works of Latin writers are imitations of Greek types. And many fiery harangues of the speakers of the French Revolution are fashioned after Cicero's invectives against Catiline and Anthony.

Every one sees that this excellent method of imitating good authors can be applied to the study of English with the greatest advantage.[2] He who takes a descriptive passage from Washington Irving, or an argument from Burke, Pitt, or Webster and works it out according to these rules of Jouvancy, will surely improve his style — provided he keeps for a long time to the same author. For changing from one author to another, as a butterfly flits from flower to flower, like all desultory work, will produce very little result.

The *correction* of the written exercises is a very troublesome and uninteresting work, the worst drudgery of the teacher's daily life. But it is, as the 21st rule says, of the greatest importance and therefore to be done conscientiously. The Ratio advises the teacher to correct the exercises in class, while the boys are writing or studying for themselves. One boy after the other is called up to the teacher's desk, and his mistakes are pointed out to him; he may himself be asked why it is wrong and correct it himself; particular instructions may be given, a word of praise or of rebuke may be added. Such private corrections afford many advantages. But much time may be lost to teaching and for this reason the rule says "those

[1] See Zielinski, *Cicero im Wandel der Jahrhunderte*.
[2] Compare the excellent observations on the value of the "Reproduction of the Thought of Others," in Genung's *Practical Rhetoric*, pp. 301—325.

themes which, owing to the great number, cannot be corrected in class, should be corrected at home." Many teachers have the following system. They correct all themes at home and return them to the students the following day, with the mistakes marked. Then, if it is a dictation, a boy is called up to translate, the other boys correct him, all comparing their own translations. The pupils will see in most cases why their translations are marked, if not, they should ask immediately, and the teacher may ask other boys why such and such a translation is a mistake. A correct copy should then be made, dictated by the teacher; in lower classes it may be well to have it written by someone on the blackboard.

It is evident that great neatness is to be insisted on in the themes. It is easier to keep paper neat and clean if the themes be exacted on single sheets. But the boys will, as a rule, be more careful, if they have copy books, which are to be used until they are filled. They do not like to see many mistakes in their copy books. In the German and Austrian gymnasia there exists an admirable system. Every exercise in the copy-book has at the top the running number, opposite on the margin the date. Corrections of the teachers and marks are made in red ink: the pupils' corrections are to be added at the end. Every month one review in Latin and one in Greek, written in ink on single sheets of the same size and kind, marked by the teacher, are to be handed in to the Director of the institution, who at any time may also ask for the copy-books of the class. The Government-Inspectors, who from time to time visit the colleges, carefully examine the copy-books, thus controlling the work of teachers and pupils alike. This system has many and great advantages. It requires hard and conscientious work on the part of the teacher especially, but is producing admirable results. A similar system exists in some Jesuit colleges. During the semi-annual examinations all the copy-books are exhibited in the class room or wherever the examination is conducted, to be inspected by the President, and the Prefect of Studies. It is very important that the copy-books be returned as soon as possible, as the work done by the pupils is still fresh in their mind. An exception to this rule must necessarily be made in the case of English composition, especially longer essays, the correction of which naturally requires more time.

This exercise of writing Latin and Greek themes, particularly free Latin compositions, has within the last decades met with great opposition. And yet, no exercise is more useful and more necessary if a solid knowledge of these languages is to be obtained. The reading of authors alone will not suffice. This is the conviction of the most experienced schoolmen. Even Greek exercises must be written, that a firmer hold may be obtained on the facts of accidence, of syntax, and of idiom.[1] And without any practice in writing the understanding of the classical authors will scarcely be more than superficial.[2] Even the writing of Latin verse may not be so useless as some represent it. Quite recently one of the most distinguished scholars of Germany, Professor von Wilamowitz, of the Berlin University, made a strong plea for this much decried

[1] Bristol, *The Teaching of Greek*, p. 301. See on pp. 298—307 some excellent remarks on Greek compositions.
[2] Bennett, *The Teaching of Latin*, p. 172.

exercise.[1] Similarly Dr. Ilberg of Leipsic, who wrote last year: "The 'antiquated' art of writing Latin verses does not deserve the contempt and the sneers with which it has been treated. It is an exercise which requires not only knowledge of the language, but also exertion of the imagination. The writing of Latin verses belongs to those exercises which challenge the pupil to produce something of his own, and which make him enjoy the pleasant sensation of having achieved something."[2] Hence Sir Joshua Fitch goes beyond the bounds of moderation when he asserts that "enormous injury is done to the rank and file of boys by this antiquated and soulless exercise; which inevitably produces weariness and disgust, and sets a false and ignoble ideal of scholarship before the pupils."[3] There is in this sweeping condemnation, as in most similar indictments of old customs, a false supposition. We doubt whether any one considers the "manufacture of Latin verses the ultimate test, the ideal and crown of scholarship." Still, it is one of the many means, although a very subordinate one, of acquiring an accomplished and all around scholarship. Above all, the writing of verses will help to appreciate more fully the classical poets.

In this connection we must say a few words on another exercise, much insisted on by the Ratio, viz. speaking Latin. Few points of the Ratio have been more misrepresented and derided than this. But this without good cause. Facility in speaking Latin is not the principal aim of the Jesuit system. This follows

[1] *Reden und Vorträge*, Berlin, 1901.
[2] *Neue Jahrbücher*, 1901, vol. VII, p. 71.
[3] *Thomas and Matthew Arnold*, p. 39.

from the tenor of the whole Ratio, and is sufficiently proved by our former statement that branches of study are merely the means to attain the one object of all instruction, the cultivation of the mind. A language — so our modern educators say — is learned much more quickly, if spoken; it becomes easy and familiar and, in a way, natural. That the speaking of Latin is, after all, not so absurd, may be seen from the fact that some of the ablest scholars of the nineteenth century have advocated it. Thus the great Latinist, Dr. Seyffert, says: "Without speaking, the writing of Latin will always remain a half-measure and patchwork." Also Dr. Dettweiler, one of the best modern authorities on the study of Latin, recommends the speaking of this language.[1] However, the attitude of the Society in this point has changed. The Society adapts itself in this respect, as in many others, to the tendency of the times. This may be inferred from a comparison between the Ratio of 1599 and that of 1832. The old Ratio enjoins the teacher to insist rigorously that the boys speak Latin in all matters pertaining to school work, except in the lowest class, where they do not know Latin.[2] The corresponding rule in the revised Ratio reads as follows: "The teacher should take great care that the pupils acquire practice in speaking Latin. For this reason he should speak Latin from the highest grammar class on, and should insist on the use of Latin, especially in explaining the precepts, in correcting Latin compositions, in the *concertationes* (contests between the boys), and in their

[1] *Didaktik des Lat. Unt.*, page 110. — See also Rollin, *Traité des études*, livre II, ch. III, art. 3.

[2] *Reg. mag. schol. inf.* 18. — See *Woodstock Letters*, 1894, p. 322 foll.

conversations." The revised rule does not prescribe the colloquial use of Latin as early as was done in former days. But still it must be remembered that the practice of speaking Latin must be gradually introduced, and, therefore, the lower classes are supposed also to have Latin in use, although not so extensively.

Be it remarked, however, that the colloquial use of Latin is, by no means, insisted on in the Ratio for its practical value; for Latin is no longer the universal language of the educated world, as it was some centuries ago. From time to time, indeed, we hear of efforts being made to restore Latin to its old place. Thus in the oration at the Leibnitz celebration of the Royal Academy of Sciences at Berlin, May 29, 1899, the chief speaker advocated the introduction of Latin as the international language of learned men. However, such efforts are too few, too sporadic, to influence the wider circles, at least for the near future. Nay more, it seems almost certain that Latin will never acquire that domineering influence which it formerly exercised. In those days the national languages and literatures were not fully developed. But now they have attained a high degree of perfection, and have gained a stronghold on the mind of the people. Besides, most of the books of great scientific value are either written in German, English, or French, or are speedily translated into one of these languages, and in our days, no one can lay claim to scholarship who does not master one or other of them besides his mother-tongue. The Society of Jesus has simply, in the words of the Jesuit Ebner, watched the trend of events, and adapted herself and her teaching in this point, as in others, to the new conditions.[1] She strives

[1] *Jesuiten-Gymnasien in Oesterreich.*

METHOD OF TEACHING IN PRACTICE.

to teach Latin thoroughly, and therefore urges the colloquial use of Latin as a most valuable means to that end, although at present not in the same degree as in former centuries when facility in speaking Latin had, moreover, a directly practical purpose.

The educational experiments of Germany during the last ten years afford an interesting illustration of what has been said in this chapter. It is known that, after the Berlin Conference of 1890, Latin lost fifteen hours a week in the nine classes of the gymnasium. The Latin compositions particularly were reduced considerably, almost completely abolished. What was the result? Very soon complaints were heard from all sides that in consequence of these changes the teaching of Latin had been greatly injured.[1] It became evident that more extensive writing of Latin was necessary to obtain the linguistic and logical training of the mind, which is one of the foremost objects of Latin instruction. Only these exercises, the practical application of the rules of etymology and syntax, the careful examination of the peculiarities of style in the higher classes, and constant comparison with the mother-tongue, by means of translations and re-translations, give a thorough knowledge and insight into the language.[2]

These are the principles on which the Ratio and Jouvancy had insisted centuries ago, and which were emphasized by the General of the Society in 1893, at the very time when the German schools saw fit to

[1] See *Verhandlungen*, 1901, pp. 282 foll.
[2] *Ibid.*, p. 286: "Vielfache Uebungen hin und her, die ein stetes Umdenken der Vorlagen erfordern, sollen sein (the pupil's) Wissen geläufig, sein Können gewandt machen und ihn allmählich zu einem sicheren Sprachgefühl verhelfen."

abandon them. But experience soon forced the German authorities to revert to what had been thrown overboard. In 1895 permission was granted to add one hour weekly in the higher classes, which was to be devoted to practice in writing and to the application and repetition of rules of grammar and style. For, as Professor Fries declared,[1] the curtailing of these exercises had proved to be the weakest point of the changes made after 1890. In the second conference, in 1900, the opinion of the most distinguished scholars was most positive in demanding a further strengthening of these exercises.[2] It was proposed[3] that a Latin composition should again be required for the last examination. Nay more, Dr. Kübler advocated — one would have thought it impossible after the vehement denunciations of this exercise — the practice of speaking Latin. "It has been exceedingly gratifying to me," he said, "to learn that the Ministry of Instruction will grant greater liberty for these exercises, especially that the speaking of Latin shall no longer be proscribed as heretofore."[4] Before him the commissary of the Government, Dr. Matthias, had declared that besides more frequent translations into Latin, more time and attention should be devoted to the practice of speaking Latin, a practice which in the Goethe-Gymnasium in Frankfurt (Reform-School) was carried on with most gratifying results.[5]

[1] *Verhandlungen*, 1901, p. 288.
[2] *Verhandlungen*, pp. 21, 129, 139.
[3] By Director Kübler and Prof. Harnack, *ibid.*, pp. 140 and 294. The latter declares Latin compositions to be absolutely necessary for a satisfactory instruction in this language.
[4] *Ib.*, p. 139.   [5] *Ib.*, p. 129.

In this reaction we may justly find a vindication of the principle maintained all along by the Society, in spite of the censures of some modern reformers.

§ 4. Contests.

Among the various school exercises mentioned by the Ratio Studiorum, we find the so-called *concertationes*, or contests between boys of the same or of different classes on matter that has been studied previously. These contests have the same end in the lower classes as the disputations in the higher: accustoming the boys to speak on the subject matter of the class, giving them readiness of reply in answering questions, in a word, making them masters of their subjects. Ribadeneira speaks of them as follows: "Many means are devised, and exercises employed, to stimulate the minds of the young, assiduous disputation, various trials of genius, prizes offered for excellence in talent and industry. As penalty and disgrace bridle the will and check it from pursuing evil, so honor and praise quicken the sense wonderfully to attain the dignity and glory of virtue."[1]

All opponents of the Jesuits try to make a capital point of "emulation" as recommended by the Ratio.[2] This "fostering of ambition" was styled "the characteristic of the corrupt Jesuitical morality." We may first ask: are the Jesuits the only educators that used this means? Professor Paulsen answers our question

---

[1] Hughes, *Loyola*, p. 90.
[2] See v. g. Compayré, p. 146. — Seeley, p. 186. — Painter, p. 171–172, where the Jesuit system is stigmatized as "stimulating baser feelings," "appealing to low motives," etc. — In France the Jesuits were attacked on this point also by M. Michel Bréal, in his *Quelques mots sur l'instruction publique.*

most appositely: "The Jesuits know better, perhaps, than others how to use declamations, contests, premiums, etc., effectively. Protestant educators are wont to express their indignation, and to inveigh against the Jesuits, for having made emulation the moving power in learning. The practice of Protestant schools never shared the disgust of these theorizers at the use of emulation, and I do not know whether this practice should be censured. It is true that the good emulation is closely related to the bad, but without the former there has never been a good school."[1]

That these exercises were by no means intended to develop the bad emulation, or false self-love in the young, is evident; this would have been little to the purpose with religious teachers. "Let them root out from themselves, in every possible way, self-love and the craving for vain glory," says the oldest code of school rules in the Society, probably from the pen of Father Peter Canisius.[2] What is appealed to, is the spirit of good and noble emulation, — *honesta aemulatio*, as the Ratio says, — and that by a world of industry which spurs young students on to excellence in whatever they undertake, and rewards the development of natural energies with the natural luxury of confessedly doing well. This makes the boys feel happy in having done well, however little they enjoyed the labor before, and will rouse them to new exertions. Gradually they may then be led to have higher motives in their endeavors. Does not the Divine teacher of mankind act similarly? He demands great sacri-

[1] *Geschichte des gelehrten Unterrichts*, p. 286. (First edition; the passage has been somewhat changed in the second edition, I, p. 430.)
[2] Hughes, *Loyola*, p. 90.

fices and arduous exertions of man: purity, humility, meekness, patience, self-denial, but he always points also to the reward, "theirs is the kingdom of heaven," "your reward in heaven is exceedingly great." God promises also earthly blessings to those that observe his commandments: "Honor thy father and thy mother, that thou mayest be long lived upon the land which the Lord thy God will give thee." Why, then, should it be unlawful and immoral to employ rewards in the education of the young, who are not yet able to grasp the highest motives of well-doing? Or is it probable that young pupils will readily be diligent, when told that *they ought to do* their work? Kant's teaching of the autonomy of human reason is not only deficient, but positively erroneous[1]; but least of all will the rule, *you ought because reason tells you so*, have any effect on the young. On this point also Professor Kemp, in his otherwise fair treatment of Jesuit education, has been led into an error, when he states that "emulation was carried to such extremes that, apparently, it must have obscured the true ends of study and cultivated improper feeling among the students."[2] Such *a priori* conclusions are very dangerous; and the "must have" is frequently only "apparent." Kant, indeed, said: "The child must be taught to act from a pure sense of duty, not from inclination." Still, in another place he declares that "it is lost labor to speak to a child of duty." Children must be treated, as St. Paul says: "as little ones in Christ, to whom I gave milk to drink, not meat; for you were not able as yet."[3] This milk, in education, is some sort of

[1] See Rickaby, S. J., *Moral Philosophy*, pp. 115—118.
[2] *History of Education*, p. 191.
[3] 1 *Cor.* 3, 1-2.

reward, a means not at all immoral. For the desire of honor is inborn in man and lawful as long as it does not become inordinate.[1] Honest emulation is therefore lawful; it is also productive of great deeds. "In all the pursuits of active and speculative life, the emulation of states and individuals is the most powerful spring of the efforts and improvements of mankind." (Gibbon.)

In speaking of reward we do not mean necessarily prizes or premiums. These are indeed more open to objections. The jealousy of pupils is more easily aroused and sometimes even the dissatisfaction of parents. However, this can not justify the general condemnation of prizes. There is hardly an appointment made to any position of honor in a city or state, but a few disappointed individuals will feel and express their disapproval, no matter how just and fair the promotion has been. Should the appointment for such adverse criticism be omitted? Further, premiums for excellence in learning, in military valor, in political ability are as old as history.. The Greeks rewarded the conqueror in their national games with a wreath; the Romans had various crowns for citizens who in different ways had deserved well of their country. And now-a-days no one objects if a victorious general or admiral is offered a token of public recognition, in the form of a precious sword, or even a more useful object. The soldiers of our generation are justly proud if their bravery is rewarded by a badge, and even the scholars of modern Europe, perhaps such as strongly denounce the corrupting influence of premi-

[1] See Thomas Aquinas, *Summa Theologiae*, 2, 2, *qu.* 131 and 132: "On Ambition and Vain Glory."

ums in Jesuit schools, do not hesitate to accept a decoration, or the title of nobility in recognition of their labors for the advance of science. Why, then, should this principle of rewarding success be so rigorously excluded from the schools? No, it is at least exceedingly difficult to prove that prizes have generally evil results, provided all injustice and even all suspicion of unfairness in the distribution is avoided. However, when speaking of reward we mean in general some public recognition, be it a word of praise or something else.[1]

Emulation may be fostered in various ways. The Ratio gives one in the contests. Each pupil may have his *aemulus* or rival. The professor questions A, while B, the aemulus of A., is on the alert to correct his rival. Or the boys question each other mutually, while the professor merely presides to see that all goes on fairly. The whole class may be divided into two sides, which are frequently called camps or armies, as boys naturally delight in anything military. Boys of the one camp, let us say the "Carthaginians," question some of the rival camps of the "Romans," and *vice versa*. The leaders of the two sides keep the record of the points gained, of the corrections made by their respective side. The leaders ought to be pupils distinguished by talent, industry and good character. Different classes may also challenge each other for an extraordinary and more solemn contest, to which other classes may be invited as witnesses.

[1] The rewarding of prizes is ably vindicated by Father R. de Scoraille, S. J., in the *Études religieuses*, Paris, August and September 1879. "Les distributions de prix dans les collèges."

It is not easy to make such contests successful, and it may require great skill and experience on the part of the teacher; and if he lacks this skill — he may be a very good teacher in other respects — it is better to find some other means of encouraging fair and successful emulation. It should not be forgotten that this emulation, in the words of Fathers Hughes and Duhr, is only one of the "subordinate elements in the Jesuit method," [1] or "only a trifling detail," as Father de Scoraille says, not the predominant element as its adversaries represent it. In general, these contests work better in the lower classes; especially in Northern countries, they will not be found as suitable for higher classes. Much of the pomp and the ceremonies which are mentioned in the Ratio and by Jouvancy, do not suit modern taste and have long ago been discarded in Jesuit colleges. But these were accidental details; the fundamental principle is sound. Father Duhr well observes: "The literary contests of the pupils brought life and action into the schools of olden times. We have become colder in such things, whether to the benefit of lively youths is another question." [2]

We quoted above the statement of Professor Paulsen to the effect that the practice of Protestant schools in regard to emulation is by no means what should be expected from their severe censures of this point in the Jesuit system. In fact Mr. Quick, writing about competitions and "class matches," says: "With young classes I have tried the Jesuits' plan of class matches and have found it answer exceedingly well." [3] In the

[1] Hughes, p. 89. — Duhr, p. 61.
[2] *Studienordnung*, p. 125.
[3] *Educational Reformers* (London edition of 1868), p. 297.

revised edition of 1890 the same author declares, in general, that there are many forms of emulation which he did not set his face against.[1] And not long ago, in 1901, Dr. Beecher of Dresden recommended for the lower classes of the gymnasium contests among the pupils, which resemble very much the *concertationes* of the Ratio. He calls them "dainties of a harmless character which make the boys relish better the dry forms of Latin grammar."[2] Still more remarkable is the fact that in the Berlin Conference, June 1900, one of the most distinguished members of that assembly, Professor Münch, pleaded for introducing a system which is not much different from the Jesuit system of the *aemuli*. He says: "It must come to it in our schools that not only the teacher asks the pupils but also that the pupils question one another."[3]

Other exercises intended to rouse the activity of the pupils are *oratorical contests* and other public exhibitions.[4] The rules for the teachers prescribe that the original productions of the pupils must be carefully corrected and polished by the teacher, but the latter should not write them in their entirety.[5] A skilful teacher can do much in stimulating interest in such entertainments, if he proposes an interesting subject and knows how to use the literary and histor-

[1] On pp. 529—532. There he also states that the New England *Journal of Education* gives an account of some interclass matches at Milwaukee, and the New York *School Journal* of contests in the McDonough School No. 12, New Orleans.

[2] *Neue Jahrbücher*, 1901, vol. VIII, p. 98.

[3] *Verhandlungen*, p. 135.

[4] See especially Father Kropf, *Ratio et Via*, chapter V, art. II. (German edition p. 426 f.).

[5] *Reg. com.* 32.

ical material treated in the class. The best entertainments will be those that treat one subject under various aspects.

In the philosophical course the contests consist in the *disputations*. The disputations of the students of philosophy in most Jesuit colleges are conducted in the same fashion as those described in a previous chapter.[1]

In the last place we must mention an exercise which has been styled a "better kind of rivalry,"[2] namely the so-called *academies*. These are voluntary associations of the students, literary societies in the middle classes, and scientific societies in Philosophy. In Philosophy, according to the rules for the academy, essays are read by the students on some scientific topic, preferably on subjects which are in some way connected with the matter studied in class, but which could not be treated there at length. At times these subjects may be given in the form of free lectures. After the essay has been read all the members of the academy are free to enter on a discussion and attack the assertion of the essayist.[3] It is clear that academies conducted in this manner afford the greatest advantages. In the essayist, the spirit of research is stimulated, and in all those who take part in the discussion, in fact, in all those present, scientific criticism is developed.

The subjects treated in the academy of the pupils of Rhetoric and Humanities are, naturally, of a literary character: criticism of rhetorical and poetical topics

[1] See above pp. 422—425.
[2] Quick, *Educ. Ref.*, p. 42.
[3] *Reg. Acad. Theolog. et Philos.*, 3.

not treated fully in class,[1] which may be illustrated from various authors; a literary and critical appreciation of a striking passage from an author; the reading of an essay or poem composed by the pupil himself; a discussion of a disputed question of literature, and other interesting and useful subjects, which are recommended by the rules of this academy.[2] An academy is to be held every week in Philosophy, and every week or every fortnight in Rhetoric and Humanities. Even the Grammar classes are to have their academies, in which similar discussions are carried on, of course less scientific than in the higher classes. At any rate, these academies are excellently fitted to stimulate the activity of the pupils.

In one Jesuit college in the United States the essays prepared in the middle classes, sometimes treated of archaeological subjects which had been alluded to in the course of the reading of the classics. This seems quite in accord with the spirit of the rules for the academy. The pupils took a great interest in such subjects and undoubtedly derived great profit from them.

When the pupil read his essay, not unfrequently drawings on the blackboard, maps and pictures served to illustrate the lecture. Then followed a short discussion of the subject and further queries of the boys, which were answered by the teacher. The following subjects were treated in this manner: The Roman Coliseum, Roman military roads, Roman aqueducts, a Roman triumph, the Romans' daily life, the Roman

[1] *Aliquid de praeceptis magis reconditis rhetoricae vel poesis*, as the 2d rule has it.
[2] *Reg. Acad. Rhet. et Hum.* 2.

family, Roman agriculture, the number and rank of early Christians, character of Greeks and Romans compared, Greek sculpture, pagan and Christian art, — this last essay was read in connection with the study of Cicero's fourth oration against Verres, "On the Statues," in which many Greek masterpieces of art are described or mentioned. — Similar subjects are: The Roman (or Greek) house, Roman (or Greek) temples, feasts, costumes, weapons, magistrates, games, theatres, slavery, education, navy, travels etc. It may be easily understood that much is requisite to conduct such "Academies" successfully, above all on the part of the teacher. For he must discuss the subject with the young writer, suggest reliable sources from which to draw material, direct the writer in his work, and lastly revise and correct the essay. But the work will be amply compensated by the result, especially by the increased interest with which the pupils study the classics.

Such, then, are the exercises of the Ratio. They are distinguished for variety: a short recitation of the memory lesson is followed by the thorough repetition of the prelection of the previous day, or of the precepts of rhetoric, poetry, and grammar. Then comes the principal work of the day, the prelection of the new passage of the author, followed by a brief repetition. Some time is devoted every day to the writing of a little theme; and lastly the contests rouse the pupils to new attention, in case the other exercises should have caused some drowsiness. Certainly this change and variety of the exercises is calculated to break the monotony which, especially with younger pupils, is apt to give rise to weariness and disgust. At the same time, the exercises are of such a character that they call into play all the faculties of the mind: memory, imagination, reasoning. Thus they are excellent means for attaining the end of education, namely the thorough and harmonious training of the mind.

Chapter XVII.

The Moral Scope.

The object of education is the harmonious development of the *whole* man. So far we have spoken of the development of the intellect. Yet the *will* needs training even more than the intellect, and the higher schools ought not to neglect this most important part of the work of education. It cannot be gainsaid that the emphasis laid upon moral training forms the most marked distinction between the true educator and the mere instructor, of whatever creed he may be. At the same time it is one of the most disquieting features of our age that so many teachers in the higher schools have lost sight of this fundamental principle of education. "I hold," writes Dr. McCosh, "that in every college the faculty should look after, not only the intellectual improvement, but also the morals of those committed to their care by parents and guardians. I am afraid that both in Europe and America all idea of looking after the character of the students has been given up by many of our younger professors."[1]

The inevitable consequence of this method must be a decline of morality among the rising generation, or to put it more mildly, and to use the expression of some writers, a lamentable disproportion between the intellectual and moral progress. The existence of this disproportion is attested to by men who have hitherto

[1] *Life of James McCosh*, p. 224.

been rather optimistic about the educational conditions of this country. Thus President Eliot has quite recently expressed himself very frankly on the "failure of our popular education." In spite of the greatest efforts of various agencies towards checking vice in every shape, he sees small results. His practical conclusion is that "we ought to spend more money on schools, because the present expenditures do not produce all the good results which were expected and may be reasonably aimed at."[1] Still, it is more than doubtful whether an increased expenditure is the needed remedy; it is not lack of money, but lack of the true method of education, which is at the root of the failure of education. This has been correctly observed in several comments on President Eliot's indictment. The defects of our people, says the Chicago *Chronicle*, lie "in morals rather than in intelligence." And the Columbia *State* remarks: "It will at least be difficult to point at any fatal exaggeration in this arraignment. But is it fair to charge all of it up to education? Would it not be better for Harvard's President to revise his views as to the power of education? Learning of itself, the mere accumulation of knowledge, can not make morally better an individual or a society. It is unfair to expect so much. Education of the mind may be a help, since it does fit the individual to understand, to distinguish right from wrong and to apprehend the consequences of evil. But education ought never to have been regarded as an insurance against immorality, a preventive of crime, a cure for cupidity, or a guaranty that the Golden Rule will be observed. The

[1] *The Literary Digest*, November 22, 1902, p. 669.

education that brings this about must be more than a mere mental training; it must be moral and spiritual."

These comments touch the sore spot in modern education. The capital error of most school reformers lies in this that they expect too much from intellectual accomplishments for the moral and social improvement of mankind. Every second word of theirs is: culture, knowledge, science, information; and yet, what is far more needed is a reform of character by training the will.[1] The plausible assertion: "Instruction is moral improvement," a principle which is repeated in many variations, is false. The neglect of the religious and moral training is the result of a false philosophy; for, there exists the closest connection between philosophy and pedagogy, so much so that a false philosophy necessarily leads to a false pedagogy, and that a false pedagogy is always the outcome of a false philosophy.[2] Pedagogy, according to the very derivation of the word, means "the guiding of children;" in order to guide them properly it is necessary to know clearly the end and goal which is to be reached. The end of man can be known only from his true nature, and this knowledge is supplied by philosophy. Philosophy, then, which is to be the foundation of sound pedagogy must correctly answer the important questions: *Whence* and *Whither?* If as the foundation of education a philosophy is chosen which gives a wrong answer to these momentous

[1] See the splendid lecture of Bishop Keppler: "Reform, True and False," (translated by the Rev. B. Guldner, S. J., in *The Catholic Mind*, No. 1, January 1903, pp. 13—14).

[2] On the "Relation of Philosophy to Pedagogy" see five articles by Father Christian Pesch, S. J., in the *Stimmen aus Maria-Laach*, volumes XIV and XV.

questions, the children will be led in a wrong direction. Now, that philosophy which considers man merely a highly developed animal, which sees in the human mind nothing but another "aspect" or "phase" of the body (Bain, Spencer, and others), and consequently denies the spirituality and immortality of the soul — such a philosophy (if it deserves this name) cannot assign any other end and object of man's life than some form of hedonism or utilitarianism. Unfortunately this philosophy has exerted a disastrous influence on many modern educational theories. It has led to the separation, more or less complete, of education from religion, and as we shall show hereafter, a solid moral training is impossible without religion. There is only one system of philosophy which can form the sound basis of true pedagogy, and that is Christian philosophy, that philosophy which is in harmony with the revealed truths of Christianity. This philosophy alone gives the correct answer to the all-important *Whence* and *Whither?* It tells us that the soul of the child is a spirit, created by a personal God to His own image and likeness, and destined for an eternal happiness in heaven; it tells us that this life is not the final stage of man, but a journey to another, higher life; that "we have not here a lasting city, but seek one that is to come."[1] A system of education based on this Christian philosophy will widely differ from those systems which are built up on "modern" philosophy, be it German pantheism, French positivism, or English and American agnosticism. The most essential difference will be this that in a Christian system the

[1] *Hebr.* 13, 14.

intellectual training is considered secondary and subordinate to the moral and religious training, whereas all other systems aim at a purely secular education, and in this again lay special stress on the intellectual, to the neglect of the moral training.

It has frequently been observed that the spirit of our age manifests many pagan tendencies. The utilitarian trend of modern education is undoubtedly a sort of neo-paganism. To the artistic mind of the Greek the "Beautiful" (καλόν) and the "Good" (ἀγαθόν) were terms almost synonymous. Greek education, accordingly, aimed at the harmonious development of body and intellect for this life. In the eyes of the Roman, the Eternal City was destined to conquer and rule the whole world. To make useful and devoted members of that mighty political fabric was the sole aim of the education imparted to Roman youths. But the aim of Christian education must be far different. Christ's life and teaching cannot be ignored and disregarded. His "seek ye first the Kingdom of God and His justice,"[1] must be the foundation of all educational principles, "for what doth it profit a man if he gain the whole world and suffer the loss of his own soul?"[2] Therefore, if "the fear of God is the beginning of all wisdom,"[3] the moral and religious training of the young must claim the special attention and care of the teacher. Whereas Greek education affected only the intellect (νοῦς, *mens*), Christian education affects the soul, (πνεῦμα, *spiritus*) as contrasted with the body, the "flesh"

[1] *Matthew* 6, 33.
[2] *Matth*, 16, 26.
[3] *Ecclesiasticus* 1, 16.

(σάρξ, caro). Pagan education aimed at mere *formation* (*Ausbildung*), at the evolution and development of the natural man; Christian education aims at *transformation* (*Umbildung*), at change, at elevation.[1] Every one, free or slave, rich or poor, white or black, is a child of God and destined to be an heir of heaven. Therefore, he is to seek first heavenly things: "*Quae sursum sunt quaerite, quae sursum sunt sapite, non quae super terram.*"[2] He must "put off the old man who is corrupted, and put on the new man who, according to God, is created in justice and holiness of truth."[3] He must listen to Christ's commendation of humility, meekness and purity, and follow His stern command: "*Abnega temetipsum, tolle crucem et sequere me:* Deny thyself, take up thy cross and follow me."[4] But this is not in accord with the natural inclinations of man; therefore, *transformation* is needed. The work of transformation must begin from the awakening of reason and must be the principal object in all education. For, as the *Following of Christ* has it, "when Christ our Master, comes for the final examination, he will not ask how well we spoke and disputed, but how well we lived, *non quid legimus, sed quid fecimus, non quam bene diximus, sed quam religiose viximus.*"[5]

In the "school of the heart" at Manresa, Ignatius had thoroughly grasped these sublime lessons. He had carried them out in his own life and made them the guiding principles of his Society. In his *Spiritual Exercises*, Ignatius has laid down a brief, but most

[1] Willmann, *Didaktik*, vol. I, ch. V.
[2] *Col.* 3, 1, 2.
[3] *Ephes.* 4, 22, 24.
[4] *Matth.* 16, 24.
[5] Book I, ch. III, 5.

comprehensive epitome of Christian philosophy. There he has expressed the whole purpose of man's life in these few lines: "Man is created to praise, reverence and serve God, and thus to save his own soul. All other things are created for the sake of man, and to aid him in the attainment of his end; therefore he should use them only with this object, and withdraw himself from them, when they would lead him from it." Apply this principle to learning, to knowledge, and you must admit that these are not man's ultimate end, they are only means to that end. Throughout the educational system of the Society, we find the application of these truths. Thus the Fourth Part of the Constitutions says: "Since the object at which the Society directly aims, is to aid its members and their fellow-men to attain the ultimate end for which they were created, learning, a knowledge of the methods of instruction, and living example are necessary." In the Ratio Studiorum the first rule of the Provincial reads: "It is one of the most important duties of the Society to teach all the sciences, which according to our Institute may be taught, in such a manner as to lead men to the knowledge and love of our Creator and Redeemer Jesus Christ." Of like import are the first rules of the Rector, the Prefect of Studies and the professors of the various grades. This great care which the Society has always bestowed on the moral and religious training of its pupils, is probably the reason that accounts for the popularity of its schools. Christian parents felt assured that the spiritual welfare of their sons would be most diligently attended to, and so sent them with the greatest confidence to Jesuit colleges. More than once have parents give expression to their sentiments on this point. The testimony of one American father, the distinguished convert from Protestantism, Orestes Brownson, may be given as an instance among many. "We ourselves have four sons in the colleges of the Jesuits, and in placing them there we feel that we are discharging our duty as a father to them, and as a citizen to this country. We rest easy, for we feel they are where they will be trained up in the way they should go; where their faith and morals will be cared for, which with us is a great thing. It is more especially for the moral and religious training which our children will receive from the good fathers that we esteem these colleges. Science, literature, the most varied and profound scholastic attainments, are worse than useless, where coupled with heresy, infidelity or impurity."[1]

However, the Society has been blamed by some for insisting too strongly upon moral and religious training, and for subordinating to it everything else. But how can any one who believes in the existence of God and an eternal life, find fault with this principle? If there is a God, if man has an immortal soul, if there is an eternity of happiness awaiting the good, and an eternity of punishment the wicked, then the "one thing necessary" on earth, and to be aimed at above everything else, is the salvation of the soul. Hence it is that men, who in their religious tenets widely differ from the Jesuits, could not help praising the latter for the attention they paid to the moral and religious education of their pupils. From numerous testimonies we may be allowed to quote a few. "As

[1] *Brownson's Review*, Jan. 1846, p. 87.

might be expected," writes Quick, "the Jesuits were to be very careful of the moral and religious training of their pupils. . . . Sacchini writes in a very high tone on this subject. Perhaps he had read of Trotzendorf's address to a school."[1] In 1879 an anti-clerical paper wrote about the Belgian higher schools: "Could not our teachers do a little more for discipline? Could they not watch more diligently over the manners and morals of the students? How often do we hear people say: 'What, I send my son to the *Athenées?*[2] God forbid! Fine manners he would learn there!' Now there is no reason why the young should acquire worse manners in the *Athenées* than in the Jesuit schools — on the contrary. However, in point of fact, only the Jesuits look after *education*, whereas our *Athenées* busy themselves only about *instruction*. I know full well that the education imparted by the clergy is bad, even dangerous. Our lay teachers should pay more attention to *education*, as it is exactly this training, however detestable, which brings to the men in the soutane the patronage of so many parents." M. Cottu, a bitter enemy of the Jesuits, had to acknowledge the same.[3]

[1] *Educational Reformers* (1890), page 47. — It is worth noting that Sacchini is supposed to have learned from Trotzendorf to esteem highly moral and religious training — by the way, Quick's edition of 1868 ascribes that address to Melanchthon! — Everything good in the Jesuit system must be traced to Protestant sources! As though Sacchini, in the teaching of the Bible and the most explicit principles of the Constitutions of his Order, had not better sources than in a school address of Melanchthon or Trotzendorf, of which he probably knew nothing!

[2] The public higher schools of Belgium.

[3] *Journal de Gand* and *La Chronique*, quoted by De Badts de Cugnac, *Les Jésuites et l'éducation*, p. 54.

Professor Kern of the University of Göttingen, a Protestant, wrote years ago: "The Jesuits attack the evil at its root: they educate boys in the fear of God and in obedience. Has it ever been heard that from Jesuit schools doctrines come forth similar to those of our modern schools? History has proved that irreligious and anarchistic doctrines spread rapidly after the suppression of the Society. Faith and science were no longer united. Reason with all its errors,—and what error is so absurd that has not had its defenders—was given the preference, faith was abandoned, ridiculed, and spoken of only under the name of superstition."[1]

By what means do the Jesuits endeavor to effect the moral training of their pupils? We may classify the means they employ under four heads: the example of a virtuous life, reasonable supervision, ethical instruction, and certain means provided by the Church, especially the sacraments. As to the first we all know that example is much more powerful than words, particularly so with the young. There is a great truth in the old Latin adage: *Verba movent, exempla trahunt.* Every teacher, therefore, should lead such a life as to be able to say with the great teacher of the Gentiles: "Be ye followers of me as I also am of Christ."[2] Above all ought this to be the case with teachers who make a profession of religion. The life of a religious is one of continual self-denial. St. Ignatius seems to have thought that daily contact with men of this stamp would be good for boys. He seems to have thought that in course of time they would assimilate some of that spirit of conscientious devotion

---

[1] Quoted by Ebner, *Jesuiten-Gymnasien.*
[2] 1. Cor. II, 1.

to duty, of generous readiness to go far beyond the limits of mere duty, of the manful and noble spirit of self-control and self-sacrifice, of that spirit which seeks not self but the good of its neighbor, that spirit which the pupils cannot help seeing exemplified in their masters, if those masters are such men as St. Ignatius intended them to be.[1] Now, St. Ignatius was very explicit on the necessity of setting a good example, and the Ratio inculcates the same in exhorting the teacher to edify the pupils by the example of a virtuous life.[2] Have the sons of Ignatius come up to the expectation of their father? Even the enemies of the Order could not help expressing their admiration for the moral purity of the lives of the Jesuits.[3] Nor can we wonder at this. The solid training in religious life, which we described in a previous chapter, and the daily practice of mental and vocal prayer, must give the religious teacher a self-control that preserves him from the more serious outbreaks of passion, which may prove detrimental to his authority and ruin all salutary influence over his pupils.[4] Professor Paulsen observes

[1] See Father Lucas, S. J., in *The Spiritual Exercises and the Education of Youth* (London, 1902).

[2] *Reg. com. mag. cl. inf.* 10.

[3] Thus the Protestant Sir Henry Howorth, who attacked the Jesuits so bitterly in recent years, must confess: "The Jesuits have been a very powerful agency in framing history. They have some things to be proud of. So far as I know, the austerity and purity of their lives was one of the greatest, probably the greatest of all, reforming agencies in the purifying of the clergy of the sixteenth century, and they strenuously leavened religious life with the stricter rules of life, which the Council of Trent tried hard to introduce into the religious world." (The London *Tablet*, Nov. 23, 1901, p. 817.)

[4] On this whole subject it is worth while to read De Badts de Cugnac, *La morale des Jésuites* (Lille, 1879).

in regard to the Jesuit teacher: "According to an old saying, he is strongest who overcomes himself. This may mean not only that the greatest effort is needed to rule one's self, but that he who is able to do so possesses the greatest strength. Now it is my conviction that there was never a body of men who succeeded better in controlling natural inclinations, and in checking individual desires, than the Jesuits. True, such qualities do not make one amiable; no one is amiable who is without human weaknesses. Perfect absence of passion in a man makes him awe-inspiring and causes others to feel uncomfortable in his presence." Then he adds: "That the Jesuits up to this day are masters in the great art of checking anger, and thus masters in the great art of ruling over men's souls, the reader may learn from a book written by a pupil of the Jesuit college of Freiburg and of the *Collegium Germanicum* in Rome, who afterwards became a Protestant minister, and who vividly and truthfully describes the impression made upon him in these Jesuit institutions."[1]

In addition to these testimonies, it will not be superfluous to cite the testimony of prominent men who as pupils in Jesuit colleges had an opportunity of watching the Jesuits closely. The first witness is Voltaire: "During the seven years," he writes, "that I lived in the house of the Jesuits, what did I see among them? The most laborious, frugal, and regular life, all their hours divided between the care they spent on us and the exercises of their austere profession. I at-

[1] *Geschichte des gelehrten Unterrichts*, pp. 282—283 (I, 408—409). The work referred to is: *Erinnerungen eines ehemaligen Jesuitenzöglings* (*Recollections of a former Jesuit pupil*). Leipzig, 1862.

test the same as thousands of others brought up by them, like myself; not one will be found to contradict me. Hence I never cease wondering how any one can accuse them of teaching corrupt morality."[1] — From Germany three men may be quoted who are considered, by friend and enemy, as equally distinguished for gifts, for noble character, and for genuine patriotism: von Ketteler, von Mallinckrodt, and Count Ballestrem. It was in the early days of the *Kulturkampf*, when the laws for expelling the Jesuits from Germany were being discussed, that among others, these three stood up to defend the persecuted Order. Freiherr von Ketteler, the celebrated Bishop of Mentz, testifies: "As a youth I was sent by my parents to an educational institution of the Jesuits, where I spent four years. From home I brought with me such independence of character and such purity of morals, that had I noticed a shadow of what the world styles Jesuitical principles, I would have turned away from them with loathing and disgust. My parents, who enjoyed an entirely independent position in life, and who were filled with the purest and strongest love for their children and their true welfare, would not for a moment have left me in that institution, had they apprehended anything of the kind. There I witnessed nothing that ever shocked my youthful spirit trained in the purest principles of Christianity. I took leave of all my teachers with deepest reverence and with the firmest conviction that they were men who daily made on themselves the demands of severest morality." — Similar testimonies were rendered by Herr von Mallinckrodt, that chivalrous spirit who, with perhaps the

[1] *Lettre*, 7 février 1746. — Hughes, *Loyola*, p. 105.

exception of Windthorst, was the greatest man in that grand Catholic organization, the German Centre Party. And Count Ballestrem, now for several years President of the German *Reichstag*, commenced one of his speeches before that assembly with the following words: "The last time I had the honor to address you here, I defended an institution which has become dear to me, and in which I have spent a great part of my life, the Prussian Army. To-day I come to defend an institution which I have known from the days of my childhood, and with whose excellences I am acquainted in every detail. I come to bear witness for my venerable teachers, for my highly esteemed friends: for the religious of the Society of Jesus."[1]

Undoubtedly the testimony of these men, who with the keen eyes of boys that so readily find fault with their teachers watched the Jesuits and scrutinized their every word and action, outweighs a thousand calumnies of prejudiced pamphleteers, who, in many cases, have never seen a Jesuit or any other religious. Moreover, these witnesses refute the oft-repeated charge of "the corrupt moral teaching of the Jesuits." Fair-minded Protestants have long since branded this charge as a slander. Thus the German Protestant Körner says in his *"History of Pedagogy"*[2]: "It is the fashion to represent the Jesuits as heartless beings, malicious, cunning, and deceitful, although it must be known perfectly well that the crimes imputed to them

[1] Duhr, *Jesuiten-Fabeln*, ch. 5 (2nd ed.), pp. 102—103.
[2] *Geschichte der Pädagogik* (Leipzig, 1857), page 12. — Quoted by Shea; *History of Georgetown College*, page 86. Italics are ours. — See also the splendid testimony rendered to the Jesuits by M. Albert Duruy in the *Revue des Deux Mondes*, January 1, 1880.

are historically groundless, and the suppression of the Order in the last century was due entirely to the tyrannical violence of Ministers of State. *It is only our duty to justice to silence the folly of such as declare the Jesuit system of education to be nothing but fanatical malice and a corruption of the young.* The Jesuits were the first educators of their time. Protestants must with envy acknowledge the fruitfulness of their labors; they made the study of the ancient classics a practical study, and training was with them as important as education. They were the first schoolmasters to apply psychological principles to education; they did not teach according to abstract principles, but they trained the individual, developed his mental resources for the affairs of practical life, and so imparted to the educational system an important influence in social and political life. From that period and from that system, scientific education takes its rise. *The Jesuits succeeded in effecting a moral purity among their pupils which was unknown in other schools during the sixteenth and seventeenth centuries.*"

Indeed, the Society has ever been most anxious to preserve her pupils from the taint of impurity, the vice to which youth most easily falls a prey. She takes most effective means to preserve what Chaucer calls the "sweet holiness of youth." She will inexorably expel a boy whose presence is dangerous to others, especially in the matter of purity. "There are some faults," says Shea,[1] "for which the Jesuit system of discipline has no mercy, and in the first place is found the vice of impurity. For this crime the only punishment is expulsion, since contamination is looked upon

---

[1] *History of Georgetown*, p. 85.

as the greatest evil that can be spread among the young. Hence the virtue of purity is fostered with all possible care and solicitude, and even Protestants have borne witness to the high moral purity of Jesuit students." (See, v. g., Mr. Körner's words quoted above.) So also another writer, the German Protestant Ruhkopf: "In Jesuit colleges a moral purity prevailed which we look for in vain in Protestant schools and universities. Such as were totally corrupt, the Jesuits did not tolerate among their pupils, but sent them away. In their colleges, impurity and demoralization could not easily arise, as with the utmost care they kept away everything that could taint the imagination of the youth committed to their charge."[1]

Boarding schools, in particular, may easily, and, if precautions are not taken, will almost invariably become hot-beds of immorality.[2] Hence the anxiety of the Jesuits in guarding their pupils. Yet they have been attacked more than once for these very precautions. Great educators, however, have been one with the Jesuits on this important question. Thus we read in the life of President McCosh: "The notion that a professor's duty began and ended with the instruction and order in the class room, was abhorrent to him. He thought it the most serious problem of the higher

[1] Janssen, *Geschichte des deutschen Volkes*, vol. VII, page 82.

[2] See, for instance, what Arnold said on this subject, in Fitch, *Thomas and Matthew Arnold*, page 77; further, the *Dublin Review*, October 1878, p. 294 foll., in the highly instructive article: "Catholic Colleges and Protestant Schools." Also "Tom Brown's School Days at Rugby," especially the Preface to the Sixth Edition, will furnish interesting material.

education to secure the oversight and unremitting care of students, without espionage or any 'injudicious interference with the liberty of the young man.' With the fine language about treating students as capable of self-government, and responsible for their own conduct, Dr. McCosh never felt the slightest sympathy, believing that the formation of good habits was more than the half of education, and that the morals of the young, like their intellect and judgment, required constant attention from the instructors."[1]

Now let us listen to what the head of an important department in one of the large institutions in this country thinks on this subject: "One way to deal with these strange, excited, inexperienced, and intensely human things called Freshmen is to let them flounder till they drown or swim; and this way has been advocated by men who have no boys of their own. It is delightfully simple, if we can only shut eye and ear and heart and conscience; and it has a kind of plausibility in the examples of men who through rough usage have achieved strong character. 'The objection,' as the master of a great school said the other day, 'is the waste; and he added, 'it is such an awful thing to waste human life!' This method is a cruel method, ignoring all the sensibilities of that delicate, high-strung instrument which we call the soul. If none but the fittest survived, the cruelty might be defended; but some, who unhappily cannot drown, become cramped swimmers for all their days. Busy and worn as a college teacher usually is, thirsty for the advancement of learning as he is assumed always to be, he cannot let hundreds of young men pass before him,

[1] *Life of James McCosh*, pp. 33 and 35.

unheeded and unfriended. At Harvard College, the Faculty, through its system of advisers for Freshmen, has made a beginning; and though there are hardly enough advisers to go round, the system has proved its usefulness. At Harvard College, also, a large committee of Seniors and Juniors has assumed some responsibility for all the Freshmen. Each undertakes to see at the beginning of the year the Freshmen assigned to him, and to give every one of them, besides kindly greeting and good advice, the feeling that an experienced undergraduate may be counted on as a friend in need." — This is excellent, but all the more surprised will the reader be to find that this author continues in the following strain: "Whether colleges should guard their students more closely than they do — whether, for example, they should with gates and bars protect their dormitories against the inroads of bad women — is an open question. For the deliberately vicious such safeguards would amount to nothing; but for the weak they might lessen the danger of sudden temptation."[1] As to the "open ques-

[1] *Atlantic Monthly*, March 1900. — A somewhat similar principle is stated in an article on Eton, in the *Edinburgh Review*, April 1861: "It was the fashion in Sydney Smith's days — it is so still — to maintain that the neglect to which boys are necessarily exposed at our public schools, in consequence of the insufficient number of assistant masters, renders them self-reliant and manly; and that the premature initiation into vice, which too often results from that cause, imparts to them an early knowledge of what are apologetically called 'the ways of the world'; and prevents their running riot when subsequently exposed at the universities to still greater temptations than those offered them in their boyhood by the public-houses and slums of Eton and Windsor." Quoted in the *Dublin Review*, October 1878, p. 308. — This

tion" we hold rather that it is a shocking principle. Must not fathers and mothers, who have sons in such schools, shudder at the thought that their children will scarcely be protected against the worst and most disgraceful of moral dangers, since the school authorities think it an "open question" whether such protection is advisable? In too many cases are youths "left to flounder till they drown or swim." And the majority will drown, or become cramped swimmers for all their days; that is, become moral, and perhaps physical wrecks. This is the end of all that specious but senseless talk about "the sanctity of the individual," "advantage of rough usage," "dangers of guarding sternly or tenderly," "free spirit of our country," and the like. The Divine Teacher of mankind, the friend of children, has clearly and sternly expressed His "views" upon these points: "He that shall scandalize" — and we may add, he that allows others to scandalize, or does not prevent from being scandalized — "one of these little ones that believe in me, it were better for him that a millstone were hanged about his neck, and that he should be drowned in the depth of the sea." Neglect of watchfulness in this regard is nothing less than treason; treason towards the souls of the pupils who should be guarded against their worst foes, their own corrupt inclinations; treason against parents who demand that their children be not exposed to such experiments.

The Jesuits do not let their pupils "flounder till they drown or swim." They consider it their most

"premature initiation into vice" was, accordingly, a frequent result of the system of the great English public schools; moreover, it was considered a positive benefit. A sad prerogative of these schools, indeed!

sacred obligation to prevent, as far as possible, their charges from coming into contact with moral contamination. "But," it is objected, "what good comes from all your protection? It usually happens that your pupil on leaving the place where he was protected against all dangers, falls the more quickly and the more shamefully. And why? For the very reason that he was shielded on all sides and never struggled with dangers and temptations. He is not prepared, he is caught unawares, and yields unconditionally and hopelessly, whereas had he been trained by daily encounter with temptation his character would have been hardened."[1] If the case were frequent, if the deeper fall inevitably followed the purer boyhood, then we may as well despair of all education and all virtue. Happily, we have here one of those sweeping generalizations and exaggerations, so common with certain writers. We answer: *First*, not all fall away after leaving the sheltering precincts of the college. Many remain good among the greatest dangers and temptations. And this perseverance they owe to the precautions taken in the college and to the virtuous habits acquired through the daily practice of observing the regulations of these institutions. The continued moral efforts required for doing this are as effective for

[1] Such objections have sometimes been made even by short-sighted Catholics who, dazzled by the outward brilliant successes of the great Protestant schools, wished some of their features to be introduced into Catholic colleges. These views have been ably refuted in various articles of the *Dublin Review*. See e. g. July and October 1878. — On the other hand, not long ago President Jones of Hobart plainly advocated *greatly increased supervision* in student life. He does not think that more stringent regulations would keep the students "milksops." *The Forum*, Jan. 1901, 592—593.

producing strength of character as the "rough usage" and, at the same time, less dangerous. *Secondly*, many of those who afterwards disgrace themselves, would have done so even had they never been inside college walls, in many cases much earlier, and perhaps more irreparably. It was college discipline that prevented them from earlier ruin. St. Ignatius used to say: "To have prevented one sin is worth all the troubles and labors of this life." *Thirdly*, many come to Catholic academies and colleges from public and private schools, where they have acquired such a knowledge of life and of the "ways of the world," that educators are sometimes horrified at discovering what boys of fourteen and sixteen years have heard and experienced. For such boys the quiet and seclusion of a Catholic college and its strict discipline are of the greatest benefit, and the spirit of piety and modesty pervading the whole atmosphere acts upon those poor boys as the healthy, pure air of Colorado and New Mexico upon consumptives. If the spiritual consumption has not progressed too far, two or three years spent in thoroughly Christian surroundings, often restore such youths to complete health of soul and body. There is scarcely a Jesuit teacher who could not recount many instances of boys whose reformation was so thorough, that they became most excellent men. Without this salutary influence their souls would have sunk into the abyss of vice and crime, and their bodies very likely into an early grave. *Fourthly*, boys who were thus protected in college, and afterwards go astray will in most cases return. Their hearts will not be happy in their pleasures and excesses; for the religious and moral principles implanted in them can never be totally destroyed. After a brief experience they become disgusted with their lives and begin to loath their vices. A young man without any previous religious training sees no way out of the quagmire of vice; he easily abandons himself the more to his evil passions. But it is very different with the young man who grew up under religious influences. In moments of disgust and remorse, at a sudden calamity that befalls him or those near him, he remembers not only the happiness of his childhood but also the salutary advice of his teacher, to whom he used to look up as a fatherly friend. Such recollections have saved more than one young man who had gone astray. *Finally*, are those young men who from early years and during college life were left to their "own experience and rough usage" of temptations, later on, in the battles of life, better and of purer morals, then those "sheltered" against dangers? An honest inquiry will assuredly be met with a decided answer in the negative.

The idea of supervision and restriction seems to be especially repugnant to people in England and America. Undoubtedly, the character of the American and English youth differs in several points from that of the youth of other countries. For this reason we may admit, with a writer in the *Dublin Review*,[1] that in dealing with English — and we add: with American—youths, it will be found beneficial to exercise a somewhat less minute supervision than that practised in some other countries. This seems to be demanded by the peculiar character and the spirit of the public and private life of the English and Amer-

[1] *Dublin Review*, October 1878, p. 285, note.

ican people. On the other hand, these differences have frequently been exaggerated, and conclusions have been drawn from these discrepancies of character which are altogether unjustified. Opinions have been uttered which seem to imply an intrinsic superiority of the American youth over those of the rest of the world, a superiority which renders laws that are necessary for good education everywhere else, superfluous in this country. Some seem to think that restrictions are little compatible with republican institutions. Professor Edward J. Goodwin, of New York, said recently: "German children are taught to submit to authority, but our boys must be taught to govern themselves."[1] We readily admit that the principle of submitting to authority can be carried to extremes, in education as well as in political life. But we think that boys will learn to govern themselves only by submitting first to authority, as in early years they possess neither the sufficient knowledge nor the necessary strength of will to govern themselves reasonably. We fasten the young tender tree to a pole, lest it grow crooked or be bent and broken by the storm; the same is necessary, and to a much higher degree, in the case of the frail human sapling in which so many perverse inclinations are hidden which tend to foster a growth in the wrong direction. Above all, educators should not forget that there is one authority to which the youths of every country must submit unconditionally, and that is the authority of the Divine Lawgiver as expressed in the precepts of morality — and obedience is one of these precepts. The same Divine authority

[1] *Report of the Commissioner of Education*, 1901, vol. I, p. 249.

imposes the sacred duty on educators to watch over their charges, and to remove, as far as lies in their power, all that endangers their morality. The Christian educator fears lest any neglect in this matter may draw upon him the dreadful words addressed to the "watchman to the house of Israel": "If thou declare it not to him [the wicked man], nor speak to him, that he may be converted from his wicked way and live: the same wicked man shall die in his iniquity, but I will require his blood at thy hand."[1] Indeed, it is the fatherly love and care for the welfare of their pupils which leads the Christian educator to exercise supervision over his pupils. He has received from the parents that treasure which is to them more precious than anything on earth; their own dearly beloved children, for whom they toil and labor, over whom they anxiously watch and pray lest they should suffer shipwreck in regard to their faith and virtue, especially the virtue of purity which is so beautiful, so priceless, and yet so difficult of securing in youth. The teacher would be guilty of the basest breach of confidence, did he not strain every nerve to avert a calamity from those so sacredly entrusted to him. We can well understand that at times this or that particular method may justly be censured, as, in reality, not being conducive to the end which is sought; but that the whole system, the very principle, should be ridiculed and condemned, spoken of in terms of invective and indignation, and stigmatized by such opprobrious names as "espionage" and the like — this, we say, is startling.[2] It can be explained only

[1] *Ezech.* 3, 18.
[2] *Dublin Review*, April 1878, p. 330.

from the false philosophical notions of such critics; particularly from their wrong conception and very low valuation of the human soul.

Many, especially such as have never stepped inside the doors of a Jesuit college, are filled with an absurd dread of the supervision exercised, as they fancy, by the Jesuits. From time to time, however, when some appalling scandals are discovered within the walls of a college where the students enjoy pretty nearly full liberty, or when scores, if not hundreds of students, exhibit most disgraceful scenes of disorder on the public streets, then the eyes of many are opened and they see that, after all, some supervision, and a pretty strict one, is necessary in a place where hundreds of hot-blooded youths live together. In 1891, an English non-Catholic paper, speaking about scandalous disclosures on board the school-ship *Britannia*, said there were two kinds of public schools, Jesuit and Gaol-bird school. "The Jesuit idea of school life is that a boy at school should, as far as possible, be in the same position as he will afterwards be in as a man in the world, that is to say, the position not of a wild beast in an African jungle, free to do what he pleases, but of a human being in a civilized country, living under the eye of the law. The Jesuits in fact police their schools, that is, what it comes to. This policing is called by people who don't like it (i. e. don't like the trouble of enforcing it) espionage and other ugly names. As a matter of fact, it amounts to no more than that ordinary care which a commonly decent and commonly sensible father exercises in his own house: It means simply reasonable supervision, aided of course by rationally constructed school buildings —

massing of boys for school as well as for play — living in the light of day, in fact. Now, neither a boy nor a man does much harm or has much harm done to him, so long as he lives in the light of day, and the consequence is that although, of course, many boys who leave Jesuit schools become bad men afterwards, yet they get no harm while they stay at school. They leave as good as they come and, moreover, if they do not come pretty reasonably good, they do not stay long. The father gets a letter to say 'the boy is doing no good at school and had better be removed.' The Goal-bird system is simplicity itself. The head master draws his salary, attends to the teaching of Greek and Latin and shuts his eyes firmly, deliberately, conscientiously, like an English gentleman, as he would say himself, to everything else going on around him."[1] This is very severe language. May it not partly apply to a number of "educators" in this country, who denounce so strongly any "paternalism" exercised over the pupils?

As regards the charges against the precautions taken in Jesuit colleges, they are usually founded upon wrong suppositions. It is believed that the Jesuit pupil is watched every moment. This is not so; he has liberty enough within a certain reasonable limit. Of course, it is a most delicate and difficult question how this limit is to be determined. It is not possible to lay down any particulars on this subject, because, in this as in other matters, there exists considerable variety in different Jesuit colleges, and Superiors assign that measure of liberty which, con-

---

[1] *Truth*, November 1891; quoted in the *Tablet*, November 14, 1891.

sidering the difference of places and circumstances, especially the age and character of the pupils, seems not to expose them to great dangers. — It is also falsely supposed that no word of necessary explanation is given concerning the dangers that await the pupil outside the college walls; that educators imperatively forbid any inquiry about matters which the students may be anxious to ask; that they never give advice and instruction on matters which at a certain age a young man may, and considering the circumstances, should know, in order not to be caught unawares by dangers and temptations, which are sure to come.[1] Necessary instruction and advice, according to age and other circumstances, will be given, above all, by the confessor; the teacher also, with moderation and discretion, will do the same. Many occasions will offer in the explanation of the catechism, of the authors, and in private conversations.

A few words must be said about the private talks with boys so much recommended in the Jesuit system. Father Jouvancy says the teacher should speak in private more frequently with those who seem to be exposed to worse and more dangerous faults.[2] Father Sacchini remarks that he should study the character and disposition of each pupil, to discover the bad outcroppings on the tender plant and nip them in the bud.[3] Father Kropf advises the teacher to go carefully over the names of his pupils every Sunday and to recommend them in prayer to our Lord and His Blessed Mother. While doing this he should reflect

[1] On this important point see Père Rochemonteix, vol. II, p. 55 foll.
[2] *Ratio Docendi*, ch. 1, art. 2.
[3] *Paraenesis*, art. 18.

especially whether it is advisable to see this boy or that in private, to correct him, to warn him against a danger, or whether it is well to communicate with his parents.[1] What should be treated of in these private conversations is plain from Jouvancy and Sacchini. And the 47th rule of the teachers says briefly, they should treat only of serious matters.[2] Speaking of conversation with the students, the Father General Vitelleschi, in 1639, gave characteristic directions: "It will be very useful if from time to time the professors treat with their auditors, and converse with them, not about vain rumors and other affairs that are not to the purpose, but about those that appertain to their well-being and education; going into the particulars that seem most to meet their wants; and showing them how they ought to conduct themselves in studies and piety. Let the professors be persuaded that a single talk in private, animated with true zeal and prudence on their part, will penetrate the heart deeper and work more powerfully, than many lectures and sermons given to all in common."[3] This keeping in touch with the individual pupil has always been considered as one of the sources of the success of the Jesuits in their educational labor. Protestant educators have not failed to recognize this and to speak of it with approval. Thus Sir Joshua Fitch writes of Arnold: "Much of the influence he gained over his scholars — influence which enabled him to dispense in an increasing degree with corporal punishment — was attributed to his knowledge of the individual char-

---

[1] *Ratio et Via*, ch. IV, art. 1, § 6.
[2] See also *Woodstock Letters*, 1896, p. 251.
[3] *Monumenta Germaniae Paedag.*, Pachtler, vol. III, p. 59. — Hughes, *Loyola*, p. 108.

acteristics of boys. . . . This is a kind of knowledge which has long been known to be characteristic of the disciplinary system of the Jesuits, but has not been common among the head masters of English public schools."[1] It is almost altogether absent in most modern systems, consistently with their principle of separating training from teaching, education from instruction, a principle which, as M. Brunetière said, "our forefathers would not have been able to understand."[2]

Supervision and exhortation are powerful means for preserving the good morals of youths, but much more powerful are the divinely appointed means, Confession and Communion. Although they are practised in all Catholic colleges, the Jesuits, following the example and advice of their founder, worked most zealously for the spread of frequent confession and communion. By doing so they incurred the special hatred of the Jansenists, whose rigorous views they vigorously opposed. We need not here refute the Protestant views of auricular confession. Every Catholic knows that it is not a "torture chamber of conscience," not an "unwarrantable invasion of the privacy of the individual," not an "intrusion into the sacred domain of domestic life," not a "source of weakness to the will," not a "dangerous and demoralizing practice." To men who use such language and hold such opinions may be applied the words of the Epistle of St. Jude the Apostle: "*Blasphemant quod ignorant,* they blaspheme things which they know not." Apart from the divine institution, the

[1] *Thomas and Matthew Arnold*, p. 102.
[2] *Revue des Deux-Mondes*, 15 février 1895.

Catholic knows that confession, the "ministry of reconciliation," the "sacrament of peace," is a source of unspeakable blessings, of consolation in distress, of encouragement in despair, of advice in perplexities. With reference to our object, the English Jesuit Father Clarke (Oxford), in an article entitled "The Practice of Confession in the Catholic Church,"[1] points out the special advantages of confession for the moral training of the young. The passage is so beautiful and so much to our purpose that it is well to quote it in its entirety.

"It has probably occurred to the mind of most Catholics, as it has often occurred to my own, that if there were no other proof of the paramount claims of the Catholic Church, we should find a sufficient one in the elaborate care with which she watches over the innocence of the young. To guard from evil and corruption the lambs of the fold is one of her chief duties and privileges. This loving care she inherits from her Divine Founder, Who was the friend and lover of little children. Now, I do not think that it is possible for any unprejudiced and well-informed person, who compares the practical working of the Catholic system with that of any other religious system in the world, to deny her unrivalled and unapproachable superiority in this respect. She shields her little ones in their early childhood with all the jealous care of the most tender mother, and when the time comes for the safe seclusion of the parental roof to be exchanged for a freer intercourse with their fellows, she provides safeguards for their purity that are unknown, or almost unknown, outside her fold. For the due education of

[1] *North American Review*, December 1899.

boys, large schools, and for those of the upper class, large boarding schools are a practical necessity. Then comes the dangerous time, and how great the dangers of that time are is well known to every one who has had an experience of the inner working of English public schools. To keep boys safe from a most perilous, if not fatal, contact with vice and sin, is a problem which has exercised the mind and troubled the conscience of every one who has taken part in the management of any of our large schools and colleges; and those among Protestant educators who have studied the subject most deeply, and who have had long experience to guide them, have had to admit, with sorrow and grief, that the task was a hopeless one.[1] They have had to submit to what they considered an inevitable evil, and their best hope has been by personal influence to mitigate to some extent that which they knew they were powerless to prevent. But is the evil one for which no remedy can be provided? God forbid! The Catholic Church provides an effective remedy for this as for every other evil incident to human life. Here I can speak from a large experience, and with a full knowledge of the subject. Again and again I have been assured by boys who have passed through Catholic colleges, from the lowest to the highest form, that during the whole of their time there they never heard one immodest word, or came into

---

[1] Compare with this the passage quoted by Arnold: "Public schools are the very seats and nurseries of vice. It may be unavoidable, or it may not, but the fact is indisputable. None can pass through a large school without being pretty intimately acquainted with vice, and few, alas! very few, without tasting too largely of that poisoned bowl." — Fitch, *l. c.*, p. 77.

contact with any sort of temptation to evil from those with whom they associated. I have known some who at the end of their school course were as innocent of moral evil as on the day they entered, and were utterly shocked and disgusted when they were thrown into the vortex of the world outside, and had to listen to the kind of talk that too often forms the common staple of conversation among those who have had a Protestant education.... I do not say that the Church is always successful in her endeavors. It is quite possible that, even in a Catholic school, evil may for a time run riot. One sinner may destroy much good. But the evil never lasts long, and the Catholic system brings about a speedy recovery. What I do assert is that the moral perils, to which a boy is exposed in a Catholic school, are infinitesimal as compared with those which will surround him in any of the Protestant public schools and colleges.

"In all this the chief engine for the good work is the confessional. There are, of course, many others. There is the personal influence and the keen sense of responsibility of those who are in authority; there is the close and intimate friendship existing between the teacher and the taught, which is something utterly different from the comparatively cold relations and official reserve which make the Protestant master far more of a stranger to his boys. But it is the weekly or fortnightly confession that is the real safeguard. It is in the confessor that he has his trusted friend, to whom he freely talks of all his dangers and temptations; it is confession that keeps the moral atmosphere healthy and pure; it is confession that maintains the high standard of life and conversation prevailing, through God's mercy, in our Catholic schools and colleges; it is confession that enables the Catholic parent to entrust his boy to the good priests, whether secular or regular, who devote themselves to the work of education, without any of those qualms or fears, that anxiety and foreboding about the future, that fill the heart of the Protestant parent when he bids farewell to his innocent child on his first plunge into the vortex of a Protestant public school.

"But there is one charge, one false and cruel charge, which some Protestant writers bring against confession. They say that it introduces the young and innocent to a knowledge of subjects which are *sacro digna silentio*, and even suggests to them evil of which they would otherwise be ignorant. I can only assure my readers (in answer to this gratuitous calumny), on the word of an honest man, that during the twenty years and more that I have been constantly hearing confessions of men and women, boys and girls, of every class and in various countries, I have never known of a single instance of any knowledge of evil having been imparted in the confessional. I am sure that I may speak for all my fellow priests all over the world, when I say that I would, with God's help, far rather be torn in a thousand pieces than say one word in the confessional that could endanger the purity of the young, or impart a knowledge of evil to one previously ignorant of it.

"But if there should be any of my readers who are not willing to accept my own personal assurance, there is another consideration which ought to convince them. If there were in this accusation the smallest element of truth, every good mother would, in her tender care for her children's innocence, have the greatest horror of seeing her little ones kneeling before the priest, and every careful father would forbid his boys and girls from incurring the risk of such contamination. Is this the case? Do we find good Catholic parents dreading the influence of the confessional for their children? On the contrary, there is nothing that gives them more hearty satisfaction than to know that their sons and daughters are, from their earliest years, regular in making their confession month by month, or week by week. They regard it as the best possible safeguard for their innocence and virtue. They are alarmed and anxious if, when boyhood emerges into youth, their sons grow irregular in frequenting the tribunal of penance. They fear there must be something wrong. They urge and entreat them not to fall away from the practice of confession. Joy fills the mother's heart when she sees her son once more returning, it may be after long absence, to that fount of mercy and of grace, where she knows that he will obtain pardon for the past, and strength and help for the struggles of the future."

It would be presumption on our part to make further comment on these beautiful words. Every Catholic will testify to the truth of Father Clarke's description of the salutary influence confession exercises over the young during the most dangerous period of life. Now let us contrast with this description a picture drawn from the life of a Protestant. Newman, in the introduction of *Loss and Gain*, describes a clergyman of the Church of England, who has just decided to send his son Charles to one of the large public schools. "Seclusion", he says to himself, "is no security for virtue. There is no telling what is in a boy's heart; he may look as open and happy as usual, and be as kind and as attentive, when there is a great deal wrong going on within. The heart is a secret with its Maker. No one on earth can hope to get at it, or to touch it. I have a cure of souls; what do I really know of my parishioners? Nothing; their hearts are sealed books to me. And this dear boy, he comes close to me; he throws his arms around me, but his soul is as much out of my sight as if he were at the antipodes. I am not accusing him of reserve, dear fellow; his very love and reverence for me keep him in a sort of charmed solitude. I cannot expect to get at the bottom of him.

> 'Each in his hidden sphere of bliss or woe,
> Our hermit spirits dwell.'

It is our lot here below. No one on earth can know Charles's secret thoughts. Did I guard him here at home ever so well, yet, in due time, it might be found that a serpent had crept into the Eden of his innocence. Boys do not fully know what is good and what is evil; they do wrong things at first almost innocently. Novelty hides vice from them; there is no one to warn them or give them rules; and they become slaves of sin while they are learning what sin is."

Is not this a most pathetic confession of a great shortcoming of the Protestant system which renounces all inward government and direction of the soul? It leaves all to the private judgment of the individual. And yet, what a blessing for young people to have one to whom they can securely disclose "their secret thoughts." Then this friend of their souls can "warn them and give them rules." The evil will be discovered and counteracted before the young are slaves of sin. The Catholic youth has all this advantage in the confession. What could an Arnold, a Thring, a McCosh do here? Indeed, does not this reserve of the Protestant system frustrate in many educators talent, zeal, kindliness, and keen-eyed affection, of their best fruits?

On the educational influence of the reception of the Holy Eucharist, a beautiful passage is found in the diary of the first American Cardinal, Archbishop McCloskey of New York, written when sojourning in Rome as a young priest. *"Feast of St. Aloysius, Rome,* June 21, 1835. This is the peculiar festivity of the students of Rome. It is observed with the greatest solemnity at the Church of the Roman College, S. Ignazio [under the care of the Jesuits]. Nearly all the students of the college, amounting to the number of 1500, receive Holy Communion together on this day. Being anxious to witness so interesting and edifying a spectacle, I took care to be at the Church of S. Ignazio at a seasonable hour. When I arrived, the students had just entered and had taken their places in ranks forming an aisle in the middle, and extending from the altar along the nave of the church to the very door. The Community Mass, a low one, was celebrated by a Cardinal, and the choir was composed of some of the choice singers among the pupils. It may have been owing to the numberless youthful associations that were connected with the scene before me, but I must confess it was to me the most edifying and most affecting ceremony I have yet witnessed in Rome. It was one which I shall never forget. To behold that spacious and beautiful edifice almost exclusively occupied by such a number of students of every rank and almost every age, arranged in such beautiful order, their countenances bespeaking a deep sense of the act they were about to perform in receiving into their bosoms their Divine Lord and Saviour, and to hear, at the same time, the solemn strains of music which filled the place with pious harmony, was certainly enough to fill a far less sensitive breast with holy enthusiasm. The moment of Communion arrived. It was a moment in which I felt the holiness and sublimity of my religion with a peculiar force. Fifteen hundred young men and boys approached the table of their Divine Master with a modesty and a fervor most marked and sincere, and, it is to be supposed, with a corresponding purity of mind and heart, all of them in the heyday of life, and most of that age, and in those exterior circumstances, which lead the youth, particularly of Protestant colleges, to the most dangerous vices. This, assuredly, I thought was a triumphant evidence of the superior moral influence of the Catholic religion. Call it Jesuitism, call it priestcraft, call it what you please, no candid mind contemplating such a spectacle can deny that as edifying a one has never been, and never will be, presented by the same number, nor one tenth of the number, of Protestant youth in any part of the world."[1]

Besides these two principal means employed for the religious and moral training of youth, there are others which are used with the most salutary results. Among them are certain *devotions* recommended to, and en-

[1] *Historical Records and Studies*, vol. II, part I: "Cardinal McCloskey," by Archbishop Farley.

couraged among, the students. Non-Catholics do not view the Catholic devotions very favorably, but their antipathy springs, for the most part, from a misunderstanding of the true nature of these devotions. Protestants think that Catholics consider these practices as the essence of religion; further, they have the opinion that these devotions are merely mechanical recitations of certain set prayers. In this they are seriously mistaken.[1] To the Catholic the religious devotions are not the essence of religion, but they are practical manifestations of religion and, at the same time, valuable helps to obtain and strengthen what is essential in religion, namely, the perfect subjection of the intellect and will to the will of God. Nor are they merely mechanical recitations of prayers; they are, if performed according to the mind of the Church, powerful means of lifting up the understanding, the imagination, the feelings and the will to the contemplation and active love of God. They all contain most potent motives for the moral elevation and betterment of man. Let us take that devotion which Jesuit educators recommend so much to their pupils: the devotion to St. Aloysius, the "Lily of Gonzaga." In this devotion the picture of the highest Christian perfection

[1] Far worse misrepresentations of Catholic devotions are due to gross ignorance of Catholic teaching. Thus we find in so learned a work as Schmid's *Geschichte der Erziehung* (vol. III, part I, page 91) the assertion that "the Society of Jesus, according to the idea of its founder, sees the end and object of all religious exercises in the adoration of Mary." Every Catholic child of seven years could have told the Leipsic Professor who wrote this calumny, that Catholics do not *adore*, but *venerate* Mary and the Saints; nor do Catholics see in the veneration of Mary and the Saints the end and object of all religious exercises.

attainable in youth is placed before the eyes of the students. They see in this Saint a noble youth who, in the midst of wealth and luxury and the allurements of a courtly life, preserved unsullied the white robe of innocence; a youth who from early childhood measured all things, as he himself expressed it, *secundum rationes aeternas, non secundum rationes temporales*, i. e. according to the value which they possess for his final destination; a youth who always followed the dictates of conscience with a chivalrous energy and steadfastness, and who heroically spurned the pleasures that prove so fatal to many young men; a youth who renounced the inheritance of a principality in order to follow the evangelical counsels, and to devote himself to the glory of God and the service of his fellow-men. Surely, a devotion which places before the admiring gaze of students such a type of youthful holiness for imitation, is a practical devotion, one that cannot fail to elevate the character of the students and make their lives purer and holier. Here we may also mention another most salutary exercise, namely, the annual retreat in which, following the directions of St. Ignatius, the end of man, the means of attaining this end, and the motives for striving after Christian sanctity are set before the mind of the pupil. What untold blessings result from these exercises, only he is able to realize who has made them.

Then there exist in every Jesuit college the *Sodalities of the Blessed Mother of God*, pious associations originated by the Jesuit Scholastic Leon, and solemnly recognized and highly eulogized by many Popes, beginning from Gregory XIII. (1584) down to Leo XIII. It is worth while to read the high commendation bestowed on them by the learned Pope Benedict XIV., who, as a former Jesuit pupil and member of the sodality, could well form a competent judgment upon their value. The influence of these sodalities on the moral life of the pupils cannot be valued too highly. Their members are usually the leaders in setting good example to others. The decline of sodalities was frequently followed by a decline of morality in Catholic colleges. In 1871 the sodalities in the thirty higher schools in Rhenish Prussia were hampered by government interference; it was said that the good they might do to individuals, should be accomplished by the schools without them. A year after, in 1872, Dr. Falk, Minister of Instruction in Prussia, ordered the dissolution of the sodalities in all higher schools in the kingdom. Not eight years had elapsed when Dr. Falk's successor, von Puttkamer, on the 20th day of May 1880, had to warn the heads of the same institutions against associations formed by the students with the avowed purpose of practising drink, dishonesty and immorality.[1]

These sodalities, instituted to advance the students in true and solid piety as well as learning, effected inestimable good. The members were exhorted to cherish above all that virtue which is the most beautiful ornament of youth, purity. They created a lofty moral tone in the colleges and sustained a healthy, manly public opinion. Thus these pious associations exerted a most powerful formative influence on the character of the students.[2] Their piety, too, was active

---

[1] *Centralblatt für die Unterrichtsverwaltung*, 1880, p. 572.
[2] See Coleman, "Old Stonyhurst" in *Messenger*, New York, 1894, p. 797 foll.

in works of charity. The sodalists of early colleges united in bands to purchase articles of food and clothing for distribution among the poor; they visited prisoners, and consoled and instructed them; they went to the hospitals and to the squalid quarters of the city to look after the sick.[1] What the students thus began to practise in college, was by many continued throughout their lives.

Nor have the sodalities ceased to achieve the same excellent results in our days. As a modern model sodality we mention that of Barcelona, consisting of seven hundred members, mostly students of the University, or members of the professions. Its *Academia* encourages excellent literary and scientific work.[2]

Another point concerning the moral training that deserves particular mention is the care of the Society with regard to reading. The press is a mighty instrument for good and evil. With it heaven and hell are contesting for a priceless treasure — the soul of man. St. Ignatius and the framers of the Ratio Studiorum knew this full well. They tell the teacher to encourage good and wholesome reading, but even more earnestly to warn the students against dangerous books, which St. Augustine calls "the hellish stream into which the children of men are daily cast."[3] Ignatius feared lest the reading of classic authors should introduce into young minds pagan tastes and

---

[1] Details may be read in the *History of the Sodalities*, Boston, Noonan & Co., 1885. — See also Rochemonteix, vol. II, p. 121 foll., where the charitable work of the Sodalities at La Flèche is related.

[2] See *The Pilgrim of our Lady of Martyrs*, New York, Sept. 1893 and Jan. 1894.

[3] *Confess.* I, c. 16.

morals. Nor was his fear groundless in view of the disastrous results that had followed the one-sided study and admiration of the classics during the latter period of the Renaissance, when people not only imitated the beautiful style of the writers of antiquity but also their shocking principles.[1] About the year 1550 Ignatius, who had thought long and deeply upon this subject, wrote to a prelate: "Seing that young people are so disposed to receive and retain first impressions, whether good or bad . . . and considering that books, especially classics as they are taught to boys, as Terence, Virgil, and others, contain amongst many things to be learnt, and not useless but profitable rather for life, some other things very profane and injurious even if only heard . . . and so much the more, if these are placed before them in books in which they study habitually, having them in their hands — this considered, it has seemed to me, as it does still seem, that it would be very expedient if we were to remove from these classic works all the parts that are unedifying or noxious, and replace them by others of a better sort, or, without adding anything leave only what is profitable. And this appears to me up to these last years most desirable for the good Christian life and good training of our youth."[2]

[1] See above chapter II, § 2: pp. 50—52 and ch. V on the theatrical performances, pp. 165—167. — Vittorino da Feltre and other representatives of the Christian Renaissance differed radically on this point from the Pagan Humanists. Thus Vittorino read certain authors to his pupils only with many excisions. Woodward, *Vittorino da Feltre*, pp. 47 and 57.

[2] In Stewart Rose, *St. Ignatius Loyola*, p. 515. — Obscene passages are meant. But *substitutions* cannot be recommended.

The principles of St. Ignatius found a practical expression in the Constitutions of the Society,[1] and later in various parts of the Ratio Studiorum.[2] There it is laid down that in the authors given into the hands of the pupils all dangerous passages should be omitted, or if certain authors, as Terence, could hardly be expurgated they ought rather not to be read at all. Many modern educators or writers on education consider this anxiety of the Jesuits mere prudery. Others who have studied the question more thoroughly and conscientiously, admit that many reasons can be given for the practice of the Jesuits. Others again declare themselves unable to speak decisively on this "perplexing" question. Thus a writer in the *St. James's Gazette*, after having mentioned the "castrated editions of the classics" used in the Jesuit college at Stonyhurst, England, says: "Our public schools go upon another principle; the argument being that the shock of introduction on entering the world, to what has been so zealously excluded would only lead to a sudden and fatal downfall. For my part I find the question a perplexing one."[3]

To those who see in the caution of the Society nothing but prudery, we may reply that even pagan writers, and those of the very highest standing, as Plato, Aristotle, Cicero and Quintilian, denounced emphatically the reading of certain authors of their own language and race. Quintilian well said: "As regards reading, great care is to be taken, above all things, that tender minds, which will imbibe deeply

---

[1] *Constit.* P. IV, c. 5. *Decl.* E.
[2] *Reg. Prov.* 34. — *Reg. com.* 8.
[3] Littell's *Living Age*, vol. CLXX (1886), p. 248.

whatever has entered them when they are ignorant of everything and, as it were, resemble empty vessels, may learn not only what is well written, but, still more, what is morally good. The reading of tragedies is beneficial, the lyric poets nourish the mind, provided that you select from them, not merely authors, but portions of their works; for the Greeks are licentious in many of their writings, and I should be loath to interpret Horace in certain passages."[1] And even Ovid, that licentious writer, warns his readers if they want to be free from the consequences of disorderly passion, not to read, nay, not to touch frivolous poetry: *Teneros ne tange poetas*, and he includes in this class some of his own works. The language of the Fathers of the Church is unmistakable on this subject. In fact, the terms of condemnation used by some Fathers against pagan writings, are actually directed against the idolatry and immorality contained therein. It would be useless to multiply quotations.

There are modern educators, also Protestants, who on this point are at one with the Society. Thus writes Quick: "It is much to the credit of the Jesuit Fathers that, though Plautus and Terence were considered very valuable for giving a knowledge of colloquial Latin and were studied and learned by heart in the Protestant schools, the Jesuits rejected them on account of their impurity."[2] Later on expurgated editions of Plautus, Terence, Horace, Juvenal, Persius and others were published by Jesuits, especially by Father Jouvancy. The words of Professor

[1] *Inst.* I, c. 8.
[2] *Educational Reformers*, p. 507. — See also von Raumer's statements above p. 166.

Paul Barth of Leipsic, written a year ago, are also well worth being summarized here.[1] "One of the truest sayings of Goethe is: 'Let no one imagine that the first impressions of youth can be effaced.' There are striking examples recorded in history how perverse reading in early years caused the greatest harm. Of course there will be wise people, even educators, who say: 'It is true, there are some offensive passages in this work, but their effect is counteracted by other instruction. Don't let us be pedantic. Don't let us make so much noise about such trifles.' These gentlemen must be answered that in education there are no trifles; that nothing is so little that it may be overlooked. For every trifle has an influence on many, very many souls of children, and in every one of these souls it can work its effect for a long time, perhaps for a whole life. Others, advocates of a 'sound realism,' as they style themselves, will say: 'Evil is after all a component part of this world, and so it is beneficial to free the young of the illusion that there is no evil in the world.' To this we reply: Belief in the moral order in this world is an energizing factor in the life of the young, and the man who robs the child of this belief, weakens its moral energy, consequently does an immoral act. Others again, granting all this, will say: 'Although there is some danger in such reading, still it gives an insight into the life and the history of the nations.' Such historians we answer: The history of

---

[1] *Neue Jahrbücher*, 1901, vol. VIII, pp. 57—59. — See also Schiller, *Handbuch der praktischen Pädagogik*, 1894, p. 172, where it is said that some satires of Horace and some passages in Homer should be left out in the school editions. The same author's opinion about the use of unabridged Bibles in schools will be quoted in the next chapter.

civilization can be learned in other ways; at any rate, it is too dearly bought if it ruins the character of children."

That no prudishness is advocated by our remarks on reading the classics, is sufficiently proved from what has been said on Homer.[1] Nor do we deny that some editors of school-texts, as well as teachers, may not have gone too far in expurgating. Here, as in other matters, the golden rule is: *Medio tutissimus ibis*. It will always remain a delicate and difficult question to decide what is to be omitted or what may be read without danger. The tact of the teacher and skill in handling such passages will often give the proper solution. But about the correctness of the general principle laid down in the Ratio Studiorum there can be no doubt.

The same principle holds good not only of the classical authors of Greece and Rome, but of the moderns as well, if not in a higher degree.[2] The ancients are direct, outspoken and straightforward, even in their obscenity; the moderns are more indirect and insinuating. The latter method is not the more harmless as might appear to the superficial, but is by far the more dangerous, since it stimulates curiosity, sets the mind thinking and leaves the reader to reflect and dwell on an unsavory and prurient subject. The Jesuit teachers are exhorted not only "not to read in class any obscene author or any book which contains matter dangerous to good morals, but also to deter most energetically their pupils from reading such

[1] See above pp. 399—400.
[2] The Rules of the Provincial 34, § 2, say: "Still greater caution is needed in regard to the vernacular authors."

books outside of class."[1] This advice about deterring pupils from bad reading, is far more necessary now-a-days than at the time when the Ratio was drawn up. How many popular books and magazines, openly, or secretly under the name of "modern science," are advocating principles which in reality are agnostic and irreligious? How many of the novels that flood the literary market, are filled with ill-disguised nastiness? How many books are borrowed by the young people from libraries, which should never be permitted to fall into their hands? God alone knows all the harm done to faith and purity by these books. For many a talented youth, the pride and joy of a happy home, the indulging in filthy novels has been the beginning of a career of sin and crime.

As a rule it is not advisable to say *this* or *that* book is bad or indecent; for some boys, either through viciousness or curiosity, will for that very reason read the book. But should an evil publication circulate among the boys, then it should be denounced in the strongest terms.

Boys should be likewise cautioned against over-indulgence in the reading of newspapers, especially of the sensational kind. There is no worse school for the mind than such papers. They not unfrequently swarm with infamous advertisements; scandalous happenings, whose very possibility ought to be unknown to young people, are there discussed in a frivolous manner and with the omission of not a single disgusting detail. If these newspapers form the daily mental food of a boy, they will dull and blunt all sense of delicacy and modesty, and disable his mind

[1] *Reg. com.* 8.

for serious application to hard study. In his "Book of the Spiritual Exercises," St. Ignatius pictures the inveterate enemy of mankind seated on a throne on the plains of Babylon, despatching innumerable demons all over the world, to every city and every person in order to ensnare and deceive men. This wily fiend has undergone a marvellous metamorphosis. He makes use of the doctrine of evolution, adapting himself to new circumstances. He is no longer the horned and hoofed monster of olden legends, but a polished, well-read gentleman, who manages thousands of printing establishments. And every mail carries countless demons, in the shape of bad novels, magazines and papers, to every city, every town, every village, every dwelling, no matter how secluded or remote. Shall we expect these envoys of Satan, "transformed into angels of light," to overlook our schools and colleges? Alas, how often do they sneak in, unnoticed by porter or janitor, to work their deeds of darkness among the young. Naught but the utmost vigilance on the part of school authorities will be able to counteract these evils. Certainly the principle of St. Ignatius and the Ratio Studiorum need not be further vindicated.[1]

We must make some remarks about *sports*, which take so important a part in our modern schools. We do this in connection with moral education for various reasons. First, because a moderate use of athletics helps to develop certain moral qualities. Secondly, because some moderns see in it a remedy for nearly all

[1] On reading see also Sacchini: *On Dangerous Reading* (In Latin); a new translation in Herder's *Bibliothek der katholischen Pädagogik*, vol. X, pp. 186—205. — Jungmann, S. J.: *Gefahren der belletristischen Lectüre*.

vicious habits of youth. They rejoice that "muscular Christianity," "a sound, practical, sensible, worldly basis of life has taken the place of the morbid asceticism and unreal superstitions and transcendentalism of former generations, which considered the flesh a burden, a clog, a snare."[1] — Thirdly, because excess in athletics leads to serious damage, moral as well as intellectual.

The physical culture of the pupils forms a most important feature in a good system of education: *sit mens sana in corpore sano*. Athletics, out-door sports and gymnastics do much for the physical health of the students. Besides, they demand, and consequently help to develop, quickness of apprehension, steadiness and coolness, self-reliance, self-control, readiness to subordinate individual impulses to a command. This is all valuable for education. Still, "in the reaction from the asceticism of our early college life there is little doubt our athletics have gone too far; so far as to direct in a noticeable degree the student's attention from his studies."[2] Indeed, it has come to pass that among students base-ball, foot-ball, boat-races and other sports form almost the exclusive topic of conversation. The favorite reading is the sporting sheet of the newspaper. Some college periodicals give almost more space to athletics than to literature. "Pray," said an Oxford Don to President McCosh, after reading several numbers of the Princetonian, "are you the president of a gymnastic institution?"[3]

---

[1] See General Walker's address in *Report of Commissioner of Education*, 1896—97, I, p. 705 foll.

[2] Prof. West of Princeton University, in *Education in the United States*, vol. I, p. 222.

[3] *Life of James McCosh*, p. 208. See also p. 223 foll.

The dangers arise not so much from athletic exercises themselves, as from their publicity and the universal admiration in which they are held. There is in our days a morbid craving for notoriety; people wish to be interviewed, to be talked about, to be kept before the eyes of the public. Many a young man thinks he cannot realize this ambition better than by athletic triumphs. Thus by competitive games much time and talent is wasted, much enthusiasm for higher aspirations is stifled. Unfortunately, some colleges, instead of checking this spirit have catered to it. No wonder that boys have changed their views of the ideal student. Their ideals are on the campus, no longer in the domain of literature and science. The hero to whom they look up with admiration is not the leading boy in the class, not the one who at the end of the year carries off the honors, but the one "who breaks the world's record" in some athletic contest. Many prefer the approving shout of thousands of spectators on the foot ball field to the earning of class honor. Indeed brain is no longer the highest human gift in the eyes of a great number of students, but muscles and muscular achievements. And a writer in a periodical for September 1901, boasted that "we are fast becoming a nation of athletes." The best educators are unanimous in condemning this excessive spirit of athleticism. They foresee the serious dangers that spring from it, to intellectual and moral culture.[1]

[1] On this keenly discussed question see: Findlay, *Arnold of Rugby*, with an *Introduction* by the Right Reverend Lord Bishop of Hereford. (1897), pp. 23 and 24. — Fitch, *Thomas and Matthew Arnold*, pp. 103—108. There it is stated that exaltation of physical powers to the same level as intellectual distinction has in late years seriously debased the ideal and

The Jesuits have never neglected the care of the health of their pupils.[1] Long ago they had introduced various games into their colleges and did much to interest all the pupils in them. This is mentioned as a laudable feature of their educational system even by men who wrote in a hostile spirit against the Society.[2] The Jesuits recognized the importance of games at a period when they were little esteemed by others. "The schools of the sixteenth and seventeenth centuries are in general noted for their gloomy neglect of

hindered the usefulness of the great public schools in England. "For the moment the type of school-boy and of manhood most in favor with the British public is Spartan rather than Athenian." Mr. Fitch states also that the famous romance of Thomas Hughes, *Tom Brown's School-days*, gives only one side and that not the best side of Rugby school life. — Some excellent remarks on athletics in college are made by Mr. Canfield in his book *The College Student and his Problems*, pp. 103—105. A very severe criticism of the excessive admiration of sport among the English public is contained in the *Contemporary Review*, Jan. 1902. — See also *Nineteenth Century*, Jan. 1903, p. 46.

[1] A document in Spanish, drawn up in the first years of the Society, contains a most interesting chapter entitled "The Preservation of Bodily Health and Strength." In seventeen paragraphs it lays down rules about moderation in studies, about food, clothing, sleep, proper bodily exercises, and sufficient recreation. Although this document was primarily written for the younger members of the Order, its principles were applied, as appears from other passages, to the pupils of the colleges, of course with necessary changes. See *Monumenta Paedagogica*, p. 68 sq. "*Para Conservar la Salud y Fuerzas del Cuerpo.*"

[2] For instance in the *Recollections of a Jesuit Pupil* (written by an apostate priest who had studied in Jesuit colleges), p. 104 foll. Bode: *Aus dem Kloster*, vol. II, p. 174 foll, quoted by Huber, *Jesuiten-Orden*, p. 370 foll.

this cheerful element in the education of youth. The schools of the Jesuits were, in this respect, conducted on more reasonable principles than most of the rest."[1] It is a well-known fact that in Germany sport in the higher schools, is, or was, until recently, neglected more than is expedient for the general development of the pupils. And yet, wherever German Jesuits opened a college, be it in Freiburg (Switzerland), Feldkirch (Vorarlberg), or Sao Leopoldo (Brazil), everywhere they introduced and encouraged plenty of healthful games, an evident sign that it is the spirit of the Society to give the pupils sufficient recreation. Of the French Jesuits, the *Figaro* wrote years ago (June 2, 1879): "Games and amusements occupy an important place in the schools of the Jesuits. They are as much interested about the place of recreation as about the study hall. The prefects induce the pupils to join in the games with the same ardor they display in stimulating them to work at their books. Two prefects, Fathers de Nodaillac and Rousseau, have written the history of games. . . . Fencing is honored and encouraged in the Jesuit schools. In the three institutions at Paris (*rue de Madrid, de Vaugirard* and *des Postes*) more than four hundred pupils take lessons in fencing under the direction of the best instructors."[2] It is not necessary to prove that in English speaking countries the Jesuit colleges do not neglect this part of training.

[1] Kiddle and Schem, *The Cyclopaedia of Education*, article "Games," p. 330.
[2] De Badts de Cugnac, *Les Jésuites et l'éducation*, pp. 25—31.

Chapter XVIII.

Religious Instruction.

The preceding chapter has shown how painstaking the Jesuits are as regards the moral training of their pupils. Other educators also insist on the necessity of this training, but the Jesuits, in fact all Catholics, differ from a great number of other educators in a most essential point, namely in that they base the moral training entirely on the religious education. They consider a moral training without the religious as defective and incomplete. Incomplete, because it disregards one of the most important obligations of man. Man's first and most sacred duty is to acknowledge his dependence on God, his Creator and Lord, and to give expression to this recognition by interior and exterior acts of worship. This is religion. Religion is a postulate of man's rational nature. This thought stood clearly before the mind of the founder of the Society of Jesus, when in his *Spiritual Exercises* he wrote down this brief summary of religion: "Man is created to praise God, to reverence and serve Him, and, by doing so, to save his soul." No system of education can be considered as harmonious which leaves this first duty of man out of consideration, and fails to implant religion into the hearts of the pupils. If it is man's duty to worship God, it is his duty likewise to know God; he can know Him from the manifestation of His works (*Romans* 1, 19), and the revelation of His word. Religion does not consist in mere sentiment and pious emotions, but in the recognition of certain truths and the subjection of the will to these truths. Hence no religion is possible without the knowledge of these truths, or let us plainly call them what they are: *dogmas*, although this word is so hateful to the ear of the rationalist and agnostic educator of the day. Dogmas must be taught and believed as the foundation of all true religion, as the Great Teacher of mankind has said: "This is life everlasting that they may know thee, the only true God, and Jesus Christ whom thou hast sent."[1] It is, indeed, the highest wisdom "to know Christ and him crucified," "in whom are hid all the treasures of wisdom and knowledge."[2] Christ, therefore, must be the centre of all true education.

The knowledge of religious truths is necessary in education for another reason, because it is the only sure foundation of morality, and without it no true moral education is possible. This is the firm conviction of Christian thinkers. I know the champions of the "unsectarian" schools cry out against such an assertion, and they ask indignantly: "Can we not teach ethics without dogmas, moral principles without religion?" Reason, history, daily experience, and our innermost conscience give a stern and emphatic answer to this question: "You cannot teach it effectively and with any satisfactory result." All motives of self-respect, honor, sense of duty, welfare of the community, etc., may deter a man from certain more revolting crimes, but they will not hold in times of fierce temptation, when neither disgrace nor civil

---

[1] *John* 17, 3.
[2] 1 *Cor.* 2, 2; and *Col.* 2, 3.

punishment is to be feared. How well has the "Father of this Country" expressed this, when he left to his people as a sacred legacy these weighty words: "Let us with caution indulge the supposition that morality can be maintained without religion. Whatever may be conceded to the influence of refined education on minds of peculiar structure, reason and experience both forbid us to expect that national morality can prevail in exclusion of religious principle." Another great military and political leader has spoken even more strongly on this subject. Lord Mahon writes of a conversation which he had with the great Duke of Wellington: "I shall never forget the earnestness and energy of manner with which he [the Duke of Wellington] deprecated mere secular education, adding, *I doubt if the devil himself could advise a worse scheme of social destruction.*" ... "Take care what you are about," he exclaimed on December 23, 1840, when speaking of the new Education Act; "for unless you base all this education on religion, you are only bringing up so many clever devils."[1] The educational legislation of the year 1902 proves that England, after many decades of experimenting, has at length realized the truth of the warning of her distinguished leader.

Alas, that the most important words of Washington have been practically forgotten in this country, and that the exclusion of religious teaching from the schools has been made one of the fundamental principles of the national system of schools, in such a degree that the Catholic Church, which all along has insisted that

---

[1] Lord Stanhope's *Conversations with the Duke of Wellington*, London, 1888, p. 180.

it was its duty to educate the children of Catholic parents in the truths of their religion, was denounced as an enemy of the country. At present the more thoughtful Protestants begin to acknowledge that this idea is the only true one. The spread of immorality and infidelity has opened the eyes of many.[1]

We may be allowed to quote one or other recent utterance of non-Catholics on this subject. Professor Gates, of the Chicago Theological Seminary, writes in the *Biblical World*, September 1902: "The great problem of life is education. The mind of the race is growing all the while, and it is for the educator to see that these mental powers are developed in the right direction. But no man's education is complete if religious instruction be omitted. One may know all mysteries of science and literature; he may sweep the heavens with the telescope, or peer into the secrets of nature with the microscope; but if in all this he see not God, he is but poorly educated after all. Now where do we find ourselves, as we confront this phase of the national problem? We have a system of public education to be proud of. Never have the various questions that meet the teacher been so well understood as to-day. But what is this great system doing

---

[1] On this subject see the following recent publications: Father Poland, S. J., "True Pedagogics and False Ethics," in *Am. Cath. Quart. Review*, April 1899; also as separate pamphlet. — Father Campbell, S. J., "The Only True American School System," *Messenger*, November 1901, and the same author's article: "Moral Teaching in French Schools," *ib.*, May 1902. — Further, Father Conway, S. J., *The Respective Rights and Duties of Family, State and Church in regard to Education.* New York, Pustet, 1890, pp. 34-60. — Father Cathrein, S. J., *Religion und Moral, oder Gibt es eine Moral ohne Gott?* Freiburg and St. Louis, Herder, 1900.

for the religious instruction of our children? Practically nothing."

It has been said time and again that religion should be taught by the Sunday school and in the family. Yet every thoughtful man must see that such instruction cannot be but insufficient. The *Biblical World*, in an editorial, October 1902, asks whether the religious and moral education is adequately achieved through the Sunday school and the home, and it gives this answer: "It has been so assumed, but each passing year shows more clearly that this is not the case... The home feels no longer the necessary responsibility, and the Sunday school has neither the time nor the instrumentalities for adequate instruction. And, in addition, the divorce of religious from secular education destroys the vital relation between the two. Therefore, it seems certain that the ideal of education, as well as the only adequate method of education, is to establish religious and moral instruction in the common schools. And we shall then find ourselves once more in accord with the status of instruction in England and Germany."

A few years ago, Mr. Amasa Thornton spoke similarly in the *North American Review*. There he said: "The questions which we have to solve then are these: How can the present decline in religious teaching and influence be checked; and how can such teaching and influence be increased to such a point as will preserve the great cities of the next century from depravity, degradation, and destruction? What can be expected of the family?" Mr. Thornton rightly adds: "If the adults of the present age are not as religious as the needs of the hour and of the future require, will the children receive the proper religious training if they receive none except in the home circle?" In fact, thousands of children do not even learn a short prayer at home. The writer then declares that one of the greatest blunders that have been made in this country is the failure of teaching religion in the public schools. He then pays a striking tribute to the Catholic Church. "The Catholic Church has insisted that it is its duty to educate the children of parents of the Catholic faith in such a way as to fix religious truths in the youthful mind. For this it has been assailed by the non-Catholic population, and Catholics have been charged with being enemies of the liberties of the people and the flag. Any careful observer in the city of New York can see that the only people, as a class, who are teaching the children in the way that will secure the future for the best civilization, are the Catholics; and although a Protestant of the firmest kind, I believe the time has come to recognize this fact, and for us all to lay aside religious prejudices and patriotically meet this question." [1]

Professor Coe of Northwestern University quite recently said in a lecture delivered in Chicago: "The position of Roman Catholics in regard to religion and education, and their policy in the establishment of parochial schools, are absolutely correct. For corroboration of this opinion I refer you to the work *Philosophy of Education*, by Dr. Arnold Tompkins, principal of the Chicago Normal School, in which he says religious character is the proper end of all education." [2]

---

[1] *North American Review*, January 1898, pp. 126–128.— See also the *Biblical World*, November 1902, p. 323.

[2] New York *Freeman's Journal*, January 24, 1903.

The Catholics object to purely secular education, because they consider it subversive of religion and true morality, subversive of "the pillars of human happiness and national security." It is not so much what is taught in the non-sectarian schools that renders them objectionable to Catholics, as what *is not* taught and cannot be taught. An education which omits Christ as its central and informing principle is an unchristian education. Such an education may not directly teach wrong principles, nor directly undermine the faith of the pupils, yet it does nothing to protect and strengthen it. The inevitable consequence of this neglect must be the weakening of faith, especially in an age in which literature and the whole domestic and social life are infected by agnosticism and a new paganism. As the non-sectarian school does not and cannot counteract these baneful tendencies, it is clear that the education which it imparts is a defective, nay, a false one.

Not unfrequently, however, Catholics must also object to what *is* taught in non-sectarian schools and colleges. It is impossible to avoid in text-books and oral instruction, in the teaching of history, literature, and natural sciences, all allusions to questions most closely connected with religion. How does the Catholic Church fare in such references? One need only examine the text-books used in many schools, to become convinced that a Catholic parent must protest against the statements contained therein about the Church, its history, its worship, the Papacy, monastic orders, etc. But if Catholic children grow weak in their love of the Church, her institutions and practices, they will gradually neglect their religious duties, and fall a prey to religious indifferentism and moral ruin. How well has this been expressed in the latest "School Order for the Higher Schools" of Prussia: "Catholic religious instruction has the specific task of grounding Catholic youth in the conviction of the truth and the divine origin of Christianity and the Church, and to teach them to preserve, foster, and steadfastly profess this conviction by living in and with Christ and His Church. Only on the solid foundation of a definite religious knowledge, of deep-rooted conviction and loyalty to the Church, can religious instruction try and expect to fulfil that other, by no means last or least important, part of its task, *viz.*, to accomplish fully and permanently the religious and the moral elevation of the pupil. According to Catholic teaching, the truly moral life rests on obedience to the Church, as the divinely attested guardian and exponent of God's ordinances, and herein is found a special protection against the false and perverse aspirations of the modern age, which endanger the moral order."[1]

For this reason, what an English Catholic said about the schools of England has also an application to our country. Dr. Windle (F. R. S.), speaking of the "Present Needs of Catholic Secondary Education," said among other things: "By the fact that we are Catholics, we are circumscribed in our choice of schools to those of our own faith. . . . I should like to add one word on this subject from my own experience. Born and brought up a Protestant I was educated at a great public school, for which I still retain considerable respect, and even affection; but I

[1] *Lehrpläne und Lehraufgaben*, 1901, pp. 15—16.

wish to say with a due sense of responsibility, that the Catholic parent who sends his son to a non-Catholic public school deliberately and without a shadow of justification exposes him to the almost certain loss of his faith, and to the grave danger of the corruption of his morals."[1]

The attitude of Catholics towards the question of religious instruction in school is, therefore, very clear. Of those Protestants that now advocate religious instruction, not a few commit a serious mistake. They recommend a sort of religious teaching which will suit all and offend none, an "unsectarian, undenominational religion," as they style it. Such a religion does not exist, and what is taught as such does not deserve the name of religion. This has been emphatically stated by many distinguished Protestants of widely differing religious opinions. Of American educators we mention President McCosh who made some very noteworthy statements on this subject.[2] Even men of most advanced liberal views condemn the teaching of an "undenominational" religion. Professor Ziegler of the University of Strassburg, who is not in the least "clerically biased," wrote two years ago in his *General Pedagogy*: "A knowledge of the religion in which one is born forms part of general culture, and the state would have to look after this part of education, as after all the rest (*sic!*). But here enters the Church as competitor, demanding that the instruction in religion be imparted to her children according to her views; an undenominational instruction in religion, which is advocated by some, is non-

[1] The London *Tablet*, September 14, 1901.
[2] See his remarks on "Boston Theology," in the sixth chapter of *Christianity and Positivism*.

sense; for every religion is denominational."[1] It would fill a large volume were we to collect the unsparing criticism passed within the last thirty years on "unsectarian" religious teaching by the most enlightened men in England, among them statesmen like Disraeli and Lord Salisbury.[2] An English agnostic, a member of the London School Board, thus described the system adopted by this Board: "The result of unsectarian teaching is to establish a new form of religion which has nothing in common with Historical Christianity or any other form of Christian teaching. By taking away everything to which any one objects, they leave something which is really worthless. They say they will have no Creed and no Catechism, and the result is that every teacher is his own Creed and his own Catechism. The result of unsectarian teaching is a colorless residuum, which I should think would be as objectionable to the earnest Christian as it is contemptible to the earnest unbeliever."[3] Other English writers were even more severe in their condemnations of this system, which they called "a misshapen beast," "a moral monster," "lifeless, boiled down, mechanical, unreal teaching of religion."[4] Needless to say, Catholics will always object to such a maimed teaching of religion.

Protestant advocates of religious instruction frequently consider the reading of the *Bible* as sufficient, and as the only admissible means of teaching religion in the schools. However, in this principle there are several serious errors. We must first mention recent

[1] *Allgemeine Pädagogik* (Leipzig, 1901), p. 107.
[2] *Fortnightly Review*, May 1896, p. 808 foll.
[3] *Ib.*, p. 814.
[4] *Ib.*, p. 815.

utterances calling for the restoration of the Bible to the schools as *literature*, as a means of literary culture. The National Educational Association that met in Minneapolis in the summer of 1902, adopted the following resolution: "It is apparent that familiarity with the English Bible as a masterpiece of literature is rapidly decreasing among the pupils in our schools. This is the direct result of a conception which regards the Bible as a theological book merely, and thereby leads to its exclusion from the schools of some states as a subject of reading and study. We hope and ask for such a change of public sentiment in this regard as will permit and encourage the English Bible, now honored by name in many school laws and state constitutions, to be read and studied as a literary work of the highest and purest type, side by side with the poetry and prose which it has inspired and in large part formed."[1] Such a study is, of course, practically useless from the religious point of view; moreover, and this is a more serious objection against the scheme advocated by the National Educational Association, it is wrong in principle and mischievous in its consequences. It is a deplorable degradation of the sacred volume to put it on a par with profane writings, be they of the highest type, as the dramas of Shakespeare or the poems of Tennyson. This scheme would tend to destroy entirely the reverence due to the Bible. Besides, no literary study is possible without explanation of the *contents* of the works studied; but it is absurd to attempt an explanation of the contents of

---

[1] *The Literary Digest*, August 2, 1902. — See also the Rev. Thomas B. Gregory, in the *New York American and Journal*, January 11, 1903.

the Bible without trespassing on religious ground. Rightly has the *Biblical World* observed that culture is not the chief end of man, nor the primary function of the Bible. The biblical books are indeed masterpieces of literature, but they have a much more important service to render to the world. The Bible is first of all for religious and moral instruction, a guidebook to religion and morality.[1] We perfectly agree with the *Biblical World* so far, but not as to the manner of reading the Bible which this review advocates. In an editorial, October 1902, we read: "The fact that the Bible is generally excluded from the public schools of the United States, where formerly it was used as a book of devotion and instruction, is not to be attributed to a growing disregard of religion. . . . This situation has been created by the friends of the Bible rather than by its enemies; for if the friends of the Bible could have agreed among themselves as to how the Bible should be taught in the schools, their influence would have secured the continuance of such instruction. But it came to pass that the Bible was used in the schools, not only for general and ethical religious instruction, but also for the inculcation of sectarian and theological ideas. Protestant teachers taught the Bible in a way which antagonized the Roman Catholics; and teachers of the several Protestant denominations interpreted the Bible to the children from their own point of view. But the public money which is raised by general taxation for the support of the common schools comes from men of widely differing ecclesiastical creeds and connections, and cannot therefore be used for the dissemination of

---

[1] *The Biblical World*, October 1902, p. 243 foll.

sectarian tenets." The writer then asks: "Can we now teach religion and morals by means of the Bible without at the same time teaching sectarian ideas? The Bible is not sectarian; Roman Catholics and all Protestant denominations equally claim it. The formal creeds and the systems of government and worship which have grown up in the centuries of Christian history are post-biblical; they are a superstructure, built upon the fundamentals of Christianity as recorded in the Bible. Can we get beneath ecclesiastical formulations, regulations, and liturgies to a fundamental religious belief and moral practice upon which all Christians can agree, and which they can unite to promote? . . . We believe that sectarianism is fast disappearing, that an era of unity in essentials is near at hand. . . . In order to restore the Bible to the schools it must be taught in the right way — the way which accords with the best modern knowledge of the Bible, the best modern science of religion and ethical teaching, and the best Christian spirit which recognizes true Christianity wherever it exists, and is able to distinguish between essentials and non-essentials." [1]

We do not want to comment on all the latitudinarian statements contained in this quotation, but confine ourselves to the following remarks. First, that religion consisting of merely the "fundamentals of Christianity without formal creeds," is no true religion. It is a distillation or a dilution of Christianity which deserves all the castigation inflicted by English writers on the "moral monster of undenominational religion." Secondly, it is said that "the Bible is not sectarian, and that Roman Catholics and

[1] *Ibid.*, pp. 243 and 246—247.

all Protestant denominations claim it." But how do they claim it? Surely not merely as a source of "general and ethical religious instruction," but as the document which is supposed to prove their particular religious tenets. It is as true now as centuries ago what the Reformed theologian Werenfels expressed in his famous distich:

> *Hic liber est in quo quaerit sua dogmata quisque;*
> *Invenit et pariter dogmata quisque sua.*
>
> Within one book each seeks to read
> The tenets of his private creed.
> And, strange to tell, each reads so well
> The selfsame words all doctrines spell.

Hence it is unreasonable to expect that the Bible will ever be taught without "sectarian" bias, or that in future it will be taught by Protestants without "antagonizing the Roman Catholics."

The objections of Catholics to the reading of the Bible in undenominational schools which are frequented by Catholic children, may briefly be summed up as follows: *First*, the Catholics must ask which translation of the Bible is to be used. Is it to be the Catholic Rheims and Douay version? To this the Protestants would undoubtedly object. Then the Protestant Bible? Against this the Catholics must protest. For the Bible of King James contains numerous errors of translation — this was candidly admitted by the authors of the Revised Version [2] — errors by no means insignificant, errors which, to a great extent, consist in rendering the Bible so as to

---

[1] On this subject see the beautiful little book *Chapters of Bible Study*, by the Reverend H. J. Heuser (New York, 1895), especially chapter XX.

justify certain Protestant tenets and to antagonize Catholic doctrines. The Revised Version has done away with some of these objectionable translations, but not with all that justly offend Catholics. Hence the very version used in the public schools is "sectarian." Besides, the Catholic acknowledges books as canonical which are rejected in the Protestant Bibles as apocryphal, and this is another reason why the Catholic cannot approve the reading of the Protestant Bible. — *Secondly,* the Catholic Church is opposed to giving the complete and unabridged Bible into the hands of children. The reason for this attitude is one that testifies to the great pedagogical wisdom of the Church. She cannot bear the thought that the most sacred of books should become a stumbling-block to the innocent, or a means of gratifying the unholy curiosity of vicious youths. There are earnest Protestants who in this matter side with the Catholic practice. It may suffice to quote one testimony, that of a Protestant educator of the first rank, namely of Professor Schiller, Director of one of the best training schools for teachers in Europe. Speaking of the causes of impurity among students, he finds one in the reading of the unabridged Bible. He affirms that a large experience has proved that most deplorable vicious habits among pupils, boys and girls, sprang up in the first place from the reading of certain passages of the Bible, the selection and knowledge of which were handed down as a tradition among the pupils. This danger, he adds, can be so easily avoided by preparing special school Bibles that the opposite practice seems unpardonable. We think it well to quote the instructive passage in the original in a note, adding here that the Catholic Church all along taught the Bible in such school editions.[1] — There is a *third* consideration which prompts Catholics to oppose the reading of the Bible as advocated by most Protestant educators. It is the following question: Is the Bible to be read with or without comment? If with comment, is this Protestant or Catholic? Evidently either Catholic or Protestant would be offended. Therefore, without comment and explanation! Now this reading is almost useless, as the young will understand very little of the meaning of the passage. Disraeli, the English statesman, has justly ridiculed this practice. "I cannot imagine," he says, "anything more absurd than that a teacher should read 'without note and comment,' as it is called, a passage from the Bible, and that children should be expected to profit by it. The 'without note and comment' people in their anxiety to ward off proselytism, seem to have forgotten that, if there is any book in the world which demands more explanation than another, it is the Bible. And so, if nothing else is possible

---

[1] "Es darf doch hier auf Grund einer reichen Erfahrung nicht unerwähnt bleiben, dass namentlich die Bibel in ihrer ursprünglichen Gestalt eine grosse Gefahr für die Sittenreinheit der Jugend ist. Es ist mehrfach konstatiert worden, dass die Onanie (self-abuse) in männlichen und weiblichen Schulen durchaus zunächst sich an die Lesung von Bibelstellen angelehnt hat, deren Auswahl und Kenntnis sich traditionell unter der Jugend fortpflanzten. Man kann dieser Gefahr insofern leicht entgegentreten, als die Herstellung von Schulbibeln schon so erfolgreich geschehen ist, dass man nicht begreift, wie man noch immer die ungekürzte Bibel den Schülern in die Hände geben kann." Schiller, *Handbuch der praktischen Pädagogik* (Leipzig, 1894, 3. ed.), pp. 171—172.

than such a feeble and useless compromise as this, I would, in the interest of the Bible itself, not have it read at all." And then he adds: "I am a great believer in the old-fashioned Church-Catechism. I wonder whether those that sneer at it, have always read it. I fancy not. It is, rightly interpreted, a most practical document, but without interpretation, not worth teaching or learning."[1]

As is to be expected, religious instruction in the widest and fullest sense received a prominent place in the educational system of the Society of Jesus. The first rule of the Ratio calls it one of the most important obligations of the Society "to teach all branches of learning in such a manner that men should be led to the knowledge and love of their Creator and Redeemer;"[2] and in the rules of the Rector, the Prefect of Studies, and the teachers, the same duty is inculcated. As regards the reading of the Bible, the old prejudice that the Church ever set her face against it is unfortunately still alive among vast numbers of non-Catholics. For our purpose it suffices to remind the reader of what was said in a former chapter, namely, that in Jesuit colleges the Gospels were read, in the higher classes the Gospels and the Acts of the Apostles in the original Greek.[3]

But above all, the Jesuits were always "great believers in the catechism." Catechetical instruction was prescribed in all classes once a week. This may seem rather little; however, it should be remembered

---

[1] *Reminiscences*, quoted in the *Fortnightly Review*, May 1896, p. 814.
[2] *Reg. Prov.* 1.
[3] See above pp. 121—124.

that there were religious instructions in the weekly meetings of the Sodalities, and, which is still more important, that the whole teaching was permeated by a religious spirit. Besides, it may be added that in many modern Jesuit colleges two full hours are devoted to religious instruction every week. In the lower classes the catechism is explained, in the higher classes a fuller explanation of the Catholic dogmas and a course of apologetics is given. Such an apologetical course was recommended by the German province of the Society of Jesus as early as 1821.[1] That in our age an apologetical treatment of the Christian religion is absolutely necessary need not be demonstrated. The words of the Apostle St. Peter: "Be ready always to satisfy every one that asketh you a reason of that hope which is in you,"[2] had, perhaps, never before a more important bearing than in this age of omnivorous reading. At a time when the literature of the day is largely infected by naturalism and agnosticism, and when the principles of Christianity are attacked in so many subtle forms, it is certainly necessary to be well instructed lest one's own faith be tainted by the prevalent scepticism, and to be ready to defend this faith against the attacks made in the name of progress, modern philosophy, and science. This readiness can be obtained only by a solid catechetical and apologetical training.

Catechetical instruction was, from the very beginning of the Society, a special ministry and a labor of love to the Jesuits. In the papal approbation of 1540

---

[1] "*Instructio catechistica, praecipue in Humanitate et Rhetorica, sit ad praeservandam contra modernos errores juventutem accommodata.*" Pachtler, IV, p. 360.

[2] 1 *Peter* 3, 15.

it is said that the Society was instituted for "the propagation of faith, and especially for the instruction of children and ignorant people in Christian doctrine." Father Sacchini has a beautiful chapter on the "Teaching of the Catechism,"[1] in which he says the Jesuit should teach languages and grammar with great diligence, but with far greater devotion and alacrity catechism, "which is the grammar of Jesus Christ."

An American prelate wrote recently on this subject: "Among religious orders established with a special view toward the religious education of youth, the first place must undoubtedly be assigned to the Society of Jesus. . . St. Ignatius himself set the example. The first forty days after the papal approbation he devoted himself to the instruction of children in Rome. When told that no one would come to his class, he answered: 'If only one child comes to my catechism, it is enough of an audience for me.' The Society followed the example of its founder with a hitherto unheard of zeal and enthusiasm. . . The Jesuits, moreover, developed a most meritorious activity in writing catechetical works, not less than one hundred and fifty having been published during the first century of their existence. The catechisms composed by Bellarmine and Canisius soon displaced all others."[2] Indeed, the writing of catechisms has been one of the glories of the Society from the first decades of its existence. Dr. Knecht, Coadjutor Bishop of Freiburg, an eminent writer on catechetics, affirms that "the Jesuit Order has un-

---

[1] *Paraenesis*, art. 13.
[2] *Spirago's Method of Christian Doctrine.* Edited by the Rt. Rev. S. G. Messmer, Bishop of Green Bay, Wis. (Benziger, N. Y., 1901.)

doubtedly produced the greatest catechists."[1] The catechism of the celebrated Bellarmine[2] was used in many countries for centuries, even at present among Romanic nations. Of great fame were also the French, Latin and Greek catechisms of Father Edmund Auger. But all were surpassed by that of Peter Canisius, the first German Jesuit; this catechism was used extensively all over Europe. The works of this eminent writer and founder of many colleges deserve to be treated at some length.

Catechetical instruction had been given from the beginning of the Church, and there existed works which guided the clergy in this sublime office. The idea of placing a summary of Christian doctrine in the hands of the people and children, appears to have been first expressed in a letter of the great Gerson, chancellor of the University of Paris (1363—1429). The first known summary of this kind was the one published at the order of the synod of Tortosa in Spain (1429). The first German catechism, so far known, was that of Dederich Coelde, a Minorite Friar of Münster in Westphalia, printed about 1470, then published in many editions.[3] There existed, besides this, other catechisms before the Reformation. Of the Protestant works of this kind Luther's "Great and

[1] *Kirchenlexikon*, vol. VII, p. 310 (2nd ed.).
[2] Pope Leo XIII., when still Cardinal Archbishop of Perugia, published a revised and enlarged edition of Bellarmine's Catechism. At the Vatican Council (1869–70), it was the wish of Pius IX. that a catechism, which should be essentially that of Bellarmine, should be adopted as the uniform and official catechism for the whole Catholic world. Messmer, *l. c.*, p. 536.
[3] Janssen, *History of the German People*, vol. I. (17th ed., p. 48 foll. — English ed., vol. I, p. 45.)

Small Catechisms" were undoubtedly those that spread most widely and had the greatest influence. Several Catholic catechisms came out shortly after, but they were, in point of language and arrangement, inferior to that of Luther. They were also either too lengthy or too difficult. The need of a new and better work, adapted to the circumstances of the times, was felt especially in Germany. Then it was, in 1554, that Canisius began to publish his three catechisms.[1] The first was the large catechism in Latin for the use of students in colleges. After this appeared a shorter one, and finally his small catechism. This last established his fame as a writer. There are about three hundred different editions extant which appeared before the death of the author in 1597. By that time the work had been translated into English, French, Greek, Italian, Bohemian, Spanish, Polish, Swedish, and many other languages. Before 1623 there existed Aethiopian, Indian, and Japanese translations. In Southern Germany, Austria, and Switzerland, up to the nineteenth century the name "Canisi" was synonymous with catechism.[2]

The merits of this work can best be judged from the innumerable recommendations which it received from Popes and bishops, and not less from the violent

---

[1] See *Kirchenlexikon*, vol. VII, p. 302. — Braunsberger, S. J., *Die Catechismen des Petrus Canisius*. Herder, St. Louis, Mo., 1893. — *Spirago's Method*, pp. 532–534. — Janssen, *Geschichte des deutschen Volkes*, vol. IV (15th ed.), pp. 436 foll. — It is to be regretted that there exists no English biography of this great Catholic reformer and educator. A sketch of his labors was published recently in the *Dublin Review*, January 1903, pp. 137–158.

[2] Janssen, vol. IV, p. 445.

attacks made upon it by Protestants. The Italian historian Cesare Cantù styles it, "the most famous Catholic catechism written since the time of Luther." Even the Protestant historian Ranke cannot help praising and admiring it. And a distinguished Protestant controversialist in Germany, Professor Kawerau, says: "The catechism of Canisius is without doubt of the same importance to the Catholic Church as Luther's was to the Church of the Reformation. It is distinguished by its clear and lucid treatment of the subject and particularly by the mild and conciliatory tone in which it is written."[1] This "mild and con-

[1] Also Chemnitz, one of the leading Reformers and a violent antagonist of Canisius, acknowledges that "the catechisms of this Jesuit are written with the greatest mildness and moderation." See his words in Braunsberger, *Canisii Epistulae et Acta*, vol. III, (Herder 1901) p. 811. — In many places of his numerous writings Canisius lays down his principles about controversies with the Protestants. "The Protestants heap the most frightful calumnies upon me. Would that we loved them the better, the more they persecute us. They deserve to be loved, although they hate us, because most of them err from ignorance. I would gladly shed my blood for them if I could thereby save their souls." He exhorts his brethren and Catholics in general to avoid all bitterness in controversies; they should argue with gravity and modesty and suffer all attacks with holy patience for the love of Christ. (See Janssen, *l. c.*, vol. IV, pp. 408—411.) — This moderation is all the more remarkable if contrasted with the shocking insults and contumelious appellations with which Canisius was loaded by his Protestant adversaries. Melanchthon calls him a "cynic." Others styled his catechism "devil's dirt," the "cursed sacrilegious book of the dog Canisius," a "heathenish work, and a product of hell." The Jesuits are styled by Chemnitz and others "scoundrels, perjurers, beasts, hell-frogs spit up by the infernal dragon, a brood of vipers born of the Babylonian . . . . .," epithets

ciliatory tone" was recommended to all Jesuit teachers. Thus Father Nadal laid it down as a rule for all teachers that "both in the subject for written exercises and in the explanation of the catechism they should proceed with the greatest moderation. Especially in Germany, France, etc., they should not use any contumelious epithets against their opponents; nay they should not even style them heretics — although in truth they may be such —, but they should call those who adhere to the Augsburg Confession, Protestants, others Anabaptists etc.[1] How, then, is Mr. Painter justified in asserting that the Jesuit system fostered religious pride and intolerance?[2]

Father Canisius gave also beautiful instructions as to the motives and methods of teaching catechism. "We who are of the Society of Jesus," he writes, "wish to provide the little ones of Christ with the salutary milk of his doctrine. It is their welfare that we love and seek to promote. To this end has our Society been instituted, to instruct youth in piety as well as in learning, as far as with the grace of Christ we can accomplish."[3] One of the most essential qualities of a good catechist is kindness of heart and manners. This quality was a marked feature of Canisius' character, one which attracted the children to his instructions. The summary of the catechetical lectures which he gave in Augsburg has been pre-

which do not bear translation here. See Janssen, *l. c.*, pp. 411—413, 441—445.

[1] *Mon. Paed.*, p. 113. Pachtler III, 470 (no. 12), 474 (no. 6). Several other documents inculcate the same moderation and spirit of Christian charity. See Janssen, *l. c.*, p. 411, note 1.

[2] *History of Education*, p. 172; see above p. 252.

[3] *Canisii Epistulae et Acta*, vol. III, p. 777.

served. Canisius began with the words of the Psalmist: "Come children hearken to me; I will teach you the fear of the Lord" (Psalm 33, 12). Then he continued: "Christ, our Lord loved the children and showed his affection for them in various ways. He blessed and embraced them and defended them against the Pharisees (Matth. 21, 15. 16) and against his own disciples (Matth. 18, 1–10). He said: 'Suffer little children to come unto me'; yea come to me, to be instructed, and to be taught the science of salvation. And to all those who are not well instructed I speak with St. Paul: 'You have need to be taught again what are the first elements of the words of God: And you are become such as have need of milk and not of strong meat.' (Hebr. 5, 11. 12.) Following the examples of the Prophets, of Christ, and of the Apostles, I shall teach you not as wise and learned ones, but as children and little ones. Come, then, with a willing and cheerful heart; be convinced that it is a matter of the greatest importance for you to be justly called and truly to be sons of God. On your part, you must imitate the Child Jesus, who, in a manner, has given you an example how to learn the doctrine of salvation, when he set aside all else, left even his parents, and remained in the temple. Watch him there, see how he sits there quietly, listens to the teachers, and asks them questions. His questions are not about silly and useless matters, but about the great things of salvation. You must imitate him in this, now and ever in the future." This simple and hearty manner of teaching found great favor with the people, and we are not surprised to hear that after a few of his catechetical instructions Canisius could write: "I am delighted at seeing the good will of the people. Even men, among them persons of distinction, set aside all other business and come to listen to the instruction for children."[1]

Throughout his life Canisius found a special delight in giving catechetical instructions. The son of a distinguished family, the celebrated Doctor of theology, and author of many learned works, the founder of the famous colleges of Prague, Ingolstadt, Munich, Dillingen, Innsbruck, and Freiburg, the man whose advice was sought by the Emperors of Germany, by the Dukes of Bavaria, by Popes and Cardinals, by Church Councils and Imperial Diets — this man devoted every spare minute to the humble work of instructing children, and that not only in the cities where he resided, but on his many journeys, from one end of Germany to the other, he performed the same work of Christian charity among the simple country people. In his old age, when worn out by incessant toils, this was his favorite occupation. A year before his death, in his seventy-eighth year, he writes that his time is spent in "instructing children and old people."[2] A touching testimony to this work of the saintly Jesuit is still extant at the present day. In a little village near Innsbruck (Tyrol) is to be seen, on the gable of an old house, a picture which represents Canisius sitting among children whom he is instructing in their catechism. It was before this house that, on his journeys to Innsbruck, he used to perform the work which the picture has immortalized. We have dwelt longer on the labors of this great

[1] *Canisii Epistulae et Acta*, vol. III, pp. 623—627.
[2] Janssen, vol. IV, p. 487.

man, because they represent so beautifully what thousands of other Jesuits have done all the world over, in their endeavors to spread the knowledge and love of Christ.

Many other Jesuits wrote catechisms after Canisius. But it will suffice to mention a more recent one, that of the German Jesuit Deharbe. The merits of Deharbe's catechism were soon recognized, and it was introduced into nearly all dioceses of Germany, and was translated into many languages. It obtained a large circulation, especially in this country.[1]

In order to give a solid and efficient religious instruction, it is not enough to teach catechism once or twice a week. The General of the Society, Father Beckx, in a letter addressed to the Austrian Minister of Instruction, July 15, 1854, maintains the following: "Religion should not only hold the first place among the various branches, but permeate and rule all, and, according to our Ratio Studiorum, the teacher should treat all subjects in such manner that the truths of the catechism are found in all branches. Now it is some wise adage, then an inspiring thought, again a remarkable incident, or a beautiful trait of character, which gives the teacher occasion to instruct, to warn, and to elevate to Christian sentiments; such hints given incidentally and, as it were, accidentally, often make an impression all the more vivid, the less they were expected. In this manner religion is not a dry and disagreeable branch, but vivifies all the rest of instruction, gives it a higher, sacred character, and

---

[1] See *Spirago's Method*, page 530 foll., where also the shortcomings of this catechism are pointed out.

makes the pupil not only more learned but also better and more virtuous."[1]

The Fathers Jouvancy and Sacchini say that the explanations of all authors, also of pagan writers, should be conducted so that they become, as it were, heralds of Christ. This is very important in our times, when pagan ideas, principles, and tendencies are praised as the spirit of the progressing human mind, as the precious fruit of modern research and civilization. From the study of the ancients, particularly the Greeks, the young may learn that mankind is on the point of going again through a circle of errors, which in a retrogressive movement shall lead our race through all the aberrations which Christianity has long ago overcome. Against the enticing sirens of "modern progress," "freedom of thought," and "independence of morality," a most salutary lesson may be learned from the ancients, who in spite of their accomplishments in art, literature, and politics, could not find in them the remedy for social evils, nor contentment of mind and heart. Such suggestions, however, must be made discreetly, with great tact and moderation, when an occasion naturally offers. Here, too, the old *ne quid nimis* is of the greatest import; if the teacher too often, in season and out of season, indulges in pious exhortations, the pupils may easily conceive disgust at them and a loathing for all kinds of spiritual and religious instruction. Therefore, the teacher should not only not molest the pupils by too frequent admonitions, but should also observe prudence in those he thinks fit to give.[2]

[1] Duhr, *Studienordnung*, p. 104.
[2] *Ratio Docendi*, chapt. I, art. 2.

The principles laid down by the Jesuits, as to the religious tone of all instruction, have recently been emphasized by Pope Leo XIII., in the Encyclical written in 1897, on occasion of the centenary of Peter Canisius. There we read: "All schools, from the elementary to the university, should be thoroughly Catholic, and one of the main duties of the pastors of the Church is to safeguard the rights of parents and the Church in this matter. It is of the very greatest importance that Catholics should have everywhere for their children not mixed schools, but their own schools, and these provided with good and well trained masters. Let no one delude himself that a sound moral training can be separated from dogmatic religious training. To separate the training in knowledge from all religious influence, is to form citizens to be the bane and pest of society instead of being the bulwark of their country. *Moreover, it is not enough for youths to be taught religion at fixed hours, but all their training must be permeated by religious principles.*"

Some Protestant educators of the highest standing have advocated a system which is practically that defended by Catholics. Thus Professor Schiller strongly insists on "concentration and unity in education." As regards religious instruction he wishes it to be given by one "who has in his hands the most important branches of instruction, those which are best suited to influence education," above all literature and history.[1] The same view is also taken in the Prussian "School Order" of 1892 and 1901, where it is said that it is of the utmost importance that religious instruction is not rent from the other branches, but

[1] *Handbuch der praktischen Pädagogik*, pp. 237-238.

intimately connected with other, particularly the *ethical* branches.[1] From this principle we may draw another argument for the advantages which can be derived, if education is in the hands of the clergy,[2] especially in the higher classes, where a thorough knowledge of theology is required in order to give that religious training needed in this stage of education. It is evident that such a course can be followed only in denominational schools. For this reason Professor Schiller deplores the fact that, in consequence of religious differences, it is almost impossible to apply this most important principle.[3]

English and American educators are not wanting who advocate the same principle on which the Jesuits have insisted for centuries. Arnold's opinion on this subject was quite explicit. Sir Joshua Fitch tells us that he dreaded any theory which would tend to view the life of the scholar as a thing apart from the life of a Christian. He protested earnestly against any attempt to divorce religious from secular instruction, or to treat them as distinct parts of an educational scheme. "The device sometimes advocated in later times for solving the religious difficulty in our common and municipal schools by confining the functions of the school teacher to secular instruction, and calling in the aid of the clergy or other specialists to give lessons on religion at separate hours, would have seemed to him wholly indefensible, and, indeed, fatal to any true conception of the relation of religious knowledge to other knowledge." In one of his ser-

[1] *Lehrpläne*, etc., p. 11.
[2] See the words of Professor Paulsen above, p. 100.
[3] *L. c.*, p. 238.

mons he said: "It is clear that neither is the Bible alone sufficient to give a complete religious education, nor is it possible to teach history, and moral and political philosophy, with no reference to the Bible, without giving an education that shall be anti-religious. For, in the one case, the rule is given without the application, and in the other the application derived from a wrong rule."[1]

But a few months ago the same view was forcibly expressed by a writer in the Chicago *Biblical World*,[2] in a leading article which is said to be inspired by the editor of this review, President Harper of the University of Chicago.[3] In this article we find the following most appropriate statements: "It is a serious phase of the present situation that the religious and moral instruction of the young is isolated from their instruction in other departments of knowledge. The correlation of the different elements of education is incomplete, because the religious and moral instruction is received in entire separation from the general instruction of the public schools. The facts and truths of religion are the foundation and the imperative of morality. Present civilization rests upon the religious and ethical ideas of the past, and the civilization of the future depends upon a due recognition of religion and morality as essential factors in the growing welfare of humanity. The knowledge and experience of religious and moral truth must underlie and penetrate all knowledge and experience. The events and the ideas of the past, as of the present, must be viewed in

[1] Fitch, *Thomas and Matthew Arnold*, pp. 95–96.
[2] *The Biblical World*, November 1902, p. 324.
[3] *The Literary Digest*, December 27, 1902.

the light of a divine hand as the creator of the universe, a divine power sustaining it, a divine wisdom guiding it, and a divine purpose accomplished in it. The physical world about us, our fellow-men, and our own selves must all be interpreted by religion truly conceived and morality properly understood. It is, therefore, impossible to accomplish the ideal education of the individual when the religious and moral element is isolated from the other elements; still worse when it is not received at all by the majority of the children. All the elements of education must be woven together into an organic unity to produce a perfect result." The writer then proposes an organization which "may seek to show how to correlate religious and moral instruction with the instruction in history, science, and literature obtained in the public schools." — A comparison with the words of Father Beckx quoted on a previous page (p. 599) will show the great similarity of the views of the President of the University of Chicago and the former General of the Society of Jesus. But we think there is one essential difference: the Jesuit draws the logical consequences of his principles, namely, that education should be imparted in denominational schools; for only in such schools can the moral and religious training be harmoniously united with the other elements of instruction. The President of the University of Chicago has not drawn this conclusion. Yet we fail to see how, except in denominational schools, the proposed correlation of religious education and instruction in the other branches is possible. However, for our present purpose it suffices to have shown that this distinguished American scholar and educator agrees with the fundamental principle of the Jesuits, namely, that religious instruction should be closely connected with the general education.

We heard that Pope Leo said all schools, from the elementary to the university, should be under the influence of religion, not only the lower schools. The student in the college and the university needs the saving and elevating influence of Christianity as well as, and perhaps even more than, the boy in the elementary course. The man who receives a higher education is to become the leader and adviser of his fellow-men. This *rôle* he will not assume to the benefit of society unless he possesses a thorough knowledge of religion. Otherwise he will be "a blind leader of the blind, and both shall fall into the pit." What dangers are to be apprehended if the religious instruction does not keep pace with the growth of secular knowledge, especially in natural sciences, has been well stated by a Catholic writer: "Catholics have the faith and a creed, but it is not an easy thing for men to bear up against the superciliousness with which high-sounding philosophy treats the doctrine of truth as puerile, effete, and obsolete. The young man leaves school or college with certain religious principles, and with certain ideas of the Being and attributes of God; he is intended for a profession to which physiological science is preparatory. His theological knowledge is stationary; his scientific is progressive. Life and motion he learns to trace to secondary causes, of which before he had heard nothing. He had been taught that life is a gift of God, and that it rests with Him to destroy or to save; but now he finds that life expresses but an aggregate of properties, attached to organization, and dependent for their exercise on the perfection of the organism and the presence of certain stimuli, as heat and light and electricity. His scientific knowledge grows into maturity; his religion is still that of his boyhood or youth! He has found other causes of the facts he sees, besides those that he knew before, and the conceit of knowledge and superiority hides from him the fact that these causes are themselves effects: and then he ascribes a real power to his generalizations, personifies abstractions, and deifies nature." [1]

For this reason the Irish Jesuit Father Delaney, Rector of University College, Dublin, believes that laymen should have a scientific training in theology. "I should like," he said in his evidence before the Royal Commission on University Education in Ireland, "that educated laymen should be given an opportunity of getting a scientific knowledge of their religion. At present boys leaving school find newspapers and pamphlets and reviews dealing with subjects vitally affecting Catholicity and Christianity itself, with the existence of a soul, and the existence of God, and where are these men to get the training and knowledge to enable them to meet difficulties which are suggested to them in this way?" [2]

Indeed, it would be not only incongruous, but even scandalous, if a Christian place of higher education imparted all sorts of secular knowledge and neglected that which is the most important, the knowledge of the Christian religion. A Catholic youth, when leav-

---

[1] *Dublin Review*, Jan. 1847, p. 383. — In this connection we would beg the reader to see the beautiful exposition of the same principle in Cardinal Newman's *Idea of a University* (pp. 372—380): "General Religious Knowledge."

[2] Quoted in *The Review*, June 19, 1902, p. 384.

ing college, should be well prepared to defend his faith against the numberless misrepresentations which are prevailing among Protestants about things Catholic. Half the controversies which go on in the world arise from ignorance and misinformation; and educated laymen that are able to remove such prejudices by a correct statement of facts of history and doctrines — and numerous questions of this kind occur in social intercourse — not only vindicate the calumniated Church, but also further peace and good feeling among men of different creeds.

Chapter XIX.

School - Management.

Holy Job says: "Man's life upon earth is a warfare." The life of a teacher is eminently such. The moment he enters his class-room where thirty pupils await him, he has to face thirty enemies. Not that the pupils cherish hostile or even unfriendly feelings towards their master. God forbid! but there is in every one of them some one more or less prominent defect or fault, which, in whole or in part, will frustrate the teacher's work in the class-room, and it is with these defects and faults, as with so many deadly foes, that the teacher must do combat. One pupil is lazy; this one is fickle; that one stubborn; and in all there is a considerable amount of ignorance. Nor does the teacher's struggle cease with the four or five hours of class work. There are other trials awaiting him on return home. The daily careful preparation of the matter to be taught is a real drudgery, while the correction of themes and compositions is very fatiguing. Over and above this there is the monotony of repeating the same matter year after year. At times, too, there may come regulations from superiors which do not suit the taste of the teacher, which, however, must be complied with; for in order to ensure unity and harmony in any educational establishment some kind of executive superintendence over persons and things is indispensable.

This presupposes, on the part of the teachers, submission and obedience. The Jesuit teachers are told by their rules to obey the Prefect of Studies in all things pertaining to studies and school discipline. It is well known that St. Ignatius insisted on nothing so much as on *obedience*.[1] The obedience demanded by the Society has frequently been censured by men who do not as much as know what this obedience really means. In an army, or in any department of government, a similar obedience is exacted as being wholly necessary for the maintenance of right order; why not much more so in a religious community whose members profess obedience to their superiors in whom they see the representatives of God? M. De Ladevèze said recently: "Military obedience has had none but vigorous apologists, obedience in religious Orders, other than the Society of Jesus, has had but rare and indulgent critics, whilst the obedience of the Jesuits has ever been the butt for attacks as numerous as — my readers would not allow me to say impartial."[2] Does

[1] "The Society of Jesus," says Cardinal Newman, "has been more distinguished than any before it for the rule of obedience.... With the Jesuits, as well as with the religious Communities which are their juniors, usefulness, secular and religious, literature, education, the confessional, preaching, the oversight of the poor, missions, the care of the sick, have been their chief object of attention; bodily austerities and the ceremonial of devotion have been made of but secondary importance. Yet it may fairly be questioned, whether in an intellectual age, when freedom both of thought and of action is so dearly prized, a greater penance can be devised for the soldier of Christ than the absolute surrender of judgment and will to the command of another." In *Development of Christian Doctrine*, ch. VIII.

[2] The *Open Court*, Jan. 1902, p. 14.

not St. Paul say: "Let every one be subject to higher powers: for there is no power but from God: and those that are are ordained by God. Therefore, he that resisteth, resisteth the power of God." It must not be forgotten that passion, especially pride, impetuosity, and stubbornness frequently blind and deceive a man to take his own conceits for absolute infallible wisdom. Therefore, St. Ignatius addresses his sons in the words of Scripture: "Lean not upon thy own prudence." Indeed, many mistakes will be avoided by the teacher who conscientiously follows the regulations of the school and the orders of the superiors. On the other hand, the teacher who is lacking in submission will sooner or later blunder most seriously.

Further, how can a teacher honestly demand obedience from his pupils unless he practises it himself? Surely, there is much truth in the old monastic maxim: "No man securely commands but he who has learned well to obey."[1] Personal obedience of the teacher, therefore, is a means to secure him the most necessary qualification for effective school-management, namely, *authority*.

§ 1. Authority.

Authority is power or influence over others derived from character, example, mental and moral superiority. How can the teacher obtain this influence? Father Jouvancy and Father Kropf have two instructive chapters on this subject, from which we draw most of the following observations. According to Jouvancy,[2] three things especially conduce to the

---

[1] *Following of Christ*, I, ch. 20.
[2] *Ratio Docendi*, ch. 3, art. 1.

acquirement of authority by the religious teachers: esteem, love, and fear.

1. The teacher must possess the *esteem* of his pupils. They must respect him for his learning and his character. He must thoroughly master the subject which he has to teach. Besides, a careful preparation of the day's lesson should be made invariably before. It is most ruinous for the teacher's authority, if the pupils detect any deficiency in his knowledge — and they will discover it very soon if there is any. The pupils cannot and will not listen to such a teacher with the respect and willingness which are necessary not only for a fruitful study, but also for school discipline. Remarks will be passed about the teacher's mistakes, or his inability to handle the subject; perhaps bolder pupils call the teacher's attention to his mistakes. In such cases the man who is master of his subject can, and mostly will, calmly admit that a slip has been made, whereas the teacher who is not sure of his subject, and who blunders frequently, is inclined to keep down any objections by frowns, scoldings or even punishment. The result will be dissatisfaction among the students, which may lead to serious breaches of discipline.

As to his character, anything like passionate or irritable behavior, abusive language, haughtiness, levity, whims, fickleness, inconsiderate or idle talk, mannerisms, peculiarities of gesture and expression which will strike the pupils as ridiculous, and any other defect of mind or character will at once be detected by the keen eyes of the students and will more or less weaken his authority. In a teacher who is a religious, the virtues expected of a religious man should appear in all words and actions, and his whole life should bespeak a mind thoroughly imbued with the lofty principles of Christianity. Such a teacher should remember the words of Christ: "So let your light shine before men that they may see your good works and glorify your Father who is in Heaven."[1] Indeed, it is absolutely necessary for him to endeavor to gain the sincere esteem of the students, not in order to gratify his vanity, nor for any other selfish purpose, but in order to manage successfully a class of petulant and mischief-loving youths.

2. The teacher must strive to gain the *affection* of his pupils.[2] This he will obtain if they see him eager for their advancement, if he possesses the mastery over his own temper, if he never appears suspicious or distrustful. While kind and obliging in private, he must show himself earnest and grave before his class. Besides, being always firm, he must moreover be friendly and kind towards all, avoiding partiality, favoritism and excessive familiarity towards individuals.[3] If the teacher yield to the not uncommon weakness, and by any sort of favoritism tries to gain the special affection of a few, he should be convinced that he will estrange all the rest from him and thus inevitably undermine his authority. — In punishments he must be considerate, just, moderate, and show that he acts only from a sense of duty and genuine love, not from passion or antipathy.[4]

The affection of his pupils will be aroused by the interest the teacher shows for their health, their diffi-

---

[1] *Matth.* 5, 16.
[2] Jouvancy, *Ratio Docendi*, ch. 3, art. 1, no. 2.
[3] See below § 3.
[4] See below § 2.

culties, their joys and troubles, and by his ceaseless efforts to help them by instruction and advice. Jouvancy says the teacher should care particularly for the more delicate, visit the sick, encourage the backward, advise those that are in any embarrassment, in short, display the earnestness of a father and the devotion of a mother, especially towards pupils recently enrolled, and those in need. He should also notify the parents of progress or remissness on the part of their children. However, in most Jesuit colleges this is done by the Prefect of Studies or the Prefect of Discipline.

The teacher will further gain the affection of his pupils if he performs his duties conscientiously, but without gloomy severity. A cheerful countenance should greet the students when they arrive for the morning session. For the teacher loses much of his authority if his pupils are forced to make a daily inspection of his face, as they would of the bulletin of the weather forecast. The teacher's lively disposition and interesting way of speaking will act like a pleasant sunny spring morning on all, and do away with sleepiness and dullness, whereas sternness and gloom on his part will influence the class like a heavy fog on a winter's day. It is possible that a whole class appears slow and spiritless, but the professor may be responsible for it, either by his own lack of spirit and alacrity, by his tedious talk, or also by his too excessive demands on the class. To be ever reaching after the absolutely unattainable, is not particularly exhilarating, yet the professor may put his pupils in such a plight by placing before them too high a standard of excellence and never admitting that their best efforts bring them nearer the ideal. Hence judicious praise is a powerful factor in the management of a class; sometimes the effort may be praised where the result cannot. "The office of a good teacher," as Quintilian prudently remarks, "is to seek and encourage the good ever to be found in children, and to supply what is wanting, to correct and change whatever needs it."

3. *Fear*, is the third element which contributes to authority.[1] This fear must be as it is styled, *timor reverentialis*, not *timor servilis*, i. e. the fear of a child, not of a slave. Gravity, firmness and prudent consistency, in a word, manliness, on the part of the teacher, will instil this salutary fear into the pupils; only few and wise regulations should be made, but these must be firmly and prudently enforced. If this is done, even the most recalcitrant will after some time surrender. Another means of preserving this wholesome fear consists in reporting to higher officials of the school, or to the parents, breaches of conduct. However, this should not be done for every trifle, but only in case of a more serious misdemeanor. This leads us to the question of punishments.

§ 2. Punishments.[2]

The saddest part of a schoolmaster's task is the necessity of punishing. Offences must be treated seriously, not lightly; but, at the same time, as they

---

[1] Jouvancy, *Ratio Docendi*, ch. 3, art. 1, no. 3.
[2] *Ratio Stud., Reg. Praef. Stud. Inf.* 38, 42. — *Reg. com.* 40. — Jouvancy, *Ratio Docendi*, ch. 3, art. 1, no. 2. — Kropf, *Ratio et Via*, ch. 6, art. 7. — Sacchini, *Paraenesis*, art. 11 and 12. — *Monumenta Paedag.*, chapter "Del Castigare," p. 277 foll. — *Woodstock Letters*, 1896, p. 244.

are in most cases the effects of levity and weakness, they must be treated with compassion and without any harshness. The teacher should never be hasty in punishing; if he is, it will appear that he is led by passion. Often, and particularly when a pupil defies the teacher and refuses obedience, it will be best to wait patiently and assign the punishment later. For, if the punishment be inflicted immediately, it will, in all probability, be often unduly severe.[1] Anger and impetuosity are bad counselors, and in such trying situations it is especially true that "silence is golden." If the teacher merely lets it be seen how much he is pained by such conduct and defers the punishment, he will gain by his self-control in the eyes of the whole class; and the offender himself, having got over his excitement, will probably be in a better disposition to accept the punishment.

The Ratio Studiorum says the teacher should not be too eager to discover occasions for punishing his pupils.[2] There are some teachers who seem always on the watch to impose tasks. If they do not find misdeeds on the surface, they make sure to ferret them out. They were born to be detectives. This is not the fatherly spirit the teacher should manifest. The Ratio is opposed to this method. "See everything but never have the appearance of prying." Know all that regards your pupils, but do not always act on your knowledge. If you can conceal your discoveries without doing harm, conceal them. In

[1] An old regulation for Jesuit schools, written in Italian, well says: "Non convien castigar subito dopo la colpa per non dar luogo alla passione che fa passar' la misura del castigo." *Monum. Paed.*, p. 279.

[2] *Reg. com. mag. cl. inf.*, 40.

general: the fewer punishments the teacher inflicts, the greater will be his success, always supposing that he keeps order without punishing. Any just reasons for pardoning, or lessening, the penance are to be welcomed.

There seems to be abroad a sentiment about corporal punishments which is evidently beyond the bounds of reason. Some contend that corporal punishment is merely a "relic of the barbarism of former ages," and that it should no longer be employed, but that the young should be governed solely by moral suasion, by an appeal to reason and the pupil's sense of right. The inspired writers thought differently. Thus we read: "He that spareth the rod hateth his son; but he that loveth him correcteth him betimes."[1] "Folly is bound up in the heart of the child, but the rod of correction shall drive it away."[2] There are some faults: flagrant violations of modesty and decency, defiance of authority, impudent insults offered to elderly persons, continued laziness, which in a younger boy are best punished by the rod, especially after exhortations have proved unsuccessful. This was the principle and practice of Jesuit educators, and the best educators are again at one with the Jesuits.[3]

[1] *Proverbs* 13, 24.
[2] *Ib.*, 22, 15.
[3] See Fitch, *Lectures on Teaching*, IV: "The proud notion of independence and dignity, which revolts at the idea of personal chastisement is not reasonable and is certainly not Christian. After all it is sin which degrades, and not punishment." — On the views of Edward Thring of Uppingham on this subject, see *Life and Letters*, by Parkin, London 1898.

The Ratio Studiorum allowed the infliction of punishment only under rigid regulations; it forbids the teacher absolutely to strike a boy.[1] Corporal punishment, if, after calm deliberation, thought necessary, is to be administered either by a trusty servant, as was the custom in former times, or by the Prefect of Discipline.[2] At any rate, this system prevents many an indeliberate act of the teachers, as there is always danger of excess in the immediate punishment of an offence. Although the rod was applied in Jesuit schools, its use was by no means as frequent as in nearly all other schools. Compared to what was done in the great public schools of England and in the gymnasia on the European continent, the practice of the Jesuit colleges was exceedingly mild. There was never anything like the brutality practised in Eton,[3] or those debasing punishments, described in *The Terrors of the Rod* (published in 1815), or in Cooper's

---

[1] *Reg. com.* 40.

[2] On this point modern views, at least in Northern countries, are different, and a punishment inflicted by a servant is considered especially disgraceful. Therefore, the unpleasant task devolves on the Prefect of Discipline. — In some Jesuit colleges punishment was administered at fixed hours, and it was left to the lad that had offended to go to apply for castigation. In this way he had an opportunity of showing his manliness and taking his punishment with a sense of having deserved it. An English writer in the *St. James's Gazette* calls it "evidence of the skill and tact of the Order to have devised this method." *Littell's Living Age*, Boston, 1886, vol. 170, p. 248. — Of the *ferula*, the instrument used at Stonyhurst, the same writer says: "Few things are more disagreeably painful and at the same time more harmless and transitory in its effects than the application of this instrument."

[3] See *The Spectator*, No. 168.

History of the Rod.[1] In the higher schools of Saxony it was the custom, even in the eighteenth century, for all the members of the faculty to punish offenders before the whole school. When, in 1703, the teachers remonstrated against this, they were told by the highest authorities to continue doing their duty.[2] Matters were different in Jesuit colleges. The offender was punished in private and only few strokes were administered. Father Nadal made a regulation in Mentz, in 1567, to the effect that not more than six strokes should be given with the rod. The boys were not to be struck in any other way.[3] The above cited Italian School Order adds that not only the poor boys should be punished but the wealthy and noble as

---

[1] As a curious illustration the case of the Suabian schoolmaster may be mentioned, who kept a diary and jotted down in the course of his fifty-one years' schoolmaster's career the number of times he administered punishment to his recalcitrant pupils. Schoolmaster John records that he distributed 911,517 strokes with a stick; 240,100 "smites" with a birchrod; 10,986 hits with a ruler; 136,715 hand smacks; 10,235 slaps on the face; 7,905 boxes on the ears; 115,800 blows on the head; 12,763 tasks from the Bible, catechism, the poets and grammar. Every two years he had to buy a Bible, to replace the one so roughly handled by his scholars; 777 times he made his pupils kneel on peas, and 5,001 scholars had to do penance with a ruler held over their hands. As to his abusive words, not a third of them were to be found in any dictionary.

[2] *Neue Jahrbücher*, 1902, vol. X, p. 296.

[3] Pachtler, vol. I, p. 160, 207, 279; IV, 164—170. — It is not improbable that the moderation required by the rules was not always observed through the fault of some individuals. Hence the one instance of excessive flogging quoted by Compayré, *Hist. of Ped.*, p. 14, was certainly an exception.

well. These should be made to understand that virtue is more highly prized than nobility.[1]

A word should be added about the famous "lines." If lines are assigned to be committed to memory they should not be such as are not fully understood. There are so many useful things that have been read or should be studied, why not give them? Catechism or Bible history should never be assigned as penalty; it might make these sacred books an object of aversion. It is advisable, however, to assign these books if the pupil has neglected to study his catechism or his Bible history. If lines are to be copied — a punishment of questionable worth — at least the same lines should not be copied more than once; it is sheer nonsense to make a student copy the same line twenty times, unless it be an exercise in penmanship for continued careless writing. The teacher should insist that all extra tasks are neatly and carefully written. It is most detrimental to the teacher's authority to assign punishments and not to see that they are done; or to assign excessive tasks and then be compelled to desist from demanding them. If, in particular cases, an extraordinary punishment is thought necessary, Jesuit educators wisely refer the matter to a Superior, either Prefect or Rector. These officials should also decide on cases where punishment has been refused, especially by older students.

§ 3. Impartiality.

Another point, important for effective school-management, is the necessity of showing strict fairness and justice. A professor accused of favoritism is

[1] *Monumenta Paedagogica*, p. 278.

sadly hindered in his work. His kindly words of good advice fall on deaf ears and his exertions for his class are viewed with coldness and distrust. The 47th rule exhorts the Jesuit teacher not to be more familiar with one boy than with the rest. Although mischievous tongues of jealous pupils will never cease to impute faults which may have no objective reality, still a strict observance of this rule will be a precious safeguard to the reputation of the teacher in a matter which is of vital importance to the proper and successful discharge of his duty. A uniform spirit of kindliness and charity should be manifested towards all, poor or rich, slow or highly gifted, uncouth or polite, uncomely or attractive. No dislike is to be shown for any pupil, no matter how great the natural aversion is which one may feel towards him. The all-embracing charity of our Lord should ever be before the eyes of the teacher, and he should strive to be "all things to all." He must not forget that in every pupil there is something good, a good side from which he may be approached. And it happens not unfrequently that in the poor workingman's son, diffident, shy, and ungainly as the boy may be, there is a nobler soul, greater talent, more prospect of great work in the future, than in the much more refined, courteous and winning boy of wealthy parents. To neglect the poor or ungainly lad would be not only unjust and cruel, but also directly opposed to the spirit of the Society, which, in the 40th rule, tells the teacher "to despise no one and to work as strenuously for the advancement of the poor as of the rich."

Another danger frequently connected with undue familiarity with some pupils has to be mentioned.

The teacher is easily inclined to speak more confidentially to them about other pupils; he may be sure that his remarks will be reported, most likely in a distorted form, to those whom he has criticized. This will destroy the good spirit among his pupils, cause bitterness, ill-feeling, factions, and little conspiracies among them, and the teacher will perhaps never be able to detect and remedy the evil.

Undue familiarity and partiality is also very harmful to the pupil himself who is thus singled out from the rest.[1] If special affection is shown to one, if his failings are tolerated more than those of the rest, if he is not reproved where he deserves it, if he is praised where he hardly deserves it, then an opening is made for jealousy; the *Benjamin* of the class will receive all sorts of names, as little flattering to him as to the teacher; and his position among his companions may become very unpleasant. The teacher's unreasonable partiality has compromised him and has placed a barrier between him and his classmates. A still more serious consequence is usually connected with such partiality: the real education of the favorite is neglected. What training of character can be expected if his whims are indulged in, if his failings are not corrected, if he is flattered and coddled, in short, if he is spoiled? Besides, such partiality invariably breeds vanity, self-conceit and stubbornness. The teacher's favorite is soon aware of the preference shown to him. He feels that he can venture what his companions dare not to do; that class regulations, class silence and the like are less severe for him than

---

[1] See: *The Little Imperfections*, by Rev. F. P. Gareschè, S. J.; chapter on "*Partialities.*" (Herder, St. Louis, 1901.)

the others. He will soon think himself a privileged being, superior to the rest: he will assume the air of authority over others and pride is nourished in his heart. Yet this is not all. The next year the pupil may pass to a teacher who is different, who does not tolerate his caprices any more than those of others and who tries to eradicate the evils that were allowed to root by his predecessor. But the spoiled child will resent any strict treatment, will peevishly refuse to be corrected. All this may lead to serious breaches of discipline and obedience, and to disagreeable punishments.

From this it should not be inferred that a teacher is forbidden to take a greater active interest in some than in others. On the contrary he must do this especially in the case of those who need it most, for instance, of those who are very bashful, and particularly of those who are exposed to greater danger. Just as a mother watches more anxiously over a delicate child, so must a good teacher look more particularly after those whose spiritual condition is more delicate. "Not the healthy ones need the physician but the sick." On this subject it may be well to quote once more the beautiful words of Father Jouvancy: "The teacher should speak in private more frequently with those who seem to be exposed to worse and more dangerous faults. If he captivates them by a wise and holy kindness, he attaches them not only to himself, but gains them for Christ." [1]

[1] *Ratio Docendi*, ch. 1, art. 2.

§ 4. Discipline in the Classroom.[1]

The effectiveness of a teacher as teacher will depend largely on his success as a disciplinarian. This holds especially of the lower classes, where the pupils are livelier and act more from their animal propensities. A few good regulations concerning order in class, as well as to the manner of entering and leaving the class room, are to be firmly insisted on. Determination is here the great factor. A classroom yields, keeps silence, remains quiet, is attentive and studious, if it learns that the professor means to insist on these points. Of course, firmness can be overdone. Too great persistence takes on the appearance of tyranny and challenges opposition. On the other hand, mildness easily gives place to weakness. The teacher has to strike the mean, which is golden here as in other things. However, it is a maxim of Jesuit educators that it will be good to be more reserved, and also stricter as to discipline, in the beginning, until the teacher knows his class and has it under perfect control. It is easy then to loosen the reins a little, whereas it is nearly impossible to draw them tight after a spirit of levity, noisiness and general disorder has started through the teacher's easy-going manner.

The following words of a French Jesuit educator on this question are most instructive. The master in charge of the boys, in his first intercourse with them, has no greater snare in his way than taking his power for granted and trusting in his strength and knowledge of the world. That master who in the very first hour

---

[1] Jouvancy, *Ratio Docendi*, ch. 3, art. 2. — Kropf, *Ratio et Via*, ch. 6, art. 3. — Sacchini, *Paraenesis*, art. 19.

has already made himself liked, almost popular with his pupils, who shows no more anxiety about his work than he must show to keep his character for good sense, that master is indeed to be pitied; he is most likely a lost man. He will soon have to choose one of two things, either to shut his eyes and put up with all irregularities or to break with a past that he would wish forgotten, and engage in open conflict with the boys who are inclined to set him at defiance. He wished to endear himself by acts of kindness, he set about crowning the edifice without making sure of the foundation. Accordingly, the first steps should be characterized by an extreme reserve, without any affectation of severity or diplomacy.[1]

Some good principles on class discipline have been laid down by Father Jouvancy.[2] The first is: *Principiis obsta:* Resist the evil from the beginning. As soon as the pupils grow restless, no matter how light the disturbance may be, it must be checked immediately. When some few are especially giddy or mischievous, they must gradually be wearied by various devices: frequent questions, repeated calling up for recitations etc., so as to become gently accustomed to bear the yoke.

Secondly: The place of the pupils in class should not be a chance affair or left to their choice and caprice.[3] If they are allowed to select their places, the light-minded and petulant will be found together in some corner, or in the rear, where they anticipate full scope for mischief. By prudent tactics many a

---

[1] Barbier, *La discipline*, Paris 1888. Quoted at greater length by Quick, *Educational Reformers*, pp. 60—62.
[2] *Ratio Docendi*, ch. 3, art. 2.
[3] Sacchini, *Paraenesis*, art. 19, no. 5.

teacher has gained the battle as before-hand, by scattering the hostile forces, by separating the talkers and mischief-makers. A petulant boy may be assigned his seat near a quiet and reserved boy; one whose morals are justly suspected near one of reliable virtue—taking care, however, lest the good boy be corrupted by the one of doubtful character.

Thirdly: No noise or confusion is to be tolerated when the students enter the class-room.[1] They should be trained to consider this room as a sacred place, "a temple of science," which ought to be entered in silence and modesty. If any come in boisterously the teacher should at the outset reprimand or punish them. This will immediately quiet their exuberant spirits.

Fourthly: The respect of the pupils for their teachers and for one another will prompt them to listen to the instructions in absolute silence.[2]

Sometimes it may happen that either all the scholars, or only a few, offend against good conduct and attention. If the former should happen, the cause of evil must be investigated and the instigators must be punished. The teacher should very rarely threaten the whole class, still less should a whole class be subjected to punishment. Such an action irritates the pupils and, feeling confidence in their number, they will be inclined to conspire against the teacher. Extraordinary tasks, like more weighty penalties, should be imposed on only a few. "Frequent ailments, unusual remedies, and continual funerals disgrace the physician,"[3] as Jouvancy wisely observes.

[1] Jouvancy, *Ratio Docendi*, ch. 3, art. 2, No. 4.
[2] *Reg. com.* 43.
[3] Jouvancy, *Ratio Docendi*, ch. 3, art. 2, 5.

Fifthly: The 44th rule gives wise directions for maintaining order at the end of class. Here the danger is greater than at the beginning of the session. The boys are not so eager to come to class as after recitation hours to rush to the yard for a game of baseball, or to hasten home for dinner. But it makes certainly a bad impression if the boys run out of class like a pack of hounds turned loose. Therefore, the teacher should be on hand and watch the boys at this critical time. These are not the minutes for correcting stray themes, or for conversation with another professor, or with one of the pupils. The teacher should, as the rule says, take his station at his desk, or at the door, and have his eye on the class room and the corridor. All are to leave the room in silence and order. There is to be no hurry, no running about, no jostling. If the teacher acts thus, all disorder will be prevented far more effectively than by punishments.

§ 5. Politeness and Truthfulness.

Another point intimately connected with discipline consists in the attention given to *politeness* and *good manners.*[1] There is nothing more attractive than a class of boys who are lively and, at the same time, truly polite. But the amusements of our boys, baseball and football especially, easily lead to a certain roughness, which is certainly the very opposite of refinement. Further, however attractive frankness and freedom of behavior may be, they frequently degenerate into want of respect. Teachers, elderly persons, and others who must claim the young man's respect, are sometimes approached without due reverence. The greeting con-

---

[1] Sacchini, *Paraenesis*, art. 14. — Kropf, *Ratio et Via*, ch. 5, art. 1, § 8.

sists in a gracious or confidential nod, or a motion of the hand in the direction of the head, without reaching to its end; then the "youngster" starts his conversation, hat on, hands in his pockets, if possible sitting or leaning on a railing, or lolling against a wall. Our boys hear so much of liberty that they easily mistake it for freedom from the obligations due to age and position, which are everywhere recognized and rightly insisted on, and which are justly considered the distinctive marks of true culture and refinement. Anything servile, cringing, or affected is, of course, to be avoided.

The teacher has many opportunities of inculcating the rules of politeness. But a most important factor is the teacher's example. Being before the eyes of his pupils four or five hours a day, his personality will naturally leave traces on their manners. He should impress his pupils not only as a scholar and a pious religious, but also as a perfect gentleman. Nor will the Jesuit teacher ever fail in this respect, if he carefully observes the "Rules on Modesty," which are laid down in the Institute, and were considered of the greatest importance by St. Ignatius and all true Jesuits. We shall quote a few of these rules: "In general, it may be said that in all outward actions there should appear modesty and humility, joined with religious gravity. There should appear outwardly a serenity, which may be the token of that which is interior. The whole countenance should show cheerfulness rather than sadness or any other less moderate affection. The apparel is to be clean, and arranged with religious decency. In fine, every gesture and motion should be such as to give edification to all men. When they have to speak they must be mindful of modesty and edification, as well in their words, as in the style and manner of speaking."

The Jesuits have always been most sedulous in cultivating in their pupils politeness, not a mere external polish, but a politeness which is the choice fruit and exterior manifestation of solid interior virtue, of sincerity of heart, humility, obedience, and charity. Protestant writers have paid homage to these endeavors of the Jesuits. Ranke writes: "The Jesuits educated well-bred gentlemen." And another Protestant, Victor Cherbuliez, is almost extravagant in his praise when he says: "However much one may detest the Jesuits, when religion is allied to intellectual charms, when it is gentle-mannered, wears a smiling face, and does all gracefully, one is always tempted to believe that the Jesuits have had a hand in the affair."[1]

Another point which deserves special care on the part of the teacher is the cultivation of *truthfulness* in the pupils. No one teaches even for a short time without recognizing the necessity of fighting the evil habit of mendacity. A boy is reprimanded for unmistakable talking, whistling, throwing paper, etc., and how often is the quick and bold answer heard: "It wasn't me," bad English being added to the moral defect. A boy fails to hand in a task. How many excuses are made which not unfrequently are more or less palpable falsehoods. Now all this is more serious than it may appear at first. How is this evil to be combated?

First by prudence. Many lies could be prevented if the teacher acted more discreetly. If a boy has been

[1] Quoted in the Chicago *Open Court,* January 1902, p. 29.

noisy, and the teacher, especially one who has the reputation of inflicting severe punishments, angrily charges him with the offence, the boy will deny the deed in sheer excitement. And one lie leads to many more; the boy assures and protests, in order not to expose his first prevarication. Therefore the master, as a rule, should not insist on arguing the case, but await a better chance, when the boy is calm. A teacher who is patient, judicious in inquiries, just and reasonable in punishments, will seldom be told a lie. If noise is going on in class, such a teacher may safely ask: Who made that noise? And in nearly all cases, as the experience of many teachers has proved, the offender will candidly acknowledge it. Sometimes this confession, with an earnest but calm word of admonition, will dispense with any further punishment. Of course, if the pardon invariably follows the confession, there will be no good effects whatever.

There are boys who, from a long practice, have acquired a most pernicious habit of lying. Such cases are hard to deal with, and it is difficult to lay down general rules. A few suggestions, however, may not be out of place. Very rarely, and only on extreme occasions, should there be shown any doubt of a pupil's word on a matter of fact. All should know that implicit confidence is placed in their assertions, and that it is considered as a matter of course that they speak the truth on facts within their knowledge. If ever a lie is found out and proved, the punishment should be severe. Dr. Arnold says, in such a case the punishment should be the loss of the teacher's confidence. But even then the teacher should try to save the offender from discouragement by holding out to him the possibility of correcting even the habit of lying. It has happened that boys given to lying, when once thoroughly convinced of the disgracefulness of their habit, conceived such a horror of it, that they became disgusted with everything dishonest, and turned out men distinguished for uprightness and truthfulness. In this as in other defects, it will be good if the teacher follows the example of the Divine Master, of whom it was said: "The bruised reed he shall not break, and smoking flax he shall not extinguish."[1]

Here again the teacher's example will exercise a powerful influence. He must be open, truthful, straightforward, strictly honest in his dealings with the pupils, not sly, crooked, and political. If he is asked a question which he cannot answer, he should say: "I do not know it," or "I am not sure about it, I will inquire and tell you next time." No one can reasonably expect the teacher to know everything, and by such honest acknowledgements he will not lose a tittle of his authority. If he has made a mistake in a statement, or in reprimanding or punishing, he should frankly admit it and apologize. No school master is infallible. The teacher need fear no detriment from such a candid retractation. On the contrary, such a

---

[1] *Matth.* 12, 20. — Father Faber remarks in his *Spiritual Conferences:* "There is a peculiar clearness about characters which have learned to be true after having been deceitful."— The humiliating consciousness of having been found guilty of deceit, and the yearning desire to be trusted again, forces them to renounce everything like untruth, and to keep guard over themselves, lest they fall again into the old habit. — See the beautiful chapter (XII): "On being true and trusty" in *Practical Notes on Moral Training*, with preface by Father Gallway, S. J., London, Burns & Oates.

teacher will gain in the esteem of his pupils, who will be more disposed to accept his admonitions.

§ 6. Some Special Helps.

The trials of the teacher are many and vexing. A few general means to endure them successfully may be suggested. One means is *patience*. Dr. Arnold, referring to the years of boyhood, once said the teacher should try to hasten out the growth of this immature and dangerous age. But in this endeavor it will be good to remember the Latin saying: *Festina lente.* Impatience, vehemence, and rashness are signs that a teacher lacks knowledge of the frail human heart. He should learn from the supreme model of teachers, who showed a Divine longanimity and forbearance in the training of his Apostles and Disciples who were not always very docile and quick of perception. From him he should learn the virtues necessary to the teacher: "Learn from me, for I am meek and humble of heart."[1] A distinguished Jesuit of our days used to say: "No one likes to settle at the foot of a volcano. And a wrathful, excitable teacher will do great harm. The outbursts of his anger will destroy all around like the eruptions of a volcano, whereas a meek, patient, and prudent man is acceptable to God, wins the hearts of men, and will work successfully." An old regulation of Jesuit schools[2] recommends especially patience: "The teachers of youths should ever remember the one perfect teacher, Christ our Lord, that they may imitate his benignity and kind forbearance toward the simple ones, that they may be unwearied in teaching and adapt themselves to the capacity of their auditors,

---

[1] *Matth.* 11, 29.
[2] Pachtler, vol. I, pp. 159—160.

admonish their pupils, practise them diligently and zealously, and *gradually* advance them, as well those of slower perception as those of ready perception, as Paul the great Apostle says: 'We became little ones in the midst of you, as if a nurse should cherish her children.'"[1]

One should, therefore, never be surprised at mistakes or moral faults; least of all should one be vexed at fickleness, unsteadiness, fits of laziness. These are defects of age, or weakness of character, not signs of bad will, consequently they are to be treated kindly. There are some things which the teacher should take good-humoredly. Many teachers feel irritated on discovering that the boys have given them a nickname. Why not take it good-naturedly and heartily laugh about it? In general, a cheerful disposition combined with a great amount of patience will make many of the troubles of school life more endurable.

Another most powerful means for overcoming the trials of teaching, and at the same time for laboring successfully, is *prayer*. The "modern" systems have little to say about it, and many educators may be inclined to sneer at such a pedagogical help. Still there is a sublime truth in what Tennyson says in his beautiful lines:

> "Pray for my soul.
> More things are wrought by prayer
> Than this world dreams of."[2]

One who believes in the fundamental truths of Christianity cannot ignore our Savior's words: "Without me you can do nothing,"[3] and the other: "What-

---

[1] 1. *Thess.* 2, 7.
[2] Words of King Arthur in *Morte d'Arthur*.
[3] *John* 15, 5.

soever you shall ask the Father in my name, that will I do,"[1] and the words of St. Paul to the Corinthians, who contended about the superiority of their teachers in the faith: "I have planted, Apollo watered, but God gave the increase;"[2] further the words of St. James: "If any one of you want wisdom, let him ask of God, and it shall be given him."[3] As we have seen, the Jesuits consider education from a supernatural point of view. They endeavor to lead the children to the knowledge, love, and service of Christ, according to Christ's words: "Suffer little children to come unto me, for of such is the Kingdom of God." This is an aim above man's nature, and can be obtained only by supernatural means. God alone can give the teacher's words the power to enter into the will, that impregnable citadel of man's nature. This power from on high is bestowed on him who humbly asks for it in prayer.

We must expect that St. Ignatius did not think lightly of this means. In the 16th rule of the *Summary of the Constitutions*, all Jesuits are exhorted "to apply to the study of solid virtues and of spiritual things; and to account these of greater moment than either learning or other natural or human gifts: for they are the interior things from which force must flow to the exterior, for the end proposed to us." This trust in God's assistance in no way lessens the earnest endeavors of the religious. As the old principle of the great order of St. Benedict was: *Ora et labora*, so St. Ignatius says: "Let this be the first rule

---

[1] *John* 14, 13.
[2] 1. *Cor.* 3, 6.
[3] *James* 1, 5.

of all your actions: trust in God, as if all success depended on him, nothing on yourself; but work, as if you had to do all and God nothing." In the Ratio Studiorum the teachers are admonished "frequently to pray for their pupils."[1] The Jesuit Sacchini has a special chapter on the importance of the teacher's prayer,[2] and exhorts him to recommend his disciples daily to Christ, and to invoke for them the intercession of the Blessed Mother of God, of the Guardian Angels and of the patrons of youth. Father Jouvancy[3] tells the teacher never to go to class without having said a fervent prayer, if possible in the Church before the Blessed Sacrament. He suggests a beautiful prayer which is almost wholly drawn from Scripture: "Lord Jesus, thou hast not hesitated to meet the most cruel death for these children; thou lovest them with an unspeakable tenderness; thou wouldst that they were led to thee (*Mark* 10, 14). Yea, whatever is done to one of these thy least brethren, thou wilt consider as done to thee (*Matth.* 25, 40): I beg and implore thee, 'keep them in thy name whom thou hast given me;' 'they are thine', 'sanctify them in truth' (*John* 17, 6. 9. 11. 17). 'Give thy words in my mouth' (*Jerem.* 1, 9), open their hearts that they may begin to love and fear thee. 'Turn away thy face from my sins '(*Psalm* 50, 11), and let not thy mercy be hindered through my faults. Give me the grace to educate these children, whom thou hast entrusted to me, with prudence, piety and firmness, to thy glory, which is all I ask." Truly, this is praying in the

---

[1] *Reg. com. mag. cl. inf.* 10.
[2] *Paraenesis*, art. 15.
[3] *Ratio Docendi*, ch. I, art. 1.

name of Jesus. And if the teacher is a man of solid piety and virtue, as the Society expects him to be after a religious training of so many years, the grace of God will surely lighten the burden of his work. "For the continual prayer of a just man availeth much."[1]

[1] *James* 5, 16.

Chapter XX.

The Teacher's Motives and Ideals.

The teacher's life is a most arduous one. Like that of the scholar and scientist it presents few attractions. It has none of the external brilliant dramatic quality that makes the soldier's and stateman's career attractive, and as its material remuneration is relatively scanty, and the chance of promotion to a lucrative position is almost excluded, it can make little impression on an age whose watchwords are exterior success and material progress.[1] Still, the teacher's mission is one of the greatest importance while touched with sublimity. It is in a way a "priestly" office, for the material on which the teacher works is the mind, the immortal soul of man; his object is truly "sacerdotal," namely to consecrate these souls to their Creator, to make them more God-like in wisdom and moral goodness. The teacher is also entrusted with the destinies of society; the children and youths whom he now trains will one day be the heads of families, the parents of a new generation, the men that powerfully influence public opinion for good or ill, in the press and from the platform, the citizens whose vote will make or mar their country. Surely, this is a profession that deserves the enthusiasm of noble hearts and the absorbing interest of the ablest minds.

[1] See *Brownson's Review*, 1860, pp. 303 and 314.

(636)

In the case of the Jesuit teacher there can be no question of a material compensation. What he needs for his sustenance is furnished by the Order; beyond this he seeks no earthly reward. In this all members of the Order are equally situated: the professor of philosophy and the teacher of the lowest grammar class, the President of the college, and the lay brother who acts as porter. What, then, are the motives that inspire him to undergo willingly and cheerfully the labors and trials of his profession? They are in the first place the consideration of the *utility* and the *dignity* of his calling. He is convinced that teaching is a grand and noble profession. St. Gregory Nazianzen says: "There is nothing more God-like than to benefit others;"[1] and what benefit can be greater than that of education, as we have described it in previous chapters: the making of man, the harmonious development of all his faculties, the fitting him for best performing the duties of this life and the preparing him for the life to come? Is not this thought a reward as well as a powerful incentive for the teacher to exert himself most strenuously in his sublime vocation?

The Jesuits Sacchini and Jouvancy have written some beautiful passages on this subject. Their comparisons may seem to some far-fetched or even fantastic, but they will appear natural and appropriate to every person who views things in the light of the teaching of the Great Master. These two Jesuits say that the school may be considered as a *garden*, a nursery,[2] in which the choicest trees and flowers are

[1] Migne, *Patrologia Graeca*, vol. XXXV, 892.
[2] Sacchini, *Paraenesis*, art. 5, no. 1—2.

cultivated, plants whose saplings are not brought from the tropics, but from heaven, whither they are again to be transplanted, when fully grown. They are, under the tender and prudent care of the teacher, to yield abundant fruit of virtues, of human and divine wisdom. They are to become the ornaments of Church, State and society. They are the plants of which the Son of Sirach said: "Hear me, ye divine offspring and bud forth as the rose planted by the brooks of waters, give ye a sweet odor as frankincense. Send forth flowers, as the lily, and bring forth leaves in grace."[1] In this garden the teacher, like him "who sowed the good seed," has to sow and to plant by instruction, to dig and to water by practice and exercise, to weed and to prune by salutary admonition, to fence and restrain by wise regulations. Besides, the virtuous example of the teacher combined with cheerfulness in performing all his duties, will be the atmosphere in which the plants grow wonderfully. However, the husbandman can plant and water, but not prevent storms and hail and frost and drought, and, therefore, implores heaven's protection for his fields; so the teacher must see the necessity of divine blessing for his class, a grace which will be given to humble and fervent prayer.

The teacher may consider himself the shepherd of the tender lambs of the flock of Christ.[2] The children, in a special sense, may be called the lambs of Christ's flock. The teacher's duty is to feed them, to lead them to the wholesome pasture and to the clear springs of divine and human knowledge. He must

---

[1] *Ecclesiasticus* 39, 17 sq.
[2] Sacchini, *Paraenesis*, art. 5, no. 8.

protect them against the wolves, especially those that "are clothed in sheepskins," that come in the garb of agnostic and infidel science, or in the glittering dress of pernicious reading. He must protect his flock without sparing himself, not fly from dangers and exertions like the hireling, but must be ready to "give his life for his sheep," that means, he must sacrifice himself, devote all his time and strength to his class. He should "go before his sheep" by his good example, attract them by kindness and meekness, that they may "know his voice and follow him, and fly not from him as from a stranger whose voice they know not."[1]

Again, is not the teacher to be compared to a sculptor, or a painter?[2] We admire the masterpieces of Phidias, Praxiteles, Lysippus, of Michael Angelo and Raphael. And yet, the teacher's art is far nobler. Those artists produced likenesses of marble or bronze, likenesses that are cold and lifeless, whereas the teacher is working at living statues. Those artists could produce only exterior likenesses of men or of superior beings; the teacher shapes the innermost nature of man. Nay, more, the Christian teacher endeavors to bring out more beautifully the image of God. Christ, the true teacher of mankind is his ideal and model. In prayer and meditation on the life of Christ, he studies line after line of him to whom he applies the words of the royal prophet: "Thou art beautiful above the sons of men, grace is poured abroad in thy lips. With thy comeliness and beauty set out, proceed prosperously and reign."[3]

[1] *John* 10, 4. 5. 11.
[2] Sacchini, *Protrepticon*, Part I, art. 8.
[3] *Psalm* 44, 3 sq.

Having grasped this beauty he tries to express in his own character, and then to embody in the hearts of his pupils that heavenly beauty of purity, humility, meekness and charity which shines forth from every word and action of the God-man. Thus he is making real living pictures of Christ, which for all eternity shall be ornaments in heaven, the trophies of the labors and struggles of the zealous teacher. And whereas the greatest artist can work only at one statue or picture at the same time, the teacher is working on as many as he has auditors.

The teacher is an *architect;* he does not build merely a splendid city hall, nor a national capitol, nor even a cathedral of stone or marble: he builds up those living temples, of which St. Paul speaks: "Know you not that you are the temple of God, and that the Spirit of God dwelleth in you?"[1]

The teacher is the *tutor of the sons of the Most High.* King Philip of Macedon chose Aristotle as preceptor to his son Alexander, an office which the great philosopher discharged for many years. The letter which Philip wrote to invite Aristotle, is said to have been couched in the following terms: "Be informed that I have a son, and that I am thankful to the gods not so much for his birth as that he was born in the same age with you; for if you will undertake the charge of his education, I assure myself that he will become worthy of his father and of the kingdom which he will inherit." King Philip's hope was not disappointed. His son, Alexander the Great, became one of the greatest figures in human history, and his success is partly due to his great teacher. At all times

---

[1] 1. *Cor.* 3, 16.

it was a much coveted honor to be the tutor to the sons of Emperors, Kings, Princes, and other high personages. Is not every Christian teacher tutor to the sons of the King of Kings?[1] St. John says: "Behold, what manner of charity the Father has bestowed upon us, that we should be called and should be the sons of God."[2]

Lastly, the teacher should consider himself the *representative* and *successor* of Christ in his love for his children. No feature in the life of the Teacher of mankind is more fascinating than his love for children. The Gospels commemorate a scene of unspeakable tenderness and sweetness. "Then little children were brought to him that he might touch them."[3] He does not bless them together, but lays his hands on every child, and takes one after the other in his arms. From this scene Christian teachers must learn an important lesson: love and reverence for children. Indeed, princes of heaven are appointed their guardians, and the teacher should be like them in watchful care for the young. This care is all the more necessary as the teacher in higher schools has to do with the young when the first and most attractive chapter of their history is already over, at the time when the storms of temptations rage most furiously in their hearts. With Christ's love for children must frequently be united the good *Samaritan's* compassion and anxious solicitude for the wayfarer who fell among the robbers. Frequently enough there is sad need of the teacher's fatherly care, not only in the

---

[1] Sacchini, *Protrepticon*, Part I, art. 12.
[2] 1 *John* 3, 1.
[3] *Mark* 10, 13.

case of the children of the poor but also of the rich. Some wealthy parents pride themselves that they do all in their power to procure for their children the best possible education, from the best instructors in elocution, music, gymnastics, etc., and yet that which above all is education — moral and religious training — is sadly neglected, owing to the indifference that pervades the family life. In consequence of this neglect of the most important part of education, it has happened that many a man ended his life in disgrace and wretchedness whose childhood was spent among the luxuries of a splendid home. <u>Fortunate is the youth who is placed under the tutelage of teachers who endeavor to counteract the baneful influences of a neglected or ill-directed home training.</u> These considerations explain the anxious care and strenuous exertions of religious teachers to promote the moral training of their charges. They realize that now is the spring-time of life when the good seed must be sown, if a rich harvest is to be hoped for in the autumn. They know that now their work is most useful, most promising of success. Now the pupil's nature is docile and pliable as wax. And if it were hard as marble, still the material is not yet spoiled and may be shaped into a beautiful statue, and it should not be forgotten, of the hardest marble the most endurable statues are made, though with greater care and labor. Similarly the most stubborn and headstrong of boys, under patient and prudent guidance, often develop into the finest character of manhood.

To the Jesuit these considerations furnish powerful incentives, the motives which inspire him in all his work. St. Ignatius, in calling his Order the

Society of Jesus, wished to impress it forcibly on the minds of his sons that they were to endeavor to imitate him whose name they bear, especially in his zeal for the glory of his Father and the welfare of men. Indeed, other educators may take as their guides and ideals Spencer, or Rousseau, or Kant, or Pestalozzi, or Herbart — the Jesuits' guide and ideal is Christ.[1] Him they are told to imitate in his devotion to his life-work, in his all-embracing zeal, in his patience and meekness. In education they behold a participation in the work of the Great Master, that work whose end and object it is to make men truly wise, good, and God-like, and thereby to lead them to true happiness. Can there be a nobler, a loftier work, a holier mission on earth?

When the teacher thus reflects on the dignity of his work, and on its necessity and utility for the individual, the family, the State and the Church, can he ever become tired and disgusted with it? Are all these considerations not most encouraging, and do they not constitute one of the rewards of the teacher? He may truly say with the sacred writer: "Wisdom I have learned without guile and communicate without envy and her riches I hide not,"[2] and again: "I have not labored for myself alone, but for all who seek discipline."[3] Such thoughts may well inspire a man with love and enthusiasm for this profession. To the Jesuit the educational work is a labor of love. We read that in the seventeenth century, in the period

---

[1] On the "Pedagogy of Our Lord" there is a beautiful article by Father Meschler, S. J., in the *Stimmen aus Maria-Laach*, vol. 38, 1890, p. 265 foll.

[2] *The Book of Wisdom* 7, 13.

[3] *Ecclesiasticus* 33, 18.

of witch panic, some Protestant writers charged the Jesuits with using secret charms in order to attach the pupils to themselves and to advance them in learning.[1] Indeed, the Jesuits as educators have a spell, and make no secret of it, but they will be glad if others wish to borrow it. This spell is nothing but ardent *devotion* to their work, a devotion which springs from the conviction of the importance and usefulness of their work. This devotion is their strongest motive to action and it urges them to use all the resources within their reach.

Although the teacher does not seek himself in his work, nevertheless he labors also for himself. What better compensation can there be than the thought of performing so important a work, the conviction that through his instrumentality noble characters are formed, that some youths are preserved in their innocence and others led back from evil paths on which they had trodden in their ignorance and levity? The teacher may not receive much recognition and gratitude for his efforts — youths do not reflect on the debts they owe to a zealous teacher —, nor is it this that he is looking for in his labors. However, some pupils will show their thankfulness by a lifelong affection for their former master. If one wishes to know with what reverence, devotion, and frequently with what attachment Jesuit pupils regard their teachers, let him read the biographies of Jesuit educators. The letters written by former pupils sufficiently testify to the impressions made by their religious teachers.

If one wishes to see beautiful specimens of the relation of Jesuit pupils to their teachers, he may read

[1] See above pp. 147—148.

the biography of Father Alexis Clerc, who left the French Navy to become a Jesuit and professor of mathematics and was shot by the Communards in Paris 1871.[1]

But it is rather the success of his pupils over which the teacher rejoices, than their tribute of gratitude. An incident is related of the life of Father Bonifacio, a distinguished Jesuit teacher of the Old Society, who for more than forty years taught the classics. One day he was visited by his brother, a professor in a university, whom he had not seen for many years. When the professor heard that the Father had spent all the years of his life in the Society in teaching Latin and Greek to young boys, he exclaimed: "You have wasted your great talents in such inferior work! I expected to find you at least a professor of philosophy or theology. What have you done that this post is assigned to you?" Father Bonifacio quietly opened a little book, and showed him the list of hundreds of pupils whom he had taught, many of whom occupied high positions in Church or State, or in the world of business. Pointing at their names, the Father said with a pleasant smile: "The success which my pupils have achieved is to me a far sweeter reward than any honor which I might have

[1] *Alexis Clerc, Sailor and Martyr*, New York, Sadlier, 1879. See especially chap. XII: "Father Clerc and his pupils." It may be interesting to add that the American edition of this biography is dedicated to the memory of Father Andrew Monroe, S. J. (grand-nephew of President Monroe), officer in the American Navy and a convert to the Catholic faith, who, after spending his religious life, like his friend Father Clerc, chiefly in the humble duties of a professor, died at St. Francis Xavier College, New York, 1871.

obtained in the most celebrated university of the kingdom."

Not all teachers may have the consolation of seeing their pupils in high positions. It happens that the best efforts of a devoted teacher seem to be lost on many pupils. Even this will not discourage the religious teacher. He will remember that his model, Jesus Christ, did not reap the fruit which might have been expected from the teaching of such a Master. Not all that he sowed brought forth fruit, a hundredfold, not even thirtyfold. Some fell upon stony ground, and some other fell among the thorns, and yet he went on patiently sowing. So a teacher ought not to be disheartened if the success should not correspond with his labors. He knows that one reward is certainly in store for him, the measure of which will not be his success, but his zeal; not the fruit, but his efforts. The Great Master has promised that "whosoever shall give to drink to one of these little ones a cup of cold water, he shall not lose his reward."[1] What, then, may he expect, who has given the little ones of Christ not a cup of cold water, but with great patience and labor has opened to them the streams of knowledge, human and divine? Indeed, "they that instruct many to justice shall shine as stars for all eternity."[2]

[1] *Matth.* 10, 42.
[2] *Daniel* 12, 3.

Conclusion.

We have examined the educational system of the Jesuits in its various aspects, its history and its principles, its theory and practice, its aims and means. There are few of its principles which have not been censured by some of its opponents. But we have also seen that there is hardly one principle in it which has not been heartily recommended by most distinguished educators, Protestants as well as Catholics. We have seen that on many lines there is, at present, a decided return to what the Jesuits defended and practised all along.[1] Can it then be said in justice that the Jesuit system is antiquated and that little can be hoped for it, and from its principles, in the improvement of education at present? Or can it be said with a modern writer that "the regulations of the Jesuit system of studies, viewed in the light of modern requirements, need not shun any comparison, and the pedagogical wisdom contained therein, is in no way antiquated"?[2] Another writer declared a few years ago, with reference to modern school systems: "Those now living may desire that in the new much of the old may be preserved which has proved of benefit."[3] May it not be said that much, very much, of the Jesuit system should be preserved, and that many of its principles and regulations could, with best advantage, be followed in the education of the present day? We leave

[1] See especially chapter XVI.
[2] See above p. 288.
[3] Dr. Nohle of Berlin, in the *Report of the Commissioner of Education*, 1897—1898, vol. I, p. 82.

it to the impartial reader to pass judgment. It is true that in our times Jesuit education is not viewed with favor by the many. To some it is too religious, too "clerical;" to others it appears old-fashioned. For this reason it is not popular; popular favor is never bestowed on what seems old. It is the novelty that attracts, and the bolder the innovations, the more captivating for the large majority of the people. This is as true now as it was 2600 years ago when old Homer sang:

> "For novel lays attract our ravished ears;
> But old, the mind with inattention hears."

And yet the novel songs are not always the best.— As to the Jesuits, they know full well that there are not many who will take the trouble to investigate thoroughly their educational system, in order to pass a fair and independent judgment on its merit, but that there are many who will content themselves with repeating the verdict passed on this system by others who were either ignorant of its true character, or were misled in their estimates by prejudice. Hence the Jesuits do not expect that the misrepresentations of their system will ever cease; their experience of three hundred years has taught them not to entertain such sanguine hopes. On the other hand, this same experience has taught them another valuable lesson, namely, not to be disheartened by the antipathy and opposition of those who do not know them, but to continue their efforts to realize, to the best of their ability, in the education of Catholic youth that which they have chosen as their motto: *The greater glory of God, and the welfare of their fellow-men.*

APPENDIX I.

Additions and Corrections.

CHAPTER I.
Observations on American Histories of Education.[1]

In the course of the present book we have frequently had occasion to point out that the histories of education by Painter, Seeley and Compayré are utterly untrustworthy in their account of the Jesuit system, and of Catholic education in general. It is natural to infer that in other respects they may be equally unreliable. Professor Cubberley, in his recent *Syllabus of Lectures on the History of Education* (New York, Macmillan, 1902), says, on page 1, that the works of "Painter, Payne, and Seeley are very unsatisfactory, and are not referred to in the Syllabus." The same should have been done as regards Compayré; for his *History of Pedagogy* is as unsatisfactory as those mentioned before; it only assumes an air of impartiality, which makes it all the more insidious. (See the present book, pp. 10-11.) Some writers quote from the Ratio Studiorum, but the quotations are often mistranslated in such a manner that they are hardly recognizable when compared with the original. Setting aside the disastrous influence which antipathy and prejudice may have had on some writers, the following reasons may account for many errors. The Ratio Studiorum is in many respects a peculiar document,

---

[1] See also the interesting article: "The History of Education. A Plea for the Study of Original Sources," by the Rev. W. Turner, D. D., in the new and promising *Review of Catholic Pedagogy*, January, 1903.

which is unintelligible unless one is acquainted with the Latin terminology of scholastic philosophy and theology, and there are exceedingly few non-Catholic writers on education who possess this knowledge. Further, numerous regulations of the Ratio are clear only when explained by other documents of the Society, which have either not been known, or not been examined by these writers. Another difficulty is to be found in the fact that the Ratio contains also the regulations for the studies of the members of the Society. Some writers have confounded rules for the novices and scholastics of the Order with regulations for the lay pupils in the colleges. Thus what is said in the *Constitutions* of the Society about the obedience to be rendered to Superiors by the Jesuits themselves, Mr. Painter has applied to the lay students. (*Hist. of Ed.*, p. 170.) Evidently an entirely false impression must be produced by such confusion.

However, in most cases it is almost certain that these writers have not taken the trouble to examine the Ratio Studiorum, but have contented themselves with copying the assertions of untrustworthy secondary authorities. Raumer's *History of Education* seems still to be considered by some a reliable source. Even Professor Cubberley styles it "still quite valuable" (*l. c.*). And yet this work is altogether antiquated. Besides, in regard to Catholic education it is so biased that fair-minded Protestants have rejected many parts of it. Thus Henry Barnard, in his translation of the chapter on the Jesuit schools, says: "We omit in this place as well as towards the close of the article, several passages of Raumer's chapter on the Jesuits, in which he discusses, from the extreme Protestant stand-point, the influence of the confessional, and the principles of what he calls 'Jesuitical' morality. These topics, and especially when handled in a partisan spirit, are more appropriate to a theological and controversial, than to an educational journal. The past as well as the present organization of the schools of the Jesuits, the course of instruction, the methods of teaching and discipline, are worthy of profound study by teachers and educators, who would profit by the experience of wise and learned men." (*American Journal of Education*, vol. V, p. 215.) However, even in the statements which Barnard accepted from Raumer, there are not a few that are incorrect. Owing to protests of Raumer, Barnard, in the VI. volume of his journal, added the passages which he had omitted in the previous translation. The misrepresentations which Raumer had borrowed from Pascal and others, need not be dwelt on here.

Nor is the estimate of the Jesuit system correct which is found in the *History of Modern Education*, by Samuel H. Williams, Professor of the Science and Art of Teaching, in Cornell University. The author evidently endeavored at times to be impartial, but he was not fortunate in the choice of his sources. They were evidently not the original documents. Otherwise he would not have been betrayed into such absurd statements as this: "The teachers were mostly novices of the Order, with a much smaller number of the fully professed brothers." Now, as the chapter on the "Training of the Jesuit Teacher" proves, novices are not employed in teaching, and the Jesuit is not engaged in teaching until after a training of five or six years succeeding the *completion* of the novitiate. The expression "fully professed brothers," also, shows that this author knows very little about Jesuit teachers.

Mr. Shoup, in his *History and Science of Education*, admits many good features in the Jesuit system; he expressly states that it has many points in common with American methods, but then his authorities lead him away into the old tirades of "neglecting mathematics, sciences, practical knowledge; suppressing of independent thought," etc.

We gladly acknowledge that the latest American book on the subject, Mr. Kemp's *History of Education* (Lippincott, 1902), is, in point of impartiality, superior to most other works. On the whole, it is free from offensive attacks on the relation of the Church to education. However, we must say that it is not free from assertions which cannot stand in the light of modern historical research. Particularly in chapter XV, many statements need considerable correction, v. g., the assertion that before the Reformation "the large majority of the people felt no need of education and took little interest in it." With this should be compared the authors from whom we quoted on p. 23 *sqq*. On p. 172, Mr. Kemp repeats Green's assertions about the Grammar schools founded by Henry VIII. But Mr. Arthur F. Leach has proved, from incontestable documents, that this is a pure myth, and that the statements of Green and Mullinger are a distortion of the historical facts. In his *English Schools at the Reformation* (Westminster, Archibald Constable, 1896), Mr. Leach says: "The records appended to this book show that close on 200 Grammar [secondary] schools existed in England before the reign of Edward VI., which were, for the most part,

APPENDIX I. 653

abolished or crippled under him. ... It will appear, however, that these records are defective .... three hundred Grammar schools is a moderate estimate of the number in the year 1535, when the floods of the great revolution were let loose. Most of them were swept away either under Henry or his son; or if not swept away, they were plundered and damaged" (pp. 5—6). Of the character of these schools the author says that they were not mere "monkish" schools, but secondary schools of exactly the same type as the secondary schools of the present day. Considering the population of England at the time, there were previous to the Reformation more higher schools in England than at present; in Herefordshire, v. g., 17 higher schools for a population of 30,000! Nearly every town had a higher school. (*Ib.*, 99—100.) Mr. Leach confesses that his researches revolutionize the traditional view of pre-Reformation schools in England, and that on this account his book was looked upon unfavorably by some people. — We call attention to these facts, because they show how the current tradition has influenced men who earnestly endeavor to be impartial. Had all American writers been animated by the spirit of fair-mindedness and zeal for correct information which distinguished that excellent American educator, and first U. S. Commissioner of Education, Henry Barnard, the cause of truth and justice would have been better served in this country.

CHAPTER II.
The Brethren of the Common Life.

What is said on pp. 31—34 about the Brethren, must partly be corrected. Recent investigations have proved that they were not, as Raumer had represented them, an order of teachers like the Jesuits. They taught, indeed, in a few schools, as in that of Liège; but in most schools with which they were connected, they received boarders and looked chiefly after their moral and religious training, while the secular instruction was in the hands of other teachers, who, however, were mostly imbued with the spirit of the Brethren. See Paulsen, *Geschichte des g. U.*, 2nd ed., vol. I, pp. 158-160, where this author modifies, in the same way, the statements expressed in the first edition of his work. Further see the recent valuable work on *Jakob Wimpfeling*, by Dr. Knepper (Herder, 1902), page 7.

CHAPTERS V AND VII.

Jesuit Scholars.

CHAPTER V, p. 156. — The importance of Father Saccheri's work is being recognized more and more. Professor Ricci of Padua contributed a highly interesting article to the *Jahresbericht der mathematischen Verbindung* (Vol. XI, October—December 1902), on the "Origin and Development of the Modern Conception of the Foundations of Geometry." There it is said that "Saccheri's works prove him a man of indisputable merit, and one of the first geometricians of his century.... The *Euclides vindicatus* alone is a work which could claim the labors of a whole life. In this work he erects an edifice of classical beauty which testifies to the extraordinary ability and geometrical taste of the architect." It is a perplexing problem to modern mathematicians how Saccheri could endeavor to refute his own arguments, with which he had so ably attacked the Euclidian system. Of this attempt

APPENDIX I. 655

Professor Ricci says: "To-day it is hard to understand that a man of so sublime an intellect did not see the truth which he almost could grasp with his hands, and that he stubbornly tried to destroy with sophisms what he had built up with so much correct geometrical skill. Able and sagacious as he is in constructing his system, he is awkward and unskilful in tearing it down." — If for once I may be allowed to venture a conjecture, I would ask: Is it not possible that Saccheri *did* grasp the truth, but did not think fit to publish it boldly? He may have feared lest his contemporaries would raise a cry of indignation against such a mathematical heresy. Besides, as at that time such hypotheses would have been looked upon as mere freaks, there may have been apprehensions that the publication of such a work would injure the reputation of the college in which Saccheri taught mathematics. The attacks on the Jesuits on account of the bold theories of Hardouin (see p. 160), and similar instances in which the whole Society was reprehended for the attitude of individuals, would have been a sufficient cause for the wariness of the author. If this explanation were the correct one, it would certainly account for the weakness of the arguments which he used to pull down his splendid structure. These arguments, accordingly, would have been merely a thin veil to hide the purport of his work. I communicated this conjecture to Father Hagen of Georgetown, and was surprised to learn that this distinguished mathematician had given the same explanation of the curious phenomenon to Professor Halsted of the University of Texas, the translator of Father Saccheri's works. However, this is only a conjecture, though not void of probability. But even if the author did not see the full truth of his deductions at the time, this has happened to many great discoverers. Professor Whewell says of Kepler, with reference to a similar instance, that it seems strange that he did not fully succeed; "but this lot of missing what afterwards seems to have been obvious, is a common one in the pursuit of truth." (*History of the Inductive Sciences*, vol. II, p. 56. Appleton's ed., 1859.)

CHAPTER VII. — Among the Jesuit scholars of the last decades mention should have been made of the sinologist Father Angelo Zottoli, who died in the College of Zi-ka-wei, near Shanghai, November 9, 1902. In 1876, Baron von Richthofen, in his work on China, expressed his regret that the Jesuit missionaries of recent times had not succeeded in regaining the scientific prestige of the Old Society. But a few years after, in 1879, the first volumes of a work appeared which inaugurated a new period in the scientific activity of the Jesuits in China. This was Father Zottoli's *Cursus Literaturae Sinicae*. When the work had been completed in five volumes, it put the humble religious in the front rank of sinologists. It has been styled "a landmark in the history of Chinese philology," and received the great prize of the *Académie des Inscriptions et des belles Lettres*. Mr. Legge, formerly a Protestant missionary in China, and one of the foremost sinologists of our age, declares that in Father Zottoli's *Cursus* "the scholarship of the earlier Jesuit missionaries has revived." (In vol. XXVII of the *Sacred Books of the East*, Preface, p. XIII.) In Father Zottoli's school some able Jesuit sinologists were trained, who now publish their researches in a special review, the *Variétés Sinologiques*, whose scholarly character has been frequently attested to by the foremost orientalists. Father Zottoli was engaged for thirty years in writing a gigantic Chinese dictionary. The ablest of his pupils are now completing this work. (See *Kölnische Volkszeitung*, Wochenausgabe, January 1, 1903.)

Some readers may be surprised at the list of Jesuit writers — we have enumerated only a small fraction of the number of scholars that well deserve to be known better than is the case —, and ask why so little is said about them in works that treat of the history of the various sciences. It is not because their works are not of great importance for science. The explanation may be found in a remarkable utterance of the celebrated Kepler, the prince of astronomers: "Alas for prejudice and hatred! If a Jesuit writes anything, it is completely ignored by the adherents of Scaliger." Allusion is made to the famous controversy on chronology between the Protestant Scaliger and the Jesuit Petavius (see page 160). The same may be said of many another scientific discussion. Kepler himself, though a Protestant, was not afraid of being a friend of Jesuit scholars, nor of asking their opinion on many of the important questions which he was investigating. (See *Johann Kepler, der Gesetzgeber der neueren Astronomie*, by Adolph Müller, S. J., Professor of astronomy in the Gregorian University in Rome [Herder, 1903]; see especially chapters 12 and 17, and page 166.)

Chapter VIII.

The Recent Educational Troubles in France.

On page 265 it is said that the non-Catholic view of the Jesuits is not based on historical facts, but largely on works of fiction. A case in point is Zola's posthumous novel, the English edition of which was issued in this country in February, 1903. The subject of this work was announced as "illustrating the keenly antagonistic influences of the *Jesuitical* and secular parties in France, as instanced in the recent educational troubles." Though the book is styled "Truth," it is in reality a tissue of falsehoods and enormous charges, not only against the religious orders, but the Catholic Church as such. The Baltimore *Sun*, February 19, 1903, says in a very judicious criticism, that the author "asserts and asserts, but, behold! of proof there is little or nothing. This, however, will make no difference to those readers to whom this diatribe appeals [among them the same paper reckons those who hate the Catholic Church, and who welcome any attack that may be made upon it]. In the present instance Zola has, seemingly, cared little about the truth of his statements." The book furnishes a strong proof of what we said on page 268, namely, that the present persecution of the teaching Congregations in France is in reality a brutal attack on Christianity and all religion. Zola says little about Jesuit education, but what is meant by secular education, is set forth in clearest light: All religious beliefs and observances are derided, every sign of religion is to be banished from the school, women are to be emancipated from the influence of the Church, experimental science is to take the place of religion in school and private life. It is the old Voltairian *Écrasez l'infâme!* This is the antagonist of "Jesuitical" education! (On this subject see the article of M. Brunetière, in the *Revue des Deux Mondes*, December 15, 1902: "The Laws of Proscription in France," translated in the *Catholic Mind*, New York, 1903, no. 2).

For the Catholic view of the educational movement in France during the last decade we refer to the *Études*, which contain many excellent articles not only on the religious side of the question, but also on modern school reforms, the classics, etc. See especially volumes 54 (page 100 *sqq.*), 57 (page 345 *sqq.*), 69 (page 224 *sqq.*), 70 (page 496 *sqq.*), 78 (page 21 *sqq.*), 79 (page 41 *sqq.*), 84 (page 654 *sqq.*), 86 (page 29 *sqq.* and 501 *sqq.*). In the volume mentioned in the last place, the article: *L'Enseignement classique en Allemagne, son rôle pédagogique*, contains interesting comparisons between the French and German secondary schools.

Chapters X—XII.

"Impressions of American Education."

Under the above title, the *Educational Review* (March, 1903) published an address delivered by Mr. Sadler, at the Annual Congress of the Educational Institute, Glasgow, Scotland, December 30, 1902. Mr. Sadler admires many features in American education: the hearty belief of Americans in the value of education, the sacrifices they make for it, etc. But he discovers also the following defects and weaknesses: 1) In some cases municipal corruption has baleful results in the sphere of educational administration. 2) There is a grave doubt whether the stricter forms of intellectual discipline have not been unduly sacrificed in many American schools. The besetting sin of some modern methods of education is that they stimulate interest without laying corresponding stress on intellectual discipline. As it were, they feed the children on sweeties and plumcake, in a strenuous revolt against an austere tradition of too much oatmeal porridge. Nor does home discipline restore the balance. The younger Americans find it difficult to focus their attention on uncongenial tasks. An insidious evil is the tendency on the part of teachers to make lessons interesting by avoiding the harder, duller, and more disciplinary parts of the subjects. Another evil is the excessive encouraging, among young children, of what is called "self-realization", even occasionally to the point of impertinence. 3) Lack of severe discipline leads to a third weakness, — superficiality, — with its attendant evils, exaggeration in language and love of excitement. The Americans do not as yet sufficiently allow for the slow percolation of ideas into the mind. They make too many short cuts. They are too fond of the last new thing. They forget that a pupil gains true independence of taste and judgment by slowly and thoroughly working his way, under guidance and with encouragement, through masterpieces as a whole, and through masses of the same kind of work, often against the grain. All true culture has in it an element of stubbornness and persistence, which must be acquired through the lessons of life, and the lessons of the school, which ought to prepare for life. 4) A fourth danger proceeds from the tendency of American men to become unduly concentrated in business pursuits. Many Americans sterilize part of their nature by too great absorption in the excitement and struggles of commercial competition. This overzeal for business forms an atmosphere which cannot but affect educational ideals. Intense absorption in commercial enterprise is not an aim worthy to dominate the thoughts and lives of the rising generation of a great people. The noble answer of the Short Catechism to the question: "What is the chief end of man?", deserves not to be forgotten in commercial pursuits.

It may be well to compare these statements with what has been said in the chapters on the "Intellectual Scope," "Prescribed Courses or Elective Studies," and "Classical Studies".

APPENDIX II.

Bibliography.

1. Primary Sources.

The Constitutions of the Society of Jesus. Numerous editions in Latin. The English translation, published by a Protestant in 1838 (London, Rivington, etc.), is very unscholarly und unreliable. — The fourth part of the Constitutions, which treats of the studies, is given in Latin and German in the work of Father Pachtler quoted further on (vol. I, pp. 9—69).

Decreta Congregationum Generalium. (Decrees of the General Congregations of the Society.) The General Congregation is the legislative assembly of the Order; the decrees of different Congregations relating to studies are contained in Father Pachtler's work, vol. I, pp. 70—125.

Ratio atque Institutio Studiorum Societatis Jesu, usually quoted as *Ratio Studiorum.* Latin text and German translation in Pachtler's vol. II, and German translation in Father Duhr's *Studienordnung*.

Pachtler, G. M., S. J. *Ratio Studiorum et Institutiones Scholasticae Societatis Jesu per Germaniam olim vigentes.* Berlin, Hofmann, 1887—1894. Volumes II, V, IX, and XVI of the great collection

APPENDIX II.

Monumenta Germaniae Paedagogica, edited by Dr. Karl Kehrbach.

This is the standard work on the educational system of the Jesuits; it contains all the most important historical documents relating to Jesuit education, particularly in Germany. The great value of the work has been acknowledged by numerous historians and writers on pedagogy. (We quote: Pachtler, I, II, III, IV.)

Monumenta Historica Societatis Jesu, Madrid, 1894 foll.

A huge collection of material relating to the early history of the Society. Published since 1894 in monthly instalments of 160 pages each; up to February 1903 there were out 110 instalments. The collection is a most valuable source of information for the history of religion and education in the sixteenth century. Of particular importance for the history of Jesuit education are instalments 93, 97, 99, 100, 101, 194, entitled:

Monumenta Paedagogica, Madrid, 1901—1902.

To be carefully distinguished from Father Pachtler's volumes in the *Monumenta Germaniae Paedagogica.*

The following works are important commentaries on the Ratio Studiorum:

Sacchini, F., S. J., *Paraenesis ad Magistros Scholarum Inferiorum Societatis Jesu,* and *Protrepticon ad Magistros Scholarum Inferiorum Societatis Jesu* (1625). — German translation by J. Stier, S. J., in Herder's *Bibliothek der katholischen Pädagogik,* 1898, vol. X, pp. 1—185.

Jouvancy, J., S. J., *Ratio Discendi et Docendi* (1703).

Of this important educational work (see above pp. 434—435) there exist eighteen editions in the original Latin, a French translation by J. Lefortier, Paris 1803, and a recent German translation: *Lern- und Lehrmethode*, by R. Schwickerath, S. J., in Herder's *Bibliothek*, etc., 1898, vol. X, pp. 207—322.

Kropf, F. X., S. J., *Ratio et Via Recte atque Ordine Procedendi in Literis Humanioribus Aetati Tenerae Tradendis* (1736). German translation: *Gymnasial-Pädagogik*, by F. Zorell, S. J., in Herder's *Bibliothek*, vol. X, pp. 323—466. (We quote Kropf, *Ratio et Via*.)

2. Works Treating Exclusively of Jesuit Education.

Hughes, T., S. J., *Loyola and the Educational System of the Jesuits.* New York, Scribners, 1892. — Belongs to the *Great Educators Series*, edited by Nicholas Murray Butler.

Duhr, B., S. J., *Die Studienordnung der Gesellschaft Jesu.* — Freiburg (Germany) and St. Louis, Mo., 1896. —

Contains the translation of the Ratio Studiorum (both of 1599 and of 1832), and a valuable commentary. Father Duhr's work is volume IX of Herder's *Bibliothek der katholischen Pädagogik.*

Maynard, Abbé, *The Studies and Teaching of the Society of Jesus at the Time of its Suppression.* Translated from the French. Baltimore, John Murphy, 1855.

De Rochemonteix, C., S. J., *Un Collège de Jésuites aux XVII. et XVIII. siècles. Le Collège Henri IV. de la Flèche.* 4 volumes. Le Mans, Leguicheux, 1889. —

This work gives the history of one of the most flourishing colleges of the Society in France; from detailed descriptions based on documentary evidence, one can learn how the Ratio Studiorum was carried into practice.

Chossat, M., S. J., *Les Jésuites et leurs oeuvres à Avignon*, 1553—1768. Avignon, Seguin, 1896.

This work, like the preceding, furnishes interesting details about the working of the Jesuit system.

De Badts de Cugnac, A., *Les Jésuites et l'éducation*. Lille, Desclée, 1879.

3. Works Having Particular Reference to Jesuit Education.

Paulsen, F., *Geschichte des gelehrten Unterrichts auf den deutschen Schulen und Universitäten vom Ausgang des Mittelalters bis zur Gegenwart*. Leipsic, Veit and Co., 1885; second edition in two volumes, 1896—1897.

Dr. Paulsen is one of the leading Professors of the University of Berlin. Of the present work the *Report of the Commissioner of Education* (1896—1897, I, p. 199) says: "It is a most thorough historical review of higher education known in the educational literature of any country." The chapter on the colleges of the Society and the educational labors of the Jesuits (vol. 1, pp. 379—432) is far more thorough, more independent, and more impartial, than most books written on the Jesuits by non-Catholics.

Schmid, K. A., *Geschichte der Erziehung vom Anfang bis auf unsere Zeit*. 5 volumes in 10 parts, by a number of scholars and educators. Stuttgart, Cotta, 1884—1901 (Part 3 of volume V, which will complete this great history of education, is not yet out).

On Jesuit education see volume III, Abteilung 1, pp. 1—109 (by Prof. Dr. Müller of Dresden); pp. 159—175 ("Jesuit Colleges in France," by Dr. E. von Sallwürk, Karlsruhe). — Volume IV, Abteilung 1, pp. 455—467; 538—543. — Volume V, Abteilung 2, pp. 176—221 ("Jesuit Education since 1600; Suppression and Restoration of the Society; the Revised Ratio Studiorum," by Dr. von Sallwürk). — The articles on the Jesuit schools are not free from some serious misinterpretations of the Ratio Studiorum. Especially Dr. Müller has misunderstood and rendered falsely several passages. In other cases, he applies to the secular students of Jesuit Colleges rules which are only for the younger members of the Society engaged in studies (*scholastics*).

Ziegler, T., *Geschichte der Pädagogik.* Munich, Beck, 1895. Is part 1, of vol. I of the *Handbuch der Erziehungs- und Unterrichtslehre für höhere Schulen*, edited by Dr. A. Baumeister.

Dr. Ziegler, Professor of Philosophy and Pedagogy in the University of Strasburg, is a prominent writer on education in Germany. In point of impartiality he is inferior to Professor Paulsen.

Willmann, O., *Didaktik als Bildungslehre.* 2 volumes, Braunschweig, Vieweg, second edition, 1894.

The author, a pupil of Herbart, became a Catholic, and is now Professor of Philosophy and Pedagogy in the University of Prague, and one of the ablest educational writers in the German tongue. His *Didaktik* is one of the most important pedagogical works published within the last decades.

Quick, H., *Educational Reformers.* London, Longmans, Green and Co., 1868. The revised edition forms part of the *International Education Series*, New York, Appleton, 1890.

Jourdain, C., *Histoire de l' Université de Paris aux 17e et 18e siècles.* 2 volumes. Paris, Didot, 1888.

A very valuable work; gives an account of the struggles of the Jesuits with the University.

Duhr, B., S. J., *Jesuitenfabeln* (Jesuit myths). Freiburg and St. Louis, Herder, 3. edition, 1899.

To this work readers must be referred who wish to see the absurdity of most legends about the Jesuits.

The book has, in the words of a non-Catholic review, "done away with a heap of calumnies against the Order." (*Literarisches Centralblatt*, Leipzig, 1899.)

Du Lac, S. J., *Jésuites*. Paris, Librairie Plon, 1901.

Huber, J., *Der Jesuiten-Orden*. Berlin, Habel, 1873.

Janssen, J., *Geschichte des deutschen Volkes seit dem Ausgang des Mittelalters*. 8 volumes. Herder, Freiburg and St. Louis. The edition used is the 18th of the first three volumes (1897—1899); 16th of vols. IV and VI; 14th of vol. V; 12th of vols. VII and VIII. The first three volumes have been translated into English:

History of the German People at the Close of the Middle Ages, by M. A. Mitchell and A. M. Christie. 6 volumes. London, Kegan Paul, 1896, 1900, 1903, and St. Louis, Mo., Herder.

It is superfluous to comment on this famous work. No historical work of the 19th century caused such a stir all over Europe as the history of the Reformation period written by Janssen from the testimony of the Reformers and their contemporaries. Unfortunately the greater part of Dr. Janssen's illustrative notes, in which the chief value of the work consists, are missing in the English version. Besides, it is not free from mistranslations; hence the German original ought to be consulted. — Jesuit education is chiefly treated in volumes IV, V and VII.

4. Miscellaneous Works.

Butler, N. M., *Education in the United States*. A Series of Monograms prepared for the United States Exhibit at the Paris Exposition, 1900. Edited by Nicholas Murray Butler. Albany, J. B. Lyon Company, 1900.

Newman, Cardinal, *Idea of a University*, and *Historical Sketches*. London and New York, Longmans.

Russell, J. E., *German Higher Schools*. New York, Longmans, 1899.
> Gives a good account of the German Gymnasium, its history, organization and practical working.

The Life of James McCosh. A Record Chiefly Autobiographical. Edited by W. M. Sloane. New York, Scribners, 1897.
> The life of the President of Princeton College is deserving of the careful study of all American teachers.

Fitch, Sir Joshua, *Thomas and Matthew Arnold and their Influence on English Education*. New York, Scribners, 1897. (*Great Educators Series*.)

Alzog, J., *Manual of Universal Church History*. Translated from the German by Dr. Pabisch and Professor Byrne. 3 volumes. Cincinnati, Clarke, 1878.

Pastor, L., *The History of the Popes from the Close of the Middle Ages*. Edited by F. I. Antrobus. 6 volumes. London, John Hodges and Kegan Paul, Trench, Trübner and Co., 1891 foll., and Herder, St. Louis, Mo. The original German edition in 3 volumes, Herder, Freiburg and St. Louis, Mo.

Guggenberger, A., S. J., *A General History of the Christian Era*. 3 volumes. St. Louis, Herder, 1900—1901.

Rashdall, H., *Universities of Europe in the Middle Ages*. 2 volumes in 3 parts. Oxford, 1895.

Drane, A. T., *Christian Schools and Scholars, or Sketches of Education from the Christian Era to the Council of Trent*. 2 volumes. London, Longmans, 1867.
> Popularly written; in many parts antiquated.

Taylor, H. O., *The Classical Heritage of the Middle Ages*. New York, Columbia University Press (Macmillan), 1900.

Einstein, L., *The Italian Renaissance in England*. New York, Columbia University Press, 1902.

Woodward, W. H., *Vittorino da Feltre and other Humanist Educators*. Cambridge, University Press, 1897.

Gasquet, F. A., O. S. B., *The Eve of the Reformation*. London and New York, 1900.

Baumgartner, A., S. J., *Geschichte der Weltliteratur*. Herder, 1897—1900.

> Of this magnificent history of Universal Literature four volumes are out so far. Volumes III and IV were used chiefly. (On this great work see pp. 233—234.)

Nägelsbach, C. F., *Gymnasial - Pädagogik*. Third edition, Erlangen, 1879.

Dettweiler, P., *Didaktik und Methodik des Lateinischen*. Munich, Beck, 1895.

—— *Didaktik und Methodik des Griechischen*. Munich, Beck, 1898.

> These two excellent books belong to Baumeister's *Handbuch der Erziehungs- und Unterrichtslehre*.

Schiller, H., *Handbuch der praktischen Pädagogik für höhere Lehranstalten*. Leipsic, Reisland, 1894, 3d edition.

Lehrpläne und Lehraufgaben für die höheren Schulen in Preussen, 1901 (The Prussian School Order). Official edition. Halle, Waisenhaus, 1901.

Verhandlungen über die Fragen des höheren Unterrichts. Berlin, 6. bis 8. Juni 1900. Halle, Waisenhaus, 1902.
    The transactions of the Berlin Conference on questions of higher education.

Report of the Commissioner of Education. Washington, Government Printing Office.
    Chiefly used were the volumes from 1888—1901.

5. Periodicals Quoted Frequently.

American: *Educational Review, Atlantic Monthly, North American Review, Forum, American Catholic Quarterly, American Ecclesiastical Review, Messenger, The Review, Woodstock Letters* (published at Woodstock College, for private circulation).

English: *Month, Tablet, Dublin Review, Fortnightly Review, Nineteenth Century, Contemporary Review.*

German: *Neue Jahrbücher für das klassische Altertum, Geschichte und deutsche Literatur und für Pädagogik* (Leipsic, Teubner), *Monatschrift für höhere Schulen* (Berlin, Weidmann), *Stimmen aus Maria-Laach* (Freiburg, Herder).

French: *Études* (Paris, Victor Retaux).

INDEX.

Academies, in Jesuit colleges, 518 *sqq.*
Accessories, in Jesuit curriculum, 118, 125, 192.
Acosta, Jesuit writer, 159.
Adaptability, of Jesuit system, 197, *sqq.*, 280—296.
Adaptation, in the Old Society, 283; since the revision of the Ratio Studiorum, 191 *sqq.*, 283 *sqq.*
Affection, of pupils, as element of teacher's authority, 612, 644.
Agricola, humanist, 33, 60, 67.
Albertus Magnus, 39, 99.
Alcala, university, 42—43, 79.
d'Alembert, 149, 174, 176.
Algué, Jesuit scientist, 230—231.
Aloysius, St., feast of students, 557; devotion to, 559—560.
Alvarez, 121 *sqq.*, grammar, 286.
America, school reforms, 1 *sqq.*, 292 *sqq.*; weaknesses of education, 293 *sqq.*, 301 *sqq.*, 307, 323 *sqq.*, 659-661; scholarship, 411—414; aid to schools, 412; classical studies, 344 *sqq.*; Jesuit colleges, 201 *sqq.*; American Histories of Education, 649 *sqq.*
Ancient authors, see "Classical Studies."
Antiquities, as taught in schools, 199, 284, 382, 451—454; method of teaching, 486 *sqq.*, 519—520; Jesuit writers on, 157—158, 233.
Appointment, of teachers according to ability, 439—442.

Aquaviva, General of the Society of Jesus, 103, 109 *sqq.*, 113.
Aquinas, St. Thomas, 39, 99; in Jesuit system, 132, 136, 193—194.
Archæology, see "Antiquities".
Aristotle, study of in Middle Ages, 45; Luther's attacks, 63; in Jesuit system, 131, 136, 193, 283; in Protestant schools, 136, note 2; in modern times, 193—194.
Arnold, Matthew, on translating, 354.
Arnold, of Rugby, on general education, 306; school exercises, 309; Latin and Greek, 351, 356; scholarship of teachers, 406; dangers of boarding schools, 537 note 2, 552 note; Jesuit methods, 549—550; on athletics, 571 note; religious instruction, 602—603; cultivating truthfulness in pupils, 629.
Arnold, Thomas, son of former, 163 note 2.
Astronomers, Jesuits, 179-180, 226—229, 232.
Astronomy, in Jesuit curriculum, 131, 194.
Athletics, in college, 569 *sqq.*
Auger, Jesuit writer, 593.
Austen, T., 321—322.
Authority of teacher, 610–614.
Avignon, Jesuit College, 127—128.
Azarias, Brother, 11 note.

Bacon, Roger, 39—40, 46.

(671)

Bacon, Francis, 39—40; on Jesuit schools, 145.
Bain, Professor, on home lessons, 475-476; teaching English, 491—492.
Balde, Jesuit writer, 130, 161—162.
Ballestrem, Count, on Jesuit teachers, 535.
Bancroft, G., on Jesuit colleges, 145; Catholics in Maryland, 203.
Barbier, Jesuit educator, 623—624.
Barnard, Henry, on Jesuit schools, 650 *sqq.*
Barnes, Dr., 323—324.
Barth, Professor, 566.
Bartoli, Jesuit writer, 137.
Baumgartner, Jesuit writer, 162, 233—234, 236, 238, 377, 381, 383, 384, 386, 387, 390, 391, 393, 396, 398, 401.
Bayer, Jesuit educator, 121 note 4.
Beaumont (England), Jesuit College, 257.
Beckx, General of the Society, 362 note 3; on national and political attitude of Jesuits, 262—263; religious instruction, 599, 604.
Beissel, Jesuit writer, 236.
Bellarmine, Robert (Cardinal), Jesuit theologian, 109; his catechism, 592, 593 note 2.
Benedict, St., 86, 633.
Benedict XIV., Pope, Jesuit pupil, 172; on the Sodalities, 561.
Benedictines, educational labors, 25—26, 86—87; as historians, 160.
Bennett, Professor in Cornell University, on experimenting in American schools, 293 note 1; on Latin, 349 note 1; on Roman pronunciation, 460 note; on compositions, 505.

Berlin Conferences on higher studies, 136 note 2, 289-291, 333 *sqq.*, 351, 356, 378, 509, 517.
Beschi, Jesuit linguist, 152.
Beirut, Jesuit University, 206.
Bible, and Reformers, 62—63; in Jesuit colleges, 121—124, 590; in Greek, 398-399; alone not sufficient for religious instruction, 583 *sqq.*; objections of Catholics to reading in public schools, 587 *sqq.*
Biblical World, on religious instruction, 577—578, 585, 603.
Bidermann, Jesuit writer, 130.
Bishops of France, on Jesuits, 273 *sqq.*
Boarding schools, of Jesuits, 250; dangers of boarding schools, 537 *sqq.*, 552, and note.
Boccaccio, humanist, 50.
Bohemia Manor, Maryland, Jesuit school, 204.
Bollandists, Jesuit historians, 161, 234—235.
Bolsius, Jesuit scientist, 233.
Bombay, St. Francis Xavier, Jesuit College, 206, 216.
Bonaventure, St., 39, 99.
Bonifacio, Jesuit educator, 163, 453, 645.
Bonvalot, Jesuit educator, 127.
Boscovich, Jesuit scientist, 179.
Boston College and President Eliot, 224 *sqq.*
Branch teacher, 442 *sqq.*
Braun, Jesuit scientist, 232.
Braunsberger, Jesuit historian, 236.
Brethren of the Common Life, 31—33, 138; see correction 653.
Briggs, Dean of Harvard College, 320, 406, 538—539.
Bristol, Professor in Cornell

INDEX.

University, 397 note 1, 398, 401 note 1, 505.
Broderick, G. C., 409–410, 415.
Brosnahan, Jesuit writer, controversy with President Eliot, 223 note 2, 224—225, 327.
Browning, O., on Jesuit education, 16, 186, 244-245, 263.
Brownson, O., 331, 529.
Brunetière, F., 550, 658.
Brunswick, laws against Jesuit schools, 240—241.
Bryce, James, 305—306, 338.
Buckle, H. T., 263.
Buffier, Jesuit geographer, 128, 448 note.
Bunyan, 265.
Busaeus, Jesuit, 44, 138.
Butler, President of Columbia University, 66—67 note, 293—294.

Caesar, 381—382.
Cajori, Professor, 155–156, 157.
Calcutta, Jesuit College, 216.
Calmette, Jesuit Sanskrit scholar, 151—152.
Cambridge, 69—70.
Campbell, Thomas, Jesuit writer, 577 note.
Canfield, President, 313—315, 572 note.
Canisius, Peter, Jesuit, 43, 109, 138; care for poor pupils, 248—250; on emulation, 512; catechisms and catechetical instructions, 593—599.
Carroll, Charles of Carrollton, 204, 260, 340.
Carroll, John, Jesuit and first Archbishop of Baltimore, 204—205, 260; founder of Georgetown College, 205.
Castelein, Jesuit writer, 235.
Catalogues of authors in Jesuit colleges, 374—375; of philological helps, 446—447, 453—454.
Catechetical training of Jesuits, 421; instruction in Jesuit schools, 590 *sqq*.
Catechisms written by Jesuits, 592 *sqq*.
Catharine II., of Russia, and the Jesuits, 177—178, 189, 258.
Catholic Church, and education, 21 *sqq*., 28, 30—31, 36—39, 50, 85—87.
Catholics, and the Bible, 587 *sqq*.; and sectarian schools, 579 *sqq*.
Cathrein, Jesuit writer, 235 note 2, 237.
Changes of teachers, 91—97, 444—445.
Character training, 317 *sqq*., 522 *sqq*.
Charlemagne, 23, 26.
Chateaubriand, 184—185.
Chevalier, Jesuit scientist, 231.
China, cartographic works of Jesuits, 129, 158; philological works, 153—154, 158, 232, 656; Jesuit mathematicians, 156, 158; Jesuit schools, 206—208.
Chossat, Jesuit writer, 128, and *passim*.
Christ, the teacher's model, 420, 631, 638, 643, 646; centre of history, 449 *sqq*.; his teaching in relation to pedagogy, 526—527, 540; Christian interpretation of authors, 365, 600.
Christian Brothers, 88, 98.
Chrysostom, St., 85.
Church and education, see "Catholic Church."
Cicero, 88, 139, 376, 377 *sqq*., 395—396, 468—471, 500.
Clarke, Jesuit writer and educator, 212, 235, 423—424, 551—555.
Classes in Jesuit schools, 118 *sqq*., 370, 372 *sqq*.
Classical studies, in Middle Ages and at time of Renais-

sance, 27 *sqq.*, 33 *sqq.*, 41—45, 47 *sqq.*; in Jesuit system, 286—287, 331 *sqq.*, 360; educational value of, 330—369; dangers of, 50—55, 367, 563 *sqq.*; the Gaume controversy, 366 *sqq.*; classical authors, 351-352, 370-401; explained in Christian spirit, 365, 600.
Class matches, 515 *sqq.*; see "Emulation."
Class teachers, 442 *sqq.*
Clavius (Klau), Jesuit, mathematician, 133—134, 155, 438.
Clement XIV., Pope, 175.
Clerc, A., Jesuit teacher, 645.
Clergymen as educators, 100, 408, 601—602.
Clerics, Regular, 80 note 3.
Cleveland, President of the United States, on patriotism of Jesuit schools, 261; on modern school reforms, 294.
Cleveland, Ohio, Jesuit College and Meteorological Observatory, 227, 229.
Coe, Professor in Northwestern University, 579.
Coeurdoux, Jesuit Sanskrit scholar, 151.
Colet, Dean, 30.
College, American, its equivalent in Jesuit system, 118, 370; function of, 304, 306 *sqq.*
Colleges of the Society, 78, 107; number, 144—146; in United States, 200—205; in other countries, 201, 205 *sqq.*; success of Jesuit colleges, 89 *sqq.*, 145—150, 207, 208—222; Roman College, 108; German College, 138.
Comenius, 292.
Communion, educational influence, 557—558.
Comparative philology, contributions by Jesuits, 149—151.
Compayré, character of his *History of Pedagogy*, 10, 11 note, 649; on primaryschools, 24; medieval universities, 40 note 2; attacks on Jesuit education, 10—11, 13 note, 77 note, 104 note, 125, 130, 135, 159, 163, 194—195, 233, 243, 245—247, 249, 250, 361, 362—363, 366 *sqq.*, 437, 489, 493, 511, 618.
Competition, see "Emulation."
Composition, see "Written exercises."
Compulsory education, 23, 29, 66.
Confession, educational influence of, 550—557.
Conservatism in Jesuit education, 288 *sqq.*; Grover Cleveland on conservatism in education, 294.
Constitutions of the Society, 74—75, 101 *sqq.*
Contests, exercises in Jesuit schools, 511 *sqq.*
Conway, James, Jesuit writer, 577 note.
Copernicus, 33, 42.
Cortie, Jesuit astronomer, 229.
Coster, Jesuit educator, 44, 138.
Cramming in modern systems, 299 *sqq.*
Cubberley, Professor, 649, 650.
Cusanus, Cardinal, 33.

Dahlmann, Jesuit scholar, 233, 236.
Dalberg, Bishop, patron of learning, 34.
Dana, C., 343.
Daniel, Jesuit writer, 128, 366.
Dante, 48—49, 387, 391.
Darjeeling, Jesuit College, 216.
Dark Ages, 21 *sqq.*
Davidson, Thomas, on Jesuit system, 13—14, 76 note.
Decline of teaching, 404—407.
Decurions, 139, 286.
Deharbe, J., Jesuit, 599.
Delaney, W., Jesuit, 606.

Demosthenes, 398.
Denis, Jesuit writer, 131, 162, 181.
Denominational schools, 580 *sqq.*
Devotions, as educational means, 558—560; devotion of teacher to work, 14, 147, 440—441, 643—644.
Dewey, Admiral, on Jesuit Observatory at Manila, 230.
Dierckx, Jesuit scientist, 233.
Discipline, in school, 537 *sqq.*, 608—635.
Disputations, in Jesuit colleges, 139, 422—425, 511, 518.
Disraeli, 583, 589—590.
Döllinger, 58, 61; on the Jesuits, 103, 189, 277.
Dominicans, 39, 56, 86—87, 99.
Dowling, M. P., Jesuit, 298.
Drama, in Jesuit colleges, 164 *sqq.*; in vernacular, 165 note 3, 192.
Draper, President, 293, 301 note, 327.
Dressel, Jesuit scientist, 236—237.
Dreves, Jesuit writer, 236.
Dufrêne, Jesuit educator, 121, 126.
Du Halde, Jesuit geographer, 159.
Duhr, Jesuit historian, 12, 112, and *passim*.
Du Pons, Jesuit linguist, 151.
Duruy, A., on Jesuit schools, 218, 260, 535 note 2.

Education, meaning of, 297—298; scope, 298—300; liberal education, 301, 305, 307, 341; commercial, 306, 337—338; professional, 303, 335; education and the Society, 87 *sqq.*, 104 *sqq.*; see "Ratio Studiorum."
Edward VI, 29, 30, 652.
Efficiency, of Jesuit schools, 89 *sqq.*, 145—150, 182 *sqq.*, 208—223; causes of, 13—14, 17—18, 89—98, 135, 415 *sqq.*, 643—644.
Ehrle, Jesuit historian, 234, 236, 238.
Einstein, L., 28, 31, 37.
Elective system, 5—6, 9—10, 310—329.
Electrical World, 293—294, 311, 339 note.
Elementary education, before Reformation, 23 *sqq.*; and the Jesuits, 104—106, 209, 247—248.
Eliot, President of Harvard University, on the Jesuit system, 5, 9, 199, 223—225, 243—244, 283, 311 *sqq.*; school reform, 293—294; elective system, 311 *sqq.*; on Roman pronunciation, 460 note; on failure of education, 523.
Elsperger, Professor, 196—197.
Emery, Abbé, 184.
Emulation, as a factor in education, 511—518.
England, education before Reformation, 29—31, 652—653; humanism, 28, 30, 37, 53; decline of learning, 69—71; penal laws against Jesuit schools, 239—240; recent attacks on Jesuits, 256 *sqq.*
England, Bishop, 330 note, 340.
English, teaching of, see "Mother-tongue."
Eobanus Hessus, 55, 61.
Epping, Jesuit scientist, 236.
Erasmus, leader of the humanists, 34, 36, 54—55; on schools in Spain, 41, 43; on decline of learning in consequence of the Reformation, 61—62; St. Ignatius and Erasmus, 140.
Erudition, part of interpretation of the authors in Jesuit system, the same as subject

explanation, 447 *sqq.*, 452, 461, 470, 485 *sqq.*
Esteem, element of teachers authority, 611 *sqq.*
Ethics, 131, 284.
Euclid, 153; non-Euclidean geometry, 156—157, cf. "Saccheri."
Example of teacher, 419, 531 *sqq.*, 627, 630.
Exercises, means of intellectual training, 308—309, 456 *sqq.*; written exercises, 499 —506; correction, 503 *sqq.*
Explanation, of authors, see "Prelection."
Expulsion of the Jesuits from various countries, 200, 225.
Expurgated editions of the classics, 363 *sqq.*, 562 *sqq.*
Eyre, Jesuit educator, 111.

Faber, F. W., 630 note.
Faber, Peter, Jesuit, 43, 60, 79.
Fabri, Jesuit writer, 349, 392.
Family, relation of Jesuit schools to, 250—251.
Fear, element of authority, 614.
Febres, Jesuit linguist, 155.
Feldkirch, Austria, Jesuit College, 411, 573.
Feltre, see "Vittorino."
Ferry, French Premier, 222, 260.
Fisher, John, Bishop, 30, 53.
Fischer, Joseph, Jesuit writer, 237.
Fitch, Sir Joshua, on clergymen as educators, 100; on home work, 475; on writing Latin verses, 506; on Jesuit education, 549—550; on religious instruction, 602; on corporal punishment, 616 note 3.
Fox, Jesuit philologist, 236.
France, success of Jesuit schools, 92, 182—184, 218—222; cause of opposition to

teaching congregations, 268 —269, 658; testimony of Bishops to Jesuits, 273—276.
Francis Xavier, St., 43, 78, 79; Jesuit College in: Bombay, 206, 216; Calcutta, 216; New York, 202.
Franciscans, 39, 56 note 2, 99.
Frederick the Great, of Prussia, 90; and the Jesuits, 176 —178, 189, 258.
Freiburg, Jesuit College, 163 note 2, 332 note 2, 573.
Friars, 39 *sqq.*, 80 note 3.
Frisbee, S. H., Jesuit, 479 *sqq.*

Gambetta, 220.
Gates, Professor, 577.
Gaubil, Jesuit sinologist, 153.
Gaume, Abbé, 366 *sqq.*
Geiler, of Kaisersberg, 34—35.
Genelli, Jesuit writer, 15, 73, 280.
General of the Society of Jesus, 101—102.
General Congregations, 101—102.
Genung, Professor, 353.
Geography, in Jesuit colleges, 127—129, 192, 447 note 2, 448; Jesuit geographers, 128 —129, 158—159, 237.
Georgetown, Jesuit College, 205, 227, 261, 411.
Gerard, J., Jesuit writer, 298, 337.
German higher schools, before Reformation, 31 *sqq.*; modern, 9, 289 *sqq.*, 333 *sqq.*; Jesuits as educators and writers, 206, 235—238, 262, 271.
Gibbon, 450, 514.
Gietmann, Jesuit writer, 236.
Gnauck-Kühne, Mrs., 96 *sqq.*
Goethe, 161; on Jesuit drama, 171; on specialization, 324; on classics, 360; on reading, 566.
Goodwin, Professor, 544.

Grammar, study of, 370 *sqq.*; Greek, 392 *sqq.*
Gratuitousness of instruction, 246, 249—250.
Greek, study of, 339 *sqq.*, 392 *sqq.*
Gretser, Jesuit writer, 121 note 3.
Grimaldi, Jesuit scientist, 157.
Grisar, Jesuit historian, 46, 234.
Groot, Gerard, 31.
Guggenberger, Jesuit historian, 54 *sqq.*
Guizot, 425.
Günther, Professor, 180—181.

Hadley, President of Yale University, 2 note 1, 339 note 1.
Hadley, Professor, 479 *sqq.*
Hagen, Jesuit mathematician, 227, 237, 655.
Hall, Stanley, President of Clark University, 307 note 1, 321, 360, 476—477, 501.
Hallam, 67—69, 71, 251.
Hanus, Professor, 310—311.
Hanxleden, Jesuit scholar, 151.
Hardouin, Jesuit historian, 160.
Harnack, Professor (Berlin), 22 note 3, 52, 60 note 1, 75—76, 83—84, 103, 290, 351.
Harris, W. T., Commissioner of Education, 330 note.
Hartmann, Edward von, 52—53.
Harvard University, 1, 203, 223, 315, 326, 327.
Health, of pupils cared for, 124, 572 *sqq.*
Hegius, humanist, 33—34, 53, 60.
Hell, Jesuit astronomer, 179.
Helmholtz, Professor, 333, 356.
Herodotus, 395.
Hervas, Jesuit linguist, 149—151, 181.

Henry VIII, 29—30, 69, 70, 652.
Herder, 161.
High school, equivalent in Jesuit system, 118, 370; function of, 303, 306; modern high school, 332.
Hildebrand, 337, 349.
Hillig, F., Jesuit, 232.
Historians, among Jesuits, 160—161, 233—234, 235.
History in Jesuit colleges, 124—126, 192, 199, 447—448; ancient, 448—451; viewpoint of Christian teacher, 448 *sqq.*, 600.
Hohenlohe, Prince, 173.
Holguin, Jesuit scholar, 154.
Holzmüller, Director, 333.
Home tasks, 475 *sqq.*
Homer, 354, 399—401, 480 *sqq.*
Horace, 391.
Howorth, Sir Henry, on the Jesuits, 175, 256 note, 532 note 2.
Huber, Professor, 77—78, 103, 104, 148, 252, 258.
Hughes, T., Jesuit writer, 200 and *passim.*
Humanism, rise and character, 26—30, 33—37, 47—49 *sqq.*; attitude of Church, 28, 30, 50, 60; radical humanists, 54—57; Luther's alliance with, 58—60; relation of the Jesuits to, 88, 138—140.
Humanities, class in Jesuit system, 119, 370.
Humphrey, W., Jesuit writer, 81 note.
Hutten, humanist, 55, 59, 60.

Ignatius of Loyola, 15; character, 73—75; studies, 32, 43, 78 *sqq.*, 137; and Luther, 59—60, 77—78, 140; and the Constitutions, 75—77, 101; as educator, 87 *sqq.*, 106; on Paris and Louvain, 137—138;

on self-activity, 308, 499; on self-conquest, 420; on individuality, 426; on dangers of reading, 51, 140, 563, 569; adaptation of his system, 15, 280, 281; prayer for persecution, 278; summary of Christian philosophy, 527—528; on good example, 532, 569; summary of religion, 574; obedience, 610; modesty, 627; prayer, 633 *sqq.*; see "Spiritual Exercises."
Imitation exercises, 500 *sqq.*
Impartiality of teacher, 612, 619—622.
India (East), Jesuit writers, 151—152; colleges, 206, 216.
Individuality, 317 *sqq.*; and Jesuit training, 367 note 1, 425—429.
Intellectual scope of education, 297 *sqq.*, 316, 322 *sqq.*; liberty, 136 note 2, 251—253, 270—271, 489.
Interpretation, see "Prelection."
Ireland, monastic schools, 26; modern Jesuit colleges, 213—216.
Italy, education, see "Humanism."

Jäger, Dr., 351, 371.
Jansenists, 164, 174.
Janssen, 23 *sqq.*, and *passim*.
Jesuits, see Society of Jesus, Constitutions, Ratio Studiorum, Colleges, Teachers, Writers, Pupils, Opposition.
Jogues, Jesuit in New York, 201—202.
Jones, President of Hobart College, 307, 321, 339, 541 note.
Jourdain, 182—184, 270—271.
Jouvancy, (Juvencius), Jesuit educator, 162, 164, 248, 331, 353, 362, 377, 382, 383—385, 387, 400, 434—435, 447, 453, 454, 461, 467 *sqq.*, 484—485, 502, 548, 565, 600, 610, 622, 624—625, 634, 637; his educational treatise: *Ratio Discendi et Docendi*, 162, 163 note 1, 434—435.
Jullien, Jesuit scientist, 232.
Juniorate, 422, 431 *sqq.*

Kant, 324, 513, 643.
Kemp, E. L., 10 note, 513, 652—653.
Kempis, Thomas a, 31, 32, 322, 527, 610.
Kepler, astronomer, on Jesuit writers, 657.
Kern, Professor, 531.
Ketteler, Bishop, 241, 534.
Kino (Kühn), Jesuit missionary and geographer, 129.
Kircher, Jesuit scholar, 157—158; *Museo Kircheriano*, 158, 226.
Knecht, Bishop, 592—593.
Kohlmann, Jesuit in New York, 202.
König, Jesuit writer, 127.
Körner, 535—536.
Kreiten, Jesuit writer, 236.
Kropf, Jesuit educator, 121 *sqq.*, 126, 163, 448, 548, 610, and *passim*.
Kübler, Dr., 290, 510.
Kugler, Jesuit scholar. 236.

Labbe, Jesuit historian, 128, 160, 448 note.
La Cerda, Jesuit philologist, 162, 163.
Ladevèze, M. de, on Jesuits, 267, 609.
La Flèche, Jesuit College, 168, 484.
Lainez, General of the Society, 79, 101.
Lalande, 179, 180, 186.
Lang, Andrew, 265.
Lang, Jesuit writer, 165.
La Rue (Ruaeus), Jesuit philologist, 163—164.

INDEX. 679

Latimer, 70.
Latin, during Middle Ages, 29, 44 sqq.; in Protestant and Jesuit schools, 6—9, 129, 345—346; in modern German schools, 290 sqq., 333 sqq., 476 sqq., 509 sqq.; in American schools, 2, 345; as means of logical training, 346—351, 357—358; speaking and writing, 6—9, 129, 422, 429—430, 498—511; "Monkish" Latin, 430 note.
Leach, A. F., 30, 430, 652—653.
Ledesma, Jesuit educator, 108, 138, 403—404, 445.
Lehmkuhl, Jesuit writer, 237.
Leibnitz, 52, 156, 161.
Lemaître, J., 368 sqq.
Leo XIII, Jesuit pupil, 278; on religious orders, 277; on Sodalities, 560; Bellarmine's catechism, 593; religious instruction, 601, 605.
Leon, Jesuit, founder of Sodalities, 560.
Leopold I., King of Belgium, on Jesuit schools, 259.
Liberal education, 301, 305, 307, 341.
Liège, school, 33, 107, 139, 140—141, 240.
Limerick, P., 276.
Lines, as punishment, 497, 619.
Literature, Jesuit writers on, 130—131, 161—163, 181, 233—234, 235.
Littledale, Canon, 73, 103, 264.
Livy, 382.
Longhaye, Jesuit writer, 234.
Louis-le-Grand, Jesuit College, 144.
Louvain, school, 33, 138.
Lowell, 323, 357.
Loyola, see "Ignatius."
Lucas, Herbert, Jesuit writer, 532.
Lugo, Jesuit theologian, 109, 427.
Luther, in Protestant tradition, 57—58; alliance with radical humanists, 58—60; and Loyola, 59—60, 77, 140; violent language against universities and Aristotle, 63—65; appalled at decline of schools, 65—66; Hallam's estimate of, 67—69; on vows and monasticism, 81; his catechism, 593—594.

Mabillon, Benedictine historian, 87.
Macaulay, 73.
Madagascar, Jesuits in, 231.
Maher, M., Jesuit writer, 235.
Mallinckrodt, von, 534.
Manare, Oliver, Jesuit, 444.
Manila, Jesuit College and Observatory, 229 sqq.
Manning, Professor, 157 note.
Marquette, Jesuit, 128—129.
Martin, Luiz, General of the Society, 286—287, 297, 509.
Martineau, 320 sqq.
Martini, Jesuit geographer, 129, 159.
Maryland, Jesuits in, 202—204.
Masen, Jesuit writer, 164.
Matches, class matches, 515 sqq.
Mathematicians, Jesuits, 155—158, 182, 227—228, 232.
Mathematics, in Jesuit colleges, 132—134, 182, 192, 194, 284; educational value compared with linguistic training, 333, 336, 355; training of Jesuit teachers of mathematics, 438—439.
Matthias, Dr., of Berlin, 4 note, 290, 510.
Maynard, Abbé, on educational labors of the Jesuits before the suppression, 178 sqq.
McCosh, President of Princeton, on liberal education, 302; on elective system at Harvard, 315—316; on Amer-

ican scholarship, 413; on moral training, 522, 537—538; on athletics, 570; on religious instruction, 582.

McCloskey, Cardinal, Archbishop of New York, 557—558.

Melanchthon, on decline of education, 61; attitude towards higher studies, 64, 67; drew inspirations from medieval schools, 72, 530 note; on Canisius, 595.

Memory lessons, 493—499.

Messina, Jesuit College, 108, 137.

Messmer, Bishop of Green Bay, 592, 593 note 2.

Metereology, cultivated by Jesuits, 227, 229—232.

Method of teaching in practice, 456 *sqq.*

Meyer, Theodore, Jesuit writer on ethics, 237.

Middle Ages, educational conditions, 21—44; character of education, 44 *sqq.*, see "Scholasticism."

Modern languages, 332; modern high school, *ib.*

Modesty, to be inculcated in pupils, 626 *sqq.*

Mommsen, Theodore, 378, 380, 381.

Monasticism, 80—84.

Monita Secreta, 102—103.

Monks, Protestant view of, 80 note 3; as educators, 84—87.

Monroe, Jesuit educator, 645 note.

Morality in Jesuit schools, 251 *sqq.*, 531—536.

Moral training, 317 *sqq.*, 522—573.

More, Thomas, 53.

Mother-tongue, studied in Jesuit colleges, 129—131, 191—192, 284, 448 note, 491 *sqq.*; and study of classics, 356 *sqq.*

Müller, Max, Professor at Oxford, on Jesuit writers, 149—151, 233.

Munich, splendor of Jesuit drama, 168—170.

Münsterberg, Professor at Harvard, on modern school reforms, 5; American teachers, 92—94; premature specialization, 303; elective system, 319—320, 325—327; preparation of teachers, 402, 403; American scholarship, 413.

Nadal, Jerome, Jesuit educator, on elementary education, 106; plan of studies, 108 note 3, 116, 117 note 2; geographical reading, 128 note 3; study of German, 130; relation to the Ratio Studiorum, 138; instruction gratuitous, 249; training of teachers, 404, 441—442; religious toleration, 596.

Nägelsbach, Professor, 385, 387, 389—390, 398, 473.

Natalis, see "Nadal."

Nation, New York, on electivism, 326; on decline of teaching, 404—406.

National questions, attitude of the Jesuits, 262—263.

Natural sciences, see "Sciences."

Neander, on monks as educators, 85—86.

Nepos, 384.

Netherlands, humanist schools, 31—32, 43; influence on formation of Ratio Studiorum, 138 *sqq.*

Newcomb, Simon, on Father Hell, 179; on American scholarship, 413.

Newman, Cardinal, on medieval education, 23 note; on monks, 81 note; religious as educators, 86—87; on clas-

INDEX. 681

sics, 355, 359—360, 378; on individuality among Jesuits, 367 note 1, 425—427; on moral training, 555 *sqq.*; Jesuit obedience, 609 note.
New York, Jesuit College, 201—202.
Nightingale, Professor, 307 note, 357.
Nobili, Robert, Jesuit, first European Sanskrit scholar, 151.
Notes, taken in class, 463—465.
Non-sectarian school, 580 *sqq.*
Noviciate, in the Society, 418—422.
Number of Jesuit colleges, 78, 107, 144 *sqq.*, 200—206; of Jesuit pupils, 13, 144—146, 206.

Obedience, of teacher, 609—610, 650; of pupil, 650.
Oberammergau, Passion play, and Jesuit drama, 169.
Observatories, of Jesuits, 180, 227, 229—232.
Odenbach, F. L., Jesuit meteorologist, 227.
Officials, in Jesuit colleges, 115—118.
Oliphant, L., 208.
Opposition, to Jesuit education, 5 *sqq.*, 146—148, 239—279; causes of, 6—13, 264 *sqq.*
Oratorians, 127, 448 note.
Ovid, 44, 385, 386, 565.
Oxford, 69—71, 212, 411.

Pachtler, Jesuit historian, 112, 283, 410, 494, and *passim.*
Painter, F. V. N., 10 note, 37, 131, 245, 252—254, 361, 511, 596.
Pantel, Jesuit scientist, 233.
Papenbroeck, Jesuit historian, 161.
Paris, University of, 32, 39, 43, 79, 99, 137; influence on Jesuit system, 137 *sqq.*; opposition to Jesuits, 182 *sqq.*, 269—271.
Patience, of teacher, 420, 630, 631—632, 646.
Patriotism, and Jesuit schools, 255—263.
Paulsen, Professor, 7, 22, 52, 59—60, 81—82, 90—91, 100, 136, 195—197, 324, 407—409, 425; on Jesuit schools, 17—18, 79—80, 193—194, 254—255, 271—272, 512, 532—533.
Peck, Professor in Columbia University, 223 note 2, 224, 327.
Pedagogy, meaning of, 524 *sqq.*; relation to philosophy, 524—525; pagan and Christian, 526; Jesuit writers on, 162—163, 434—435.
Permanent teachers, 435 *sqq.*
Perpinian, Jesuit writer, 162.
Perry, Jesuit astronomer, 228.
Pesch, Henry, Jesuit writer, 237.
Petavius, Jesuit scholar, 160, 427, 448 note.
Petrarch, 49—50.
Phaedrus, 385, 472—473.
Philology, in the Society of Jesus, 149—155, 199, 446—447, 453—454; Jesuit contributions to comparative philology, 149—150.
Philosophy, Aristotelian, see "Aristotle"; in Jesuit system, 131, 193—197; philosophy neglected in modern systems, 195—197; philosophical training of Jesuits, 422 *sqq.*; philosophy in relation to pedagogy, 524—525.
Physics, in Jesuit curriculum, 131, 134, 194.
Pitt, on classics, 358.
Plans of studies, previous to the Ratio Studiorum, 108—109.

Plato, 396—398, 451.
Plautus, 165—166, 391, 565.
Polanco, Jesuit, 137.
Poland, W., Jesuit writer, 11 note, 577 note.
Politeness, of pupils, 626 *sqq.*
Politics, attitude of Jesuits, 262—263.
Pombal, 174.
Pompadour, 174.
Pontanus, Jesuit philologian, 110, 121 note 2, 162.
Poor pupils, care of, in Jesuit schools, 247—250.
Porée, Jesuit educator, 181.
Porter, Noah, of Yale, on Jesuit schools, 245, 246, 269.
Port Royal, 127, 164.
Portugal, suppression of Society, 174.
Postgate, Professor, 498 note.
Poulton, Jesuit, founder of school in Maryland, 203.
Prayer, educational help, 632 *sqq.*
Prefect of Discipline, 117.
Prefect of Studies, 117, 609.
Prelection, i. e. interpretation of authors, etc., 457—493; preparation of, 464—466.
Prémare, Jesuit sinologist, 153.
Prescribed courses, 310—329.
Primary education, see "Elementary."
Prince Henry, and the Jesuits in China, 207—208.
Private talks with pupils, 548 *sqq.*
Prizes, 514; see "Emulation."
Pronunciation, correct, 459—461; Roman, of Latin, 460 note.
Protestant, Reformation and education, 57—72; schools in 16. and 17. centuries, 89—91; view of Jesuits, 264—267; moral training in Protestant and Catholic schools, 538 *sqq.*, 541 note, 551—557; reading of Bible, 583 *sqq.*
Provincial, 101.
Prussia, Jesuit colleges after suppression, 176.
Prussian School Order, 9, 289, 291, 392, 394 note 1; on class teachers, 443; on translations, 478; on written exercises, 500; religious instruction, 581, 601—602.
Psychology, in Jesuit course, 131, 194.
Punishments, 614—619; corporal, 616.
Pupils, of Jesuit schools, number, 13, 144—146, 206; distinguished, 172, 204—205, 258.

Quick, on Jesuit system, 10, 13, 98, 135—136, 241, 243, 246—249, 265, 431, 437, 466, 489, 516—517, 518, 530, 565, 624.
Quigley, Archbishop of Chicago, 302.
Quintilian, 419, 564, 614.

Ranke, 18, 89, 145, 246, 322, 595, 628.
Rashdall, H., 21 *sqq.*, 29—30, 39—40, 41, 430.
Ratio Discendi et Docendi, of Jouvancy, 162, 163 note 1, 434—435.
Ratio Studiorum, 107—143, 189—199; modern criticism on, 5—16; drawn up, 109—111; name, 111; seized by Spanish Inquisition, 112 *sqq.*; character, 114 *sqq.*; classes, 118, 121 *sqq.*; school hours, 124; branches: languages, 118, 331 *sqq.*, 345—360; mother-tongue, 129, 284, 491 *sqq.*; history, 125 *sqq.*, 447 note 2; geography, 127 *sqq.*; archaeology, see "Antiquities"; philosophy, 131 *sqq.*, 193—197; mathematics,

132—134; sciences, 134, 192, 194—195, 197—199; successive teaching, of branches, 132; class teachers, 442 *sqq.*, sources of Ratio, 19—20, 136—143; revision, 191 *sqq.*; results, see "Efficiency", adaptability, 280 *sqq.*; essentials, 286 *sqq.*; defects, 14, 92 note 1, 444—445.
Raumer, 17, 166, 251—252; character of his history of education, 650 *sqq.*
Reading, according to sense, 458—461, 498; amount of, 482 *sqq.*; dangers of reading, 51, 166, 367, 562 *sqq.*
Rector, President in Jesuit colleges, 115—116.
Reformation, and education, 57 *sqq.*; decline of schools, 60—66; in England, 69—71; elementary school not child of Reformation, 24; Jesuit system not borrowed from Protestant schools, 19—20, 140 *sqq.*; compulsory education and state-monopoly result of, 66.
Reform-Gymnasium, 291—292, 336.
Reforms, modern, 1—5; in Germany, 289—292; in America, 292—296; towards elective system, 310—312.
Relations, of Jesuits, 128.
Religious, name, 80 note 3; as educators, 84 *sqq.*, 96—98, 209; opposition to, 89, 98-100; success of, 92—98, 221 *sqq.*
Religious instruction, 574—607; necessity, 574—578; Catholic position, 578—582; undenominational religion, 582—583; reading of Bible, 583 *sqq.*; catechism, 590 *sqq.*; correlation of all branches with religion, 599—605; religious instruction in higher schools, 605 *sqq.*

Renaissance, see "Humanism."
Repetition, in Jesuit system, 466—467, 474.
Resistance, value of, in education, 319—322.
Rethwisch, C., 7 *sqq.*
Revival of Learning, see "Humanism."
Revision of the Ratio Studiorum, 191 *sqq.*
Rhetoric, class in Jesuit system, 120, 370; meaning of, 432.
Ribadeneira, Peter, Jesuit writer, 102, 138, 511.
Ribot, M., on secondary schools in France, 218—219.
Ricci, Jesuit scholar, 153, 156.
Richelieu, Cardinal, Jesuit pupil, 172; on Jesuit colleges, 271.
Richthofen, Baron, on Jesuit scholars, 129, 158—159.
Rickaby, Joseph, Jesuit writer, 235.
Rivals, see "Class matches."
Rogers, Thorold, 30.
Roman College, 108, 110, 144, 227.
Roman history, 448—451.
Roothaan, General of the Society, 191, 197—198, 296, 329, 360—361.
Roth, Jesuit, author of first European Sanskrit grammar, 151.
Rousseau, 175, 643.
Rowland, Professor in Johns Hopkins University, 413.
Ruaeus (La Rue), Jesuit scholar, 163—164.
Ruhkopf, on morality in Jesuit schools, 537.
Ruiz, Jesuit linguist, 155.
Russell, Dr., Columbia University, 8—9, 19, 20, 141, 244, 313.
Russia, Society preserved in, 177, 189.

Sabatier, P., 209.
Saccheri, Jesuit mathematician, 156—157, 654—655.
Sacchini, Jesuit writer. 162, 249, 436, 438, 497, 530, 548, 592, 600, 624, 634, 637.
Sadler, Mr., 659.
Saintsbury, on Southwell, 162.
Saint-Vincent, Gregory, 156.
Salamanca, University, 41, 43, 79.
Salisbury, Lord, on undenominational religion, 583.
Sallust, 382—383.
Sallwürk, Dr. von, 435, 448 note.
Sanskrit, Jesuit scholars, 151—152.
Sanson, geographer, 448 note.
Sarbiewski, Jesuit poet, 161.
Savonarola, 51, 60.
Scaliger, 160, 657.
Schall, Jesuit mathematician, 156.
Scheiner, Jesuit scientist, 157.
Schiller, Director, 478, 566 note, 588—589, 601—602.
Scholars, Jesuits, see "Writers."
Scholarship, among Jesuits, 198—199, 226—238, 410—411; in America, 411 sqq.; scholarship and teaching ability, 402—414.
Scholasticism, 45—57; defects of, 46 sqq.; humanists on, 52; relation of Jesuit system to, 136.
School drama, 164 sqq.
School management, 608—635.
Schopenhauer, 325.
Sciences, in Jesuit curriculum, 134, 192, 194—195, 197—198, 199, 283; and classics, 359.
Scientists, among Jesuits, 157, 178—181, 226—233, 654—656.
Scoraille, Jesuit writer, 515—516.
Scotland, education before Reformation, 28—29.

Scope of education, intellectual, 297 sqq.; injured by electivism, 316 sqq.; moral, 317 sqq., 522 sqq.
Scotus, 39, 193, 425.
Secchi, Angelo, Jesuit astronomer, 226—227.
Secondary schools before Reformation, 26 sqq., 652—653.
Sectarian schools, 580 sqq.
Seeley, Levi, 10 note, 37, 246—247, 511, 649.
Selfishness, alleged of Jesuits, 251, 254—255.
Seminary of teachers in Society, 433—434, 453.
Seneca, 384—385.
Seyffert, M., 309, 379, 507.
Shea, Gilmary, 536—537.
Shoup, W. J., 652.
Sirmond, Jesuit historian, 448 note.
Sixtus V., and the Ratio Studiorum, 112—113.
Sloane, Rev. M., on Jesuits, 243.
Smith, Clement L., 304—305.
Smith, Sydney, Jesuit writer, 173 note 1.
Snyder, Carl, 413.
Society of Jesus, name, 75; foundation and aim, 75—77, 79 sqq.; and education, 80 sqq.; constitutions, 101 sqq.; suppression, 173—175, 189—190.
Socrates, 253, 397.
Sodalities, 560—562.
Sommervogel, Jesuit writer, 148.
Sources, of Ratio Studiorum, 136—143.
Southwell, Robert, Jesuit poet, 162.
Spahn, Deputy, on Jesuit scholars, 235—237.
Spain, schools, 40—44; suppression of Society, 174.
Spanish Inquisition. seized Ratio Studiorum, 112 sqq.

INDEX. 685

Spe, Frederick, Jesuit writer, 130 and note 4.
Speaking Latin, 506 *sqq*.
Specialization, 303, 317, 322—325; in Society, 198–199, 440.
Spencer, 525, 643.
Spiritual Exercises, of St. Ignatius, 75, 420, 426, 527, 532 note 1, 560, 574.
Sport, see "Athletics."
St. Boniface, Jesuit College, 216.
Stephens, Jesuit linguist, 152.
Stiglmayr, Jesuit scholar, 237, 397.
Stonyhurst, Jesuit College, 228, 229, 257—258, 564, 617.
Strassmaier, Jesuit assyriologist, 233, 236.
Stryker, President of Hamilton College, on liberal education, 341.
Studia inferiora, 118 *sqq*.
Sturm, Reformer and schoolman at Strasburg, 19—20, 72; his system not model of Ratio Studiorum, 140 *sqq*.
Suarez, Jesuit theologian, 81 note, 88, 109, 426, 427.
Success, of Jesuit colleges, see "Efficiency."
Successive teaching, preferred to simultaneous, 118, 132.
Sunday schools, and religious training, 578.
Supervision in college, 537 *sqq*., 541 *sqq*., 546–547.
Suppression of the Society, 173—175; effects on education, 184—186.
Sydney Smith, discipline in English public schools, 539 note.
Syria, Jesuit schools, 106, 206—207, 209.

Tacitus, 383—384.
Taunton, E., 427—428.
Taylor, H. O., 45, 49, 82—83.
Teaching, in relation to

scholarship, see "Scholarship."
Teachers of the Society, 91—98, 415 *sqq*.; permanent teachers, 435, 437 *sqq*.; changes of teachers, 92 note 1, 444—445; training of, 415—455; direct training for teaching, 431—434; cf. 410; continued self-training, 446 *sqq*.; training of teachers of mathematics in the Old Society, 133, 438—439; appointment according to ability, 439—442; qualities requisite: in general, 415—416; in particular: mastery of the subject, 403—404, 410, 446 *sqq*., 453 *sq* ., 611; see also "Scholarship"; qualities of character: authority, 610—614; submission, 608—610; self-control, 419—420, 531—533, 611—612, 615; impartiality, 420, 612, 619 *sqq*.; politeness, 627—628; truthfulness, 630; patience, 420, 630, 631—632, 646; kindness, 420, 612—613, 622; firmness, 612, 614, 619, 623 *sqq*.; prudence, 418—419, 615, 624—625, 628—629; zeal and devotion to work, 94, 98, 420, 436—438, 528—531, 535—537, 540—543, 545—547, 548—550, 562 *sqq*., 637—644; piety, 419—421, 643 *sqq*.; perseverance, 95 *sqq*., 435—438, 642; motives and ideals, 636—648.
Terence, 165—166, 391, 565.
Tetlow, Principal, 327—328.
Text-books, of Jesuits, 163—164, 393.
Theiner, 173, 178, 185.
Thomas, see "Aquinas" and "Kempis."
Thornton, A., 578—579.
Thring, E., 337, 616.
Thucydides, 395.

686 JESUIT EDUCATION.

Tiraboschi, Jesuit writer, 181.
Times, London, 222, 256—257.
Tolerance, religious and the Jesuits, 252—254, 595—596.
Tom Brown's School Days, 537, 572.
Tragedies, 401.
Training of teachers, see "Teachers."
Translation, of classical authors, 353 *sqq.*; by the teacher, 462—463; in class, 474—478.
Trendelenburg, Professor, 193.
Trent, Council of, and reform of education, 71.
Trichinopoli, Jesuit College, 206.
Trivium and *Quadrivium*, 27, 44.
Trotzendorf, 530.
Truth, on "Jesuit and Gaol-Bird System," 546—547.
Truthfulness, 628 *sqq.*
Tursellini, Jesuit writer, 126 note 2, 164.

Undenominational school, 579 *sqq.*
Universities, before Reformation, 38—44; denounced by Luther, 63—64; opposition of, to Jesuits, 182 *sqq.*, 269 *sqq.*

Valla, humanist, 51.
Vasquez, Jesuit theologian, 109, 426, 427.
Vatican library, 28.
Vest, Senator, on Jesuit schools among the Indians, 209—211.
Viger, Jesuit philologist, 164.
Virchow, Professor, 290, 334.
Virgil, 44, 49, 387—391, 471.
Visconti, General of the Society, 431—432, 434, 442.
Vitelleschi, General of the Society, 549.

Vittorino da Feltre, 26—28, 60, 563 note.
Vives, Luiz, humanist, 141—142.
Vogt, Professor, 336.
Voltaire, 152, 174, 435; on Jesuit colleges, 174—175, 181, on morality in Jesuit colleges, 533—534.

Wagner, Jesuit writer, 126.
Waldeck-Rousseau, and Jesuit schools, 186, 219.
Washington, George, at Georgetown College, 205; on religion, 576.
Wasmann, Jesuit entomologist, 232—233, 236, 238.
Weissenfels, Professor, 306 note 3, 317.
Wellington, Duke of, on effects of suppression of Society, 185; on schools without religion, 576.
Werenfels, Reformed theologian, 587.
West, Professor in Princeton, 344.
Whitton, Professor, 251, 406.
Wiese, Dr., 309, 356.
Wilamowitz, von, (University of Berlin), 369, 378, 505.
William of St. Amour, 99.
Williams, Professor in Cornell University, 651.
Willmann, Professor, 4 note, 468 *sqq.*, 473, 485.
Wimpheling, humanist, 35—36, 54, 60.
Windle, Dr., 581.
Winsor, Justin, on Jesuit writers, 154—155, 159.
Witchcraft, charges against Jesuit teachers, 148.
Women, education of in Middle Ages, 41, and note 2.
Writers of the Society, 148—164, 179—182, 225—238; why often ignored, 154, 657.

Written exercises, see "Exercises."

Xavier, see "Francis."
Xenophon, 394—395.
Ximenez, Cardinal, 42.

Yenni, Jesuit educator, 438.

Zahorowski, 103.
Zallinger, three Jesuit scientists, 180—181.
Ziegler, Professor, 82 note, 140, 255, 270, 433, 582.
Zi-ka-wei, Jesuit College and observatory, 207—208, 232.
Zottoli, Jesuit sinologist, 656.